Mechanics 3 & 4

Mechanics 3 & 4

Douglas Quadling

Series editor Hugh Neill

CAMBRIDGE
UNIVERSITY PRESS

CAMBRIDGE
UNIVERSITY PRESS

University Printing House, Cambridge CB2 8BS, United Kingdom

Cambridge University Press is part of the University of Cambridge.

It furthers the University's mission by disseminating knowledge in the pursuit of education, learning and research at the highest international levels of excellence.

www.cambridge.org
Information on this title: www.cambridge.org/9780521549028

© Cambridge University Press 2005

First published 2001
Second edition 2005
8th printing 2015

Printed in Italy by Rotolito Lombarda S.p.A.

A catalogue record for this publication is available from the British Library

ISBN 978-0-521-54902-8 Paperback

Contents

Introduction

Cambridge Advanced Mathematics has been written especially for the OCR modular examination. It consists of one book or half-book corresponding to each module. This book contains the third and fourth Mechanics modules, M3 and M4.

The books are divided into chapters roughly corresponding to specification headings. Occasionally a section includes an important result that is difficult to prove or outside the specification. These sections are marked with an asterisk (*) in the section heading, and there is usually a sentence early on explaining precisely what it is that the student needs to know.

It is expected that most students using the M3 module will already have completed C4; for these students the chapters can be followed in the order in which they appear. Those who are taking M3 and C4 in parallel may prefer to begin with Chapters 4, 5 and 7, which extend topics already introduced in M2, before tackling earlier chapters which require familiarity with differential equations and additional integration techniques. In M4 Chapter 1 is independent of the other chapters, and may be taken at any stage of the course. It is recommended that the remaining chapters of M4 should be studied in the order in which they appear, although the later sections of Chapter 3 could, if desired, be taken after Chapter 4.

Occasionally within the text, paragraphs appear in a grey box. These paragraphs are usually outside the main stream of the mathematical argument, but may help to give insight, or suggest extra work or different approaches.

Numerical work is presented in a form intended to discourage premature approximation. In ongoing calculations inexact numbers appear in decimal form like 3.456... , signifying that the number is held in a calculator to more places than are given. Numbers are not rounded at this stage; the full display could be, for example 3.456 123 or 3.456 789. Final answers are then stated with some indication that they are approximate, for example '3.46 correct to 3 significant figures'.

The value of g is taken as $9.8\,\mathrm{m\,s^{-2}}$.

There are plenty of straightforward exercises to provide immediate reinforcement of material in the preceding text. Each chapter also contains a Miscellaneous exercise which includes some questions of examination standard, many from recent past OCR or MEI papers. Some of these are from three-hour papers, and may therefore be longer (but not necessarily more demanding) than the questions likely to be set in a modular examination. A few questions which go beyond examination requirements are marked by an asterisk. There are sets of Revision exercises in the middle and at the end of both M3 and M4, and two practice examination papers for each of M3 and M4.

The author thanks Peter Thomas and Steve Green, who read the books very carefully and made many extremely useful and constructive comments. The author also thanks OCR and Cambridge University Press for their help in producing this book. However, the responsibility for the text, and for any errors, remains with the author.

Module M3

Mechanics 3

1 Linear motion with variable forces

This chapter is about the motion of a particle along a straight line when the forces acting on it depend on time or on its velocity or position. When you have completed the chapter, you should

- know how to describe the motion by a differential equation involving two or more of the quantities displacement, velocity and time
- be able to solve the differential equation in cases where the variables are separable, and interpret the solution
- know that acceleration can be expressed as $v\dfrac{dv}{dx}$
- know that the work done by a force can be expressed as $\displaystyle\int F\,dx$ and the impulse of a force as $\displaystyle\int F\,dt$.

To use this chapter you need to be familiar with the methods of solving differential equations described in C4 Chapter 7 and with integration using partial fractions and the form $\displaystyle\int \dfrac{f'(x)}{f(x)}\,dx$ (C4 Section 2.4). Sections 1.3 and 1.5 use the method of separable variables described in C4 Section 8.3.

1.1 Velocity–time equations

When an object is moving in a straight line under the action of constant forces, you know from Newton's second law that the acceleration is constant. You can then use the standard methods for constant acceleration to get equations relating the velocity, displacement and time.

But often the forces on an object are not constant. For example, if you push a table across the floor, you may push hard to get it started and then reduce the force once the table is moving. On the other hand, if you are driving a car, you may apply a light touch on the accelerator as you move off from rest and then increase the pressure as the car gains speed. In such cases the acceleration will not be constant.

You know, however, from M1 Section 11.2, that the acceleration can be written as $\dfrac{dv}{dt}$. So if you have a formula for the force in terms of the time, you can express the acceleration as a function of the time, and then integrate this to find an expression for the velocity.

Example 1.1.1
A milk float of mass 800 kg is powered by an electric motor. Starting from rest, the driver applies a gradually increasing accelerating force, given by $60\sqrt{t}$ newtons after t seconds. How long does the float take to reach its maximum speed of $10\,\mathrm{m\,s^{-1}}$?

By Newton's second law the acceleration of the float is $\dfrac{60\sqrt{t}}{800}\,\mathrm{m\,s^{-2}}$. So if the velocity after t seconds is $v\,\mathrm{m\,s^{-1}}$, the motion is described by the differential equation

$$\frac{dv}{dt} = \tfrac{3}{40}\sqrt{t}.$$

This can be integrated directly to give

$$v = \tfrac{1}{20}t^{\frac{3}{2}} + k.$$

Since t denotes the time after the float starts to move, $v = 0$ when $t = 0$, so $k = 0$. The (t, v) equation is therefore

$$v = \tfrac{1}{20}t^{\frac{3}{2}}.$$

You are told that this equation holds for velocities up to the maximum value $v = 10$. When $v = 10$, $t^{\frac{3}{2}} = 200$, so $t = 200^{\frac{2}{3}} = 34.19\dots$.

The milk float takes 34.2 seconds to reach its maximum speed.

Variable acceleration does not always appear as a function of t. Another cause of variation is that the force may depend on how fast an object is moving. One example is air resistance, which increases as speed increases. Another is when an engine is working at constant power, in which case the driving force decreases as the speed increases.

Examples like this lead to differential equations which give $\dfrac{dv}{dt}$ in terms of v. These can be solved by the method described in C4 Section 7.2, using the property that $\dfrac{dv}{dt} \times \dfrac{dt}{dv} = 1$. A differential equation of the form $\dfrac{dv}{dt} = f(v)$ can then be written as $\dfrac{dt}{dv} = \dfrac{1}{f(v)}$, and this can then be integrated directly.

Example 1.1.2
A particle of mass 5 kg is projected along a smooth straight horizontal tube with a speed of $250\,\mathrm{m\,s^{-1}}$. When it is moving at a speed of $v\,\mathrm{m\,s^{-1}}$, the air resistance slowing it down is $\tfrac{1}{500}v^2$ newtons. Find an expression for the speed of the particle after t seconds.

The equation $F = ma$ applied to the motion of the particle, writing a as $\dfrac{dv}{dt}$, is

$$-\tfrac{1}{500}v^2 = 5\frac{dv}{dt},$$

which gives the differential equation

$$\frac{dv}{dt} = -\tfrac{1}{2500}v^2.$$

To solve this, note that $\dfrac{dv}{dt}$ is given in terms of v, so write

$$\frac{dt}{dv} = 1 \div \frac{dv}{dt} = 1 \div \left(-\frac{1}{2500}v^2\right) = -\frac{2500}{v^2}.$$

This can be integrated with respect to v, to give

$$t = \frac{2500}{v} + k.$$

To find k, use the fact that the speed of projection is $250\,\mathrm{m\,s^{-1}}$. This is the speed after 0 seconds, so that $v = 250$ when $t = 0$. Therefore

$$0 = \frac{2500}{250} + k,$$

which gives $k = -10$. The equation connecting t and v is therefore

$$t = \frac{2500}{v} - 10.$$

The question asks for the speed after t seconds, so you now have to express v in terms of t. So write

$$t + 10 = \frac{2500}{v},$$

$$v = \frac{2500}{t + 10},$$

which is in the form required.

Example 1.1.3

A cyclist and her bicycle have total mass $100\,\mathrm{kg}$. She is working at constant power of 80 watts. Calculate how long it takes her to accelerate from $4\,\mathrm{m\,s^{-1}}$ to $8\,\mathrm{m\,s^{-1}}$ along a level road,

(a) if air resistance is neglected,

(b) making allowance for air resistance of $0.8v$ newtons when her speed is $v\,\mathrm{m\,s^{-1}}$.

    (a) Power can be calculated as force $\times$ velocity, so at $v\,\mathrm{m\,s^{-1}}$ her efforts produce a driving force of $\dfrac{80}{v}$ newtons. Writing her acceleration as $\dfrac{dv}{dt}$, Newton's second law gives

$$\frac{80}{v} = 100\frac{dv}{dt}, \quad \text{that is,} \quad \frac{dv}{dt} = \frac{4}{5v}.$$

To solve this differential equation, write

$$\frac{dt}{dv} = 1 \div \frac{dv}{dt} = 1 \div \frac{4}{5v} = \tfrac{5}{4}v.$$

This can be integrated with respect to v, to give

$$t = \tfrac{5}{8}v^2 + k.$$

Suppose that time is measured from the instant when the cyclist's speed is $4\,\mathrm{m\,s^{-1}}$. Then $t = 0$ when $v = 4$, so

$$0 = \tfrac{5}{8} \times 4^2 + k, \quad \text{giving} \quad k = -\tfrac{5}{8} \times 16 = -10.$$

Therefore

$$t = \tfrac{5}{8}v^2 - 10.$$

To find how long it takes her to accelerate to $8\,\mathrm{m\,s^{-1}}$, put $v = 8$. This gives

$$t = \tfrac{5}{8} \times 64 - 10 = 30.$$

    (b) The original equation now includes an extra term to take account of the resistance, and becomes

$$\frac{80}{v} - 0.8v = 100\frac{dv}{dt}.$$

The left side is $\dfrac{0.8(100 - v^2)}{v}$, and $\dfrac{0.8}{100} = \frac{1}{125}$, so the equation can be written

$$\frac{dv}{dt} = \frac{100 - v^2}{125v}.$$

Inverting this to express $\dfrac{dt}{dv}$ as a function of v gives

$$\frac{dt}{dv} = \frac{125v}{100 - v^2},$$

so $t = \displaystyle\int \frac{125v}{100 - v^2}\, dv.$

The key to finding this integral is to notice that it can be written as $-62.5 \times \displaystyle\int \frac{-2v}{100 - v^2}\, dv$. In this form the numerator of the integrand is the derivative of the denominator with respect to v. This is the special type of integral referred to in C4 Section 2.4, and gives the solution

$$t = -62.5 \ln(100 - v^2) + k.$$

Substituting $t = 0$ when $v = 4$ gives

$$0 = -62.5 \ln 84 + k, \quad \text{so} \quad k = 62.5 \ln 84.$$

Therefore, when $v = 8$,

$$\begin{aligned} t &= -62.5 \ln(100 - 64) + 62.5 \ln 84 \\ &= 62.5(\ln 84 - \ln 36) \\ &= 52.95\ldots. \end{aligned}$$

The time to accelerate from $4\,\mathrm{m\,s^{-1}}$ to $8\,\mathrm{m\,s^{-1}}$ is calculated as

(a) 30 seconds if resistance is neglected, or

(b) 53.0 seconds taking resistance into account.

It is worth noticing that the answers in Example 1.1.3 could have been obtained directly as definite integrals

$$\text{(a)}\ \int_4^8 \tfrac{5}{4}v\, dv \quad \text{and} \quad \text{(b)}\ \int_4^8 \frac{125v}{100 - v^2}\, dv.$$

The reason for not doing this will appear when you come to Example 1.2.3, where algebraic expressions for v in terms of t are needed.

1.2 Displacement–time equations

Often you don't just want to know the velocity of an object at a given time, but also where it is. Once you have the connection between v and t, this can be found by using the fact that $v = \dfrac{dx}{dt}$, where x is the displacement of the object from a fixed point on the line.

Example 1.2.1

It was shown in Example 1.1.2 that, for the particle projected along the tube against air resistance, the speed $v\,\mathrm{m\,s^{-1}}$ after t seconds is given by $v = \dfrac{2500}{t+10}$. Find an expression for the distance, x metres, travelled by the particle in t seconds.

Writing v as $\dfrac{\mathrm{d}x}{\mathrm{d}t}$, the differential equation

$$\frac{\mathrm{d}x}{\mathrm{d}t} = \frac{2500}{t+10}$$

can be integrated directly to give

$$x = 2500\ln(t+10) + k.$$

What information do you need to find k? In this example, x metres is the distance travelled by the particle in t seconds. Obviously, in 0 seconds the particle has travelled 0 metres. So $x = 0$ when $t = 0$. Substituting these values in the equation,

$$0 = 2500\ln 10 + k.$$

Therefore $k = -2500\ln 10$, so

$$x = 2500\ln(t+10) - 2500\ln 10.$$

This is the expression required, but it can be written more neatly in the form

$$x = 2500(\ln(t+10) - \ln 10) = 2500\ln\frac{t+10}{10}.$$

Example 1.2.2 extends Example 1.1.1 to find how far the milk float travels.

Example 1.2.2

A milk float of mass 800 kg is powered by an electric motor. Starting from rest, the driver applies a gradually increasing accelerating force, given by $60\sqrt{t}$ newtons after t seconds. How far does the milk float travel before it reaches its maximum speed of $10\,\mathrm{m\,s^{-1}}$?

The velocity of the float after t seconds was found to be $v = \frac{1}{20}t^{\frac{3}{2}}$. This equation can be written as

$$\frac{\mathrm{d}x}{\mathrm{d}t} = \tfrac{1}{20}t^{\frac{3}{2}},$$

where x metres is the displacement after t seconds. Integrating,

$$x = \int \tfrac{1}{20}t^{\frac{3}{2}}\,\mathrm{d}t = \tfrac{1}{50}t^{\frac{5}{2}} + k.$$

Since $x = 0$ when $t = 0$, $k = 0$ and the (t, x) equation is simply $x = \frac{1}{50}t^{\frac{5}{2}}$.

The question asks for the displacement when $v = 10$, that is when $t = 34.19...$ (see Example 1.1.1). Substituting this value for t gives $x = 136.7...$.

The float travels 137 metres in reaching its maximum speed.

Notice that, if you aren't interested in knowing the (t, x) equation, but only in the total distance travelled, the answer in Example 1.2.2 could be calculated as the definite integral $x = \int_0^{34.19...} \frac{1}{20} t^{\frac{3}{2}} \, dt$. This method is used in the next example, which extends Example 1.1.3 to calculate the distance travelled.

Example 1.2.3
A cyclist and her bicycle have total mass 100 kg. She is working at constant power of 80 watts. How far does the cyclist travel in increasing her speed from $4 \, \text{m s}^{-1}$ to $8 \, \text{m s}^{-1}$

(a) if air resistance is neglected,

(b) making allowance for air resistance of $0.8v$ newtons when her speed is $v \, \text{m s}^{-1}$?

(a) It was shown in Example 1.1.3(a) that, if resistance is neglected, t and v are connected by the equation $t = \frac{5}{8}v^2 - 10$. Before this can be used to find an expression for the displacement, the equation must be rearranged to show v as a function of t. You can easily see that $v^2 = \frac{8}{5}(t + 10)$, so

$$v = \sqrt{1.6t + 16}.$$

There is no need to include a $\pm$ sign when taking the square root, since all the motion takes place in one direction, which will obviously be chosen to be the positive direction.

The total distance travelled can be found by integrating this with respect to t over the appropriate interval of time. Example 1.1.3(a) shows that this time is from 0 to 30 seconds. The distance is therefore given by

$$x = \int_0^{30} (1.6t + 16)^{\frac{1}{2}} \, dt,$$

which can be evaluated as

$$\left[\frac{1}{1.6} \times \frac{2}{3} (1.6t + 16)^{\frac{3}{2}} \right]_0^{30} = \frac{1}{2.4} \left(64^{\frac{3}{2}} - 16^{\frac{3}{2}} \right)$$
$$= \frac{1}{2.4} (512 - 64) = 186\frac{2}{3},$$

using the rule for integration in C3 Section 4.2.

> The answer has been found by using a definite integral, because you are not going to need the algebraic equation connecting x and t.

(b) Using a similar method to part (a), the (t, v) equation when resistance is taken into account is $t = 62.5(\ln 84 - \ln(100 - v^2))$, which can be rearranged as

$$-0.016t = \ln \frac{100 - v^2}{84},$$

which gives

$$\frac{100 - v^2}{84} = e^{-0.016t},$$
$$100 - v^2 = 84e^{-0.016t},$$
so $$v = \sqrt{100 - 84e^{-0.016t}}.$$

From Example 1.1.3(b), the range of time is now from 0 to 52.95... seconds, so the distance is given by

$$x = \int_0^{52.95...} \sqrt{100 - 84e^{-0.016t}}\, dt.$$

This is a difficult integral to evaluate exactly, so you can use an approximate method such as the trapezium rule (see C2 Chapter 10). With four intervals, this gives the value of the integral as approximately

$$\tfrac{1}{2} \times \tfrac{52.95...}{4} \times (4 + 2(5.659... + 6.708... + 7.450...) + 8),$$

which is about 342.

The distance covered by the cyclist is calculated as (a) 187 metres if resistance is neglected, or (b) approximately 342 metres if resistance is taken into account.

Exercise 1A

Keep your solutions to Questions 6, 7, 10, 11 and 12 for use in Exercise 1B.

1 A car of mass 1200 kg is at rest on a level road. Two people push it, producing a total force given by $(240 - 12t)$ newtons, where t is the time in seconds, until this becomes zero after 20 seconds. How fast is the car then moving, and how far does it move while it is being pushed?

2 A racing car of mass 2000 kg accelerates from rest with a driving force of $480(t - 10)^2$ newtons until it reaches its maximum speed after 10 seconds. Find its maximum speed, and the distance it travels in reaching this speed.

3 A particle of mass 2 kg is at rest at the origin. It is acted on by a force which varies periodically according to the law $F = 8 \sin 2t$ newtons. Find expressions for the velocity and position of the particle after t seconds. Draw sketches of the (t, x) and (t, v) graphs.

4 A car of mass 900 kg is travelling at $24\,\mathrm{m\,s^{-1}}$ when the brakes are suddenly applied. The braking force is given by $(4500 - kt^2)$ newtons, where t is the time in seconds and k is a constant, and the car comes to a stop in 6 seconds. Find the value of k, and the distance the car travels in coming to a stop.

5 A particle of mass m is at rest at the origin. It is acted on by a force which decreases exponentially according to the law $F = Ke^{-ct}$. Find expressions for its velocity and position after time t. Draw sketches of the velocity–time and displacement–time graphs.

6 A rollerblader of mass 50 kg is moving at $8\,\mathrm{m\,s^{-1}}$ and slows down against a resistance given by v newtons, where v is her speed in $\mathrm{m\,s^{-1}}$. Find how fast she is moving 20 seconds later, and how far she has gone in that time.

7 An aircraft of mass 4000 kg lands on the deck of a stationary aircraft carrier with a speed of $50\,\mathrm{m\,s^{-1}}$. It is brought to rest with the help of air brakes and a parachute, which slow it down with a resisting force of $50v^2$ newtons, where v is the speed in $\mathrm{m\,s^{-1}}$. Find how long it takes for the speed to drop to $10\,\mathrm{m\,s^{-1}}$, and how far the aircraft travels in this time. Why shouldn't the aircraft rely on this means alone to bring it to rest?

8 In first gear a car of mass 900 kg accelerates from rest to $5\,\mathrm{m\,s^{-1}}$ with a constant driving force of 3000 newtons. Assuming air resistance of $30v$ newtons when the car's speed is $v\,\mathrm{m\,s^{-1}}$, calculate how long the car takes to gain speed, and how far it travels in doing so. Compare your answers with those obtained by neglecting the resistance.

9 The car in Question 8 accelerates from $5\,\mathrm{m\,s^{-1}}$ to $15\,\mathrm{m\,s^{-1}}$ in second gear, with the engine developing constant power of 15 kW. Neglecting resistance, calculate how long it takes to gain speed, and how far it travels in doing so. Hence find its average speed in this gear. Find how long it takes to gain speed if there is air resistance of $30v$ newtons when the speed is $v\,\mathrm{m\,s^{-1}}$.

10 A car of mass 1250 kg is taking part in a fuel economy trial. It is conjectured that, if it is travelling at $v\,\mathrm{m\,s^{-1}}$ with the engine disengaged and without the brakes being applied, the resistance is given by $(5v + v^2)$ newtons. If it is initially moving at $20\,\mathrm{m\,s^{-1}}$, how long does it take for the speed to drop to $5\,\mathrm{m\,s^{-1}}$? Show that, if the car has travelled x metres and has speed $v\,\mathrm{m\,s^{-1}}$ after t seconds, then $v = \dfrac{20\mathrm{e}^{-0.004t}}{5 - 4\mathrm{e}^{-0.004t}}$ and $x = 1250\ln(5 - 4\mathrm{e}^{-0.004t})$. Hence find how far the car travels while slowing down to $5\,\mathrm{m\,s^{-1}}$.

11 An airliner of mass 500 tonnes is powered by engines developing 25 000 kW. Resistance to motion at a speed of $v\,\mathrm{m\,s^{-1}}$ is $0.8v^2$ newtons. Write as a definite integral the time it takes to reach a speed of $80\,\mathrm{m\,s^{-1}}$ from rest on take-off. Use the trapezium rule to find this time approximately.

12 A tube train of mass 1000 tonnes is accelerated from rest with a driving force of 200 000 newtons. At a speed of $v\,\mathrm{m\,s^{-1}}$ the air in the tunnel produces a resisting force of $500v^2$ newtons. Find how long the train takes to reach a speed of $10\,\mathrm{m\,s^{-1}}$.

If the speed of the train after t seconds is $v\,\mathrm{m\,s^{-1}}$, show that $v = 20\dfrac{\mathrm{e}^{0.01t} - \mathrm{e}^{-0.01t}}{\mathrm{e}^{0.01t} + \mathrm{e}^{-0.01t}}$. Hence find the distance travelled by the train in accelerating to a speed of $10\,\mathrm{m\,s^{-1}}$.

1.3   Velocity–displacement equations

When the acceleration is constant, the equation $v^2 = u^2 + 2as$ can be obtained by eliminating t between the two equations $v = u + at$ and $s = ut + \frac{1}{2}at^2$. What happens when the acceleration is not constant?

You are familiar with using displacement–time and velocity–time graphs to show the motion of objects along a line. For example, for the milk float in Examples 1.1.1 and 1.2.2 these graphs have the forms shown in Fig. 1.1 and Fig. 1.2. The velocity–time graph is the graph of the gradient of the displacement–time graph, and the acceleration is the gradient of the velocity–time graph.

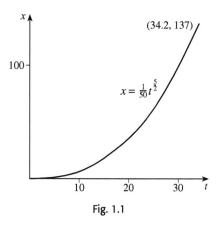

Fig. 1.1

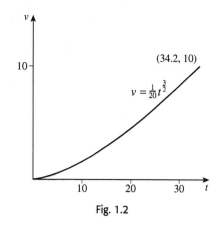

Fig. 1.2

There is another way of describing the motion, using a velocity–displacement graph. In the milk float example, from the two equations

$$x = \tfrac{1}{50}t^{\frac{5}{2}} \quad \text{and} \quad v = \tfrac{1}{20}t^{\frac{3}{2}}$$

found in Examples 1.1.1 and 1.2.2, you can eliminate the variable t.

From $x = \tfrac{1}{50}t^{\frac{5}{2}}$, it follows that $t = (50x)^{0.4}$. So

$$t^{\frac{3}{2}} = \left((50x)^{0.4}\right)^{\frac{3}{2}} = (50x)^{0.4 \times \frac{3}{2}} = (50x)^{0.6}$$
$$= 10.456...x^{0.6},$$

which gives

$$v = \tfrac{1}{20}t^{\frac{3}{2}} = 0.5228...x^{0.6}.$$

This graph is shown, for values of v from 0 to 10, in Fig. 1.3.

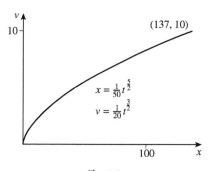

Fig. 1.3

How can you find the acceleration from a velocity–displacement graph? To answer this, notice that the (t, x) and (t, v) equations above can be regarded as parametric equations for the (x, v) graph, with t as the parameter. So the gradient of the (x, v) graph can be found by the rule proved in C4 Section 3.3, as

$$\frac{dv}{dx} = \frac{dv}{dt} \bigg/ \frac{dx}{dt}.$$

Since $\dfrac{dv}{dt} = a$ and $\dfrac{dx}{dt} = v$, this is $\dfrac{dv}{dx} = \dfrac{a}{v}$,

so $a = v\dfrac{dv}{dx}$.

This is an important result, which you should remember alongside $v = \dfrac{dx}{dt}$ and $a = \dfrac{dv}{dt} = \dfrac{d^2x}{dt^2}$ which were established in M1 Chapter 11.

> For an object moving in a straight line, if x denotes the displacement from a fixed point O of the line, v denotes the velocity and a the acceleration, then $a = v\dfrac{dv}{dx}$.

Example 1.3.1

A particle moves along a straight line in such a way that the velocity when it has travelled a distance x is given by $v = \dfrac{1}{p+qx}$, where p and q are constants. Find expressions for the acceleration   (a) in terms of x,   (b) in terms of v.

(a) $\dfrac{dv}{dx} = -\dfrac{q}{(p+qx)^2}$, so $a = v\dfrac{dv}{dx} = -\dfrac{q}{(p+qx)^3}$.

(b) $\dfrac{1}{(p+qx)^3} = v^3$, so $a = -qv^3$.

If you have an expression for the acceleration in terms of either x or v (or both), you can use the form $v\dfrac{dv}{dx}$ to make a differential equation connecting x and v, without bringing in time.

Example 1.3.2

A particle of mass $5\,\text{kg}$ is projected along a smooth straight horizontal tube with a speed of $250\,\text{m s}^{-1}$. When it is moving at a speed of $v\,\text{m s}^{-1}$, the air resistance slowing it down is $\frac{1}{500}v^2$ newtons. Find an expression for the speed of the particle after it has travelled x metres.

This is the same situation as in Example 1.1.2, but now you are asked to find an expression for v in terms of x rather than t. So write a as $v\dfrac{dv}{dx}$; the equation $F = ma$ then takes the form

$$-\tfrac{1}{500}v^2 = 5v\dfrac{dv}{dx}.$$

The differential equation to be solved is therefore

$$\dfrac{dv}{dx} = -\tfrac{1}{2500}v.$$

Since this gives $\dfrac{dv}{dx}$ in terms of v rather than x, use the fact that $\dfrac{dv}{dx} \times \dfrac{dx}{dv} = 1$ to write the differential equation in the form

$$\dfrac{dx}{dv} = -\dfrac{2500}{v}.$$

This can be integrated directly to give

$$x = -2500 \ln v + k.$$

To find k, use the information that the speed of projection is $250 \, \mathrm{m\,s^{-1}}$, so that $v = 250$ when $x = 0$. Substituting these values in the integrated equation,

$$0 = -2500 \ln 250 + k,$$

which gives $k = 2500 \ln 250$. Therefore

$$x = -2500 \ln v + 2500 \ln 250,$$

which can be written more neatly as

$$x = 2500(\ln 250 - \ln v) = 2500 \ln \frac{250}{v}.$$

You can easily check for yourself that this equation could also be obtained by eliminating t between the equations $v = \dfrac{2500}{t + 10}$ and $x = 2500 \ln \dfrac{t + 10}{10}$ found in Examples 1.1.2 and 1.2.1. But by using $v \dfrac{dv}{dx}$ for the acceleration, you can get the answer with just one integration rather than two.

The solution is not yet quite complete. The question asks for v in terms of x, but so far you only have x in terms of v. So a little more algebra is needed.

$$\ln \frac{250}{v} = \frac{x}{2500} = 0.0004x,$$

$$\frac{250}{v} = e^{0.0004x},$$

$$v = 250 e^{-0.0004x}.$$

This is in the form required. After the particle has travelled x metres, its speed is $250 e^{-0.0004x} \, \mathrm{m\,s^{-1}}$.

Example 1.3.3
A vehicle of mass $500 \, \mathrm{kg}$ is moving at $25 \, \mathrm{m\,s^{-1}}$ along a straight horizontal road when the engine cuts out. It is slowed down by air resistance of amount $5v^{\frac{3}{2}}$ newtons, where v is the speed in $\mathrm{m\,s^{-1}}$. How far does it travel in coming to rest?

If the vehicle has travelled x metres when the speed is $v \, \mathrm{m\,s^{-1}}$,

$$-5v^{\frac{3}{2}} = 500 \times v \frac{dv}{dx},$$

so that

$$100 \frac{dv}{dx} = -v^{\frac{1}{2}}.$$

Writing $\dfrac{dv}{dx}$ as $1 \div \dfrac{dx}{dv}$, this differential equation can be rearranged as

$$\frac{dx}{dv} = -100v^{-\frac{1}{2}}.$$

Integrating,

$$x = -200v^{\frac{1}{2}} + k.$$

Since $v = 25$ when $x = 0$,

$$0 = -200 \times \sqrt{25} + k, \quad \text{so that} \quad k = 1000.$$

The equation connecting v with x is therefore

$$x = 1000 - 200v^{\frac{1}{2}}.$$

To find how far the vehicle travels in coming to rest, put $v = 0$ in this equation, which gives $x = 1000$. So the vehicle travels 1000 metres in coming to rest.

Example 1.3.4
A projectile is launched vertically upwards from the surface of the moon with initial speed u. The radius of the moon is R. When the projectile is at a height x above the surface, the gravitational attraction produces an acceleration $\dfrac{C}{(R+x)^2}$ towards the centre of the moon, where C is a positive constant. Find an expression for the speed of the projectile when it is at height x. How large must u be for the projectile never to return to the surface?

Taking the upward direction to be positive,

$$v\frac{dv}{dx} = -\frac{C}{(R+x)^2}.$$

This is a differential equation of the separable variables type (see C4 Section 8.3), but it is already arranged so that it can be directly integrated with respect to x.

Since $v\dfrac{dv}{dx} = \dfrac{d}{dx}\left(\tfrac{1}{2}v^2\right)$ by the chain rule,

$$\tfrac{1}{2}v^2 = \int -\frac{C}{(R+x)^2}\,dx = \frac{C}{R+x} + k.$$

It is given that $v = u$ when $x = 0$, so

$$\tfrac{1}{2}u^2 = \frac{C}{R} + k.$$

Therefore $\tfrac{1}{2}v^2 - \tfrac{1}{2}u^2 = \dfrac{C}{R+x} - \dfrac{C}{R}$, giving $v = \pm\sqrt{\dfrac{2C}{R+x} - \dfrac{2C}{R} + u^2}$.

There are now two possibilities according to the value of u. The term $\dfrac{2C}{R+x}$ gets smaller as x increases, but it always stays positive. So if $u^2 \geqslant \dfrac{2C}{R}$, v never becomes zero; and since it has the positive value u to start with, it is always positive. This means that if $u \geqslant \sqrt{\dfrac{2C}{R}}$ the projectile goes on moving away from the moon indefinitely, and never returns to the surface.

If $u < \sqrt{\dfrac{2C}{R}}$, v becomes zero when $\dfrac{2C}{R+x} - \dfrac{2C}{R} + u^2 = 0$. This equation can be solved to give $x = \dfrac{u^2 R}{\dfrac{2C}{R} - u^2}$. Because the expression inside the square root sign can't be negative, x can never be greater than this. So what happens is that the velocity changes sign from $+$ to $-$, which means that the projectile falls back to the surface of the moon. Notice that, since x is the only variable in the expression for v, the value of $|v|$ is the same at any given height whether the projectile is going up or coming down. When it hits the surface, it is again moving with speed u.

For the problem of the cyclist in Example 1.1.3, you can use the form $v\dfrac{dv}{dx}$ for the acceleration to find the distance travelled directly, without first finding the time. You should compare the answers in the next example with those found in Example 1.2.3.

Example 1.3.5
A cyclist and her bicycle have total mass 100 kg. She is working at constant power of 80 watts. Calculate how far she travels in increasing her speed from $4\,\text{m\,s}^{-1}$ to $8\,\text{m\,s}^{-1}$ along a level road,

(a) if air resistance is neglected,

(b) making allowance for air resistance of $0.8v$ newtons when her speed is $v\,\text{m\,s}^{-1}$.

The differential equations are formed in just the same way as in Example 1.1.3, but writing the acceleration as $v\dfrac{dv}{dx}$ rather than $\dfrac{dv}{dt}$.

(a) If resistance is neglected, the accelerating force is $\dfrac{80}{v}$ newtons, so

$$\frac{80}{v} = 100v\frac{dv}{dx},$$

which gives $\dfrac{dv}{dx} = \dfrac{4}{5v^2}$.

Since v appears in this equation but x doesn't, you want the derivative to appear as $\dfrac{dx}{dv}$ rather than $\dfrac{dv}{dx}$. So using $\dfrac{dx}{dv} = 1 \div \dfrac{dv}{dx}$, the differential equation can be arranged as

$$\frac{dx}{dv} = \tfrac{5}{4}v^2.$$

Only the total distance is asked for, so this can be calculated as the definite integral

$$\int_4^8 \tfrac{5}{4}v^2\,dv = \left[\tfrac{5}{12}v^3\right]_4^8 = \tfrac{5}{12}(512 - 64) = 186\tfrac{2}{3}.$$

(b) Taking resistance into account,

$$\frac{80}{v} - 0.8v = 100v\frac{dv}{dx}.$$

The left side is $\dfrac{0.8(100 - v^2)}{v}$, so the differential equation can be arranged as

$$\frac{dx}{dv} = \frac{125v^2}{100 - v^2}.$$

The distance is then calculated as

$$\int_4^8 \frac{125v^2}{100 - v^2}\, dv.$$

The key to finding this integral is to write the v^2 in the numerator as $100 - (100 - v^2)$, so that the integrand then becomes

$$\frac{125(100 - (100 - v^2))}{100 - v^2} = \frac{12\,500}{100 - v^2} - 125$$

$$= \frac{12\,500}{(10 + v)(10 - v)} - 125.$$

The first term can then be split into partial fractions as $\dfrac{625}{10 + v} + \dfrac{625}{10 - v}$. The integral then becomes

$$\int_4^8 \left(\frac{625}{10 + v} + \frac{625}{10 - v} - 125\right) dv = [625\ln(10 + v) - 625\ln(10 - v) - 125v]_4^8$$

$$= 625(\ln 18 - \ln 14 - \ln 2 + \ln 6) - 125(8 - 4)$$

$$= 625\ln \tfrac{27}{7} - 500 = 343.7\dots.$$

The distance covered by the cyclist is calculated as 187 metres if resistance is neglected, or as 344 metres if resistance is taken into account.

Notice that the answer to part (b) of Example 1.2.3, 342 metres, is very close to the value given by this exact method. This suggests that using the trapezium rule was quite acceptable, bearing in mind that the model on which the calculation is based is itself only approximate.

1.4   Reintroducing time

Sometimes you want to reverse the process described at the beginning of Section 1.3, and find the (t, x) or the (t, v) relation from an equation connecting velocity and displacement. This can be done by writing v as $\dfrac{dx}{dt}$ and solving a differential equation involving x and t.

Example 1.4.1

A car is travelling at $10\,\mathrm{m\,s^{-1}}$ when the driver applies the brakes and brings the car to rest in a distance of 20 metres. The velocity–displacement relationship is modelled by a straight line graph. Find an expression for the distance the car has travelled t seconds after the brakes are applied.

Fig. 1.4 shows the velocity–displacement graph, which has equation $2v + x = 20$.

Writing v as $\dfrac{dx}{dt}$, this gives the differential equation

$$\frac{dx}{dt} = \tfrac{1}{2}(20 - x).$$

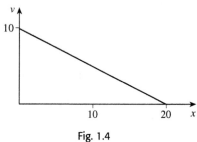

Fig. 1.4

Since the right side is a function of x rather than t, use $\dfrac{dt}{dx} = 1 \div \dfrac{dx}{dt}$ to rewrite the differential equation as

$$\frac{dt}{dx} = \frac{2}{20 - x}.$$

This has solution

$$t = -2\ln(20 - x) + k.$$

Since t is measured from the instant when the brakes are applied, $t = 0$ when $x = 0$. So $0 = -2\ln 20 + k$, and

$$t = -2\ln(20 - x) + 2\ln 20,$$

or more conveniently

$$t = -2\ln\frac{20 - x}{20} = -2\ln\left(1 - \tfrac{1}{20}x\right).$$

The question asks for x in terms of t, so the equation must now be rearranged in the form $x = \dots$. This can be done by writing the equation in exponential form as

$$e^{-\frac{1}{2}t} = 1 - \tfrac{1}{20}x, \quad \text{giving} \quad x = 20\left(1 - e^{-\frac{1}{2}t}\right).$$

It is a good idea to check the answer by differentiating this equation with respect to t, to get

$$v = \frac{dx}{dt} = 10e^{-\frac{1}{2}t}, \quad \text{so} \quad 2v + x = 20e^{-\frac{1}{2}t} + 20\left(1 - e^{-\frac{1}{2}t}\right) = 20,$$

which brings you back to the original (x, v) equation.

The (t, x) and (t, v) equations show that, with the suggested model, x never reaches the value 20 in finite time, and v never becomes zero. So this is not a plausible model for the complete braking operation, although it might be valid over most of the distance.

1.5 Impulse and work

The momentum equation

$$Ft = mv - mu \qquad \text{(see M1 Chapter 8)}$$

and the work–energy equation

$$Fs = \tfrac{1}{2}mv^2 - \tfrac{1}{2}mu^2 \qquad \text{(see M2 Chapter 2)}$$

were both obtained by combining the equation $F = ma$ with one of the constant acceleration formulae. So in this form they only apply to situations in which the force is constant. Using the expressions $\dfrac{dv}{dt}$ and $v\dfrac{dv}{dx}$ for the acceleration, these equations can be generalised to cover situations in which the force is variable.

Writing Newton's second law as $F = m\dfrac{dv}{dt}$, you can integrate to obtain

$$\int F\,dt = \int m\frac{dv}{dt}\,dt.$$

Then, using the principle of substitution (see C4 Chapter 2), the integral on the right can be replaced by $\int m \, dv$.

It is most useful to work with definite integrals. Suppose that under the action of the force F the velocity changes from v_1 when $t = t_1$ to v_2 when $t = t_2$. Then

$$\int_{t_1}^{t_2} F \, dt = \int_{v_1}^{v_2} m \, dv = [mv]_{v_1}^{v_2} = mv_2 - mv_1.$$

The last expression is the increase in the momentum of the object on which the force acts. So the impulse–momentum principle (M2 Section 7.1) still holds when the force varies over time, but with the impulse defined as $\int_{t_1}^{t_2} F \, dt$ instead of $F(t_2 - t_1)$.

In a similar way, Newton's second law in the form $F = mv\dfrac{dv}{dx}$ leads to

$$\int_{x_1}^{x_2} F \, dx = \int_{x_1}^{x_2} mv \, \frac{dv}{dx} \, dx = \int_{v_1}^{v_2} mv \, dv = [\tfrac{1}{2}mv^2]_{v_1}^{v_2} = \tfrac{1}{2}mv_2^2 - \tfrac{1}{2}mv_1^2.$$

The last expression is the gain in the kinetic energy of the object as it moves from $x = x_1$ to $x = x_2$, so $\int_{x_1}^{x_2} F \, dx$ is the work done by the force.

> If an object modelled as a particle moving in a straight line changes its position from x_1 at time t_1 to x_2 at time t_2 under the action of a force F, the impulse of the force is $\int_{t_1}^{t_2} F \, dt$, and the work done by the force is $\int_{x_1}^{x_2} F \, dx$.

Exercise 1B

1 For the following equations and intervals, express v in terms of t. Hence find equations connecting v with x. Draw sketches of the (t, x), (t, v) and (x, v) graphs.

    (a) $x = 4t^2 + t$ for $0 \leqslant t \leqslant 2$ (b) $x = 3 \sin 2t$ for $0 \leqslant t \leqslant 2\pi$

    (c) $x = 5e^{-2t}$ for $0 \leqslant t \leqslant \ln 2$ (d) $x = \dfrac{1}{t + 1}$ for $0 \leqslant t \leqslant 4$

2 A particle is at the origin at time $t = 0$, and its velocity is given by the following equations. Find equations connecting x with t, and v with x, and find expressions for the acceleration

    (i) in terms of x,   (ii) in terms of v.

    (a) $v = \sec^2 t$ for $0 \leqslant t \leqslant \tfrac{1}{2}\pi$ (b) $v = e^{\frac{1}{4}t}$ for $t \geqslant 0$

    (c) $v = \sin \tfrac{1}{2}t$ for $t \geqslant 0$ (d) $v = e^t + e^{-t}$ for $t \geqslant 0$

3 For the rollerblader in Exercise 1A Question 6, find an equation connecting v with x.

4 For the aircraft in Exercise 1A Question 7, use a direct method to find the distance travelled as the speed drops from $50 \, \text{m s}^{-1}$ to $10 \, \text{m s}^{-1}$.

5 For the car in Exercise 1A Question 10, use a direct method to find the distance travelled while the speed drops from $20 \, \text{m s}^{-1}$ to $5 \, \text{m s}^{-1}$.

6 For the tube train in Exercise 1A Question 12, use a direct method to find the distance travelled in reaching a speed of $10\,\mathrm{m\,s^{-1}}$ from rest.

7 A motorcycle with its rider has mass 300 kg. The power of the engine is 5 kW, and the air resistance is given by $0.5v^2$ newtons when the speed is $v\,\mathrm{m\,s^{-1}}$. Find how far it travels in increasing its speed from $5\,\mathrm{m\,s^{-1}}$ to $15\,\mathrm{m\,s^{-1}}$.

8 For the airliner in Exercise 1A Question 11, find the distance travelled in reaching the take-off speed of $80\,\mathrm{m\,s^{-1}}$ from rest.

9 On joining a motorway a car of mass 1800 kg accelerates from $10\,\mathrm{m\,s^{-1}}$ to $30\,\mathrm{m\,s^{-1}}$. The engine produces a constant driving force of 4000 newtons, and the resistance to motion at a speed of $v\,\mathrm{m\,s^{-1}}$ is $0.9v^2$ newtons. Find how far the car travels while accelerating.

10 A car of mass 4000 kg, trying to beat the land speed record, reaches a speed of $300\,\mathrm{m\,s^{-1}}$. In order to slow down from this speed, the driver first deploys a small parachute, which produces a resistance of $2v^2$ newtons at a speed of $v\,\mathrm{m\,s^{-1}}$. When the speed has dropped to $100\,\mathrm{m\,s^{-1}}$, mechanical brakes are applied which increase the retarding force by a further 8000 newtons. What is the total distance required to bring the car to a complete stop?

11 The (x, v) equation for a particle is $v = 10 - 0.1x^2$ for $0 < x < 10$. Find the (t, x) equation, given that $x = 0$ when $t = 0$. Check your answer by finding an expression for v both as $\dfrac{\mathrm{d}x}{\mathrm{d}t}$ and as $10 - 0.1x^2$.

12 The (x, v) equation for a particle is $v = \sqrt{p + qx}$. Show that the acceleration is constant. Find the (t, x) equation, given that $x = 0$ when $t = 0$, and express it in as simple a form as possible.

By making suitable substitutions for p and q, identify your equations with the standard equations for motion with constant acceleration.

13 If $x = c\sin(nt + \varepsilon)$, where c, n and ε are constants, obtain the (x, v) equation and express the acceleration in terms of x. Draw sketches of the (t, x), (t, v) and (x, v) graphs.

14* When a golf ball is hit, the ball is in contact with the club for 0.02 seconds, and over that time the force is modelled by the equation $F = kt(0.02 - t)$ newtons, where $k = 1.2 \times 10^6$. Calculate the impulse given to the ball.

15* As part of the development trials of a new railcar, a prototype is set in motion by means of a rocket which burns for 6 seconds. The force provided by the rocket t seconds after the start of the burn is given by $500t^2(6 - t)$ newtons. Calculate the momentum imparted to the railcar.

16 A piston is used to compress the air in a cylinder 0.2 metres long. When the piston has moved x metres, the force opposing it is $\dfrac{10}{0.2 - x}$ newtons. Calculate the work done in moving the piston a distance of 0.18 metres.

17 A girl sets a gyroscope spinning by means of a thread 80 cm long. When she has pulled it through x cm, she is exerting a force of $(20 + \frac{1}{4}x)$ newtons. Find the kinetic energy of the gyroscope when the whole thread has been pulled through.

1.6   Vertical motion with air resistance

You have now done enough about linear motion to follow the rest of the M3 course, so if you like you can now go on to the next chapter and return to this section as revision later on.

A particular application of the methods described in Sections 1.1 to 1.4 is to objects moving vertically under gravity and opposed by air resistance depending on the speed. The basic ideas were explained in M1 Section 6.3, but at that stage it was only possible to give a descriptive treatment. Now you can find equations which fit each of the most commonly used models. These models are that the resistance is proportional to the square of the speed, and that it is proportional to the speed.

In this section these models are applied to the problem discussed in M1 Example 6.2.3 without air resistance.

Example 1.6.1

A cannonball is projected vertically upwards from a mortar with an initial speed of $49 \, \mathrm{m \, s^{-1}}$. The mortar is situated at the edge of a cliff 180 metres above the sea. On the way down, the cannonball just misses the cliff. In vertical fall the cannonball would have a terminal speed of $70 \, \mathrm{m \, s^{-1}}$. Assuming that air resistance is proportional to the square of the speed, find how high the cannonball rises and how long it is in the air before falling into the sea.

Suppose that the mass of the cannonball is $M \, \mathrm{kg}$, and that the air resistance at speed $v \, \mathrm{m \, s^{-1}}$ is kv^2 newtons. The constant k can be found from the terminal speed; at this speed the weight of the cannonball is equal to the resistance, so

$$9.8M = k \times 70^2, \quad \text{which gives} \quad k = 0.002M.$$

The resistance $0.002Mv^2$ is always positive or zero. So because it acts downwards when the cannonball is going up, and upwards when it is going down, the problem must be split into two stages: the motion upwards to the highest point, and the drop from the highest point into the sea.

Upward stage   While the cannonball is on the way up, it is opposed by both the weight and the resistance. Newton's second law then gives

$$-9.8M - 0.002Mv^2 = Ma,$$

where $a \, \mathrm{m \, s^{-2}}$ is the acceleration and upwards is taken as the positive direction.

Therefore

$$a = -0.002(4900 + v^2).$$

To find the height, you want an equation connecting velocity and displacement, so write a as $v\dfrac{dv}{dx}$. Then

$$v\frac{dv}{dx} = -0.002(4900 + v^2),$$

which can be rearranged as

$$\frac{\mathrm{d}x}{\mathrm{d}v} = -\frac{500v}{4900 + v^2}.$$

Initially v is 49, and at maximum height this has dropped to zero. So the total height is given by the definite integral

$$\int_{49}^{0} -\frac{500v}{4900 + v^2} \, \mathrm{d}v.$$

The minus sign in the integrand can be used to reverse the order of the limits of integration, and the integral can then be calculated as

$$\int_{0}^{49} \frac{500v}{4900 + v^2} \, \mathrm{d}v = \left[250\ln(4900 + v^2)\right]_{0}^{49} = 250\left(\ln 7301 - \ln 4900\right)$$

$$= 250\ln\left(\tfrac{7301}{4900}\right) = 250\ln 1.49 = 99.69\ldots.$$

You also need to find how long the cannonball takes to reach its highest point. To do this, write a as $\dfrac{\mathrm{d}v}{\mathrm{d}t}$, so

$$\frac{\mathrm{d}v}{\mathrm{d}t} = -0.002(4900 + v^2),$$

which can be rearranged as

$$\frac{\mathrm{d}t}{\mathrm{d}v} = -\frac{500}{4900 + v^2}.$$

The time up to the highest point is therefore given by

$$\int_{49}^{0} -\frac{500}{4900 + v^2} \, \mathrm{d}v, \quad \text{which is} \quad \int_{0}^{49} \frac{500}{4900 + v^2} \, \mathrm{d}v.$$

You can evaluate this integral by using the substitution $v = 70\tan\theta$ (see C4 Chapter 2). Then $\dfrac{\mathrm{d}v}{\mathrm{d}\theta} = 70\sec^2\theta$, so

$$\int_{0}^{49} \frac{500}{4900 + v^2} \, \mathrm{d}v = \int_{0}^{\tan^{-1}0.7} \frac{500}{4900 + 4900\tan^2\theta} \times 70\sec^2\theta \, \mathrm{d}\theta$$

$$= \int_{0}^{\tan^{-1}0.7} \frac{500}{4900\sec^2\theta} \times 70\sec^2\theta \, \mathrm{d}\theta$$

$$= \int_{0}^{\tan^{-1}0.7} \frac{50}{7} \, \mathrm{d}\theta = \tfrac{50}{7}\tan^{-1}0.7 = 4.362\ldots.$$

Downward stage When the cannonball starts to come down, the direction of the resistance is reversed, and new equations are needed. It is also best to choose the positive direction to be downwards, and to measure x and t from the instant when the cannonball is at its highest point. The equations then become

$$\frac{\mathrm{d}x}{\mathrm{d}v} = \frac{500v}{4900 - v^2} \quad \text{and} \quad \frac{\mathrm{d}t}{\mathrm{d}v} = \frac{500}{4900 - v^2},$$

with $x = 0$ and $v = 0$ when $t = 0$.

You now know that the cannonball has to fall a distance $(99.69... + 180)$ metres into the sea, and you want to know the time this takes. That is, you want the value of t when $x = 279.69...$. So it seems best to begin by using the equation which involves t. Splitting the right side into partial fractions gives

$$\frac{dt}{dv} = \frac{25}{7} \left(\frac{1}{70+v} + \frac{1}{70-v} \right),$$

which can be integrated as

$$t = \tfrac{25}{7}(\ln(70+v) - \ln(70-v)) + k = \tfrac{25}{7} \ln \frac{70+v}{70-v} + k.$$

Since $v = 0$ when $t = 0$, $0 = \tfrac{25}{7} \ln 1 + k = 0 + k$. So $k = 0$, and

$$t = \tfrac{25}{7} \ln \frac{70+v}{70-v}.$$

This is halfway to the answer, but to find the (t, x) equation you have to write v as $\dfrac{dx}{dt}$ and integrate a second time. First, put the equation into exponential form as

$$\frac{70+v}{70-v} = e^{0.28t},$$

and then rearrange this to get

$$\frac{dx}{dt} = v = 70 \frac{e^{0.28t} - 1}{e^{0.28t} + 1}.$$

At this point you may hit a snag. Further progress depends on being able to integrate the right side of this equation, which requires a small trick. In case you can't spot this, it is useful to have an alternative method up your sleeve. So here are two ways of finishing off the problem.

Method 1   The clue you need is to divide top and bottom of the fraction on the right side by $e^{0.14t}$, so the equation becomes

$$\frac{dx}{dt} = 70 \frac{e^{0.14t} - e^{-0.14t}}{e^{0.14t} + e^{-0.14t}}.$$

You now have a fraction in which the numerator is almost (apart from a constant factor) the derivative of the denominator, and it isn't hard to see that

$$x = \frac{70}{0.14} \ln(e^{0.14t} + e^{-0.14t}) + k.$$

Since $x = 0$ when $t = 0$, $0 = 500 \ln 2 + k$, so $k = -500 \ln 2$.

Therefore $x = 500 \ln \left(\tfrac{1}{2}(e^{0.14t} + e^{-0.14t}) \right)$.

If you have met hyperbolic functions in FP2 Chapter 4, you will recognise this equation as $x = 500 \ln (\cosh 0.14t)$. The solution can then be completed by writing $0.14t = \cosh^{-1}(e^{\frac{279.69...}{500}})$.

All that remains is to solve this equation for t when $x = 279.69...$. So put the equation into exponential form as

$$e^{0.14t} + e^{-0.14t} = 2e^{\frac{279.69...}{500}} = 3.499...,$$

and notice that if you multiply this by $e^{0.14t}$ you get a quadratic equation with $e^{0.14t}$ as the unknown:

$$(e^{0.14t})^2 - 3.499...e^{0.14t} + 1 = 0.$$

The solution of this is $e^{0.14t} = 3.185...$ or $0.313...$, giving

$$t = \frac{\ln 3.185...}{0.14} = 8.275...   \text{or}   t = \frac{\ln 0.313...}{0.14} = -8.275....$$

Since t must be positive, the required value of t is $8.275...$.

Method 2   Instead of trying to connect t and x directly, this method links the two variables by finding the speed when the cannonball enters the sea. To do this, go back to the (x, v) equation

$$\frac{dx}{dv} = \frac{500v}{4900 - v^2},$$

which can be integrated directly as

$$x = -250\ln(4900 - v^2) + k.$$

Since $v = 0$ when $x = 0$, $0 = -250\ln 4900 + k$. So $k = 250\ln 4900$, and

$$x = -250\ln(4900 - v^2) + 250\ln 4900 = -250\ln\left(1 - \tfrac{1}{4900}v^2\right).$$

This can be rearranged to give

$$1 - \tfrac{1}{4900}v^2 = e^{-0.004x},   \text{so}   v = 70\sqrt{1 - e^{-0.004x}}.$$

You can now calculate that, when $x = 279.69...$, $v = 57.439...$. This value of v can then be substituted in the equation for t found above, to give

$$t = \tfrac{25}{7}\ln\frac{70 + v}{70 - v} = \tfrac{25}{7}\ln\frac{70 + 57.439...}{70 - 57.439...} = 8.275....$$

Whichever method you use, this value of t now has to be added to the time found earlier for the upward stage to give a total time of $(4.362... + 8.275...)$ seconds, which is $12.637...$ seconds.

So, with this model, the cannonball rises to a height of 99.7 metres and then falls into the sea after being in the air for 12.6 seconds.

Example 1.6.2

A cannonball is projected vertically upwards from a mortar with an initial speed of $49\,\mathrm{m\,s^{-1}}$. The mortar is situated at the edge of a cliff 180 metres above the sea. On the way down, the cannonball just misses the cliff. In vertical fall the cannonball would have a terminal speed of $70\,\mathrm{m\,s^{-1}}$. Assuming that air resistance is proportional to the speed, find how high the cannonball rises and how long it is in the air before falling into the sea.

If the air resistance at speed $v \,\mathrm{m\,s^{-1}}$ is kv newtons, equating the weight to the resistance at terminal speed gives

$$9.8v = k \times 70, \quad \text{so} \quad k = 0.14M.$$

For the upward stage, Newton's second law then gives

$$-9.8M - 0.14Mv = Ma, \quad \text{so} \quad a = -9.8 - 0.14v.$$

What about the downward stage? As in Example 1.6.1, the direction of the resistance is reversed when the cannonball starts to fall. But, if a, v, x and t keep the same meaning as they had for the upward stage, the velocity v changes sign from positive to negative at the same instant. So the equation for the acceleration for the downward stage becomes

$$a = -9.8 + 0.14 \,|v|, \quad \text{where} \quad v = -|v|;$$

that is,

$$a = -9.8 - 0.14v,$$

the same equation as for the upward stage.

What this shows is that, if the air resistance is proportional to the speed, you can use the same equation for the downward stage as for the upward stage, with all the variables having the same meaning for both stages.

It is now very easy to complete the solution. The differential equation

$$\frac{dv}{dt} = -0.14(70 + v)$$

can be rearranged as

$$\frac{dt}{dv} = -\tfrac{50}{7} \times \frac{1}{70 + v}, \quad \text{which integrates as} \quad t = -\tfrac{50}{7}\ln(70 + v) + k.$$

You know that $v = 49$ when $t = 0$, so $0 = -\tfrac{50}{7}\ln 119 + k$. Therefore

$$t = -\tfrac{50}{7}\ln\frac{70 + v}{119}.$$

In exponential form, this is

$$v = 119\mathrm{e}^{-0.14t} - 70.$$

Writing v as $\dfrac{dx}{dt}$, a second integration gives

$$x = -850\mathrm{e}^{-0.14t} - 70t + c.$$

Since $x = 0$ when $t = 0$, $c = 850$, so

$$x = -850\mathrm{e}^{-0.14t} + 850 - 70t.$$

These equations can now be used to find the greatest height and the time that the cannonball is in the air. The greatest height is reached when $v = 0$, that is when

$$e^{-0.14t} = \tfrac{10}{17}, \quad \text{or} \quad t = \frac{\ln 1.7}{0.14}.$$

Then $x = -850 \times \tfrac{10}{17} + 850 - 500\ln 1.7 = 84.68...$.

The cannonball enters the sea when $x = -180$, which leads to the equation

$$850e^{-0.14t} + 70t = 1030.$$

This can't be solved exactly, but you can use an approximate numerical method (see C3 Chapter 8) to find that the solution is 12.6 correct to 3 significant figures.

So, with this model, the cannonball rises to a height of 84.7 metres and falls into the sea after being in the air for 12.6 seconds.

It is interesting to notice that, although the values found for the maximum height are very different for the two models and for the calculation which ignores the resistance entirely (99.7 metres and 84.7 metres, compared with 122.5 metres), those for the total time are very close (12.6 seconds in both these examples, compared with 12.9 seconds if resistance is ignored).

Exercise 1C

1 A rock of mass 10 kg falls over a cliff and drops vertically on to a field 200 metres below. The air resistance is given by $0.0392v^2$ newtons when the speed is $v\,\mathrm{m\,s}^{-1}$. Find

   (a) the terminal speed for a fall of indefinite distance,

   (b) the speed with which the rock hits the field,

   (c) the time that the rock takes to fall.

2 A bullet of mass 50 grams is fired vertically into the air with a speed of $600\,\mathrm{m\,s}^{-1}$. At a speed of $v\,\mathrm{m\,s}^{-1}$ it experiences air resistance of kv^2 newtons, where $k = 4.9 \times 10^{-5}$. Find

   (a) how high the bullet rises,

   (b) the speed of the bullet at half this height,

   (c) the time taken by the bullet to reach its maximum height.

3* A stone of mass 100 grams will fall with terminal speed $35\,\mathrm{m\,s}^{-1}$. A boy catapults the stone vertically upwards with a speed of $25\,\mathrm{m\,s}^{-1}$. Assuming that the resistance to motion is proportional to the speed, find

   (a) how high the stone rises,

   (b) how fast the stone is moving just before it hits the ground,

   (c) how long it takes for the stone to return to ground level.

4* Repeat Question 3 if the air resistance is proportional to the square of the speed.

Miscellaneous exercise 1

1   A particle P of mass $0.4\,\text{kg}$ is initially at rest at a point O on a horizontal surface. In a simple model it is assumed that the surface is smooth. A horizontal force of magnitude $2t$ newtons is applied to P, where t seconds is the time after the force first begins to act. Given that the force is always directed away from O and that P moves in a straight line, calculate the speed of P when $t = 3$.

A more realistic model takes account of friction. State the effect of this on the initial behaviour of P. (OCR)

2   A cyclist and her bicycle have a total mass of $60\,\text{kg}$. The cyclist rides her bicycle up a straight slope inclined at $7°$ to the horizontal, starting from rest. At time t seconds after starting, she is moving with velocity $v\,\text{m\,s}^{-1}$ up a line of greatest slope. In a mathematical model for the motion, the cyclist creates a force of magnitude $150e^{-\frac{1}{30}t}$ newtons in the direction of motion, and all resisting forces are ignored. The cyclist with her bicycle is treated as a particle.

(a) Show that $\dfrac{dv}{dt} = \frac{5}{2}e^{-\frac{1}{30}t} - 1.2$, approximately.

(b) Find v, correct to 2 significant figures, when $t = 12$.

Explain how the mathematical model corresponds to the fact that the cyclist tires as she rides up the slope. (OCR)

3   A particle of mass $2\,\text{kg}$ is acted on by a single force of magnitude $8x$ newtons, where x metres is its displacement from a fixed point O. The force is directed away from O. The particle is at rest when it is 2 metres from O.

(a) Show that $v\dfrac{dv}{dx} = 4x$, where $v\,\text{m\,s}^{-1}$ is the velocity of the particle when its displacement is x metres.

(b) Find v in terms of x. (OCR)

4   A particle of mass $0.5\,\text{kg}$ moves on the positive x-axis under the action of a variable force of magnitude $\dfrac{4}{x^3}$ newtons, where x metres is the distance of the particle from O. The force is directed towards O. The particle is released from rest at a point A, where $OA = 8$ metres. The speed of the particle is denoted by $v\,\text{m\,s}^{-1}$. Show that $v^2 = \dfrac{64 - x^2}{8x^2}$. (OCR)

5   An object of mass $1\,\text{kg}$ falls vertically from rest. A resisting force of magnitude $2v$ newtons acts on the object during its descent, where $v\,\text{m\,s}^{-1}$ is the speed of the object at time t seconds after it begins to fall. The object is modelled as a particle. Show that $v = 4.9(1 - e^{-2t})$. Calculate the increase in speed of the object during the fifth second of its descent.

Sketch the (t, v) graph for the motion of the object, showing clearly the behaviour of v as t becomes large. (OCR)

6 A skier S of mass 60 kg moves down a straight line of greatest slope, which is inclined at 30° to the horizontal, on a snow-covered mountain. She starts from rest at a point O. At time t seconds after starting, her displacement from O is x metres down the slope. For $0 \leqslant x \leqslant 20$, the resisting force due to the snow has magnitude kx newtons. The acceleration of the skier is zero when she is 20 metres from O. In a model for the skier's motion, air resistance on the skier is ignored. Find the value of k.

Show that, for $0 \leqslant x \leqslant 20$, the acceleration of the skier is $4.9\left(1 - \frac{1}{20}x\right) \mathrm{m\,s^{-2}}$. Hence find the speed of the skier when $x = 20$.

In a refined model for the skier's motion, air resistance is included and the acceleration of the skier is still zero when she is 20 metres from O. State, without further calculation, what effect this would have on the value of k. (OCR)

7 A ball-bearing is at rest at a point O on the horizontal base of a large tank containing oil. The ball-bearing is projected horizontally from O, and after t seconds its velocity is $v \mathrm{\,m\,s^{-1}}$. It may be assumed that the resistance to motion is proportional to v. Given that $v = 4$ when $t = 0$ and that $v = 2$ when $t = 1$, show that $v = 4\mathrm{e}^{-t\ln 2}$.

Find the displacement, x metres, of the ball-bearing from O in terms of t and show that it can be written as $x = \dfrac{4}{\ln 2}(1 - 2^{-t})$. Find the time when the displacement from O is 1 m.

Comment on the value of x when t is large. (OCR)

8 A car of mass 800 kg is moving along a straight horizontal road. The engine of the car is working at a constant power of 20 kW. The frictional resistance to motion has magnitude 500 newtons. After t seconds the speed of the car is $v \mathrm{\,m\,s^{-1}}$. Show that $8\dfrac{\mathrm{d}v}{\mathrm{d}t} = \dfrac{5(40 - v)}{v}$.

Show that this differential equation may be written in the form $\dfrac{\mathrm{d}t}{\mathrm{d}v} = \dfrac{64}{40 - v} - \dfrac{8}{5}$, and find, to the nearest 0.1 seconds, the time taken for the speed of the car to increase from $10 \mathrm{\,m\,s^{-1}}$ to $15 \mathrm{\,m\,s^{-1}}$. (OCR, adapted)

9 A car of mass 1200 kg is travelling on a straight horizontal road, with its engine working at a constant rate of 25 kW. Given that the resistance to motion of the car is proportional to the square of its velocity and that the greatest constant speed the car can maintain is $50 \mathrm{\,m\,s^{-1}}$, show that $125\,000 - v^3 = 6000v^2 \dfrac{\mathrm{d}v}{\mathrm{d}x}$, where $v \mathrm{\,m\,s^{-1}}$ is the velocity of the car when its displacement from a fixed point on the road is x metres. Hence find the distance covered by the car in increasing its speed from $30 \mathrm{\,m\,s^{-1}}$ to $45 \mathrm{\,m\,s^{-1}}$, giving your answer to the nearest metre. (OCR)

10 A 120 tonne locomotive is working at constant power 1000 kW on a level track. When it is moving at speed $v \mathrm{\,m\,s^{-1}}$, the air resistance is kv^2 newtons. The maximum speed of the locomotive is $30 \mathrm{\,m\,s^{-1}}$. Show that $k = \frac{1000}{27}$.

By writing down the equation of motion, show that $3240v\dfrac{\mathrm{d}v}{\mathrm{d}t} = 27\,000 - v^3$. Show that the time T seconds taken by the locomotive to increase its speed from $10 \mathrm{\,m\,s^{-1}}$ to $20 \mathrm{\,m\,s^{-1}}$ is

$$T = 3240 \int_{10}^{20} \frac{v}{27\,000 - v^3}\,\mathrm{d}v.$$ Use an approximate method to obtain a 1 decimal place approximation to T. (OCR, adapted)

11* A train of mass 3000 tonnes starts from rest on a horizontal track. The driving force is 200 kN and the total resistance to motion is $4v$ kN when the speed is $v\,\mathrm{m\,s^{-1}}$. The driving force is constant until the power of the train reaches 2500 kW, after which point the power remains constant. Write down the speed of the train at the instant when the power reaches 2500 kW, and show that the time, t_1 seconds, taken to reach this speed is $t_1 = 750 \ln \frac{4}{3}$.

Show that, for $t > t_1$, v satisfies the differential equation $750\dfrac{\mathrm{d}v}{\mathrm{d}t} = \dfrac{625}{v} - v$. Solve this differential equation to show that, for $t > t_1$, $v = 25\left(1 - \frac{4}{3}\mathrm{e}^{-\frac{1}{375}t}\right)^{\frac{1}{2}}$.   (OCR)

12* A parachutist jumps from a helicopter which is hovering at a height of several hundred metres, and falls vertically. The air resistance is proportional to his speed. Assume that, before the parachute is opened, the terminal velocity is $50\,\mathrm{m\,s^{-1}}$. Assume also that, after the parachute is opened, the terminal velocity is $10\,\mathrm{m\,s^{-1}}$. The parachutist opens the parachute 10 seconds after jumping.

(a) For the parachutist's motion before the parachute opens, express the velocity in terms of the time, and hence show that the parachutist is falling at approximately $43\,\mathrm{m\,s^{-1}}$ just before the parachute opens.

(b) Assuming that the time taken for the parachute to open fully is negligible, find the parachutist's speed 2 seconds after the parachute opens.

(c) Sketch the (t, v) graph for the parachutist's descent.   (OCR)

13* Particles of mass 1.5 kg and 0.5 kg are attached to the ends of a light inextensible string which passes over a fixed smooth peg. The system is released from rest in a position where both parts of the string hanging from the peg are vertical. Assume that there is a resisting force on each particle due to its motion through the air and that the magnitude of this force is $\frac{1}{40}v^2$ newtons, where $v\,\mathrm{m\,s^{-1}}$ is the speed of the particle when it has moved a distance x metres from its original position. Show that $40v\dfrac{\mathrm{d}v}{\mathrm{d}x} = 196 - v^2$, and find v in terms of x.

Show that the tension T newtons in the string is given by $T = 9.8\left(1 - \frac{1}{4}\mathrm{e}^{-0.05x}\right)$.

(OCR, adapted)

2 Elastic strings and springs

This chapter introduces a model to describe the behaviour of strings and springs whose length depends on the force applied to them. When you have completed it, you should

- be able to use Hooke's law as a model relating to the extension of a string, or to the extension and compression of a spring
- understand the terms 'stiffness' and 'modulus of elasticity'
- be able to derive and use the formula for the work done in stretching a string, or in stretching and compressing a spring
- understand that elastic forces are conservative, and know how to include elastic potential energy in energy calculations.

2.1 The elastic string model

So far, when dealing with mechanical systems which include strings, ropes, chains or cables, there has been no suggestion that these might stretch when pulled. In fact, in M1 Section 7.3, the model of an 'inextensible' cable was introduced, with the property that the two trucks connected by the cable move with the same speed and acceleration.

This is a very good approximation to reality in many cases, but every cable will stretch a bit when its ends are pulled apart, and some materials are made intentionally so that they stretch a lot. This doesn't just apply to substances called 'elastic', but also for example to the synthetic materials used in making ropes for rock climbers and bungee jumpers.

How does the force pulling the ends apart affect the length of a piece of elastic? You already have enough experience to know some basic facts.

- The harder you pull, the greater the length.
- If you don't pull excessively hard, the same pull will produce the same stretch each time you apply it, and the elastic will revert to its original length when you stop pulling.
- If you pull too hard, the material will be permanently distorted and lose its elastic property.

These observations now have to be converted into a mathematical model.

A few definitions are needed. The original length is called the **natural length**, usually denoted by l. The amount by which the length exceeds the natural length is the **extension**. Also, the force pulling the ends is equal to the tension. Denoting the extension by x and the tension by T, the first two points are equivalent to stating that

$T = f(x)$, where f is an increasing function and $f(0) = 0$.

The third point states that this rule only holds so long as T, and therefore x, is not too large. That is, for any piece of elastic there is a length b such that the rule holds provided that $0 \leqslant x \leqslant b$.

To find the form of the function f, and the value of *b*, you need to do precise experiments.

For materials which stretch easily, the simplest method is to fix one end, to hang weights of various magnitudes from the other end, and to measure the corresponding lengths, as in Fig. 2.1. For tougher materials more elaborate testing machinery is needed, but the principle is the same.

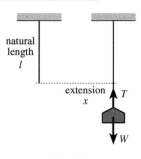

Fig. 2.1

These experiments show that, for a wide variety of materials, the results fit pretty well a model of the form $T = kx$ for some constant *k*. The value of *k*, called the 'stiffness' or the 'elastic constant', is small for materials which stretch easily, and much larger for materials which seem to be almost inextensible.

This model is known as Hooke's law. It is named after Robert Hooke, a brilliant inventor and physical scientist who lived at about the same time as Isaac Newton.

Hooke's law
If forces are applied at the ends of a string, rope, chain or cable, then over some range of values the tension is proportional to the extension beyond the natural length.

But there is a drawback in using the equation $T = kx$ to describe this law. If you take two pieces of elastic, one twice as long as the other but otherwise identical, then the value of *k* would be half as big for the longer piece. This is because, if the same forces are applied to both, the value of *T* is the same; but the longer piece, which you can think of as two of the shorter pieces joined together, will stretch twice as much. Generalising this argument, you can say that *k* is inversely proportional to the natural length. That is, $k = \dfrac{\lambda}{l}$, where λ has the same value whatever the length. This gives the usual form in which Hooke's law is used:

For an elastic string of natural length *l*, the tension *T* and extension *x* are connected by the equation $T = \dfrac{\lambda x}{l}$. The constant λ is called the **modulus of elasticity** of the string.

Notice that, if $x = l$, then $T = \lambda$. In this case the total length of the string is $l + l = 2l$. So a physical interpretation is that the constant λ is the force that has to be applied to the ends of the string to double its length. This shows too that the modulus of elasticity can be interpreted as a force, so it is measured in the same units as force, that is in newtons.

Example 2.1.1
A climber of mass 70 kg hangs from a rope secured at its upper end by a belay. The natural length of the rope is 20 metres, and it stretches to 22 metres when supporting the climber. What is the modulus of elasticity of the rope?

The tension in the rope is 70×9.8 newtons, and the extension of the rope is 2 metres. Substitution in the equation $T = \dfrac{\lambda x}{l}$ gives

$$70 \times 9.8 = \frac{2\lambda}{20}, \quad \text{so} \quad \lambda = 6860.$$

The modulus of elasticity of the rope is 6860 newtons.

Example 2.1.2

A spider of mass 2 grams hangs from a thread which it is spinning. This has length 8 cm. A typical piece of the web has modulus of elasticity 0.05 newtons. What is the natural length of the thread from which the spider is hanging?

It is safest to convert all the data to basic SI units. Let the natural length of the thread be l metres, and let the extension be x metres. Then

$$0.002 \times 9.8 = \frac{0.05x}{l}, \quad \text{and} \quad l + x = 0.08.$$

From the first equation,

$$x = \frac{0.002 \times 9.8 l}{0.05} = 0.392 l.$$

So

$$l + 0.392 l = 0.08, \quad \text{which gives} \quad l = \frac{0.08}{1.392} = 0.0575.$$

Converting back to more suitable units, the natural length of the thread is 5.75 cm.

Example 2.1.3

A student uses a 40 cm length of curtain wire as a washing line. One end is attached to a hook H on the wall. When he has some laundry to dry, he stretches the wire so that the other end reaches another hook K at the same level 48 cm away. The tension in the wire is then 10 newtons. When the student hangs a wet shirt at the mid-point M of the wire, the wire stretches further so that M is 7 cm below the mid-point N of HK. How much does the wet shirt weigh? (The weight of the hangar is small and can be neglected.)

In metre units the natural length of the wire is 0.4 m, and when the extension is 0.08 m the tension is 10 newtons. From this you can calculate the modulus of elasticity, using the equation $10 = \dfrac{0.08\lambda}{0.4}$ which gives $\lambda = 50$ (in newtons).

Now since the modulus of elasticity is defined so that it is independent of the length of the wire, you can use this value of λ for each of the two parts of the wire, HM and MK in Fig. 2.2.

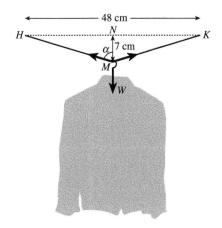

Fig. 2.2

By Pythagoras' theorem, each of these has length $\sqrt{24^2 + 7^2}\,\text{cm} = 25\,\text{cm}$. The natural length of each part is 0.2 m, so the extension is 0.05 m and the tension is $\dfrac{50 \times 0.05}{0.2}$ newtons, which is 12.5 newtons.

If the weight of the shirt is W newtons, and the angle NMH is α,

$$\mathcal{R}(\uparrow) \qquad 2 \times 12.5 \times \cos\alpha = W.$$

Since $\cos\alpha = \tfrac{7}{25}$, $\quad W = 7$.

The wet shirt weighs 7 newtons.

Example 2.1.4

Fig. 2.3 shows the design for an adjustable desk lamp in which the light bulb can rest in various positions. O is a point of the base, and a vertical column fixed at O has a small pulley P at the top. A rigid arm OL is hinged at O so that it can rotate in a vertical plane. A lamp is attached to the arm at L. An elastic cord passes round the palley; it has one end fixed at O and the other end fixed to the arm at L. The natural length of the cord is equal to the height of the column OP, so that the extension of the cord is equal to PL.

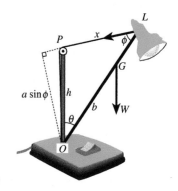

Fig. 2.3

The column OP has height h, and the arm OL has length a. The arm and the lamp together have weight W, and the centre of mass is at a point G of OL such that $OG = b$. The modulus of elasticity of the cord is λ. Show that, if a certain relation holds connecting λ, W, a and b, the arm OL can rest in equilibrium at any angle to the vertical.

Denote the angle POL by θ, the angle OLP by ϕ and the length PL by x. The tension in the cord is $\dfrac{\lambda x}{h}$, so for the arm OL to be in equilibrium,

$$\mathcal{M}(O) \qquad \frac{\lambda x}{h} \times a\sin\phi = W \times b\sin\theta.$$

This can be rearranged as

$$\frac{x}{\sin\theta} \times \lambda a = \frac{h}{\sin\phi} \times Wb.$$

But by the sine rule in triangle OLP, $\dfrac{x}{\sin\theta} = \dfrac{h}{\sin\phi}$.

So the arm will be in equilibrium if $\lambda a = Wb$.

This equation doesn't involve θ, so if it is satisfied the arm will be in equilibrium at any angle to the vertical. It is interesting to notice that the equation also doesn't involve h, so the column can be made of any convenient height provided that the cord is also cut to this natural length.

2.2 Springs and rods

You will find springs in many household objects, such as door catches, mattresses, lamp holders and clocks. They come in a variety of shapes, but this section is concerned only with 'helical springs', which are in the shape of a helix (see Fig. 2.4) and which expand and contract in a direction along the axis of the helix. (A helix is the path followed if you climb up the curved surface of a cylinder at a constant angle.)

Fig. 2.4

From the point of view of mechanics, the essential difference between springs and elastic strings is that springs can be used in either tension or compression. Where a spring is used only in tension, for example in a spring balance (see M1 Section 3.5), it would be possible to replace the spring by a length of stiff elastic. But this would not be true of springs such as those in a mattress, which are used only in compression. Some exercise devices contain springs which are used both in tension and compression.

Hooke's law also applies to springs, but with the difference that both T and x can be either positive or negative. When x is negative, the spring is compressed and it exerts a thrust outwards at each end. So the equation $T = kx$ can be applied for values of x in an interval $-c \leqslant x \leqslant b$, where b and c are positive constants. It is more common to express the strength of a spring in terms of the stiffness k (in units such as newtons per metre) rather than the modulus of elasticity, although the constant λ may still appear in more theoretical examples.

A metal rod can also exert forces of either tension or compression, and will expand or contract slightly according to Hooke's law, with a very large value of k.

Example 2.2.1
Fig. 2.5 shows the design of the bar in a toilet-roll holder, which fits between the two arms of a metal frame 134 mm wide. When out of the frame, the cylindrical part of the bar just fits between the two arms. The projections at the ends are 6 mm long, and they fit into cavities 2 mm deep in the frame. To compress the bar so as to get it out of the frame requires a force of 12 newtons. How much force does the bar exert on each arm when it is in place?

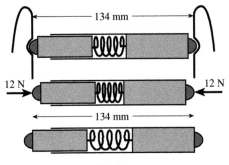

Fig. 2.5

To get the bar out of the frame its length must be reduced by 12 mm, the length of the two projections. This requires a force of 12 N, so the stiffness of the spring is 1 newton per millimetre.

When the bar is in place in the frame, there is a gap of 4 mm at each end, so the bar is compressed by 8 mm. The force exerted by the bar on each arm is therefore 8 newtons.

Notice that, since the spring is concealed inside the bar, its length isn't known. It is therefore impossible to determine the modulus of elasticity. But you only need to know the stiffness to answer the question.

Example 2.2.2

A uniform square platform of mass 60 kg is supported by identical vertical springs at each corner. Each spring has natural length 10 cm and modulus of elasticity 4900 N.

(a) Find the height of the underside of the platform above the ground.

(b) A person now stands on the platform at its centre, and the springs are compressed by a further 0.4 cm. Find the mass of the person.

(a) The weight of the platform is 60×9.8 N, and each spring bears one-quarter of this weight, which is 147 N. The natural length is 0.1 m. If the spring is then compressed by x metres, the thrust is $4900 \times \dfrac{x}{0.1}$. Therefore

$$4900 \times \frac{x}{0.1} = 147,$$

which gives $x = 0.003$. The underside of the platform is therefore $(0.1 - 0.003)$ m above the ground, that is 0.097 m, or 9.7 cm.

Since $\dfrac{x}{l}$ is a ratio of lengths, any unit of length could be used for x and l in the equation $T = \lambda \dfrac{x}{l}$. In this example the compression and the natural length could have been measured in centimetres rather then metres, giving the ratio as $\dfrac{0.3}{10}$ instead of $\dfrac{0.003}{0.1}$, but it is safer to stick to SI units.

(b) The total compression of each spring is now $(0.3 + 0.4)$ cm, which is 0.007 m. So the thrust in each spring is $4900 \times \dfrac{0.007}{0.1}$ N $= 343$ N. The thrust from the four springs therefore supports a weight of 4×343 N, which is 1372 N. So the total mass of the platform and the person is $\dfrac{1372}{9.8}$ kg $= 140$ kg. Since the mass of the platform is 60 kg, the mass of the person standing on it is 80 kg.

Example 2.2.3

Fig. 2.6 shows the design for a diving board. The board is uniform, 2 metres long and has mass 30 kg. It is hinged at one end, and is supported in a horizontal position by a spring of natural length 50 cm which is 1.4 metres from the hinge. When it is just supporting the weight of the board, the spring is compressed by 0.7 cm.

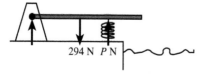

$294\text{ N } P\text{ N}$

Fig. 2.6

(a) Find the modulus of elasticity of the spring.

(b) A boy of mass 48 kg now stands at the pool end of the board. Modelling the board as rigid, find by how much his weight lowers the end of the board.

(a) Let the thrust from the spring be P newtons. The weight of the board is 30×9.8 newtons, which is 294 newtons.

$$\mathcal{M}(\text{hinge}) \quad P \times 1.4 = 294 \times 1,$$

so that $P = 210$.

This is the force from the spring on the board, so by Newton's third law the force from the board on the spring is 210 newtons downwards. Let the modulus of elasticity of the spring be λ newtons. Then, since the natural length is 0.5 metres and the spring is compressed by 0.007 metres,

$$210 = \frac{\lambda \times 0.007}{0.5}.$$

This gives $\lambda = \dfrac{210 \times 0.5}{0.007} = 15\,000.$

The modulus of elasticity of the spring is 15 000 newtons.

(b) The weight of the boy is 48×9.8 newtons, which is 470.4 newtons. If the spring is now compressed by x metres, the thrust in the spring is $\dfrac{15\,000 \times x}{0.5}$ newtons, which is $30\,000x$ newtons. The forces on the board are now as shown in Fig. 2.7.

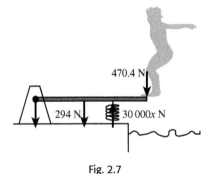

470.4 N

294 N   30 000x N

Fig. 2.7

$$\mathcal{M}(\text{hinge}) \quad 30\,000x \times 1.4 = 294 \times 1 + 470.4 \times 2,$$

so that $x = 0.0294$.

The compression of the spring is therefore 2.94 cm. Since it was previously 0.7 cm, the point of the board to which the spring is attached drops by 2.24 cm when the boy stands on the board. So the end of the board drops by $\dfrac{2}{1.4} \times 2.24$ cm, which is 3.2 cm.

Notice that the force from the hinge on the board changes direction when the boy stands at the other end.

Exercise 2A

1   A light elastic cord AB has natural length 0.4 metres and modulus of elasticity 200 newtons. The end A is attached to a hook. The end B is pulled with a horizontal force of magnitude 60 newtons. By how much is the cord stretched?

2   An elastic string of natural length 20 cm hangs from a hook in the ceiling. When an ornament of mass 0.5 kg is hung from the lower end of the string, the length increases to 24 cm. Calculate the modulus of elasticity.

3   A cable 20 metres long is being used to raise a container of mass 25 tonnes. After the cable has been pulled taut, the upper end has to move a further 1.6 cm before the container lifts clear of the ground. Calculate the modulus of elasticity of the cable.

4   A ring of mass 20 grams is lifted gently off a table at a steady speed by an elastic thread of natural length 25 cm and modulus of elasticity 7 newtons. What is the length of the thread while it is lifting the ring?

5   A crate of mass 50 kg stands on the floor of a warehouse. The ends of a light spring are attached to the top of the crate and to a beam 4.3 metres above it. The spring has natural length 4 metres and modulus of elasticity 5000 newtons. Find the normal contact force between the crate and the floor.

6   In a cafeteria a cylindrical container for plates stands on the floor. Its height is 0.8 metres. A spring of negligible mass and modulus of elasticity 420 newtons stands on the base of the container. With no plates in the container the top of the spring just reaches the top of the container. When a flat plate of thickness 0.7 cm is placed on top of the spring, its upper surface comes level with the top of the container. Find the mass of the plate.

Show that if several such plates are piled on top of the spring, the upper surface of the top plate will still come level with the top of the container.

7   Four children split into two teams for a tug-of-war. They use a rope 6 metres long with modulus of elasticity 10 000 newtons. The two back children are at the ends of the rope, and the front children are 1 metre in front of their team-mates. They start to pull, each with a force of 50 newtons. How much does the rope stretch

(a) between the two front children,

(b) between the two back children?

8   A box of weight 20 newtons is placed on a table. It is to be pulled along by an elastic string with natural length 15 cm and modulus of elasticity 5 newtons. The coefficient of friction between the box and the table is 0.4. Holding the string horizontally by its loose end, and beginning with the string just taut, how far would you have to pull before the box starts to move?

9   A mattress is 18 cm deep. When a 75 kg sleeper lies on it, 14 of the springs are compressed by an average of 0.7 cm. Calculate the force needed to compress each spring by 1 cm.

10 A new bulb with a bayonet fitting is to be inserted into a standard lamp. The mass of the bulb is 40 grams. To insert the bulb it is first placed in the holder so that it rests on the pins. It then has to be pushed down 6 mm against the pins and twisted; then, when it is released, it rises 2 mm and is held firm by the pins in the slots in the holder. The maximum force you need to exert during the process is 2 newtons. Find the force holding the bulb in position.

11 A uniform rod AB of weight W and length l is hinged to a wall at A and has a small ring at B. An elastic string of natural length l and modulus of elasticity λ has one end tied to the hinge at A, passes through the ring at B and is then attached to a point C on the wall at a distance c vertically above A. Show that the rod can rest horizontally in equilibrium provided that $\lambda c = \frac{1}{2}lW$.

12 An elastic string of natural length l and modulus of elasticity λ has its two ends attached to pegs a distance a apart. It is pulled aside by a force applied at the mid-point of the string at right angles to the line of the pegs. Find the force necessary to hold it in position when the two parts of the string and the line joining the pegs form an equilateral triangle.

13 An elastic band is made of material with modulus of elasticity 2 newtons. The natural length of the band is 12 cm, and a lucky mascot of weight 10 newtons hangs from it. The band is supported in two ways:

(a) from a single peg,

(b) stretched over two pegs at the same level 12 cm apart.

In each case, find how far the point of attachment of the mascot is below the peg(s) when it is in equilibrium.

14* The ends of an elastic string of natural length $2l$ and modulus λ are attached to two pegs a distance $4l$ apart. It is held firmly at its mid-point H, and this point is then moved along the line between the pegs. Find expressions for the force needed to hold it steady at a distance x from its original position

(a) when $x < l$,   (b) when $l < x < 3l$,   (c) when $x > 3l$.

Illustrate your answer with a graph.

15* Two elastic strings, each of natural length l and modulus of elasticity λ, are clamped together at their ends to form a single string of natural length l. What is its modulus of elasticity?

16* A point A of the ceiling is directly above a point B of the floor 2.5 metres below. A and B are joined by a light spring of natural length 2 metres; the tension in the spring is then 20 newtons. A lump of putty of weight 4 newtons is now attached to the spring at the point 1 metre above the floor. At what height above the floor will the putty rest in equilibrium?

2.3 Work done in stretching and compressing

When you stretch a piece of elastic, you are not just concerned to provide the force needed to hold it steady once it is stretched. You also have to stretch it to that length in the first place, and to do that you have to do work.

It was shown in Section 1.5 that, when a variable force F acts on an object, then the work done is $\int_{x_1}^{x_2} F \, dx$. Applying this when x is given by Hooke's law $F = kx$, the work done in stretching the string from its natural length to an extension of x_2 is

$$\int_0^{x_2} kx \, dx = \tfrac{1}{2}kx_2^2.$$

This is true for any extension x_2, so it is simpler to drop the suffix, and to say that the work done in giving a string an extension x is $\tfrac{1}{2}kx^2$. In terms of the modulus of elasticity, this is $\dfrac{\lambda x^2}{2l}$.

Another way of expressing this formula is as $\tfrac{1}{2}kx \times x$. Since kx is the tension when the string is stretched to extension x, this is $\tfrac{1}{2} \times$ final tension $\times$ extension. It sometimes happens that you know the tension and the extension, but have not calculated the stiffness, and this is then the simplest way of finding the work done.

The formula also holds when you compress a spring. Although F and x are then both negative, $\tfrac{1}{2}kx^2$ is positive. Whether you are stretching or compressing a spring, you have to do a positive amount of work.

> When a string is stretched, or a spring is stretched or compressed, starting at its natural length l, the work done in changing its length by an amount x is
>
> $$\tfrac{1}{2}kx^2 = \frac{\lambda x^2}{2l},$$
>
> where k is the stiffness and λ is the modulus of elasticity. This is $\tfrac{1}{2} \times$ final tension $\times$ extension, or $\tfrac{1}{2} \times$ final thrust $\times$ reduction in length.

Example 2.3.1

In Example 2.1.3, the student uses a 40 cm length of curtain wire as a washing line. One end is attached to a hook H on the wall. When he has some laundry to dry, he stretches the wire so that the other end reaches another hook K at the same level 48 cm away. The tension in the wire is then 10 newtons. How much work does he do in fixing the curtain wire to the second hook?

To get the answer in joules, it is important to begin by converting the lengths from centimetres to metres. It was shown in Example 2.1.3 that the modulus of elasticity is 50 newtons. The work can then can be calculated as

$$\frac{\lambda x^2}{2l} = \frac{50 \times 0.08^2}{2 \times 0.4} = 0.4,$$

or as $\tfrac{1}{2} \times$ final tension $\times$ extension $= \tfrac{1}{2} \times 10 \times 0.8 = 0.4$.

The work done in fixing the wire to the second hook is 0.4 joules.

2.4   Elastic potential energy

What have a bow-and-arrow and a watch in common? Both of them use the elastic properties of materials as a source of energy. An archer does work in flexing the bow, and the energy thus created is converted into the kinetic energy of the arrow. Winding up a watch stores energy in the mainspring, which is then used to operate the time-keeping mechanism.

The same principle holds when you stretch or compress a helical spring, or stretch an elastic string. Elastic forces, like gravity, are conservative. This means that the work you do in deforming the spring or string is not wasted, but stored up as 'elastic potential energy' for possible use later. The formulae in Section 2.3 can then be restated as follows:

> A string or spring, stretched or compressed by a distance x, possesses
> **elastic potential energy** of amount $\frac{1}{2}kx^2 = \frac{\lambda x^2}{2l}$.

When you have a mechanical system which includes elastic materials, elastic potential energy has to be included alongside kinetic energy and gravitational potential energy in the total energy equation. The conservation of energy principle (see M2 Chapter 3) then becomes:

> If no work is done by non-conservative forces, the total energy (kinetic and potential, both gravitational and elastic) remains constant.

Example 2.4.1

In a pop-gun a cork of mass 4 grams is shot out of the barrel by the release of a spring, which is compressed through a distance of 5 cm. A force of $6x$ newtons is needed to keep the spring compressed by x cm. Find the speed with which the cork leaves the barrel.

> Converting the data to basic SI units, the mass of the cork is 0.004 kg, the stiffness is $600\,\mathrm{N\,m^{-1}}$ and the compression of the spring is 0.05 m. The potential energy of the compressed spring is $\frac{1}{2} \times 600 \times 0.05^2\,\mathrm{J}$, and this is converted into kinetic energy of $\frac{1}{2} \times 0.004 \times v^2\,\mathrm{J}$, where $v\,\mathrm{m\,s^{-1}}$ is the speed of the cork. Assuming that the barrel is smooth, and that the gun is held still as it is fired, there are no other forces which do work. So
>
> $$0.75 = 0.002v^2,$$
>
> which gives
>
> $$v = 19.36...\,.$$

The cork leaves the barrel at a speed of $19.4\,\mathrm{m\,s^{-1}}$.

Example 2.4.2

A straight track PQ of length $5a$ is fixed with P at a height $3a$ above Q. A particle of mass m is attached to P by an elastic string of natural length $2a$ and modulus of elasticity $2mg$. The coefficient of friction between the particle and the track is $\frac{1}{2}$.

(a) How far down the track from P can the particle be placed to remain in equilibrium?

(b) If the particle is placed on the track at Q and released, will it reach P?

The angle α which the track makes with the horizontal has $\sin\alpha = \frac{3}{5}$ and $\cos\alpha = \frac{4}{5}$.

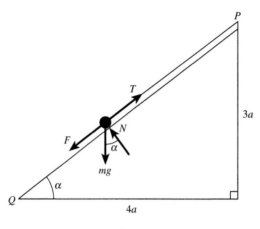

Fig. 2.8

(a) Fig. 2.8 shows the forces on the particle in equilibrium at the furthest possible distance from P. The frictional force F then acts down the track with its limiting value. If N is the normal contact force,

$\mathcal{R}(\perp$ to track$)$ $N = mg\cos\alpha.$

So $N = \frac{4}{5}mg$ and $F = \frac{1}{2}N = \frac{2}{5}mg.$

If the distance of the particle from P is x, the extension of the string is $x - 2a$. The tension T is therefore $\dfrac{2mg(x - 2a)}{2a} = \dfrac{mg}{a}(x - 2a)$. Since

$\mathcal{R}(\text{up the track})$ $T = mg\sin\alpha + F,$

$$\frac{mg}{a}(x - 2a) = \tfrac{3}{5}mg + \tfrac{2}{5}mg,$$

which gives $x = 2a + a = 3a.$

The greatest distance from P down the track at which the particle can remain in equilibrium is $3a$.

(b) If the particle is to reach P from Q it will need to gain gravitational potential energy of amount $mg \times 3a = 3mga$.

Also, while the particle is moving up the track, the frictional force will have the limiting value of $\frac{2}{5}mg$ calculated in part (a). In moving from Q to P work would be done against friction of amount $\frac{2}{5}mg \times 5a = 2mga$.

So to reach P, the total energy needed at Q is $3mga + 2mga = 5mga$.

When the particle is placed at Q the extension of the string is $3a$, so the elastic energy stored in the string is $\dfrac{2mg \times (3a)^2}{2 \times 2a} = \frac{9}{2}mga$, which is less than $5mga$. It follows that the particle will not reach P after it is released.

Example 2.4.3

One end of an elastic string, of natural length 1.5 metres and modulus of elasticity 49 newtons, is attached to a hook in the ceiling. A particle of mass 2 kg is attached at the other end, and hangs in equilibrium, as shown in Fig. 2.9. The particle is then pulled down a distance of b metres, and released. Find how high it rises

(a) if $b = 0.4$,   (b) if $b = 0.9$.

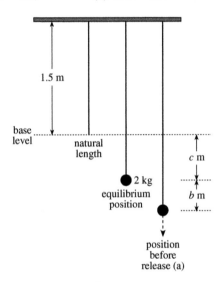

Fig. 2.9

If the extension of the string is c metres when the particle is in equilibrium, the tension in the string is equal to the weight, so

$$\mathcal{R}(\uparrow) \quad \frac{49c}{1.5} = 2 \times 9.8, \quad \text{which gives} \quad c = 0.6.$$

(a) If $b = 0.4$, the extension of the string is 1 metres when the particle is released. There is then no kinetic energy, so the total energy is the sum of the gravitational and the elastic potential energy.

You need to choose a base level from which to measure the gravitational energy, and a convenient choice is 1.5 metres below the hook, which is the level of the bottom of the string if there is no particle attached to it. Then the gravitational energy is $-2 \times 9.8 \times 1\,\text{J}$ and the elastic energy is $\dfrac{49 \times 1^2}{2 \times 1.5}\,\text{J}$.

Since there is a common factor of 49, the arithmetic is simpler using fractions; the total energy is then $49\left(-\frac{2}{5} + \frac{1}{3}\right)\text{J}$, which can be simplified to $-\frac{49}{15}\,\text{J}$.

Now there is a problem. It is not obvious whether, at the top of its path, the particle rises above the base level or not. You can settle this by thinking how much energy there would be at that level if the particle rises that far. There would be no gravitational energy, and also no elastic energy (because the string would be unstretched in that position). So the only possible energy is kinetic, which must be positive. But since you already know that the total energy is negative, that is impossible. It follows that the string is still stretched at the top of the path.

So let the extension be x metres where the particle comes to rest at its highest point. There is then no kinetic energy, and the total energy is made up of gravitational energy of $-2 \times 9.8 \times x$ J and elastic energy of $\dfrac{49 \times x^2}{2 \times 1.5}$ J, making a total of $49\left(-\frac{2}{5}x + \frac{1}{3}x^2\right)$ J.

Equating this to the energy when the particle is released,

$$-\tfrac{49}{15} = 49\left(-\tfrac{2}{5}x + \tfrac{1}{3}x^2\right).$$

This can be written as $5x^2 - 6x + 1 = 0$, which factorises as $(5x - 1)(x - 1) = 0$, so $x = 0.2$ or $x = 1$.

You may be surprised to get a quadratic equation with two roots, but of course $x = 1$ corresponds to the point where the particle was released, when there is also no kinetic energy. So the root required is $x = 0.2$.

The particle rises by $(1 - 0.2)$ metres, which is 0.8 metres.

(b) If $b = 0.9$, the extension is 1.5 metres, so the gravitational energy when the particle is released is $-2 \times 9.8 \times 1.5$ J, and the elastic energy is $\dfrac{49 \times 1.5^2}{2 \times 1.5}$ J. The total energy is therefore $49\left(-\frac{3}{5} + \frac{3}{4}\right)$ J, which can be simplified to $49 \times \frac{3}{20}$ J.

Because this is positive, the particle now still has positive energy at the base level where the string is unstretched; since both gravitational and elastic energy are zero at this level, this is kinetic energy. At the highest point therefore the string is unstretched, and there is no elastic energy. If the top of the path is y metres above the base level, the gravitational potential energy is $2 \times 9.8 \times y$ J, which is $49 \times \left(\frac{2}{5}y\right)$ J.

The energy equation now has the form

$$49 \times \tfrac{3}{20} = 49 \times \left(\tfrac{2}{5}y\right)$$

with solution $y = 0.375$.

The particle rises by $(1.5 + 0.375)$ metres, which is 1.875 metres.

In Example 2.4.3, it is important to notice that if the string is replaced by a spring, then the answer to part (a) would be the same, but the answer to part (b) would be different. This is because, once the particle rises above the base level, the spring would be compressed, and there would be elastic energy of $\dfrac{49 \times y^2}{2 \times 1.5}$ J to add to the gravitational energy. You can check for yourself that this would lead to the quadratic equation $\frac{1}{3}y^2 + \frac{2}{5}y - \frac{3}{20} = 0$ and the relevant solution is $y = 0.3$.

The particle would therefore rise by $(1.5 + 0.3)$ metres, which is 1.8 metres.

Exercise 2B

1 An elastic cord has natural length 3 metres and modulus of elasticity 60 newtons. How much work must be done to fix it between two hooks 5 metres apart?

2 A spring has natural length 40 cm. A force of 18 newtons is needed to compress it by 5 cm. How much energy is needed to push it down into a box of height 15 cm?

3 A muscle strengthener consists of a spring of length 0.5 metres with handles at each end. A man takes one handle in each hand and stretches his arms so that the spring extends across his chest to a length of 1.3 metres. To hold it in this position requires him to exert a force of 120 newtons with each arm. Find the modulus of elasticity of the spring, and the work done by the man in performing the exercise.

4 An elastic string has natural length 2 metres and modulus of elasticity 45 newtons. One end is fastened to a fixed point O on a smooth table. A particle of mass 0.1 kg is attached to the other end. The particle is placed on the table 2.5 metres from O, with the string stretched, and then released. How fast is the particle moving when the string becomes slack?

How far is the particle from O when it next comes to rest? Describe the motion after that.

5 Repeat Question 4 with the elastic string replaced by a spring with the same natural length and modulus of elasticity.

6 The ceiling of a room is 2 metres above the floor. A ball of mass m kg hangs from an elastic string attached to the ceiling. The natural length of the string is 0.8 metres, and in equilibrium the ball rests 1 metre below the ceiling. The ball is now pulled down and placed on the floor with the string stretched. Find the speed with which the ball hits the ceiling after it is released.

7 A piston of mass 0.5 kg moves in a horizontal cylinder which is closed at one end. The piston is pushed along the cylinder against the thrust from a spring which is attached to the base of the cylinder at its other end. A force of $1500x$ newtons is required to compress the spring by x metres. The motion of the piston is opposed by a frictional force of 10 newtons from the walls of the cylinder. In the initial position the spring is unstressed, and the piston is then pushed through a distance of 6 cm and released.

(a) How much work is done in pushing the piston?

(b) With what speed does the piston emerge from the open end of the cylinder?

8 A particle of mass m hangs in equilibrium from a fixed point by an elastic string, which stretches a distance x under the weight of the particle. If you place your hand underneath the particle and raise it gently until the string is unstretched, how much work do you do?

9 A bungee jumper of mass 80 kg is attached to a bridge by a rope 30 metres long. The river runs 45 metres below the bridge. If the jump is designed to bring him to rest 1 metre above the water level, what should be the modulus of elasticity of the rope?

10 A steeplejack of mass 80 kg is wearing a safety harness with modulus of elasticity 3920 newtons. He loses his footing, and when he has fallen 2 metres the harness becomes taut. How much further does he fall before he is brought to rest?

11 An elastic string of natural length 2 metres and modulus of elasticity 40 newtons is stretched between two fixed pegs 4 metres apart on a smooth horizontal table. A particle of mass 0.1 kg is attached to the string at its mid-point, and pulled aside through a distance of 1 metre at right angles to the line joining the pegs. After the particle is released, how fast is it moving when it crosses the line joining the pegs?

12 The prongs of a catapult are 18 cm apart. An elastic string of unstretched length 15 cm is attached to each prong, and the strings are joined together by a small leather pouch in which the stone is placed. The pouch is pulled back horizontally, symmetrically between the prongs, until it is 40 cm behind the vertical plane of the prongs, and then let go. If the force holding the pouch in position is 30 newtons, and the mass of the stone is 50 grams, find the speed with which the stone is projected when the strings become slack.

13 In a circus act an elastic rope of natural length 8 metres is stretched between two fixed points 10 metres apart at the same level. An acrobat, of mass 50 kg, grabs the rope at its mid-point and descends vertically. She comes to rest when she has dropped 12 metres. Find the modulus of elasticity of the rope, and how fast she is moving when she has dropped 6 metres.

14 A particle of mass m is attached to an elastic string of natural length l and modulus of elasticity λ. The upper end of the string is fixed, and the particle is falling with speed u when the string becomes taut.

(a) Find an expression for the speed when the string has extension x.

(b) Find how far the string stretches before it comes to rest.

(c) Show that the speed is greatest when the particle passes through the equilibrium position. How could this be predicted without doing any calculation?

15* An elastic rope of natural length l hangs from a tree branch. A monkey of mass m grasps the rope at its lower end, and rests in equilibrium at a distance $l + a$ below the branch. How much work does the monkey do if he climbs slowly up the rope to the branch?

Miscellaneous exercise 2

1 A light spring of natural length 0.2 m has modulus of elasticity 400 N. One end of the spring is attached to a fixed point O, and a particle of mass 5.5 kg is attached to the other end. The system is in equilibrium with the spring hanging vertically from O. Calculate the extension of the spring.   (OCR)

2 A light elastic spring of modulus of elasticity 1.10 N rests in a vertical position supporting a small block of mass 0.020 kg. In the equilibrium position the length of the spring is 0.14 m. Find the natural length of the spring.

The block is replaced by one of mass 0.030 kg. Find the length of the spring in the new equilibrium position.   (OCR)

3 A particle P of mass 0.13 kg moves on a smooth horizontal table. The particle is attached to one end of a light elastic string with natural length 1.5 m and modulus of elasticity 78 N. The other end of the string is attached to a fixed point O of the table. The particle is released from rest at a distance 2.2 m from O. Ignoring air resistance, calculate the speed of P when the string becomes slack. (OCR)

4 A uniform rectangular lamina of weight 5 N has sides of lengths 5 cm and 12 cm. One end of a light elastic string, of natural length 16 cm and modulus of elasticity 10 N, is attached to a corner of the lamina. The other end of the string is attached to a fixed point O and the lamina hangs in equilibrium below O. Given that the lamina does not touch the ground, show that the height of O above the ground is greater than 37 cm. (OCR)

5 One end of a light elastic spring of natural length 0.28 m and modulus of elasticity 9.9 N is attached to a fixed point O. The spring hangs vertically below O with a particle of mass 0.23 kg attached to its lowest point. The particle hangs freely at rest. Calculate

(a) the extension of the spring,

(b) the elastic potential energy of the spring. (OCR)

6 A light elastic string of natural length 0.4 m has one end A attached to a fixed point and carries a particle of mass 0.5 kg at the other end B. When the particle hangs in equilibrium the length of AB is 1 m. Find the modulus of elasticity of the string.

An upward vertical force is applied at B, raising the particle through a distance of 0.2 m, starting and finishing at rest. Find the work done by this force. (OCR)

7 One end of a light elastic string of natural length 1.8 m and modulus of elasticity 1.2 N is attached to a point O of a plane which is inclined at $70°$ to the horizontal. The other end of the string is attached to a particle P of mass 0.05 kg. The particle P is released from rest at the point A of the plane, which is below O and on the same line of greatest slope as O. The distance OA is 1.8 m. State a necessary property of the plane for the principle of the conservation of energy to apply in the subsequent motion.

Use the principle to find

(a) the speed of P when the extension of the string is 0.5 m,

(b) the extension of the string when P is at its lowest point. (OCR)

8 One end of a light elastic string, of natural length 1.5 m and modulus of elasticity 30 N, is attached to a fixed point A of an inclined plane. The other end of the string is attached to a particle P of weight 25 N which lies on the plane. The plane makes an angle α with the horizontal, where $\tan \alpha = \frac{3}{4}$, and the string is parallel to a line of greatest slope of the plane. The coefficient of friction between P and the plane is 0.15.

(a) P is in equilibrium, and the extension of the string is x metres. Find the greatest and least possible values of x.

(b) P is released from rest in the position where $AP = 2$ m. By considering energy and work, find the distance AP when P first comes to rest. (OCR)

9 The diagram shows a uniform rod AB of length 0.4 m and mass 0.8 kg which is smoothly hinged at A to a vertical wall. The rod is kept in equilibrium at an angle of 60° to the vertical, being supported by a light elastic string of natural length 0.5 m. One end of the string is attached to B, and the other end is attached to the wall at the point C which is 0.4 m above A.

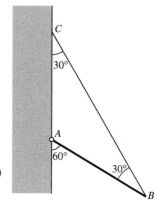

(a) Show that the tension in the string is approximately 6.8 N.

(b) Find the modulus of elasticity of the string.   (OCR)

10 A nylon rope has the property that, when stretched by x metres, its tension is $1890x$ newtons. Find an expression for the work done in stretching it by this length.

The unstretched length of the rope is 28 m. Francesca is climbing on a vertical cliff-face. She fixes one end of the rope to a piton hammered into the cliff-face, and has the other end attached to her waist belt. She is vertically above the piton, with the rope fully paid out, when she slips and falls. The total mass of Francesca and her equipment is 75 kg. If the mass of the rope can be neglected, calculate by what length it will stretch in absorbing the energy of her fall.   (OCR)

11 Two small objects A and B, of masses 3 kg and 2 kg respectively, are connected by a light inextensible string passing over a fixed smooth pulley. A light vertical spring, of natural length 1 m and modulus of elasticity 50 N, connects B to the ground (see diagram). Find the extension of the spring when the system is in equilibrium.
The system is released from rest, with the string taut, from the position in which A and B are each 1 m above the ground. Air resistance may be neglected.

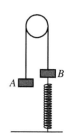

(a) Show that A descends a distance of 0.39 m, correct to 2 significant figures, before first coming instantaneously to rest.

(b) Find the speed of A as it passes through the equilibrium position.   (OCR)

12 A light elastic string has natural length 0.5 m and modulus of elasticity 49 N. The end A is attached to a point on a ceiling. A small object of mass 3 kg is attached to the end B of the string and hangs in equilibrium. Calculate the length AB.

A second string, identical to the first one, is now attached to the object at B and to a point C on the floor, 2.5 m vertically below the point A. The system is in equilibrium with B a distance x metres below A. Find the tension in each of the strings in terms of x and hence show that $x = 1.4$. Calculate the elastic potential energy in the strings when the object hangs in equilibrium.

The object is now pulled down 0.1 m from its equilibrium position and released from rest. Calculate the speed of the object when it passes through the equilibrium position. Any resistances to motion may be neglected.   (MEI)

13 A light elastic string has natural length 10 m and modulus of elasticity 130 N. The ends of the string are attached to fixed points A and B, which are at the same horizontal level and 12.6 m apart. Calculate the tension in the string.

An object is attached to the mid-point of the string and hangs in equilibrium at a point 1.6 m below AB. Calculate

(a) the elastic energy in the string when the object is in this position,

(b) the weight of the object. (OCR)

14 A baby bouncer consists of a seat hung from an elastic rope AB, of natural length 0.8 m, suspended in a doorway of height 2 m. The end A is fixed to the top of the doorway. The first diagram shows the elastic rope hanging from the doorway.

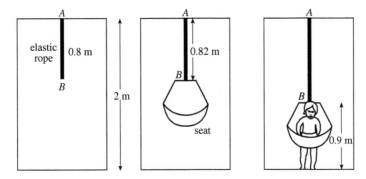

The end B is attached to a seat of mass 0.5 kg.

When the empty seat hangs in equilibrium, as shown in the second diagram, the rope is 0.82 m long. Show that the stiffness of the rope is 245 N m^{-1}.

A baby is placed in the seat. The combined mass of baby and seat is 6.5 kg. Her feet are 0.87 m below B. Show that the clearance between the baby's feet and the floor is 0.07 m.

When the baby is a few months older, the combined mass of baby and seat is 9 kg. Her feet can now reach the floor and she rests in equilibrium with B a distance 0.9 m above the floor, as shown in the third diagram. Calculate the reaction of the floor on the baby.

She pushes up on the floor to bounce vertically. She leaves the floor when B is 0.9 m above the floor and her speed at this point is u m s^{-1}. If she rises by 0.08 m to the top of her bounce, calculate u. (MEI)

15 An elastic string is of unstretched length 20 cm and, when stretched by a distance x cm, has a tension of $\frac{1}{4}x$ newtons. Find an expression for the work done (in N cm) in stretching it by this distance.

The string is fastened between two pegs A and B, 20 cm apart. Its mid-point, M, is pulled aside in a direction perpendicular to AB and is held a distance y cm from the mid-point of AB by a force of F newtons. Show that the string is stretched a distance $2(\sqrt{100 + y^2} - 10)$ cm. Hence show that $F = y - \dfrac{10y}{\sqrt{100 + y^2}}$.

Find the work done by the force F newtons as y increases from 0 to 10. (OCR)

16* In a safety drill, a raft is dropped from rest on a boat-deck into the sea, supported by two light elastic ropes, one at each end. Under the tension in these ropes, the raft comes instantaneously to rest just above the water. The raft is modelled by a uniform rod AB, of mass m kg and length 6 m, which remains horizontal. The ropes CA and DB are attached to A and B and to two fixed points, C and D, on the edge of the deck, so that AB is vertically below CD. The natural length of each rope is 3 m, and each is unstretched when AB is at $A_0 B_0$ on the deck. The ropes each have modulus of elasticity $\frac{15}{16}mg$, and the vertical distance of AB below CD is denoted by x metres, as shown in the diagram.

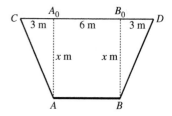

(a) The raft comes to instantaneous rest when $x = x_1$. Show by energy considerations that
$$5\left(\sqrt{x_1^2 + 9} - 3\right)^2 = 16x_1,$$
and verify that this equation is satisfied by $x_1 = 7.2$.

(b) The raft hangs in equilibrium at a vertical distance x_2 below CD. Show that
$$5x_2\left(1 - \frac{3}{\sqrt{x_2^2 + 9}}\right) = 8,$$
and verify that this equation is satisfied by $x_2 = 4$.

(c) Find, to 3 significant figures, the speed with which the raft first passes through its equilibrium position. (OCR)

17* The point O is mid-way between two small smooth pegs A and B which are fixed at the same horizontal level a distance $2a$ apart. Two light elastic strings, each of natural length a and modulus of elasticity λ, have one end fixed at O and are attached at the other end to a particle P of mass m. One of the strings passes over peg A and the other passes over peg B. The particle hangs in equilibrium at a distance h vertically below O, as shown in the diagram. Express the tension in each string in terms of λ, a and h, and show that
$$h = \frac{mga}{2\lambda}.$$

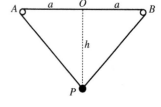

The particle is held at O, and released from rest. In the subsequent motion any resistances can be neglected.

(a) Express in terms of λ and a the total elastic potential energy in the strings at the instant when the particle is released.

(b) Show that, when the particle is at its lowest point, $OP = 2h$.

(c) Express in terms of m, g, a and λ the speed of P as it passes the equilibrium position. (OCR)

18 An elastic string, which obeys Hooke's law, is of natural length 0.2 m. When it has a tension of 3 N it has a total length of 0.3 m. Show that, in general, the tension, T newtons, is related to the total length, r metres, by the formula $T = 6(5r - 1)$.

A particle of mass 0.2 kg is attached to one end of the string and is lying on the horizontal surface of a smooth table. The other end is attached to a fixed point O on the table. The particle is set in motion so that it moves in a circle centre O, radius r metres, with a speed of $v\,\mathrm{m\,s^{-1}}$. Find an expression for v^2 in terms of r.

If the speed of the particle is $6\,\mathrm{m\,s^{-1}}$, what is the radius of the circle in which it moves?

Show that, whatever the speed of the particle in circular motion, its angular velocity is less than $5\sqrt{6}\,\mathrm{rad\,s^{-1}}$.   (OCR)

3 Simple harmonic motion

This chapter is about oscillations, and mechanical systems which produce them. When you have completed the chapter, you should

- recognise (t, x) equations for simple harmonic motion, and know the terms 'amplitude' and 'period'
- know the forms of the (t, v) and (x, v) equations, and that the acceleration is negatively proportional to the displacement from the centre of oscillation
- recognise differential equations for simple harmonic motion, and be able to find solutions satisfying given initial conditions
- be able to obtain a differential equation for simple harmonic motion for a vibrating mechanical system, and deduce the period of vibration.

From this chapter onwards, regular use will be made of the 'dot notation' for velocity and acceleration, in which a dot placed over a letter indicates differentiation with respect to time. In this notation $\dot{x}$ stands for $\dfrac{\mathrm{d}x}{\mathrm{d}t}$, $\dot{v}$ for $\dfrac{\mathrm{d}v}{\mathrm{d}t}$, and $\ddot{x}$ for $\dfrac{\mathrm{d}^2 x}{\mathrm{d}t^2}$. (See M1 Section 11.6.)

3.1 Models for oscillation

Suppose that a particle is oscillating forwards and backwards along a straight line about a centre O. Then its (t, x) graph will have the shape of a wavy line like Fig. 3.1. The equations which immediately come to mind for such a graph are $x = \cos t$ and $x = \sin t$. With these equations you know that x takes values between -1 and $+1$, and that if you increase t by 2π the graph repeats itself.

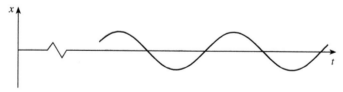

Fig. 3.1

What is the equation for an oscillation in which x takes values between $-a$ and $+a$, where a is some positive constant? You can get this by a one-way stretch with factor a in the x-direction, which changes the equation to $x = a \cos t$ or $x = a \sin t$. The constant a (not to be confused with the acceleration!) is called the **amplitude** of the oscillation.

Notice that the amplitude is the maximum distance of the particle from O in the oscillation; the particle is actually oscillating through a total distance of $2a$ forwards and backwards.

In a similar way, if you replace t by nt in the equations, where n is a positive constant, this produces a one-way stretch with factor $\dfrac{1}{n}$ in the t-direction. So graphs with equations like $x = a \cos nt$ and $x = a \sin nt$ repeat themselves if t is increased by $\dfrac{2\pi}{n}$.

This is called the **period** of the oscillation. The larger value of n, the shorter the period, and the more rapid the oscillation.

Oscillations with equations like $x = a \cos nt$ and $x = a \sin nt$ are called **simple harmonic** oscillations. The word 'harmonic' is a reminder that oscillations like these are the basis of musical sounds; and a 'simple' harmonic oscillation is one which produces a pure musical tone, rather than a mixture of tones.

These equations are special examples of simple harmonic oscillation, because of their particular properties at time $t = 0$. If $x = a \cos nt$, then when $t = 0$ the particle is at its maximum displacement $x = a$ from the centre O. In this position the particle is stationary; you can check this by differentiation, since the velocity $\dot{x} = -na \sin nt$, which is zero when $t = 0$. This would be the equation to use if the motion is started off by displacing the particle from its position of equilibrium and releasing it.

The other equation, $x = a \sin nt$, applies to a particle for which $x = 0$ when $t = 0$. In this case, the velocity $\dot{x} = na \cos nt$, and this has its maximum value na when $t = 0$. So you would use an equation like this for a particle which is set in motion by a sudden impulse applied while it is in its central position.

> The greek letter ω is sometimes used instead of n in simple harmonic equations. The reason for this is explained in Section 3.6.

Example 3.1.1
Write down equations for the motion of particles which oscillate in the following ways.

(a) The particle is released from rest at 2 metres from O in the positive direction, and first returns to this position after 4 seconds.

(b) The particle is initially at O, and is set in motion with velocity $6\,\mathrm{m\,s^{-1}}$ in the positive direction, and oscillates with period $\frac{1}{2}\pi$ seconds.

    (a) The equation has the form $x = a \cos nt$, and the amplitude $a = 2$. The period is $\dfrac{2\pi}{n} = 4$, so $n = \frac{1}{2}\pi$. The equation is therefore $x = 2 \cos \frac{1}{2}\pi t$.

    (b) The equation has the form $x = a \sin nt$. The period is $\dfrac{2\pi}{n} = \frac{1}{2}\pi$, so $n = 4$. For an equation of this form the velocity $\dot{x} = na \cos nt$ when $t = 0$ is na, so $4a = 6$, which gives $a = \frac{3}{2}$. The equation is therefore $x = \frac{3}{2} \sin 4t$.

3.2 Properties of simple harmonic oscillations

The two equations $x = a \cos nt$ and $x = a \sin nt$ have some important properties in common. To show the similarities and differences, these properties are developed in this section in parallel columns for the two equations.

For the oscillation given by

$$x = a \cos nt, \qquad\qquad x = a \sin nt,$$

expressions for the velocity are given by differentiation:

$$v = \dot{x} = -na \sin nt. \qquad\qquad v = \dot{x} = na \cos nt.$$

To find the (x, v) equation, eliminate t between the (t, x) and (t, v) equations using $\cos^2 nt + \sin^2 nt = 1$:

$$\left(\frac{x}{a}\right)^2 + \left(-\frac{v}{na}\right)^2 = 1, \qquad\qquad \left(\frac{v}{na}\right)^2 + \left(\frac{x}{a}\right)^2 = 1,$$

which can be simplified to give $v^2 + n^2 x^2 = n^2 a^2,$

which is
$$v^2 = n^2(a^2 - x^2),$$
$$v = \pm n\sqrt{a^2 - x^2}.$$

You need the $\pm$ sign here, because during the oscillation v is positive for one half of the period and negative for the other half.

From this equation it is easy to draw the (x, v) graph. You know that the equation of a circle with centre $(0, 0)$ and radius a has equation $x^2 + y^2 = a^2$, or $y = \pm\sqrt{a^2 - x^2}$. So you can get the graph of v from this by a one-way stretch of factor n in the y-direction. This produces the ellipse in Fig. 3.2, with semi-axes of lengths a and na across the page and up the page.

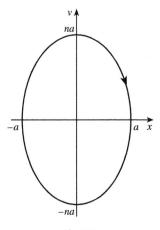

Fig. 3.2

Although the (x, v) graph is the same for both equations, the starting points are different. You can see from the (t, x) and the (t, v) equations that, at the starts and ends of quarter-periods of the first complete oscillation, the values of x and v are as shown in Table 3.3.

	$x = a \cos nt$						$x = a \sin nt$				
t	0	$\frac{\pi}{2n}$	$\frac{\pi}{n}$	$\frac{3\pi}{2n}$	$\frac{2\pi}{n}$	t	0	$\frac{\pi}{2n}$	$\frac{\pi}{n}$	$\frac{3\pi}{2n}$	$\frac{2\pi}{n}$
x	a	0	$-a$	0	a	x	0	a	0	$-a$	0
v	0	$-na$	0	na	0	v	na	0	$-na$	0	na

Table 3.3

The table shows that, for either equation, as t increases the point (x, v) moves clockwise round the (x, v) graph. This is indicated by the arrow in Fig. 3.2. A complete circuit of the (x, v) graph corresponds to one period of the oscillation.

To find the acceleration, differentiate a second time:

$$\ddot{x} = -n^2 a \cos nt. \qquad \Big| \qquad \ddot{x} = -n^2 a \sin nt.$$

You will notice that, although these two equations are different, it is true in both cases that

$$\ddot{x} = -n^2 x.$$

This differential equation describes a fundamental property of simple harmonic oscillation. Notice first the negative sign, indicating that the acceleration is always in the opposite direction to the displacement. When the particle is to the right of O the acceleration is towards the left, and vice versa. Also, the magnitude of the acceleration is proportional to the magnitude of the displacement; the further the particle is from O, the greater the acceleration (and therefore the force) tending to bring it back.

3.3 General definitions

The equations $x = a \cos nt$ and $x = a \sin nt$ are just two of any number of possible equations for simple harmonic oscillations, with initial values $x = a$, $v = 0$ and $x = 0$, $v = na$ respectively. In general the particle might start at time $t = 0$ at some displacement x_0 from O with velocity v_0. In that case the oscillation will have an equation such as $x = a \cos(nt + \varepsilon)$, where the extra '$+ \varepsilon$' in the equation corresponds to a translation of the (t, x) graph in the t-direction.

Differentiating this more general equation,

$$v = \dot{x} = -na \sin(nt + \varepsilon) \quad \text{and} \quad \ddot{x} = -n^2 a \cos(nt + \varepsilon).$$

Notice that it is still true that

$$v^2 + n^2 x^2 = n^2 a^2 \quad \text{and that} \quad \ddot{x} = -n^2 x.$$

This can all be summarised in the following definition.

> A particle which moves so that its position on the x-axis at time t is given by an equation $x = a \cos(nt + \varepsilon)$, where a, n and ε are constants (a and n positive), is oscillating with **simple harmonic motion** about the origin.
>
> For a particle moving with simple harmonic motion,
> $$v^2 = n^2(a^2 - x^2), \quad \ddot{x} = -n^2 x, \quad \text{and the period is} \quad \frac{2\pi}{n}.$$

These properties are important, and you should remember them.

Example 3.3.1

A particle is performing simple harmonic oscillations about O, with amplitude 10 metres and period 4 seconds. Find

(a) the greatest speed,   (b) the greatest acceleration

of the particle during the oscillation.

Using the formula $\dfrac{2\pi}{n}$ for the period gives the equation $\dfrac{2\pi}{n} = 4$, so $n = \tfrac{1}{2}\pi$.

The constant n is measured in units of s^{-1}.

(a) From the equation $v^2 = n^2(a^2 - x^2)$, the speed is greatest when $x = 0$, in which case $v^2 = n^2 a^2$, so $|v| = na$. With the given figures $n = \tfrac{1}{2}\pi$ and $a = 10$, so the greatest speed is $5\pi\ \mathrm{m\,s}^{-1}$, which is $15.7\ \mathrm{m\,s}^{-1}$ correct to 3 significant figures.

(b) The magnitude of the acceleration is n^2 times the distance of the particle from O. So it is greatest when the particle is at its greatest distance from O, which is the amplitude of the oscillation. The greatest acceleration is therefore $\left(\tfrac{1}{2}\pi\right)^2 \times 10\ \mathrm{m\,s}^{-2}$, which is $24.7\ \mathrm{m\,s}^{-2}$ correct to 3 significant figures.

Example 3.3.2

A and B are points on the x-axis with coordinates $x = 25$ and $x = 20$, the units being centimetres. A particle oscillating with simple harmonic motion about the origin O starts from rest at A. When it reaches B, its speed is $30\ \mathrm{cm\,s}^{-1}$. Find the time it takes to get from A to B.

Since the particle is at rest at A, the amplitude of the oscillation is 25 cm. At B it is given that $x = 20$ and $v = -30$. (Note the minus sign, because at this stage the particle is moving in the negative x-direction.) Substituting in the equation $v^2 = n^2(a^2 - x^2)$,

$$(-30)^2 = n^2(25^2 - 20^2), \quad \text{which gives } n^2 = 4, \text{ so } n = 2.$$

When $t = 0$ the particle is at its greatest displacement from O, so the (t, x) equation has the form $x = a \cos nt$ with $a = 25$ and $n = 2$. So, when $x = 20$, t satisfies

$$20 = 25 \cos 2t.$$

This equation has infinitely many roots. In this example the smallest positive root is required. Since $\cos^{-1} 0.8 = 0.643...$ radians, $t = \tfrac{1}{2} \times 0.643... = 0.322...$.

The particle takes 0.322 seconds, correct to 3 significant figures, to get from A to B.

You can use the equation $v^2 + n^2 x^2 = n^2 a^2$ to find the amplitude of the general oscillation $x = a \cos(nt + \varepsilon)$ from the given initial values x_0 and v_0 of the displacement and velocity when $t = 0$:

$$n^2 a^2 = v_0^2 + n^2 x_0^2, \quad \text{so} \quad a = \sqrt{x_0^2 + \left(\dfrac{v_0}{n}\right)^2}.$$

(Remember that the amplitude is positive by definition.) Having found a, you can find ε by putting $t = 0$ in the equations for x and v, which gives

$$\cos \varepsilon = \frac{x_0}{a} \quad \text{and} \quad \sin \varepsilon = -\frac{v_0}{na}.$$

If you take ε to be $-\frac{1}{2}\pi$, you get $x = a \cos\left(nt - \frac{1}{2}\pi\right)$, which can be simplified to $x = a \sin nt$. So the forms $x = a \cos nt$ and $x = a \sin nt$ are just special cases of the general equation $x = a \cos(nt + \varepsilon)$ with $\varepsilon = 0$ and $\varepsilon = -\frac{1}{2}\pi$ respectively.

One further generalisation should be mentioned. It is possible for the oscillation not to be centred on the origin, but on a point C such that $x = c$. The equations in this case become

$$x = c + a\cos(nt + \varepsilon), \quad v^2 = n^2(a^2 - (x - c)^2), \quad \ddot{x} = -n^2(x - c),$$

and the period is still $\dfrac{2\pi}{n}$. These results are not worth committing to memory, though you should be aware of the possibility and know how to deal with it.

Example 3.3.3
A particle is oscillating on the x-axis about the point $x = 5$ with simple harmonic motion, the units being centimetres. The period of the oscillation is 6π seconds. At a certain instant the particle is at the point $x = 12$ and moving away from the origin with velocity $8 \, \mathrm{m\,s^{-1}}$. Find the greatest distance of the particle from the origin during the oscillation, and the time that will elapse before the particle reaches this position.

The simplest method is to introduce a new variable $z = x - 5$, so that the particle oscillates about the point where $z = 0$. The equation of the oscillation can then be written in the form $z = a\cos(nt + \varepsilon)$.

Take the instant of the given observation to be the time $t = 0$. Notice that $\dot{z} = \dot{x}$, so the value of v is not affected by the change of variable.

Since the period is 6π seconds, $\dfrac{2\pi}{n} = 6\pi$, which gives $n = \frac{1}{3}$. To find the amplitude, substitute the initial velocity and displacement $v_0 = 8$, $z_0 = 12 - 5 = 7$ into the equation $v_0^2 = n^2(a^2 - x_0^2)$. This gives

$$64 = \tfrac{1}{9}(a^2 - 49),$$

so that $a^2 = 49 + 9 \times 64 = 625$, and $a = 25$.

From the equations $z = a\cos(nt + \varepsilon)$ and $v = \dot{z} = -na\sin(nt + \varepsilon)$ with $t = 0$ it follows that $z_0 = a\cos\varepsilon$ and $v_0 = -a\sin\varepsilon$. So

$$\cos\varepsilon = \frac{z_0}{a} = \tfrac{7}{25} \quad \text{and} \quad \sin\varepsilon = -\frac{v_0}{na} = -\frac{8}{\frac{1}{3} \times 25} = -\tfrac{24}{25}.$$

A solution of these equations is $\varepsilon = -1.287\ldots$, so the equation of the oscillation can be written as

$$z = 25\cos\left(\tfrac{1}{3}t - 1.287\ldots\right) \quad \text{or} \quad x = 5 + 25\cos\left(\tfrac{1}{3}t - 1.287\ldots\right).$$

> Don't forget that your calculator must be set in radian mode.

From these equations you can see that the value of z varies between -25 and $+25$, so the value of x varies between $5 - 25 = -20$ and $5 + 25 = 30$.

The variable z takes its greatest value 25 when $\cos\left(\frac{1}{3}t - 1.287...\right)$ is equal to 1, which occurs when $\frac{1}{3}t - 1.287... = 0$, 2π, 4π, ... The smallest such value of t is given by $\frac{1}{3}t - 1.287... = 0$, so $t = 3.861...$.

The particle reaches its greatest distance of $30\,\text{cm}$ from the origin after 3.86 seconds.

Exercise 3A

1. Find the amplitude, the period and the maximum speed of the oscillations given by

   (a) $x = 3\sin 5t$,   (b) $x = 2\cos\frac{1}{3}\pi t$,   (c) $x = -5\sin\pi t$,

   the units being metres and seconds.

2. Find (t, x) equations to represent simple harmonic oscillations about O with the following properties.

   (a) A particle is released from rest 4 metres from O and first returns to this position after 5 seconds.

   (b) A particle at O is set in motion with speed $2\,\text{m s}^{-1}$ and oscillates with period 4 seconds.

   (c) A particle is released from rest 2 metres from O and passes through O at a speed of $6\,\text{m s}^{-1}$.

3. A particle situated at O is given a speed of $3\,\text{m s}^{-1}$, and oscillates with simple harmonic motion about O with amplitude 6 metres. Find the period of the oscillation, and the greatest acceleration of the particle during the oscillation.

4. A particle is in simple harmonic oscillation about O with period 2 seconds. When it is $10\,\text{cm}$ from O it is moving at $8\,\text{cm s}^{-1}$. Find the amplitude of the oscillation, and the greatest speed attained by the particle.

5. A particle is performing simple harmonic oscillations about O. When it is at its greatest distance of $50\,\text{cm}$ from O, its deceleration is $2\,\text{cm s}^{-2}$. Find the period of the oscillation, and the speed and acceleration of the particle when it is $40\,\text{cm}$ from O.

6. A particle is in simple harmonic oscillation about O. When it is 6 metres from O its speed is $4\,\text{m s}^{-1}$ and its deceleration is $1.5\,\text{m s}^{-2}$. Find the amplitude of the oscillation, and the greatest speed of the particle as it oscillates.

7. A particle is oscillating with simple harmonic motion about O. At time $t = 0$ it is 8 metres from O in the positive direction, moving at $3\,\text{m s}^{-1}$ away from O and decelerating at $2\,\text{m s}^{-2}$. Find the (t, x) equation for the motion, and sketch the (t, x) graph. Also sketch the (x, v) graph, and mark on your sketch the point corresponding to $t = 0$.

8 For the oscillations with the following equations, find the period, the initial position when $t = 0$, the initial velocity and the coordinates of the extreme points. The units are metres and seconds.

(a) $x = 2\sin\left(\frac{1}{2}t + \frac{1}{6}\pi\right)$

(b) $x = 3\cos\left(\pi t - \frac{1}{4}\pi\right)$

(c) $x = 2 + 5\cos 3t$

(d) $x = 5(1 - \sin(2t + 1))$

(e) $x = 4\cos(t - 3)\pi$

(f) $x = c + a\cos(nt + \varepsilon)$ $(a, n > 0)$

9 A particle is describing simple harmonic oscillations about $x = 2$ with period 2π seconds, the unit of length being the metre. When $x = 7$ the speed of the particle is $12\,\mathrm{m\,s}^{-1}$. Find the values of x at the extreme points of the oscillation, and the speed of the particle as it passes through the origin.

10 A particle is oscillating with simple harmonic motion. When $x = 1$, $v = \pm 7$ and when $x = 5$, $v = \pm 2$, the units being millimetres and seconds. Find the amplitude and the period

(a) if the centre of oscillation is O,

(b) if the centre of oscillation is $x = 1$,

(c) if the centre of oscillation is $x = 2$.

11 A balloon is performing simple harmonic oscillations in a vertical line with period 40 seconds. Its height varies between 800 metres and 850 metres. Find the speed of the balloon when its height is 820 metres.

In the balloon basket a woman of mass 60 kg weighs herself with a spring balance. What is the reading on the balance when the height of the balloon is 820 metres?

12 A boat is riding the waves in high seas, oscillating with simple harmonic motion in a vertical line. The period of the oscillation is 8 seconds, and the height of the boat varies between 5 metres and 11 metres below the pinnacle of a nearby rock. Find the maximum vertical speed and the maximum acceleration of the boat during the oscillation.

There is an unsecured box of mass 20 kg on the deck of the boat. Find the normal contact force from the deck on the box

(a) at the top,   (b) at the bottom,   (c) in the middle

of the oscillation.

3.4 Mechanical oscillations

One further important step is needed before you can make use of the theory of simple harmonic motion in mechanical problems. This is the converse of the 'acceleration is negatively proportional to displacement' property.

> If a variable x satisfies the differential equation $\ddot{x} = -kx$, where k is a positive constant, then $x = a\cos(nt + \varepsilon)$ for some constants a and ε, where $n = \sqrt{k}$.

For the time being this will be assumed, so that it can be used to investigate various practical problems. You will find a proof in Section 3.7.

Since acceleration is proportional to force, the problems to which this result can be applied are those where the force always acts to bring an object back towards its equilibrium position, with a magnitude proportional to the distance from the equilibrium position. Such situations often arise in mechanical systems which include elastic strings and springs.

Example 3.4.1

A spring of natural length 0.6 metres is attached to a fixed point A on a smooth horizontal table. A force of $10x$ newtons is needed to keep the spring extended by x metres. A block of mass 0.1 kg is attached to the other end. The block is pulled away from A until it is 0.75 metres from A, and then let go. Describe the subsequent motion.

The block will oscillate about the point O which is 0.6 metres from A, where the spring is unstretched. When the block is further from A than this, the spring is in tension; when it is closer to A, the spring is in compression. Either way, the spring will act so as to bring the block back towards O. So let x metres denote the displacement of the block from O, and take the positive direction to be away from A.

When you draw a diagram for a problem like this, it is important not to show the block in any special position, such as the one where it is set in motion, but in a general position at some stage of the oscillation. It is simpler to use the diagram if it shows a position where the displacement is positive, as in Fig. 3.4.

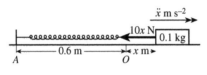

Fig. 3.4

Clearly the weight of the block is balanced by the normal contact force from the table. To simplify the diagram these forces are not shown.

The only horizontal force on the block is from the spring, of magnitude $10x$ newtons. Since this is in the negative direction when x is positive, and vice versa,

$$\mathcal{R}(\rightarrow) \qquad -10x = 0.1\ddot{x}.$$

This gives $\ddot{x} = -100x$, which you will recognise as an equation of simple harmonic motion with $n = \sqrt{100} = 10$.

Now initially the block is stationary with $x = 0.75 - 0.6 = 0.15$, so the appropriate solution equation is $x = 0.15 \cos 10t$.

The block oscillates with simple harmonic motion of amplitude 0.15 metres about O. It reaches a maximum speed of $10 \times 0.15 \, \mathrm{m\,s^{-1}}$, which is $1.5 \, \mathrm{m\,s^{-1}}$, each time it passes through O. The period of the oscillation is $\dfrac{2\pi}{10}$ seconds, which is $\frac{1}{5}\pi$ seconds.

It is often acceptable to leave the answer for the period in this form, as a multiple of π. However, it will give a better idea of the physical situation if you evaluate it, as 0.628 seconds correct to 3 significant figures.

An important feature of simple harmonic motion illustrated by Example 3.4.1 is that the value of the period, which depends only on n, comes directly from the equation $-10x = 0.1\ddot{x}$, and isn't affected by the initial conditions. If the block had been released at a different distance from A, the amplitude of the oscillation would have been different but the period would still have been $\frac{1}{5}\pi$ seconds.

Example 3.4.2
The spring in Example 3.4.1, with the 0.1 kg block attached to it, is hung vertically from a fixed point B. The block is pulled down from its equilibrium position until it is 0.75 metres from B, and then released. Describe the subsequent motion.

Suppose that when the block is in equilibrium the extension of the spring is z metres. Then the tension of $10z$ newtons is equal to the weight of 0.98 newtons. So $z = 0.098$, which means that in equilibrium the block hangs a distance 0.698 metres below B.

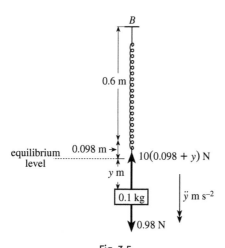

Fig. 3.5

You will probably guess, correctly, that the block will oscillate about the equilibrium position. So instead of using the extension of the spring as the variable, it may be simpler to measure the displacement of the block from the equilibrium position. If y metres denotes this displacement, then the total extension of the spring is $(0.098 + y)$ metres. The only forces acting on the block are the weight and the tension. Taking the downward direction as positive (see Fig. 3.5),

$$\mathcal{R}(\downarrow) \qquad 0.98 - 10(0.098 + y) = 0.1\ddot{y}.$$

After multiplying out the bracket, this can be simplified to

$$\ddot{y} = -100y.$$

This is the same equation as in Example 3.4.1, with y in place of x. This shows that the value of n, which determines the period of the oscillation, depends only on the stiffness of the spring and the mass of the block, and is unaffected by the presence of the gravitational force.

What is different though is that, when the block is released at time $t = 0$, the displacement from the centre of oscillation is only $(0.75 - 0.698)$ metres. The oscillation therefore has amplitude 0.052 metres, and the (t, y) equation is $y = 0.052 \cos 10t$. This means that, after t seconds, the extension of the spring is $(0.098 + 0.052 \cos 10t)$ metres.

The block therefore oscillates with simple harmonic motion of amplitude 0.052 metres about the equilibrium position, so that the extension of the spring varies between 0.046 metres and 0.15 metres. The maximum speed of the block is $0.52 \, \text{m s}^{-1}$, and the period of the oscillation is $\frac{1}{5}\pi$ seconds.

In Example 3.4.2, not only is the period unaffected by the presence of the gravitational force, it also doesn't depend on the value of g. The apparatus would oscillate with the same period even if it were used on the surface of the moon.

Example 3.4.3
A and B are two points on a smooth floor 9.2 metres apart. A disc of diameter 0.2 metres and mass 2 kg is attached to A by an elastic string of natural length 4 metres and modulus of elasticity 30 newtons, and to B by an elastic string of natural length 2 metres and modulus of elasticity 10 newtons. While at rest in equilibrium, the disc is hit in the direction of B. What is the largest impulse that it can be given if neither of the strings becomes slack in the resulting motion?

Fig. 3.6 shows the disc in equilibrium. The total length of the strings is $(9.2 - 0.2)$ metres, so take the two lengths to be z metres and $(9 - z)$ metres respectively. Then

$$\mathcal{R}(\rightarrow) \qquad \frac{10((9-z)-2)}{2} - \frac{30(z-4)}{4} = 0.$$

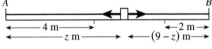

Fig. 3.6

Simplifying,

$$2(7 - z) - 3(z - 4) = 0,$$

which gives $z = 5.2$. So in this position the extensions of the strings are 1.2 metres and 1.8 metres respectively.

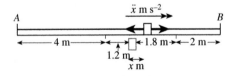

Fig. 3.7

Now consider the forces on the disc after it has been hit, at an instant when its displacement from the equilibrium position towards B is x metres (see Fig. 3.7).

Then, if neither string is slack,

$$\mathcal{R}(\to) \quad \frac{10(1.8 - x)}{2} - \frac{30(1.2 + x)}{4} = 2\ddot{x},$$

so

$$10(1.8 - x) - 15(1.2 + x) = 4\ddot{x}.$$

This leads to the differential equation $\ddot{x} = -\frac{25}{4}x$.

This shows that the disc oscillates with simple harmonic motion about the equilibrium position, with $n = \frac{5}{2}$. Since the motion starts with $x = 0$, the (t, x) equation has the form $x = a \sin \frac{5}{2}t$ for some value of a.

> The fact that there is no constant term in the differential equation is a useful check that the equilibrium position has been correctly calculated.

Since the oscillation is symmetrical about the equilibrium position, the string most likely to become slack is the one attached to A, so the amplitude a must not exceed 1.2 metres. This means that the value of $\dot{x} = \frac{5}{2}a \cos \frac{5}{2}t$ when $t = 0$, which is $\frac{5}{2}a$, must not exceed $\frac{5}{2} \times 1.2 = 3$. The impulse which would give the 2 kg disc a speed of $3 \, \mathrm{m \, s^{-1}}$ is $6 \, \mathrm{N \, s}$.

The largest impulse with which the disc can be hit without either string becoming slack is $6 \, \mathrm{N \, s}$.

The next example brings together a number of processes which you have already met. The oscillation is started by a collision, so the initial velocity has to be found from a conservation of momentum equation. After that the period of the oscillation is obtained by a method which is essentially the same as that used in Example 3.4.2. The amplitude is then calculated by a method similar to that used in Example 3.3.3. You will probably find it helpful to read the whole example through once without paying too much attention to the algebraic detail. Then read it again to make sure that you fully understand each of the equations which contribute to the solution. It is left to you to draw your own diagrams for this example.

Example 3.4.4*
A ball of mass M hangs in equilibrium from the ceiling by a spring of natural length l and modulus of elasticity mg. A ring of mass m which surrounds the spring at ceiling level is dislodged, falls and strikes the ball. After the collision the ring and the ball move together in simple harmonic motion. Show that the amplitude of the oscillation is $\sqrt{3}l$.

Before embarking on the solution it pays to plan a strategy. There are three stages to consider.

Stage 1 The ring falls from rest through a distance $l + c$, where c is the extension of the spring with the ball hanging from it.

Stage 2 The collision, during which momentum is conserved.

Stage 3 The ring and ball oscillate about a new equilibrium position. This motion will start at a displacement x_0 from this equilibrium position with velocity v_0, and the amplitude will be found from the equation $a^2 = x_0^2 + \left(\dfrac{v_0}{n}\right)^2$ (see Section 3.3).

So it will be necessary to calculate three quantities:

x_0, which is the difference between the two equilibrium positions;
v_0, by combining results of Stages 1 and 2;
n, from the simple harmonic motion equation for the ring and ball.

For both x_0 and n you need to know the equilibrium positions, so this is a good place to start.

Equilibrium positions   When just the ball hangs from the spring, the tension $\dfrac{\lambda c}{l}$ must balance the weight Mg, so the extension is $c = \dfrac{Mgl}{\lambda}$. This is $c = \dfrac{Ml}{m}$ because λ is given to be mg.

By a similar argument with the combined weight $(m + M)g$ after the collision, the new equilibrium position has extension $\dfrac{(m + M)l}{m}$.

It follows that x_0, the displacement from the new equilibrium position when the collision takes place, is $\dfrac{Ml}{m} - \dfrac{(m + M)l}{m}$, which is $-l$.

Stages 1 and 2   The ring drops a distance $l + \dfrac{Ml}{m}$, which is $\dfrac{(m + M)l}{m}$, before the collision. Using the equation $v^2 = u^2 + 2as$ with $u = 0$ and $a = g$, the speed just before the collision is $\sqrt{\dfrac{2g(m + M)l}{m}}$.

The combined speed of ring and ball after the collision is v_0. Since momentum is conserved,

$$m\sqrt{\dfrac{2g(m + M)l}{m}} = (m + M)v_0,$$

so

$$v_0 = \sqrt{\dfrac{m^2}{(m + M)^2} \times \dfrac{2g(m + M)l}{m}}$$

$$= \sqrt{\dfrac{2mgl}{m + M}}.$$

Simple harmonic motion   If in a general position the ring and ball are a distance x below their equilibrium position with extension $\dfrac{(m + M)l}{m}$, then there are two forces acting, the weight $(m + M)g$ and the tension $\dfrac{mg}{l}\left(\dfrac{(m + M)l}{m} + x\right)$.

$\mathcal{R}(\downarrow)$ $(m + M)g - \dfrac{mg}{l}\left(\dfrac{(m + M)l}{m} + x\right) = (m + M)\ddot{x},$

that is,

$$(m+M)g - (m+M)g - \frac{mg}{l}x = (m+M)\ddot{x}.$$

This can be simplified to $\ddot{x} = -\frac{mg}{(m+M)l}x$,

which is the equation for simple harmonic motion with $n^2 = \frac{mg}{(m+M)l}$.

Everything is now in place. Since $x_0 = -l$ and $\frac{v_0^2}{n^2} = \frac{2mgl}{(m+M)} \bigg/ \frac{mg}{(m+M)l} = 2l^2$, it

follows that $a^2 = l^2 + 2l^2 = 3l^2$,   so $a = \sqrt{3}l$.

Exercise 3B

1 A spring has natural length 0.5 metres and modulus of elasticity 10 newtons. One end is attached to a fixed point A on a smooth table, and a particle of mass 0.05 kg attached to the other end rests on the table in equilibrium. The particle is given a velocity of $2\,\mathrm{m\,s^{-1}}$ towards A. Find the period and the amplitude of the oscillation which results.

2 A spring rests on a smooth table with one end attached to a fixed point A. A block of mass $\frac{1}{2}$ kg is attached to the other end. The block is now pulled away from A through a distance of 0.1 metres, and the tension in the stretched spring is then 20 newtons. Find the period with which the block will oscillate when it is released.

3 A toy truck of mass 2 kg with smooth wheel bearings is placed on a floor facing a wall. An elastic string of natural length 2 metres and modulus of elasticity 25 newtons has one end attached to the truck and the other to the wall. The truck is released from rest at a point 5 metres from the wall.

(a) Describe the motion of the truck from the time when it is released until it hits the wall.

(b) Find the speed of the truck when it hits the wall.

(c) Find how much time elapses before the truck hits the wall.

4 Two identical elastic strings each have natural length 40 cm and modulus of elasticity 18 newtons. They are joined together end-to-end, and a particle of mass 100 grams is attached at the knot. The other ends of the strings are attached to points of a smooth table 1 metre apart. Whilst the particle is at rest in equilibrium, it is given an impulse and starts to move along the line of the strings with speed $1.2\,\mathrm{m\,s^{-1}}$. Find the period and amplitude of the resulting oscillation, and show that neither string becomes slack.

5 A piston of mass 75 grams is free to move without friction in a tube of length 5 metres. The piston is attached to the end A of the tube by a spring of natural length 1.5 metres and modulus of elasticity 30 newtons, and to the end B by a spring of natural length 2 metres and modulus of elasticity 20 newtons. Find the distance from A at which the piston can rest in equilibrium.

The piston is positioned at the centre of the tube and then released. In the subsequent oscillation, find

(a) the amplitude,   (b) the period,   (c) the greatest speed of the piston.

6 A vertical spring is placed inside a smooth cylindrical tube which stands on the floor. A stone sphere of mass 2 kg is placed on top of the spring; this depresses it by a distance of 0.2 metres. The sphere is then struck vertically downwards with a hammer, so that it starts to move with speed $0.7\,\mathrm{m\,s^{-1}}$. Find the period with which it oscillates, and the amplitude of the oscillation. Write down an equation for the amount by which the spring is compressed after t seconds.

7 An elastic string has one end attached to the ceiling, and a particle of mass 0.1 kg is attached to the other end. The string has natural length 1.6 metres and modulus of elasticity 49 newtons. The particle is pulled downwards until it is 1.65 metres below the ceiling and released. Find the amplitude and the period of the resulting oscillation.

8 The ceiling of a hall is 15 metres above the floor. A vertical elastic string of natural length 5 metres and modulus of elasticity 6 newtons has one end attached to the ceiling and the other end attached to the floor. A lamp of mass 0.5 kg is held at a height of 9 metres above the floor, and attached to the string. When the lamp is let go, find the heights between which it will oscillate, and the period of the oscillation.

9 A table top, 80 cm above the floor, has a very small hole in the middle. A small ball of mass 10 grams sits on top of the hole, and an elastic string attached to the ball passes through the hole and is fixed to a point in the floor directly below the hole. The natural length of the string is 80 cm, and its modulus of elasticity is 20 newtons. The ball is then moved across the table away from the hole and released. Find the period of its oscillations on the table.

10 A particle of mass m is attached to one end of a piece of elastic with natural length l and modulus of elasticity λ. The particle rests on a smooth table, and the other end of the elastic is pinned to a point in the middle of the table. The particle is held at a distance $l + a$ from the pin and then released. Show that it will next come to rest, on the opposite side of the pin, after a time $\left(\pi + \dfrac{2l}{a}\right)\sqrt{\dfrac{ml}{\lambda}}$.

11 The figure shows a hydrometer, which is an instrument for measuring relative density, floating in a liquid. The tube has cross-sectional area $A\,\mathrm{m^2}$, and the hydrometer has mass M kg. If the hydrometer is depressed by an additional distance x metres, the buoyancy force increases by an amount $1000Argx$ newtons, where r is the relative density of the liquid. Show that the hydrometer can perform vertical simple harmonic oscillations about the position of equilibrium, and find an expression for the period in terms of A, r, g and M.

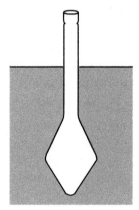

12* The roof of a circus tent is 40 metres above the floor. An elastic rope of length 25 metres hangs from the roof. An acrobat of mass 64 kg stands on a platform 15 metres above the floor facing the lower end of the rope. He hooks the rope on to his waistband and, on a drum-roll signal, steps off the platform. He descends by 10 metres and then starts to rise again. As he does so he picks up his assistant, of mass 48 kg, who is standing on a platform 10 metres above the floor. As they then move together, how high are they above the floor at the top and bottom of their oscillation?

At the lowest point the assistant disengages herself and drops to the floor. How high does the acrobat then rise? How fast is he rising when he passes the platform on which he was originally standing?

3.5 Shifting the origin

Look back at Examples 3.4.1 and 3.4.2. Both examples are about the same spring, but different variables were used in the solutions. In Example 3.4.1 the variable was the extension of the spring, x metres, but in Example 3.4.2 it was the displacement beyond the equilibrium position, y metres. What happens if Example 3.4.2 is worked using the extension x metres as the variable?

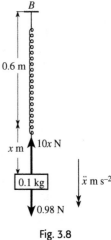

Fig. 3.8

The forces on the block would then be as shown in Fig. 3.8, which lead to the equation

$$\mathcal{R}(\downarrow) \qquad 0.98 - 10x = 0.1\ddot{x}.$$

This differs from the standard simple harmonic motion equation by the addition of the constant term 0.98. You can get rid of this by using a simple substitution.

Notice that $0.98 - 10x$ can be written as $-10(x - 0.098)$. If you write $x - 0.098$ as y, then the left side of the differential equation is $-10y$. Also, since x and y differ only by a constant, which disappears when you differentiate, $\dot{x} = \dot{y}$ and $\ddot{x} = \ddot{y}$. The differential equation can therefore be written in terms of y as

$$-10y = 0.1\ddot{y}, \quad \text{which gives} \quad \ddot{y} = -100y.$$

This is precisely the equation obtained in Example 3.4.2; not surprisingly, since $(x - 0.098)$ metres is in fact the displacement beyond the equilibrium position, which was denoted by y metres in Example 3.4.2. But here the equation has been derived without first locating the equilibrium position.

You therefore have a choice of ways for dealing with problems involving masses supported by vertical strings or springs. Either you can begin by finding the equilibrium position and get the simple harmonic equation in its simplest form, or you can choose a simpler variable but solve a slightly more complicated differential equation by using a substitution.

The general result can be stated as follows.

> The differential equation $\ddot{x} = c - kx$, where c and k are constants and
> $k > 0$, can be rearranged in the form $\ddot{x} = -k\left(x - \dfrac{c}{k}\right)$ and reduced to the
> standard simple harmonic equation $\ddot{y} = -ky$ by means of the substitution
> $y = x - \dfrac{c}{k}$.

It is important to understand the method, but don't bother to remember the algebraic details.

Example 3.5.1

A spring supports a platform of mass 2 kg, which can move up and down inside a cylindrical container. When the spring is compressed by x metres, the thrust in the spring is 490x newtons. A package of mass 8 kg is placed gently on the platform, so that it begins to oscillate vertically. Find the greatest contact force between the package and the platform as it oscillates.

Fig. 3.9 shows the platform before the package is placed on it. The spring then supports the weight of the platform, which is 2×9.8 N, that is 19.6 N. So the spring is compressed by x metres where

$$490x = 19.6,$$

giving $x = 0.04$.

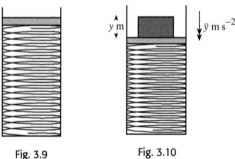

Fig. 3.9   Fig. 3.10

Fig. 3.10 shows the platform with the package on it after it has descended a distance of y metres. Considering the package and the platform together, with total mass 10 kg and weight 98 N, the acceleration is $\ddot{y}$ m s^{-2}. In this position the spring is compressed by $(0.04 + y)$ metres, so

$$98 - 490(0.04 + y) = 10\ddot{y}$$

giving

$$\ddot{y} = 7.84 - 49y.$$

This is not a standard simple harmonic motion equation, but it can be transformed into one by writing it as

$$\ddot{y} = -49\left(y - \frac{7.84}{49}\right) = -49(y - 0.16)$$

and substituting $y - 0.16 = z$. Since $\ddot{y} = \ddot{z}$, the equation then becomes

$$\ddot{z} = -49z.$$

This shows that the package oscillates with simple harmonic motion. Since the package is placed gently on the platform, the velocity $\dot{y} = 0$ when $y = 0$, so that $\dot{z} = 0$ when $z = 0 - 0.16 = -0.16$. The amplitude of the oscillation is therefore 0.16 metres, the greatest value of z in the oscillation is 0.16, and the greatest value of y is $0.16 + 0.16 = 0.32$. In this position, $\ddot{y} = \ddot{z} = -49 \times 0.16 = -7.84$.

To find the contact force between the package and the platform you must consider the forces on the package alone, which are shown in Fig. 3.11. The weight of the package is 8×9.8 N, that is 78.4 N. If the contact force is P newtons, where

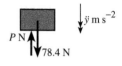

Fig. 3.11

$$78.4 - P = 8\ddot{y},$$

so $\qquad P = 78.4 - 8\ddot{y}.$

The greatest value of P is when $\ddot{y}$ is least, that is when $\ddot{y} = -7.84$. Then

$$P = 78.4 - 8 \times (-7.84) = 141.12.$$

The greatest contact force between the platform and the package is 141 newtons.

Equations of this kind sometimes arise in oscillation problems where there is no obvious equilibrium position. In the next example, Example 3.4.1 is reworked when the motion takes place on a rough table.

Example 3.5.2
A spring of natural length 0.6 metres is attached to a fixed point A on a horizontal table. A force of $10x$ newtons is needed to keep the spring extended by x metres. A block of mass 0.1 kg is attached to the other end. The coefficient of friction between the block and the table is $\frac{5}{7}$. The block is pulled away from A until it is 0.75 metres from A, and then let go. Describe the subsequent motion.

The normal contact force is equal to the weight of the block, which is 0.98 N. So the greatest possible friction force is $\frac{5}{7} \times 0.98$ N, or 0.7 N.

As in Example 3.4.1, denote the extension of the spring by x metres. When the block is released with $x = 0.15$, the tension in the spring is 10×0.15 N, which is 1.5 N. Since this is greater than the limiting friction, the block will begin to move towards A.

Fig. 3.12 shows the horizontal forces on the block, still moving towards A, when the extension is x metres. Notice that the acceleration must still be shown as $\ddot{x}$ in the positive direction, even though the velocity is in the opposite direction.

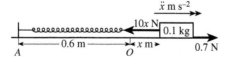

Fig. 3.12

Newton's second law then gives

$$\mathcal{R}(\rightarrow) \qquad 0.7 - 10x = 0.1\ddot{x}.$$

This can be solved by writing $0.7 - 10x$ as $-10(x - 0.07)$ and making the substitution $y = x - 0.07$. The differential equation then becomes

$$-10y = 0.1\ddot{y}, \quad \text{so} \quad \ddot{y} = -100y.$$

This represents simple harmonic motion about a centre of oscillation given by $y = 0$, or $x = 0.07$. Since initially $x = 0.15$, the amplitude is 0.08 metres, and after the first half-period the value of x is $(0.07 - 0.08)$ metres, which is -0.01 metres.

Also, as in Example 3.4.1, the complete period of this oscillation is $\frac{1}{5}\pi$ seconds. So after $\frac{1}{10}\pi$ seconds the block is stationary with the spring compressed by 0.01 metres. In this position the thrust from the spring is 10×0.01 N, which is 0.1 N. This is less than the limiting friction of 0.7 N, so the block will stay in this position and there will be no further motion.

The block will move towards A from its initial position until it is 0.59 metres from A, where it will remain at rest. The block will be in motion for $\frac{1}{10}\pi$ seconds, and over this time the (t, x) equation is $x = 0.67 + 0.08 \cos 10t$.

Example 3.5.3
A car tows a trailer of mass m with a rope of natural length l and modulus of elasticity mln^2 where n is a positive constant. The car and the trailer both start at rest and the rope is just taut. The car then accelerates at a constant rate c. Describe the motion of the trailer.

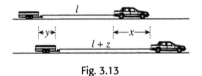

Fig. 3.13

In Fig. 3.13 the upper diagram shows the initial position, and the lower diagram shows the position after time t, when the car has moved a distance x, the trailer has moved a distance y, and the extension of the rope is z. The diagram shows that $l + x = y + (l + z)$, so

$$x = y + z.$$

Differentiating twice, and using the given fact that $\ddot{x} = c$,

$$\ddot{y} + \ddot{z} = c.$$

By Hooke's law, the tension in the rope is $\dfrac{(mln^2)z}{l}$, so Newton's second law applied to the motion of the trailer gives

$$mn^2 z = m\ddot{y}.$$

Eliminating $\ddot{y}$ between the last two equations,

$$\ddot{z} = c - n^2 z.$$

This can be rearranged as

$$\ddot{z} = -n^2 \left(z - \frac{c}{n^2} \right),$$

so make the substitution $z - \dfrac{c}{n^2} = w$ to obtain the standard simple harmonic differential equation

$$\ddot{w} = -n^2 w.$$

To solve this equation, the initial conditions for w need to be found. You are given that, when $t = 0$, $z = 0$. Also, when $t = 0$, $\dot{x} = 0$ and $\dot{y} = 0$; since $\dot{x} = \dot{y} + \dot{z}$, this means that $\dot{z} = 0$. So initially $w = -\dfrac{c}{n^2}$ and $\dot{w} = 0$. It follows that

$$w = -\frac{c}{n^2} \cos nt, \quad \text{so} \quad z = \frac{c}{n^2} - \frac{c}{n^2} \cos nt = \frac{c}{n^2}(1 - \cos nt).$$

At this point it is important to notice that the factor $1 - \cos nt$ is never negative, so the rope never becomes slack. This equation therefore continues to hold as long as the car is accelerating.

Now the question asks for the motion of the trailer rather than the extension of the rope. This can be found by using $x = y + z$, so $y = x - z$. The constant acceleration equations give $x = \frac{1}{2}ct^2$; combining this with the equation for z just found,

$$y = \tfrac{1}{2}ct^2 - \frac{c}{n^2}(1 - \cos nt).$$

This solution is illustrated by the graph in Fig. 3.14.

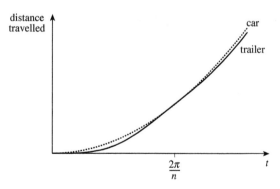

Fig. 3.14

The broken and solid lines show the distances travelled by the car and the trailer respectively. The trailer lags behind the car by an amount which oscillates between the values 0 and $\dfrac{2c}{n^2}$ with period $\dfrac{2\pi}{n}$.

3.6*   A geometrical illustration

The illustration of simple harmonic motion described in this section is especially useful when only a part of each oscillation is simple harmonic. It is also often used in physics to illustrate alternating current.

You will remember that the definition of cosine in C2 Section 1.1 was based on the idea of projecting a point of a circle of unit radius on the x-axis. A small generalisation suggests that the equation $x = a\cos(nt + \varepsilon)$ can be illustrated by drawing a circle of radius a, and taking a point P on it such that OP makes an angle $nt + \varepsilon$ with the x-axis. You then get Fig. 3.15, in which the x-coordinate of P is $a\cos(nt + \varepsilon)$, so that its projection N describes a simple harmonic oscillation along the x-axis. The point P starts at S when $t = 0$ and rotates round the circle with angular speed n. This shows that:

Simple harmonic motion along a line can be illustrated as the projection on the line of a point which moves round a circle with its centre at the centre of the oscillation, radius the amplitude, with constant angular speed n, where the period of the oscillation is $\dfrac{2\pi}{n}$.

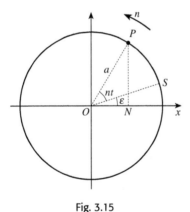

Fig. 3.15

Because n appears as the angular speed of P, the letter ω is sometimes used in place of n for this constant, especially in applications to electricity. You then get equations such as $x = a\cos(\omega t + \varepsilon)$, $v^2 = \omega^2(a^2 - x^2)$ and $\ddot{x} = -\omega^2 x$. The disadvantage of this is that you will soon meet examples of simple harmonic oscillation in which the variable is not a displacement but an angle, and using ω as the constant can then lead to confusion. So in this book the letter n has been chosen as the standard notation for this constant.

This illustration suggests another way of finding the acceleration of N. The formula for the acceleration of a particle moving in a circle is $r\omega^2$, which in the notation of Fig. 3.15 is an^2, in the direction $\overrightarrow{PO}$. So the acceleration of N is the resolved part of this in the x-direction, which is $an^2\cos(\omega t + \varepsilon)$, or $n^2 x$, in the direction opposite to the displacement. Therefore $\ddot{x} = -n^2 x$.

The illustration can sometimes be useful in solving problems, especially when the motion of a particle is simple harmonic for only part of the time.

Example 3.6.1
A particle is oscillating with simple harmonic motion of amplitude 5 units about the centre $x = -2$. For what proportion of the period is $x > 0$?

The motion can be regarded as the projection on the x-axis of a point moving round the circle in Fig. 3.16, with centre C and radius 5, at constant angular speed. The x-coordinate is positive when the point is on the minor arc AB.

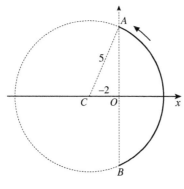

Fig. 3.16

The angle ACO is $\cos^{-1} 0.4 = 66.42...°$, so the minor arc AB is $\dfrac{2 \times 66.42...}{360} = 0.369...$ of the total circumference of the circle.

The x-coordinate is positive for 0.369 of the period, correct to 3 significant figures.

Example 3.6.2
A particle hangs from a fixed point by an elastic string of natural length l. The extension of the string when the particle hangs in equilibrium is $\frac{1}{2}l$. The particle is pulled down a further distance l below its equilibrium position and released from rest. Find the period of the subsequent oscillations.

If the particle has mass m, and the modulus of elasticity of the string is λ, then in equilibrium $mg = \dfrac{\lambda(\frac{1}{2}l)}{l}$, so $\lambda = 2mg$.

When the particle is a distance y below its equilibrium position, the tension in the string is $\dfrac{2mg(\frac{1}{2}l + y)}{l}$, which is $mg + \dfrac{2mgy}{l}$. Therefore

$$\mathcal{R}(\downarrow) \quad mg - \left(mg + \frac{2mgy}{l}\right) = m\ddot{y},$$

which gives the simple harmonic motion equation

$$\ddot{y} = -\frac{2g}{l}y.$$

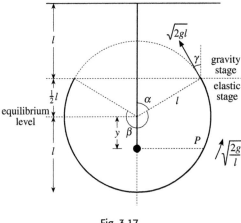

Fig. 3.17

Fig. 3.17 shows this motion illustrated as the projection, on the vertical line of the string, of a point P moving round a circle of radius l with angular speed $\sqrt{\dfrac{2g}{l}}$.

But this applies only for the part of the motion until the string becomes slack, which occurs when the particle is $\frac{1}{2}l$ above the centre of oscillation. At heights above this, the particle moves in a vertical line under the effect of gravity alone. The oscillation therefore splits into two stages, an 'elastic stage' and a 'gravity stage', which must be considered separately.

Elastic stage   The angle labelled α in Fig. 3.17 is $\cos^{-1}\frac{1}{2}$, which is $\frac{1}{3}\pi$, so the angle labelled β is $\frac{4}{3}\pi$. The time for the point to rotate through this angle at angular speed $\sqrt{\dfrac{2g}{l}}$ is $\frac{4}{3}\pi \Big/ \sqrt{\dfrac{2g}{l}}$, which can be written as $\frac{2}{3}\pi\sqrt{\dfrac{2l}{g}}$.

Gravity stage   During the elastic stage the point goes round the circumference of the circle with speed $l \times \sqrt{\dfrac{2g}{l}}$, which is $\sqrt{2gl}$. As the string becomes slack the speed of the particle is the vertical resolved part of $\sqrt{2gl}$; since the angle labelled γ is $\frac{1}{6}\pi$, this speed is $\sqrt{2gl} \times \frac{1}{2}\sqrt{3}$.

Now the time for a particle thrown upwards with speed u to return to the point from which is was thrown is found from the equation $0 = ut - \frac{1}{2}gt^2$, which gives $\dfrac{2u}{g}$. So the time taken for the gravity stage is $\dfrac{2\sqrt{2gl}}{g} \times \frac{1}{2}\sqrt{3}$, which can be written as $\sqrt{3} \times \sqrt{\dfrac{2l}{g}}$.

The total time for a complete oscillation is therefore $\left(\frac{2}{3}\pi + \sqrt{3}\right)\sqrt{\dfrac{2l}{g}}$.

3.7   Solving the differential equation

The last three sections have used the result that, if x and t are related by the differential equation $\ddot{x} = -n^2x$, then $x = a\cos(nt + \varepsilon)$ for some constants a and ε. But this hasn't yet been proved. You can do this by using some of the methods introduced in Chapter 1.

A first integration can be done by writing the acceleration $\ddot{x}$ in the form $v\dfrac{dv}{dx}$ (see Section 1.3). This gives a differential equation,

$$v\dfrac{dv}{dx} = -n^2 x,$$

in which the variables v and x are separable. Since $v\dfrac{dv}{dx} = \dfrac{d}{dx}(\tfrac{1}{2}v^2)$, it can be integrated directly as

$$\tfrac{1}{2}v^2 = -\tfrac{1}{2}n^2 x^2 + k,$$

where the constant k is obviously positive (or, uninterestingly, zero), since it is the sum of two terms involving squares. You could therefore write k as $\tfrac{1}{2}n^2 a^2$, where a is a positive number. The equation then takes the form

$$v^2 = n^2(a^2 - x^2),$$

an equation you are already familiar with.

This is halfway to the solution. To get an equation connecting x and t, you can now write v as $\dfrac{dx}{dt}$ and integrate the equation

$$\left(\dfrac{dx}{dt}\right)^2 = n^2(a^2 - x^2).$$

The rest of the solution uses a substitution technique which you may not have met. If so, you can omit what follows and simply check for yourself that $x = a\cos(nt + \varepsilon)$ is a solution of the differential equation for any value of the arbitrary constant ε.

* Notice that the right side involves only the variable x, so this is a differential equation which can be solved using the method in Section 1.4, writing $\dfrac{dt}{dx}$ as $1\left/\dfrac{dx}{dt}\right.$. But before embarking on the details it is worth noting that it will be necessary to take a square root, and that this will lead to an expression involving $\sqrt{a^2 - x^2}$. It is shown in C4 Chapter 2 that in such cases the substitution $x = a\sin u$ or $x = a\cos u$ is often useful.

It turns out to be neater to make such a substitution in the differential equation straight away. If $x = a\cos u$, then by the chain rule $\dfrac{dx}{dt} = -a\sin u\dfrac{du}{dt}$. This converts the differential equation to

$$\left(-a\sin u\dfrac{du}{dt}\right)^2 = n^2(a^2 - a^2\cos^2 u).$$

This can be simplified to

$$a^2\sin^2 u\left(\dfrac{du}{dt}\right)^2 = n^2 a^2\sin^2 u,$$

so $$\left(\dfrac{du}{dt}\right)^2 = n^2.$$

One reason for proceeding in this way is to put off as long as possible taking a square root, which introduces the ambiguity of a $\pm$ sign. But this can't be deferred any longer, and the next step is to deduce that

$$\text{either } \frac{du}{dt} = n \quad \text{or} \quad \frac{du}{dt} = -n.$$

In fact it doesn't matter which choice you make, so long as you stick to one or the other throughout the motion. The reason for this is that you want to make a substitution so that $\frac{dx}{dt}$ and $\frac{dx}{du}$ vary continuously, so $\frac{du}{dt}$ must do the same.

Suppose you choose the positive sign. Then

$$\frac{du}{dt} = n \quad \Rightarrow \quad u = nt + \varepsilon, \text{ for some constant } \varepsilon.$$

And since $x = a \cos u$, it follows that

$$x = a \cos(nt + \varepsilon),$$

which is the solution required.

What would happen if you chose the negative sign?

Another method of solving the differential equation is suggested in Exercise 3C Question 16, in which you can go directly from $\ddot{x} = -n^2 x$ to the (t, x) equation $x = A \cos nt + B \sin nt$, which can be written alternatively as $x = a \cos(nt + \varepsilon)$ (see C3 Section 6.6). Yet another method, using complex numbers, is given in FP3 Chapter 8. With these alternative methods, the difficulty of the ambiguous square root doesn't arise.

Exercise 3C

1 A particle is oscillating with simple harmonic motion on the x-axis about the centre $x = 7$. It starts from rest at $x = 20$, and the period of a complete oscillation is 10 seconds. After what time does x first become negative?

2 A particle is in simple harmonic oscillation of amplitude 3 cm about a centre O. For what proportion of the time is it more than 2 cm from O?

3 A marker buoy has the form of a cylinder of height 1.2 metres with its axis vertical. It is performing simple harmonic oscillations in a vertical line with period 6 seconds, and the depth of the base varies between 0.4 metres and 1 metre. Find the length of time in each oscillation for which more than half of the buoy is visible above the surface.

4 In a child's toy a face oscillates up and down behind a screen with period 5 seconds and amplitude 2 cm. The top of the face is visible above the top of the screen for 4 seconds of the period. If the face is 3 cm high, find for how long in each period the whole face can be seen, assuming that the oscillation is simple harmonic.

5 A flexible metal strip is pushed horizontally into a crack in a wall, and a cherry pip is placed on it at its free end. This free end is depressed by 2 cm and then released, so that it oscillates with simple harmonic motion 5 times a second. After what time will contact be broken between the pip and the metal strip, and with what speed will it then be moving?

6* Use the geometrical illustration of simple harmonic motion described in Section 3.6 to demonstrate the equation $v^2 = n^2(a^2 - x^2)$.

7 Solve the following differential equations with the given initial conditions.

(a) $\ddot{x} = -25(x - 1.6)$, $x = 6$ and $\dot{x} = 0$ when $t = 0$

(b) $\ddot{x} = -4x - 12$, $x = 0$ and $\dot{x} = 0$ when $t = 0$

8 Rework Example 3.4.3 using the length of the string attached at A as the variable.

9* Rework Example 3.5.2 if the coefficient of friction is $\frac{1}{7}$.

10 An elastic string of natural length 50 cm and modulus of elasticity 0.9 newtons hangs from a fixed point. While the string is unstretched, a ring of mass 50 grams is attached to the free end and then released from rest. Show that, if the extension of the string is x metres after t seconds, then x satisfies the differential equation $\ddot{x} = 9.8 - 36x$. Hence find the period of oscillation of the ring, and the extension of the string when the ring is in equilibrium.

11 A particle of mass 10 grams hangs in equilibrium from the roof of a stationary lift by an elastic string of natural length 80 cm and modulus of elasticity 20 newtons. The lift starts to move upwards with acceleration $0.2 \, \text{m s}^{-2}$. Find an expression for the extension of the string after t seconds.

12 A bungee jumper falls a total distance of 48 metres, of which the first 20 metres are free fall under gravity alone before the rope becomes taut. Find the total time she takes to fall to the lowest point of her jump, and the greatest speed she attains.

13 A weather balloon has mass 25 kg. Since the density of air decreases with height, the force of buoyancy supporting the balloon at a height x metres above the ground is modelled by the formula $(400 - 0.04x)$ newtons. The balloon oscillates in a vertical line with amplitude 200 metres. Show that the motion is simple harmonic, and find the period of the oscillation.

The cloud base is at a height of 4000 metres. Find for how long the balloon disappears from view during each oscillation.

14 An elastic band has natural length l and modulus of elasticity λ. It is hooked round two smooth pegs a distance l apart at the same level. A particle of mass m is attached to the band, as shown in the diagram, so that the band takes the form of an isosceles triangle with the particle at its apex. Show that, when the particle is at a distance x below the pegs, the tension produces a force vertically upwards of $\dfrac{4\lambda x}{l}$.

If the particle is disturbed from its equilibrium position and oscillates in a vertical line, show that the equilibrium position is the centre of the oscillation and find the period.

15* A particle of mass m moves along a straight line. When the particle is at P, it is acted on by a force $F = mn^2x$ directed towards a point O of the line, where x denotes the displacement OP. The velocity of the particle at P is v. At the point A where x has the value a, $v = 0$. Find the work done against F as the particle moves from P to A. Hence show that the equation $v^2 = n^2(a^2 - x^2)$ can be derived from a work–energy equation.

16* Show that the substitution $x = w \cos nt$, where w is a function of t, converts the equation $\ddot{x} = -n^2x$ to $\ddot{w} \cos nt - 2n\dot{w} \sin nt = 0$. Hence show that $\dfrac{d}{dt}(\dot{w} \cos^2 nt) = 0$.
Deduce that $x = A \cos nt + B \sin nt$, where A and B are arbitrary constants.

Miscellaneous exercise 3

1 A particle moves in a straight line with simple harmonic motion. At time t seconds the velocity of the particle is $6 \cos 3t \ \mathrm{m\,s}^{-1}$. Calculate the speed of the particle when $t = 7$, and the amplitude of the motion. (OCR)

2 A particle is moving in a straight line with simple harmonic motion. The maximum speed of the particle is $4 \ \mathrm{m\,s}^{-1}$, and the amplitude of the motion is 8 metres. Calculate the period of the motion. (OCR)

3 A particle of mass 0.3 kg is moving in a straight line with simple harmonic motion. The period of the motion is π seconds and the amplitude is 0.2 metres. Calculate the maximum speed of the particle, and the maximum magnitude of the resultant force on the particle. (OCR)

4 An engineer is observing a machine component performing simple harmonic motion about a fixed point O. She uses x to denote the displacement (in cm) of the component from O, and t to denote the time (in seconds) from the first observation.

She first observes the component when $x = 3$ and it is moving away from O. Two seconds later she observes it pass through O for the first time. She observes that the period of the motion is 6 seconds. Sketch a graph of x against t for $0 \leqslant t \leqslant 6$, showing the values of x and t where the graph crosses the axes.

An expression for x in terms of t of the form $x = a \cos(\omega t + \varepsilon)$ is to be found.

(a) Calculate ω and a value of ε between $-\pi$ and π.

(b) Calculate the amplitude of the motion and hence, or otherwise, calculate the speed of the component when it was first observed.

(c) Find the greatest acceleration of the component. (MEI, adapted)

5 A student is investigating simple harmonic motion in a laboratory. She makes measurements using a scale pan suspended by an elastic spring and carrying a small particle. She uses the following notation to describe the simple harmonic motion:

x is the displacement upwards in metres from the centre of the oscillation,

t is the time, measured in seconds from an instant when the pan is at its highest point,

a is the amplitude,

T is the period.

Sketch the graph of x against t.

She notes that, at time $t = 0$, the scale pan is 0.1 m above a mark on an adjacent wall. At $t = 2.5$ s, the pan passes the mark for the first time and at $t = 12.5$ s the pan passes the mark for the second time. Explain how this information tells you that $T = 15$ s.

By writing down an expression for x as a function of t, deduce the value of the amplitude a.

In another experiment, she uses a different spring and particle but ensures that the amplitude of the motion remains the same as before. She notes that the particle just breaks contact with the scale pan for one instant in every complete oscillation. Find the period of the oscillation in this case.   (MEI)

6 A particle P of mass 0.2 kg is attached to fixed points A and B on a smooth horizontal table by two light elastic strings, each of natural length 0.3 metres and modulus of elasticity 12 newtons. The distance AB is 1 metre, and O is the mid-point of AB. The particle is projected horizontally from O towards B with initial speed $2\,\mathrm{m\,s^{-1}}$. At time t seconds after projection, the displacement of P from O towards B is x metres and both strings are taut. Show that the tension in the string PB is $(8 - 40x)$ newtons, and find the corresponding expression for the tension in the string PA. Hence show that the particle moves with simple harmonic motion of period 0.1π seconds and amplitude 0.1 metres.

Calculate the speed of the particle when $x = 0.08$, and the displacement of the particle towards O when $t = 0.15$.   (OCR)

7 A particle of mass 0.2 kg is connected by two equal light elastic springs, each of natural length 0.5 metres and modulus of elasticity 5 newtons, to two points A and B on a smooth horizontal table. The mid-point of AB is O and the length of AB is 1 metre. The particle is displaced from O, towards B, through a distance of 0.3 metres to a point C and released from rest. In the subsequent motion air resistance may be neglected. After t seconds the displacement of the particle from O is x metres. Show that $\dfrac{d^2x}{dt^2} = -100x$.

The particle moves a distance 0.1 metres from C to D. Find, to 3 significant figures, the speed of the particle at D, and the time taken to reach D.

When the particle reaches D the spring joining the particle to A breaks. Find the speed of the particle as it passes through O.   (OCR)

8 *AB* and *BC* are two light springs each of natural
   length *l* but with modulus of elasticity *kl* and *2kl*
   respectively, as shown in the diagram. The ends *A*
   and *C* are attached to fixed points *A* and *C* a
   distance *5l* apart. The other end of each spring is
   attached to a mass *m* and oscillations can take place

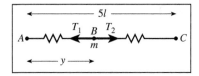

   along the line *ABC* on a smooth horizontal table. The variable *y* gives the distance of the
   mass *m* from *A* at time *t*.

   The mass *m* is held at rest at the mid-point of *AC*, when $y = \frac{5}{2}l$, and is then released.

   (a) Find the tensions T_1 and T_2 in the two springs *AB* and *BC* respectively, in terms of *y*, at
       any later time.

   (b) Write down the equation of motion of the mass at time *t*. Show that the motion is
       simple harmonic and that the centre of the motion is at the point where $y = 3l$.

   (c) Write down the period and amplitude, showing that the period is independent of *l*.

   (d) Whilst the mass is once again held at rest when $y = \frac{5}{2}l$, the end *C* is moved a further
       distance $\frac{5}{2}l$ away from *A* in the same line. The distance *AC* is now $\frac{15}{2}l$. The mass is then
       released from rest. Show that the period of the resulting oscillation is unaltered but
       that the amplitude is increased by $\frac{5}{3}l$.   (MEI, adapted)

9 A particle of mass *m* is attached to one end of a light elastic string of modulus *3mg* and
   natural length *3l*. The other end of the string is attached to a fixed point *A*. The particle
   can move freely under gravity in the vertical line containing *A*. Let *y* be the displacement
   below *A* of the particle at time *t*.

   (a) Show that $y = 4l$ when the particle hangs in equilibrium.

   (b) The particle is pulled down a distance $\frac{1}{2}l$ from the equilibrium position and released
       from rest. Show that the motion is simple harmonic. Find the period and amplitude
       and explain why the string does not become slack.

   (c) The particle is now pulled down a distance *2l* from the equilibrium position and
       released from rest when the time *t* is zero. Show that the string first becomes slack

       when $t = \frac{2}{3}\pi\sqrt{\dfrac{l}{g}}$. Find the value of *y* when the particle is at its greatest height.   (MEI)

10 A small block, which may be modelled as a particle of mass 0.8 kg, is attached to one end
   of a light elastic string of natural length 0.5 metres and modulus of elasticity 10 newtons.
   The other end of the string is attached to a point *O* of a rough horizontal table. The block
   rests in limiting equilibrium at a point *A* of the table, where *OA* = 0.7 metres. Calculate
   the coefficient of friction between the block and the table.

   The block is given a speed of $2\,\mathrm{m\,s^{-1}}$ in the direction $\overrightarrow{AO}$. After *t* seconds the block has
   moved *x* metres.

   (a) Show that, while the string is extended, $\dfrac{d^2x}{dt^2} = -25x$.

   (b) Calculate the speed of the block at the instant when the string becomes slack.

   (c) Given that the block does not reach *O*, calculate the length of time during which the
       block is in motion.   (OCR)

11 A light elastic string, of natural length 1 metre and modulus of elasticity 20 newtons, has one end attached to a point O of a rough horizontal table. The other end is attached to a small block P of mass 0.50 kg. Initially the block is at rest on the table with the string just taut. The block is then pulled by a force of constant magnitude 10 newtons in the direction $\overrightarrow{OP}$. The block comes to instantaneous rest after moving 0.8 metres. Neglecting air resistance, show, by consideration of work and energy, that the coefficient of friction between the block and the table is approximately 0.41.

At any time before first coming to instantaneous rest the block has moved x metres in t seconds.

(a) Show that $\dfrac{d^2x}{dt^2} = 16 - 40x$.

(b) Find the value of x when the speed is greatest.

(c) Show that the substitution $y = x - 0.4$ transforms the differential equation in part (a) to $\dfrac{d^2y}{dt^2} = -40y$. Find the time taken for the block to move the first 0.8 metres.

State, giving a reason, whether the differential equation in part (a) applies after the block comes to instantaneous rest.   (OCR, adapted)

12 A cylindrical tube of length 0.25 metres is closed at one end. Fixed to the closed end of the tube is a light spring of modulus 0.49 newtons and natural length 0.25 metres. The tube is fixed in a vertical position with its open end uppermost. A small ball of mass 0.01 kg is placed on the spring. The internal surface of the tube is smooth. The ball and the spring may be assumed to move vertically and to remain in contact while the ball is wholly or partly in the tube.

(a) Show that when the ball is in equilibrium the length of the spring is 0.2 metres.

(b) The ball is pushed down a short distance and released. Show that the resulting motion may be modelled by the simple harmonic motion equation $\ddot{x} + 196x = 0$, where x metres is the displacement of the base of the ball above the equilibrium position at time t seconds.

(c) The ball is struck sharply with a stick, so that when it loses contact with the stick it has a velocity of $0.126\,\mathrm{m\,s^{-1}}$ downwards and its displacement is 0.04 metres below the equilibrium position. Show that the amplitude of the resulting motion is 0.041 metres. Hence use the general solution of the simple harmonic motion equation in part (b), in the form $x = a\sin(\omega t + \varepsilon)$, to find an expression for x in terms of t, the time after it loses contact with the stick.

(d) The ball can be retrieved from the tube when the displacement above the equilibrium position is at least 0.04 metres. Find the time at which this is first possible.   (MEI)

13 A light elastic string, of natural length 1.2 metres and modulus of
    elasticity λ newtons, has one end attached to a point O of a smooth
    horizontal plane. The string passes through a small smooth ring
    fixed at a height 1.2 metres above O.

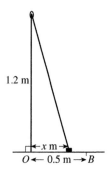

    A small block of mass 0.4 kg is attached to the other end of the
    string. The block is held on the plane at the point B, where
    $OB = 0.5$ metres (see diagram). The block is released from rest and
    moves along the straight line BO without leaving the plane. Show
    that the vertical component of the force on the block due to the
    string is constant, and hence show that the greatest possible value
    of λ is approximately 3.92.

    While the block moves from B to O, its displacement from O after t seconds is x metres.
    Show, neglecting air resistance, that $\ddot{x} = -\dfrac{25\lambda}{12}x$.

    The block passes through the point C, where $BC = 0.11$ metres, when $t = 0.27$. Find the
    value of λ, and the speed of the block at C.   (OCR)

14 The diagram shows a particle P of mass 0.1 kg on a pan Q of mass
    0.2 kg which is attached to one end of a light spring. The spring is
    suspended from a fixed point O. The spring has natural length
    0.5 metres and modulus of elasticity 9.8 newtons. Show that, when the
    system is in equilibrium, the total length of the spring is 0.65 metres.

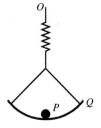

    Q is raised 0.15 metres above the equilibrium position and is released
    from rest with P lying in the pan. Air resistance may be ignored in the
    subsequent motion.

    Modelling P together with Q as a single particle, prove that the motion is simple
    harmonic with period 0.78 seconds approximately. Find the distance from the equilibrium
    position when the speed is $1 \, \text{m s}^{-1}$.

    Hence, or otherwise, find the two values for the magnitude of the force exerted by Q on P
    when they are moving with speed $1 \, \text{m s}^{-1}$.   (OCR)

Revision exercise 1

1 A particle is moving with simple harmonic motion in a straight line. The period is 0.2 s and the amplitude of the motion is 0.3 m. Find the maximum speed of the particle. (OCR)

2 An aircraft of mass 80 000 kg travelling at 90 m s^{-1} touches down on a straight horizontal runway. It is brought to rest by braking and resistive forces which together are modelled by a horizontal force of magnitude $(27\,000 + 50v^2)$ newtons, where v m s^{-1} is the speed of the aircraft. Find the distance travelled by the aircraft between touching down and coming to rest. (OCR)

3 For a bungee jump, a girl is joined to a fixed point O of a bridge by an elastic rope of natural length 25 m and modulus of elasticity 1320 N. The girl starts from rest at O and falls vertically. The lowest point reached by the girl is 60 m vertically below O. The girl is modelled as a particle, the rope is assumed to be light, and air resistance is neglected.

(a) Use energy considerations to find the mass of the girl.

(b) Find the tension in the rope when the girl is at the lowest point.

(c) Find the acceleration of the girl when she is at the lowest point. (OCR)

4 Two points A and B lie on a vertical line with A at a distance 2.6 m above B. A particle P of mass 10 kg is joined to A by an elastic string and to B by another elastic string (see diagram). Each string has natural length 0.8 m and modulus of elasticity 196 N. The strings are light and air resistance may be neglected.

(a) Verify that P is in equilibrium when P is vertically below A and the length of the string PA is 1.5 m.

The particle is set in motion along the line AB with both strings remaining taut. The displacement of P below the equilibrium position is denoted by x metres.

(b) Show that the tension in the string PA is $245(0.7 + x)$ newtons, and the tension in the string PB is $245(0.3 - x)$ newtons.

(c) Show that the motion of P is simple harmonic, and find the period. (OCR)

5 A particle of mass 0.2 kg is released from rest and falls vertically. At time t seconds after release, the speed of the particle is v m s^{-1} and the air resistance acting on the particle has magnitude $0.07v$ newtons.

(a) Show that $\left(\dfrac{1}{28 - v}\right)\dfrac{dv}{dt} = 0.35$, and hence find v in terms of t.

(b) Find the distance fallen by the particle during the first 3 seconds after release. (OCR)

6 A light spring with modulus of elasticity $259\,\mathrm{N}$ is placed in a vertical line with its lower end on the ground. A block of mass $5\,\mathrm{kg}$ rests on the upper end of the spring (see diagram). The block is in equilibrium when the length of the spring is $0.6\,\mathrm{m}$.

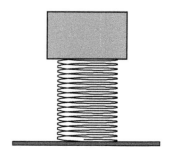

(a) Find the natural length of the spring.

(b) Find the elastic potential energy stored in the spring when the block is in equilibrium.

The block starts at rest in the equilibrium position. A constant force F newtons, acting vertically upwards, is now applied to the block. The block moves upwards, and first comes to instantaneous rest in the position where the spring has its natural length.

(c) By considering work and energy, or otherwise, find F.   (OCR)

7 A particle Q of mass m moves along the straight line between two fixed points A and B, where $AB = 3a$. The only forces acting on Q are $F_1 = \dfrac{4\,mk}{x^2}$ towards A and $F_2 = \dfrac{mk}{(3a - x)^2}$ towards B, where x is the distance of Q from A and k is a positive constant (see diagram).

(a) Express the acceleration of Q in terms of x, a and k.

(b) Show that $x = 2a$ is the only value of x between 0 and $3a$ for which the acceleration is zero.

When $x = a$, Q is moving towards B with speed $\sqrt{\dfrac{8k}{a}}$.

(c) Express the speed of Q in terms of x, a and k.

(d) Find the minimum speed of Q.   (OCR)

8 A particle P of mass $2\,\mathrm{kg}$ is connected to a fixed point O by a light elastic string of natural length $1.5\,\mathrm{m}$. The particle hangs in equilibrium at a distance of $1.7\,\mathrm{m}$ vertically below O.

(a) Find the modulus of elasticity of the string.

Starting in the equilibrium position, P is struck so that it begins to move vertically downwards at $2.8\,\mathrm{m\,s^{-1}}$. In the subsequent motion the only forces acting on P are its weight and the tension in the string. At time t seconds later, the string is still taut and P is x metres below the equilibrium position.

(b) Show that $\dfrac{\mathrm{d}^2 x}{\mathrm{d}t^2} = -49x$.

(c) Express x in terms of t.

(d) Find the time between the start of the motion and the instant when the string first becomes slack.   (OCR)

9 The fixed points A and B are on the same horizontal level at a distance 1.2 m apart. A rock of mass 3 kg is joined to A and B by two elastic strings, each of natural length 0.5 m and modulus of elasticity 900 N. The rock is held at a point 0.25 m vertically below the mid-point M of AB (see diagram). The rock is released from rest in this position and it then moves vertically upwards.

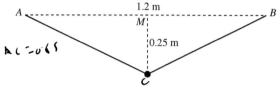

(a) Find the tension in each string at the instant when the rock is released.

(b) Find the acceleration of the rock immediately after it is released.

(c) Use energy considerations to find the speed of the rock when it passes through M.

(d) State three modelling assumptions made when answering this question.   (OCR)

10 A uniform plank AB, of length 3 m and mass 30 kg, is freely hinged at the end A. A light elastic rope, of natural length 3 m, has one end attached to the end B of the plank and the other end attached to a fixed point C vertically above A. In equilibrium the plank is horizontal and the rope makes an angle of $35°$ with the horizontal. Find

(a) the tension in the rope,

(b) the modulus of elasticity of the rope,

(c) the horizontal and vertical components of the force acting on the plank at A.   (OCR)

11 A piston of mass m kg can move inside a fixed cylindrical tube. There is a force on the piston due to the pressure of the gas in the region G of the tube; this force is inversely proportional to x, where x metres is the displacement of the piston from the end of the tube. The velocity of the piston, in the direction of increasing x, is $v\,\mathrm{m\,s^{-1}}$ (see diagram). It may be assumed that the region A of the tube is a vacuum, thus containing no gas, and that there is no friction between the piston and the tube.

(a) Write down a differential equation relating v and x.

(b) Given that $v = 0$ when $x = 0.01$ and that $v = 10$ when $x = 1$, show that
$$v^2 \ln 100 = 100 \ln(100x).$$

In a more realistic model, the contact between the piston and the tube cannot be assumed to be smooth. Write down a modified differential equation corresponding to (a) to take this into account.   (OCR)

12 A china vase rests on a horizontal shelf. The coefficient of friction between the vase and the shelf is 0.4. The effects of an earthquake are simulated by vibrating the shelf horizontally with simple harmonic motion, making 3 complete oscillations per second. Through what distance must the shelf vibrate for the vase to slip?

13 A child's toy consists of a bat of mass 0.12 kg attached to a small ball of mass 0.03 kg by a light elastic string of natural length 0.5 m.

(a) When the ball hangs vertically in equilibrium, the string is 0.6 m long. Show that the modulus of elasticity of the string is 1.47 N.

(b) The child now holds the ball and lets the bat hang vertically in equilibrium. Calculate the length of the string.

(c) The child holds the bat and hits the ball vertically upwards. It leaves the bat with speed $7 \, \text{m s}^{-1}$. Assuming that the bat is stationary from the moment the ball loses contact with it, find the greatest height of the ball above the bat.

(d) Another child has an identical toy. The children manage to entangle the strings at the ends connected to the balls. They slowly pull the bats apart until they are at rest on the same horizontal level. The balls hang in equilibrium and both strings are at an angle of 30° to the horizontal. Calculate the distance between the bats.   (MEI)

14 One end of a light elastic spring, of natural length 0.3 m and modulus of elasticity 150 N, is attached to a fixed point O on a smooth horizontal table. A particle P of mass 0.2 kg is attached to the other end of the spring. The particle P is released from rest at a point on the table such that the distance OP is 0.2 m. It subsequently collides with a particle Q, of mass 0.25 kg, which is at rest at a distance of 0.3 m from O. Immediately after the collision the speed of P is $0.5 \, \text{m s}^{-1}$. Calculate the two possible values of the speed with which Q starts to move.   (OCR)

15 A light elastic string of natural length 1.6 m and modulus of elasticity 2 N has a small metal ball of mass 0.09 kg attached to one end, the other end being attached to a point on the ceiling of a room. The ball hangs freely at rest under gravity. Find the least possible height of the ceiling.

The ball is set in motion in such a way that it moves with constant speed in a horizontal circle with the string inclined at an angle of 30° to the vertical. Find

(a) the tension in the string,

(b) the time for the ball to make one complete revolution.   (OCR)

16 Each of two equal particles A and B has a mass of 0.25 kg. The particles are at rest on a smooth horizontal table, with B attached to one end of a light horizontal spring. The other end of the spring is fixed to a point O on the table, and A, B and O lie in a straight line in that order. The spring has natural length 2 m and modulus of elasticity 16 N. The particle A is projected across the table towards B. When A strikes B the particles coalesce, and the combined particle initially moves towards O with speed $3 \, \text{m s}^{-1}$. Calculate the speed of A immediately before the collision.

Ignoring air resistance, show that, after the collision, the combined particle moves with simple harmonic motion. Hence

(a) show that the period of the motion is approximately 1.57 s,

(b) show that the shortest length of the spring during the subsequent motion is 1.25 m,

(c) find the time which elapses before the length of the spring is first 2.1 m.   (OCR)

17 The diagram shows a child's toy, which is cylindrical in shape, and 10 cm high. Inside the cylinder is a horizontal plastic plate, of mass 30 grams, whose diameter is equal to the internal diameter of the cylinder. The plate is supported by three springs, each of natural length 12 cm and modulus of elasticity 24 newtons. At the top of the cylinder the rim projects inwards, so that the plate is prevented from rising above it.

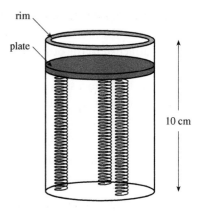

The child places a woolly ball of mass 50 grams on the plate, pushes it down until the plate is 3 cm below the rim of the cylinder, and then releases it. Calculate

(a) the height to which the ball rises above the base of the toy,

(b) the impulse on the projecting rim when the plate hits it.

18 A cyclist free-wheels down a hill that makes a constant angle of 5° with the horizontal. The total mass of the cyclist and the bicycle is 85 kg. The cyclist travels at a constant speed. Calculate the resistance to the motion.

While still travelling down this hill, the cyclist begins to pedal, working at a constant rate of 150 W. Assuming that the resistance to motion retains the same constant value as before,

(a) write down a differential equation relating the distance, x metres, moved since the cyclist began pedalling, and the cyclist's speed, $v \, \text{m s}^{-1}$,

(b) show that the distance moved while the cyclist's speed increases from $8 \, \text{m s}^{-1}$ to $12 \, \text{m s}^{-1}$ is 230 m, correct to 2 significant figures.

On another occasion, the same cyclist is cycling up the same hill. At a certain instant the cyclist's speed is $5 \, \text{m s}^{-1}$ and the resistance to motion has the same value as before. The cyclist is again working at a constant rate of 150 W. Calculate the deceleration of the cyclist at this instant.

Show that the time, in seconds, taken for the cyclist's speed up the hill to drop from $5 \, \text{m s}^{-1}$ to $2 \, \text{m s}^{-1}$ is $\displaystyle\int_2^5 \frac{85v}{145v - 150} \, dv$, approximately, assuming that the cyclist's rate of working and the resistance to motion remain unchanged.   (OCR)

19* A microlight aircraft of mass m is in steady level flight with speed v_0 at a height h_0 above the ground. The lift force on the wings is given by an equation of the form $L = kv^2$, where v is the forward speed of the aircraft, and in steady flight $kv_0^2 = mg$.

The aircraft momentarily experiences some turbulence which gives it a small velocity upwards. As it rises to a height h, it gains potential energy, so that the forward speed is reduced to v, where $\frac{1}{2}mv^2 = \frac{1}{2}mv_0^2 - mg(h - h_0)$. Show that the subsequent height of the aircraft is given by the equation $\ddot{h} = -\dfrac{2kg}{m}(h - h_0)$.

According to this model, describe how the turbulence will affect the subsequent motion of the microlight.

20 The end A of an inextensible light string of length l is attached to a fixed point, and an object of mass m is attached to the other end B. A light spring of natural length $\frac{1}{4}l$ and modulus of elasticity $mg\sqrt{3}$ is attached to B and to a smooth pivot at the point O. The system rotates with angular speed ω about the vertical line OA. The angle $OAB = 30°$ and OB is horizontal, as shown in the figure.

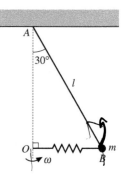

(a) Find the tension in the string AB and show that the tension in the spring OB is $\frac{1}{4}mg\sqrt{3}$.

(b) Deduce that $\omega^2 = \dfrac{7g\sqrt{3}}{6l}$. (MEI, adapted)

21 A man of mass $80\,\text{kg}$, wearing a parachute, falls from rest from the edge of a high cliff. When his speed is $20\,\text{m s}^{-1}$ he pulls the cord which releases the parachute. While the parachute is opening the resistance to motion is $32v$ newtons, where $v\,\text{m s}^{-1}$ is the man's speed. It takes 6 seconds for the parachute to open fully. Show that, t seconds after pulling the cord, v is given by

$$v = 24.5 - 4.5e^{-0.4t}, \qquad 0 \leqslant t \leqslant 6.$$

Find the distance moved by the man while the parachute is opening. (OCR)

22 A glider and its pilot have total mass $230\,\text{kg}$. The glider lands on a horizontal airstrip and when its speed is $16\,\text{m s}^{-1}$ it hooks on to the mid-point of a light elastic rope of natural length $40\,\text{m}$ and modulus of elasticity $4000\,\text{N}$. The ends of the rope are fixed to points A and B of the airstrip, where $AB = 40\,\text{m}$. When the glider hooks on to the rope, the glider is moving in a direction perpendicular to AB. The modelling assumptions are that the glider may be treated as a particle moving horizontally, and that the only horizontal force acting results from the tension in the rope. Find

(a) the speed of the glider when it has moved $15\,\text{m}$ past the mid-point of AB,

(b) the displacement from the mid-point of AB when the glider first comes instantaneously to rest,

(c) the acceleration of the glider when it first comes instantaneously to rest. (OCR)

23 A particle P of mass $0.5\,\text{kg}$ is free to move in the straight line OA, where $OA = 6\,\text{m}$. The particle is joined to A by a light elastic string of natural length $2\,\text{m}$ and modulus of elasticity $20\,\text{N}$. In addition the particle is attracted towards O by a force of magnitude $\dfrac{k}{x^2}\,\text{N}$, where k is a constant and the distance OP is x metres. The equilibrium position of the particle is E, where $OE = 2\,\text{m}$. Show that $k = 80$.

The particle is pulled to the point B, between O and A, where $OB = 4\,\text{m}$, and released from rest. The velocity of P when $OP = x$ metres is denoted by $v\,\text{m s}^{-1}$. Obtain a differential equation relating v and x.

Find the speed of P as it passes through the mid-point of OA.

24* A particle of mass m is attached to a fixed point O on a smooth horizontal table by a light elastic string of natural length a and modulus of elasticity λ. The particle moves on the table in a circle, centre O, with constant angular speed ω.

(a) Show that the extension of the string is $\dfrac{ma^2\omega^2}{\lambda - ma\omega^2}$.

(b) The kinetic energy of the particle is K and the elastic potential energy of the string is V. Show that $\dfrac{K}{V} = \dfrac{\lambda}{ma\omega^2}$, and deduce that $K > V$.

(c) If the extension of the string exceeds a, the particle will fall off the table. Show that the greatest value of ω that allows the particle to remain on the table is given by $\omega^2 = \dfrac{\lambda}{2ma}$.

(d) The particle is moving with the extension of the string equal to a. It is brought to instantaneous rest, and immediately begins to move towards O under the tension in the string. Show that its speed when it reaches O is $a\omega\sqrt{2}$.   (OCR)

25* A hailstone falls vertically from a cloud. Two models are suggested to describe the resistance of the air to its motion:

Model 1   The resistance is proportional to the speed.
Model 2   The resistance is proportional to the square of the speed.

With both models, the terminal speed has the same value v_T.

(a) Find expressions, in terms of v_T, g and λ, for the times, t_1 and t_2, predicted by the two models for the hailstone to reach a speed of λv_T, where $0 < \lambda < 1$. Determine whether t_1 is greater or less than t_2.

(b) Repeat the questions in part (a) for the distances, x_1 and x_2, predicted by the two models for the hailstone to reach a speed of λv_T. (Use the fact that $\ln \dfrac{1+\lambda}{1-\lambda} > 2\lambda$ for $0 < \lambda < 1$.)

(c) Which model will predict the greater time for the hailstone to fall to earth from the cloud, and which model will predict the greater speed for the hailstone when it hits the ground?

4 Systems of rigid objects

This chapter is about structures made up of two or more rigid objects in contact with each other. When you have completed it, you should

- understand that Newton's third law applies to the forces between rigid objects
- understand the principles underlying the application of the law to objects connected by pin joints
- be able to formulate equations for the equilibrium of each object separately or for the structure as a whole
- be able to select good strategies for solving problems involving such structures.

4.1 Newton's third law

Example 4.1.1

An archaeologist is working on a site on which there is a fallen stone of mass 1200 kg. She wants to move it, but it is far too heavy to lift unaided. She manages to dig out a shallow channel 5 cm long under one end of the stone, into which she can insert the end of a wooden plank of mass 4 kg and length 210 cm as illustrated in Fig. 4.1. If she can lever the stone up with this plank, her assistant can get a cable underneath it, so that the stone could be raised with a crane. How much force will be needed to achieve this?

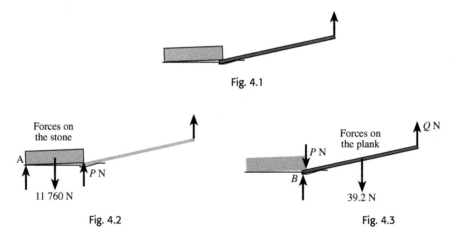

Fig. 4.1

Fig. 4.2

Fig. 4.3

The force which actually lifts the stone is the contact force from the plank, denoted in Fig. 4.2 by P newtons. The other forces on the stone are its weight of 1200×9.8 newtons and the force supporting it from the ground at A. Suppose that the stone has length l cm. Then, assuming that it can be modelled as a uniform cuboid, its centre of mass will be $\frac{1}{2}l$ cm horizontally from A, so

$$\mathcal{M}(A) \quad Pl = 11\,760\left(\tfrac{1}{2}l\right), \quad \text{which gives} \quad P = 5880.$$

Now consider the forces on the plank, shown in Fig. 4.3. Assume the plank to be uniform, so that its weight acts at its mid-point. The effect of the stone will be communicated in the form of the contact force from the stone on the plank, which acts at 5 cm from the end B. By Newton's third law (see Ml Section 7.1) this has the same magnitude as the force from the plank on the stone, but in the opposite direction. The other forces are the plank's weight of 4×9.8 newtons, the lifting force of Q newtons from the archaeologist, and the force from the ground supporting the plank at its other end B. So

$$\mathcal{M}(B) \quad Q \times 210 = 5880 \times 5 + 39.2 \times 105,$$

from which it follows that $Q = 159.6$.

The stone can be lifted off the ground with a force of approximately 160 newtons.

This method of solving a problem involving two objects which interact with each other is just the same as you used in M1 Chapter 7. The only difference is that there Newton's law was applied to objects modelled as particles, but in Example 4.1.1 the stone and the plank are modelled as rigid objects, and equations of moments are used in the solution. This means that you have to consider not only the magnitude and direction of the forces, but also the lines along which they act. A few extra words therefore have to be added to the statement of Newton's third law given in M1 Chapter 7.

Newton's third law

If an object A exerts a force on an object B, then B exerts a force on A of the same magnitude along the same line but in the opposite direction.

Example 4.1.2
A uniform rod of weight 100 newtons and length 4 metres is hinged at one end to a point on the floor. It is raised at an angle of 60° to the horizontal, and kept in position by a wheel of radius 1 metre with a smooth rim which stands on the floor. The wheel is prevented from moving by a horizontal force applied to the rim at the level of the hub, as shown in Fig. 4.4. Find the magnitude of this force.

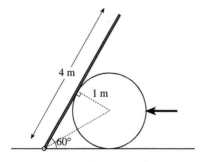

Fig. 4.4

There are two questions: what is holding the rod up, and why would the wheel move if the force was not applied? The answer to both questions is the same, the contact force between the wheel and the rod. Since the wheel is smooth, this force is at right angles to the rod, at 60° to the vertical. It acts upwards from the wheel on the rod, downwards from the rod on the wheel. Fig. 4.5 shows the forces on the rod, Fig. 4.6 the forces on the wheel.

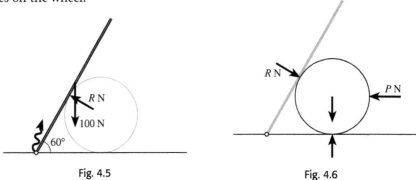

Fig. 4.5   Fig. 4.6

Let the horizontal force applied to the wheel be P newtons, and the contact force R newtons. The distance from the hinge to the point of contact of the rod with the wheel can be calculated from the triangle in Fig. 4.4 as $1 \times \cot 30°$ metres, which is $\sqrt{3}$ metres.

For the rod:

$\mathcal{M}(\text{hinge}) \quad R \times \sqrt{3} = 100 \times (2 \cos 60°).$

For the wheel:

$\mathcal{R}(\rightarrow) \quad R \cos 30° = P.$

From the first equation,

$$R = \frac{100 \times (2 \times \frac{1}{2})}{\sqrt{3}} = \frac{100}{\sqrt{3}}.$$

Then, from the second equation,

$$P = \frac{100}{\sqrt{3}} \times \tfrac{1}{2}\sqrt{3} = 50.$$

The force needed to prevent the wheel from moving is 50 newtons.

In Examples 4.1.1 and 4.1.2 the forces between the plank and the stone, and between the rod and the wheel, are normal contact forces, but Newton's third law applies to any kind of force. In the next example it is also applied to frictional forces.

Example 4.1.3
Two cylindrical logs, each of weight W and radius $3a$, rest side-by-side on horizontal ground, just touching each other. A third log, of weight w and radius $2a$, rests symmetrically on top of them in equilibrium, as shown in Fig. 4.7. What can be said about the coefficients of friction at the points of contact?

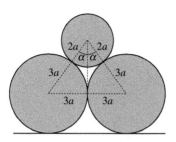

Fig. 4.7

Notice that, in referring to 'points of contact' rather than lines of contact, the question is implicitly modelling the three-dimensional problem in two dimensions, treating the logs as circular laminas rather than cylinders.

Because of the symmetry of the structure, the magnitudes of the forces on the two larger logs are the same. In the cross-section shown, the centres of the circles form an isosceles triangle with sides $5a$, $5a$ and $6a$, so the sides of length $5a$ make an angle α with the vertical such that $\sin\alpha = \frac{3}{5}$, $\cos\alpha = \frac{4}{5}$.

Either an algebraic or a geometrical method can be used. You may, if you wish, read just one of the solutions now, and come back to the other solution later.

Algebraic method   Fig. 4.8 and 4.9 show the forces on the upper log and on the left lower log. R and S are normal contact forces, F and G are the corresponding frictional forces. Notice that, at the contact between these two logs, both the forces from the lower log on the upper have equal magnitude and opposite direction to the forces from the upper log on the lower. Because the two lower logs are only just touching each other, and the addition of the upper log will tend to push them apart, there is no contact force between these two logs.

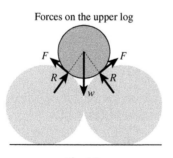

Forces on the upper log

Fig. 4.8

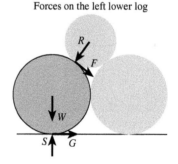

Forces on the left lower log

Fig. 4.9

For the upper log:

$\mathcal{R}(\uparrow)$ $2R \times \frac{4}{5} + 2F \times \frac{3}{5} = w.$

For the left lower log:

$\mathcal{R}(\uparrow) \quad S = R \times \frac{4}{5} + F \times \frac{3}{5} + W,$

$\mathcal{R}(\rightarrow) \quad G + F \times \frac{4}{5} = R \times \frac{3}{5},$

$\mathcal{M}(\text{centre}) \quad F(3a) = G(3a).$

Using these four equations in reverse order, you can find that $F = G$, $R = 3F$, $S = 3F + W$ and $w = 6F$, so $G = \frac{1}{6}w$, $S = \frac{1}{2}w + W$, $F = \frac{1}{6}w$ and $R = \frac{1}{2}w$.

It follows that

$$\frac{F}{R} = \frac{1}{3} \quad \text{and} \quad \frac{G}{S} = \frac{1}{3}\frac{w}{w+2W}.$$

Geometrical method   If the normal and frictional forces are combined as total contact forces X and Y, you get Figs. 4.10 and 4.11.

Notice first that, in Fig. 4.11, there are just three forces on the left lower log. It was shown in M2 Section 9.2 that if a rigid body is in equilibrium under the action of three non-parallel forces, then their lines of action must be concurrent. Since Y and W pass through the point of contact with the ground, the line of action of X must also pass through this point. Fig. 4.12 shows this line of action as AE, where (by the properties of similar triangles) E is the highest point of the upper log, so that the isosceles triangle ABE has base $6a$ and height $3a + 4a + 2a = 9a$. The angles marked β therefore have $\tan \beta = \frac{1}{3}$.

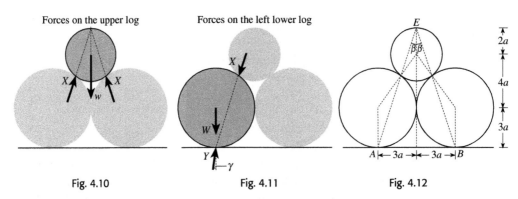

Fig. 4.10   Fig. 4.11   Fig. 4.12

To find the angle made by the force Y with the vertical, labelled γ in Fig. 4.11, you can draw triangles of forces for each log, as in Fig. 4.13.

Notice that the sides representing the force X in these two triangles have the same length; the two triangles can therefore be fitted together along these sides, as in Fig. 4.14.

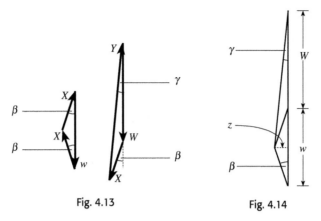

Fig. 4.13   Fig. 4.14

The length marked z in Fig. 4.14 is $\frac{1}{2}w(\tan \beta) = \frac{1}{6}w$, so

$$\tan \gamma = \frac{\frac{1}{6}w}{\frac{1}{2}w + W} = \frac{w}{3(w + 2W)}.$$

Since $\dfrac{F}{R}$, or $\tan \beta$, cannot be greater than the coefficient of friction between the logs, it follows that this coefficient of friction must be at least $\frac{1}{3}$. Similarly, the coefficient of friction between the lower logs and the ground cannot be less than $\frac{1}{3}\dfrac{w}{w + 2W}$.

4.2   Pin joints

One way in which rigid objects, particularly rigid rods, are often joined together is by means of a pin joint, as illustrated in Fig. 4.15. A hole is drilled into each of the objects, and they are then secured together by driving a pin, or rivet, through the two holes. In this way the two objects can rotate relative to each other at a common point.

Fig. 4.15

Notice that, with this mechanism, the objects are not in contact with each other, but both are in contact with the pin. Suppose that the pin exerts a force **P** on one object and **Q** on the other. Then the two objects exert forces $-\mathbf{P}$ and $-\mathbf{Q}$ respectively on the pin, as shown in Fig. 4.16. Now these are the only two forces on the pin (which is assumed to be so light that its weight can be neglected), so $(-\mathbf{P}) + (-\mathbf{Q}) = \mathbf{0}$. It follows that $\mathbf{P} + \mathbf{Q} = \mathbf{0}$; that is, the forces which the pin exerts on the two objects have equal magnitude but opposite directions.

Forces from pin   Forces on pin

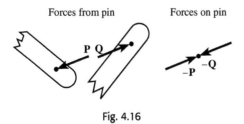

Fig. 4.16

What this means is that, although the objects are not actually in contact, the effect of the forces exerted on them through the pin is the same as if Newton's third law applied between them directly.

> When two objects are joined to each other through a pin joint, the forces exerted on them by the pin have equal magnitudes and opposite directions.

Objects joined through a smooth pin joint are sometimes described as **freely jointed**.

Example 4.2.1

In the mechanism illustrated in Fig. 4.17, two levers AB and BC are connected by a pin joint at B. A vertical spring has one end on a fixed base and is attached to the lever AB at D. The lever BC rests on a fixed smooth support at E, and AB is attached to a vertical wall by a fixed hinge at A. The weight of the levers is negligible by comparison with the other forces acting. Each lever has length a, and $AD = BE = \frac{1}{4}a$. When C is depressed by a force P, the tension in the spring is T. Find an equation connecting P and T.

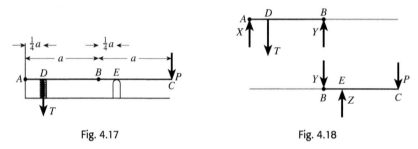

Fig. 4.17   Fig. 4.18

Fig. 4.18 shows the forces on the levers AB and BC separately. The pin at B exerts a force of Y downwards on BC, and a force of Y upwards on AB. The forces from the hinge at A and the support at E are X and Z respectively; neither of these forces is required, so these are the points to take moments about.

For the lever AB:

$\mathcal{M}(A) \qquad T\left(\tfrac{1}{4}a\right) = Ya.$

For the lever BC:

$\mathcal{M}(E) \qquad Y\left(\tfrac{1}{4}a\right) = P\left(\tfrac{3}{4}a\right).$

The connection between T and P can be found by eliminating Y from these two equations:

$$P = \tfrac{1}{3}Y = \tfrac{1}{3}\left(\tfrac{1}{4}T\right), \quad \text{so} \quad P = \tfrac{1}{12}T.$$

Example 4.2.2

Two uniform rods AB and BC are freely jointed to each other at B. The rod AB has length $80\,\text{cm}$ and weight 16 newtons; BC has length $60\,\text{cm}$ and weight 12 newtons. There are small rings on the rods at A and C which can slide on a horizontal rail. The system is set up as shown in Fig. 4.19 with the rings $100\,\text{cm}$ apart, so that angle ABC is a right angle. Find the least coefficient of friction between the rings and the rail for the rods to remain in this position.

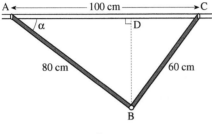

Fig. 4.19

In a problem like this it is often simplest to split the forces on the rods at the pin joint into horizontal and vertical components. Let these be X newtons and Y newtons respectively. The forces on AB and BC separately are shown in Fig. 4.20. The normal forces between the rings and the rail at A and C are P newtons and Q newtons, and the frictional forces are F newtons and G newtons.

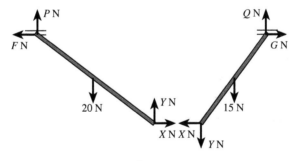

Fig. 4.20

It is helpful to begin by calculating the lengths which will be needed in the equations of moments. In Fig. 4.19 the line BD has been drawn perpendicular to AC, and the angle BAC is denoted by α. Then $\sin\alpha = \dfrac{60}{100} = 0.6$ and $\cos\alpha = \dfrac{80}{100} = 0.8$, so that (in centimetres)

$$AD = 80\cos\alpha = 64, \quad BD = 80\sin\alpha = 48 \quad \text{and} \quad CD = 100 - AD = 36.$$

You can find equations connecting X and Y for each rod by taking moments about A and C respectively. (The units are N cm.)

For the rod AB:

$$\mathcal{M}(A) \qquad Y \times 64 + X \times 48 = 20 \times \left(\tfrac{1}{2} \times 64\right).$$

For the rod BC:

$$\mathcal{M}(C) \quad Y \times 36 + 15 \times \left(\tfrac{1}{2} \times 36\right) = X \times 48.$$

Equating the values of $48X$ from the two equations,

$$640 - 64Y = 36Y + 270$$

giving $100Y = 370$, so $Y = 3.7$.

Then, substituting back in the first equation,

$$48X = 640 - 3.7 \times 64,$$

which gives $X = 8.4$.

It is now easy to find the frictional and normal forces. Resolving horizontally for each rod gives

$$X = F \quad \text{and} \quad G = X,$$

so that $F = G = 8.4$. The normal forces are found by resolving vertically,

$$P + Y = 20 \quad \text{and} \quad Q = Y + 15,$$

which give

$$P = 20 - 3.7 = 16.3 \quad \text{and} \quad Q = 3.7 + 15 = 18.7.$$

Since the frictional forces are equal, the ring which is more likely to slip is the one at which the normal force is less. The ring A is therefore more likely to slip. If this is not to happen, the coefficient of friction must be at least $\dfrac{8.4}{16.3} = 0.515$.

Example 4.2.3

Two rectangular boards are pin-jointed together along a pair of edges. One board lies flat on the floor, with the other board on top of it, as shown in Fig. 4.21. A rope is attached to the middle of the edge of the upper board opposite to the jointed edge. The rope rises vertically and passes over a fixed pulley. The rope is slowly wound in over the pulley. Show that the lower board can't start to lift off the floor immediately.

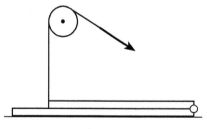

Fig. 4.21

The method used to solve this example is proof by contradiction (see C3 Section 0.4). The argument is to suppose that the lower board *does* start to lift off the floor immediately, and to show that this leads to an impossible conclusion. It follows that the opposite supposition must be true.

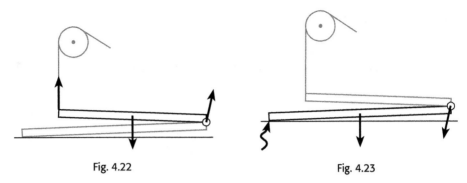

Fig. 4.22   Fig. 4.23

Figs. 4.22 and 4.23 show how the mechanism would look if the lower board started to lift off the floor as soon as the rope is wound in. From Fig. 4.22, which shows the forces on the upper board, taking moments about the left end shows that the force from the joint would initially have an upward component. So the force at the joint on the lower board would have a downward component. But from Fig. 4.23, which shows the forces on the lower board, this is clearly impossible, since both the weight and the force from the joint would then have clockwise moments about the point of contact with the floor.

So, using proof by contradiction, the lower board will not start to lift off the floor immediately.

Exercise 4A

1 A light beam AB of length 4 m rests horizontally on two supports, one at each end of the beam. A light beam BC of length 8 m rests horizontally on a support at C and on the beam AB, which it slightly overlaps at B. The beam AB carries a load of 100 N at its mid-point and BC carries a load of 200 N at its mid-point. Show, in separate diagrams, the forces acting on AB and on BC.

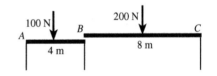

2 Three uniform rods AB, BC and CD, each of weight W and length a, are connected by pin joints at B and C. They rest horizontally in line on supports at E, F and G, where $AE = BF = CG = \frac{1}{3}a$. What force must be exerted at A to keep the rods in equilibrium?

Show that, if this force is applied, equilibrium can be maintained with the support at F removed.

3 Two uniform rods AB and BC, each 1 metre long and of equal weight, are connected at B through a pin joint. They are in equilibrium in a horizontal line, with each rod resting on just one support. These supports are at distances x metres and y metres from B respectively. Prove that $x + y = 4xy$.

4 Two uniform planks AB and BC, of weights 400 N and 300 N respectively, are arranged to facilitate the crossing of a stream. The heavier plank is 3 m long and the lighter plank is 2 m long. The plank AB rests horizontally on two supports, one at each end of the beam. The plank BC rests horizontally on a support at C and on the plank AB, which it slightly overlaps at B. A woman of weight 600 N walks slowly across the planks. The diagram shows her at a distance x metres from A.

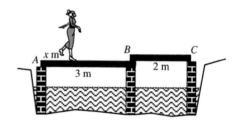

(a) Find R in terms of x, where R N is the magnitude of the upward force exerted by the support at B on the plank AB.

(b) Find F in terms of x, where F N is the magnitude of the upward force exerted by the plank AB on the plank BC at B.

(c) Sketch the graphs of R against x and of F against x, for $0 \leqslant x \leqslant 5$.

5 Two uniform rods AB and BC, each of weight 120 newtons and length 5 metres, are connected by a smooth pin joint at B. There are rings at A and C, which slide on a rough horizontal rail. The rods rest in limiting equilibrium with B vertically below the rail and with A and C 6 metres apart.

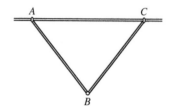

(a) Draw a diagram to show the forces acting on the rod AB, and explain why the force from the pin at B on AB is horizontal.

(b) Calculate the coefficient of friction between the ring and the rail at A.

6 Two uniform planks AB and BC, each of weight 60 newtons and length 2.6 metres, are smoothly pin-jointed to each other at B. They rest with their ends A and C on a smooth floor and with B vertically above the mid-point of AC. To prevent the structure from collapsing, A and C are connected by a rope of length 2 metres. Calculate the tension in the rope.

7 Two uniform rods XY and YZ, each of weight 20 newtons and length 80 cm, are connected by a smooth pin joint at Y. They rest symmetrically on two smooth pegs P and Q at the same level, with angle $XYZ = 90°$, as shown in the diagram. Show that P and Q are approximately 28 cm apart, and find the magnitude of the force from the pin on each rod.

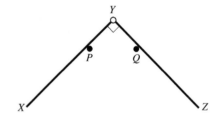

8 XY and YZ are uniform rods of equal length smoothly pin-jointed together at Y. They are hinged to a horizontal beam at X and Z respectively, and hang below the beam with angle $XYZ = 90°$. The rod XY has weight 8 newtons, and the rod YZ has weight 12 newtons. Find the horizontal and vertical components of the force from the pin at Y on the rod XY.

9 In the diagram AB and BC are uniform rods connected by a smooth pin joint at B. The rod AB has length 200 cm and weight 50 newtons, and the rod BC has length 120 cm and weight 30 newtons. The rods are hinged to a vertical wall at A and C, where A is 160 cm above C, so that angle ACB is a right angle. The pin at B exerts a force on the rod BC with horizontal and vertical components X and Y. Determine the directions and magnitudes of the components X and Y.

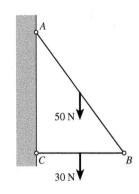

10 Uniform rods AB and BC are connected by a smooth pin joint at B. The rods hang from a horizontal beam, and are smoothly hinged to the beam at A and C. If the rod AB is vertical, what can you say about the force which the pin at B exerts on the rod BC?

11 A heavy uniform cylindrical drum is placed, with its axis horizontal, on a slope inclined at an angle α to the horizontal. It is prevented from sliding or rolling down the slope by a triangular wedge, as shown in the diagram. The weight of the wedge is negligible compared with the weight of the drum. The angle at the point of the wedge is β, and the coefficient of friction between the wedge and the slope is μ, where $\mu > \tan \alpha$. Show that, however smooth the surface of the drum, the wedge will keep it in equilibrium provided that β is between α and $\tan^{-1} \mu$.

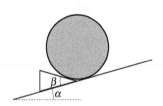

12 A hemispherical bowl of weight 20 newtons and radius 45 cm rests with its rim in contact with the floor and its curved surface upwards. A uniform rod of weight 50 newtons and length 90 cm rests against the bowl, with one end on the floor at a point 75 cm from the centre of the bowl. The contact between the rod and the curved surface of the bowl is smooth. Find the least acceptable coefficients of friction between the rod and the floor, and between the rim of the bowl and the floor, if equilibrium is to be maintained.

13 A man is trying to push a chest of weight W up a slope inclined at an angle α to the horizontal, by exerting a force parallel to the slope. The coefficient of friction between the soles of his shoes and the floor is μ and the coefficient of friction between the feet of the chest and the floor is ν. Show that the force pushing the chest must exceed $W(\sin \alpha + \mu \cos \alpha)$. Hence prove that the man has no hope of succeeding unless his weight is more than $\dfrac{\nu + \tan \alpha}{\mu - \tan \alpha} W$.

14 Two uniform rods AB and BC, each of length 1 metre and weight W newtons, are connected at B by a smooth pin joint. The rods rest symmetrically in equilibrium in contact with a smooth cylindrical drum of radius 0.8 metres with its axis fixed and horizontal. Explain why the force from the pin on each rod is horizontal, and calculate the angle between the rods.

15* A mass-produced machine component has the shape
of a half cylinder, with semicircular cross-section.
Three of these components are stacked on the floor
as shown in the diagram. Find the least coefficients
of friction to maintain equilibrium if

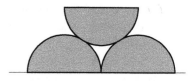

(a) the curved surfaces are rough and the plane surfaces are smooth,

(b) the plane surfaces are rough and the curved surfaces are smooth.

Is equilibrium possible if all the surfaces are rough, and the coefficients of friction at each
contact are one-half of the values calculated in parts (a) and (b) respectively?

16 Two identical prisms with square cross-section and
weight W stand side-by-side on the floor a small
distance apart. A prism with equilateral triangular
cross-section is placed symmetrically above the gap.
The weight of the triangular prism is w. The contacts
between the prisms are smooth, but the contact
between the square prisms and the floor is rough, with
coefficient of friction μ. Find the largest acceptable
value of w

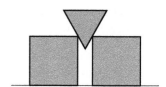

(a) if the square prisms are not to slide outwards,

(b) if the square prisms are not to topple about their outside lower edges.

17 A cylindrical drum of weight 400 newtons and radius 35 cm
stands on the floor of a warehouse. Its axis is horizontal and
parallel to a vertical wall, at a distance of 55 cm from it. A
second cylindrical drum, of weight 300 newtons and radius
30 cm, is laid gently on top, with its axis horizontal,
touching the wall and the first drum as shown in the
diagram. By considering the forces on each drum, show that
equilibrium is impossible if the contacts at A, B and C are
all smooth.

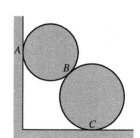

Find the least values of the coefficients of friction at A, B and
C for equilibrium to be possible.

4.3   Internal and external forces

Look back to Example 4.1.3. One result which emerged from the equations was that
$S = \frac{1}{2}w + W$. It will probably have occurred to you that this could have been written down
straight away, since the two normal contact forces of S have to support the weight of all three
logs, so $2S = w + 2W$.

The essence of this argument is that, since the complete structure of the three logs is in equilibrium, the external forces on the structure must be in equilibrium. The only external forces are the weights of the logs, and the normal and frictional forces S and G at the contacts with the ground. The forces F and R, which are internal forces between the objects which make up the structure, don't come into the equations.

For problems involving more than one rigid object, the most efficient solution often uses a mixture of equations for the separate objects and for the structure as a whole.

Example 4.3.1
Two uniform rods OX and XY, pin-jointed together at X, hang from a fixed hinge at O. The rods have length a and b, and weight ka and kb respectively. The lower end Y is now pulled aside with a horizontal force F. Find the angles α and β which the rods make with the vertical in equilibrium.

The unknowns in this problem are the angles α and β, and the magnitude and direction of the forces from the pin at X and the hinge at O. The first of these forces is an internal force for the pair of rods, the second is an external force.

Now the force at a hinge doesn't appear in an equation if you take moments about that hinge. This suggests that you take moments about X for the rod XY, and about the hinge at O for the system as a whole. Fig. 4.24 shows the forces on the rod XY, and Fig. 4.25 the external forces on the system.

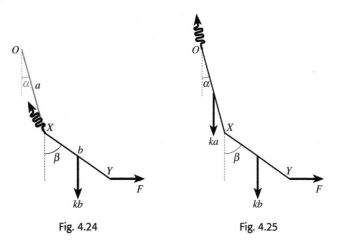

Fig. 4.24   Fig. 4.25

For the rod XY:

$$\mathcal{M}(X) \qquad F(b\cos\beta) = kb(\tfrac{1}{2}b\sin\beta),$$

so that

$$2F\cos\beta = kb\sin\beta.$$

For the whole system:

$$\mathcal{M}(O) \qquad F(a\cos\alpha + b\cos\beta) = ka(\tfrac{1}{2}a\sin\alpha) + kb(a\sin\alpha + \tfrac{1}{2}b\sin\beta).$$

Notice that one term on each side of the second equation also appears in the first, so you can subtract to get the simpler equation

$$F(a \cos \alpha) = ka(\tfrac{1}{2}a \sin \alpha) + kb(a \sin \alpha),$$
$$2F \cos \alpha = k(a + 2b) \sin \alpha.$$

So, using the identity $\dfrac{\sin \theta}{\cos \theta} \equiv \tan \theta,$

$$\tan \beta = \frac{2F}{kb} \quad \text{and} \quad \tan \alpha = \frac{2F}{k(a + 2b)}.$$

In Example 4.3.1, notice that the $\mathcal{M}(O)$ equation for the whole system is exactly the same as it would be if OXY were a single rigid, bent rod. When you write equations of resolving or moments for the equilibrium of the external forces on a system, it makes no difference whether the system is rigid or flexible. However, the $\mathcal{M}(X)$ equation for the rod XY holds only because there is a pin joint at X.

Example 4.3.2
A step-ladder is 6 metres long and weighs 40 newtons, with its centre of mass halfway up. At 5 metres from the foot it is pin-jointed to a uniform prop, which is 4.8 metres long and weighs 10 newtons. The ladder is set up at 70° to the horizontal, as shown in Fig. 4.26. A man of weight 750 newtons climbs the ladder up to a height of 4.5 metres. Find the least coefficients of friction at the foot of the steps and the prop if neither is to slip as he climbs.

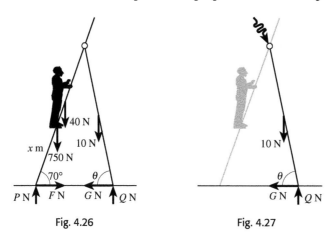

Fig. 4.26   Fig. 4.27

If the prop makes an angle θ with the horizontal, then by the sine rule

$$\frac{5}{\sin \theta} = \frac{4.8}{\sin 70°},$$

so $\theta = 78.19...°$.

Much of the information you need can be got by considering the external forces on the ladder, so that the internal forces at the pin don't come into the equations. These are the forces shown in Fig. 4.26. Let the normal contact and frictional forces at the foot of the steps be P newtons and F newtons, and let the corresponding forces at the foot of the prop be Q newtons and G newtons. Consider the situation when the man has climbed x metres up the ladder. Then

$\mathcal{R}(\rightarrow)$ $F = G,$

$\mathcal{R}(\uparrow)$ $P + Q = 40 + 750 + 10,$

$\mathcal{M}(\text{foot of steps})$ $Q(5 \cos 70° + 4.8 \cos \theta)$
$$= 40(3 \cos 70°) + 750(x \cos 70°) + 10(5 \cos 70° + 2.4 \cos \theta).$$

From the last two equations,

$$2.692...Q = 63.05... + 256.5... \, x \quad \text{and} \quad P = 800 - Q,$$

so

$$Q = 23.42... + (95.28...) \, x \quad \text{and} \quad P = 776.57... - (95.28...) \, x.$$

You also know from the first equation that the two frictional forces are equal, but you don't know their value. To get this, consider the forces on the prop alone. These include the force from the pin (see Fig. 4.27); you aren't interested in this, so take moments about the pin.

$\mathcal{M}(\text{pin})$ $Q(4.8 \cos \theta) = 10(2.4 \cos \theta) + G(4.8 \sin \theta).$

Dividing by $4.8 \cos \theta$ and using $\dfrac{\sin \theta}{\cos \theta} \equiv \tan \theta$ gives $Q = 5 + G \tan \theta$; so

$$G = \frac{Q - 5}{\tan \theta}.$$

Substituting the values of Q and θ which you already know gives

$$G = \frac{18.42... + (95.28...) \, x}{\tan 78.19...°}$$
$$= 3.85... + (19.91...) \, x.$$

Therefore, since $F = G$,

$$\frac{F}{P} = \frac{3.85... + (19.91...)x}{776.57... - (95.28...)x} \quad \text{and} \quad \frac{G}{Q} = \frac{3.85... + (19.91...)x}{23.42... + (95.28...)x}.$$

If you plot these expressions for values of x from 0 to 4.5, you find that $\dfrac{F}{P}$ increases from 0.005 to 0.269, and $\dfrac{G}{Q}$ from 0.164 to 0.206, correct to 3 decimal places.

So the ladder is increasingly likely to slip at both contacts with the ground as the man climbs the ladder, but the effect of his ascent is much greater at the steps than at the prop. If there is to be no slipping, the coefficient of friction must be at least 0.269 at the foot of the steps, and 0.206 at the foot of the prop.

4.4   The light rod model

The rigid objects which make up structures often support forces which are very much larger than their own weight. For example, in a high wind the light aluminium poles supporting a tent are subjected to very large stresses. When you write equations for the equilibrium of structures like this, it is often legitimate to neglect the weight of such components.

Suppose for example that a gardener makes a wind-break from a rectangular panel of light plastic, freely hinged at the top edge and with the opposite edge in contact with the ground, facing directly into the wind (see Fig. 4.28). Then if the weight is neglected, there are just three forces on the panel: the resultant force of the wind, the force from the hinge pin and the contact force from the ground. You can then use the special conditions for the equilibrium of three forces (concurrency of the lines of action and triangle of forces; see M2 Section 9.2) to investigate the forces to which the panel is subjected.

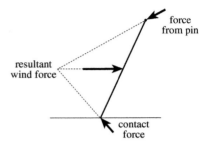

Fig. 4.28

The situation is even simpler if the only forces on a component, modelled as a light rod, are applied at the ends. For example, in Example 4.3.2, you might decide that the weight of the prop is so small that it can be neglected. Then the forces on the prop are simply the force from the pin at the top and the force from the ground (see Fig. 4.29). Both these forces must therefore act along the line of the prop, which is at 78.19...° to the horizontal, or 11.80...° to the vertical. Treating the force from the ground as a total contact force in this direction, the least acceptable coefficient of friction is tan 11.80...°, which is 0.209 correct to 3 decimal places. Notice that this is independent of where the man is standing on the steps.

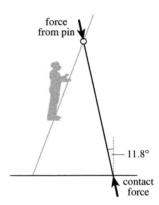

Fig. 4.29

The force on the prop from the pin is equal and opposite to the contact force. This means that the force from the pin on the other component, the steps, is equal to the contact force from the ground. Fig. 4.30 shows the forces on the steps, and the solution can be completed by writing equations of moments and resolving for these forces. It is not difficult to calculate that the distance labelled p is 2.635... metres, from which it can be shown that $F = 3.18... + (19.91...)x$ and $P = 786.88... - (95.28...)x$. The ratio $\dfrac{F}{P}$ increases from 0.004 to 0.259 as the man climbs the steps to a height of 4.5 metres.

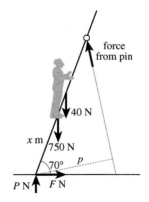

Fig. 4.30

If you compare these answers with those in Example 4.3.2, you will see that the error which results from neglecting the weight of the prop is quite small; but the calculations are a lot easier. (But don't bank on this always being so. See, for example, Exercise 4B Question 3.)

Example 4.4.1

Figure 4.31 shows a simplified model of a girl doing press-ups. *OAB* represents her body, with its centre of mass at *G*, and *AC* represents her arms. Her body is at 20° to the horizontal, $OG = 0.9$ m and $OA = OC = 1.2$ m. The weight of her body is 500 N, and the weight of her arms can be neglected. Using this model, calculate

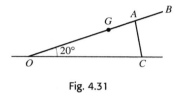

Fig. 4.31

(a) the thrust in each arm,

(b) the normal and friction forces at her feet and at each hand.

The forces in one arm are shown in Fig. 4.32. Because the weight is negligible, there are just three forces: the force *T* N from her body at the shoulder (which is equal to the thrust in her arm), and the normal and friction forces on her hand, *R* N and *F* N.

Their lines of action are concurrent, so that the force from her body acts along the line of her arm. Since $OA = OC$, the triangle *OAC* is isosceles, and her arms are at 80° to the horizontal.

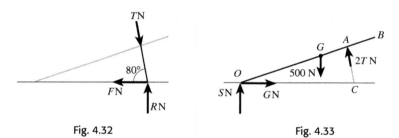

Fig. 4.32   Fig. 4.33

Fig. 4.33 shows the forces on her body: the combined thrust of $2T$ N from her arms, her weight, and the normal and friction forces *S* N and *G* N at her feet.

(a) The force from her arms can be found by taking moments about *O* for the forces on her body. The perpendicular distance from *O* to the line *AC* is $1.2 \cos 10°$ m (since *OAC* is isosceles), and from *O* to the vertical through *G* is $0.9 \cos 20°$ m.

$$\mathcal{M}(O) \quad 2T \times 1.2 \cos 10° = 500 \times 0.9 \cos 20°$$

which gives $T = 178.9...$.

The thrust in each arm is 179 N, correct to 3 significant figures.

(b) The remaining forces can now be found by resolving. For her arms,

$$\mathcal{R}(\uparrow) \quad R = T \cos 10°,$$
$$\mathcal{R}(\leftarrow) \quad F = T \cos 80°.$$

Substituting 178.9... for T, these equations give $R = 176.1...$ and $F = 31.0...$.

The normal and friction forces on each hand are 176 N and 31 N respectively.

To find the forces at her feet, you now have a choice. You could either resolve vertically and horizontally for the forces on her body alone, or (slightly more simply) resolve for the external forces on the girl, taking her body and arms together. Using the second method, the equations are

$\mathcal{R}(\uparrow)$ $2R + S = 500$ and $\mathcal{R}(\rightarrow)$ $G = 2F$.

So $S = 500 - 2 \times 176.1... = 147.6...$ and $G = 2 \times 31.0... = 62.1...$.

The normal and friction forces at her feet are 148 N and 62 N respectively.

Example 4.4.2
A structure consists of two congruent right-angled triangular laminas, OAB and COD, each of weight W, and a light rod pin-jointed at its ends to the laminas at B and C. The lengths $OB = CD = 3a$, $OA = OC = 4a$ and $AB = BC = OD = 5a$ (see Fig. 4.34). The laminas are independently hinged to a fixed point at O, and the structure hangs in stable equilibrium in a vertical plane. Investigate the forces in the structure.

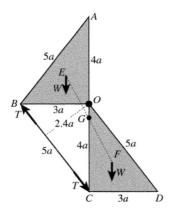

Fig. 4.34

Begin by noting that, if E and F are the centres of mass of the two laminas, then the centre of mass G of the whole structure is the mid-point of EF, which lies on the edge OC. So in stable equilibrium the structure hangs with AOC vertical and C below O.

Now consider the light rod BC. The only forces on this are from the pins at B and C so these forces act along the line of the rod. The rod therefore exerts on the pin at B a force in the direction $\overrightarrow{CB}$; let its magnitude be T.

Next consider the lamina OAB, and take moments about O. The line of action of the weight is a distance a from O. Also, since the sine of angle OBC is $\dfrac{4a}{5a} = 0.8$, the distance from O to BC is $(3a) \times 0.8 = 2.4a$. So

$\mathcal{M}(O)$ $Wa = T(2.4a)$,   which gives $T = \tfrac{5}{12}W$.

You can now resolve for the forces on the lamina OAB, and find that the force from the pin at O has a horizontal component of $T \times \frac{3}{5}$, which is $\frac{1}{4}W$, to the right; and a vertical component of $W - T \times \frac{4}{5}$, which is $\frac{2}{3}W$, upwards.

If instead you took moments about O for the forces on the lamina OCD, you would find that the $\mathcal{M}(O)$ equation gives no fresh information; in fact, the equation is exactly the same as for the lamina OAB. This is because the argument in the first paragraph, that G is vertically below O, is based in effect on an $\mathcal{M}(O)$ equation for the structure as a whole.

Resolving for the forces on the lamina OCD then shows that the pin at O exerts a force on it of $T \times \frac{3}{5}$ to the left and $W + T \times \frac{4}{5}$ upwards; that is, $\frac{1}{4}W$ to the left and $\frac{4}{3}W$ upwards.

So, as you would expect, the resultant force from the pin at O on the structure as a whole is zero horizontally and $\frac{2}{3}W + \frac{4}{3}W = 2W$ upwards.

Notice that, in Fig. 4.34, the forces labelled T in the rod BC are not the forces *on* the rod, but the forces exerted *by* the rod, through the pins at B and C, on the laminas. When you have light rods in a structure, with forces acting only at the ends, it is common practice to draw diagrams which show the forces on the pins (or whatever), rather than the forces on the rod itself. This convention is summarised in Fig. 4.35.

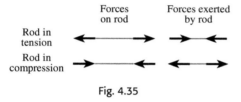

Fig. 4.35

Examples 4.4.3 and 4.4.4 show how this convention is applied to frameworks made up entirely of light rods pin-jointed together. The tensions and thrusts in these rods are found by considering in turn the equilibrium of the forces on the various pins. Rather than drawing separate diagrams for the forces on each pin, the usual practice is to combine these in a single diagram; in Example 4.4.3 blue dotted circles have been drawn round the various pins to indicate that the forces inside each circle are the forces which act on the corresponding pin.

Example 4.4.3
A load of weight 500 newtons is suspended from a point C by means of two pin-jointed rods AC and BC, whose weight can be neglected. The other ends of the rods are hinged to a vertical wall, with A 2.5 metres above B. The lengths of the rods are 1.8 and 1.6 metres respectively. Find the forces with which the wall supports the structure at A and B.

The forces shown in Fig. 4.36 are the forces exerted by the rods, the wall and the load on the pins at A, B and C. The problem is solved by considering the equilibrium of the three pins.

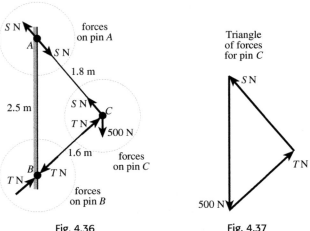

Fig. 4.36   Fig. 4.37

At C there are three forces, and the condition for their equilibrium can be expressed by drawing a triangle of forces (Fig. 4.37). Notice that the sides of this triangle are parallel to the sides of the triangle ABC, so the forces of S newtons in AC, T newtons in BC and the load of 500 newtons are proportional to the lengths of AC, BC and AB. That is,

$$\frac{S}{1.8} = \frac{T}{1.6} = \frac{500}{2.5}, \quad \text{which gives} \quad S = 360 \quad \text{and} \quad T = 320.$$

At both A and B there are only two forces, so these must be equal in magnitude and opposite in direction. The force from the wall at A is therefore 360 newtons in the direction $\overrightarrow{CA}$ and the force at B is 320 newtons in the direction $\overrightarrow{BC}$. The rod AB is in tension, and the rod BC in compression.

Example 4.4.4

The structure in Fig. 4.38 is used to support a load of weight 1000 newtons. The weights of the four rods can be neglected; the lengths of BC, CD and BD are each 1 metre, and the length of AD is 0.5 metres. The rod DA is hinged to the wall at A, and DB and CB are hinged to the wall at B. Find the stresses in the four rods.

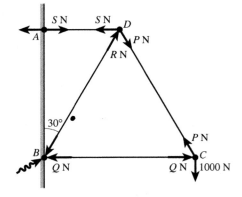

Fig. 4.38

All the forces required can be found by considering the equilibrium of the forces on the pins at C and D. You can do the calculations either by resolving or by drawing triangles of forces.

Fig. 4.39 shows triangles of forces for the forces at C and D. These give

$$P = 1000\sec 30° = 1155,$$
$$Q = 1000\tan 30° = 577,$$
$$R = S = P = 1155.$$

The rods CD and AD are in tension, the rods BC and BD are in compression.

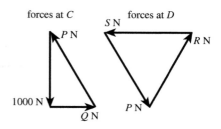

Fig. 4.39

Exercise 4B

1 Two fixed points A and B on a horizontal beam are 4 metres apart. Two rods, AC and BC, of length 5 metres and 3 metres and weight 100 newtons and 60 newtons, are connected to each other by a pin joint at C, and to the beam by pins at A and B. Find the forces on the rods from the pins at A, B and C.

2 Two identical uniform rods, OX and XY, each of weight W, are connected through a pin joint at X. They hang from a fixed hinge at O. The end Y is grasped and held at the same level as O, so that both rods make an angle of $30°$ with the horizontal. Find the magnitude and direction of the force needed to hold the rods in this position.

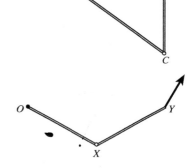

3 A rectangular window, of weight 50 newtons, whose centre of mass is at its geometrical centre, is hinged along its top edge. It is opened to an angle of $50°$ to the vertical, and kept in place by a metal rod of weight 4 newtons. The rod is hinged to the window at one end, and rests against the wall at the other end at a point just below the lower edge of the window frame. Find the least coefficient of friction necessary to keep the rod in this position.

Compare your answer with that which you would get by modelling the rod as having negligible weight.

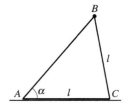

4 Two uniform beams, AB and BC, are connected by a pin joint at B. They are set up in a vertical plane, with A and C on a smooth floor, and A and C are connected by a rope equal in length to BC, as shown in the diagram. The beam AB makes an angle α with the horizontal. The weight of each beam is k times its length. Investigate whether the beams can rest in equilibrium

(a) if $\alpha = 60°$,   (b) if $\alpha = 45°$,   (c) if $\alpha = 30°$,   (d) if $\alpha = 15°$.

If so, calculate the tension in the rope in terms of k and the length l of BC. Find also the horizontal and vertical components of the force from the pin on BC.

5 A paving stone of length 1 metre is lying flat on the
ground. One edge is raised, and the stone is
supported at a point 0.2 metres from that edge and
halfway across its width by a light metal bar of
length 0.6 metres. The bar is at right angles to the
plane of the stone, and rests on the ground at its
lower end, as shown in the diagram. Find the least
possible coefficients of friction

(a) between the metal bar and the ground,

(b) between the paving stone and the ground,

for equilibrium to be maintained.

6 A pub puts up a rectangular signboard on the
pavement, supported by two light struts hinged to it
at the two upper corners. The board and the struts
are at angles of 80° to the horizontal, and the struts
are in the same vertical planes as the side edges of
the board. The mass of the board is 5 kg. Find the
force on the board from each strut, and the least
possible coefficient of friction between the board
and the pavement.

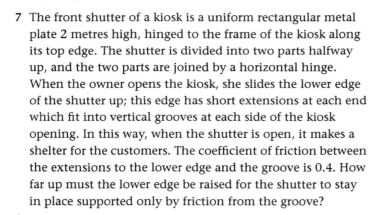

7 The front shutter of a kiosk is a uniform rectangular metal
plate 2 metres high, hinged to the frame of the kiosk along
its top edge. The shutter is divided into two parts halfway
up, and the two parts are joined by a horizontal hinge.
When the owner opens the kiosk, she slides the lower edge
of the shutter up; this edge has short extensions at each end
which fit into vertical grooves at each side of the kiosk
opening. In this way, when the shutter is open, it makes a
shelter for the customers. The coefficient of friction between
the extensions to the lower edge and the groove is 0.4. How
far up must the lower edge be raised for the shutter to stay
in place supported only by friction from the groove?

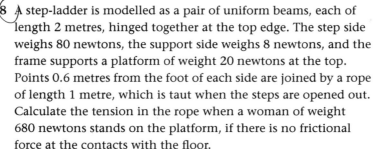

8 A step-ladder is modelled as a pair of uniform beams, each of
length 2 metres, hinged together at the top edge. The step side
weighs 80 newtons, the support side weighs 8 newtons, and the
frame supports a platform of weight 20 newtons at the top.
Points 0.6 metres from the foot of each side are joined by a rope
of length 1 metre, which is taut when the steps are opened out.
Calculate the tension in the rope when a woman of weight
680 newtons stands on the platform, if there is no frictional
force at the contacts with the floor.

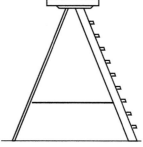

9 A temporary road sign is displayed on a metal frame, hinged along its top edge. When closed up, each half of the frame is 2 metres high, weighs 20 newtons, and has its centre of mass 0.8 metres from the hinge. The sign is a rectangular board weighing 40 newtons, and its centre of mass is 0.5 metres below the hinge. The frame is now opened up, as shown in the diagram. If the coefficient of friction between the feet of the frame and the road is 0.6, what is the greatest possible distance apart of the feet of the two halves of the frame?

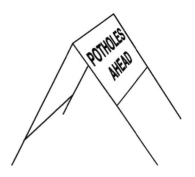

10 A shopkeeper wants to suspend a hanging basket of mass 3 kg at a distance of 0.6 metres from the wall of her premises. It hangs from the pin which connects two rods AC and BC, whose other ends are pinned to the wall at A and B, where A is 1 metre above B. Show that one of the rods is in tension and the other in compression, and state which is which. Find the lengths of the rods, and the forces of tension and compression,

(a) if the forces in the two rods are to be equal in magnitude,

(b) if the force in the rod which is in compression is to be as small as possible.

11 A simple crane is fixed to horizontal ground at the points A and B. The dimensions of the members BC, CD and DB are $5L$, $5L$ and $8L$ respectively, and the crane supports a load of weight $15X$ as shown in the diagram.

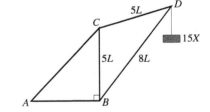

(a) By considering the equilibrium of D, find the magnitude of the thrust exerted on D by the member BD, and the tension in the member CD.

(b) Given that the force at A exerted on the crane by the ground acts vertically downwards and has magnitude $16X$, and the force at B acts vertically upwards and has magnitude $31X$, find the distance AB in terms of L.

12 A and B are pins fixed in a horizontal beam, at a distance 1 metre apart. Four rods AD, BC, BD and DC are connected by pin joints to form a structure which hangs from A and B. The lengths $AD = BC = 2.6$ metres, $BD = 2.4$ metres and $DC = 1$ metre. A load of 1200 newtons hangs from C, as shown in the diagram. Calculate the stresses in the four rods, and the magnitude and direction of the forces on the structure from the pins at A and B.

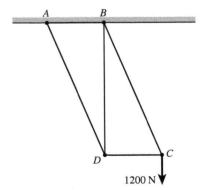

Miscellaneous exercise 4

1   The diagram shows two rectangular blocks A and
B, with masses 8 kg and 5 kg respectively, resting in
equilibrium on a rough plane inclined at $25°$ to the
horizontal. The blocks A and B are in contact, and
A is above B. Both blocks are on the point of
slipping down the plane. The contact between A
and B is smooth and the coefficient of friction
between block A and the plane is 0.35.

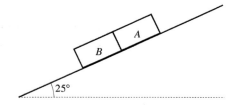

   (a) Calculate the magnitude of the contact force between the blocks A and B.

   (b) Calculate the coefficient of friction between block B and the plane.   (OCR)

2   A rectangular block of mass 5 kg is at rest on a plane
inclined at $30°$ to the horizontal. A smooth circular
cylinder of mass 2 kg rests (with its axis horizontal) in
contact with the plane and a face of the block. The
diagram shows the vertical cross-section through the
centres of mass of the two bodies; this cross-section lies
in a vertical plane through a line of greatest slope. The
system is in equilibrium.

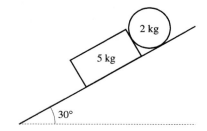

   (a) Find the magnitude of the contact force on the cylinder due to the block.

   (b) Find the least possible coefficient of friction between the rectangular block and the
       inclined plane.   (OCR)

3   Two uniform beams AB and BC, each of length $5a$, have masses $3m$ and $2m$ respectively. The
beams are freely jointed to fixed points at A and C, and to each other at B. The points A and
C are on the same horizontal level at a distance $8a$ apart, and the beams are in equilibrium
with B vertically below the mid-point of AC.

   (a) Find the vertical component of the force acting on BC at C, and show that the
       horizontal component of this force is $\frac{5}{3}mg$.

   (b) Find the magnitude and direction of the force acting on AB at B.   (OCR)

4   Three identical square boards, each of weight
200 newtons and side 2 metres, are joined together by
two hinges and rest on the floor. The middle board is
then raised, remaining horizontal, with the edges of
the outer boards resting on the floor, until the outer
edges are 4 metres apart, as shown in the diagram.
How large must the coefficient of friction be for the
framework to remain unsupported in this position?

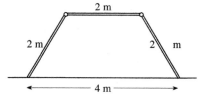

   A gradually increasing force is now applied vertically upwards at the centre of the middle
board. If the coefficient of friction has the value calculated in the first part, find how large
a force could be applied without breaking the equilibrium of the framework.

5 A uniform cylinder of radius 25 cm and weight 20 newtons rests on a rough floor. A uniform rod of length 50 cm and weight 60 newtons is hinged to a fixed point 50 cm above the centre of the cylinder. The rod rests against the surface of the cylinder. Find the minimum coefficients of friction between the rod and the cylinder, and between the cylinder and the floor, if the cylinder is to remain in equilibrium.

6 The diagram shows a mechanism for raising a heavy beam AB, which is hinged to a fixed point at A. The beam has length l and weight W. It is pin-jointed at B to a lighter rod BC, also of length l but of weight w. A small ring on this rod at C runs on a smooth horizontal rail at the same level as A. A cord CD, attached to the rod at C, runs along the rail to a smooth pulley and then hangs vertically. The beam is raised by pulling on the cord at D. When the beam is at an angle θ to the vertical, find the force that has to be applied to the cord at D to raise the beam at a slow steady rate.

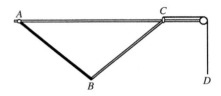

Suppose now that the rail is rough, and that the coefficient of friction between the ring and the rail at C is μ. Show that this adds a fixed amount $\frac{1}{4}\mu\,(W+3w)$ to the force at D needed to raise the beam.

7 Three uniform rods AB, AC, BC, have lengths 2.0 m, 2.0 m and 2.4 m, and weights 480 N, 560 N and 400 N respectively. The rods are freely jointed at A, B, C, and hang in equilibrium in a vertical plane with BC horizontal, supported by vertical wires attached to points P on AB and Q on AC, where $AP = AQ = 0.5$ m. The tensions in the wires at P and Q are T_1 and T_2 respectively (see diagram).

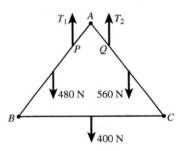

(a) Show that $T_1 = 640$ N.

(b) Find the magnitude and direction of the force acting on BC at B.   (OCR)

8* The figure shows the cross-section of a conservatory attached at A to the vertical wall of a house. The glass sections AB, BC and CD are each of uniform thickness and weigh 250 N, 100 N and 200 N respectively. These sections are pin-jointed at A, B, C and D whose coordinates are $(0, 5)$, $(2, 4)$, $(3, 3)$ and $(4, 1)$ respectively, referred to horizontal and vertical axes Ox and Oy. The structure is held rigid by a light tie-rod AC.

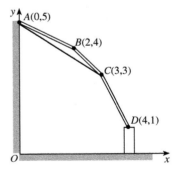

By taking moments about A for the complete structure and about C for section CD, determine the horizontal and vertical components of the reaction at D. Find also the components of the reaction at A.

Show that the magnitude of the tension in the tie-rod AC is $50\sqrt{13}$ N.   (OCR)

9) A framework consists of three light, rigid rods AB, BC and AC, freely pin-jointed to each other at A, B and C. The framework is freely attached to a vertical wall at A. AB is horizontal and C rests on a smooth plane inclined at 45° to the vertical. AB has length 2 m, $AC = BC$ and C is 2 m vertically below the line AB, as shown in the figure, so that angle $CAB =$ angle $CBA = \alpha$, where $\sin\alpha = \dfrac{2}{\sqrt{5}}$ and $\cos\alpha = \dfrac{1}{\sqrt{5}}$. A load of 300 N is attached at B, and the figure shows the external forces U N, V N and R N.

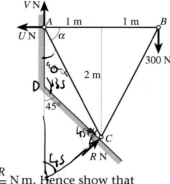

(a) Show that the anticlockwise moment of R about A is $\dfrac{3R}{\sqrt{2}}$ N m. Hence show that $R = 200\sqrt{2}$.

(b) Calculate the values of U and V.

(c) By considering the equilibrium of the forces acting at points A and B, or otherwise, calculate the magnitude of the internal force in each of the rods, stating whether it is in tension or compression. (MEI)

10) A framework used for supporting loads is modelled as five light rods AB, BC, CD, AD and DB freely pin-jointed together. $ABCD$ is a parallelogram with $AB = CD = 4$ m and $AD = BC = 2$ m; angle $DAB = 60°$. The framework rests on smooth horizontal supports at A and B which are at the same height. The framework supports vertical loads of 200 N and 100 N at the points D and C respectively, as shown in the diagram.

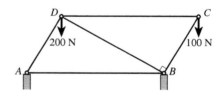

(a) Show that the supports at A and B exert forces of 125 N and 175 N vertically upwards respectively on the framework.

(b) Calculate the magnitudes of the internal forces in the rods and state for each rod whether it is in tension or compression. (MEI)

5 Motion round a circle with variable speed

This chapter extends the theory of circular motion to situations in which the angular speed is not constant. When you have completed the chapter, you should

- know what is meant by angular velocity and angular acceleration
- know that the acceleration has radial and transverse components, and how to find them
- be able to apply the theory to problems in which a particle moves in a vertical circle
- know that the equation of transverse motion can be integrated to obtain the equation of energy.

5.1 Angular velocity and angular acceleration

One of the first steps in studying mechanics mathematically is to generalise motion with constant speed in a straight line, by introducing the idea of velocity which can not only vary with time but also take positive and negative values. Velocity is then defined as $\dfrac{\mathrm{d}x}{\mathrm{d}t}$, where x is the displacement from a fixed point of the line in whichever direction you have chosen to be positive.

For motion round a circle, angular speed can be generalised in a similar way. Instead of a fixed point on a straight line you need to choose a fixed direction from O, the centre of the circle. Also, instead of a positive direction you need to choose a positive sense of rotation.

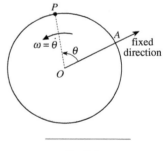

Fig. 5.1

Then, if θ is the angle (in radians) measured in the positive sense from the fixed direction to the radius OP on which the rotating particle P is located, the angular velocity is defined to be $\dfrac{\mathrm{d}\theta}{\mathrm{d}t}$, often written as $\dot{\theta}$. This is shown in Fig. 5.1. The Greek letter ω is almost always used for angular velocity.

You can take the comparison further by introducing the idea of angular acceleration. For a particle moving in a straight line with velocity v, the acceleration is defined as $\dfrac{\mathrm{d}v}{\mathrm{d}t}$. Similarly, for motion round a circle, angular acceleration is defined as $\dfrac{\mathrm{d}\omega}{\mathrm{d}t}$, often written as $\dot{\omega}$. The Greek letter α is usually chosen to denote angular acceleration.

> For a particle P moving round a circle with centre O, if θ denotes the angular displacement of the radius OP from a fixed direction at time t, measured in radians in the positive sense, then
>
> the **angular velocity** $\omega = \dot{\theta}$,
>
> and   the **angular acceleration** $\alpha = \dot{\omega} = \ddot{\theta}$.

5.2 Velocity and acceleration in circular motion

If you know the angular velocity and angular acceleration for the particle P, how can you find its actual velocity and acceleration?

The velocity is obviously directed along the tangent to the circle. You know from M2 Section 8.2 that, for the special case when the angular speed ω is constant, the speed of the particle is $r\omega$.

You will probably guess that this still holds when ω varies with time; and this is in fact correct, though it needs to be proved. Notice that $r\omega$ can also be written as $r\dot\theta$, which is $\frac{\mathrm{d}}{\mathrm{d}t}(r\theta)$ since r is constant; and $r\theta$ is the displacement of P from the point A measured round the circumference, where OA is the radius in the fixed direction.

You might be tempted to think that you could get the acceleration by differentiating a second time, as $\frac{\mathrm{d}}{\mathrm{d}t}(r\omega) = r\dot\omega$. But this is obviously wrong. You already know that, if ω is constant, the particle's acceleration is not zero, but $r\omega^2$ directed towards the centre of the circle.

In fact, the correct answer combines these two ideas. The acceleration of the particle has two components. There is one component, $r\dot\omega$, directed along the tangent, because the speed is changing; and a second component, $r\omega^2$, directed from P towards the centre O, because the direction of motion is changing. This is illustrated in Fig. 5.2.

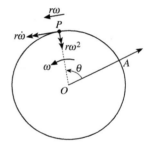

Fig. 5.2

A practical example of this is driving a car round a bend. A good driver goes into the bend slowly, then begins to apply pressure on the accelerator pedal as she rounds the bend. The effect is that the car accelerates in the direction in which it is moving but, for the car to continue to move in a circle, there is also acceleration towards the centre of the bend.

> A particle moving round a circle of radius r with variable angular velocity ω has velocity $r\omega$ directed along the tangent, and acceleration which is the resultant of two components:
>
> a **transverse component** $r\dot\omega$, directed along the tangent,
>
> and   a **radial component** $r\omega^2$, directed towards the centre of the circle.

You will find proofs of these results in Section 5.5, but the statement in the blue box gives all you need to know to solve practical problems about circular motion.

The word 'transverse' means at right angles to the radius. For motion in a circle, the 'transverse direction' and the 'tangential direction' are the same. But for a particle moving round any other curve, the tangent is not usually at right angles to the radius, so the two terms then have different meanings. The radial component of acceleration is sometimes given as $-r\omega^2$ in the direction of the radius vector.

Notice that $r\dot{\omega}$ can also be written as $r\ddot{\theta}$, and $r\omega^2$ as $r\dot{\theta}^2$. Also since the speed v is equal to $r\omega$, and r is constant, $r\dot{\omega}$ can be written as $\dot{v}$, and $r\omega^2$ as $\dfrac{v^2}{r}$. You will sometimes find it convenient to use these alternative expressions for the components of acceleration.

Example 5.2.1
At an athletics meeting a hammer-thrower rotates through three complete revolutions in getting up speed before releasing the hammer. If θ denotes the angle (in radians) through which he has rotated t seconds after he starts his throw, this rotation is modelled by the equation $\theta = 5t^{\frac{3}{2}}$. The motion of the hammer is modelled as rotation in a circle of radius 2 metres. Calculate the velocity and the acceleration of the hammer after 1, 2 and 3 revolutions.

The angular velocity and angular acceleration are given by

$$\omega = \dot{\theta} = 7.5t^{\frac{1}{2}} \quad \text{and} \quad \alpha = \dot{\omega} = 3.75t^{-\frac{1}{2}}.$$

The values of these are required at the values of t for which $\theta = 2\pi$, 4π and 6π. To find these, the equation for θ is rearranged in the form $t = \left(\frac{1}{5}\theta\right)^{\frac{2}{3}}$. The results of the calculations can then be tabulated.

angle turned through (rad)	θ	2π	4π	6π
time (s)	t	1.16	1.85	2.42
angular velocity (rad s^{-1})	ω	8.09	10.19	11.67
angular acceleration (rad s^{-2})	α	3.48	2.76	2.41
transverse velocity (m s^{-1})	$r\omega$	16.2	20.4	23.3
acceleration { transverse component (m s^{-2})	$r\alpha$	6.9	5.5	4.8
acceleration { radial component (m s^{-2})	$r\omega^2$	131.0	208.0	272.5

Notice that, with this model, the first revolution takes almost half the time of the throw, by which time the hammer is already moving at about two-thirds of its final speed. As the throw proceeds, the radial component of the acceleration increases rapidly, while the small transverse component decreases. Since the hammer has a mass of over 7 kg, the force which the thrower has to produce just before he releases the hammer is about 1900 newtons.

Example 5.2.2

A motorcyclist is rounding a bend of radius 20 metres. She enters the bend travelling at $10 \, \text{m s}^{-1}$, and increases speed at a constant rate of $2 \, \text{m s}^{-1}$ per second for each of the next 3 seconds. Find the angle which her acceleration makes with the direction of motion at the beginning and end of this time, and the angle through which she has turned.

It is convenient to use the expressions $\dot{v}$ and $\dfrac{v^2}{r}$ for the components of acceleration. It is given that $\dfrac{dv}{dt} = 2$, and $v = 10$ when $t = 0$, so $v = 10 + 2t$. The components of acceleration after t seconds are $\dot{v} = 2$ and $\dfrac{v^2}{20} = \dfrac{(10 + 2t)^2}{20}$. When $t = 0$ the components of acceleration are $2 \, \text{m s}^{-2}$ in the direction of the tangent and $5 \, \text{m s}^{-2}$ towards the centre of the bend, so the acceleration vector makes an angle of $\tan^{-1} \frac{5}{2}$, which is $68.2°$, with the direction of motion. When $t = 3$ the corresponding components are $2 \, \text{m s}^{-2}$ and $12.8 \, \text{m s}^{-2}$, so the angle is $\tan^{-1} 6.4$, which is $81.1°$.

Since $v = r\dot{\theta}$, the angle through which the motorbike has turned is given by the differential equation $\dot{\theta} = \frac{1}{20}(10 + 2t) = 0.5 + 0.1t$. Taking $\theta = 0$ when $t = 0$, this gives $\theta = 0.5t + 0.05t^2$; so when $t = 3$, $\theta = 1.5 + 0.45 = 1.95$. The motorbike has therefore turned through 1.95 radians, which is about $112°$, in the 3 seconds.

5.3 Motion round a vertical circle

A familiar example of motion round a circle with variable speed is when an object travels round a circular path in a vertical plane under the action of the force of gravity. On the upward part of the motion the object gains height, so it gains potential energy and loses kinetic energy. So the speed of the object varies as it moves round the circle.

Example 5.3.1

A bead B of mass 10 grams is threaded on a smooth circular wire of radius 2.5 metres, which is fixed in a vertical plane with its centre at O. Initially the bead is at rest at the lowest point of the wire. It is then hit with an impulse of $0.1 \, \text{N s}$ horizontally, so that it starts to travel round the wire. Describe the subsequent motion of the bead, and find an expression for the force which the wire exerts on the bead when the radius OB makes an angle θ with the downward vertical.

The bead, whose mass is 0.01 kg, gains momentum of $0.1 \, \text{N s}$ from the impulse, so it starts to move with speed $10 \, \text{m s}^{-1}$. Its initial kinetic energy is therefore $\frac{1}{2} \times 0.01 \times 10^2 \, \text{J}$, which is $0.5 \, \text{J}$.

When the radius has turned through an angle θ, the bead has gained height of $(2.5 - 2.5 \cos \theta)$ metres (see Fig. 5.3), so it has gained potential energy of amount $0.01 \times 9.8 \times 2.5(1 - \cos \theta) \, \text{J}$, which is $0.245(1 - \cos \theta) \, \text{J}$. If its speed in this position is $v \, \text{m s}^{-1}$, its kinetic energy is $\frac{1}{2} \times 0.01 \times v^2 \, \text{J}$. Since the wire is smooth, there is no frictional force. The force from the wire on the bead is then at right angles to the direction of motion, and therefore does no work.

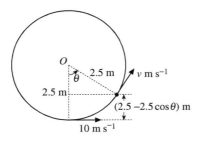

Fig. 5.3

So the conservation of energy principle can be applied to give the equation

$$0.5 = 0.245(1 - \cos\theta) + 0.005v^2.$$

When rearranged, this gives

$$v^2 = 51 + 49\cos\theta.$$

Initially θ has the value 0, and the equation gives the known value $v^2 = 100$, so $v = 10$. As the bead moves up the wire, so that θ increases, $\cos\theta$ decreases until, when $\theta = \pi$, $v^2 = 51 - 49 = 2$, so $v = \sqrt{2} = 1.414...$.

This shows that the bead has sufficient energy to reach the highest point of the wire, where the speed is about 1.41 m s^{-1}. After that $\cos\theta$ starts to increase until, when $\theta = 2\pi$, $v^2 = 51 + 49 = 100$ again. That is, the bead is again at the lowest point and moving with a speed of 10 m s^{-1}. This cycle is then repeated indefinitely. Fig. 5.4 shows a graph of v against θ for the first circuit and part of the second.

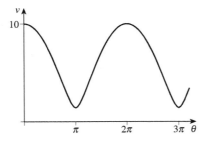

Fig. 5.4

Now that you know the velocity of the bead in any position, you can use this to find the radial component of acceleration, and hence the force from the wire on the bead. In Fig. 5.5 the figure on the left shows the two forces on the bead when OB makes an angle θ with the downward vertical: its weight of 0.098 newtons, and the contact force of R newtons from the wire. The figure on the right shows the two components of acceleration, $\dfrac{dv}{dt} \text{ m s}^{-2}$ (which must of course be negative in the position shown) and $\dfrac{v^2}{2.5} \text{ m s}^{-2}$ towards O.

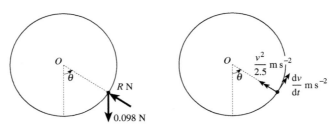

Fig. 5.5

The most awkward term to cope with would be the derivative $\dfrac{dv}{dt}$, and you can avoid bringing this in by applying the equation $\mathbf{F} = m\mathbf{a}$ in the direction of the radius. Substituting the expression already found for v^2 in terms of θ, this gives

$\mathcal{R}$(towards O) $R - 0.098\cos\theta = 0.01 \times \dfrac{51 + 49\cos\theta}{2.5}$,

so

$$R = 0.204 + 0.294\cos\theta.$$

How does this force vary as the bead travels round the wire? Before the impulse the wire simply had to support the weight of the bead, which is 0.098 newtons. But substituting $\theta = 0$ in the expression for R shows that, immediately after the bead starts to move, the force increases to 0.498 newtons. As θ increases from 0 to π, $\cos\theta$ decreases, so that at the top of the wire $R = 0.204 - 0.294 = -0.09$. This means that, somewhere between the lowest and the highest points of the wire, the direction of the contact force changes, so that at the top the wire is pushing the bead away from O.

To find just where this occurs, put $R = 0$ in the equation, which gives $\cos\theta = -\dfrac{0.204}{0.294} = -0.693...$ so, $\theta = 2.33...$ rad. This shows that, when the radius OB makes an angle of about 134° with the downward vertical, which is 46° with the upward vertical, the contact force changes from acting inwards to acting outwards. This is illustrated in Fig. 5.6, which shows the graph of R against θ for the first circuit of the bead round the wire.

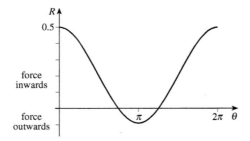

Fig. 5.6

You will see from Example 5.3.1 that it is only possible for the bead to make complete circuits of the wire because the force which the wire exerts on the bead can act either inwards or outwards. What would happen if the wire were replaced by a string? This is investigated in the next example.

Example 5.3.2

A small ball B of mass 10 grams hangs from a fixed point O by a string of length 2.5 metres. While the ball is in equilibrium it is hit horizontally with an impulse of 0.1 N s. Describe the subsequent motion of the bead.

At the start, the motion of the ball is the same as that of the bead in Example 5.3.1. The only difference is that the force which keeps the ball moving in a circle is the tension in the string, whereas for the bead it is the contact force from the wire.

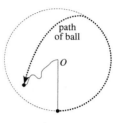

The two particles start to behave differently when θ reaches the value $\cos^{-1}\left(-\dfrac{0.204}{0.294}\right)$, when the contact force on the bead changes direction. This is impossible for the ball on the string, which can only be in tension. So at this point the ball no longer continues to move in a circle; the string becomes slack, and the ball follows the path of a projectile moving freely under gravity. This is illustrated in Fig. 5.7.

Fig. 5.7

Eventually the string will again become taut, after which the ball may again start to move in a circular path.

It is important to understand that the ball has enough energy to reach the top of the circular path, just as the bead has in Example 5.3.1. The reason why it doesn't do so is that, at the top of the circle, the ball would not be moving fast enough to maintain the circular motion without some force acting outwards along the radius.

Example 5.3.3

The roof of an arena is a dome in the shape of a hemisphere of radius 30 metres. A lump of ice at the top of the dome starts to slide down the surface. Where will it hit the ground?

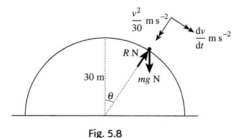

Fig. 5.8

Fig. 5.8 shows the ice, of mass m kg, at a point where the radius makes an angle θ with the vertical. It has then fallen a distance of $30(1 - \cos\theta)$ metres, so its speed v m s^{-1} can be found from an equation of energy:

$$\tfrac{1}{2}mv^2 = mg \times 30(1 - \cos\theta),$$

which gives $v^2 = 60g(1 - \cos\theta).$

You will find in this example that it is simpler not to substitute 9.8 for g. It turns out that the answer to the question asked is the same whatever value is taken for g.

The next step is to find the contact force, R newtons, from the surface of the hemisphere, by resolving inwards along the radius. The component of acceleration in this direction is $\dfrac{v^2}{30}\,\mathrm{m\,s^{-2}}$, which is $2g(1 - \cos\theta)\,\mathrm{m\,s^{-2}}$.

$$\mathcal{R}(\text{along radius}) \qquad mg\cos\theta - R = m \times 2g(1 - \cos\theta),$$

so $R = mg(3\cos\theta - 2)$.

This shows that initially, when $\theta = 0$ and the ice is not moving, R is equal to mg. But as θ increases, R decreases until, when θ reaches the value $\beta = \cos^{-1}\frac{2}{3}$, R becomes zero and the ice leaves the surface of the dome.

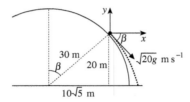

Fig. 5.9

From this point onwards the ice falls freely under gravity. To describe its path, take axes through the point at which the ice leaves the surface (see Fig. 5.9). This point is at a height of $30\cos\beta$ metres, which is 20 metres, above the ground, and $\sqrt{30^2 - 20^2} = 10\sqrt{5}$ metres horizontally from the centre of the dome.

For the projectile motion, the angle of projection is $-\beta$. The initial speed can be found from the equation for v given above, with $\frac{2}{3}$ for $\cos\theta$, so $v^2 = 60g(1 - \frac{2}{3}) = 20g$. You also need to know $\tan\beta$, which is $\frac{1}{2}\sqrt{5}$. The standard equation of the trajectory,

$$y = x\tan\alpha - \frac{gx^2}{2u^2\cos^2\alpha}, \qquad\qquad \text{(see M2 Section 1.3)}$$

with $\tan\alpha = -\frac{1}{2}\sqrt{5}$, $u^2 = 20g$ and $\cos\alpha = \frac{2}{3}$ gives

$$y = -x \times \tfrac{1}{2}\sqrt{5} - \frac{gx^2}{2 \times 20g \times \left(\frac{2}{3}\right)^2}.$$

This can be written more simply as $y = -\frac{1}{2}\sqrt{5}x - \frac{9}{160}x^2$.

Notice that g has now disappeared from the equation.

To find where the ice hits the ground, you want to know the value of x when $y = -20$. This gives the quadratic equation

$$-20 = -\tfrac{1}{2}\sqrt{5}x - \tfrac{9}{160}x^2, \quad \text{or more simply} \quad 9x^2 + 80\sqrt{5}x - 3200 = 0.$$

Solving this by the usual formula,

$$x = \frac{-80\sqrt{5} + \sqrt{32\,000 + 4 \times 9 \times 3200}}{18} = \frac{40(\sqrt{23} - \sqrt{5})}{9}.$$

Notice that x must be positive, so there is no need for the $\pm$ sign.

To find how far the ice lands from the centre of the dome, you must add the horizontal distance of $10\sqrt{5}$ metres found earlier, to give a total of $\frac{1}{9}(40\sqrt{23} + 50\sqrt{5})$ metres, which is $33.737...$ metres.

The ice hits the ground 3.74 metres, correct to 3 significant figures, from the outside wall of the dome.

Exercise 5A

1 A car, starting from rest, travels in a circular path of radius 45 metres. It moves so that, after t seconds, its speed increases at a rate $0.3(12 - t)\,\mathrm{m\,s^{-1}}$ per second, until it reaches its maximum speed after 12 seconds. Find the magnitude and direction of the acceleration of the car

(a) at the start,   (b) after 6 seconds,   (c) after 12 seconds.

2 A particle P moves round the circumference of a circle with centre O and radius 1.6 metres. The radius OP makes an angle θ radians with a fixed radius, so that, after t seconds, $\theta = 0.2 \sin 5t$. Find expressions for the velocity, and for the radial and transverse components of acceleration, after t seconds. Describe the motion.

If the fixed radius is taken to be vertically downwards, suggest a physical situation which might be modelled by this equation.

3 A yacht Y goes round a buoy B in a circle of radius 10 metres, in such a way that the angle made by the radius with a fixed direction after t seconds is modelled by $\theta = a \ln(1 + bt)$, where a and b are constants. Find a and b if the yacht is initially moving at $5\,\mathrm{m\,s^{-1}}$ due south, and its speed after 10 seconds is $2.5\,\mathrm{m\,s^{-1}}$. Hence find how long it takes before the yacht is moving due north.

Show that the angle between the directions of the yacht's velocity and its acceleration is constant, and calculate this angle in degrees.

4 An astronaut is conducting an experiment on a spaceship under conditions of zero gravity. A bead is threaded on a circular wire, and set in motion with angular velocity ω_0 about the centre. If the coefficient of friction between the bead and the wire is μ, show that the angular velocity ω at time t satisfies the differential equation $\dot{\omega} = -\mu\omega^2$. Solve this equation, and hence find an expression for θ, the angle turned through after time t. Show that, according to this model, the bead will never come to a complete stop.

5 A particle of mass 50 grams hangs by a thread of length 2 metres from a fixed point. It is pulled aside until the thread makes an angle of 60° with the downward vertical, and then released. Find the magnitude and direction of the acceleration of the particle, and the tension in the thread,

(a) as the particle passes through its equilibrium position,

(b) just after the particle is released.

6 A particle hangs from a fixed point. It is given a horizontal velocity $u\,\mathrm{m\,s^{-1}}$ so that it moves round the fixed point in a vertical circle. What is the least value of u for this to be possible if the particle is connected to the fixed point by

(a) a light rod of length 80 cm,   (b) a string of length 80 cm?

7 A circular disc of radius 40 cm is fixed in a vertical plane. A track runs round the outside of the rim. A bead of mass m kg is placed at a point on the track and released from rest. The bead slides down the track until the radius to the bead makes an angle of 60° to the vertical. It then loses contact with the track.

(a) Find the speed at which the bead is moving when it leaves the surface.

(b) Find the angle which the radius to the bead makes with the vertical at the point where the bead is released.

8 A ball of mass 100 grams is hanging from a fixed point by a string 2.5 metres long. It is struck with a bat so that it starts to describe a circle in a vertical plane. When the ball has risen a height of 4 metres the string becomes slack. Find the speed of the ball immediately after it was struck, and the tension in the string at that instant.

9 The diagram shows the design for a table game. It consists of a smooth metal groove fixed in a vertical plane. Part of the groove is straight, and part is bent into an arc of a circle of radius 25 cm. There is a spring at the start of the straight section, which is used to project a small ball of mass 20 grams along the groove. Find expressions for the speed of the ball, and the normal contact force from the groove, at the point of the circular section at which the radius is at an angle θ to the downward vertical, if the ball is projected with a speed of

(a) $2\,\mathrm{m\,s^{-1}}$,   (b) $3\,\mathrm{m\,s^{-1}}$,   (c) $4\,\mathrm{m\,s^{-1}}$.

In each case give a brief description of the motion of the ball.

10 A 'try your strength' competition at a village fete consists of a metal ball of mass 10 kg suspended by a light rod of length 2.4 metres from a fixed point. Contestants strike the ball with a mallet, and they win a prize if the ball makes a complete circle. The blacksmith has a go, but the ball comes to rest when the rod makes an angle of 10° with the upward vertical. Calculate the horizontal impulse with which he strikes the ball, and the force in the rod

(a) immediately after the ball is struck,   (b) when the ball is at its highest point.

11 A small bob of mass m is swinging as a pendulum from a fixed point by a string of length l. At the bottom of its swing it has speed u. Show that, if $u \leqslant \sqrt{2gl}$, the string remains taut throughout the oscillation. Find an expression for the tension in the string

(a) when the string makes an angle θ with the downward vertical,

(b) when the bob momentarily becomes stationary.

What happens if $u = \sqrt{3gl}$?

12 A small round island is modelled as the top 40 metres of a smooth sphere of radius 100 metres. A person standing on top of the island kicks a football along the ground. When the ball is 20 metres above sea level it leaves the surface of the island and ends up in the sea. Find

  (a) how fast the ball is kicked,

  (b) how far out from the shore the ball enters the sea.

13 A small ball of mass m hangs by a string of length l from a fixed point A. It is given a velocity $\sqrt{\frac{7}{2}gl}$ horizontally, so that it starts to move in a vertical circle.

  (a) Find the speed of the ball and the tension when the string makes an angle θ with the upward vertical, provided that the string has not become slack.

  (b) Find the value of θ when the string becomes slack, and the speed at which it is then moving.

  (c) Taking x- and y-axes through the point at which the string becomes slack, show that the equation of the trajectory of the ball is $y = \sqrt{3}x - \dfrac{4}{l}x^2$.

  (d) Show that the trajectory passes through the point where the ball was originally.

5.4* Resolving along the tangent

You may think it surprising that none of the examples in Section 5.3 made use of the transverse acceleration $r\dot{\omega}$. Would this have given any additional information?

Before answering this question, it will be useful to find another way of writing the angular acceleration, similar to the expression $v\dfrac{dv}{dx}$ which you have used for acceleration along a straight line (see Section 1.3). In devising definitions for angular velocity and angular acceleration the linear quantities x, v and a have been replaced by the angular quantities θ, ω and α. For example, equations corresponding to $v = \dot{x}$ and $a = \dot{v}$ are $\omega = \dot{\theta}$ and $\alpha = \dot{\omega}$. You would therefore expect that, corresponding to $a = v\dfrac{dv}{dx}$ there is an angular equivalent

$$\alpha = \omega\frac{d\omega}{d\theta}.$$

This is easy to prove, since $\dfrac{d\omega}{d\theta} = \dfrac{d\omega}{dt} \Big/ \dfrac{d\theta}{dt}$, which is $\dfrac{\dot{\omega}}{\omega}$. So $\omega\dfrac{d\omega}{d\theta} = \dot{\omega} = \alpha$.

Now consider a typical question on motion in a vertical circle. Fig. 5.10 shows a particle of mass m moving round a smooth vertical tube, having speed u at the highest point. In a general position, when the radius to the particle makes an angle θ with the upward vertical, there are two forces, R and mg, and two components of acceleration $r\dot{\omega}$ and $r\omega^2$. If you resolve in the direction of the tangent, neither R nor $r\omega^2$ comes into the equation, so

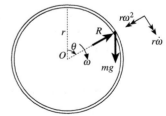

Fig. 5.10

$\mathcal{R}$(along tangent) $mg\sin\theta = m(r\dot{\omega})$.

Now write $\dot{\omega}$ as $\omega\dfrac{\mathrm{d}\omega}{\mathrm{d}\theta}$. You then get the differential equation

$$mr\omega\frac{\mathrm{d}\omega}{\mathrm{d}\theta} = mg\sin\theta.$$

This is of the separable variables type. Notice that $\omega\dfrac{\mathrm{d}\omega}{\mathrm{d}\theta}$ is $\dfrac{\mathrm{d}}{\mathrm{d}\theta}\left(\tfrac{1}{2}\omega^2\right)$, by the chain rule, so the equation can be integrated directly to give

$$\tfrac{1}{2}mr\omega^2 = -mg\cos\theta + k, \quad \text{where } k \text{ is constant.}$$

To find k, note that, when $\theta = 0$, $\omega = \dfrac{u}{r}$, so

$$\tfrac{1}{2}mr\left(\frac{u}{r}\right)^2 = -mg + k,$$

which gives

$$k = \tfrac{1}{2}mr\left(\frac{u}{r}\right)^2 + mg.$$

The equation connecting ω with θ is therefore

$$\tfrac{1}{2}mr\omega^2 = -mg\cos\theta + \tfrac{1}{2}mr\left(\frac{u}{r}\right)^2 + mg.$$

Multiplying by r and rearranging,

$$\tfrac{1}{2}mr^2\omega^2 + mgr\cos\theta = \tfrac{1}{2}mu^2 + mgr.$$

You should recognise this equation. The terms $mgr\cos\theta$ and mgr are the potential energy of the particle in the general position and at the top of the tube respectively, taking the centre of the circle as base. The term $\tfrac{1}{2}mr^2\omega^2$ can be written as $\tfrac{1}{2}m(r\omega)^2$, which is $\tfrac{1}{2}mv^2$, so this and $\tfrac{1}{2}mu^2$ are the kinetic energy in the two positions. This equation is therefore just the conservation of energy equation.

So the answer to the question at the beginning of this section is no. When you used an energy equation to find the speed at a general point of the circular motion, you were in fact using the transverse equation of motion without realising it, but in an integrated form. Conversely, if you differentiate the energy equation, you get an equation which is essentially the same as the equation for resolving in the tangential direction.

5.5 Proof of the velocity and acceleration formulae

All that remains is to prove the formulae for velocity and acceleration given in Section 5.2. You may, if you wish, omit this section and go straight to Miscellaneous exercise 5.

Since motion round a circle is two-dimensional, the theory can conveniently be investigated using vector notation. (Compare M2 Chapter 1, where vectors were used to describe the motion of a projectile in two dimensions.) The new feature is that the vector which describes the position of the moving particle relative to the centre is rotating.

So it will be useful to begin by seeing what happens when you differentiate a rotating vector. To keep things as simple as possible, begin with a rotating unit vector, which has constant magnitude 1.

Theorem   If a unit vector $\mathbf{p}$ is rotating with angular velocity ω, then $\dfrac{d\mathbf{p}}{dt} = \omega\mathbf{q}$, where $\mathbf{q}$ is the unit vector in a direction $\frac{1}{2}\pi$ in advance of the direction of $\mathbf{p}$.

Two proofs are given. The first is technically simpler, but the second gives a clearer idea of what the result means. It is worth trying to understand both.

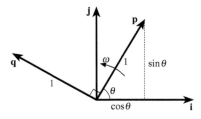

Fig. 5.11

First proof   Set up a coordinate system in the plane of the rotation, and use the x-axis as the 'fixed direction' in the definition of angular velocity. Suppose that the vector $\mathbf{p}$ makes an angle θ with the x-axis, as shown in Fig. 5.11. Since it has magnitude 1, it has components $\cos\theta$ and $\sin\theta$ in the x- and y-directions. It can therefore be expressed in terms of the basic unit vectors $\mathbf{i}$ and $\mathbf{j}$ as

$$\mathbf{p} = \cos\theta\,\mathbf{i} + \sin\theta\,\mathbf{j}.$$

Since $\mathbf{i}$ and $\mathbf{j}$ are constant,

$$\frac{d\mathbf{p}}{dt} = \frac{d}{dt}\cos\theta \times \mathbf{i} + \frac{d}{dt}\sin\theta \times \mathbf{j} = -\sin\theta \times \dot\theta\,\mathbf{i} + \cos\theta \times \dot\theta\,\mathbf{j}.$$

You know that $-\sin\theta = \cos(\theta + \frac{1}{2}\pi)$ and $\cos\theta = \sin\left(\theta + \frac{1}{2}\pi\right)$. Also $\dot\theta = \omega$, so the expression for $\dfrac{d\mathbf{p}}{dt}$ can be written as

$$\frac{d\mathbf{p}}{dt} = \omega\mathbf{q}, \quad \text{where} \quad \mathbf{q} = \cos(\theta + \tfrac{1}{2}\pi)\,\mathbf{i} + \sin(\theta + \tfrac{1}{2}\pi)\,\mathbf{j}.$$

You can see that the expression for $\mathbf{q}$ is similar to that for $\mathbf{p}$, but with $\theta + \frac{1}{2}\pi$ in place of θ. It therefore represents a unit vector in a direction $\frac{1}{2}\pi$ in advance of that of $\mathbf{p}$.

Second proof   Fig. 5.12 shows the vector $\mathbf{p}$ at times t and $t + \delta t$, represented by $\overrightarrow{AB}$ and $\overrightarrow{AC}$ respectively. Both AB and AC have length 1, and angle BAC is the angle $\delta\theta$ through which $\mathbf{p}$ has turned in time δt. The change in $\mathbf{p}$ over this time is represented by $\overrightarrow{AC} - \overrightarrow{AB}$, which is $\overrightarrow{BC}$. It is easy to see that this represents a vector with magnitude $2\sin\frac{1}{2}\delta\theta$ making an angle $\phi = \frac{1}{2}\pi + \frac{1}{2}\delta\theta$ in advance of $\overrightarrow{AB}$. Denote this vector by $\delta\mathbf{p}$. To find $\dfrac{d\mathbf{p}}{dt}$, you need to find $\dfrac{\delta\mathbf{p}}{\delta t}$ and then consider what happens to this as δt tends to 0.

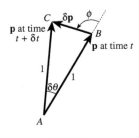

Fig. 5.12

Now dividing by δt involves dividing the magnitude of $\delta\mathbf{p}$ by δt, but doesn't affect the direction. So $\dfrac{\delta\mathbf{p}}{\delta t}$ is a vector which is also at an angle ϕ in advance of $\overrightarrow{AB}$, with magnitude $\dfrac{2\sin\frac{1}{2}\delta\theta}{\delta t}$, which can be written as $\dfrac{\sin\frac{1}{2}\delta\theta}{\frac{1}{2}\delta\theta} \times \dfrac{\delta\theta}{\delta t}$.

The point of writing the magnitude in this form is that you know that, as $\delta\theta$ tends to 0, $\dfrac{\sin\frac{1}{2}\delta\theta}{\frac{1}{2}\delta\theta}$ tends to 1 (see C4 Section 1.2). Since $\delta\theta$ tends to 0 as δt tends to 0, the limit of the expression for the magnitude of $\dfrac{\delta\mathbf{p}}{\delta t}$ is $1 \times \dfrac{\mathrm{d}\theta}{\mathrm{d}t}$, which is just $\dot\theta$, or ω.

Since $\dfrac{\delta\mathbf{p}}{\delta t}$ is a vector, you also have to consider the limit of its direction. Clearly ϕ tends to $\frac{1}{2}\pi$ as $\delta\theta$ tends to 0, so $\dfrac{\mathrm{d}\mathbf{p}}{\mathrm{d}t}$ has direction $\frac{1}{2}\pi$ in advance of that of $\mathbf{p}$. This is the direction of the unit vector $\mathbf{q}$.

Putting all this together, it follows that $\dfrac{\mathrm{d}\mathbf{p}}{\mathrm{d}t} = \omega\mathbf{q}$.

There is no reason why you shouldn't use 'dot notation' with vectors, so this result could be written as $\dot{\mathbf{p}} = \omega\mathbf{q}$. Notice that $\mathbf{q}$ is also rotating with angular velocity ω, and that the unit vector $\frac{1}{2}\pi$ ahead of $\mathbf{q}$ is π ahead of $\mathbf{p}$, which is $-\mathbf{p}$. So the theorem can be used to show also that $\dot{\mathbf{q}} = -\omega\mathbf{p}$.

> If $\mathbf{p}$ and $\mathbf{q}$ are unit vectors rotating with angular velocity ω, and $\mathbf{q}$ is $\frac{1}{2}\pi$ ahead of $\mathbf{p}$, then $\dot{\mathbf{p}} = \omega\mathbf{q}$ and $\dot{\mathbf{q}} = -\omega\mathbf{p}$.

The hard work is now done. To get the formulae for velocity and acceleration of a particle in a circular path, take the origin at the centre of the circle and note that the position vector of the particle can be written as

$\mathbf{r} = r\mathbf{p}$, where r is the radius, which is constant.

Then $\mathbf{v} = \dot{\mathbf{r}} = r\dot{\mathbf{p}} = r\omega\mathbf{q}$.

This shows that the velocity of the particle has magnitude $r\omega$, and that it has the direction of $\mathbf{q}$, perpendicular to $\mathbf{p}$, which is the direction of the tangent.

A second differentiation, using the product rule, gives

$$\begin{aligned}\mathbf{a} = \dot{\mathbf{v}} &= r\dot\omega\mathbf{q} + r\omega\dot{\mathbf{q}} \\ &= r\dot\omega\mathbf{q} + r\omega(-\omega\mathbf{p}) \\ &= r\dot\omega\mathbf{q} + (-r\omega^2)\mathbf{p}.\end{aligned}$$

So the acceleration has two components: $r\dot\omega$ in the direction of the tangent, and $r\omega^2$ in the direction of the radial vector reversed, that is towards the centre.

This establishes the results stated in the blue box in Section 5.2.

Exercise 5B*

1 In Example 5.3.3, the energy equation while the ice is in contact with the surface of the dome is $\frac{1}{2}mv^2 = mg \times 30(1 - \cos\theta)$. By differentiating this equation, show that the result is equivalent to the equation $\mathbf{F} = m\mathbf{a}$ resolved in the transverse direction.

2 Two particles, of mass m and M where $m < M < 3m$, are connected by a string of length πr. They are initially at rest at the two ends of the horizontal diameter of a smooth circular peg of radius r, with the string in contact with the upper half of the circumference. At time t later, when the heavier particle has descended a distance $r\theta$, the tension in the string is T and the normal contact force on the lighter particle from the peg is R.

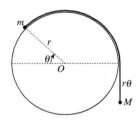

   (a) Write three equations to describe the motion of the particles.

   (b) Write an equation of energy for the motion of the particles. By differentiation, show how the result is related to the equations found in part (a).

   (c) Show that the lighter particle loses contact with the peg when $(M + 3m)\sin\theta = 2M\theta$.

3 A hemispherical bowl of radius r has a smooth inside surface. It is fixed with its rim horizontal and uppermost. A pair of particles, each of mass m, are joined by a light rod of length $\sqrt{2}r$. Initially one of the particles is at the lowest point of the bowl and the other is at a point of the rim, as shown in the diagram. Use an equation of energy to find the speed of the particles when they have rotated through an angle θ about the centre of the bowl. By differentiation, find an expression for the transverse acceleration of each particle in this position.

Write down the equations obtained by resolving along the tangent for each of the particles. Show that you can also use these to obtain the expression for the transverse acceleration. Find the thrust in the rod in terms of θ. In what position is the thrust in the rod

   (a) greatest,   (b) least?

Find also expressions for the contact forces on the two particles from the bowl in the general position.

4 A hemisphere of radius r is fixed with its rim on the ground. A particle of mass m is placed at a point on the surface where the radius makes an angle α with the vertical, and then released. Its motion is opposed by a constant resisting force of magnitude F, which is less than $mg\sin\alpha$. Write down an equation of energy and an equation of transverse motion in a general position where the radius makes an angle θ with the vertical and $\theta > \alpha$. Show how one of these equations can be obtained from the other.

Investigate whether it is possible, for suitable values of α and F, for the particle to remain in contact with the surface until it hits the ground.

5 A particle is forced to move in a circle of radius r so that its acceleration is always at right angles to the direction of its initial velocity, which has magnitude u. By writing $\dot{\omega}$ as $\omega\dfrac{d\omega}{d\theta}$, find an expression for the angular velocity when it is moving at an angle θ to its original direction. Hence find the time that it takes to change direction by $\frac{1}{6}\pi$ radians. Find also an expression for the magnitude of the acceleration in terms of u, r and θ.

6 A bead is threaded on a horizontal circular wire of radius r and set in motion with angular velocity ω_0 about the centre. If the coefficient of friction between the bead and the wire is μ, show that the angular velocity ω when the bead has rotated through an angle θ satisfies the differential equation $\omega\dfrac{d\omega}{d\theta} = -\mu\sqrt{\omega^4 + \left(\dfrac{g}{r}\right)^2}$. Deduce that the angle through which the bead rotates about the centre of the wire before coming to rest is given by

$$\dfrac{1}{2\mu}\int_0^{\omega_0^2} \dfrac{1}{\sqrt{z^2 + k^2}}\, dz, \text{ where } z = \omega^2 \text{ and } k = \dfrac{g}{r}.$$

Show that $\dfrac{d}{dz}(\ln(z + \sqrt{z^2 + k^2})) = \dfrac{1}{\sqrt{z^2 + k^2}}$. Hence calculate the angle through which the bead rotates if $\mu = 0.5$, the radius of the wire is 2 metres, and the initial velocity of the bead is $14\,\text{m s}^{-1}$.

7 The equation $\mathbf{r} = r\mathbf{p}$, where r is not constant but varies with time, can be used to find the velocity and acceleration for a particle moving in a curve which is not a circle. Obtain the equation $\mathbf{v} = \dot{r}\mathbf{p} + r\omega\mathbf{q}$. Illustrate this with a diagram, and interpret it.

Differentiate again to find an expression for the acceleration, and interpret it.

Miscellaneous exercise 5

1 A point P moves in a circle with centre O and radius 0.4 m. After t seconds OP has turned through θ radians, where $\theta = 5t^2$. Find the transverse component of the acceleration of P. (OCR)

2 A particle P of mass 0.2 kg moves in a vertical circle of radius 0.5 m. The centre of the circle is the fixed point O, and P is attached to O by a light inextensible string of length 0.5 m. When the angle between the string and the downward vertical is 60° the speed of P is $4\,\text{m s}^{-1}$. Calculate the tension in the string at this instant. (OCR)

3 The diagram shows a particle P moving on the smooth inner surface of a fixed hollow cylinder of radius 0.6 m. The axis of the cylinder is horizontal. P travels along an arc of a vertical circle, centre O, until it loses contact with the cylinder at the point B. Given that OB makes an angle of 30° with the horizontal, calculate the speed of the particle at B. (OCR)

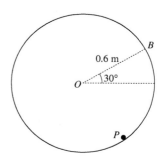

4 A bead B of mass m kg is threaded on a smooth circular hoop fixed in a vertical plane. The radius of the circle is 0.25 m and the centre is O. The bead is projected with initial speed $3 \, \text{m s}^{-1}$ from the lowest point of the hoop. The bead is modelled as a particle, and any forces on it, other than the force of gravity and the contact force between the bead and the hoop, can be ignored. The speed of the bead is $v \, \text{m s}^{-1}$ when the angle between OB and the downward vertical is θ.

(a) Show that $v^2 = 4.1 + 4.9 \cos \theta$.

(b) Calculate the value of θ when the bead is first at instantaneous rest, and find the magnitude and direction of the transverse component of acceleration of the bead at this position.

(c) Find the value of θ at the position where the contact force between the bead and the hoop is first zero. (OCR)

5 One end of a light inextensible string is attached to a fixed point O. The other end of the string is attached to a particle P of mass 0.2 kg which moves in a vertical circle of radius 0.3 m. Air resistance is ignored. When the particle has speed $4 \, \text{m s}^{-1}$ the string makes an acute angle θ with the downward vertical. At this instant the magnitude of the transverse component of acceleration of P is $6.3 \, \text{m s}^{-2}$. Show that $\theta = 40°$ approximately.

At a later instant the string makes an angle of 30° with the upward vertical. Calculate the tension in the string at this instant. (OCR)

6 The diagram shows the circular cross-section of a smooth fixed cylinder of radius r, whose horizontal axis of symmetry passes through O. A particle P, of mass m, is free to move on the surface of the cylinder in a plane which is perpendicular to the axis through O. The speed of P is v when OP makes an angle θ with the upward vertical through O. The particle is released from rest after being slightly displaced from its initial position on top of the cylinder. For the motion while the particle is in contact with the cylinder,

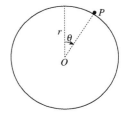

(a) find v^2 in terms of g, r and θ,

(b) show that the magnitude of the force exerted on the particle by the cylinder is $mg(3 \cos \theta - 2)$.

Given that $r = 0.5$, find the speed of the particle at the instant when it leaves the surface of the cylinder. (OCR)

7 A particle P of mass 0.2 kg is attached to a fixed point O by a light inextensible string of length 0.4 m. The particle is projected with horizontal speed $7 \, \text{m s}^{-1}$ from a position 0.4 m directly below O and makes complete vertical circles. Air resistance may be ignored. Show that the particle has speed $5.8 \, \text{m s}^{-1}$ approximately when it is vertically above O, and calculate the corresponding tension in the string.

State the greatest and least magnitudes of the transverse component of acceleration of P after it has been set in motion. State also the corresponding positions of P in relation to O. (OCR)

8 A toy 'speed-racing' track consists of a slope smoothly joined at A to part of a vertical circular loop of track of radius a that rests upon the ground at B (see diagram). A small toy car is released from rest at point D on the slope. Assume the motion to be modelled by a point mass sliding around a smooth track. D is at height $2a$ above the ground.

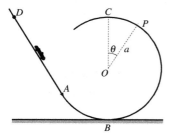

(a) Find the speed of the car when it reaches B.

(b) Show that, if it is still in contact with the track at P, where angle $COP = \theta$, then the speed v at P is given by $v^2 = 2ga(1 - \cos\theta)$.

(c) Draw a diagram showing the forces acting on the car at P. By using the component of '$\mathbf{F} = m\mathbf{a}$' in the radial direction, find a formula for the reaction R between the car and the track, and show that R vanishes when $\cos\theta = \frac{2}{3}$.

(d) With the help of the equation in part (b), find the vertical component of the car's velocity at the point where R vanishes. Deduce that, after it has passed B, the maximum height of the car above the ground is $\frac{50}{27}a$. (OCR)

9 A water chute consists of two portions, AB and BC, each in the shape of an arc of a circle. One has radius 3 m and the other has radius 9 m. The arcs subtend angles of $60°$ and $40°$ at their respective centres E and D, and EBD is a vertical straight line (see diagram). A child of mass 20 kg starts from rest at A and slides down the chute. The water level is 0.5 m below C. The child may be modelled as a particle, and resistances may be neglected.

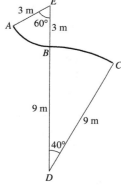

(a) Calculate the speed with which the child reaches B and the speed of impact with the water.

(b) Show that the child loses contact with the chute shortly before reaching C.

State with brief reasons whether there would be any change in the results of parts (a) and (b) if the mass of the child is 30 kg rather than 20 kg.

Give a reason why taking resistances into account might indicate that the child does not lose contact before reaching C. (OCR)

10 One end of a light inextensible string of length 0.5 m is attached to a fixed point O and a particle of mass 0.2 kg is attached to the other end. When hanging in equilibrium under gravity the particle is projected horizontally. In the subsequent motion, air resistance may be neglected. When the string has turned through an angle θ without going slack, the tension in the string is T newtons and the speed of the particle is $v\,\mathrm{m\,s^{-1}}$. Show that $T = 1.96\cos\theta + 0.4v^2$. Explain why the greatest value of T occurs when the particle is vertically below O.

The initial speed of the particle is $u\,\mathrm{m\,s^{-1}}$.

(a) Find the greatest value of u for the tension in the string not to exceed 80 N.

(b) For the case $u = 3.7$, find the height of the particle above O at the instant when the string slackens.   (OCR)

11 A particle of mass m is attached to one end A of a light, inelastic string of length l. The other end B of the string is attached to a ceiling so that the particle is free to swing in a vertical plane; the angle between the string and the downward vertical is θ radians. You may assume that air resistance on the particle is negligible. Initially $\theta = \frac{1}{3}\pi$ and the particle is released from rest.

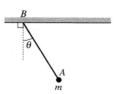

(a) Show that the potential energy lost by the particle since leaving its initial position is $\frac{1}{2}mgl(2\cos\theta - 1)$. Hence find an expression for v^2, where v is the linear speed of the particle, in terms of l, g and θ.

(b) Show that the tension in the string at any point of the motion is $mg(3\cos\theta - 1)$.

(c) Find the greatest tension in the string. What is the position of the particle when the tension in the string is greatest?

Before its release with $\theta = \frac{1}{3}\pi$, the particle is held in position by means of a second light string inclined at an acute angle α to the downward vertical, as shown in the diagram. The second string is cut to allow the particle to swing.

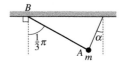

(d) What is the direction of the acceleration of the particle just after the string is cut?

(e) Find the value of α for which the tension in AB remains unchanged when the string is cut.   (MEI)

12 A ball B of mass 0.12 kg is attached to the mid-point of a light inextensible string AC of length 3.6 m. The ends A and C are attached to fixed points at the same horizontal level. In equilibrium AB and CB are each inclined at an angle α to the horizontal (see diagram). The string BC is cut.

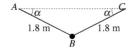

(a) Find the range of values of α for which the tension in AB before the string is cut is greater than the tension in AB just after it is cut.

(b) Neglecting air resistance, find, in terms of α, the tension in the string AB when it is vertical.

(c) State, giving a reason, the effect on the answer to part (b) if air resistance were taken into account. (OCR)

13 A stone of mass 0.4 kg is attached to one end of a light inextensible string of length 1.2 m. The other end of the string is attached to a fixed point. The stone is released from rest with the string taut and at an angle of 60° to the vertical. In the subsequent motion, air resistance may be neglected. For the instant when the string has turned through an angle of 30°,

(a) show that the speed of the stone is 2.93 m s^{-1}, to 3 significant figures,

(b) find the tension in the string,

(c) find the radial and transverse components of the acceleration of the stone, and hence find the magnitude of the acceleration of the stone.

If air resistance were taken into account, state briefly what effect this would have on the answer to part (b). (OCR)

6 Oscillations with small amplitude

Some mechanical systems, such as pendulums, oscillate in a way which approximates to simple harmonic motion, but only when the amplitude is small. When you have completed the chapter, you should

- know how to use linear approximation to obtain equations of simple harmonic form
- be able to use this method to investigate the motion of a simple pendulum
- understand that in simple harmonic motion the dependent variable may represent angular displacement
- understand the similarities and differences between the behaviour of an oscillating system and its simple harmonic approximation.

6.1 Equations approximating to simple harmonic form

This chapter is mostly about the oscillation of pendulums, which is almost but not exactly simple harmonic. By way of introduction, this section looks at a problem of a more familiar kind which exhibits rather similar behaviour.

Suppose that an elastic string is stretched between two pegs on a horizontal table, and that a particle is attached at its mid-point, You met some examples in Chapter 3 in which the particle is displaced along the line joining the pegs (for example, Miscellaneous exercise 3 Question 7) and you know that in such cases the particle oscillates with simple harmonic motion.

What will happen if the particle is displaced at right angles to the line joining the pegs?

Example 6.1.1
An elastic string, of natural length 1.6 metres and modulus of elasticity 20 newtons, has a particle of mass 0.1 kg attached at its mid-point. The ends of the string are attached at two fixed points, A and B, 2 metres apart on a smooth horizontal table. The particle is pulled aside in a horizontal direction perpendicular to AB, and released. Find a differential equation describing the motion of the particle.

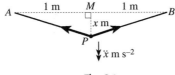

Fig. 6.1

Obviously the particle will oscillate so that its position P at any time is on a line perpendicular to AB through the mid-point M of AB, as shown in Fig. 6.1. Denote the displacement MP along this line after t seconds by x metres. Then the acceleration of the particle is $\ddot{x}$ m s^{-2} in the positive direction; that is, away from M if x is positive.

The lengths AP and BP are $\sqrt{1 + x^2}$ metres, so the tension in each of the parts AP and BP of the string is $\dfrac{20(\sqrt{1 + x^2} - 0.8)}{0.8}$ newtons.

Also $\cos \angle APM = \cos \angle BPM = \dfrac{x}{\sqrt{1 + x^2}}$.

Therefore

$$\mathcal{R}(\text{direction } MP) \qquad -2 \times \frac{20(\sqrt{1 + x^2} - 0.8)}{0.8} \times \frac{x}{\sqrt{1 + x^2}} = 0.1\ddot{x}.$$

The left side of this equation can be simplified as

$$-\frac{2 \times 20}{0.8} x \times \frac{\sqrt{1 + x^2} - 0.8}{\sqrt{1 + x^2}} = -50x \left(1 - \frac{0.8}{\sqrt{1 + x^2}}\right).$$

The motion is therefore described by the differential equation

$$\ddot{x} = -500x \left(1 - \frac{0.8}{\sqrt{1 + x^2}}\right).$$

The point to notice about Example 6.1.1 is that the motion of the particle is obviously an oscillation about M. But the differential equation is not of the form $\ddot{x} = -n^2x$, so it is not a simple harmonic oscillation. The equations found for simple harmonic motion in Chapter 3 therefore don't apply to it. Not all oscillations are simple harmonic.

There is no elementary way of solving the differential equation in Example 6.1.1. You can do it by numerical methods, and print out a (t, x) graph, but you can't find an equation for it. The question is, can you get any further by algebraic methods?

Look again at the differential equation. You can see that the problem lies in the factor in brackets; if that were constant, then you would have a simple harmonic equation. Now this factor could be written as $1 - 0.8(1 + x^2)^{-\frac{1}{2}}$, and you can expand this using the binomial series as

$$1 - 0.8 \left(1 - \tfrac{1}{2}x^2 + \tfrac{3}{8}x^4 - \tfrac{5}{16}x^6 + \ldots\right)$$
$$= 0.2 + 0.4x^2 - 0.3x^4 + 0.25x^6 - \ldots.$$

If you twang a string as described in Example 6.1.1, in practice you will probably only pull the particle aside through quite a short distance, perhaps about 0.1 metres. In that case the magnitude of x will never be greater than 0.1, so the largest magnitudes of the second, third, fourth, ... terms of the expansion are 0.004, 0.000 03, 0.000 000 25,.... These are all very small compared with the first term 0.2, so you might get a good approximation to the solution by ignoring them and replacing the factor in the bracket by 0.2. You could then write

$$\ddot{x} \approx -500x \times 0.2, \quad \text{which is} \quad \ddot{x} \approx -100x.$$

Now you do have an 'equation' of simple harmonic motion, from which you can make the usual deductions. The most important of these is that the period of the oscillation is $\dfrac{2\pi}{10}$ seconds, which is $\tfrac{1}{5}\pi$ seconds.

But this is only valid because the oscillation has small amplitude. If you pulled the particle aside by, say, 1 metre, so that the strings start at 45° to AB, then you couldn't expect this approximation to give you a reasonable answer.

> You should be warned that, although the argument used above is all right for this particular example, making a small change in a term of a differential equation can't always be guaranteed to produce a change in the solution which is also small.
>
> (Compare, for example, the solution curves through $(1, 0)$ for $\dfrac{dy}{dx} = x^n$ with $n = -1.01$, $n = -1$ and $n = -0.99$.)

6.2 The simple pendulum

The swing of a pendulum is another example of an oscillation which is only approximately simple harmonic.

The simplest kind of pendulum consists of a very small sphere or disc (called a 'bob') which hangs by a thread attached to a fixed point. This is called a **simple pendulum**.

Let the bob have mass m, and let the thread have length l. Then, when the thread has angular displacement θ from the vertical, the forces and accelerations are as shown in Fig. 6.2.

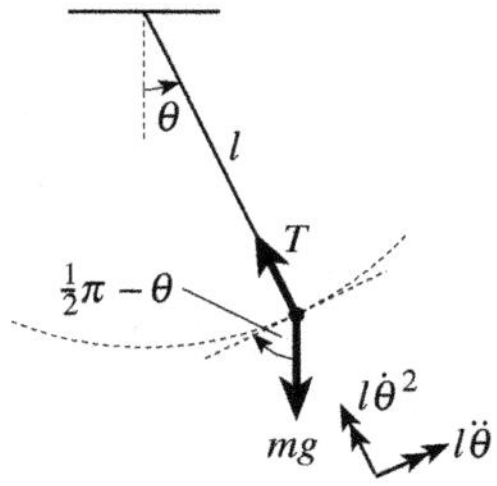

$\mathcal{R}(\perp$ to thread$)$ $-mg \sin \theta = ml\ddot{\theta}$,

Fig. 6.2

which can be written more simply as

$$\ddot{\theta} = -\frac{g}{l} \sin \theta.$$

The reason why this can be approximated as a simple harmonic equation is that, when θ is a small angle (measured in radians), θ is a good approximation to $\sin \theta$. (This is discussed in C4 Section 1.2.) So, for swings of sufficiently small amplitude, the differential equation may be replaced by

$$\ddot{\theta} \approx -\frac{g}{l} \theta.$$

Now the exact differential equation $\ddot{\theta} = -\frac{g}{l} \theta$ represents simple harmonic oscillation with period $2\pi \Big/ \sqrt{\dfrac{g}{l}} = 2\pi \sqrt{\dfrac{l}{g}}$. So you can expect this expression to give a good approximation to the period of swing of the pendulum.

> A simple pendulum consisting of a bob at the end of a thread of length l, swinging through a small angle on either side of the vertical, oscillates with period of approximately $2\pi \sqrt{\dfrac{l}{g}}$.

Notice that in this application the oscillating variable is not a displacement x but an angular displacement θ. If the motion is started by pulling the bob aside until the thread makes an angle a with the vertical, and then releasing it, then the (t, θ) graph for the simple harmonic equation has the form of Fig. 6.3, with θ taking values between $-a$ and $+a$.

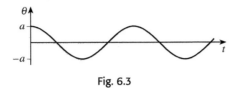

Fig. 6.3

Example 6.2.1

A particle of mass 100 grams hangs from a fixed point O by a string of length 5 metres. It is struck by a horizontal blow of impulse 0.07 N s, so that the string starts to oscillate about the vertical through O. Use a simple harmonic approximation to find values for

(a) the period of one complete swing,

(b) the maximum angle which the string makes with the vertical,

(c) the greatest and least tension in the string during the oscillation.

Fig. 6.4 shows the initial motion of the particle. If the string starts to rotate with angular velocity $\omega \, \text{rad}\, \text{s}^{-1}$, the initial speed of the particle is $5\omega \, \text{m}\, \text{s}^{-1}$. The mass of the particle is 0.1 kg, so the initial momentum is $0.1 \times 5\omega \, \text{N}\, \text{s}$. Equating this to the impulse of the blow,

$$0.5\omega = 0.07,$$

which gives $\omega = 0.14$.

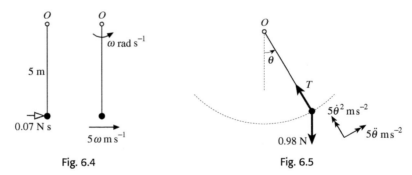

Fig. 6.4   Fig. 6.5

Fig. 6.5 shows the forces and acceleration components t seconds after the motion starts, with the string making an angle θ radians with the vertical. The weight of the particle is 0.98 newtons, and the transverse acceleration is $5\ddot{\theta} \, \text{m}\, \text{s}^{-2}$. Therefore, by Newton's second law,

$$\mathcal{R}(\perp \text{ to string}) \qquad -0.98 \sin\theta = 0.1 \times 5\ddot{\theta},$$

so that $\ddot{\theta} = -1.96 \sin \theta$. If θ is small, this can be replaced by the approximate equation

$$\ddot{\theta} \approx -1.96\theta.$$

The answers to the question are based on this approximation.

(a) The equation represents simple harmonic motion $\ddot{\theta} = -n^2\theta$ with $n^2 = 1.96$ so $n = 1.4$.

The period of one complete swing is $\dfrac{2\pi}{n} = \dfrac{2\pi}{1.4}$ seconds, which is 4.49 seconds correct to 3 significant figures.

(b) Since the oscillation begins with the string vertical, where $\theta = 0$, the (t, θ) equation has the form

$$\theta = a \sin 1.4t,$$

where a is the maximum angle with the vertical. Differentiating this,

$$\dot{\theta} = 1.4a \cos 1.4t.$$

Since when $\theta = 0$, $\dot{\theta} = \omega$, it follows that $1.4a = 0.14$, so $a = 0.1$.

This is the maximum angle in radians; in degrees it is about $5.7°$. This justifies treating this as a small angle oscillation, approximating $\sin \theta$ to θ.

(c) If the tension in the string is T newtons, using Fig. 6.5 again,

$$\mathcal{R}\,(\text{towards } O) \qquad T - 0.98 \cos \theta = 5\dot{\theta}^2,$$

so $T = 0.98 \cos \theta + 5\dot{\theta}^2$.

Both terms on the right side of this equation are greatest when $\theta = 0$, where $\dot{\theta} = \omega$, so the greatest value of T is $0.98 + 5 \times 0.14^2 = 1.078$.

They are least when $\theta = a$, where $\dot{\theta} = 0$, so the least value of T is

$$0.98 \times \cos 0.1 + 0 = 0.9751\ldots.$$

The greatest and least values of the tension are 1.078 newtons and 0.975 newtons.

It is worth remarking that, in Example 6.2.1, it is possible to answer parts (b) and (c) exactly using the methods of Chapter 5. The exact equation of energy at any point of the oscillation (taking O as the base level for potential energy) is

$$\tfrac{1}{2} \times 0.1 \times (5\dot{\theta})^2 - 0.98 \times 5 \cos \theta = \tfrac{1}{2} \times 0.1 \times (5\omega)^2 - 0.98 \times 5.$$

With $\omega = 0.14$, this can be simplified to

$$\dot{\theta}^2 = 3.92 \cos \theta - 3.9004.$$

This shows that $\dot{\theta} = 0$ when $\cos \theta = \dfrac{3.9004}{3.92} = 0.995$, giving $\theta = 0.1004\ldots$. Compare this with the value 0.1 for the amplitude with the simple harmonic approximation.

In part (c), the resolving equation remains valid, and the calculation of the greatest tension is unchanged. But the least value of T is now

$$0.98 \cos 0.1004... = 0.98 \times \frac{3.9004}{3.92},$$

giving the least tension as 0.9751 newtons. So for a swing of this size, the answers given by the simple harmonic approximation hardly differ at all from those given by the exact method.

Example 6.2.2

A bead of mass 50 grams is threaded on a fixed smooth vertical wire of radius 32 cm. The apparatus is taken into a lift and set oscillating about the lowest point of the wire. Describe the motion of the bead on the wire

(a) when the lift is stationary,

(b) when the lift is descending with acceleration $1.8 \, \text{m s}^{-2}$.

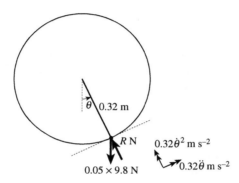

Fig. 6.6

(a) Fig. 6.6 shows the forces and components of acceleration when the lift is stationary and the radius through the bead has angular displacement θ from the vertical. Notice that these are similar to those in Fig. 6.2, with the tension T in the thread replaced by the contact force R from the wire, and the length l of the thread replaced by the radius of the wire, which is 0.32 metres. The weight of the bead is 0.05×9.8 newtons.

$\mathcal{R}$(along the tangent) $-0.05 \times 9.8 \sin \theta = 0.05 \times 0.32 \ddot{\theta},$

which gives

$$\ddot{\theta} = -30.625 \sin \theta.$$

This represents oscillation about the lowest point of the wire. If the amplitude is small, the period of oscillation is approximately equal to that of the simple harmonic oscillation $\ddot{\theta} = -30.625\theta$, which is $\dfrac{2\pi}{\sqrt{30.625}}$ seconds, or 1.14 seconds correct to 3 significant figures.

(b) When the lift starts accelerating downwards, the acceleration of the lift must be included with the other two components of acceleration, as shown in Fig. 6.7. The forces are the same as in part (a).

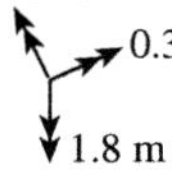

$0.32\dot\theta^2$ m s^{-2}
$0.32\ddot\theta$ m s^{-2}
1.8 m s^{-2}

Fig. 6.7

$\mathcal{R}$ (along the tangent) $\qquad -0.05 \times 9.8 \sin\theta = 0.05 \times (0.32\ddot\theta - 1.8\sin\theta)$.

When rearranged, this becomes

$$\ddot\theta = -25\sin\theta.$$

For oscillations of small amplitude, the period is approximately equal to that of the simple harmonic oscillation $\ddot\theta = -25\theta$, which is $\dfrac{2\pi}{5}$ seconds, or 1.26 seconds correct to 3 significant figures.

6.3 A note on accuracy

To make use of the simple pendulum formula you need to know for what amplitude of swing it gives a reasonable approximation. To answer this, it is helpful to know that $\sin\theta$ can be expressed as a series of powers of θ by means of its Maclaurin expansion,

$$\sin\theta = \theta - \tfrac{1}{6}\theta^3 + \tfrac{1}{120}\theta^5 - \dots .$$

You will find this in FP2 Section 3.3; the numbers 6, 120, ... , which appear in the coefficients, are in fact 3!, 5!, ... Suppose for example that the pendulum swings through an angle of 0.3 radians on either side of the vertical, which is just over 17°. Then the largest magnitudes of the first, second, third, ... terms of the expansion are 0.3, 0.0045, 0.000 020 25, ... In order of magnitude these are roughly comparable with the values found in Section 6.1 for the particle on the elastic string oscillating with amplitude 0.1 metres (for which angle *MAP* is about 5.7°). Both in fact give answers for the period which are accurate within a margin of less than 1% if the function is replaced by the first term of the series.

> You can investigate the approximation for yourself by using a calculator to plot graphs of $y = x$ and $y = \sin x$ for values of x from about 0 to 1. For what values of x can you distinguish between the two graphs?

6.4* What does 'approximation' mean?

This section probes in greater depth what is meant by saying that the solution of one differential equation approximates to the solution of another. You may omit the details if you wish, and go straight to the summary at the end of the section.

The difference between the equations

$$\ddot{\theta} = -\frac{g}{l}\sin\theta \qquad \text{(the 'exact equation'),}$$

and $\qquad \ddot{\theta} = -\frac{g}{l}\theta \qquad$ (the 'approximate equation')

is that $\sin\theta$ in the first is replaced by θ in the second. Since the magnitude of $\sin\theta$ is always smaller than the magnitude of θ (except when $\theta = 0$), the effect of the approximation is to make the size of the angular acceleration too large. So if you consider solutions of the two equations with the same amplitude, the approximate equation overestimates the speed of the bob. It therefore underestimates the period of the oscillation.

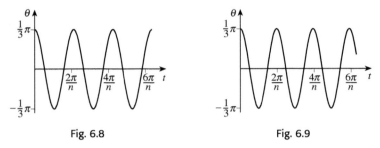

Fig. 6.8   Fig. 6.9

This is illustrated by Figs. 6.8 and 6.9, which are both drawn for oscillations with amplitude $\frac{1}{3}\pi$, that is for a pendulum swinging through 60° either side of the vertical. These (t, θ) graphs have been drawn by a numerical method, though in fact you know that Fig. 6.9, for the approximate equation, has equation $\theta = \frac{1}{3}\pi\cos nt$, where $n = \sqrt{\frac{g}{l}}$. Fig. 6.8, for the exact equation, could be mistaken for a cosine graph, but it isn't one; it is too wide near the maxima and minima. You can see that by time $\frac{6\pi}{n}$, when the solution of the approximate equation has completed three periods, the exact solution has run for only just over $2\frac{3}{4}$ periods.

So it is certainly not true that, if the solution of the exact equation is $\theta = \frac{1}{3}\pi\, f(t)$, then $f(t) \approx \cos\left(\sqrt{\frac{g}{l}}\,t\right)$ for all values of t. If you set the real pendulum in motion alongside a 'virtual' bob obeying the approximate equation, the two would soon get out of phase with each other.

There is more mileage in comparing the (θ, ω) graphs for the two equations, where ω is the angular velocity $\dot{\theta}$. You know from Section 5.4 that you can often integrate a differential equation for motion round a circle by writing $\ddot{\theta}$ as $\omega\dfrac{d\omega}{d\theta}$. So the exact equation can be written as

$$\omega\frac{d\omega}{d\theta} = -\frac{g}{l}\sin\theta.$$

This can be integrated with respect to θ as

$$\tfrac{1}{2}\omega^2 = \frac{g}{l}\cos\theta - \frac{g}{l}\cos a,$$

where the constant has been found using the fact that $\omega = 0$ when $\theta = a$. As in Section 5.4, this could also have been obtained from the energy equation, $\frac{1}{2}m(l\omega)^2 = mgl(\cos\theta - \cos a)$.

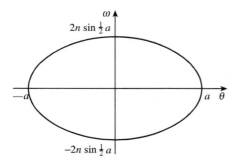

Fig. 6.10

The graph of this equation is shown in Fig. 6.10. You will recognise it as being a shape like Fig. 3.2 in Section 3.2, though that was an ellipse and this isn't. It does, however, have the same symmetries as the graph for simple harmonic motion, and it describes the oscillation in just the same way.

Notice that, writing n^2 for $\frac{g}{l}$, the value of ω when $\theta = 0$ is given by

$$\omega^2 = 2n^2(\cos 0 - \cos a) = 2n^2(1 - \cos a) = 4n^2 \sin^2 \tfrac{1}{2}a,$$

so $\omega = \pm 2n \sin \tfrac{1}{2}a$.

You can get the corresponding result for the approximate differential equation by replacing v by ω and x by θ in the standard simple harmonic equation $v^2 = n^2(a^2 - x^2)$ (see Section 3.2), which gives

$$\omega^2 = n^2(a^2 - \theta^2).$$

For this equation, $\omega = \pm na$ when $\theta = 0$.

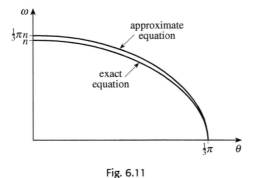

Fig. 6.11

Fig. 6.11 shows the (θ, ω) graphs for the two differential equations for the case $a = \tfrac{1}{3}\pi$. (Because of the symmetry, only the parts in the first quadrant, for which θ and ω are both positive, need be shown.) The values of ω when $\theta = 0$ are then $2n \sin \tfrac{1}{6}\pi = n$ for the exact equation, and $na = \tfrac{1}{3}\pi n$ for the approximate equation. You can see again from this figure that, throughout the motion, the approximate equation overestimates the value of the angular velocity, and therefore underestimates the period. (You can get an idea of the degree of inaccuracy by working Miscellaneous exercise 6, Question 10.)

To sum up:

- The exact differential equation and the corresponding approximate equation both have solutions which represent oscillations about a point at which the acceleration changes sign.
- The solution of the exact equation is not a cosine function, but it is periodic. The period depends on the amplitude. The (t, θ) equation cannot be found exactly.
- The solution of the approximate equation is a cosine function. The period is independent of the amplitude.
- The period for the approximate equation is a good approximation to the period for the exact equation when the amplitude is sufficiently small.
- The (t, θ) equation for the approximate equation does not give a good approximation to the exact value of θ for a particular value of t.

Exercise 6

1 Find the length of a pendulum which takes 1 second to swing between two successive positions of rest.

2 For a science exhibition it is decided to suspend a pendulum from the roof of a tall building so that it makes a complete oscillation once every 10 seconds. By what length of wire must it be suspended?

3 The acceleration due to gravity on the earth is 6.13 times the acceleration due to gravity on the moon. A pendulum oscillates with a period of 2 seconds on the earth. What would its period of oscillation be on the moon?

4 A clock is operated by a pendulum which consists of a bob hanging from a fixed point by a metal wire. In normal conditions at sea level it keeps perfect time. Will the period increase, decrease or neither if

(a) it is used in extreme tropical temperatures,

(b) it is taken to the top of a mountain,

(c) it is carried in a ship travelling at a steady speed,

(d) a thick layer of dust accumulates evenly on the surface of the bob,

(e) it is taken up in a lift which is accelerating upwards,

(f) it is used in a space station orbiting the earth?

If the period increases, does the clock run fast or slow?

5 The bob of a simple pendulum is drawn aside until the string makes an angle of 10° with the vertical, and released from rest in this position. The length of the thread is 1.25 metres. Use a simple harmonic approximation to find the time that it will take the bob to reach the lowest point of its path, and its speed at that point.

Check your answer by using an energy method to calculate the speed.

6 For a simple pendulum, if s denotes the displacement of the bob along its circular path from the lowest point, show that s satisfies the differential equation $\ddot{s} = -\dfrac{g}{l}s$.

A sphere of mass 2 kg hangs from a high beam by a rope of length 7.2 metres. It is set in motion by a horizontal blow of impulse 1.4 N s. Use a simple harmonic approximation to find how far it moves before coming to rest, and the angle that the rope then makes with the vertical. After how long is the rope again vertical?

7 A simple pendulum is swinging through an angle of 0.3 radians on either side of the vertical. At its lowest point the bob is moving with a speed of $2\,\mathrm{m\,s}^{-1}$. Use a simple harmonic approximation to calculate the length of the thread. Find also the speed of the bob when the thread is at 0.18 radians to the vertical.

8 The vertical section of a valley bottom has the shape of a circular arc of radius 980 metres. A skier of mass 60 kg is crossing the valley. At one instant she is descending at 5° to the horizontal with a speed of $20\,\mathrm{m\,s}^{-1}$. The snow surface is smooth and she exerts no additional force while descending. Show that, if the angle to the horizontal t seconds later is θ radians, then θ satisfies approximately the differential equation $\ddot{\theta} = -0.01\theta$. Use this equation to find approximately

(a) how long she will take to reach the bottom of the valley,

(b) the speed at which she is then moving,

(c) the normal force on the skier in this position.

9 Immediately after launch a space shuttle accelerates vertically upwards at a rate of $90.2\,\mathrm{m\,s}^{-2}$. Describe the motion of a pendulum of length 1 metre set oscillating inside the capsule.

10 A small ball of mass m kg hangs from the roof of a stationary railway carriage by a string of length 2 metres. The carriage starts to accelerate at a rate of $0.98\,\mathrm{m\,s}^{-2}$. If after t seconds the string makes an angle θ with the vertical (towards the rear of the carriage), obtain the differential equation $\ddot{\theta} = -4.9\left(\sin\theta - \frac{1}{10}\cos\theta\right)$. By writing $\sin\theta - \frac{1}{10}\cos\theta$ in the form $R\sin(\theta - \varepsilon)$, and then substituting $\phi = \theta - \varepsilon$, show that ϕ satisfies approximately a simple harmonic equation. Find the values of ϕ and $\dot{\phi}$ when $t = 0$, and hence find the amplitude and the period of the oscillation.

11 A pendulum swings through an angle a radians on either side of the vertical. The length of the thread is l and the mass of the bob is m. Find an expression for the tension in the thread when the bob is at its lowest point.

Find also the tension predicted by using the simple harmonic approximation. Is this an overestimate or an underestimate?

Miscellaneous exercise 6

1   A particle P is suspended from a fixed point O by a light inextensible string of length 4 m. The particle is displaced so that the taut string makes an angle α with the downward vertical through O. The particle is then released from rest. By considering the transverse component of acceleration of the particle at time t seconds after release, when the string makes an angle θ with the downward vertical, obtain a differential equation expressing $\dfrac{d^2\theta}{dt^2}$ in terms of θ.

By using an approximation based on the assumption that α is small, and ignoring air resistance, deduce that the motion of the particle will be approximately simple harmonic, and calculate its approximate period.   (OCR)

2   Part of an adventure playground consists of a bowl excavated out of the ground and coated with a layer of concrete, in the form of part of a sphere. The rim is a horizontal circle of radius 18 metres, and the lowest point of the bowl is 2 metres below the level of the rim. A skateboarder starts at a point of the rim and, under the action of gravity alone, travels through the lowest point of the bowl and up to the rim on the other side. Find the radius of the bowl, and how long she takes to skate across it.

3   A smooth wire in the form of a circle of radius 0.8 metres is fixed in a vertical plane. A bead of mass 50 grams is threaded on the wire and rests in equilibrium at the lowest point. It is set in motion by a blow of impulse 0.021 N s. Show that the bead will oscillate on the wire with approximate simple harmonic motion. Use this approximation to calculate how far the bead travels along the wire before coming to rest, and the time that it will take to do so.

4   A ball of mass 150 grams hangs by a thread 5 metres long from a hook fixed into a vertical wall. The ball rests against the wall with the thread vertical. It is now pulled away from the wall until the thread makes an angle of 10° with the vertical and then released. The coefficient of restitution between the ball and the wall is 0.6. On the rebound, find the greatest angle which the thread makes with the vertical. Find also the approximate time that elapses between the two positions of rest.

5   Two spheres of mass m and $2m$ hang by strings of equal length from points at the same level. In equilibrium the strings are just touching and the strings are parallel. The lighter sphere is pulled aside by a small distance with the string taut and then released. Explain why collisions between the spheres will occur at equal intervals of time with the strings vertical.

If the coefficient of restitution is 0.8, and the lighter sphere is released with the string at 10° to the vertical, use a simple harmonic approximation to find how far from the vertical each string will swing after the first collision.

6   Near the bottom of a hill the shape of a road is an arc of a circle in a vertical plane with radius 3920 metres. A cyclist is at a point of the road where the gradient is 10% (that is, the angle of descent δ is such that $\sin\delta = 0.1$). He is then travelling at 5 m s^{-1}, and he freewheels down to the bottom of the hill. Use a simple harmonic approximation to find how long he will take to get to the bottom of the hill, and how fast he will then be moving. If he continues to freewheel, how far will he get up the other side of the hill before coming to a stop?

7* Three light rods, each of length l, are pin-jointed together to form an equilateral triangle ABC. Particles of mass m are attached to the pins at B and C. The pin at A is driven into a wall, so that the framework is free to swing about A in its own vertical plane. It is displaced by a small angle from its position of stable equilibrium and then released. Find an approximation to the period of the oscillation.

Find also the thrust in the rod BC when it makes an angle θ with the horizontal.

8* A laboratory cubicle is taken to a great height and then released, so that it falls freely under gravity. There is a pendulum inside the cubicle with a thread of length 1 metre. Describe the motion of the pendulum, and find the period of oscillation where appropriate, at the following stages of the fall.

(a) At the point of release, the acceleration due to gravity is $9.5\,\mathrm{m\,s^{-2}}$ and there is no air resistance.

(b) After falling some distance, the acceleration due to gravity is $9.6\,\mathrm{m\,s^{-2}}$ but air resistance reduces the acceleration of the cubicle to $6.1\,\mathrm{m\,s^{-2}}$.

(c) When the parachute is deployed, the acceleration due to gravity is $9.8\,\mathrm{m\,s^{-2}}$ and the cubicle decelerates at $34.2\,\mathrm{m\,s^{-2}}$.

9* A pendulum has a bob of mass m at the end of a light rod of length l. The pendulum is mounted on a frame which moves horizontally with acceleration $g\tan\beta$. Show that it can hang with the rod at a constant angle β to the vertical.

If the pendulum is slightly displaced from this position, find an approximate expression for the period with which it oscillates.

10* A simple pendulum with length l swings through an angle of a radians on either side of the vertical, where $a < \frac{1}{2}\pi$. By writing an energy equation, and considering the quarter-period for which both θ and ω are positive, show that the total period can be calculated as

$$2\sqrt{\frac{l}{g}}\int_0^a \frac{1}{\sqrt{\sin^2\frac{1}{2}a - \sin^2\frac{1}{2}\theta}}\,\mathrm{d}\theta.$$

Use the substitution $\sin\frac{1}{2}\theta = \sin\frac{1}{2}a\sin u$ to show that this is equal to

$$4\sqrt{\frac{l}{g}}\int_0^{\frac{1}{2}\pi}\frac{1}{\sqrt{1 - k^2\sin^2 u}}\,\mathrm{d}u, \text{ where } k = \sin\tfrac{1}{2}a.$$

Use the trapezium rule with 3 intervals to find an approximate value of the integral when $a = \frac{1}{3}\pi$. Hence estimate the percentage error in using the approximate value $2\pi\sqrt{\dfrac{l}{g}}$ for the period when $a = \frac{1}{3}\pi$.

11* For the particle in Example 6.1.1, suppose that the speed when the displacement is x metres is $v\,\mathrm{m\,s^{-1}}$, and that the motion is started by releasing the particle at a distance of a metres from M. By writing $\ddot{x}$ as $v\dfrac{dv}{dx}$ or otherwise, show that, as the particle oscillates about M, the value of $v^2 + 500x^2 - 800\sqrt{1 + x^2}$ remains constant. Write an expression for this constant in terms of a.

Write down the equivalent (x, v) equation for a particle oscillating according to the simple harmonic approximation $\ddot{x} = -100x$ with the same amplitude.

Hence, for both the exact equation and the simple harmonic approximation, find an expression for v_0^2 in terms of a, where v_0 is the value of v when $x = 0$. Investigate which of the expressions for v_0 has the greater value, and hence make a conjecture whether the period given by the approximate simple harmonic equation overestimates or underestimates the true period.

12* In Example 6.1.1, suppose that the elastic string is replaced by another string with natural length 2 metres and the same modulus of elasticity. Show that an approximation to the differential equation describing the motion is then $\ddot{x} = -200x^3$. If the amplitude is a metres, deduce an (x, v) equation for this approximation.

Show that, using this approximation, the quarter-period for which $x > 0$ and $v > 0$ has duration given by the integral $\displaystyle\int_0^a \frac{0.1}{\sqrt{a^4 - x^4}}\,dx$. Use the substitution $x = au$ to show that the total period for one oscillation is $\dfrac{K}{a}$ seconds, where $K = \displaystyle\int_0^1 \frac{0.4}{\sqrt{1 - u^4}}\,du$.

By considering the physical situation modelled by this equation, suggest why it might be expected that oscillations with larger amplitude would have a shorter period.

7 Impulse and momentum in two dimensions

This chapter extends the theory of impulse, momentum and restitution to objects free to move in two dimensions. When you have completed it, you should

- understand the vector nature of the impulse–momentum and conservation of momentum equations
- understand the standard models for collisions and restitution in two dimensions
- be able to use these models to solve problems on collisions between two smooth spheres or discs, or between one smooth sphere or disc and a fixed plane surface.

7.1 The impulse–momentum equation

In M1 Chapter 8 the momentum equation $Ft = mv - mu$ was obtained by eliminating the acceleration a between the two equations $F = ma$ and $v = u + at$. You now know that both of these equations are in fact vector equations, written as $\mathbf{F} = m\mathbf{a}$ and $\mathbf{v} = \mathbf{u} + \mathbf{a}t$. (The second of these equations was used in the form $\mathbf{v} = \mathbf{u} + \mathbf{g}t$ in M2 Section 1.1, but the argument given there applies equally to any constant acceleration.)

Just as in the one-dimensional case, you can write

$$\mathbf{F}t = m\mathbf{a}\,t = m(\mathbf{v} - \mathbf{u}) = m\mathbf{v} - m\mathbf{u}.$$

You can use this to solve problems in which a moving object is deflected through an angle by applying a force. Because the impulse $\mathbf{F}t$ and the momentum $m\mathbf{v}$ are vector quantities, the equation can be applied either by using a vector triangle or by writing the vectors in component form.

Example 7.1.1
When a footballer receives the ball it is moving at $8\,\mathrm{m\,s}^{-1}$. He kicks it so that its direction is diverted through $60°$ and its speed is increased to $20\,\mathrm{m\,s}^{-1}$. In what direction does the player kick the ball?

If the mass of the ball is M kg, the magnitude of the momentum changes from $8M$ N s to $20M$ N s. If arrows $\overrightarrow{AB}$ and $\overrightarrow{AC}$ are drawn representing the initial and final momentum respectively, as in Fig. 7.1, then $\overrightarrow{BC}$ represents the change in momentum, which is equal to the impulse; that is $m\mathbf{v} - m\mathbf{u} = \mathbf{F}t$. Its direction is given by the angle θ.

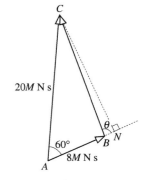

You can find this by drawing a perpendicular CN to AB produced. Then, in newton-second units,

$$CN = 20M \sin 60° = 10M\sqrt{3}, \text{ and}$$
$$BN = 20M \cos 60° - 8M = 2M.$$

Fig. 7.1

So $\tan\theta = \dfrac{10M\sqrt{3}}{2M} = 5\sqrt{3}$, which gives $\theta = 83.4°$.

The ball is kicked at an angle of $83.4°$ to the original direction of motion.

Example 7.1.2

In cricket a batsman receives the ball, of mass 160 grams, travelling horizontally and directly down the line of the wickets at $30\,\mathrm{m\,s^{-1}}$. He hits it with an impulse of $4\,\mathrm{N\,s}$ at $40°$ to the line of the wickets (see Fig. 7.2). In which direction, and at what speed, does the ball leave the bat?

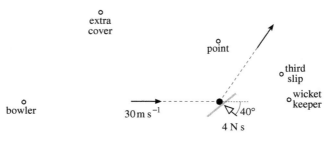

Fig. 7.2

Taking x- and y-axes along and perpendicular to the line of the wickets, and the initial direction of the ball as positive, the initial momentum is $m\mathbf{u} = 0.16\begin{pmatrix} 30 \\ 0 \end{pmatrix}\,\mathrm{N\,s}$, which is $\begin{pmatrix} 4.8 \\ 0 \end{pmatrix}\,\mathrm{N\,s}$. The impulse from the bat is $\mathbf{I} = \begin{pmatrix} -4\cos 40° \\ 4\sin 40° \end{pmatrix}\,\mathrm{N\,s}$. Using the impulse–momentum equation in the form $m\mathbf{v} = m\mathbf{u} + \mathbf{I}$, the final momentum is $\begin{pmatrix} 4.8 - 4\cos 40° \\ 4\sin 40° \end{pmatrix}\,\mathrm{N\,s}$. Dividing by m, the final velocity is

$$\mathbf{v} = \frac{1}{0.16}\begin{pmatrix} 4.8 - 4\cos 40° \\ 4\sin 40° \end{pmatrix}\,\mathrm{m\,s^{-1}}, \text{ which is } \begin{pmatrix} 10.848... \\ 16.069... \end{pmatrix}\,\mathrm{m\,s^{-1}}.$$

To complete the calculation, this must be converted to a magnitude and direction. Using the rectangular–polar conversion, this is a velocity of $19.4\,\mathrm{m\,s^{-1}}$ at $56.0°$ to the original direction of motion, both correct to one decimal place.

So although the batsman makes a stroke towards extra cover, the ball actually passes between point and third slip.

7.2 Conservation of momentum

In M1 Section 8.2 you used the conservation of momentum principle to find what happens after two objects moving in the same line collide. The principle applies just as well to collisions in which the objects are not moving in the same line.

When two objects collide, each gives an impulse to the other, and these impulses are equal in magnitude and opposite in direction. So you can write an impulse–momentum equation for each,

$$\mathbf{I} = m_2\mathbf{v}_2 - m_2\mathbf{u}_2 \quad \text{and} \quad -\mathbf{I} = m_1\mathbf{v}_1 - m_1\mathbf{u}_1,$$

where $\mathbf{u}$, $\mathbf{v}$ denote velocity before and after the collision, and $\mathbf{I}$ is the impulse from object 1 on object 2. So, eliminating $\mathbf{I}$ and rearranging,

$$m_1\mathbf{v}_1 + m_2\mathbf{v}_2 = m_1\mathbf{u}_1 + m_2\mathbf{u}_2.$$

This is the conservation of momentum principle you already know, but in vector form, which shows that it holds equally well in two or three dimensions as in one. It has very general application, because the forces between the objects can be of any kind. Also, the principle can be extended to cases where the force between the objects is not constant, but varies in magnitude and direction; this can be justified by applying the principle repeatedly over a succession of short intervals of time in which the force can be regarded as constant.

Example 7.2.1
A car of mass 1200 kg is skidding out of control on an icy surface. Whilst travelling at $6\,\mathrm{m\,s}^{-1}$ it strikes a stationary car of mass 800 kg. The moving car is deflected through 10°, and the other car starts moving at an angle of 50° to the original direction of motion of the car that hit it. Calculate the speeds with which the cars move after the impact, and the magnitude of the impulse between them.

The situation before and after the collision is illustrated in Fig. 7.3. The speeds of the cars after the impact are denoted by $x\,\mathrm{m\,s}^{-1}$ and $y\,\mathrm{m\,s}^{-1}$.

Only the heavier car has momentum before the collision, of amount 1200×6 N s.

After the collision the cars have momentum $1200x$ N s and $800y$ N s respectively.

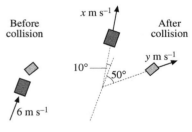

Fig. 7.3

The fact that the total momentum is unchanged by the collision can be expressed by drawing the vector triangle in Fig. 7.4.

From this it follows, by the sine rule, that

$$\frac{1200x}{\sin 50°} = \frac{800y}{\sin 10°} = \frac{7200}{\sin 120°},$$

so $x = 5.307\ldots$ and $y = 1.804\ldots$.

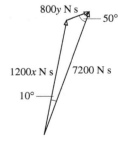

Fig. 7.4

To find the impulse, it is best to consider the smaller car, since that was stationary to start with. The impulse is therefore in the direction in which that car starts to move, and of magnitude $800y$ N s, which is 1443.6... N s.

After the collision the cars move with speeds $5.31\,\mathrm{m\,s^{-1}}$ and $1.80\,\mathrm{m\,s^{-1}}$. The impulse has magnitude 1440 N s, correct to 3 significant figures.

It is often easier to use component methods to solve problems on the conservation of momentum.

Example 7.2.2
A small hovercraft, of mass 45 kg, is being used for naval target practice. It is moving across a lake on a course due north at $30\,\mathrm{m\,s^{-1}}$. It is struck by a missile of mass 5 kg, moving horizontally with a speed of $200\,\mathrm{m\,s^{-1}}$ on a bearing of 040°. The missile is designed to stick to the hovercraft on impact. Find the combined velocity of the hovercraft and the missile after the impact.

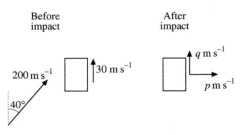

Fig. 7.5

Take x- and y-directions east and north respectively, as shown in Fig. 7.5. Then the momentum of the hovercraft is $45\begin{pmatrix} 0 \\ 30 \end{pmatrix}$ N s, and the momentum of the missile is

$5\begin{pmatrix} 200\sin 40° \\ 200\cos 40° \end{pmatrix}$ N s. So the total momentum (in N s) before the impact is

$$\begin{pmatrix} 0 \\ 1350 \end{pmatrix} + \begin{pmatrix} 1000\sin 40° \\ 1000\cos 40° \end{pmatrix} = \begin{pmatrix} 642.7... \\ 2116.0... \end{pmatrix}.$$

Suppose that the components of velocity east and north after the impact are $p\,\mathrm{m\,s^{-1}}$ and $q\,\mathrm{m\,s^{-1}}$. The total mass moving at this velocity is 50 kg, so the momentum after the impact is $50\begin{pmatrix} p \\ q \end{pmatrix}$ N s. Since momentum is conserved,

$$50\begin{pmatrix} p \\ q \end{pmatrix} = \begin{pmatrix} 642.7... \\ 2116.0... \end{pmatrix},$$

so that $\begin{pmatrix} p \\ q \end{pmatrix} = \tfrac{1}{50}\begin{pmatrix} 642.7... \\ 2116.0... \end{pmatrix} = \begin{pmatrix} 12.85... \\ 42.32... \end{pmatrix}.$

Fig. 7.6 shows these components combined to produce a single velocity vector. The magnitude is $\sqrt{p^2 + q^2} = 44.23\ldots$, and the angle with the north direction is $\tan^{-1}\frac{p}{q}$, which is $16.89\ldots°$.

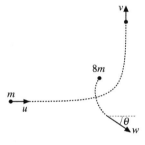

The combined velocity after the impact is $44.2\,\text{m s}^{-1}$ on a bearing of $016.9°$.

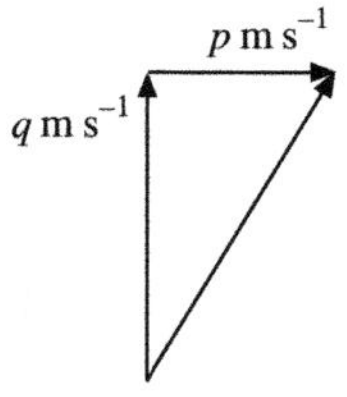

Fig. 7.6

The conservation of momentum principle doesn't only apply when the interaction between the objects takes place over a short time. So long as there are no other forces acting on the objects, the total momentum remains constant indefinitely, as in the next example.

Example 7.2.3*

A star of mass m approaches from a great distance at speed u. Its course passes close to a heavier star of mass $8m$, which can be regarded as 'stationary'. Once the lighter star has passed and is again at a great distance, its course has turned through a right angle. Find the speed at which it is then moving, and the velocity given to the heavier star.

Fig. 7.7 shows the paths of the two stars during the encounter. Denote their final speeds by v and w, and suppose that the heavier star is then moving at an angle θ to the original course of the lighter star. Take axes in the initial and final directions of motion of the lighter star.

The conservation of momentum equation then gives

$$m\begin{pmatrix} u \\ 0 \end{pmatrix} = m\begin{pmatrix} 0 \\ v \end{pmatrix} + 8m\begin{pmatrix} w\cos\theta \\ -w\sin\theta \end{pmatrix},$$

Fig. 7.7

which can be split into the two equations

$$mu = 8mw\cos\theta \quad \text{and} \quad 0 = mv - 8mw\sin\theta,$$

so that

$$u = 8w\cos\theta \quad \text{and} \quad v = 8w\sin\theta.$$

The problem now is that there are three unknowns (u, v and θ) but you have only two equations. A third equation can be found by using ideas of energy. As the two stars come closer together, the gravitational force between them does work, so the total kinetic energy increases. But later, as stars separate, work is done against the gravitational force, so the kinetic energy decreases again. At a large distance the kinetic energy is the same as it was at the start. Therefore

$$\tfrac{1}{2}mu^2 = \tfrac{1}{2}mv^2 + \tfrac{1}{2}(8m)w^2,$$

so that $u^2 = v^2 + 8w^2$.

To solve the three equations, note that from the first two equations

$$u^2 + v^2 = 64w^2 \cos^2 \theta + 64w^2 \sin^2 \theta$$
$$= 64w^2(\cos^2 \theta + \sin^2 \theta)$$
$$= 64w^2.$$

So you now have two equations for v and w in terms of u:

$$64w^2 - v^2 = u^2, \quad \text{and} \quad 8w^2 + v^2 = u^2.$$

Adding these equations,

$$72w^2 = 2u^2,$$

so that $w^2 = \frac{1}{36}u^2$, and $w = \frac{1}{6}u$.

Substituting $\frac{1}{6}u$ for w in the equation $8w^2 + v^2 = u^2$,

$$v^2 = u^2 - 8\left(\frac{1}{6}u\right)^2 = \frac{7}{9}u^2,$$

so $v = \frac{1}{3}\sqrt{7}u.$

To find θ, go back to the first two equations, to obtain

$$\tan \theta = \frac{v}{u} = \frac{1}{3}\sqrt{7}, \quad \text{which gives} \quad \theta = 41.4°.$$

The lighter star ultimately moves with speed $\frac{1}{3}\sqrt{7}$, and the heavier star acquires a speed $\frac{1}{6}u$ at an angle 41.4° to the original direction of motion of the lighter star.

Exercise 7A

1 A football of mass 450 grams is kicked along the ground. It strikes a vertical wall with a velocity of $18\,\mathrm{m\,s^{-1}}$ at 50° to the wall, and rebounds at 35° to the wall. Given that the impulse from the wall is perpendicular to the wall, calculate the speed of the rebound, and the magnitude of the impulse.

2 A cricket ball of mass 160 grams is thrown on to the ground with a velocity of $25\,\mathrm{m\,s^{-1}}$ at 40° to the horizontal. Because of friction the total impulse from the ground is at 10° to the vertical. The ball rebounds at 25° to the horizontal. Calculate the speed of the ball on the rebound, and the magnitude of the total impulse.

3 A cricketer receives a ball of mass 160 grams travelling horizontally at $24\,\mathrm{m\,s^{-1}}$ and deflects it through 70° without change of speed. Calculate the impulse given to the ball from the bat.

4 A tennis player receives a ball of mass 60 grams travelling horizontally at $55\,\mathrm{m\,s^{-1}}$ perpendicular to the net, and returns it at $28\,\mathrm{m\,s^{-1}}$ in a direction at 20° to the line along which she received it. Calculate the impulse given to the ball.

5 A yacht of mass 1.2 tonnes is sailing north at $8\,\mathrm{m\,s^{-1}}$. A little later it is sailing on a bearing of 030° at $6\,\mathrm{m\,s^{-1}}$. What resultant impulse is needed to effect this change?

6 A footballer receives the ball, of mass 450 grams, when it is travelling at $12 \, \text{m s}^{-1}$. To get it into the goal he has to deflect it through an angle between 20° and 26°. He kicks it in a direction at 70° to the line of motion. Within what limits must the magnitude of the impulse lie if the ball is to go in the direction of the goal?

7 An ice-hockey puck, of mass 160 grams, is moving over the ice at $50 \, \text{m s}^{-1}$. What is the greatest angle through which it can be deflected by an impulse of magnitude $1 \, \text{N s}$? In which direction should the impulse be applied to achieve the greatest deflection?

8 In an acrobatic show two performers, of mass 70 kg and 50 kg, are swinging on ropes. As they come together they are moving horizontally in directions at 60° to each other, both with speed $10 \, \text{m s}^{-1}$. At this instant the heavier acrobat transfers himself to the other one's rope. At what speed, and in what direction, do they go on together?

9 In a fast-food restaurant, plates of mass 200 grams are delivered on a conveyor belt travelling at $2 \, \text{m s}^{-1}$, and burgers of mass 250 grams are delivered on a perpendicular conveyor belt at $3 \, \text{m s}^{-1}$. Where they meet, a burger lands on a plate and is taken away on a third belt. In what direction, and at what speed, should the third belt move to avoid any frictional impulse between the belt and the under-side of the plate?

10 A satellite of mass 500 kg, travelling in orbit at $8 \, \text{km s}^{-1}$, is struck by a piece of space debris of mass 10 kg, travelling at $6 \, \text{km s}^{-1}$ and approaching the satellite from a direction 60° to the left of its forward line of sight. After the impact the debris disintegrates and starts to fall vertically to earth. Through what angle is the velocity of the satellite deflected, and how is its speed affected by the impact?

11 A ball of mass 0.5 kg is floating on a pond just out of its owner's reach. In an attempt to recover it, a stone of mass 0.2 kg is thrown at the ball horizontally with a speed of $4 \, \text{m s}^{-1}$. It ricochets off the ball at $3 \, \text{m s}^{-1}$ in a perpendicular direction. How fast, and in what direction, does the ball start to move?

12* Two particles, each of mass 1 kg, rest on a smooth table. They are joined by an elastic string which is just taut. One of the particles is struck a blow with an impulse of $2 \, \text{N s}$ in a direction at 30° to the line of the string, so that the string starts to stretch. When the string first returns to its natural length, the particle which was struck is moving at right angles to the original line of the string. Use equations of momentum and energy to find the direction in which the other particle is then moving.

7.3 Impacts with a fixed surface

So far the laws involving impulse, momentum and restitution have been applied to objects of a variety of shapes, which may have been attached to strings or moving over a surface. But their motion has always been modelled as that of particles, which is not realistic for rolling objects such as snooker balls. Because of this, many of the calculations you have done give answers which are only approximations to what would happen in practice.

When the possibility of motion is extended to two dimensions, it is even more important to recognise the limitations of the model. For example, you know that by using the friction between a tennis racket and a ball you can get the ball to spin; and that when a spinning ball hits the ground there is friction between the ball and the ground, which can cause the ball to move in unexpected directions. It is possible to devise mathematical models to include spin, but the mathematics is very complicated, and it won't be attempted here.

So before extending the theory to two dimensions it is important to clarify the model on which it is based. First, it will be restricted to uniform objects with spherical or circular symmetry, such as balls or discs. Secondly, it is assumed that all surfaces are smooth, and that all objects move without rotation.

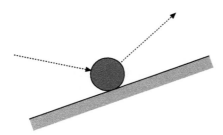

Fig. 7.8

With these restrictions in mind, consider what happens when a ball strikes a flat surface and bounces off it, as illustrated in Fig. 7.8. Its velocity changes, so its momentum also changes, and this change is caused by the impulse from the surface. Since the surfaces are smooth, this impulse acts along a normal to the surface.

The relation between the velocities after and before the impact is then governed by two principles.

> When a smooth ball strikes a flat surface,
>
> the impulse on the ball acts along the line through the centre of the ball perpendicular to the surface, and
>
> Newton's law of impact, that $\dfrac{\text{separation speed}}{\text{approach speed}}$ is constant, applies to the component of the velocity of the ball perpendicular to the surface.

As for impacts in one dimension, the second of these principles is equivalent to the hypothesis that the impulse during the restitution is e times the impulse during the compression stage; in the notation of M2 Section 7.6, $I_{\text{rest}} = eI_{\text{comp}}$.

To see the effect of applying the first principle, set up axes in the plane of the motion, with the x-axis parallel to the surface through the centre of the ball, and the y-axis pointing away from the surface, as in Fig. 7.9. Let the initial velocity of the ball be $\begin{pmatrix} u_x \\ -u_y \end{pmatrix}$, and let the velocity after the impact be $\begin{pmatrix} v_x \\ v_y \end{pmatrix}$. Let the impulse be $\begin{pmatrix} 0 \\ I \end{pmatrix}$, and the mass of the ball be m.

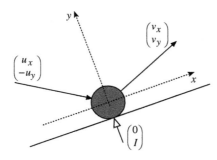

Fig. 7.9

Then the impulse–momentum equation is

$$\begin{pmatrix} 0 \\ I \end{pmatrix} = m\begin{pmatrix} v_x \\ v_y \end{pmatrix} - m\begin{pmatrix} u_x \\ -u_y \end{pmatrix}.$$

This gives two equations for the separate components. For the x-component,

$$0 = mv_x - mu_x, \quad \text{which is just} \quad v_x = u_x.$$

That is, the component of velocity parallel to the surface is unchanged by the impact.

For the y-component,

$$I = mv_y + mu_y.$$

This is just the one-dimensional impulse–momentum equation, $I = mv_y - m(-u_y)$, applied at right angles to the surface.

So, in practice, the effect of applying the principles is as follows.

> When a smooth ball strikes a flat surface,
>
> the component of its velocity parallel to the surface is unchanged by the impact,
>
> Newton's law of impact applies to the component of velocity perpendicular to the surface before and after impact,
>
> the impulse is perpendicular to the surface and equal to the change in the component of momentum perpendicular to the surface.

In this statement, the 'smooth ball' could be replaced by a smooth disc sliding across the floor and striking a vertical wall. But the model couldn't be used with confidence for objects with less regular shapes.

Example 7.3.1

In the Basque game of pelota, a ball of mass 70 grams hits the floor of the court with a speed of $12\,\mathrm{m\,s^{-1}}$ at $40°$ to the horizontal, and rebounds at $30°$ to the horizontal, as shown in Fig. 7.10. Assuming that the contact between the ball and the floor is smooth, calculate

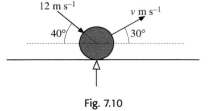

Fig. 7.10

(a) the speed of the ball as it rebounds,

(b) the coefficient of restitution, e,

(c) the impulse given to the ball from the floor.

(a) Suppose that the speed of the ball after the impact is $v\,\mathrm{m\,s^{-1}}$. Since the horizontal component of velocity is unchanged by the impact,

$$v\cos 30° = 12\cos 40°, \quad \text{so} \quad v = 10.61\ldots.$$

The ball rebounds with a speed of $10.6\,\mathrm{m\,s^{-1}}$, correct to 3 significant figures.

(b) The vertical components of velocity before and after the impact are $12\sin 40°\,\mathrm{m\,s^{-1}}$ and $v\sin 30°\,\mathrm{m\,s^{-1}}$, so

$$e = \frac{10.61\ldots \times \sin 30°}{12\sin 40°} = 0.688, \text{ correct to 3 significant figures.}$$

(c) The impulse is equal to the change in the vertical momentum, which is (in newton seconds)

$$0.07 \times v\sin 30° - 0.07 \times (-12\sin 40°)$$
$$= 0.07 \times (10.61\ldots \times \sin 30° + 12\sin 40°)$$
$$= 0.911\ldots.$$

The impulse from the floor on the ball is $0.911\,\mathrm{N\,s}$, correct to 3 significant figures.

Example 7.3.2

In ice-hockey the playing area is bounded by a vertical wooden barrier. A puck strikes the barrier at an angle of $63°$ and rebounds at an angle of $49°$. Calculate the coefficient of restitution.

Let u and v denote the speed of the puck before and after the impact. Considering motion parallel and perpendicular to the barrier,

$$v\cos 49° = u\cos 63° \quad \text{and} \quad v\sin 49° = eu\sin 63°.$$

Dividing each side of the second equation by the corresponding side of the first,

$$\frac{v\sin 49°}{v\cos 49°} = \frac{eu\sin 63°}{u\cos 63°}, \quad \text{so} \quad e\tan 63° = \tan 49°,$$

which gives $e = 0.586$, correct to 3 significant figures.

7.4   Colliding spheres in two dimensions

The principles governing collisions between two smooth spheres (or sliding discs) in two dimensions are very similar to those for collisions between one sphere and a fixed surface. The line along which the impulse acts now passes through the centres of both spheres as well as their point of contact. This is called the **line of centres**.

> When a collision occurs between two smooth spheres,
>
> > the impulse from each sphere on the other acts along the line of centres, and Newton's law of impact applies to the components of velocity along the line of centres.

You can follow through the consequences of applying these principles, in the same way as was done in Section 7.3.

Fig. 7.11 shows a collision between two spheres, with the velocities of each sphere before and after the collision and the impulse from each on the other. The line of centres has been taken as the x-direction, with the y-direction at right angles to this.

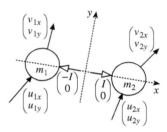

Fig. 7.11

The notation looks complicated, but it is quite easy to understand. The letters u, v denote velocity components before and after the collision; the first suffix, 1 or 2, indicates which sphere it applies to; and the second suffix, x or y, indicates which component is referred to. All the velocity components are shown in the positive x- and y-directions, although in a particular example some of these components may be negative.

The impulse–momentum equations for the two spheres are

$$\begin{pmatrix} -I \\ 0 \end{pmatrix} = m_1 \begin{pmatrix} v_{1x} \\ v_{1y} \end{pmatrix} - m_1 \begin{pmatrix} u_{1x} \\ u_{1y} \end{pmatrix} \quad \text{and} \quad \begin{pmatrix} I \\ 0 \end{pmatrix} = m_2 \begin{pmatrix} v_{2x} \\ v_{2y} \end{pmatrix} - m_2 \begin{pmatrix} u_{2x} \\ u_{2y} \end{pmatrix}.$$

Equating the y-components in each equation gives

$$0 = m_1 v_{1y} - m_1 u_{1y} \quad \text{and} \quad 0 = m_2 v_{2y} - m_2 u_{2y},$$

which is simply $v_{1y} = u_{1y}$ and $v_{2y} = u_{2y}$. That is, the components of velocity of each sphere at right angles to the line of centres are unchanged by the collision.

Equating the x-components gives

$$-I = m_1 v_{1x} - m_1 u_{1x} \quad \text{and} \quad I = m_2 v_{2x} - m_2 u_{2x}.$$

Adding the two equations and rearranging,

$$m_1 u_{1x} + m_2 u_{2x} = m_1 v_{1x} + m_2 v_{2x}.$$

This has just the same form as the one-dimensional conservation of momentum equation, applied to the components of velocity along the line of centres.

When a collision occurs between two smooth spheres,

the component of the velocity of each sphere perpendicular to the line of centres is unchanged by the impact, and

the components of velocity along the line of centres after the impact are determined from the components before the impact by applying the conservation of momentum principle and Newton's law of impact.

It is a little more complicated to apply these rules than those for impacts with a flat surface, because there are two moving objects rather than one, so twice as many velocity vectors to deal with. But once you have learnt to visualise the situation and draw a suitable diagram, it is a simple matter to convert the rules into equations for the motion along and at right angles to the line of centres, and to solve them.

Example 7.4.1

In a game of shove-ha'penny, one coin is already at rest on the board. A second coin of the same mass is moving along the board at a speed of $10\,\text{cm}\,\text{s}^{-1}$ when it clips the first coin at an angle. At the instant when the coins come into contact, the second coin is moving at $60°$ to the line of centres. The coefficient of restitution is 0.6. Find how the two coins are moving immediately after the collision.

Let each coin have mass m grams. It is simplest to use units of grams and centimetres throughout.

Most people find it helpful always to draw diagrams with the line of centres across the page, as in Fig. 7.12. You can then, if you want to, take x- and y-directions along and perpendicular to the line of centres.

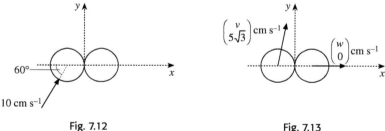

Fig. 7.12   Fig. 7.13

In this example the velocity before the impact can then be written as $\begin{pmatrix} 5 \\ 5\sqrt{3} \end{pmatrix}\,\text{cm}\,\text{s}^{-1}$. Since the impulse acts along the line of centres, the coin which was stationary will start to move along that line, so its velocity can be written as $\begin{pmatrix} w \\ 0 \end{pmatrix}\,\text{cm}\,\text{s}^{-1}$. For the second coin, the y-component is unchanged by the impact, so its velocity can be written as $\begin{pmatrix} v \\ 5\sqrt{3} \end{pmatrix}$. This is shown in Fig. 7.13.

To find the components v cm s^{-1} and w cm s^{-1} along the line of centres, you can write two equations:

conservation of momentum $m \times 5 = mv + mw$,
Newton's law of impact $w - v = 0.6 \times 5.$

These can be simplified as

$$v + w = 5 \quad \text{and} \quad w - v = 3.$$

Adding them gives $2w = 8$, so $w = 4$ and $v = 1$.

So the velocities of the coins after the impact are $\begin{pmatrix} 4 \\ 0 \end{pmatrix}$ cm s^{-1} and $\begin{pmatrix} 1 \\ 5\sqrt{3} \end{pmatrix}$ cm s^{-1}. The second of these represents a speed of 8.72 cm s^{-1} at $83.4°$ to the line of centres.

So after the impact the coin which was stationary starts to move at 4 cm s^{-1} at $60°$ to the original direction of the moving coin. The speed of the moving coin is reduced to 8.72 cm s^{-1} and its direction of motion is deflected through an angle of $23.4°$.

Example 7.4.2
Two spheres A and B, of mass 1 kg and 2 kg and equal radii, just touch each other as they hang by vertical strings of equal length from fixed points in the ceiling. The spheres are then pulled aside in perpendicular vertical planes, and released. When they again make contact, they are in their original equilibrium positions and moving in perpendicular directions with speeds 2.5 m s^{-1} and 2.0 m s^{-1} (see Fig. 7.14). At that instant sphere A is moving at an angle α to the line of centres, where $\sin \alpha = 0.6$ and $\cos \alpha = 0.8$. The coefficient of restitution is 0.5. Find

(a) the angle between the directions of motion after the collision,

(b) the magnitude of the impulse from each sphere on the other,

(c) the amount of kinetic energy lost as a result of the collision.

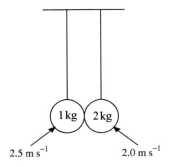

Fig. 7.14

(a) Fig. 7.15 shows a plan view of the collision, which takes place in a horizontal plane. Taking axes along and perpendicular to the line of centres as shown, the velocity components (in $m\,s^{-1}$) of A and B before the collision are $\begin{pmatrix} 2.5\cos\alpha \\ 2.5\sin\alpha \end{pmatrix} = \begin{pmatrix} 2.0 \\ 1.5 \end{pmatrix}$ and $\begin{pmatrix} -2.0\sin\alpha \\ 2.0\cos\alpha \end{pmatrix} = \begin{pmatrix} -1.2 \\ 1.6 \end{pmatrix}$ respectively. Since the y-components are unchanged after the collision, denote the velocity components after the collision by $\begin{pmatrix} -v \\ 1.5 \end{pmatrix}$ and $\begin{pmatrix} w \\ 1.6 \end{pmatrix}$.

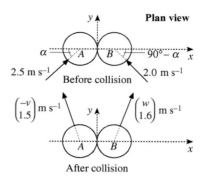

Fig. 7.15

Fig. 7.16 shows the x-components of velocity before and after the collision, and the impulse between the spheres. To find v and w, you can write two equations:

conservation of momentum

$$2.0 - 2 \times 1.2 = -v + 2w,$$

Newtons law of impact

$$v + w = 0.5 \times (2.0 + 1.2).$$

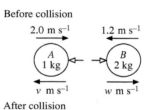

Fig. 7.16

Simplifying,

$$-v + 2w = -0.4 \quad \text{and} \quad v + w = 1.6.$$

Adding these gives $3w = 1.2$, so $w = 0.4$ and $v = 1.2$.

The velocities after the collision are therefore $\begin{pmatrix} -1.2 \\ 1.5 \end{pmatrix} m\,s^{-1}$ and $\begin{pmatrix} 0.4 \\ 1.6 \end{pmatrix} m\,s^{-1}$, which make angles of $128.6...°$ and $75.9...°$ with the x-direction. The angle between the paths after the collision is therefore $128.6...° - 75.9...°$, which is $52.7°$ correct to one decimal place.

(b) Since the impulse acts along the line of centres, it is calculated using the x-components of velocity. Sphere B had velocity $-1.2\,m\,s^{-1}$ before and $0.4\,m\,s^{-1}$ after the collision. So the impulse from sphere A on sphere B is $(2 \times 0.4 - 2 \times (-1.2))\,N\,s$, which is $3.2\,N\,s$.

(c) The total kinetic energy after the collision, in joules, is

$$\tfrac{1}{2} \times 1 \times ((-1.2)^2 + 1.5^2) + \tfrac{1}{2} \times 2 \times (0.4^2 + 1.6^2).$$

The total kinetic energy before the collision could be written either as $\tfrac{1}{2} \times 1 \times 2.5^2 + \tfrac{1}{2} \times 2 \times 2.0^2$, using the given original speeds, or as

$$\tfrac{1}{2} \times 1 \times (2.0^2 + 1.5^2) + \tfrac{1}{2} \times 2 \times ((-1.2)^2 + 1.6^2),$$

using the velocity components.

The form which uses the components in fact leads to a slightly simpler calculation, because the velocity components perpendicular to the line of centres are the same before and after the collision, so these terms are irrelevant when calculating the loss of energy. The difference in the two expressions is

$$\tfrac{1}{2} \times (2.0^2 - (-1.2)^2) + \tfrac{1}{2} \times 2 \times ((-1.2)^2 - 0.4^2)$$
$$= \tfrac{1}{2}(4 - 1.44) + (1.44 - 0.16)$$
$$= 2.56.$$

The loss of kinetic energy as a result of the collision is 2.56 joules.

Exercise 7B

In questions 1 and 2 mass, speed and impulse are measured in basic SI units.

1 In this question a smooth sphere of mass m strikes a fixed plane surface with speed u at an angle α to the plane, and rebounds with speed v at an angle β. The coefficient of restitution is e, and the impulse from the surface on the sphere has magnitude I.

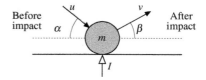

(a) Given that $\alpha = 70°$, $u = 20$, $\beta = 55°$, find v and e.

(b) Given that $\alpha = 55°$, $u = 12$, $v = 10$, find β and e.

(c) Given that $m = 2$, $u = 15$, $v = 12$, $\beta = 45°$, find e and I.

(d) Given that $m = 5$, $\alpha = 60°$, $u = 10$, $I = 60$, find β, v and e.

(e) Given that $\alpha = 75°$, $u = 18$, $e = 0.7$, find β and v.

2 In this question two smooth spheres, of mass m_1 and m_2, collide. Before the collision the sphere of mass m_1 has speed u_1 at an angle α to the line of centres, and the sphere of mass m_2 has speed u_2 at an angle β to the line of centres. After the collision the corresponding velocities are v_1 at an angle γ and v_2 at an angle δ. The coefficient of restitution is e, and the impulse between the spheres has magnitude I.

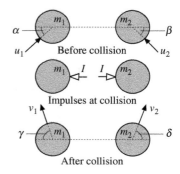

(a) Given that $m_1 = 2$, $m_2 = 3$, $u_1 = 5$, $\alpha = 0°$, $u_2 = 4$, $\beta = 90°$, $e = 0.6$, find v_1, γ, v_2 and δ.

(b) Given that $m_2 = 1$, $u_1 = 6$, $\alpha = 40°$, $u_2 = 4$, $\beta = 65°$, $\gamma = 55°$, $\delta = 80°$, find v_1, v_2, e, I and m_1.

(c) Given that $u_1 = 10$, $\alpha = 20°$, $u_2 = 5$, $\beta = 120°$, $\gamma = 90°$, $\delta = 45°$, find $m_1 : m_2$ and e.

(d) Given that $m_1 = 4$, $m_2 = 3$, $u_1 = 6$, $\alpha = 30°$, $u_2 = 4$, $\beta = 60°$, $e = 0.5$, find v_1, v_2, γ, δ and I.

3 A ball strikes a flat surface at an angle α, and rebounds at an angle β. Show that the coefficient of restitution is $\dfrac{\tan \beta}{\tan \alpha}$.

4 The coefficient of restitution between a smooth ball and a plane surface is e. The ball strikes the surface at an angle θ and rebounds at right angles to its original direction of motion. Express θ in terms of e.

5 The diagram shows part of a billiard-table. The ball is at B. The player hits the ball so that it rebounds off the cushion at X and lands in the pocket at P. The coefficient of restitution is e. Modelling the ball as smooth, find an expression for θ in terms of a, b, c and e.

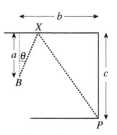

6 A ball is projected from ground level, and bounces along a smooth floor. The horizontal and vertical components of the initial velocity are p and q. The coefficient of restitution is e. If the ball goes a distance R horizontally before hitting the floor for the first time, express R in terms of p, q and g. Hence show that it goes a further distance eR before hitting the floor a second time. How far does it go before it stops bouncing completely? What happens after that?

7 A squash ball is hit up against a smooth vertical wall. After striking the wall, it comes back to the place from which it was hit. The coefficient of restitution is e, and the wall is modelled as smooth. If the ball was hit at a distance d from the wall, and the horizontal and vertical components of the initial velocity are u and v, show that $\dfrac{2uv}{g} = \dfrac{(1+e)d}{e}$.

8 Two smooth, perfectly elastic spheres of equal mass collide with each other. Show that after the collision the components of velocity along the line of centres are interchanged. If each was moving at 45° to the line of centres before the collision, show that their paths are still perpendicular to each other after the collision.

9 In a snooker shot, the moving white ball hits the stationary black ball. The black ball starts to move at 60° to the original direction of motion of the white ball. Show that it moves with speed between one-quarter and one-half of the initial speed of the white ball.

If it moves with speed 0.4 times the initial speed of the white ball, find through what angle the path of the white ball is deflected.

Miscellaneous exercise 7

1 A crash barrier along the central reservation of a motorway is struck by a vehicle of mass 3000 kg travelling at 29 m s^{-1} at an angle of 22° with the barrier. After the collision the path of the vehicle makes an angle of 5° with the barrier (see diagram). The impact can be modelled by the impact of a particle on a fixed smooth vertical wall. Find

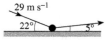

(a) the speed of the vehicle immediately after the collision,

(b) the coefficient of restitution for the collision between the vehicle and the barrier. (OCR)

2 In the corner of a room two vertical walls meet at right angles. A smooth disc slides across the floor and bounces off each wall in turn. Show that it is then moving along a line parallel to its original direction of motion, but in the opposite direction.

3 A horizontal snooker table is 1.78 m wide from Q to R. A player strikes the ball B, which has mass 0.15 kg, so that it hits the cushion of the table once before travelling in a straight line to the pocket at R. The point of impact between the ball and the cushion is at P, which is 1.30 m from the corner Q of the table. The situation may be modelled by the impact of a smooth particle with a smooth vertical wall. It is given that before the ball hits the cushion at P its speed is u m s^{-1}, and its path makes an angle of 30° with the normal (see diagram).

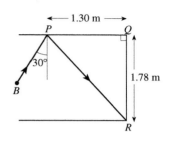

(a) Prove that the coefficient of restitution for the impact of the ball with the cushion is 0.79, correct to 2 significant figures.

(b) Calculate, in terms of u, the magnitude of the impulse on the cushion at P.

(c) Show that the time between the ball hitting the cushion and entering the pocket is at least $\dfrac{2.6}{u}$ seconds. State an assumption which must be included in the model for this time to be equal to $\dfrac{2.6}{u}$ seconds. (OCR)

4 Two smooth spheres, A and B, of equal radius, have the same speed of 14 m s^{-1} immediately before they collide. The mass of A is 0.8 kg and the mass of B is 0.7 kg. Before the collision the path of each sphere makes an angle of 60° with the line of centres, and immediately after the collision A moves perpendicular to the line of centres (see diagram). Calculate

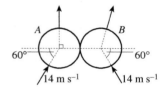

(a) the speed of A immediately after the collision,

(b) the coefficient of restitution. (OCR)

5 A collision occurs between two uniform smooth spheres A and B, of equal radius and unequal mass, which move on a smooth horizontal plane. Immediately before the collision A is moving with speed 12 m s^{-1} at an angle of 30° with the line of centres, and B is moving with speed 7 m s^{-1} perpendicular to the line of centres. Immediately after the collision the directions of motion of A and B make angles of 90° and 45° respectively with the line of centres (see diagram).

(a) Show that the speed of B immediately after the collision is 9.9 m s^{-1} approximately.

(b) Calculate the coefficient of restitution.

(c) Given that the mass of A is 0.3 kg, calculate the magnitude of the impulse on A during the collision.

(d) It is given that the radius of each sphere is 5 cm and that after the collision each sphere moves in a straight line with constant speed. Calculate the time taken, from the collision, until the centres of the spheres are 110 cm apart. (OCR)

6 Two uniform smooth spheres A and B, of equal radius, are free to move on a smooth horizontal table. The mass of B is twice the mass of A. Initially B is at rest and A is moving with speed $5\,\mathrm{m\,s^{-1}}$. The spheres collide, and immediately before impact the direction of motion of A makes an angle of 30° with the line of centres. After the collision A moves at right angles to its original direction.

(a) Show that the speed of B immediately after the collision is $\frac{5}{3}\sqrt{3}\,\mathrm{m\,s^{-1}}$.

(b) Hence show that the collision is perfectly elastic.   (OCR)

7 An ice hockey puck strikes the vertical barrier surrounding the playing area and rebounds. The coefficient of restitution is e. The angles made by the path of the puck with the barrier before and after the impact are θ and ϕ respectively. Find an equation connecting θ, ϕ and e. Deduce that, if the direction of motion of the puck is deflected by an angle δ as a result of the impact, then $\tan\delta = \dfrac{(1+e)\tan\theta}{1 - e\tan^2\theta}$.

If $e = \frac{2}{3}$, and the direction of motion of the puck is deflected by 45° as a result of the impact, find the angles θ and ϕ.

8 A collision occurs between two uniform smooth spheres A and B, of equal radius and of masses 2 kg and 3 kg respectively. Immediately before the collision A is moving along the line of centres with speed $5\,\mathrm{m\,s^{-1}}$, and B is moving perpendicular to the line of centres with speed $4\,\mathrm{m\,s^{-1}}$. Given that the spheres are perfectly elastic, find the speed and direction of motion of each sphere immediately after the collision.   (OCR)

9* In one version of the Basque game of pelota the players hit a hard ball with a bat against a high vertical wall. A player practising by himself stands at a distance d from the wall and hits the ball in a plane at right angles to the plane of the wall; he hits it just hard enough and in such a direction that the ball continually returns to him after bouncing off the wall and the floor. The path of the ball is shown in the figure. The coefficient of restitution between the ball and both the wall and the floor is e.

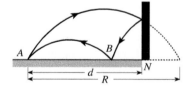

The points at which the ball is hit and at which it bounces off the floor are denoted by A and B respectively, and N is the point in the plane of the motion at the foot of the wall. Denote by R the distance that the ball would travel before returning to floor level if the wall were not in the way. By considering the horizontal and vertical components of velocity before and after each impact, establish the following properties of the path of the ball. You may assume that the player hits the ball each time at the level of the floor.

(a) $BN = e(R - d)$.

(b) When the ball bounces off the floor at B, the angle which its velocity makes with the floor is the same as the angle at which it was hit by the player at A.

(c) $AB = e^2 R$.

(d) The player should stand at a distance eR from the wall.

(e) The player starts a rally by holding the ball stationary in his hand and hitting it with an impulse of magnitude I. Show that, in order to keep the ball in the same path after each return, he must subsequently hit it with an impulse of magnitude $(1 + e)I$.   (OCR, adapted)

10 A ball of mass m moving with velocity $\mathbf{u}$ is hit with an impulse $\mathbf{I}$, which changes its velocity to $\mathbf{v}$. Show that the ball gains kinetic energy of amount $\frac{1}{2}\mathbf{I} \cdot (\mathbf{u} + \mathbf{v})$.

11* The quadrilateral $ABCD$ represents a vector diagram to demonstrate the conservation of momentum principle for two colliding objects. What quantity is represented by

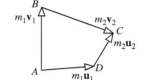

   (a) the diagonal $\overrightarrow{AC}$,

   (b) the diagonal $\overrightarrow{BD}$?

12 In M2 Section 7.8 it is proved that, when two objects collide, the loss of kinetic energy is $\frac{1}{2}\dfrac{m_1 m_2}{m_1 + m_2}(1 - e^2)A^2$, where A is the approach speed. Prove that the result applies in two dimensions to collisions between two smooth spheres, where A denotes the approach speed for the components of velocity in the direction of the line of centres.

Revision exercise 2

1 A cricket ball of mass 0.16 kg is travelling with speed 28 m s^{-1} when it is struck by a bat. The ball leaves the bat travelling with speed 16.5 m s^{-1} in a direction perpendicular to its original direction of motion. Find the magnitude of the impulse on the ball. (OCR)

2 Two uniform rods, AB and BC, are freely jointed to each other at B and to fixed points A and C, where A is 2.4 m vertically above C. The rods are in equilibrium with AB horizontal. The rod AB has length 0.8 m and weight 56 N, and the rod BC has weight 214 N (see diagram). Find the magnitude and direction of the force acting on AB at B. (OCR)

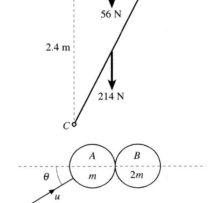

3 A sphere A of mass m, moving on a horizontal surface, collides with another sphere B of mass $2m$, which is at rest on the surface. The spheres are smooth and uniform, and have equal radius.

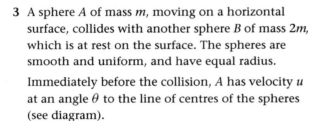

Immediately before the collision, A has velocity u at an angle θ to the line of centres of the spheres (see diagram).

Immediately after the collision, the spheres move in directions that are perpendicular to each other.

(a) Find the coefficient of restitution between the spheres.

(b) Given that the spheres have equal speeds after the collision, find θ. (OCR)

4 A smooth sphere of mass 0.25 kg bounces on a fixed horizontal surface. Immediately before the sphere bounces, it has velocity 15 m s^{-1} in a direction 30° below the horizontal. The coefficient of restitution between the sphere and the surface is 0.6. Find the magnitude and direction of the impulse on the sphere. (OCR)

5 One end of a light inextensible string of length 0.9 m is attached to a fixed point O. A particle of mass 0.5 kg is attached to the other end of the string. With the string taut and horizontal, the particle is projected vertically downwards at 6 m s^{-1}. The particle then moves without resistance in a vertical circle with centre O. Find the minimum tension in the string. (OCR)

6 A particle P is joined to a fixed point O by a light inextensible string of length a. The particle hangs in equilibrium vertically below O. It is then projected with horizontal speed u and moves in a vertical circle. Air resistance may be neglected. Find, in terms of a and g, the least value of u for which P reaches the highest point of the circle.   (OCR)

7 Two uniform rods AB and BC have weights $40\,\text{N}$ and $30\,\text{N}$ respectively. The rods are freely jointed to each other at B and to fixed points at A and C. The points A and C are on the same horizontal level, and B is $1.2\,\text{m}$ vertically below AC. The horizontal distance between A and B is $1.6\,\text{m}$, and the horizontal distance between B and C is $0.9\,\text{m}$ (see diagram).

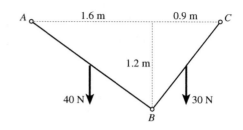

The rods are in equilibrium. Find the horizontal and vertical components of the force acting on AB at B.   (OCR)

8 Two uniform smooth spheres A and B, of equal radius, have masses $3\,\text{kg}$ and $2\,\text{kg}$ respectively. They are moving on a horizontal surface when they collide. The diagram shows the situation immediately before the collision; A has velocity $9\,\text{m s}^{-1}$ at $25°$ to the line of centres, and B has velocity $5\,\text{m s}^{-1}$ at $60°$ to the line of centres.

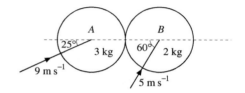

The coefficient of restitution between the spheres is 0.7. Find the magnitude and direction of the velocity of A immediately after the collision.   (OCR)

9 A particle P of mass $0.3\,\text{kg}$ is moving in a vertical circle. It is attached to the fixed point O at the centre of the circle by a light inextensible string of length $1.5\,\text{m}$. When the string makes an angle of $40°$ with the downward vertical, the speed of P is $6.5\,\text{m s}^{-1}$ (see diagram). Air resistance may be neglected.

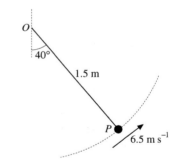

(a) Find the radial and transverse components of the acceleration of P at this instant.

In the subsequent motion, with the string still taut and making an angle θ with the downward vertical, the speed of P is $v\,\text{m s}^{-1}$.

(b) Use conservation of energy to show that $v^2 \approx 19.7 + 29.4\cos\theta$.

(c) Find the tension in the string in terms of θ.

(d) Find the value of θ at the instant when the string becomes slack.   (OCR)

10 A step-ladder is modelled as two uniform rods AB and AC, freely jointed at A. The rods are in equilibrium in a vertical plane with B and C in contact with a rough horizontal surface. The rods have equal lengths; AB has weight 150 N and AC has weight 270 N. The point A is 2.5 m vertically above the surface, and $BC = 1.6$ m (see diagram).

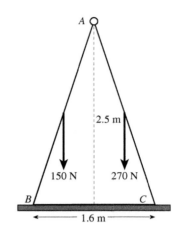

(a) Find the horizontal and vertical components of the force acting on AC at A.

(b) The coefficient of friction has the same value μ at B and at C, and the step-ladder is on the point of slipping. Giving a reason, state whether the equilibrium is limiting at B or at C, and find μ.   (OCR)

11 The diagram shows the situation just before a collision between two uniform smooth spheres A and B, of equal radius, moving on a horizontal surface. The velocity of A is $6\,\mathrm{m\,s^{-1}}$ at an angle of 40° to the line of centres of the spheres, and the velocity of B is $9\,\mathrm{m\,s^{-1}}$ at an angle of 25° to the line of centres. The mass of A is 3 kg, the mass of B is 2 kg, and the coefficient of restitution between the spheres is 0.75. Find the speed of B after the collision.   (OCR)

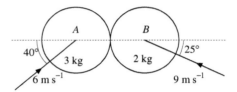

12 A simple pendulum consists of a particle attached to a fixed point by a light inextensible string of length 1.25 m, swinging in a vertical plane. Air resistance may be neglected. The angle between the string and the downward vertical is denoted by θ radians.

(a) By considering the transverse acceleration of the particle, or otherwise, show that $\ddot{\theta} = -7.84\sin\theta$.

(b) Hence show that, for small oscillations, the particle is in approximate simple harmonic motion, and find its period.

(c) The pendulum is released from rest with the string making an angle of 0.1 radians with the downward vertical. Using the simple harmonic approximation, find the time after release when the particle first reaches a speed of $0.3\,\mathrm{m\,s^{-1}}$.   (OCR)

13 A house is being demolished with the help of a stone ball, of mass 2 tonnes, which hangs from a crane by a cable of length 12 metres. The ball is pulled aside in a plane at right angles to a wall of the house, until the cable makes an angle of 20° with the vertical, and is then released. The impact between the ball and the wall, which is inelastic, occurs when the cable is vertical. Calculate

(a) the impulse from the ball on the wall,

(b) the approximate time that elapses between the release of the ball and its impact with the wall,

(c) the tension in the cable just before the ball hits the wall.

14 On a roller-coaster a car of mass m, starting from rest, descends from a height h and then performs a vertical loop of radius r. Find an expression, in terms of m, h, r and g, for the contact force between the car and the rails at the top of the loop.

15 The diagram shows an easel used to support a display board, which stands on a smooth floor. The main frame AB has weight 100 newtons. A prop CD, of weight 20 newtons, is hinged to the main frame at C, where $CA = CD$. The easel is set up with AB and DC at 75° to the horizontal. It is prevented from collapsing by a rope joining a point G on the frame to a point H on the prop. The centres of mass of the frame and the prop are at the mid-points of AB and CD. The lengths $AB = 2$ metres, $AC = 1.6$ metres, $AG = DH = 0.4$ metres. Find the tension in the rope before the display board is placed on the easel.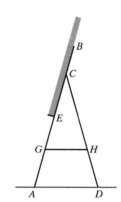

A uniform display board, of height 1.4 metres and weight 80 newtons, is now placed on the frame with its lower edge at E, where $AE = 1$ metre. Find the tension in the rope when the display board is in place.

16 A particle is suspended from a fixed point A by a light inextensible string of length l. The particle is set in motion in a vertical plane through A so that it performs small oscillations with the string taut, At time t the string makes an angle θ with the downward vertical through A.

(a) Show that the approximate equation of motion of the particle is $\ddot{\theta} = -\dfrac{g}{l}\theta$.

(b) The period of small oscillations is 2 seconds. Find the value of l, giving your answer correct to 3 significant figures.

(c) (i) Find the period when the mass of the particle is doubled, but the length of the string is unchanged.

    (ii) Find the period when the length of the string is doubled, but the mass of the particle is unchanged. (OCR)

17 A simple pendulum consists of a light inextensible string of length 1.5 m with a small bob of mass 0.2 kg at one end. When suspended from a fixed point and hanging at rest under gravity the bob is given a horizontal speed of $u\,\mathrm{m\,s^{-1}}$ and it comes instantaneously to rest when the string makes an angle of 0.1 rad with the vertical. At time t seconds after projection the string makes an angle θ with the vertical. Show that, neglecting air resistance, $\left(\dfrac{\mathrm{d}\theta}{\mathrm{d}t}\right)^2 = 13.1(\cos\theta - \cos 0.1)$, where the numerical coefficient is given to 3 significant figures. Find, correct to 2 significant figures, the value of u and the tension in the string when $\theta = 0.05$ rad.

By differentiating the above equation for $\left(\dfrac{\mathrm{d}\theta}{\mathrm{d}t}\right)^2$, show that the motion of the bob can be modelled approximately by simple harmonic motion, and hence find the value of t at which the bob first comes instantaneously to rest. (OCR)

18 A particle P of mass m is attached to a fixed point O by a light inextensible string of length a. P is released from rest with $OP = a$ and the line OP inclined at an angle of $30°$ above the horizontal. P falls vertically under gravity in the absence of any resisting forces until the string becomes taut. Show that the speed of P immediately before the string becomes taut is $\sqrt{2ga}$.

Immediately the string becomes taut, the particle moves in a vertical circle with centre O and radius a.

(a) By using conservation of linear momentum, perpendicular to the string, show that the speed of the particle immediately after the string becomes taut is $\sqrt{\frac{3}{2}ga}$.

(b) Calculate the magnitude of the impulse acting on P at the instant when the string becomes taut.

Find, in terms of g, the magnitude of the transverse component of the acceleration of P immediately after the string becomes taut.

Find, in terms of m and g, the tension in the string when P is vertically below O.   (OCR)

19* The diagram shows the side view of a design for a deck chair. $ABB'A'$ and $CDD'C'$ are rectangular metal frames, hinged together at H and H'. (A, B, C, D, H are on the left side of the person sitting in the chair, A', B', C', D', H' are on the right.) The chair is kept rigid by struts FG and $F'G'$ on the two sides of the chair. The canvas seat is looped round the horizontal parts BB' and CC' of the two frames. When the seat is occupied, the forces from the canvas have horizontal and vertical components 200 newtons and 400 newtons on BB',

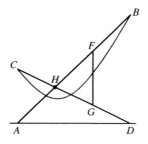

and 200 newtons and 300 newtons on CC'. AB is at $45°$ to the horizontal, $AH = HF = FB$ and $CH = HG = GD$, and CC' and BB' are vertically above AA' and DD' respectively. Assume that the weight of the chair can be neglected in comparison with the weight of the occupant, and that there is no frictional force at A or D. Calculate

(a) the normal contact forces at A, A', D and D',

(b) the thrust in each of the struts FG and $F'G'$.

20* A smooth metal sphere, of mass 3 kg and radius 5 cm, rests on a smooth horizontal floor. A wooden sphere, of mass 1 kg and also of radius 5 cm, descends along a vertical line 6 cm from the centre of the metal sphere. The wooden sphere is moving at $2\,\mathrm{m\,s^{-1}}$ when it strikes the metal sphere. After the impact the wooden sphere rebounds horizontally. Calculate

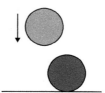

(a) the speed at which the wooden sphere rebounds,

(b) the impulse between the spheres,

(c) the speed at which the metal sphere starts to move,

(d) the impulse from the floor on the metal sphere,

(e) the coefficient of restitution between the two spheres.

21 A smooth sphere is sliding along a horizontal plane surface with speed u when it strikes a small plate fixed at 30° to the horizontal, as shown in the diagram. If the coefficient of restitution between the sphere and the plate is e, find the horizontal and vertical components of the velocity of the sphere immediately after the impact. Show that the horizontal distance that the sphere travels before hitting the surface again is between $\frac{3}{8}\sqrt{3}\,\dfrac{u^2}{g}$ and $\frac{1}{2}\sqrt{3}\,\dfrac{u^2}{g}$.

22* An engineer is analysing the running of a machine round a circular, horizontal track. The motor in the machine runs at constant power P, and the engineer reckons that the main resistance to motion comes from the friction force between wheels and rails due to the acceleration of the machine towards the centre of the circle.

(a) Explain why the engineer might take the equation of motion of the machine to be
$m\dfrac{\mathrm{d}v}{\mathrm{d}t} = \dfrac{P}{v} - \dfrac{\mu m v^2}{R}$, where R is the radius of the track and μ is the coefficient of friction.

(b) State the terminal speed of the machine for this equation of motion.

(c) The machine starts from rest. Determine how its speed v increases with distance s round the track.

(d) At a later instant the speed of the machine is V and the motor is switched off (and remains off). Find an expression for its speed at time t after that instant.

Criticise any one aspect of the engineer's modelling of the situation; suggest an improved model for the aspect you have criticised.   (OCR)

23* The figure shows a smooth circular wire, whose centre is O and whose radius is a, which is fixed in a vertical plane. A small bead B of mass m is threaded on the wire. A small smooth ring is attached to the wire at its top point A. A light elastic string has one end fixed at the point K, at a distance ka vertically above A; the natural length of the string is ka and its modulus of elasticity is cmg.

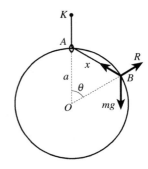

The other end of the string is fixed to the bead B, and the string passes through the ring at A. The length AB is denoted by x, and the angle AOB by θ. Calculate x in terms of a and θ, and show that the elastic energy of the string is given by $\dfrac{cmga(1 - \cos\theta)}{k}$.

Initially the value of θ is very small and positive, and the bead is released from rest. Show that θ begins to increase provided that $c < k$.

Use conservation of energy (explaining why it is applicable in this case) to show that the speed v of the bead is $v = \sin\frac{1}{2}\theta\sqrt{4ga\left(1 - \dfrac{c}{k}\right)}$.

Find the normal reaction R of the wire on the bead, in terms of m, g, k, c and θ.

(OCR, adapted)

24 This question models the action of a tumble drier in which clothes are carried without slipping up the wall of the drum before falling back through the interior of the drum. The cylindrical drum of the drier has internal radius 0.4 metres and is rotated about a fixed horizontal axis through O at a steady angular speed of $3.5 \, \text{rad} \, \text{s}^{-1}$. A wet sock, moving with the drum, is about to leave the surface of the drum at the position P shown in the first figure. The angle between OP and the upward vertical is θ. The wet sock is modelled as a particle of mass 0.1 kg. After it leaves the drum at P it falls freely under gravity (see the second figure).

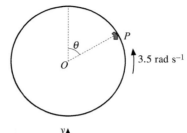

(a) By using Newton's equation in the radial direction OP, show that $\theta = 60°$.

(b) Using the axes indicated in the second figure, give the coordinates of the point P at which the sock leaves the drum. Show that the initial components of the velocity of the sock as it leaves the drum are given by the vector $\begin{pmatrix} -0.7 \\ 0.7\sqrt{3} \end{pmatrix} \, \text{m} \, \text{s}^{-1}$.

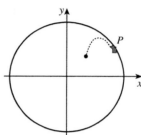

(c) Find the velocity and position vectors of the sock t seconds after leaving the drum while it is still in the air.

(d) Verify that at time $t = \frac{2}{7}\sqrt{3}$ the sock will hit the drum again, and find the position of the point of impact.

(e) If the sock sticks to the drum on impact, find in magnitude and direction the impulse exerted by the drum on the sock.

(OCR, adapted)

Practice examination 1 for M3

Time 1 hour 30 minutes

Answer all the questions.

Graphic calculators are permitted.

1 The rise and fall of the water level in a tidal stretch of a river can be modelled, on a particular day, as simple harmonic motion with period 12 hours and amplitude 1.5 m. The water is at its lowest level at 9 a.m.

   (i) Find by how much the water level has risen by 1 p.m. [4]

   (ii) Find how fast the level is rising at 1 p.m. [3]

2 Two identical snooker balls, A and B, are free to move on a horizontal table. Initially, B is at rest and A is moving with speed V. The balls collide; immediately before the collision the velocity of A makes an angle α with the line of centres, and immediately after the collision the velocity of A makes an angle β with the line of centres (see diagram).

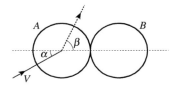

The coefficient of restitution is e, and the balls are modelled as being smooth. Show that $\tan \beta = \dfrac{2 \tan \alpha}{1 - e}$. [7]

3 A particle P of mass 0.5 kg is attached by light elastic strings to points A and B which are at the same horizontal level and a distance 1.2 m apart. Each string has natural length 0.6 m and modulus of elasticity 30 N. The particle is projected vertically downwards with speed v m s^{-1} from the mid-point of AB (see diagram).

$$A \bullet \quad \underset{0.6 \text{ m}}{\rule{2cm}{0.4pt}} \quad \overset{P}{\bullet} \quad \underset{0.6 \text{ m}}{\rule{2cm}{0.4pt}} \quad \bullet B$$
$$\downarrow v \text{ m s}^{-1}$$

Subsequently P comes to instantaneous rest at the point C which is at a distance of 0.8 m below the level of AB.

   (i) Find the value of v. [6]

   (ii) Find also the upward acceleration of P when it is at C. [3]

4 When a gun is fired, the shell is propelled along the barrel by the pressure of the gas generated by the explosive charge. When the shell is at a distance x m from the closed end of the barrel, the speed is v m s^{-1} (see diagram).

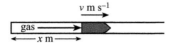

In a simple model of the motion, the force exerted by the gas on the shell is taken to be proportional to $x^{-\frac{3}{2}}$, and all resistances to the motion of the shell are neglected. The barrel is assumed to be horizontal.

(i) Write down a differential equation relating v and x, and hence show that
$v^2 = A - \dfrac{B}{\sqrt{x}}$, where A and B are constants.   [4]

(ii) The shell starts from rest at a distance of 0.1 m from the closed end of the barrel. The shell emerges from the barrel, which is 2 m long, at a speed of 300 m s^{-1}. Find the initial acceleration of the shell.   [6]

5 The diagram shows a vertical cross-section through the centre O of a fixed smooth hollow sphere of radius r. The points A and B are such that OAB is an equilateral triangle, with AB vertical.

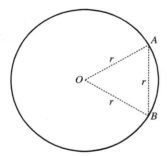

A particle of mass m is held on the inner surface of the sphere at A, and released from rest.

(i) Write down the speed of the particle just before it hits the sphere at B.   [1]

(ii) When the particle hits the sphere at B, an impulse directed along the radius acts. The particle does not rebound, but immediately begins to move along the surface of the sphere with speed u. Find the magnitude of the impulse, and show that $u = \sqrt{\frac{3}{2}gr}$.   [4]

(iii) Show that the particle subsequently loses contact with the surface of the sphere at an instant when its speed is $\sqrt{\frac{1}{6}gr}$.   [7]

6 A particle P of mass 0.5 kg rests on a smooth horizontal table. A light inextensible string, passing over a smooth pulley at the edge of the table, connects P to a particle Q, also of mass 0.5 kg, which hangs freely. P is attached to a fixed point A of the table by a light elastic spring; A, P, Q and the pulley are in the same vertical plane (see diagram).

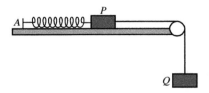

The spring has natural length 0.2 m and modulus of elasticity 49 N.

(i) Find the extension of the spring when P and Q are in equilibrium.   [2]

(ii) The system is displaced from the equilibrium position, and is released from rest. At time t s the displacement of P from its equilibrium position is x m. Assuming that the string connecting the particles remains taut, write down equations of motion for P and for Q, and hence show that the particles move in simple harmonic motion with period just over 0.4 s.   [7]

(iii) Find the largest amplitude of the motion in part (ii) for which the assumption about the string remaining taut is valid.   [4]

7 Two identical uniform cylinders rest in equilibrium, in contact with each other and with their axes parallel. The lower cylinder is in contact with horizontal ground and the upper cylinder is in contact with a vertical wall. The diagram shows a vertical cross-section through the centres of mass A and B of the cylinders; AB makes an angle of 45° with the horizontal. Each cylinder weighs 100 N.

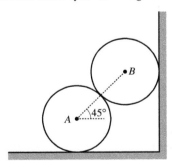

(i) By considering the forces on the lower cylinder, show that this cylinder cannot be smooth.   [2]

(ii) The friction force acting on the lower cylinder at its contact with the ground has magnitude F N. Show that there must be a friction force, also of magnitude F N, acting on the upper cylinder at its contact with the wall.   [4]

(iii) By resolving horizontally for the lower cylinder and vertically for the upper cylinder, or otherwise, find F.   [4]

(iv) Determine the least possible value for the coefficient of friction between the lower cylinder and the ground.   [4]

Time 1 hour 30 minutes

Answer all the questions.

Graphic calculators are permitted.

1 *A* and *B* are fixed points, with *A* a distance of 3 m vertically above *B*. A particle *P* of weight 10 N is attached to *A* and *B* by means of two light elastic strings, each of natural length 1 m and modulus of elasticity 20 N (see diagram).

    (i) *P* hangs in equilibrium between *A* and *B*, with both strings taut. Show that the distance *AP* is 1.75 m.   [3]

    (ii) *P* is released from rest at *B*. Find the speed of *P* when it is at a height of 2 m above *B*.   [4]

2 Uniform beams *AB*, of length 5*a* and weight *W*, and *BC*, of length 4*a* and weight 8*W*, are freely jointed to a fixed vertical wall at *A* and *C*, and to each other at *B*. The distance *AC* is 3*a*. The beams are in equilibrium with *CB* horizontal (see diagram).

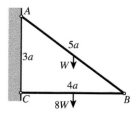

    (i) By considering the equilibrium of the beam *CB*, find the vertical component of the force acting on the beam at *C*.   [2]

    (ii) Find the horizontal and vertical components of the force acting on the beam *AB* at *A*.   [6]

3 A particle moves in a straight line in simple harmonic motion with centre O. The speed of the particle when it is at a distance of 1 m from O is $4\,\mathrm{m\,s^{-1}}$, and its speed when it is at a distance of 2 m from O is $2\,\mathrm{m\,s^{-1}}$.

  (i) Find the period and amplitude of the motion. [6]

  (ii) Find also the greatest acceleration of the particle. [2]

4 A smooth ball of mass m bounces on horizontal ground. Immediately before impact the ball has speed u in a direction making an angle θ with the vertical. Immediately after impact the direction of motion makes an angle θ with the horizontal (see diagram). The coefficient of restitution is $\frac{1}{3}$.

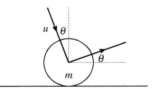

Find

  (i) the value of θ, [4]

  (ii) the magnitude of the impulse acting on the ball at the impact, [2]

  (iii) the proportion of the ball's kinetic energy that is lost in the impact. [4]

5 A simple pendulum consists of a particle attached to one end of a light inextensible string of length l, the other end of which is attached to a fixed point.

  (i) Prove that small oscillations of the pendulum are approximately simple harmonic with period $2\pi\sqrt{\dfrac{l}{g}}$. [5]

The greatest angle that the pendulum makes with the vertical in its motion is α radians. Using the simple harmonic approximation,

  (ii) find the time taken for the pendulum to swing from an angle $\frac{1}{2}\alpha$ on one side of the vertical to $\frac{1}{2}\alpha$ on the other side, [4]

  (iii) show that the greatest speed of the particle during its motion is $\alpha\sqrt{gl}$. [3]

6 A car of mass 750 kg travels along a straight horizontal road. Its engine has constant power 20 kW and the resistance to motion has magnitude kv, where k is a constant and $v\,\mathrm{m\,s^{-1}}$ is the speed of the car at time $t\,\mathrm{s}$.

  (i) The greatest steady speed that the car can maintain is $80\,\mathrm{m\,s^{-1}}$. Find the value of k. [2]

  (ii) Show that the equation of motion can be expressed in the form
$$\frac{2v}{6400 - v^2}\frac{\mathrm{d}v}{\mathrm{d}t} = \frac{1}{120}.$$ [3]

  (iii) Given that the car starts from rest at time $t = 0$, find v in terms of t. [5]

  (iv) Find the acceleration of the car when it has been moving for 1 minute. [3]

7 Particles P, of mass m, and Q, of mass $2m$, are joined by a light inextensible string of length πa. Initially P and Q are at opposite ends of the horizontal diameter of a fixed smooth sphere with centre O and radius a, with the string on the upper surface of the sphere (see the first diagram). The particles are released from rest. At time t, particle P is still in contact with the sphere, with OP making an angle θ with the horizontal, and Q has fallen a distance $a\theta$ (see the second diagram).

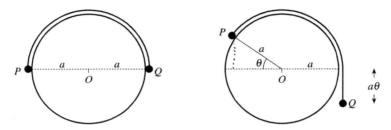

(i) By considering the transverse motion of P, show that the tension T in the string is given by $T = m(g\cos\theta + a\ddot{\theta})$. [2]

(ii) Write down the equation of motion for Q, and hence express $\ddot{\theta}$ in terms of a, g and θ. [4]

(iii) By considering energy, or otherwise, show that $a\dot{\theta}^2 = \frac{2}{3}g(2\theta - \sin\theta)$. [3]

(iv) Find an expression, in terms of m, g and θ, for the magnitude of the reaction between P and the sphere, and verify that P loses contact with the surface when θ is between 1.13 and 1.14 radians. [5]

Module M4

Mechanics 4

1 Relative motion

Whenever you have described the velocity of an object modelled as a particle, it has always been relative to some frame of reference regarded as fixed. This chapter deals with situations in which velocity is described relative to some frame which is itself moving. When you have completed it, you should

- understand the idea of relative displacement and relative velocity
- know how to combine relative velocities as vectors
- be able to use relative velocities to solve problems on relative displacement
- appreciate the effect of using mechanical systems in an accelerating frame.

1.1 Combining velocities

Imagine a canoeist out on a river. Fig. 1.1 shows three stages of her trip. In Stage 1 she is canoeing in still water close to the bank, at a speed of $3 \, \text{m s}^{-1}$. Then at Stage 2 she moves out into mid-stream, where she is helped by a current flowing at $2 \, \text{m s}^{-1}$. If she stopped paddling, the water would carry her 2 metres downstream in each second. But if she continues to paddle as she did at Stage 1, she will also move 3 metres downstream by her own efforts. So a person standing on the bank would see that she actually moves 5 metres downstream in each second.

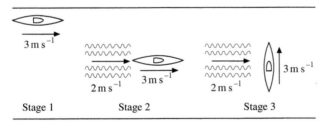

Stage 1   Stage 2   Stage 3

Fig. 1.1

This is described by saying that her velocity 'relative to the water' is $3 \, \text{m s}^{-1}$, but her velocity 'relative to the bank' is $5 \, \text{m s}^{-1}$. You get the velocity relative to the bank by adding the velocity of the water to her velocity relative to the water.

In Stage 3 she turns the canoe through a right angle so as to return to the bank. If she continues to paddle as before, she moves 3 metres closer to the bank in each second. But in that second the stream will carry her 2 metres downstream. This is illustrated in Fig. 1.2, which shows that her total displacement is at an angle to the direction in which she is facing. This displacement has magnitude $\sqrt{3^2 + 2^2}$ metres, which is about 3.6 metres, and it is at an angle $\tan^{-1} \frac{2}{3}$, about 34°, to the direction in which she is facing.

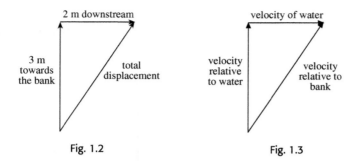

Fig. 1.2   Fig. 1.3

So her velocity relative to the bank is still the sum of her velocity relative to the water and the velocity of the water. But now the word 'sum' must be understood as the vector sum of the two velocities, illustrated by the vector triangle in Fig. 1.3.

Example 1.1.1

When a cyclist is travelling at $6\,\text{m s}^{-1}$ the pedals go round once in 2 seconds. If the pedal levers are 20 cm long, how fast and in what direction is her front foot moving when the pedals are horizontal?

If the bike were not moving (for example, if she was on an exercise bike) her foot would be moving vertically downwards. The pedals rotate through 2π radians in 2 seconds, so the angular speed of her foot would be $\dfrac{2\pi}{2}$ rad s^{-1}. The pedal levers are 0.2 metres long, so the speed would be $0.2\pi\ \text{m s}^{-1}$, which is about $0.628\,\text{m s}^{-1}$. This is given by the equation $v = r\omega$, as the velocity of her foot 'relative to the bike'.

But, since the bike is moving, the velocity of her foot relative to the bike has to be combined with the velocity of the bike itself. Because velocity is a vector quantity, the actual velocity of the cyclist's foot can be found from the vector triangle in Fig. 1.4.

Fig. 1.4

You can calculate that her foot is moving at $6.03\,\text{m s}^{-1}$ at an angle of $6.0°$ below the horizontal.

This is how her foot would seem to be moving as observed by a bystander on the pavement as she passes him. It is the velocity 'relative to the road'.

Figure 1.4 illustrates that the velocity of the cyclist's foot relative to the road is the vector sum of the velocity of her foot relative to the bike and the velocity of the bike relative to the road.

Example 1.1.2

A car is moving along a straight road at $15\,\mathrm{m\,s^{-1}}$. A child sitting in the back seat throws his teddy bear out of the side window with a velocity of $3\,\mathrm{m\,s^{-1}}$ horizontally at right angles to the velocity of the car. The teddy is in the air for 0.4 seconds. Describe how the motion of the ball will look.

(a) to the child,   (b) to a girl standing on the pavement.

(a) The teddy appears to the child to be moving sideways. By the time it hits the ground it has moved 1.2 metres, and the child will see it land by looking sideways out of the window.

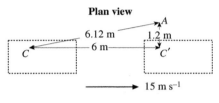

Fig. 1.5

(b) The girl can see that in the 0.4 seconds the car has moved forwards 6 metres. In the notation of Fig. 1.5, which shows the incident viewed from above, the teddy in fact lands at A. If C denotes the child at the instant when the teddy is thrown, and C' denotes the child when the teddy lands, then $C'A = 1.2$ metres, so by Pythagoras' theorem $CA = 6.12$ metres.

This means that, viewed from the pavement, the teddy goes 6.12 metres in 0.4 seconds, at a horizontal speed of $\dfrac{6.12}{0.4}\,\mathrm{m\,s^{-1}}$, which is $15.3\,\mathrm{m\,s^{-1}}$. The direction of this velocity is at an angle of $\tan^{-1}\dfrac{1.2}{6}$ which is $11.3°$, to the direction of motion of the car.

This velocity is represented by the hypotenuse of the vector triangle in Fig. 1.6. The sides of this triangle are the initial velocity of the teddy relative to the car, the velocity of the car relative to the road, and the initial velocity of the teddy relative to the road.

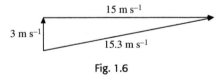

Fig. 1.6

An additional feature in Example 1.1.2 is that, as well as moving horizontally, the teddy is also falling. The child will see it moving as a projectile with an initial horizontal velocity of $3\,\mathrm{m\,s^{-1}}$. The girl will also see it moving as a projectile, but following a much flatter trajectory with an initial horizontal velocity of $15.3\,\mathrm{m\,s^{-1}}$.

Example 1.1.3

A microlight aircraft is capable of flying at a speed of $40\,\text{km h}^{-1}$ in still air. The pilot wants to fly on a northerly course. There is a wind blowing at $30\,\text{km h}^{-1}$ from a direction of $120°$.

(a) If the aircraft points due north, how far off course will it be blown by the wind?

(b) In what direction should the aircraft be pointed so that it travels due north? At what speed will it then be moving over the ground?

(a) Fig. 1.7 is a vector triangle in which the two known velocities are combined: the velocity of the aircraft relative to the air, which is $40\,\text{km h}^{-1}$ due north; and the velocity of the air relative to the ground, which is the wind velocity of $30\,\text{km h}^{-1}$ on a bearing of $300°$. The resultant velocity is the velocity of the aircraft relative to the ground, which determines the aircraft's actual course.

This resultant velocity can be calculated using components. Taking axes east and north, the resultant $\begin{pmatrix} u \\ v \end{pmatrix}$ km h^{-1} is given by the equation

$$\begin{pmatrix} u \\ v \end{pmatrix} = \begin{pmatrix} 0 \\ 40 \end{pmatrix} + \begin{pmatrix} -30\sin 60° \\ 30\cos 60° \end{pmatrix} = \begin{pmatrix} -25.98... \\ 55 \end{pmatrix}.$$

The aircraft is therefore blown off course by an amount $\tan^{-1}\dfrac{25.98...}{55}$ to the west, which is $25.3°$ to the nearest $0.1°$.

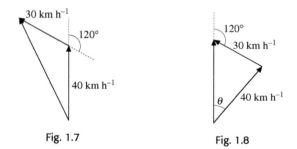

Fig. 1.7   Fig. 1.8

(b) To achieve a northerly course, the pilot must head at some angle, θ, east of north, so that in the velocity vector triangle (Fig. 1.8) the side representing the resultant velocity points due north. The value of θ is easily found from the sine rule, $\dfrac{30}{\sin\theta} = \dfrac{40}{\sin 60°}$, which gives $\theta = 40.50...°$.

The vector triangle shows that the magnitude of the resultant velocity over the ground is $(40\cos\theta + 30\cos 60°)\,\text{km h}^{-1}$, which is $45.4\,\text{km h}^{-1}$ correct to 3 significant figures.

The aircraft should therefore be pointed on a bearing of $040.5°$. It will then travel due north over the ground with a speed of $45.4\,\text{km h}^{-1}$.

1.2   Definitions and notation

The examples in the last section make the point that every velocity is measured relative to some 'frame of reference'; that is, an origin and a set of axes which can be used to establish the coordinates of points and the components of vectors. Often this frame of reference is simply 'the earth', or more precisely that little bit of the earth's surface currently under observation, and there is a tendency to think of this as 'fixed'. But of course, to an observer on a distant star or another planet, the earth would not look at all fixed.

On the other hand, you may be on some vehicle which is certainly not fixed, but on which mechanical laws appear to be just the same as on 'terra firma'. If you swim in the pool on a cruise ship, or pour a cup of coffee on an aircraft travelling at a constant velocity, you don't experience anything different from the same activity on the ground. You could describe what is happening by choosing an origin and coordinate system fixed in the ship or the aircraft rather than the sea or the ground.

The velocity of an object, or a frame of reference, A relative to a frame of reference B is denoted by the symbol $_A\mathbf{v}_B$. For example, Example 1.1.3 deals with the velocity of the microlight (m) relative to two frames of reference, the ground (g) and the air (a), which could be denoted by $_m\mathbf{v}_g$ and $_m\mathbf{v}_a$ respectively. But the air is moving relative to the ground with the wind velocity $_a\mathbf{v}_g$. The vector triangles in Fig. 1.7 and Fig. 1.8 correspond to the vector equation $_m\mathbf{v}_a + {_a\mathbf{v}_g} = {_m\mathbf{v}_g}$.

This is a special case of a general rule.

> If P, Q, R are objects or frames of reference which are moving relative to each other, then $_P\mathbf{v}_Q + {_Q\mathbf{v}_R} = {_P\mathbf{v}_R}$.

> It should be mentioned for completeness that, if Q and R stand for frames of reference, then this law assumes that the motion of Q relative to R doesn't involve rotation. If the microlight in Example 1.1.3 were caught in a tornado, and the frame of reference for the air rotated with the tornado, then the equation would have to include the angular velocity of the tornado. Rotating frames are specially important when you need to consider the effect of the spin of the earth about its axis. Rotating frames of reference are too complicated to be considered at this stage.

Example 1.2.1
As a jogger runs up a straight road at $4\,\mathrm{m\,s^{-1}}$ on a bearing of $050°$, the wind appears to be coming from the north. When he turns round and runs in the opposite direction at the same speed, the wind appears to be from the west. In fact the wind hasn't changed. What is the actual speed and direction of the wind?

> There are three velocities involved in this situation: the velocity of the jogger (j) relative to the ground (g); the velocity of the air (a) relative to the jogger; and the actual wind velocity, which is the velocity of the air relative to the ground. Denote

these by $_j\mathbf{v}_g$, $_a\mathbf{v}_j$ and $_a\mathbf{v}_g$ respectively. Then look for the symbol which occurs once before and once after the $\mathbf{v}$, which is j. The equation linking the three velocities is therefore

$$_a\mathbf{v}_j + {_j}\mathbf{v}_g = {_a}\mathbf{v}_g.$$

Now you know $_j\mathbf{v}_g$ in both magnitude and direction. You also know the direction of $_a\mathbf{v}_j$, which is from the north when he runs one way and from the west after he turns round. So you can tentatively draw vector triangles for the two runs. These are shown in Fig. 1.9.

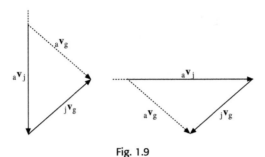

Fig. 1.9

In both triangles the arrow representing $_a\mathbf{v}_j$ is shown with broken ends because you don't know how far it extends. And the arrow representing $_a\mathbf{v}_g$ is shown dotted, because you don't know either its magnitude or direction.

But what you do know is that the wind doesn't change when the jogger turns round. So the dotted arrows in both triangles must be the same. This means that, if you superimpose one triangle on the other, the two triangles will have this arrow in common. This is done in Fig. 1.10.

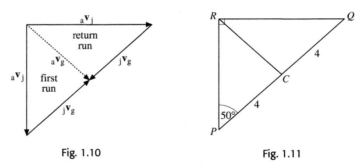

Fig. 1.10   Fig. 1.11

The solution is completed by a simple piece of geometry. Fig. 1.11 is the same as Fig. 1.10 but lettered as an ordinary geometric figure with the known lengths (i.e. speeds) and angles marked. Since angle PRQ is a right angle, R lies on the circle with diameter PQ. Also C is the mid-point of PQ, so it is the centre of this circle. So triangles CPR and CQR are isosceles, angle $PRC = 50°$ and $CR = RP = 4$.

Now go back to Fig. 1.10 to interpret these results. The vector $_a\mathbf{v}_g$ points on a bearing of $180° -$ angle PRC, which is $130°$, and its magnitude is $4\,\text{m s}^{-1}$.

The wind velocity is $4\,\text{m s}^{-1}$ on a bearing of $130°$.

Exercise 1A

1 A passenger steps off a bus when it is moving at $3\,\mathrm{m\,s^{-1}}$, with a speed of $1\,\mathrm{m\,s^{-1}}$ relative to the bus at right angles to its direction of motion. What is the passenger's velocity relative to the ground?

2 A parachute jumper launches herself from an aircraft at a speed of $4\,\mathrm{m\,s^{-1}}$ at right angles to the direction of motion of the aircraft. If the aircraft is travelling horizontally at $30\,\mathrm{m\,s^{-1}}$, what is her velocity as observed by someone standing on the ground?

3 A bag of rubbish is thrown off a ferry travelling at $12\,\mathrm{m\,s^{-1}}$, with a horizontal velocity of $6\,\mathrm{m\,s^{-1}}$ at $50°$ to the direction of motion of the ship. If it lands in the sea 3 seconds later, what horizontal distance does it appear to travel before hitting the sea

(a) as observed by a passenger on the ferry,

(b) as observed by a person standing on the harbour wall?

4 A seagull takes off due astern from the deck of a liner travelling at $15\,\mathrm{m\,s^{-1}}$. Relative to the liner, its velocity is $5\,\mathrm{m\,s^{-1}}$ at $20°$ to the horizontal. What is its velocity relative to the sea?

5 An athlete can throw a discus from a standing position at a speed of $20\,\mathrm{m\,s^{-1}}$ at an angle of $30°$ to the horizontal. How much further will the discus travel if, at the instant when the discus is released, the athlete is rotating at a rate of half a revolution per second, the discus is 80 cm from the axis of rotation, and the athlete exerts the same force as in the standing position?

6 A motor cruiser capable of a speed of $8\,\mathrm{m\,s^{-1}}$ in still water sets course on a bearing of $040°$. There is a tide running at $4\,\mathrm{m\,s^{-1}}$ from due west. In what direction, and at what speed, does the boat actually travel?

7 The parallel banks of a river are 60 metres apart, and there is a current running at $0.6\,\mathrm{m\,s^{-1}}$. A woman capable of swimming at $1\,\mathrm{m\,s^{-1}}$ in still water wants to cross from one bank to the other.

(a) If she swims at right angles to the current, how far will she be carried downstream, and how long will she be in the water?

(b) If she wants to cross between points on the two banks directly opposite each other, at what direction to the current must she swim, and how long will she be in the water?

8 A light aircraft, flying at $200\,\mathrm{km\,h^{-1}}$ relative to the air, flies from Aberdeen to Birmingham, a distance of 520 km due south. There is a wind of $80\,\mathrm{km\,h^{-1}}$ blowing from a direction of $125°$ throughout the flight. Find, either by accurate drawing or by calculation,

(a) what course the pilot must set relative to the air,

(b) how long the flight will take.

9 An aircraft flies at a speed of $120\,\mathrm{km\,h^{-1}}$ in still air. When it is set on a course due north it is blown $10°$ to the east by the wind. When it is set on a course due west it is blown $10°$ to the north. Find the speed and the direction of the wind.

10 A cyclist is travelling due east at a speed of $30\,\mathrm{km\,h^{-1}}$. The wind is blowing from $160°$, but to the cyclist it appears to be blowing from $110°$. What is the speed of the wind?

1.3 Relative displacement

Suppose that two aircraft are travelling in cloud at the same height. Air traffic control will know at any time the ground coordinates and the velocity of each aircraft. But the pilots, concerned to avoid a near miss or worse, don't need to know these details. What each pilot needs to know is the position and velocity of the other aircraft relative to his own. The examples in this section show how you can investigate problems which involve two moving objects.

Example 1.3.1
An aircraft A is flying at $500 \, \text{km h}^{-1}$ on a bearing of 070°, and an aircraft B is flying at $450 \, \text{km h}^{-1}$ on a bearing of 010° at the same height. At a particular instant the aircraft are 20 km apart, and the bearing of A from B is 315°. If both aircraft continue to fly on the same course at the same speed, how close will they come to each other, and when will this occur?

You can choose to look at the situation from the point of view of the pilot of either aircraft. If you choose aircraft B, then you want to find the velocity of A relative to B, which is denoted by $_A\mathbf{v}_B$. You know the velocities of each aircraft relative to the ground, so the relevant equation is

$$_A\mathbf{v}_{\text{ground}} = {_A}\mathbf{v}_B + {_B}\mathbf{v}_{\text{ground}}.$$

The calculations can be done using either a vector triangle or components.

Vector triangle method   Fig. 1.12 is a vector triangle XYZ corresponding to the relative velocity equation, with sides proportional to the speeds in km h^{-1}. It is given that $XZ = 500$, $YZ = 450$ and from the known bearings the angle XZY is $70° - 10° = 60°$. You can then use the cosine rule to find that $XY = 476.96...$, which is the speed of A relative to B in km h^{-1}. Then, from the sine rule, angle ZXY is $54.79...°$. Since $\overrightarrow{XZ}$ representing $_A\mathbf{v}_{\text{ground}}$ has a bearing of 070°, $_A\mathbf{v}_B$ has a bearing of $70° + 54.79...°$, which is $124.79...°$.

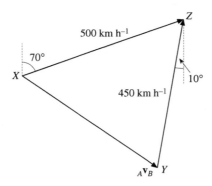

Fig. 1.12

Component method   The relative velocity equation can be arranged as

$$_A\mathbf{V}_B = {}_A\mathbf{V}_{\text{ground}} - {}_B\mathbf{V}_{\text{ground}}.$$

Taking axes in the directions east and north, this gives

$$_A\mathbf{V}_B = \begin{pmatrix} 500\sin 70° \\ 500\cos 70° \end{pmatrix} - \begin{pmatrix} 450\sin 10° \\ 450\cos 10° \end{pmatrix} = \begin{pmatrix} 391.70... \\ -272.15... \end{pmatrix}.$$

Converting this from cartesian to polar form, this is a velocity of $476.96...\,\text{km}\,\text{h}^{-1}$ on a bearing of $124.79...°$.

Whichever method you use, these results can now be transferred to Fig. 1.13, which shows the motion of aircraft A relative to aircraft B. Initially A is 20 km from B on a bearing of 315°, and the arrow shows the velocity of A relative to B. This arrow defines the course of A as observed by the pilot of B, and the point C on this course such that BCA is a right angle shows the situation when the distance between the two aircraft is smallest.

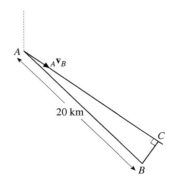

Fig. 1.13

The bearing of $\overrightarrow{AB}$ is 135°, and the calculation above shows that the bearing of $\overrightarrow{AC}$ is $124.79...°$, so angle BAC is $(135° - 124.79...°)$, which is $10.20...°$. Therefore the distance BC is $20\sin 10.20...°$ km, which is 3.54 km correct to 3 significant figures.

You can also calculate that AC is $20\cos 10.20...°$ km, which is $19.68...$ km. This is the distance that A travels relative to B until the time when the aircraft are closest together, and this distance is covered at a relative speed of $476.96...\,\text{km}\,\text{h}^{-1}$. The time taken is therefore $\dfrac{19.68...}{476.96...}$ hours, which is 2.48 minutes correct to 3 significant figures.

So the closest distance between the aircraft is 3.54 km; this occurs after 2.48 minutes.

Example 1.3.2

A car is speeding due south down a motorway at $80\,\text{m}\,\text{s}^{-1}$. It is observed passing due east of a police base, and a helicopter immediately sets off to intercept it. The helicopter can fly at $100\,\text{m}\,\text{s}^{-1}$. On what bearing should it fly?

For the helicopter (h) to intercept the car (c), the velocity of the helicopter relative to the car should be in a direction due east. But since the car is speeding south, the helicopter must head in a more southerly direction if it is to achieve the interception. Both the given velocities are relative to the ground (g).

There are three velocities involved:

$_h\mathbf{v}_c$ due east

$_c\mathbf{v}_g$ $80\,\mathrm{m\,s^{-1}}$,   due south

$_h\mathbf{v}_g$ $100\,\mathrm{m\,s^{-1}}$,   direction unknown.

These are related by the equation

$$_h\mathbf{v}_c + {_c\mathbf{v}_g} = {_h\mathbf{v}_g}.$$

A triangle has to be drawn to fit the data. See Fig. 1.14.

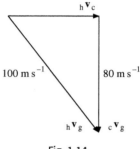

Begin by drawing the side representing the completely known velocity, $_c\mathbf{v}_g$. The velocity $_h\mathbf{v}_c$ which has to be added to this is due east but of unknown amount. The triangle is therefore right-angled.

The third side, representing $_h\mathbf{v}_g$, is the hypotenuse of this triangle, of magnitude $100\ \mathrm{m\,s^{-1}}$. This completes the triangle, and you can now use this to answer the question about the course of the helicopter.

Fig. 1.14

This course is at an angle $\sin^{-1}\frac{80}{100} = 53.1°$ south of east; that is, the helicopter should fly on a bearing of $090° + 53.1°$, which is $143.1°$.

Example 1.3.3

A fisheries protection vessel, P, observes a trawler, T, at a distance of 5 nautical miles due north. The trawler is steaming at a steady speed of 10 knots on a bearing of $130°$. The captain of P sets a course to try to intercept T.

(a) What is the least speed which will enable P to intercept T?

(b) What course should P set to intercept T, and how long will it take, if its speed is

    (i) 12 knots,   (ii) 8 knots?

(c) If the speed of P is 6 knots, how close can it get to T, and how long will it take to reach this position?

> Speeds at sea are traditionally measured in knots. A knot is a speed of 1 nautical mile per hour; a nautical mile is approximately 1.15 land miles.

Relative to P, the trawler T is initially due north. So to achieve an interception, the velocity of P relative to T must be due north. You therefore want to connect this velocity, $_P\mathbf{v}_T$, with the velocities of P and T relative to the sea, using the vector equation

$$_P\mathbf{v}_T + {_T\mathbf{v}_{sea}} = {_P\mathbf{v}_{sea}}.$$

Notice, however, that $_T\mathbf{v}_{sea}$ is known completely, but you only know the direction of $_P\mathbf{v}_T$. So it is slightly simpler to reverse the order of the terms on the left of the equation, and to base the solution on the equation

$$_T\mathbf{v}_{sea} + {_P\mathbf{v}_T} = {_P\mathbf{v}_{sea}}.$$

This is illustrated by the vector triangle XYZ in Fig. 1.15.

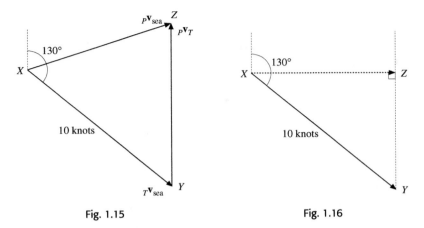

Fig. 1.15   Fig. 1.16

(a) You know the side XY completely, but only the direction of the side YZ. The question is, what is the smallest length for the side XZ, representing $_P\mathbf{v}_\text{sea}$, for it to be possible to complete the triangle. If you imagine trying to draw the triangle, as in Fig. 1.16, you can see that this is given by drawing XZ perpendicular to the northerly line through Y. Since angle XYZ is 50°, the least magnitude of $_P\mathbf{v}_\text{sea}$ for the construction to be possible is $10\sin 50°$ knots, which is 7.66 knots.

(b) Fig. 1.17 shows how you would construct the triangle if it is known that $_P\mathbf{v}_\text{sea}$ has magnitude (i) 12 knots or (ii) 8 knots. Notice the difference between the two cases: in case (i) there is only one position for Z, but in case (ii) there are two possibilities.

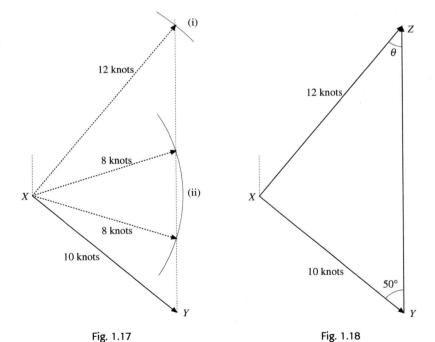

Fig. 1.17   Fig. 1.18

(i) If angle XZY is θ, as in Fig. 1.18, then by the sine rule $\dfrac{\sin\theta}{10}=\dfrac{\sin 50°}{12}$, which gives $\theta = 39.67...°$. So P should steer a course on a bearing of $039.7°$.

Also, by projection in a northerly direction, YZ represents a speed of $(10\cos 50° + 12\cos\theta)$ knots, which with $\theta = 39.67...°$ is $15.66...$ knots. This is the speed of P relative to T; and since initially T is 5 nautical miles north of P, the time taken for the interception is $\dfrac{5}{15.66...}$ hours, which is 19.2 minutes correct to 3 significant figures.

(ii) Fig. 1.17 shows that there are two possible courses on which P can steer to intercept T. Which is better? Presumably the quicker, so you want the larger of the two possible lengths for YZ, which represents the speed of P relative to T. This means choosing Z so that angle XZY is acute rather than obtuse.

The calculation then proceeds just as in case (i). Denoting angle XZY by θ, the sine rule gives $\theta = 73.24...°$ or $106.75...°$. Since the acute angle is wanted, P should steer a course on a bearing of $073.2°$.

Continuing the calculation as before gives $YZ = 8.73...$ knots. So the time taken for the interception is $\dfrac{5}{8.73...}$ hours, which is 34.3 minutes.

(c) You know from part (a) that interception is impossible at a speed of 6 knots. This means that the velocity of P relative to T can't be due north, so the motion relative to T will have the form of Fig. 1.19. This shows that, for P to come as close to T as possible, the angle between $_P\mathbf{v}_T$ and north should be as small as possible.

The size of this angle can be found from the velocity triangle, which now has the form of Fig. 1.20. The point Z has to lie on a circle with radius XZ representing 6 knots; so for $\overrightarrow{YZ}$ to be as near north as possible, YZ should be a tangent to this circle.

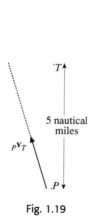

Fig. 1.19

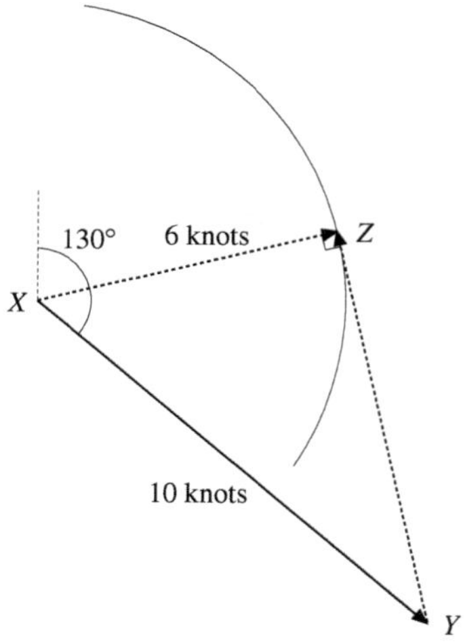

Fig. 1.20

This means that XZY is a right angle, so angle XYZ is $\sin^{-1} 0.6$, which is $36.86...°$. The angle that $_P\mathbf{v}_T$ is west of north is then $(50 - 36.86...)° = 13.13...°$.

Now go back to Fig. 1.19, from which it is easy to see that the closest approach is a distance of $5 \sin 13.13...°$ nautical miles, which is 1.14 nautical miles correct to 3 significant figures.

The velocity triangle in Fig. 1.20 also shows that $_P\mathbf{v}_T$, represented by $\overrightarrow{YZ}$ has magnitude 8 knots. Since the closest approach occurs when P has gone a distance relative to T of $5 \cos 13.13...°$ nautical miles, the time taken to reach this is $\dfrac{5 \cos 13.13...°}{8}$ hours, which is 36.5 minutes.

Notice how, in the examples in this section, the argument oscillates between the velocity vector triangle, in which the sides are proportional to the relative speeds, and the space triangle representing the motion of one of the moving vehicles relative to the other. Learning to switch between these two diagrams is the key to solving problems on interception and closest approach.

Exercise 1B

1 At a clay pigeon shoot, a clay is projected horizontally at a speed of $15\,\mathrm{m\,s^{-1}}$. A competitor fires a shot with a speed of $200\,\mathrm{m\,s^{-1}}$ when the line of sight is in a direction at $110°$ to the velocity of the clay. At what angle to the line of sight should she aim off to allow for the motion of the clay?

2 Two boats B and C are initially $48\,\mathrm{km}$ apart in still water, with C due west of B. The boat B is sailing due north with a constant speed. The boat C is sailing on a fixed bearing of $030°$ at a constant speed. Given that the boats meet after three hours, calculate

   (a) the magnitude of their relative velocity,

   (b) the speed of each boat.   (OCR)

3 Two tanks are manoeuvring in flat open country. Tank A is at the point $(5, 7)$ and moving with velocity $\begin{pmatrix} 15 \\ 5 \end{pmatrix}$, and tank B at $(6.5, 9)$ and moving with velocity $\begin{pmatrix} 7 \\ -10 \end{pmatrix}$, the units being kilometres and hours. Find, in magnitude and direction, the displacement and the velocity of B relative to A.

   Assuming that they continue to move with these velocities, find how close the tanks come to each other. Find also the coordinates of each tank when this occurs.

4 Ron is walking due north at $1\frac{1}{2}\,\mathrm{m\,s^{-1}}$. He sees his friend Sue 200 metres away to the north-west, walking due east at $2\,\mathrm{m\,s^{-1}}$. If both continue to walk with the same velocity, how close will they come to each other?

   In fact, as soon as he sees Sue, Ron changes direction without changing speed so as to intercept Sue. In what direction does he walk, and how long is it before they meet?

5 In a rugby game a wing three-quarter is running with the ball just inside the touch-line at $8 \, \text{m s}^{-1}$; he is 20 metres short of the goal-line. The opposing full back is on the goal-line, 10 metres in from the touch-line. The full back must try to prevent the man with the ball from reaching the goal-line. If he runs at $5 \, \text{m s}^{-1}$, at what angle to the touch-line should the full back run to intercept the wing three-quarter?

6 A hockey ball is hit from a point on the side-line with a speed of $18 \, \text{m s}^{-1}$ at $15°$ to the side-line. A player standing further along the side-line wants to intercept the ball. What is the least speed at which she must run?

If she runs at $6 \, \text{m s}^{-1}$, at what angle to the side-line should she run so as to intercept the ball as quickly as possible?

7 A yacht is 500 metres north-west of a motorboat. Both are moving at $6 \, \text{m s}^{-1}$; the yacht is travelling east and the motorboat north-east. How close to each other do they come?

8 A smuggler is steering a ship on a southerly course at $25 \, \text{km h}^{-1}$. A police launch, with maximum speed of $35 \, \text{km h}^{-1}$, spots the smuggler 3 km away on a bearing of $130°$. What course should the police launch steer to intercept the smuggler, and how long will it take to do so?

9 Two children stand at adjacent corners of a playground 40 metres square. They each have a ball, and they play a game in which they both roll their balls across the playground. Dot begins by rolling her ball along the diagonal with a speed of $5 \, \text{m s}^{-1}$. Two seconds later Ed rolls his ball with a speed of $6 \, \text{m s}^{-1}$. Find, either by accurate drawing or by calculation, the direction in which Ed should roll his ball so as to hit Dot's.

10 A frigate is steaming on a bearing of $110°$ at a speed of 25 knots. A submarine, 5 nautical miles away from the frigate on a bearing of $040°$, wants to get as close to the frigate as possible. If the maximum speed of the submarine is 15 knots, how close can it get? On what course should the submarine be steered?

11 In a game of football a striker is 30 metres directly in front of the opposing goal with the ball at his feet. The goalkeeper is 8 metres in front of the goal-line, and 6 metres to the side of the line from the striker to the goal. If the striker kicks the ball at $27 \, \text{m s}^{-1}$, and the goalkeeper can run at $7 \, \text{m s}^{-1}$, show that the goalkeeper can't prevent the striker from scoring.

If the striker kicks the ball at $15 \, \text{m s}^{-1}$, and the goalkeeper runs at $7 \, \text{m s}^{-1}$, at what angle to the ball's path should the goalkeeper move to intercept the ball?

12* The President's aircraft is flying due west at $600 \, \text{km h}^{-1}$. An airliner, flying at $500 \, \text{km h}^{-1}$, is 50 km away on a bearing of $250°$. The airliner is instructed to keep at least 10 km away from the President's aircraft. On what courses is the airliner forbidden to fly?

1.4 Connected objects

Ideas of relative velocity can often be used to find the connection between the velocities of objects which are rigidly connected to each other.

The basic idea is that, since the distance between the objects remains constant, the motion of one object relative to the other is round a circle. This means, in particular, that the relative velocity is at right angles to the line connecting them.

Example 1.4.1

A connecting rod AB, which forms part of a mechanism, moves in a vertical plane. At a particular instant this rod is horizontal and the end A is moving at 5 m s^{-1} at 20° to the rod in the upward direction, as shown in Fig. 1.21. At the same instant the end B is moving at 130° to the rod in the downward direction. Find the speed at which B is moving.

Suppose that the speed of B is v m s^{-1}. Since the rod AB is rigid, the end B moves in a circle relative to A, so the relative velocity $_B\mathbf{v}_A$ is at right angles to AB. The rod AB is horizontal at this instant, so $_B\mathbf{v}_A$ is vertical.

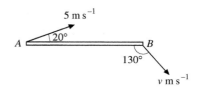

Fig. 1.21

The separate velocities of A and B are both shown relative to a fixed frame of reference. Denote this by F, so that the velocities are $_A\mathbf{v}_F$ and $_B\mathbf{v}_F$. These, with the relative velocity $_B\mathbf{v}_A$, are connected by the equation

$$_B\mathbf{v}_A + {_A\mathbf{v}_F} = {_B\mathbf{v}_F}.$$

You can complete the solution by using either a vector triangle or components.

Vector triangle method   Since the quantity that is completely known is $_A\mathbf{v}_F$, it is slightly more convenient to write the relative velocity equation in the form

$$_A\mathbf{v}_F + {_B\mathbf{v}_A} = {_B\mathbf{v}_F},$$

with the completely known velocity first. This is drawn first, and the triangle can then be completed by drawing lines in the directions of $_B\mathbf{v}_A$ (which is vertical) and $_B\mathbf{v}_F$ (whose direction is given). Where these intersect determines the lengths of the corresponding arrows. The completed vector triangle is shown in Fig. 1.22.

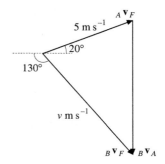

Fig. 1.22

It is easy to calculate the angles opposite the $_A\mathbf{v}_F$ and $_B\mathbf{v}_F$ arrows as 40° and 70° respectively. Then, by the sine rule,

$$\frac{v}{\sin 70°} = \frac{5}{\sin 40°},$$

which gives $v = 7.31$, correct to 3 significant figures.

Component method   Taking axes horizontal and vertically upwards,

$$_A\mathbf{v}_F = \begin{pmatrix} 5\cos 20° \\ 5\sin 20° \end{pmatrix} \quad \text{and} \quad _B\mathbf{v}_F = \begin{pmatrix} v\cos 50° \\ -v\sin 50° \end{pmatrix}.$$

Writing the vector equation in the form

$$_B\mathbf{v}_A = {_B\mathbf{v}_F} - {_A\mathbf{v}_F},$$

$$_B\mathbf{v}_A = \begin{pmatrix} v\cos 50° \\ -v\sin 50° \end{pmatrix} - \begin{pmatrix} 5\cos 20° \\ 5\sin 20° \end{pmatrix}$$

$$= \begin{pmatrix} v\cos 50° - 5\cos 20° \\ -v\sin 50° - 5\sin 20° \end{pmatrix}.$$

Since $_B\mathbf{v}_A$ is vertical, its horizontal component is zero. Therefore

$$v\cos 50° - 5\cos 20° = 0,$$

which gives

$$v = \frac{5\cos 20°}{\cos 50°} = 7.31, \quad \text{correct to 3 significant figures.}$$

The end B of the rod is moving at a speed of $7.31\,\mathrm{m\,s^{-1}}$.

The next example shows how this relative velocity argument can be combined with the principles of energy and momentum to find how two connected objects move in a plane over a period of time, if left to their own devices.

Example 1.4.2

Two particles A and B, of mass $2m$ and m respectively, are connected be a light rod and placed on a smooth table. The particle B is hit by a blow of impulse J at a angle of $45°$ to $\overrightarrow{AB}$ where $J = 3mk\sqrt{2}$ (see Fig. 1.23). Find the velocities of A and B

(a) immediately after the blow,

(b) when the rod has turned through $90°$.

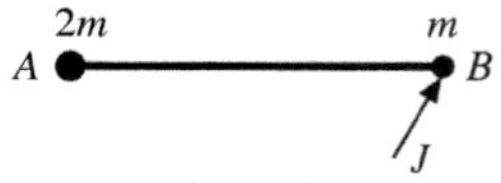

Fig. 1.23

(a) When B is hit, there is also an impulsive tension in the rod. The particle B is therefore subjected to two impulses, but A receives only the impulse from the rod. It follows that A begins to move in the direction $\overrightarrow{AB}$.

By using component notation in directions along and perpendicular to the rod, the velocity of A can be denoted by $\begin{pmatrix} u \\ 0 \end{pmatrix}$.

Now, as B is connected to A by a rigid rod, its motion relative to A is round a circle. Its velocity relative to A is therefore at right angles to AB; denote this velocity by $\begin{pmatrix} 0 \\ v \end{pmatrix}$. Then the velocity of B relative to the table is the sum of $\begin{pmatrix} u \\ 0 \end{pmatrix}$

and $\begin{pmatrix} 0 \\ v \end{pmatrix}$, that is $\begin{pmatrix} u \\ v \end{pmatrix}$. These velocities are shown in Fig. 1.24.

Fig. 1.24

The two unknown quantities u and v can be found from an impulse–momentum equation for the complete system. The impulsive tension is an internal impulse, so it doesn't come into the equation. The components of the external impulse are $\begin{pmatrix} J \cos 45° \\ J \sin 45° \end{pmatrix}$; since $\cos 45° = \sin 45° = \dfrac{1}{\sqrt{2}}$, this impulse is $\begin{pmatrix} 3mk \\ 3mk \end{pmatrix}$. So

$$\begin{pmatrix} 3mk \\ 3mk \end{pmatrix} = 2m \begin{pmatrix} u \\ 0 \end{pmatrix} + m \begin{pmatrix} u \\ v \end{pmatrix},$$

giving the equations $3mk = 2mu + mu$ and $3mk = mv$, with solution $u = k$ and $v = 3k$.

Immediately after the blow A moves in the direction $\overrightarrow{AB}$ with speed k, and B has velocity $\begin{pmatrix} k \\ 3k \end{pmatrix}$, which is a speed of $\sqrt{10}\,k$ at $\tan^{-1} 3 = 71.6°$ to $\overrightarrow{AB}$.

(b) Fig. 1.25 shows the velocities of the particles when the rod has turned through 90°. By this time A may have acquired a component of velocity perpendicular to its original direction of motion, so its velocity could be described by the vector $\begin{pmatrix} s \\ t \end{pmatrix}$.

But, relative to A, B is still moving round a circle, so its velocity can only differ from that of A in the component at right angles to AB. Its velocity can therefore be written as $\begin{pmatrix} w \\ t \end{pmatrix}$.

The problem is to find the three unknowns s, t and w.

Fig. 1.25

Two equations connecting these unknowns can be found from an impulse–momentum equation, since there has been no external force to change the total momentum of the system. So

$$\begin{pmatrix} 3mk \\ 3mk \end{pmatrix} = 2m \begin{pmatrix} s \\ t \end{pmatrix} + m \begin{pmatrix} w \\ t \end{pmatrix},$$

giving the two equations $3mk = 2ms + mw$ and $3mk = 2mt + mt$. So $t = k$, and $2s + w = 3k$.

A third equation comes from the conservation of kinetic energy between the positions shown in Fig. 1.24 and Fig. 1.25. This gives

$$\tfrac{1}{2}(2m)\,u^2 + \tfrac{1}{2}m(u^2 + v^2) = \tfrac{1}{2}(2m)(s^2 + t^2) + \tfrac{1}{2}m(w^2 + t^2).$$

Dividing each term by $\tfrac{1}{2}m$, and setting $u = k$ and $v = 3k$, this is

$$12k^2 = 2s^2 + 3t^2 + w^2.$$

Now substitute $t = k$ and $w = 3k - 2s$, as found above, to get

$$12k^2 = 2s^2 + 3k^2 + (3k - 2s)^2, \quad \text{which is} \quad 6s^2 - 12ks = 0.$$

So there are two possibilities: either $s = 2k$ and $w = -k$, or $s = 0$ and $w = 3k$.

The first corresponds to the time when the rod has turned through 90°, the second to the time when the rod has turned through 270°.

When the rod has turned through 90°, A has velocity $\begin{pmatrix} 2k \\ k \end{pmatrix}$ and B has velocity $\begin{pmatrix} -k \\ k \end{pmatrix}$.

Exercise 1C

1. Ann and Ben are holding the two ends of a skipping rope. Ann is running at $2\,\mathrm{m\,s^{-1}}$ directly away from Ben. Ben is running at $3\,\mathrm{m\,s^{-1}}$ in a direction such that the rope remains taut. At what angle to the rope is Ben running?

2. The diagram shows a flagpole being raised by a cable from a crane. When the pole is at 20° to the horizontal, the cable is pulling the top of the pole in a direction 10° to the vertical at a speed of $2\,\mathrm{m\,s^{-1}}$. Find the speed of the foot of the pole along the ground.

3. The diagram shows the rectangular plan view $ABCD$ of a coach negotiating a right-angled corner XOY. The coach has length 10 m and width 2 m. When A is 8 m from O and B is 6 m from O, A and B are moving parallel to XO and OY respectively, and B is moving at $5\,\mathrm{m\,s^{-1}}$.

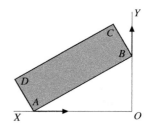

   (a) What is the direction of the velocity of B relative to A?

   (b) Calculate the speed of A.

   (c) Relative to A, B is moving in a circle. Calculate the angular speed of B relative to A.

   (d) The angular speed of C relative to B is the same as the angular speed of B relative to A. Find the velocity of C relative to B.

   (e) Find the components of the velocity of C in the directions OX and OY. Hence find the magnitude and direction of the velocity of C.

(4) The diagram shows a rigid rod AB. The end A is moving with a speed of $6\,\mathrm{m\,s^{-1}}$ at $60°$ to the direction $\overrightarrow{AB}$. The end B is moving at $30°$ to the direction $\overrightarrow{AB}$. Calculate

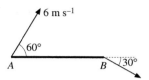

(a) the speed with which B is moving,

(b) the velocity of the mid-point of AB.

5 A light rod connects two particles of mass m and $2m$, which move on a smooth horizontal surface. The rod is rotating clockwise. The first figure shows the velocities, $2u$ and u at right angles to the rod, of the particles at a particular instant.

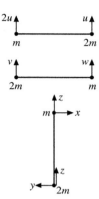

(a) The second figure shows the situation when the rod has rotated through $180°$. Use conservation of momentum and energy to find the velocities v and w in terms of u.

(b) The third figure shows the situation when the rod has rotated through $90°$. Find the velocity components x, y and z in terms of u.

6 A light rod AB has particles of mass m and $3m$ attached at A and B respectively. The particle at A is struck with a blow of impulse I at an angle of $60°$ to the direction $\overrightarrow{AB}$. Find the direction in which the particle at A starts to move.

7* The ends A and B of a rigid rod are in contact with a smooth floor and a smooth vertical wall respectively. The rod is slipping so that it moves in a plane perpendicular to the wall and the floor. When the rod makes an angle θ with the vertical, the end A has speed u and the end B has speed v. By considering the velocity of B relative to A, prove that $v = u\tan\theta$.

The rod is light and has length l. Particles of mass m are attached to the rod at each end. Initially the rod is vertical, and it is slightly displaced from this position so that it starts to slip. Find expressions for u and v in terms of l, θ and g. What angle does the rod make with the vertical when A has its greatest speed?

1.5* Mechanics in an accelerating frame

So far in this chapter the relative velocity equation has been applied only to objects moving with constant velocity. But if this is not the case, you can differentiate $_P\mathbf{v}_Q + {}_Q\mathbf{v}_R = {}_P\mathbf{v}_R$ with respect to t, to get an equation connecting relative accelerations,

$$_P\mathbf{a}_Q + {}_Q\mathbf{a}_R = {}_P\mathbf{a}_R.$$

This section investigates some of the implications of this equation. You may omit it if you wish.

At various stages in the course you have met problems involving mechanical systems which operate inside compartments which are themselves accelerating horizontally or vertically. Compare the results of the following three examples, which all take place inside a lift accelerating downwards with acceleration f.

Example 1.5.1

A case of mass m is placed on the floor of a lift. Find the contact force from the floor on the case when the lift has downward acceleration f.

> The only forces on the case are the contact force R and its weight mg. Since the case is stationary relative to the lift, it has acceleration f downwards. Therefore
>
> $$\mathcal{R}(\downarrow) \qquad mg - R = mf, \quad \text{so} \quad R = m(g - f).$$

Example 1.5.2

A particle of mass m hangs from the roof of a lift by a spring whose tension is kx (k is a constant) when its extension is x. The lift has downward acceleration f. Find the period with which the particle oscillates relative to the lift, and the position of the centre of oscillation.

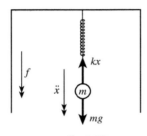

Fig. 1.26

> When the extension of the spring is x, the forces on the particle are its weight mg and the tension kx (see Fig. 1.26). The acceleration of the particle is $\ddot{x}$ relative to the lift, and to this must be added the acceleration of the lift relative to the ground, so the acceleration of the particle relative to the ground is $\ddot{x} + f$ downwards.
>
> $$\mathcal{R}(\downarrow) \qquad mg - kx = m(\ddot{x} + f),$$
>
> which can be rearranged as
>
> $$\ddot{x} = -\frac{k}{m}\left(x - \frac{m}{k}(g - f)\right).$$
>
> Writing $x - \frac{m}{k}(g - f)$ as y, this equation takes the standard simple harmonic form
>
> $$\ddot{y} = -\frac{k}{m}y.$$
>
> It follows that the particle oscillates relative to the lift with period $2\pi\sqrt{\dfrac{m}{k}}$ about a centre of oscillation in which the spring has extension $\dfrac{m}{k}(g - f)$.

Example 1.5.3

A particle hangs from the roof of a lift by an inextensible string of length l. Relative to the lift it rotates as a conical pendulum with constant angular speed ω. The lift has downward acceleration f. Find the angle θ which the string makes with the vertical as it rotates, and the tension in the string.

The forces on the particle are its weight mg and the tension T. Relative to the lift the acceleration of the particle is $l \sin \theta\, \omega^2$ horizontally; to find the acceleration relative to the ground this must be combined with the acceleration of the lift, which is f vertically downwards (see Fig. 1.27).

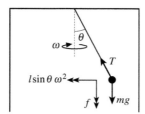

Fig. 1.27

You can resolve the equation $\mathbf{F} = m\mathbf{a}$ in any two directions, not necessarily at right angles to each other. The neatest solution probably comes by using the equations

$\mathcal{R}(\perp \text{ to string}) \qquad mg \sin \theta = m(l \sin \theta\, \omega^2 \times \cos \theta + f \sin \theta)$, and
$\mathcal{R}(\leftarrow) \qquad\qquad\quad T \sin \theta = ml \sin \theta\, \omega^2$.

After dividing both equations by $m \sin \theta$, the first equation leads directly to $\cos \theta = \dfrac{g - f}{l\omega^2}$ and the second gives $T = ml\omega^2$.

Notice a feature common to the answers in all these examples. Some of them involve g, others don't (the period in Example 1.5.2 and the tension in Example 1.5.3). All those which involve g do so in the combination $g - f$. This means that the effect of carrying out the experiment in a lift which has a downward acceleration f, as against carrying it out in a stationary laboratory, is simply to replace the constant g by $g - f$ wherever it appears.

So, if you were to carry out the experiments in a sealed room with no windows, there would be no way of telling from the results whether the room was accelerating downwards or whether the room was stationary but the force of gravity had got smaller.

This doesn't apply only to vertical acceleration. Imagine that you are placed in a large spherical capsule in which there is a pendulum of length l swinging from a point O fixed in the capsule, and that the capsule has acceleration $\mathbf{f}$ relative to the ground. Suppose that the bob has position vector $\mathbf{r}$ relative to O; its acceleration relative to the capsule is then $\ddot{\mathbf{r}}$, so its acceleration relative to the ground is $\ddot{\mathbf{r}} + \mathbf{f}$. The forces on the bob are the tension $\mathbf{T}$ and the weight $m\mathbf{g}$, where $\mathbf{g}$ as usual denotes the acceleration due to gravity. So, by Newton's second law,

$\mathbf{T} + m\mathbf{g} = m(\ddot{\mathbf{r}} + \mathbf{f})$.

This can be rearranged as $\mathbf{T} + m(\mathbf{g} - \mathbf{f}) = m\ddot{\mathbf{r}}$.

So, if you couldn't see out of the capsule, you might think that the laboratory is stationary and that the acceleration of gravity is $\mathbf{g} - \mathbf{f}$.

For example, if the capsule is accelerating horizontally with acceleration of magnitude f, it would appear that the 'vertical' is at an angle $\tan^{-1}\dfrac{f}{g}$ behind the true vertical, and that the acceleration of gravity has magnitude $\sqrt{g^2 + f^2}$ rather than g. This is illustrated in Fig. 1.28.

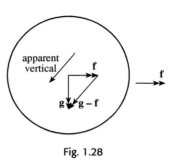

Fig. 1.28

Exercise 1D*

1 In a parachute display, two people jump from an aircraft together, holding on to each other. They remain linked for several seconds, and then push each other apart so that they continue the drop independently of each other.

   (a) Neglecting air resistance, find the acceleration of one parachutist relative to the other.

   (b) Describe how the displacement of one parachutist relative to the other varies from the time when they separate until they open their parachutes.

2 A person in a lift, descending with acceleration f, holds a ball at a height h above the floor of the lift. If the ball is released, find how long it will take to fall to the floor.

3 Model the earth as a perfect sphere of radius R rotating about its axis with angular speed ω, which exerts a gravitational force mg on a particle of mass m directed along a radius. Let P be a point on the surface at latitude λ. Because of the rotation a particle falls to the earth at P with acceleration g' at an angle δ to the geometrical vertical at P. Show that

$$\frac{g'}{\sin \lambda} = \frac{g}{\sin(\lambda + \delta)} = \frac{R\omega^2 \cos \lambda}{\sin \delta}$$

Given that $R\omega^2$ is small compared with g, deduce that δ is approximately $\dfrac{R\omega^2 \sin 2\lambda}{2g}$ radians.

The circumference of the earth is 40 000 km. Show that, in middle latitudes, the mechanical vertical differs from the geometrical vertical by about 0.1°; and that at the equator g' is about 0.03 m s^{-2} less than g.

Miscellaneous exercise 1

1 A yacht is sailing due east with a constant speed of 10 km h^{-1}, in a steady wind of speed 20 km h^{-1}. The magnitude of the velocity of the wind relative to the yacht is 12 km h^{-1}. Calculate the angle between the direction of the wind and the easterly direction in which the yacht is moving. (OCR)

2 Ship A is sailing due north at a constant speed of 41 km h^{-1}. Ship B is sailing at a constant speed of 40 km h^{-1} on a fixed bearing. The magnitude of the velocity of B relative to A is 9 km h^{-1}. Show that the velocity of B relative to A is perpendicular to the path of B. (OCR)

3 A woman can swim at a maximum speed of $1.6\,\mathrm{m\,s^{-1}}$ in still water. She swims across a river 48 m wide in the shortest possible time. The river flows with uniform speed $1.2\,\mathrm{m\,s^{-1}}$ between parallel banks. Find the time the woman takes to cross the river.

Show that, when the woman reaches the opposite bank, she is 60 m from her starting point.   (OCR)

4 A man wishes to row a boat across a river which flows with uniform speed $2\,\mathrm{m\,s^{-1}}$ between parallel banks. The man keeps his boat pointed at an angle θ to the direction AB in which he travels. Given that the man can row at $3\,\mathrm{m\,s^{-1}}$ in still water, and that the line AB is perpendicular to the banks, calculate the value of θ.   (OCR, adapted)

5 Instruments on an aircraft show that, relative to the air, it is moving directly east with a speed of $500\,\mathrm{km\,h^{-1}}$. Ground-based radar shows that it actually is moving with speed $530\,\mathrm{km\,h^{-1}}$ in a direction $10°$ north of east. Unit vectors $\mathbf{i}$ and $\mathbf{j}$ are defined in the easterly and northerly directions respectively. Express both the above velocities in the form $a\mathbf{i}+b\mathbf{j}$, where a and b are scalars. Hence express the air velocity in the same form and find the speed of the air.   (OCR)

6 A river flows between parallel banks at a uniform speed of $2\,\mathrm{m\,s^{-1}}$. Two boats A and B, each travelling at a fixed speed $u\,\mathrm{m\,s^{-1}}$ relative to the water, leave a point O on one bank. Boat A travels in a straight line from O to P, and boat B travels in a straight line from O to Q. The lines OP and OQ each make an angle of $60°$ with the bank. The velocities of A and B relative to the water make acute angles α with OP, and β with OQ, respectively (see diagram). Prove that $\alpha = \beta$.

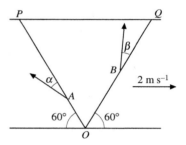

It is given that $\alpha = \beta = 30°$. Calculate the value of u. Show that B crosses the river in half the time taken by A.   (OCR)

7 A student, A, walking in the park sees a friend, B, strolling due north at $1.2\,\mathrm{m\,s^{-1}}$. Student A is 100 metres due west of student B. He decides to intercept B by hurrying at $2.5\,\mathrm{m\,s^{-1}}$ in a direction at an angle θ to the northerly path taken by B. Find the angle θ, and the time that it will take A to reach B.   (OCR)

8 A party of tourists on safari in a minibus spot an antelope 200 metres north of them. The antelope is travelling with velocity $15\mathbf{i}\,\mathrm{m\,s^{-1}}$ and the minibus is travelling at a velocity of $(10\mathbf{i}+10\mathbf{j})\,\mathrm{m\,s^{-1}}$, where $\mathbf{i}$ is a unit vector in an easterly direction and $\mathbf{j}$ is a unit vector in a northerly direction. The antelope and the minibus continue to travel with these velocities. Calculate

(a) the velocity of the antelope relative to the minibus,

(b) the displacement of the antelope relative to the minibus t seconds after it is sighted,

(c) the distance of closest approach of the minibus to the antelope.   (OCR)

9   The position vectors of two ships, P and Q, at time t hours after noon are given respectively by $\mathbf{r}_P$ and $\mathbf{r}_Q$ where $\mathbf{r}_P = 11\mathbf{j} + t(9\mathbf{i} - 12\mathbf{j})$ and $\mathbf{r}_Q = -6\mathbf{j} + t(-5\mathbf{i} + 12\mathbf{j})$, and the units are kilometres. Write down expressions, in terms of $\mathbf{i}$ and $\mathbf{j}$, for the velocity of ship P, the velocity of ship Q, and the velocity of ship Q relative to ship P.

Both ships continue moving with these velocities. Find the least distance between the ships in their subsequent motion.   (OCR)

10 Unit vectors $\mathbf{i}$ and $\mathbf{j}$ are defined in the directions due east and due north respectively. Two ships, A and B, move on the open sea with velocities $\mathbf{v}_A = (12\mathbf{i} + 16\mathbf{j})\,\mathrm{km\,h^{-1}}$ and $\mathbf{v}_B = (8\mathbf{i} + \alpha\,\mathbf{j})\,\mathrm{km\,h^{-1}}$ respectively where α is a scalar constant.

(a) Write down, in terms of $\mathbf{i}$ and $\mathbf{j}$, an expression for the velocity of ship A relative to ship B.

When the two ships first sight each other, A is $10\,\mathrm{km}$ due west of B. Find

(b) the value of α for which the two ships would collide if their present courses were maintained,

(c) the time between the ships first sighting each other and their collision.   (OCR)

11 A ship S is sailing due north at a constant speed of $20\,\mathrm{km\,h^{-1}}$. At 12 noon an oil tanker T is sighted, $10\,\mathrm{km}$ from S on a bearing of $090°$. At 1 p.m. T is $16\,\mathrm{km}$ from S on a bearing of $150°$. Given that T sails at a constant speed on a fixed bearing, find, in either order,

(a) the magnitude and direction of the velocity of T relative to S,

(b) the speed of T.   (OCR)

12 A cyclist is riding directly into the wind in a shower of rain. When he cycles at $5\,\mathrm{m\,s^{-1}}$ the rain appears to be coming at an angle of $60°$ to the horizontal. When he cycles at $12\,\mathrm{m\,s^{-1}}$ the rain appears to be coming at $40°$ to the horizontal. At what angle to the horizontal is the rain actually falling, and with what speed?

13 An oil tanker, sailing with constant speed $16\,\mathrm{km\,h^{-1}}$ on a course bearing $060°$, sends a request for medical help to a lifeboat station $10\,\mathrm{km}$ away due east. A small rescue boat is immediately despatched from the lifeboat station. It travels in a straight line at $20\,\mathrm{km\,h^{-1}}$, to intercept the oil tanker. Find

(a) the bearing on which the rescue boat should sail,

(b) the distance from the lifeboat station to the meeting point.   (OCR)

14 Two aircraft T and R, flying at the same altitude, are taking part in a mid-air refuelling exercise. T is a tanker aircraft flying horizontally with a constant velocity of $300\,\mathrm{km\,h^{-1}}$ on a bearing of $030°$. Aircraft R is initially $8\,\mathrm{km}$ due east of T and flies horizontally with a constant velocity of magnitude $500\,\mathrm{km\,h^{-1}}$. Modelling the aircraft as particles which arrive simultaneously at the refuelling point, find the bearing on which R travels.

Calculate the distance between the initial position of R and the refuelling point.   (OCR)

15) A coastguard boat C spotted a launch due north at a distance of 5000 m. The launch L was moving at full speed in a fixed direction towards a point P. The coastguard calculated that, if C moved at $15\,\mathrm{m\,s^{-1}}$ in the direction with bearing 045°, it would intercept L as it arrived at P, 10 minutes later. Find the distance of L from P, and find also the speed of L.

In fact, C moved at $20\,\mathrm{m\,s^{-1}}$ in a different direction and intercepted L, which did not change speed or direction. In what direction did C move, and how far from P did the interception take place?   (MEI)

16) A coastguard boat C on patrol was moving at a steady speed of $5\,\mathrm{m\,s^{-1}}$. When C was moving due east, the wind appeared to come from a direction with bearing 060°. When C was moving on a bearing of 330°, but still at $5\,\mathrm{m\,s^{-1}}$, the wind appeared to come from the north. Find the wind speed, and the direction from which it was blowing.   (MEI)

17) The noise of a car travelling along a straight road with constant speed V startles a rabbit which then darts across the road. A plan view of the situation is shown in the diagram. The rectangular car $ABCD$ has width a and the corner B is initially at the origin O of cartesian coordinates (x, y). The rabbit starts running from R with constant speed W at an angle θ to the x-axis. Unit vectors in the x- and y-directions are denoted by $\mathbf{i}$ and $\mathbf{j}$.

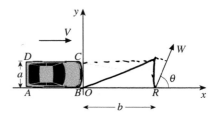

(a) If $\theta = \frac{1}{2}\pi$, show that the rabbit is safe provided $W > \dfrac{aV}{b}$.

The rabbit is safe however for smaller values of W provided the angle θ is suitably chosen.

(b) Explain why the position vector $\mathbf{r}_C$ of C at time t is given by $\mathbf{r}_C = vt\mathbf{i} + a\mathbf{j}$, and find the position vector $\mathbf{r}_R$ of the rabbit at the same time.

(c) Show that the rabbit is safe for an angle θ provided $W > \dfrac{aV}{a\cos\theta + b\sin\theta}$.

(d) Deduce the value of the lowest speed with which the rabbit can run to safety. Find also the corresponding direction in which the rabbit must run.

(e) Illustrate these results geometrically by using a relative velocity diagram, which should show how the relative velocities are related to the original positions of the car and rabbit.   (MEI)

2 Rotational energy

In this chapter the theory of energy is applied to rigid objects rotating about a fixed axis. When you have completed it, you should

- know how to calculate the kinetic energy of a rotating rigid object
- know the definition of moment of inertia, and some formulae for calculating it
- know how to calculate the work done by a force applied to a rotating rigid object
- know what is meant by a couple, and how to calculate the work done by a couple
- know how to calculate the gravitational potential energy of large objects.

2.1 Kinetic energy

When you mend a bicycle, you often turn it upside down so that it rests on the saddle and the handlebars. Suppose that you then spin the front wheel round so that it rotates with angular speed $10\,\text{rad}\,\text{s}^{-1}$. If the rim has mass 1.6 kg and radius 0.35 metres, how much kinetic energy does it have?

The only formula you know for kinetic energy is $\frac{1}{2}mv^2$. But what is v in this case? The bicycle is not moving, so the centre of mass of the wheel is stationary. But obviously putting $v = 0$ won't give the answer.

It is the points of the rim which are moving, and all of these points have speed $0.35 \times 10\,\text{m}\,\text{s}^{-1}$, which is $3.5\,\text{m}\,\text{s}^{-1}$. But they are all moving in different directions.

But imagine the rim cut up into a lot of small pieces – say n pieces, each of mass $\dfrac{1.6}{n}$ kg. Then if n is a large number, each piece could be modelled as a particle, moving along the tangent to a circular path with speed $3.5\,\text{m}\,\text{s}^{-1}$. The kinetic energy of each particle would be $\frac{1}{2} \times \dfrac{1.6}{n} \times 3.5^2$ joules, which is $\dfrac{9.8}{n}$ joules.

Now because kinetic energy is a scalar quantity, the total energy can be found by adding up the energy of all the separate pieces. There are n pieces, each with energy $\dfrac{9.8}{n}$ joules, so the total kinetic energy is 9.8 joules.

2.2 Rigid objects and rotation

This idea of modelling an object as a large number of pieces, each small enough to be modelled as a particle, can be generalised. If there are n particles in all, they can be numbered 1, 2,... , n. Particle i can then be identified as having mass m_i and located at the point P_i. The total mass M of the object is then $m_1 + m_2 + ... + m_n$; this can be abbreviated using sigma notation, as $\sum m_i$, where i takes successively the values 1, 2,... , n.

This model can be used whether or not the object is rigid. What distinguishes a rigid object from one which is not rigid? This is a geometrical property, that the distance between each pair of particles making up the object remains constant. This model is illustrated in Fig. 2.1.

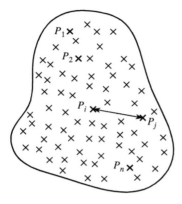

Fig. 2.1

A rigid object is modelled as a set of n particles. A typical particle has mass m_i and is located at a point P_i where $1 \leqslant i \leqslant n$, such that the distance $P_i P_j$ between each pair of particles remains constant.

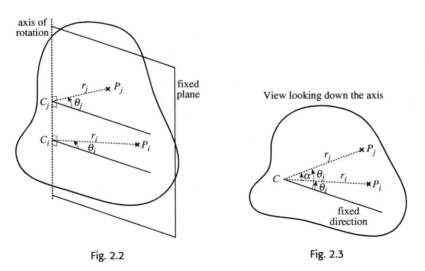

Fig. 2.2   Fig. 2.3

Now suppose that such an object is rotating about an axis, as shown in Fig. 2.2. (In general this is three-dimensional, but you may find it simpler to follow the argument with the two-dimensional version in Fig. 2.3, which is a projection of Fig. 2.2 on a plane perpendicular to the axis of rotation.) $P_i C_i$ and $P_j C_j$ are drawn perpendicular to the axis of rotation, so C_i and C_j are fixed points as the object rotates. Since these lengths are constant, P_i and P_j move in circles with centres C_i and C_j. Their angular velocities are $\dot{\theta}_i$ and $\dot{\theta}_j$, where θ_i and θ_j are the angles made by $C_i P_i$ and $C_j P_j$ with a fixed plane containing the axis.

Now since the rotating object is rigid, the length $P_i P_j$ is constant, and you can then see from Fig. 2.3 that θ_i and θ_j differ by a fixed angle α. It follows that $\theta_i + \alpha = \theta_j$, so that $\dot{\theta}_i = \dot{\theta}_j$. That is, each particle making up the rigid object rotates in a circle about the axis with the same angular velocity.

> If a rigid object rotates about an axis which is fixed relative to the object and in space, each particle making up the object rotates about the axis with the same angular velocity. This is called the **angular velocity** of the rigid object.

> It is not necessary to call it the angular velocity of the object 'about the axis'. In fact, you can talk about the angular velocity of a rigid object whether or not it is rotating about a fixed axis. But in this book you will only be dealing with rigid objects which rotate about a fixed axis.

You can now find an expression for the kinetic energy of any rigid object rotating about an axis with angular velocity ω. If the radius $C_i P_i$ is denoted by r_i, the particle at P_i moves round a circle with speed $r_i \omega$, so the kinetic energy of this particle is $\frac{1}{2} m_i (r_i \omega)^2$. The total kinetic energy of the rotating object is therefore

$$\frac{1}{2} m_1 r_1^2 \omega^2 + \frac{1}{2} m_2 r_2^2 \omega^2 + \ldots + \frac{1}{2} m_n r_n^2 \omega^2$$
$$= \frac{1}{2} \left(m_1 r_1^2 + m_2 r_2^2 + \ldots + m_n r_n^2 \right) \omega^2.$$

This can be written in a shorter form as $\frac{1}{2} I \omega^2$, where I denotes the sum in brackets, which can be expressed as $\sum m_i r_i^2$.

> A rigid object rotating about a fixed axis with angular velocity ω has kinetic energy $\frac{1}{2} I \omega^2$, where $I = \sum m_i r_i^2$. The quantity I is called the **moment of inertia** of the rigid object about the axis.

The rather odd term 'moment of inertia' needs a word of explanation. 'Inertia' was an old-fashioned word for mass. (Nowadays it is used in everyday speech in the associated sense of 'reluctance to move'.) The word 'moment' is linked in mechanics with the idea of turning. So moment of inertia has a role in the theory of rotation comparable with that of mass in linear motion. You can see this by comparing the formulae $\frac{1}{2} I \omega^2$ and $\frac{1}{2} m v^2$ for the kinetic energy in the two situations.

Since the basic SI units for m_i and r_i are kilograms and metres, the unit for moment of inertia is the 'kilogram metre squared', abbreviated to kg m^2. For small objects it is convenient to use the 'gram centimetre squared' (gram cm^2).

> The standard abbreviation for grams is g. In print g (grams) is distinguished from g (gravitational acceleration) by using a different style of type. But in handwriting there is danger of confusion, so it may be safer to represent the unit by gram rather than g.

Example 2.2.1

Find the moment of inertia for the rim of the bicycle wheel in Section 2.1, and use this to calculate the kinetic energy when the wheel rotates at $10 \, \text{rad s}^{-1}$.

Since all the points of the rim are at a distance 0.35 metres from the axis, the moment of inertia can be calculated as $\sum m_i (0.35)^2$. You can take out the constant factor and write this as $\sum m_i \times 0.35^2$, which is the total mass times 0.35^2.

The mass of the rim is $1.6 \, \text{kg}$, so the moment of inertia is $1.6 \times 0.35^2 \, \text{kg m}^2$, which is $0.196 \, \text{kg m}^2$.

When the angular speed is $10 \, \text{rad s}^{-1}$, the kinetic energy is $\frac{1}{2} \times 0.196 \times 10^2$ joules, which is 9.8 joules.

Example 2.2.2

A cheer-leader spins a twirling stick, which consists of a rod 60 cm long with a small metal ball attached at each end. The mass of each ball is 200 grams. As a modelling simplification the balls can be treated as point masses, and the mass of the rod may be neglected.

(a) Find the moment of inertia of the twirling stick about its mid-point.

(b) Find the kinetic energy of the stick if it makes 2 revolutions per second about its mid-point.

(a) The twirling stick is modelled as a pair of particles, each of mass 0.2 kg at a distance of 0.3 metres from the mid-point. The moment of inertia is therefore $(0.2 \times 0.3^2 + 0.2 \times 0.3^2) \, \text{kg m}^2$, which is $0.036 \, \text{kg m}^2$.

(b) A revolution is 2π radians, so the angular speed of the stick is 4π rad s^{-1}. The kinetic energy is given by the formula $\frac{1}{2} I \omega^2$ to be $\frac{1}{2} \times 0.036 \times (4\pi)^2$ joules, which is 2.84 joules.

Example 2.2.3

A light square lamina $ABCD$, whose mass can be neglected, has diagonals of length 1 metre. Particles of mass 1 kg, 2 kg, 3 kg, 2 kg are attached to the lamina at A, B, C and D respectively. A small hole is drilled in the lamina at a point O on AC such that $AO = \frac{1}{4}$ metre.

(a) Find the moment of inertia of the weighted lamina about O.

(b) The lamina is fastened to a wall by a nail at O, so that it can rotate freely about O in a vertical plane. Initially the lamina is held with C vertically above O, as in Fig. 2.4, and then released. If it is slightly disturbed from this position of unstable equilibrium (see M2 Section 10.3), find its angular speed in the position when C is vertically below O.

(a) The expression $\sum m_i r_i^2$ takes the form

$$1 \times \left(\tfrac{1}{4}\right)^2 + 2\left(\left(\tfrac{1}{4}\right)^2 + \left(\tfrac{1}{2}\right)^2\right) + 3 \times \left(\tfrac{3}{4}\right)^2 + 2\left(\left(\tfrac{1}{4}\right)^2 + \left(\tfrac{1}{2}\right)^2\right)$$
$$= \tfrac{1}{16} + \tfrac{5}{8} + \tfrac{27}{16} + \tfrac{5}{8} = 3,$$

so the moment of inertia is $3 \, \text{kg m}^2$.

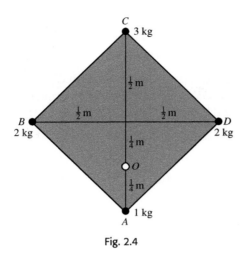

Fig. 2.4

(b) In the initial position, taking O as the base level, the potential energy is

$$1 \times 9.8 \times \left(-\tfrac{1}{4}\right) + 2 \times 9.8 \times \tfrac{1}{4} + 3 \times 9.8 \times \tfrac{3}{4} + 2 \times 9.8 \times \tfrac{1}{4} \text{ joules,}$$

which is 29.4 joules. When C is vertically below O, each height is reversed in sign, so the potential energy is –29.4 joules. The loss of potential energy is therefore 58.8 joules.

This is converted into kinetic energy of amount $\tfrac{1}{2} \times 3 \times \omega^2$ joules, where ω rad s^{-1} is the angular speed. So $\omega = \sqrt{\dfrac{2 \times 58.8}{3}} = 6.26$ correct to 3 significant figures.

The angular speed when C is vertically below O is 6.26 rad s^{-1}.

2.3   Formulae for moment of inertia

The method used in Example 2.2.1 to calculate the moment of inertia of the rim of bicycle wheel could be applied more generally to a rim of radius r with mass M. If the rim is modelled as a set of n particles of mass $m_1, m_2, \ldots, m_n$, each at a distance r from the axis, the moment of inertia is

$$m_1 r^2 + m_2 r^2 + \cdots + m_n r^2 = (m_1 + m_2 + \cdots + m_n) r^2 = M r^2.$$

This is a particularly easy moment of inertia to calculate because all the particles are at the same distance from the axis. For objects with other simple shapes you can find formulae for the moment of inertia; these are all of the form

$$\text{constant} \times \text{total mass} \times \text{length}^2.$$

Here are some examples; proofs of these are given in Chapter 3. In each formula M stands for the total mass of the object.

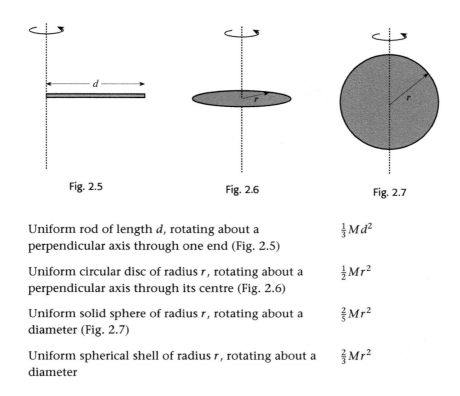

Fig. 2.5   Fig. 2.6   Fig. 2.7

Uniform rod of length d, rotating about a perpendicular axis through one end (Fig. 2.5)	$\frac{1}{3}Md^2$
Uniform circular disc of radius r, rotating about a perpendicular axis through its centre (Fig. 2.6)	$\frac{1}{2}Mr^2$
Uniform solid sphere of radius r, rotating about a diameter (Fig. 2.7)	$\frac{2}{5}Mr^2$
Uniform spherical shell of radius r, rotating about a diameter	$\frac{2}{3}Mr^2$

Formulae like these are listed in a variety of reference books, so it isn't necessary to remember them. But most people find that it is worth knowing those which are used most often; these would certainly include the first three on the above list.

Example 2.3.1
The wheel of a cart is modelled as a set of 10 rods (the spokes), each of mass 4 kg and length 0.75 metres, and a rim of mass 24 kg and radius 0.75 metres. Find the moment of inertia about the axle.

The axle is perpendicular to each spoke, so the moment of inertia of a spoke is $\frac{1}{3} \times 4 \times 0.75^2 \, \text{kg m}^2$, which is $0.75 \, \text{kg m}^2$. The moment of inertia of the rim is given by the formula Mr^2, which is $24 \times 0.75^2 \, \text{kg m}^2$, or $13.5 \, \text{kg m}^2$.

The moment of inertia of the whole is the sum of the moments of inertia of the separate parts, which is $(10 \times 0.75 + 13.5) \, \text{kg m}^2$.

The moment of inertia of the wheel is therefore $21 \, \text{kg m}^2$.

Example 2.3.2
Find the moment of inertia of a uniform rod of mass M and length $2l$ about a perpendicular axis through its centre.

You could think of the rod as made up of two half-rods, each of mass $\frac{1}{2}M$ and length l, and each rotating about a perpendicular axis through its end (see Fig. 2.8). The moment of inertia of each half-rod is $\frac{1}{3}\left(\frac{1}{2}M\right)l^2$, so the moment of inertia of the complete rod is $2 \times \left(\frac{1}{6}Ml^2\right) = \frac{1}{3}Ml^2$.

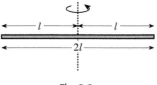

Fig. 2.8

The result of Example 2.3.2 is important, and is usually included in reference lists. Notice that it is given for a rod of length $2l$ rather than length l; you will quite often meet this in questions with algebraic data, so it is worth familiarising yourself with all the following results for a rod of mass M rotating about a perpendicular axis.

length d, about one end (from list above)	$\frac{1}{3}Md^2$
length $2l$, about one end (substitute $d = 2l$)	$\frac{4}{3}Ml^2$
length $2l$, about the centre (Example 2.3.2)	$\frac{1}{3}Ml^2$

Notice that the moment of inertia is much smaller about the centre of the rod than it is about the end. This is because the particles of which the rod is composed cluster much more closely around the centre of the rod. It is in fact true that the moment of inertia is always smaller about an axis through the centre of mass than about any other parallel axis. The proof of this for a rod is in Exercise 2A Question 14, and the general proof for any rigid object is in Section 3.8.

Example 2.3.3

A uniform solid sphere of radius 0.8 metres and mass 100 kg can rotate without friction about a horizontal axis through its centre. A particle of mass 9 kg is attached at the top of the sphere, where it rests in unstable equilibrium. When the sphere is slightly disturbed, equilibrium is broken and the particle descends. Find the angular speed of the sphere when it has rotated through half a revolution, so that the particle is at the lowest point.

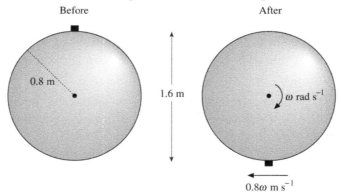

Fig. 2.9

Fig. 2.9 shows the particle in its initial position and at the lowest point of the sphere. As it descends from one position to the other, a distance of 1.6 metres, it loses potential energy of amount $(9 \times 9.8) \times 1.6$ joules, which is 141.12 joules. The potential energy of the sphere stays the same. Since there is no loss of energy due to friction, the potential energy lost is converted into kinetic energy of the sphere and the particle.

The moment of inertia of the sphere is given by the formula $\frac{2}{5}Mr^2$ as $\frac{2}{5} \times 100 \times 0.8^2$ kg m^2, which is 25.6 kg m^2. If its angular speed in the second position is ω rad s^{-1}, the kinetic energy is $\frac{1}{2} \times 25.6\omega^2$, which is $12.8\omega^2$.

At the lowest point the particle also has kinetic energy. The tangential speed of the particle is 0.8ω m s^{-1}, so its kinetic energy is $\frac{1}{2} \times 9 \times (0.8\omega)^2$ joules, which is $2.88\omega^2$ joules.

Equating the total kinetic energy gained to the potential energy lost,

$$12.8\omega^2 + 2.88\omega^2 = 141.12,$$

which gives $\omega^2 = 9$ and hence $\omega = 3$.

The angular speed of the sphere after it has rotated through half a revolution is 3 rad s^{-1}.

Exercise 2A

1 Calculate the moment of inertia of

(a) a pikestaff, of mass 6 kg and length 4 metres, about a perpendicular axis at one end,

(b) a spherical meteorite, of mass 4000 tonnes and radius 5 metres, about a diameter,

(c) the turntable in a microwave oven, of mass 250 grams and diameter 20 cm, about its vertical axis,

(d) a hollow beach ball, of mass 100 grams and radius 15 cm, about a diameter.

2 Calculate the kinetic energy of

(a) a solid flywheel of mass 20 kg and radius 40 cm, rotating at 3000 revolutions per minute,

(b) the propeller of a model aircraft, modelled as three rods each of mass 30 grams and length 4 cm, rotating at 25 revolutions per second,

(c) a hovering frisbee of mass 80 grams and radius 10 cm, rotating at 10 revolutions per second.

3 An orange is modelled as a uniform sphere of mass 100 grams and radius 4 cm, covered with a thin peel of mass 6 grams. Find the moment of inertia of the orange about a diameter

(a) in gram cm^2,   (b) in kg m^2.

4 A wheel of radius 25 cm is made of a solid uniform disc of mass 16 kg, bound round the circumference by a thin iron band of mass 4 kg. Find the moment of inertia of the wheel.

5 A mass of metal could be formed into either a sphere of radius r or a disc of radius r. Which will have the larger moment of inertia? Give a physical explanation for your answer.

6 A square metal aerial, of total mass 6 kg and side 1.6 metres, is mounted on a vertical axis as shown in the diagram. By modelling it as four rods joined together, find its moment of inertia.

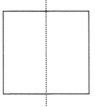

7   The toy gyroscope shown in the diagram consists of a disc of mass 150 grams and radius 3 cm which can rotate about an axis fixed in a spherical skeletal frame. The disc is set spinning by pulling on a thread of length 1.2 metres wound round the axis, with a constant force of 0.2 newtons. Calculate the angular speed of the disc when the whole of the thread has unwound.

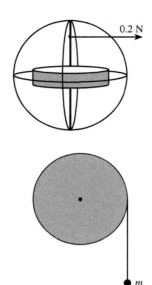

8   A uniform disc of mass m and radius r is mounted on a horizontal axle. A thread is fixed to a point of the circumference, wound several times round the disc, and then hangs vertically as shown in the diagram. A particle of mass m is attached to the free end of the thread. Find the speed with which the particle is moving when it has fallen a distance h from rest.

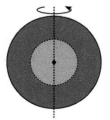

9   On a building site a wheel in the form of a uniform disc of mass 2 kg and radius 10 cm is mounted on a horizontal axle through its centre. A long, rough rope of mass 1 kg and length 25 metres is placed over the top half of the circumference and hangs down symmetrically on either side. Buckets of mass 5 kg and 4 kg are attached to the two ends of the rope. Find the speed of the buckets, and the angular speed of the wheel, when the heavier bucket has fallen a distance of 10 metres.

10 A uniform disc of mass m and radius r has a particle of mass $\frac{1}{2}m$ attached at a point of its circumference. The disc is mounted on a horizontal axle through its centre, and set spinning. At an instant when the particle is at the highest point of the disc the angular speed of the disc is ω. Find the angular speed when the particle is at the lowest point of the disc.

11 A solid hemisphere of mass m and radius r can rotate about its axis of symmetry. By considering the moment of inertia of the sphere formed by joining two such hemispheres together over their plane surfaces, find a formula for the moment of inertia of the hemisphere about its axis of symmetry.

12 Use a method similar to that in Question 11 to find a formula for the moment of inertia of a solid hemisphere about a diameter of its plane face.

13 The diagram represents the cross-section through the centre of a uniform hollow sphere of mass m, with internal radius $\frac{1}{2}r$ and external radius r. If the central core were filled up with material of the same density, what would its mass be? Use your answer to find a formula for the moment of inertia of the hollow sphere about the vertical diameter.

14 A rod of length $2l$ and mass m can rotate about a
perpendicular axis at a distance a from its centre, as
shown in the diagram. By regarding the rod as a
combination of two rods, each rotating about an axis
through one end, show that the moment of inertia of
the rod is $\frac{1}{3}ml^2 + ma^2$. For what value of a is this least?

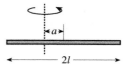

15* A square lamina of negligible mass and sides of length $2l$ has particles of mass $\frac{1}{4}m$
attached at each corner. P is a point of the lamina at a distance a from the centre O,
where OP makes an angle θ with the direction of one pair of sides. Find the moment of
inertia of the set of particles about an axis through P perpendicular to the plane of the
lamina. Do you notice anything surprising about the answer?

2.4 Work done in rotation

Fig. 2.10 shows a plan view of a heavy door being
opened by a person exerting a force F at right angles to
the door. The distance from the hinge to the handle is
a, and the force is applied while the door turns through
an angle θ.

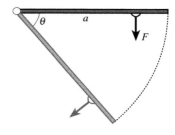

The force is applied through a distance $a\theta$, and at each
instant the displacement is in the direction of the force,
so the work done by the force is $F(a\theta)$. This can be
written as $(Fa)\theta$, and you will recognise the factor Fa as
the moment of the force about the hinge. Denoting
this moment by C, the work done by the force is $C\theta$.

Fig. 2.10

This last formula applies even if the force exerted on the door handle is not at right angles to
the door. If there is also a component of force directed towards the hinge, then this won't
contribute to the work done, because it is perpendicular to the direction of motion. Also, it has
no moment about the hinge. So the rule for calculating the work done is not affected.

> If a rigid object rotates about a fixed axis, the work done by a force
> applied to it is equal to the product of the moment of the force and the
> angle through which the object turns (measured in radians).

If the moment of inertia of the door about the hinge is I, and the door is rotating with angular
velocity ω when it has turned through an angle θ, the work–energy equation takes the form

$$C\theta = \tfrac{1}{2}I\omega^2.$$

> Notice the similarity between the equation $C\theta = \frac{1}{2}I\omega^2$ and the equation $Fs = \frac{1}{2}mv^2$ for an object modelled as a particle moving in a straight line.

2.5 Couples

Imagine a merry-go-round on a children's playground. A group of children push it round to get it started, and then they jump on, hoping that it will go on turning. But after a little while it comes to a stop. Why?

The only force affecting the rotation (apart from air resistance, which would be very small) comes from friction at the bearings of the vertical axle. But this friction doesn't produce a force in any particular direction. Its effect is to produce a kind of 'pure turning force'. This is called a **couple**.

You know lots of examples of couples. When you use a screwdriver or a corkscrew, or when a motor drives a power drill or a food blender, the forces combine to produce an effect which is purely rotational.

The size of a couple is measured by its moment; but instead of calculating this as a force times a distance, it will simply be given as a certain number of newton metres. The couple doesn't have a direction, but you do need to specify its sense of rotation; in two dimensions, this will be simply anticlockwise or clockwise. So, for example, you might refer to a couple of 20 N m clockwise.

The simplest example of a couple is a pair of forces of equal magnitude in opposite directions, not acting in the same line. A good approximation to this is when you apply forces with your thumb and finger to screw a corkscrew into a cork (Fig. 2.11). If forces of 4 newtons are applied at 3 cm from the shaft of the corkscrew, then each force has moment 12 N cm, or 0.12 N m; so the total moment of the couple is 0.24 N m, clockwise.

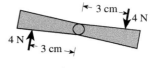

Fig. 2.11

But many couples are produced by more complicated systems of forces. For example, when you use a screwdriver you grip the handle in the palm of your hand, and the turning is produced by a lot of small forces at the points of contact between your hand and the handle of the screwdriver.

Now look back at the corkscrew in Fig. 2.11. If in one movement the handle turns through θ radians, then the work done by each of the forces is 0.12θ joules, so the total work done by the couple is 0.24θ joules. You can see this is $C\theta$, where C is the moment of the couple.

> A couple is a system of forces which has zero resultant but which produces a turning effect.
>
> If a couple is applied to a rigid object rotating about a fixed axis, the work done is the product of the moment of the couple and the angle through which the object turns.

The definition refers to 'the moment of the couple' rather than 'the moment of the couple about the axis'. This is because the moment of a couple is in fact the same, whatever point you take moments about. (See Exercise 2B Question 12.) But for the purpose of this course you can take it to be simply the moment about the axis.

Example 2.5.1

The bicycle wheel in Example 2.2.1 comes to rest after it has turned through 30 revolutions. Assuming that the frictional couple slowing it down is constant, calculate its moment.

The kinetic energy of the rim when rotating at $10 \, \text{rad s}^{-1}$ was calculated as 9.8 joules. This takes no account of the kinetic energy of the spokes and the hub, but these will be comparatively small (why?), and will be neglected in the calculation.

A rotation of 30 revolutions is 60π radians. If the frictional couple has moment $C \, \text{N m}$, the work done against the friction as the wheel slows down is $C \times 60\pi$ joules.

So $C \times 60\pi = 9.8$, which gives $C = 0.051\,9\ldots$.

The frictional couple is $0.052 \, \text{N m}$, correct to 3 decimal places.

Example 2.5.2

A revolving door has moment of inertia $25 \, \text{kg m}^2$ about its vertical central axis. A woman passing through the door exerts a horizontal force on one of the panels while it turns through an angle of $60°$, so that the angular speed of the door reaches $1.8 \, \text{rad s}^{-1}$. The force is exerted at a distance 0.8 metres from the axis at right angles to the panel. She then reduces the force, so that the door goes on rotating at this speed until she has passed through it. After that the door goes on rotating through a further two revolutions before friction brings it to rest. Find

(a) the frictional couple opposing the rotation (assumed constant),

(b) the force the woman exerts to start with,

(c) the force she exerts once the door has got up speed.

(a) At its greatest angular speed the kinetic energy of the door is $\frac{1}{2} \times 25 \times 1.8^2$ joules, which is 40.5 joules. This is reduced to zero by the frictional couple acting through 4π radians. If the moment of the frictional couple is $C \, \text{N m}$, the work done against this couple is $4\pi C$ joules. Therefore $4\pi C = 40.5$, which gives $C = 3.22\ldots$.

(b) While the door is gaining speed, the moment of the force F newtons is opposed by the frictional couple. The moment of the force is $F \times 0.8 \, \text{N m}$, and the door turns through $\frac{1}{3}\pi$ radians, so the work–energy equation for this stage of the motion is

$$0.08F \times \tfrac{1}{3}\pi - C \times \tfrac{1}{3}\pi = 40.5, \quad \text{so} \quad 0.08F - C = \frac{40.5}{\frac{1}{3}\pi}.$$

Substituting $C = 3.22\ldots$, this gives $F = 52.4$ correct to 1 decimal place.

(c) Once the door is rotating at its greatest angular speed, the moment of the force is balanced by the frictional couple. So, if the force is then F' newtons, $0.8F' = 3.22...$, and $F' = 4.0$ correct to 1 decimal place.

The woman pushes the door with a force of 52.4 newtons to start with, reducing this to 4.0 newtons once the door reaches the required angular speed. The frictional couple has moment $3.22\,\mathrm{N\,m}$.

2.6   Potential energy

To apply the conservation of energy principle to an object modelled as a collection of particles, you need to be able to calculate its gravitational potential energy in any position.

To find potential energy, you first have to choose a base level. Then, for a particle of mass m at a height y above this base level, the potential energy is mgy. (See M2 Section 3.4.)

To apply this to an object modelled as a set of particles, with masses $m_1, m_2, ... , m_n$, suppose that the particle of mass m_i is at a height y_i above the base level. Then the total potential energy is

$$m_1 g y_1 + m_2 g y_2 + \cdots + m_n g y_n.$$

Taking out the common factor g, this is

$$g(m_1 y_1 + m_2 y_2 + \cdots + m_n y_n).$$

You should recognise the expression in brackets. You have seen it previously in the formula for the centre of mass,

$$\bar{y} = \frac{m_1 y_1 + m_2 y_2 + \cdots + m_n y_n}{M}$$

where M is the total mass. (See M2 Section 5.2.) It follows that the total potential energy can be written as $g(M\bar{y})$ or $Mg\bar{y}$.

> The potential energy of an object modelled as a set of particles is equal to $Mg\bar{y}$, where M is the total mass and $\bar{y}$ is the height of the centre of mass above the base level.

You won't be surprised by this result, but that doesn't mean that it shouldn't be proved.

Notice that the proof makes no reference to the object being rigid. It holds equally well for rigid and for non-rigid objects. For example, you can apply it to the motion of a dancer who changes the shape of her body in executing a movement.

Example 2.6.1
A uniform rod of length $2l$ is hinged to a fixed horizontal axis at one end and hangs vertically in stable equilibrium. It is set rotating in a vertical plane with initial angular speed ω. How large must ω be for the rod to perform complete revolutions?

To perform complete revolutions, the centre of mass of the rod must move from a position l below the fixed axis to a position l above the fixed axis. In doing this, it gains potential energy of amount $mg(2l)$, where m is the mass of the rod.

When it reaches its highest position, the rod must still have positive kinetic energy. The moment of inertia of the rod about one end is $\frac{4}{3}ml^2$ (see Section 2.3). Therefore, using the conservation of energy principle,

$$\tfrac{1}{2}\left(\tfrac{4}{3}ml^2\right)\omega^2 - 2mgl > 0, \quad \text{which gives} \quad \omega^2 > \frac{3g}{l}.$$

The initial angular speed must be greater than $\sqrt{\dfrac{3g}{l}}$.

Example 2.6.2
Four uniform rods are pin-jointed together at A, B, C and D. The rods AB and CD each have length 80 cm and weight 5 newtons; BC and DA each have length 60 cm and weight 4 newtons. The pin A is fixed to a beam. Initially the rods hang below A under their own weight (Fig. 2.12). A force is now applied vertically upwards to the pin at C, so that the rods slowly open out into a parallelogram shape (Fig. 2.13). This continues until the rods form a rectangle (Fig. 2.14). Find the work done in raising the rods to this position.

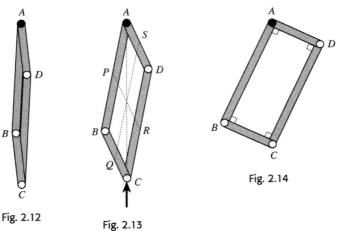

Fig. 2.12

Fig. 2.13

Fig. 2.14

There is no need to consider each rod separately. Although the framework is not rigid, the work done can be calculated as the product of the total weight and the distance through which the centre of mass is raised.

Let the mid-points of the rods be P, Q, R and S (Fig. 2.13). The rods AB and CD have equal weight, so their combined centre of mass is at the mid-point of PR. Similarly the combined centre of mass of BC and DA is at the mid-point of QS. These two mid-points coincide at the centre of the parallelogram, which is also the mid-point of AC. So the centre of mass of the whole framework is at the mid-point of AC.

In Fig. 2.12 C is a distance $(80 + 60)$ cm below A, which is 140 cm. In Fig. 2.13 C is a distance $\sqrt{80^2 + 60^2}$ cm below A, which is 100 cm. So C rises by 40 cm, and the mid-point of AC rises by 20 cm, or 0.2 metres.

The total weight of the framework is $(2 \times 5 + 2 \times 4)$ newtons, which is 18 newtons.

So the work done in raising the centre of mass by 0.2 metres is 18×0.2 joules, which is 3.6 joules.

Exercise 2B

1 A fan has moment of inertia 0.005 kg m^2 about its axis. It is rotating at 200 rad s^{-1} when the power is switched off. It is brought to rest by a frictional couple of moment 0.4 N m. Through how many revolutions does it turn in coming to rest?

2 A door has moment of inertia 8 kg m^2 about the line of the hinges. An automatic door closer applies a force of constant magnitude 2 newtons perpendicular to the door at a distance of 12 cm from the hinge. If the door is opened to an angle of 80° and allowed to close under the action of the door closer, what is its angular speed when it hits the door frame?

3 A flying saucer has moment of inertia 60 kg m^2 about its vertical axis of symmetry. While flying, to assist stability, it rotates about its axis at a rate of 1 revolution per second. As it lands, it rotates through an angle of 270° in contact with the ground before coming to rest. Find the magnitude of the frictional couple slowing it down.

4 The diagram shows a circular platform which can rotate about a vertical axis through its centre. It is made to rotate by applying a constant horizontal force to a handle 20 cm from the axis, in a direction perpendicular to the radius. The moment of inertia of the platform (including the handle) is 0.6 kg m^2. The rotation is opposed by a frictional couple of moment 0.3 N m. After 4 turns of the handle the platform is rotating at 10 rad s^{-1}. Find the force applied to the handle.

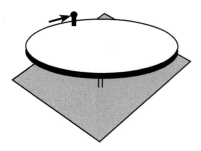

If the force is now removed, how many more revolutions will the platform make before it comes to rest?

5 A uniform solid sphere of radius 5 cm and mass 2.5 kg can rotate about a vertical axis through its centre on smooth bearings. Find its moment of inertia in kg m^2.

When a motor is switched on, the sphere is accelerated by a couple of moment 2 N m. How many revolutions does the sphere turn through before it is rotating at 50 revolutions per second?

6 In a molasses mill a vertical shaft has a pine trunk inserted through it horizontally, to produce two arms each of length 6 metres; the diagram shows a view of the mechanism from above. A horse is harnessed to each arm, and each horse pulls with a force of 200 newtons at an angle of 70° to its arm. Find

(a) the work done by each horse in one revolution of the shaft,

(b) the moment of the couple produced by the two horses.

7 The figure shows a plastic toy called a 'tippe top'. This has a hemispherical base of radius 20 mm and mass 10 grams. The top part consists of a hollow part-hemisphere and a cylindrical handle of radius 4 mm with a rough curved surface; these are of negligible mass. The top is set spinning by friction from the thumb and index finger on the curved surface of the handle. Each of these exerts a force of 0.1 newtons through a distance of 15 mm. Find the angular speed with which the top starts to spin.

8 An egg-beater is operated by means of a handle which rotates in a circle of radius 4 cm. A cook turns the handle at the rate of 1.2 revolutions per second exerting a force of 2 newtons perpendicular to the radius. At what power is she working?

9 An engine developing power of 40 kW drives a rotating shaft at 3000 revolutions per minute. Calculate the moment of the couple transmitted through the shaft. (This is sometimes called the *torque* of the engine.)

10 A turntable is modelled as a disc of mass 0.5 kg and radius 12 cm. It is rotating about a vertical axis at 200 rad s^{-1} and it is brought to rest by a constant frictional couple. When it has completed one revolution its angular speed has fallen to 180 rad s^{-1}. Calculate the magnitude of the frictional couple, and find how many more revolutions the turntable will make before it comes to rest.

11 A light rope hangs over a wheel which can rotate about a horizontal axle. The wheel has radius 0.1 metres and moment of inertia 0.02 kg m^2, and its rotation is resisted by a frictional couple of moment 0.6 N m. Objects of mass 3 kg and 5 kg are attached to the two ends of the rope. Find the angular speed of the wheel when the heavier object has fallen 5 metres.

12* The diagrams show two examples of sets of forces which form couples. Show that, in each case, the moment about every point in the plane is the same. If the two couples have equal moments, find an expression for Q in terms of P.

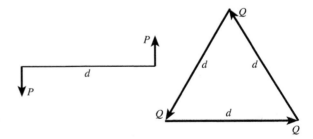

Miscellaneous exercise 2

1 The three blades of a helicopter rotor are modelled as rods of length 6 metres and mass 15 kg. Find the total kinetic energy when the rotor is turning at 20 revolutions per second.

2 A generator is started by pulling a handle attached to a cable with a force of 6 newtons through a distance of 80 cm. This sets up rotation in a flywheel, which is a uniform disc of mass 2 kg and radius 5 cm. Find the angular speed of the flywheel.

3 The Ferris wheel at a fairground is modelled as a rigid body rotating without resistance about a fixed horizontal axis. On one occasion when it is loaded, its mass is 3200 kg, its moment of inertia about the axis is 220 000 kg m², and the centre of mass G is 0.06 m from the axis. The wheel starts at rest with G vertically below the axis. When the motor is switched on, a couple of constant moment 1800 N m is applied to the wheel. Find the angular speed of the wheel after $1\frac{1}{2}$ revolutions.   (OCR)

4 A uniform disc can rotate freely in a vertical plane about a horizontal axis through its centre. The disc has radius 40 cm and mass 2 kg. A particle of mass 1 kg is attached at a point on the rim of the disc. When the particle is directly below the axis the disc is rotating at 25 rad s⁻¹. At what angular speed is it rotating when the particle is directly above the axis?

5 A hollow spherical shell of mass 2 kg and radius 60 cm is rotating about a vertical axis with angular speed 24 rad s⁻¹. The rotation is opposed by a constant frictional couple so that after 5 revolutions the angular speed has dropped to 21 rad s⁻¹. Find

(a) the moment of the frictional couple,

(b) the angular speed after a further 15 revolutions.

6 In a zoo a wheel is mounted on a horizontal axle. The rim is modelled as the circumference of a circle, with mass 100 kg and radius 2 metres. This is fixed to the hub by 20 uniform spokes, each 2 metres long and of mass 6 kg. A small monkey of mass 10 kg climbs on the wheel at a point where the radius makes an angle of 60° with the upward vertical, as shown in the diagram. The monkey clings on to the wheel, which starts to rotate.

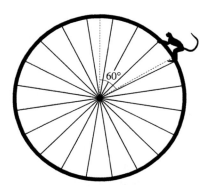

(a) Calculate the moment of inertia of the wheel. (Assume that the moment of inertia of the hub is negligible.)

(b) If the wheel rotated on smooth bearings, what would its angular speed be when the monkey reaches the lowest point?

(c) In fact the angular speed is only 0.9 rad s⁻¹ when the monkey reaches the lowest point. Assuming that the frictional couple at the bearings is constant, find its moment.

7 A smooth tube is fixed in a vertical plane. It is bent into the shape of a semicircle of radius r. A chain of mass m and length $\frac{1}{3}\pi r$ is inserted into the tube and held with the end of the chain at one end of the tube, as shown in the diagram. The chain is then released and slides down the tube. When the middle of the chain reaches the bottom of the tube, find

(a) the potential energy lost,

(b) the speed with which the chain is moving.

8) A sphere of radius r is constructed in two parts. One part is a uniform solid hemisphere of mass $5m$, the other is a uniform hemispherical shell of mass m; the two parts are joined round their the common circular rims. A needle is passed through the sphere along a diameter of the plane common to the two parts, and mounted horizontally on V-shaped supports held on either side of the sphere. The sphere is in its position of unstable equilibrium and released. A slight disturbance causes it to fall. Find its angular speed when it has rotated through half a revolution. (Use the results of Exercise 2A, Questions 11 and 12 and the centre of mass formulae on the inside back cover.)

9 A narrow ruler of length $2l$ has a hole drilled through it at a distance a from the centre. The rod hangs vertically with a fixed horizontal nail passing through the hole. The rod is then turned through 60° and released from rest in this position. Find its angular speed when it is again vertical. (Use the result of Exercise 2A, Question 14.)

Find the value of a for which this angular speed has its largest possible value.

10*) A rod of length 1.4 metres and mass 4 kg is attached to a fixed point at one end by a rusty hinge. The rotation of the rod is opposed by a frictional couple of constant magnitude. The rod is held in a horizontal position and then released. Friction brings the rod to rest just as it reaches its vertical position. Calculate the moment of the frictional couple.

What is the greatest angle to the vertical at which the rod can rest in equilibrium?

The rod is now raised through an angle of 120° from its vertical position and released from rest. Find the angular speed with which it will subsequently pass through its vertical position. Will it swing back after it has come to rest?

11* The figure shows a man hitting a post with a sledgehammer. This is modelled by assuming that his arms and the handle of the hammer are in a straight line, which rotates about his shoulder joints S. His arms are modelled as two uniform rods of length 60 cm, each of mass 2 kg. The sledgehammer has a handle of length 80 cm and mass 0.6 kg, and the metal hammer at the end of the handle has mass 5 kg. The man raises his arms to an angle of 50° with the horizontal. As the hammer falls he exerts a couple of constant moment 4 N m with his shoulder muscles.

(a) Calculate the potential energy of his arms and the hammer above the level of S when the hammer is at its highest point.

(b) Calculate the moment of inertia of his arms and the hammer about S. (Assume that the formula in Exercise 2A Question 14 can be used to find the moment of inertia of the handle.)

(c) If the top of the post is at the same height as S, calculate the speed with which the hammer hits the post.

3 Moments of inertia

This chapter describes various ways of finding formulae for moments of inertia. When you have completed it, you should

- know and be able to apply the stretch rule
- know and be able to apply the perpendicular axes rule
- understand the idea of symmetrical partitioning
- understand the use of integration in applying the summation principle
- know how to use integration to find moments of inertia
- know how to prove the most important formulae for moments of inertia of standard shapes
- know and be able to apply the parallel axes rule.

This is a long chapter, but you will need most of the results given here to do some of the questions in Chapter 5. You can, if you wish, omit the starred proofs in Sections 3.4 and 3.7, and you may like to omit Section 3.9 at a first reading and come back to it for revision at a later stage of the module.

3.1 The stretch rule

In Chapter 2 you were given a short list of standard formulae for moments of inertia. In fact, these formulae can be used for more shapes than are included in that list.

Moment of inertia is defined as $\sum m_i r_i^2$, where r_i is the distance of the ith particle from the axis of rotation. So, if you move the particle parallel to the axis, the moment of inertia doesn't change.

Take for example the rim of the bicycle wheel, whose moment of inertia was shown in Section 2.3 to be Mr^2. If you stretch this out parallel to the axis to make a tube of radius r, this is equivalent to moving some of the particles parallel to the axis, so the moment of inertia of the tube is still Mr^2.

> **Stretch rule**
>
> If a rigid object is transformed by a one-way stretch parallel to the axis of rotation, without changing the distribution of mass at various distances from the axis, the moment of inertia is unchanged.

If you apply this rule to the formulae for the moment of inertia of a rod, a disc and a solid sphere given in Section 2.3, you get formulae for a rectangle, a cylinder and a spheroid.

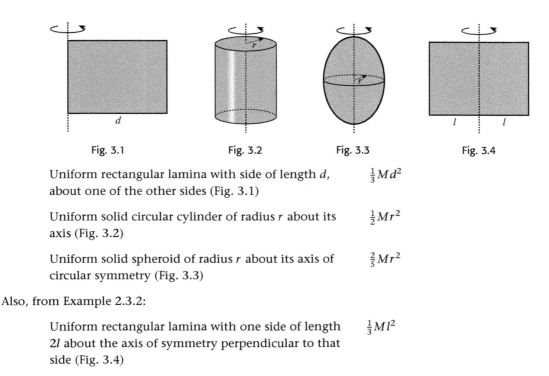

Fig. 3.1   Fig. 3.2   Fig. 3.3   Fig. 3.4

Uniform rectangular lamina with side of length d, $\frac{1}{3}Md^2$
about one of the other sides (Fig. 3.1)

Uniform solid circular cylinder of radius r about its $\frac{1}{2}Mr^2$
axis (Fig. 3.2)

Uniform solid spheroid of radius r about its axis of $\frac{2}{5}Mr^2$
circular symmetry (Fig. 3.3)

Also, from Example 2.3.2:

Uniform rectangular lamina with one side of length $\frac{1}{3}Ml^2$
$2l$ about the axis of symmetry perpendicular to that
side (Fig. 3.4)

But notice one omission from the list in Section 2.3. If you stretch a hollow
sphere parallel to the axis of rotation to form a hollow spheroid, the parts of the
surface near the ends of the axis will get stretched much less than those near the
central cross-section. The effect of stretching is therefore that the surface is no
longer uniform. That is the reason for including the words 'without changing the
distribution of mass' in the statement of the rule.

3.2   The perpendicular axes rule

Suppose that an object lies entirely in a plane; it
could be either a lamina or a wire (such as a ring),
and it needn't be uniform. The perpendicular axes
rule gives a method of calculating the moment of
inertia of the object about an axis perpendicular to
the plane.

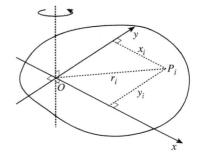

Suppose that the axis cuts the plane at O (Fig. 3.5). Then
the moment of inertia I is defined as $\sum m_i r_i^2$, where r_i is
the distance of the point P_i from O.

Fig. 3.5

To find r_i, you could take x- and y-axes in the plane, and define the position of P_i by its coordinates (x_i, y_i). Then $r_i^2 = x_i^2 + y_i^2$, so

$$I = \sum m_i(x_i^2 + y_i^2),$$

and this sum can be split into two parts as

$$I = \sum m_i x_i^2 + \sum m_i y_i^2.$$

Now x_i is the displacement of P_i from the y-axis, so $\sum m_i x_i^2$ is the moment of inertia of the object about the y-axis; this can be denoted by I_y. Similarly $\sum m_i y_i^2$ is I_x, the moment of inertia about the x-axis. The equation then becomes

$$I = I_y + I_x.$$

> **Perpendicular axes rule**
>
> For a rigid object which lies entirely in one plane, the moment of inertia about an axis at right angles to the plane, through a point O of the plane, is equal to the sum of the moments of inertia about two perpendicular axes in the plane through O.

You can use this rule to find more formulae for moments of inertia for special shapes.

Rectangles and cuboids

Fig. 3.6 shows a rectangular lamina having sides of length $2a$ and $2b$, with its axes of symmetry. It was shown in Section 3.1, using the stretch rule, that the moment of inertia about the axis up the page is $\frac{1}{3}Ma^2$; similarly, the moment of inertia about the axis across the page is $\frac{1}{3}Mb^2$. The perpendicular axes rule then shows that the moment of inertia of the lamina about the axis through the centre perpendicular to the plane is $\frac{1}{3}M(a^2 + b^2)$.

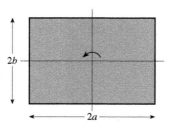

Fig. 3.6

Now stretch the lamina parallel to this axis, so that it becomes a uniform solid cuboid with edges of length $2a$, $2b$ and $2c$ (Fig. 3.7). This doesn't change the moment of inertia, so the moment of inertia of the cuboid about the axis through its centre parallel to the edges of length $2c$ is $\frac{1}{3}M(a^2 + b^2)$.

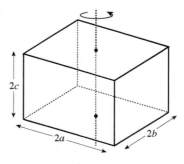

Fig. 3.7

Circular and elliptical laminas

You already know that, for a circular lamina, the moment of inertia about the axis through the centre perpendicular to the plane is $\frac{1}{2}Mr^2$. Now draw two perpendicular diameters of the disc (Fig. 3.8). Obviously, by symmetry, the moment of inertia of the disc about each of these diameters is the same; denote it by I. Then, using the perpendicular axes rule, $\frac{1}{2}Mr^2 = I + I$. It follows that $I = \frac{1}{4}Mr^2$.

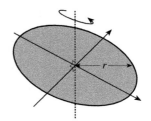

Now suppose that you have a uniform elliptical lamina, with axes of length $2a$ and $2b$ in the x- and y-directions respectively (Fig. 3.9). Denote the moments of inertia about these axes by I_x and I_y. If you stretch the lamina in the y-direction in the ratio $\frac{a}{b}$, it is transformed into a circular lamina of radius a. Since stretching doesn't change the moment of inertia I_y about the y-axis, it follows that $I_y = \frac{1}{4}Ma^2$. By a similar argument, $I_x = \frac{1}{4}Mb^2$.

Fig. 3.8

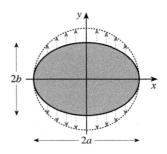

You can now apply the perpendicular axes rule again, to the elliptical lamina, to show that the moment of inertia about the axis through the centre perpendicular to the plane is $\frac{1}{4}M(a^2 + b^2)$.

Fig. 3.9

> It is very important to remember that the perpendicular axes rule applies only to objects which lie in a plane. You cannot use it for objects in three dimensions.

3.3 Symmetrical partitioning

Take a uniform shape whose moment of inertia you know about some axis, and cut it into two or more identical pieces. The shape can be a wire, a lamina, a shell or a solid. Then if all the pieces are related to the axis in the same way, you can find a formula for the moment of inertia of one of the pieces about the axis.

The method is best described by an example.

You know that the moment of inertia of a uniform solid sphere about a diameter is $\frac{2}{5}Mr^2$, where M is the mass and r the radius. (This is proved in Section 3.7.) Now partition the sphere into four quarters by perpendicular planes through the diameter; think of the way you cut up a tomato or an apple. Suppose that each quarter has mass m. What is the moment of inertia of one of the quarters about the diameter, in terms of m and r?

Clearly each of the quarters is related to the diameter in the same way; the diameter is the line in which the two cutting planes meet. So the moment of inertia of each of the quarters about the diameter is the same. If this moment of inertia is I, then the moment of inertia of the whole sphere is $4I$. Also, the mass of the whole sphere is $4m$. It follows that

$$4I = \frac{2}{5}(4m)r^2,$$

so that

$$I = \tfrac{2}{5}mr^2.$$

That is, the moment of inertia of one portion, of mass m, cut out of a sphere of radius r, is $\tfrac{2}{5}mr^2$.

> You may be surprised that the formula for the moment of inertia looks the same for one portion as for the whole sphere. But, of course, the mass m of the portion is not the same as the mass M of the sphere from which it is cut.

3.4*　Spherical shells

It was stated in Section 2.3 that the moment of inertia of a uniform hollow spherical shell of radius r is given by the formula $\tfrac{2}{3}Mr^2$. This can be proved by an argument similar to those used above, so it is convenient to give it here. You may omit this section if you wish.

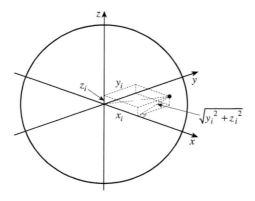

Fig. 3.10

Fig. 3.10 shows a spherical shell, with x-, y- and z-axes through its centre. If a typical particle with mass m_i is at a point (x_i, y_i, z_i) on the surface of the shell, and a perpendicular is drawn to the x-axis, the foot of the perpendicular is at $(x_i, 0, 0)$. The perpendicular distance to the x-axis is therefore $\sqrt{y_i^2 + z_i^2}$, so the moment of inertia I_x of the shell about the x-axis is $\sum m_i(y_i^2 + z_i^2)$. Similarly $I_y = \sum m_i(z_i^2 + x_i^2)$ and $I_z = \sum m_i(x_i^2 + y_i^2)$.

Now obviously the moment of inertia of the shell is the same about any diameter; denote it by I. Writing $I_x = I_y = I_z = I$,

$$\begin{aligned}
3I &= I_x + I_y + I_z \\
&= \sum m_i(y_i^2 + z_i^2) + \sum m_i(z_i^2 + x_i^2) + \sum m_i(x_i^2 + y_i^2) \\
&= \sum m_i(2x_i^2 + 2y_i^2 + 2z_i^2).
\end{aligned}$$

But (x_i, y_i, z_i) is on the surface of the sphere, $x_i^2 + y_i^2 + z_i^2 = r^2$, so

$$3I = \sum m_i(2r^2) = 2r^2 \sum m_i = 2Mr^2,$$

which gives $I = \frac{2}{3}Mr^2$.

This is the formula given in Section 2.3.

Exercise 3A

Some of these questions depend on answers to earlier questions in the exercise. This dependence is indicated by numbers in square brackets at the end of these questions.

1 A ring of radius r is formed from a length of uniform wire of mass M. Find its moment of inertia about a diameter.

Explain why you can't use the stretch rule to deduce from this the moment of inertia of an elliptical ring about its major axis.

2 A length of uniform wire of mass m is bent into the shape of a semicircle of radius r with ends A and B. By combining two such wires to make a complete ring, find the moment of inertia of the wire about the axis AB. [Q1]

3 A uniform solid cylinder of mass M has elliptical cross-section with axes of length $2a$ and $2b$. The central axis of the cylinder is perpendicular to this cross-section. Use the formula for the moment of inertia of an elliptical lamina to find the moment of inertia of the cylinder about this central axis.

4 A uniform square lamina of mass M has sides of length $2a$. Find its moment of inertia about

(a) an axis of symmetry parallel to one side,

(b) an axis through the centre perpendicular to its plane,

(c) a diagonal.

5 A uniform lamina of mass M in the shape of a rhombus has diagonals of length $2p$ and $2q$. Find its moment of inertia for rotation about

(a) the diagonal of length $2p$,

(b) the line through the centre perpendicular to its plane. [Q4]

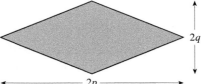

6 A uniform lamina of mass m in the shape of an isosceles triangle has base of length $2c$ and height h. Find formulae for its moment of inertia about

(a) the base,

(b) an axis through the mid-point of the base perpendicular to its plane. [Q5]

7 A wire of mass M is bent into the shape of a square of side $2a$. Find its moment of inertia about a diagonal.

8* In a plane, a *shear* is a transformation in which points move parallel to a fixed line through a distance which is proportional to their displacements from that line. If the x-axis is taken as the fixed line, the point (x, y) moves to $(x + ky, y)$ where k is a constant. For example, a shear transforms a rectangle with sides parallel to the axes into a parallelogram.

Prove the *shear rule*, that the moment of inertia of a lamina about any axis is unchanged by a shear transformation parallel to that axis.

9* State a formula for the moment of inertia of a parallelogram of mass M about an axis along one side, in terms of M and the distance h between that side and the parallel side. [Q8]

10* Use the shear rule to show that the moment of inertia of a uniform triangular lamina about its base depends only on the mass and the height. [Q6, Q8]

11* (a) The diagram shows a uniform square lamina with two axes at right angles to each other in the plane of the lamina through its centre. Explain why the moment of inertia of the lamina is the same about both axes. If the lamina has mass M and side $2a$, use the perpendicular axes rule to show that this moment of inertia is $\frac{1}{3}Ma^2$. [Q4]

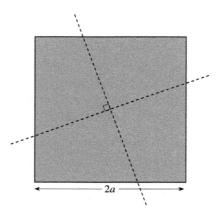

(b) This shows that the moment of inertia of a uniform square lamina is the same about any line in its plane through the centre of the square. Are there any other regular polygons with this property?

3.5 The summation principle

Many of the moments of inertia found in Sections 3.1 and 3.2 were derived from the formulae for the moment of inertia of a rod and of a circular disc, but these formulae haven't yet been proved. To do this, you need a new technique which involves integration. This is based on an idea called the 'summation principle'.

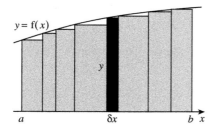

Fig. 3.11

Consider the area under a curve. If you didn't know about differentiation, you might try to find such areas as the sum of the areas of a lot of thin rectangles, as illustrated by the shaded region in Fig. 3.11. A typical one of these rectangles has been blacked in; it has height y (for that particular value of x) and width a small bit of the x-axis, which you could denote by δx. Then the area of this typical rectangle would be $y \times \delta x$, and the total area of all the rectangles could be written as $\sum y \delta x$.

This would not of course give you the area under the curve exactly, because of the small near-triangular bits that don't fit in. But you could argue that, if the number of rectangles were increased indefinitely, and the width of every rectangle correspondingly decreased, then in the limit the sum would tend to the required area. Symbolically, you could write

$$\lim \sum y \delta x = \int_a^b y \, dx.$$

The essential feature of the argument is that the bits that were left out were very small compared with the whole, and that they can be made as small as you like by making the widths of the rectangles small enough.

This is the basis of the **summation principle**, which can be applied to many calculations other than areas.

> If an interval of the x-axis $a < x < b$ is split into a large number of small pieces, of which a typical one has width δx; and if a quantity can be expressed approximately as a sum $\sum f(x) \delta x$, where the size of the error tends to zero as the widths of the rectangles tend to 0, then in the limit the sum $\sum f(x) \delta x$ tends to the integral $\int_a^b f(x) \, dx$.

As a second example, take the volume of a solid such as a loaf of bread. If you slice this up and then trim the crusts off square, then you get a situation like Fig. 3.11 but in three dimensions. A typical slice would have area A (which is a function of x) and thickness δx, so its volume would be $A \delta x$. The total volume would then be $\sum A \delta x$. The thinner you slice the bread, the less crust would be wasted, and in the limit the total volume of the loaf would be $\int_a^b A \, dx$. For the special case of a solid of revolution, for which $A = \pi y^2$, you get the familiar formula $\int_a^b \pi y^2 \, dx$ for the volume.

Example 3.5.1

A geographer makes a relief map on a scale of 1:1000. This includes the hill shown in Fig. 3.12, which has the shape formed by rotating the parabola with equation $y = 10 - \frac{1}{40}x^2$ about the y-axis. In the model the units are centimetres. Find the volume of the hill in the model.

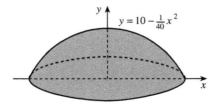

Fig. 3.12

From the equation, when $x = 0$ $y = 10$, so the height of the hill in the model is 10 cm.

One way of making such a model is to build it up as a pile of 'stepped discs', and then to file down the surface to get the smooth shape required. The thinner the discs, the less material has to be removed. Fig. 3.13 shows one such disc, whose lower surface has radius x cm, at a height y cm above the base. The thickness of the disc is δy cm, so its volume is $\pi x^2 \delta y$ cm^3. The total volume of the model before the edges are filed down can then be written as $\sum \pi x^2 \, \delta y$ cm^3.

The limiting value of $\sum \pi x^2 \, \delta y$ as the thickness of the discs tends to 0 is $\int_0^{10} \pi x^2 \, dy$. Notice that the limits of integration correspond to the interval of values of y needed to make the complete model hill.

The integral can be calculated using the equation $y = 10 - \frac{1}{40} x^2$ in the form $x^2 = 40(10 - y)$. Then

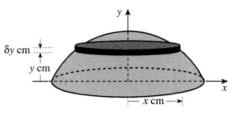

Fig. 3.13

$$\int_0^{10} \pi x^2 \, dy = \int_0^{10} \pi(400 - 40y) \, dy$$
$$= \left[\pi(400y - 20y^2) \right]_0^{10}$$
$$= \pi(4000 - 2000)$$
$$= 2000\pi.$$

In the model the volume of the hill is 2000π cm^3, which is approximately 6280 cm^3.

3.6 Finding moments of inertia by integration

Since the definition of moment of inertia involves splitting objects into a lot of small parts and summing $m_i r_i^2$ for each part, the summation principle can be used to find moments of inertia. This section and the next give a variety of examples. These include the standard results for uniform rods, circular discs and solid spheres.

Rods

The method will be used to find the moment of inertia of a uniform rod of mass M and length $2l$ about a perpendicular axis, first at one end and then at the centre.

Fig. 3.14a shows the rod rotating about an axis through the end O, which is taken as the origin. Imagine this rod split into a lot of small pieces, of which a typical one has length δx at a displacement between x and $x + \delta x$ from O, shaded black in the figure. Since the mass per unit length of the rod is $\frac{M}{2l}$, this typical piece has mass $\frac{M\delta x}{2l}$. Its moment of inertia about the axis is therefore approximately $\frac{M\delta x}{2l} x^2$, so the moment of inertia of the whole rod about O is $\sum \frac{M}{2l} x^2 \, \delta x$.

In the limit, as the length of the pieces tends to 0, this becomes

$$\int_0^{2l} \frac{M}{2l} x^2 \, dx = \left[\frac{M}{6l} x^3 \right]_0^{2l} = \frac{M}{6l} \times 8l^3 = \tfrac{4}{3} M l^2.$$

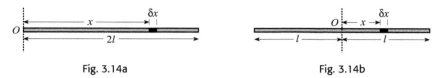

Fig. 3.14a   Fig. 3.14b

The only difference for the rod rotating about an axis through its centre is that the origin is taken at the centre of the rod, so that the integration is from $-l$ to l rather than from 0 to $2l$ (see Fig. 3.14b). The moment of inertia is therefore

$$\int_{-l}^{l} \frac{M}{2l} x^2 \, dx = \left[\frac{M}{6l} x^3 \right]_{-l}^{l} = \frac{M}{6l} \times 2l^3 = \tfrac{1}{3} M l^2.$$

These are the results which were given without proof at the end of Section 2.3.

General laminas

The shape of a lamina is often defined by giving the equation of the graph forming its boundary. The method of finding the moment of inertia in such cases is illustrated by three examples.

Example 3.6.1

A ceremonial gateway is surmounted by a decorated signboard having the shape of Fig. 3.15. The curve has equation $y = 3 \sin x$ for values of x from 0 to π, the units being metres. It is made of plywood of mass 2 kg per square metre. Calculate its moment of inertia about its lower edge.

To find the moment of inertia you don't need to break the lamina down into its basic small particles. The technique is to split it into small elements whose moment of inertia you already know how to find. In this case, you can approximate to the shape of the board by strips parallel to the y-axis of width δx; a typical strip is shaded black in the figure. This is a rectangle of length $3 \sin x$ metres.

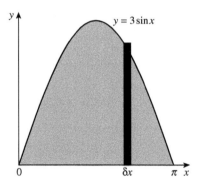

Fig. 3.15

The area of this rectangle is $3 \sin x \, \delta x \, \text{m}^2$, so its mass is $2 \times 3 \sin x \, \delta x \, \text{kg}$. Using the formula $\tfrac{1}{3} M d^2$ for the moment of inertia of a rectangle of length d about a perpendicular side, the moment of inertia is $\tfrac{1}{3} (2 \times 3 \sin x \, \delta x) \times (3 \sin x)^2 \, \text{kg m}^2$. So the moment of inertia of the complete signboard can be approximated as $\sum 18 \sin^3 x \, \delta x \, \text{kg m}^2$.

To get the exact moment of inertia, let the width of the strips tend to 0, which smooths out the boundary of the board. The sum then becomes $\int_0^\pi 18\sin^3 x\,dx$, which can be evaluated as

$$\int_0^\pi 18(1 - \cos^2 x)\sin x\,dx = \int_0^\pi 18\sin x\,dx - \int_0^\pi 18\cos^2 x\sin x\,dx.$$

The first of these integrals can be evaluated directly, and the second can be found by substituting $u = \cos x$, so that $\dfrac{du}{dx} = -\sin x$. This gives

$$\left[-18\cos x\right]_0^\pi + \int_1^{-1} 18u^2\,du = 18 - (-18) + \left[6u^3\right]_1^{-1} = 36 + (-6 - 6) = 24.$$

The moment of inertia of the signboard about the lower edge is therefore $24\,\text{kg m}^2$.

Example 3.6.2

Find a formula for the moment of inertia about the y-axis of a uniform triangular lamina of mass M with vertices at the points $(0, 0)$, $(2a, 0)$ and $(0, a)$.

Notice that the area of the lamina is $\frac{1}{2} \times 2a \times a = a^2$, so the mass per unit area is $\dfrac{M}{a^2}$.

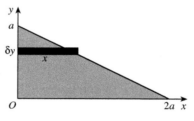

Fig. 3.16

Since you want the moment of inertia about the y-axis, you could draw rectangles parallel to the x-axis, as shown in Fig. 3.16. A typical rectangle has width δy and length x. The mass is therefore $\dfrac{M}{a^2} x\,\delta y$, and the moment of inertia about the y-axis is $\frac{1}{3} \times \left(\dfrac{M}{a^2} x\,\delta y\right) \times x^2$. The moment of inertia of all the rectangles is therefore given by $\sum \dfrac{M}{3a^2} x^3\,\delta y$.

In the limit, as the width of the strips tends to 0, the exact value of the moment of inertia of the triangle is given by $\int_0^a \dfrac{M}{3a^2} x^3\,dy$.

Before you can evaluate this, you have to express x in terms of y. The equation of the line joining $(0, a)$ to $(2a, 0)$ is $y = a - \frac{1}{2}x$. This must be rearranged as $x = 2(a - y)$ and then substituted in the integral to give the moment of inertia as

$$\int_0^a \dfrac{M}{3a^2} \times 8(a - y)^3\,dy = \dfrac{M}{3a^2}\left[-2(a - y)^4\right]_0^a = \dfrac{M}{3a^2} \times 2a^4 = \tfrac{2}{3}Ma^2.$$

The moment of inertia of the triangular lamina about the y-axis is $\frac{2}{3}Ma^2$.

In Example 3.6.2 it was quite easy to rearrange the equation of the line to express x as a function of y. However, this isn't always so easy, and it may be impossible. In such cases it is better to split the region into rectangles parallel to the y-axis, as was done in Example 3.6.1. The next example illustrates the method.

Example 3.6.3

The rudder of a ship is in the shape of the region bounded by the positive x- and y-axes and the curve $y = 3 - x - \frac{1}{4}x^2$, the units being metres. The rudder is uniform and of mass 200 kg. It can turn about hinges along the y-axis. Find the moment of inertia of the rudder about the hinges. (See Fig. 3.17.)

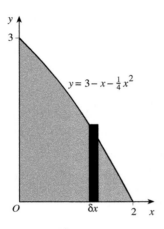

Fig. 3.17

At some stage in the calculation you will need to know the mass per unit area of the rudder, so it helps to begin by finding the area. This is given, in m^2, by

$$\int_0^2 (3 - x - \tfrac{1}{4}x^2)\, dx = \left[3x - \tfrac{1}{2}x^2 - \tfrac{1}{12}x^3\right]_0^2 = 6 - 2 - \tfrac{2}{3} = \tfrac{10}{3}.$$

The mass per unit area is therefore $200 \div \frac{10}{3}\ kg\,m^{-2}$, which is $60\ kg\,m^{-2}$.

From the equation you will notice that, to express x as a function of y, you would have to solve a quadratic equation, and the resulting expression would involve square roots. It is simpler to split the region into rectangles parallel to the y-axis, of width δx and area $y\,\delta x$. The mass of a typical rectangle is then $60y\,\delta x$ kg.

It is very easy to find the approximate moment of inertia of the rectangle about the y-axis, since all points are at approximately the same distance, x metres, from that axis. The moment of inertia of the rectangle is therefore approximately $(60y\,\delta x) \times x^2\ kg\,m^2$, and the moment of inertia of the whole rudder is $\sum 60x^2 y\,\delta x\ kg\,m^2$.

Taking the limit in the usual way, the sum becomes

$$\int_0^2 60x^2 y\, dx = \int_0^2 60x^2(3 - x - \tfrac{1}{4}x^2)\, dx = \int_0^2 (180x^2 - 60x^3 - 15x^4)\, dx$$
$$= \left[60x^3 - 15x^4 - 3x^5\right]_0^2 = 480 - 240 - 96 = 144.$$

The moment of inertia of the rudder about the hinges is $144\ kg\,m^2$.

Exercise 3B

1 A uniform lamina is bounded by the positive x- and y-axes and the portion of the graph of $y = \cos x$ for which $0 < x < \frac{1}{2}\pi$, the units being metres. The mass per unit area is $3\,\text{kg}\,\text{m}^{-2}$. Find the moment of inertia of the lamina about

   (a) the x-axis,   (b) the y-axis.

2 A uniform lamina has the form of the region between $y = 1 - x^2$ and the x-axis, the units being metres. The total mass of the lamina is $4\,\text{kg}$. Find its moment of inertia about

   (a) the x-axis,   (b) the y-axis,

   (c) the axis through the origin perpendicular to its plane.

3 A lamina is bounded by the lines $x = 0$, $y = 0$, $x = a$ and part of the curve $y = a\,e^{-x/a}$. The mass per unit area is k. Find, in terms of a and k, the moment of inertia of the lamina about

   (a) the x-axis,   (b) the y-axis.

4 A billiard cue of length 1 metre is tapered so that, at a distance x metres from one end, the mass per unit length is given by the formula $\frac{1}{4}(3 - 2x)^2 \,\text{kg}\,\text{m}^{-1}$. Find its mass, and the moment of inertia about a perpendicular axis at its heavy end.

5 Use integration to find the moment of inertia of a uniform rod of length a and mass M about an axis through one end at an angle α to the line of the rod.

   The rod is supported by a universal joint at one end. It rotates about a vertical axis at an angle α to the downward vertical with constant angular speed ω. Find an expression for its kinetic energy.

6 Solve Example 3.6.2 by the method used in Example 3.6.3.

7 A uniform semicircular lamina of mass M is defined by the region between the curve $x^2 + y^2 = r^2$ and the y-axis for $0 < x < r$. By considering a typical rectangle of width δx parallel to the y-axis, show that the moment of inertia of the lamina about the y-axis is given by $\dfrac{4M}{\pi r^2} \displaystyle\int_0^r x^2\sqrt{r^2 - x^2}\,dx$. Use the substitution $x = r\sin u$ to find the integral, and deduce a formula for the moment of inertia.

8 A uniform lamina of mass M is in the form of an isosceles triangle with base of length $2c$ and height h. By considering a typical rectangle parallel to the base, find formulae for the moments of inertia

   (a) about the base,   (b) about the axis of symmetry.

9 A uniform lamina occupies the region under the graph of $y = f(x)$ between $x = a$ and $x = b$, which lies entirely in the first quadrant. If the mass per unit area is k, write expressions as integrals for the moment of inertia about the x- and y-axes.

3.7 Shapes with circular symmetry

Solids of revolution

It was shown in Section 3.5 that to find the volume of an object in the form of a solid of revolution, you can imagine it to be split into thin slices perpendicular to the axis of symmetry, so that each slice can be approximated as a disc. The same method is used to find the moment of inertia.

Example 3.7.1

A solid piece of wood is carved into the shape formed by rotating about the y-axis that part of the parabola $y = \frac{1}{10}(1 - x^2)$ for which $y \geqslant 0$. The units are metres and the density of the wood is $600\,\mathrm{kg\,m^{-3}}$. Find the moment of inertia about the y-axis.

You can begin by considering a solid made up of thin discs with centres on the y-axis, similar to that in Example 3.5.1. Find an expression for the moment of inertia of this solid, and then consider the limit as the thickness of the discs tends to 0.

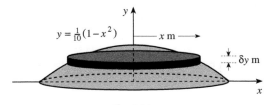

Fig. 3.18

Fig. 3.18 (which is not drawn to scale) shows a typical disc with radius x m and thickness δy m. Its volume is $\pi x^2 \delta y \,\mathrm{m^3}$. Therefore, since $1\,\mathrm{m^3}$ of the wood has mass $600\,\mathrm{kg}$, the mass of the disc is $600\pi x^2 \delta y\,\mathrm{kg}$. You can now use the formula $\frac{1}{2} \times$ mass $\times$ radius^2 for the moment of inertia of a disc about a perpendicular axis through its centre; this gives the moment of inertia of the disc about the y-axis as $\frac{1}{2} \times (600\pi x^2 \delta y) \times x^2\,\mathrm{kg\,m^2}$, which is $300\pi x^4 \delta y\,\mathrm{kg\,m^2}$. The moment of inertia of the solid made up of all the discs is therefore $\sum 300\pi x^4 \delta y\,\mathrm{kg\,m^2}$.

The interval of values of y in which the solid lies is $0 \leqslant y \leqslant 0.1$. Therefore, in the limit, the expression $\sum 300\pi x^4 \delta y$ tends to $\int_0^{0.1} 300\pi x^4 \,\mathrm{d}y$ with $y = \frac{1}{10}(1 - x^2)$, so that $x^2 = 1 - 10y$. That is,

$$
\begin{aligned}
\int_0^{0.1} 300\pi x^4 \,\mathrm{d}y &= \int_0^{0.1} \pi(300 - 6000y + 30\,000y^2)\,\mathrm{d}y \\
&= \left[\pi(300y - 3000y^2 + 10\,000y^3)\right]_0^{0.1} \\
&= \pi(30 - 30 + 10) \\
&= 10\pi.
\end{aligned}
$$

The moment of inertia of the solid about the y-axis is $10\pi\,\mathrm{kg\,m^2}$, which is approximately $31.4\,\mathrm{kg\,m^2}$.

There is no easy way of checking the answer to a calculation like this, but you can sometimes see if it is of the right order of magnitude by comparing it with the moment of inertia of a similar solid of standard shape. For example, you might guess that the solid in Example 3.7.1 is not too different from a cylinder of radius 1 m and height $\frac{1}{20}$ m (half the height of the solid), whose volume is $\pi \times 1^2 \times \frac{1}{20}$ m^3. If made of the same material as the solid, its mass would be $\frac{1}{20}\pi \times 600$ kg, which is 30π kg. The moment of inertia of the cylinder is therefore given by the formula $\frac{1}{2}Mr^2$ as $\frac{1}{2} \times 30\pi \times 1^2$ kg m^2, which is 15π kg m^2. This suggests that the answer to Example 3.7.1 is about the right size, especially since the mass of the solid is concentrated rather more towards the y-axis than the mass of the cylinder.

The summation method can be used to prove some of the formulae for solids of standard shapes, such as cones and spheres.

Example 3.7.2

Find a formula for the moment of inertia of a uniform circular cone with height h and base radius r about its axis of symmetry.

Although the question refers to the 'height' and the 'base', you will probably find it simplest to work with the vertex of the cone at the origin and the axis of symmetry along the x-axis, as shown in Fig. 3.19. The cone is then the solid formed by rotating about the x-axis the region contained inside the triangle with vertices at $(0, 0)$, $(h, 0)$ and (h, r).

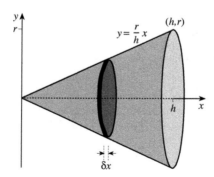

Fig. 3.19

A typical disc, of thickness δx, at a distance x along the axis, has radius $\dfrac{rx}{h}$. Its volume is therefore $\pi \left(\dfrac{rx}{h} \right)^2 \delta x$.

The volume of the cone is $\frac{1}{3}\pi r^2 h$; so, if its mass is M, the mass per unit volume is $\dfrac{3M}{\pi r^2 h}$. It follows that the mass of a typical disc is $\dfrac{3M}{\pi r^2 h} \times \pi \dfrac{r^2 x^2}{h^2} \delta x$, which can be simplified to $\dfrac{3M}{h^3} x^2 \delta x$.

You can now use the formula for the moment of inertia of a disc about the perpendicular axis of circular symmetry, to show that the moment of inertia about the x-axis of the typical disc is $\frac{1}{2} \times \left(\dfrac{3M}{h^3} x^2 \delta x \right) \times \left(\dfrac{rx}{h} \right)^2$, which is $\dfrac{3Mr^2}{2h^5} x^4 \delta x$.

From this, by the usual argument, it follows that the moment of inertia of the whole cone about the x-axis is

$$\int_0^h \frac{3Mr^2}{2h^5} x^4 \, dx = \frac{3Mr^2}{2h^5} \left[\tfrac{1}{5} x^5 \right]_0^h = \frac{3Mr^2}{2h^5} \times \frac{h^5}{5} = \tfrac{3}{10} Mr^2.$$

The moment of inertia of the cone about its axis of symmetry is $\tfrac{3}{10} Mr^2$.

Solid spheres

A solid sphere of radius r is a special case of a solid of revolution, so you can find its moment of inertia about a diameter by the method used in Example 3.7.2. There is another method of getting the answer which uses the formula $\tfrac{2}{3} Mr^2$ for a spherical shell, proved in Section 3.4; both are given here, but you can omit the second method if you wish.

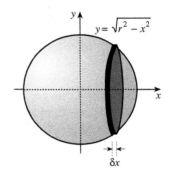

Method 1 Fig. 3.20 shows the sphere regarded as a solid formed by rotating the region under the curve $y = \sqrt{r^2 - x^2}$ from $x = -r$ to $x = r$ about the x-axis.

Fig. 3.20

Notice first that the mass per unit volume is $M \div \tfrac{4}{3} \pi r^3$, which is $\dfrac{3M}{4\pi r^3}$. You can then list the various stages in the calculation as follows.

Dimensions of typical disc: radius $\sqrt{r^2 - x^2}$, thickness δx

Volume of typical disc: $\pi \left(\sqrt{r^2 - x^2} \right)^2 \delta x = \pi (r^2 - x^2) \, \delta x$

Mass of typical disc: $\dfrac{3M}{4\pi r^3} \times \pi (r^2 - x^2) \, \delta x = \dfrac{3M}{4r^3} (r^2 - x^2) \, \delta x$

Moment of inertia of typical disc: $\tfrac{1}{2} \times \left(\dfrac{3M}{4r^3} (r^2 - x^2) \, \delta x \right) \times \left(\sqrt{r^2 - x^2} \right)^2$

$$= \frac{3M}{8r^3} (r^2 - x^2)^2 \, \delta x.$$

It follows that the moment of inertia for the whole solid sphere is

$$\int_{-r}^r \frac{3M}{8r^3} (r^2 - x^2)^2 \, dx = \int_{-r}^r \frac{3M}{8r^3} (r^4 - 2r^2 x^2 + x^4) \, dx = \frac{3M}{8r^3} \left[r^4 x - \tfrac{2}{3} r^2 x^3 + \tfrac{1}{5} x^5 \right]_{-r}^r$$

$$= \frac{3M}{8r^3} \times \left(2 - \tfrac{2}{3} \times 2 + \tfrac{1}{5} \times 2 \right) r^5 = \frac{3M}{8r^3} \times \tfrac{16}{15} r^5 = \tfrac{2}{5} Mr^2.$$

Method 2* Instead of imagining the sphere as made up of discs, you can think of it as a collection of spherical shells, one inside another, with radii varying from 0 to r, rather like the structure of an onion.

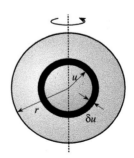

This is illustrated in Fig. 3.21, which you must try to visualise in three dimensions; the black region represents a typical spherical shell, of radius u and thickness δu. The surface area of this shell is $4\pi u^2$, so its volume is approximately $4\pi u^2 \, \delta u$.

Fig. 3.21

The mass per unit volume is of course the same as for Method 1, so the mass of the typical shell is $\dfrac{3M}{4\pi r^3} \times 4\pi u^2\,\delta u$, which can be simplified as $\dfrac{3M}{r^3}u^2\,\delta u$. From this, using the formula proved in Section 3.4, the moment of inertia of the typical shell is approximately $\tfrac{2}{3} \times \dfrac{3M}{r^3}u^2\,\delta u \times u^2$ which is $\dfrac{2M}{r^3}u^4\,\delta u$.

Therefore, for the whole sphere, the moment of inertia is

$$\int_0^r \frac{2M}{r^3}u^4\,du = \frac{2M}{r^3}\left[\tfrac{1}{5}u^5\right]_0^r = \frac{2M}{r^3} \times \tfrac{1}{5}r^5 = \tfrac{2}{5}Mr^2.$$

Whichever method you use, you will recognise the answer as the formula listed in Section 2.3.

Discs*

There is still one gap in the reasoning. The solid of revolution calculations earlier in this section made use of the formula for the moment of inertia of a circular lamina about a perpendicular axis, but this hasn't yet been proved. You could do this by the methods of Section 3.6 (see Exercise 3B Question 7) and then use the perpendicular axes rule, but it is much easier to use the two-dimensional equivalent of Method 2 for the solid sphere.

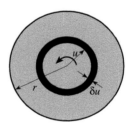

Fig. 3.22

Fig. 3.22 looks very like Fig. 3.21, but this time it is two-dimensional, and the black region represents a ring of radius u and width δu. This ring has circumference $2\pi u$, so its area is approximately $2\pi u\,\delta u$. Also, the mass per unit area is $\dfrac{M}{\pi r^2}$, so the mass of the ring is $\dfrac{M}{\pi r^2} \times 2\pi u\,\delta u$, which is $\dfrac{2M}{r^2}u\,\delta u$.

Now all the points of the ring are approximately at a distance u from the axis of rotation, so the moment of inertia of the ring is approximately $\dfrac{2M}{r^2}u\,\delta u \times u^2$, which is $\dfrac{2M}{r^2}u^3\,\delta u$. So if you sum and take the limit in the usual way, you get the moment of inertia of the disc to be

$$\int_0^r \frac{2M}{r^2}u^3\,du = \frac{2M}{r^2}\left[\tfrac{1}{4}u^4\right]_0^r = \frac{2M}{r^2} \times \tfrac{1}{4}r^4 = \tfrac{1}{2}Mr^2.$$

This proves the last of the entries in the list in Section 2.3, and validates the proofs for the cone and the sphere given above.

Exercise 3C

1 A spindle is made of wood of density $0.0008\,\text{kg cm}^{-3}$. It has the shape formed by rotating about the x-axis the region bounded by the x-axis and by the part of the curve $y = \tfrac{1}{10}\sqrt{x(30-x)}$ for which y exists, the units being centimetres. Find the moment of inertia of the spindle about the axis of rotation.

2 The diagram shows a solid formed by rotating the region under the curve $y = \sqrt{16 + x^2}$ for $-3 \leqslant x \leqslant 3$ about the x-axis. The units are centimetres. The solid is made of metal with density $0.005\,\text{kg}\,\text{cm}^{-3}$. Calculate its moment of inertia about the x-axis in $\text{kg}\,\text{cm}^2$.

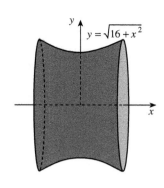

3 The diagram shows a solid formed by rotating about the y-axis the region bounded by the curve $y = \sqrt{16 + x^2}$ for $-3 \leqslant x \leqslant 3$ and the line $y = 5$. The units are centimetres. The solid is made of metal with density $0.005\,\text{kg}\,\text{cm}^{-3}$. Calculate its moment of inertia about the y-axis in $\text{kg}\,\text{cm}^2$.

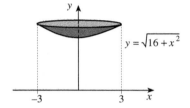

4 A spinning top has a shape obtained by rotating the graph of $y = \frac{1}{2}x\sqrt{4 - x}$ for $0 \leqslant x \leqslant 4$ about the x-axis, the units being centimetres. Its density is 0.9 gram cm^{-3}. Find, in gram cm^2, the moment of inertia of the top about its axis of symmetry.

5 A small machine component is made of solid metal of density 5 gram cm^{-3}. Its shape is obtained by rotating the graph of $y = 2^{-x}\ (= e^{-kx}$, where $k = \ln 2)$ from $x = 0$ to $x = 1$ about the x-axis, the units being centimetres. Find the mass of the component in grams, and its moment of inertia about the x-axis in gram cm^2.

6 A uniform solid is formed by rotating about the x-axis the curve $y = \sqrt{ax}$ from $x = 0$ to $x = a$. If the mass of the solid is M, find an expression for its moment of inertia about the x-axis in terms of M and a.

7 A uniform solid of mass M has the shape obtained by rotating the ellipse with equation $\dfrac{x^2}{a^2} + \dfrac{y^2}{b^2} = 1$, where $a > b$, about the y-axis (see diagram). Use integration to find a formula for the moment of inertia of the solid about the y-axis, in terms of M and a. Why does the formula not involve b?

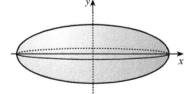

8 The diagram shows a design for an artillery shell. The curved nose has the shape of $y = 5(1 - 0.01x^2)$ from $x = 0$ to $x = 10$, the units being centimetres, rotated about the x-axis. The interior of the shell is uniform with density 4 gram cm^{-3}. Find the mass of the shell in kg, and the moment of inertia about its axis in $\text{kg}\,\text{m}^2$.

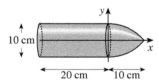

9 A uniform solid of mass M is formed by rotating the region under $y = f(x)$ between $x = a$ and $x = b$ about the x-axis. Show that its moment of inertia about the axis is

$$\tfrac{1}{2} M \frac{\displaystyle\int_a^b (f(x))^4 \, dx}{\displaystyle\int_a^b (f(x))^2 \, dx}.$$

Use this formula to obtain the answer to Example 3.7.2.

3.8 The parallel axes rule

There is one more rule which is useful when you want to find moments of inertia. This connects the moment of inertia about any axis with the moment of inertia about the parallel axis through the centre of mass.

> **Parallel axes rule**
>
> If I denotes the moment of inertia of a rigid object of mass M about some axis, and I_G denotes the moment of inertia about the parallel axis through the centre of mass, then $I = I_G + Ma^2$, where a is the perpendicular distance between the two axes.

Before proving this rule, here are two examples to show how it can be used.

Example 3.8.1

A uniform circular lamina of radius r and mass M has a small hole at a distance $\tfrac{1}{2}r$ from its centre. The lamina rotates about an axis perpendicular to its plane through the hole. Find the moment of inertia.

> The centre of mass of the lamina is at the centre of the circle, and you know that the moment of inertia about the perpendicular axis through the centre is $\tfrac{1}{2}Mr^2$. The parallel axes rule shows that the moment of inertia about the parallel axis through the hole is $\tfrac{1}{2}Mr^2 + M\left(\tfrac{1}{2}r\right)^2$, which is $\tfrac{3}{4}Mr^2$.

Unlike the perpendicular axes rule, applications of the parallel axes rule are not restricted to laminas. However, it is important to notice that the parallel axes rule only holds if one of the axes passes through the centre of mass. In the next example you want to link the moments of inertia about two parallel axes neither of which passes through the centre of mass. To do this, you have to introduce a third parallel axis through the centre of mass, and link the moment of inertia about this third axis with the moment of inertia about each of the other two.

Example 3.8.2

On a uniform solid hemisphere, O is the centre and T is the point where the axis of symmetry meets the curved surface. The hemisphere rotates about an axis which is a tangent to the hemisphere at T. Find the moment of inertia of the hemisphere about this axis in terms of the mass M and the radius r.

You know, from M2 Section 10.3, that the centre of mass of the hemisphere is at a point G on OT such that $OG = \frac{3}{8}r$, so $GT = \frac{5}{8}r$ (see Fig. 3.23). But it would be very complicated to try to find the moment of inertia about the axis through G parallel to the axis of rotation through T. However, it is easy to find the moment of inertia about a parallel axis through O by using the method of symmetrical partitioning (see Section 3.3).

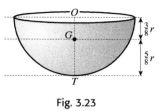

Fig. 3.23

If you take another identical hemisphere and place it upside down on the given one, then the two hemispheres would together make a sphere of mass $2M$. The moment of inertia of this sphere about any axis through O is $\frac{2}{5}(2M)r^2$, which is $\frac{4}{5}Mr^2$. As both hemispheres clearly have the same moment of inertia about an axis in their common plane, the moment of inertia for each must be one-half of $\frac{4}{5}Mr^2$, which is $\frac{2}{5}Mr^2$.

Let the moments of inertia of the hemisphere about the three parallel axes through O, G and T be denoted by I_O, I_G and I_T. You can't use the parallel axes rule to connect I_O and I_T directly, but you can connect both with I_G. The equations are

$$I_O = I_G + M\left(\tfrac{3}{8}r\right)^2 \quad \text{and} \quad I_T = I_G + M\left(\tfrac{5}{8}r\right)^2.$$

Subtracting the first equation from the second then gives

$$I_T - I_O = \tfrac{25}{64}Mr^2 - \tfrac{9}{64}Mr^2 = \tfrac{1}{4}Mr^2.$$

Therefore, substituting $I_O = \frac{2}{5}Mr^2$, $I_T = \frac{2}{5}Mr^2 + \frac{1}{4}Mr^2 = \frac{13}{20}Mr^2$.

The moment of inertia about the tangent to the hemisphere at T is $\frac{13}{20}Mr^2$.

The parallel axes rule can be proved directly from the definition of moment of inertia given in Section 2.2 as $\sum m_i r_i^2$. Fig. 3.24 represents a rigid object, modelled as a set of particles, with an axis of rotation through G and a parallel axis of rotation at a distance a from it. Let A be the point on the second axis of rotation such that GA is perpendicular to the two parallel axes.

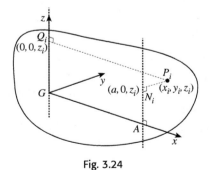

Fig. 3.24

Now set up a coordinate system. Take G as origin, GA as the x-axis, and the axis of rotation through G as the z-axis. This fixes the y-axis, perpendicular to the x- and z-axes. Since $GA = a$, the coordinates of A are $(a, 0, 0)$.

Let P_i with coordinates (x_i, y_i, z_i) be the position of a particle of mass m_i. If you draw lines $P_i Q_i$ and $P_i N_i$ perpendicular to the two axes of rotation, the coordinates of Q_i are $(0, 0, z_i)$ and the coordinates of N_i are $(a, 0, z_i)$.

Denote the moments of inertia of the object about the two axes of rotation by I_G and I_A. Then, from the definition,

$$I_G = \sum m_i P_i Q_i^2 = \sum m_i (x_i^2 + y_i^2), \quad \text{and}$$

$$I_A = \sum m_i P_i N_i^2 = \sum m_i ((x_i - a)^2 + y_i^2)$$
$$= \sum m_i (x_i^2 - 2ax_i + a^2 + y_i^2)$$

which you can write as

$$I_A = \sum m_i (x_i^2 + y_i^2) - \sum 2am_i x_i + \sum m_i a^2$$
$$= I_G - 2a \sum m_i x_i + a^2 \sum m_i.$$

The proof has not yet used the fact that G is the centre of mass. To do this, you can make use of the general formula for the centre of mass given in M2 Section 5.2, which can be written in sigma notation as

$$\bar{x} = \frac{\sum m_i x_i}{M} \quad \text{where} \quad M = \sum m_i.$$

In this proof, the centre of mass has been taken to be the origin, so $\bar{x} = 0$. It follows that $\sum m_i x_i = 0$. So the equation for I_A becomes

$$I_A = I_G - 2a \times 0 + a^2 M, \quad \text{or more simply} \quad I_A = I_G + Ma^2.$$

This is the parallel axes rule.

An important consequence of the rule is that, if $a \neq 0$, then $I_A > I_G$. That is, of all the possible axes of rotation in a given direction, the moment of inertia is least for rotation about the axis through the centre of mass.

If you have done module S1, it may have occurred to you that moment of inertia about an axis through G is rather like variance in statistics. The former measures how closely the particles cluster round the axis through G; the latter measures how closely the data cluster round the mean. The parallel axes rule is the equivalent in mechanics of the rule

$$\text{variance} = \frac{1}{n} \sum x_i^2 - \bar{x}^2,$$

given in S1 Section 3.6.

3.9   Integration using the parallel axes rule

Sometimes, when you use integration to find a moment of inertia, you need to apply the parallel axes rule before integrating. This occurs, for example, when you have a cylinder, cone or pyramid which rotates about an axis at right angles to the axis of symmetry. The method is best explained with an example.

Example 3.9.1

A uniform cylinder of mass 900 grams has radius 4 cm and height 12 cm. Find its moment of inertia about a diameter p of the base.

Imagine the cylinder to be made of a pile of thin uniform discs. A typical disc, with radius 4 cm and height δy cm, is shown in Fig. 3.25. Because the cylinder is uniform, its mass is a fraction $\dfrac{\delta y}{12}$ of the total mass of the cylinder, which is 900 grams. The mass of the disc is therefore $75\,\delta y$ grams.

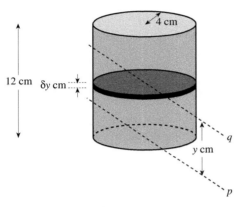

Fig. 3.25

Now if you can find the moment of inertia of this disc about a diameter q parallel to p (see Fig. 3.25), you can use the parallel axes rule to find its moment of inertia about p.

If δy is small enough, you could say that the disc is approximately a lamina of no thickness, with mass $75\,\delta y$ grams and radius 4 cm. The moment of inertia of such a lamina about a diameter is given by the formula $\frac{1}{4} \times$ mass of lamina $\times$ radius^2 (see Section 3.2) to be $\frac{1}{4} \times (75\,\delta y) \times 4^2$ gram cm^2, which is $300\,\delta y$ gram cm^2.

The distance between the axes p and q is y cm, so by the parallel axes rule the moment of inertia of the disc about the axis p is

$$(300\,\delta y + 75\,\delta y \times y^2)\ \text{gram cm}^2.$$

To get the moment of inertia of the whole cylinder about p you must add the contributions from all the discs, which gives the approximate expression

$$\sum (300\,\delta y + 75\,\delta y \times y^2)\ \text{gram cm}^2.$$

In the limit, as the thickness of the discs tends to 0, the sum tends to

$$\int_0^{12} (300 + 75y^2)\,\mathrm{d}y = \left[300y + 25y^3\right]_0^{12}$$
$$= 3600 + 43\,200$$
$$= 46\,800.$$

The moment of inertia of the cylinder about the axis p is $46\,800$ gram cm^2, or 46.8 kg cm^2.

Example 3.9.2

For the circular cone in Example 3.7.2, find the moment of inertia about an axis through the vertex perpendicular to the axis of symmetry.

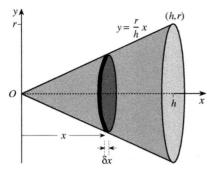

Fig. 3.26

Fig. 3.26 is similar to Fig. 3.19. The question now asks for the moment of inertia about an axis through the vertex O perpendicular to the x-axis; it makes no difference which axis of rotation you choose, so it is simplest to follow the argument by finding the moment of inertia about the y-axis.

Taking a typical disc of width δx as in Example 3.7.2, you want to begin by finding the moment of inertia of the disc about the y-axis. Now, approximating the thin disc as a circular lamina, you know how to find its moment of inertia about the diameter parallel to the y-axis; but to find its moment of inertia about the y-axis you have to use the parallel axes rule.

It was shown in Example 3.7.2 that the typical disc has mass $\dfrac{3M}{h^3}x^2\,\delta x$ and radius $\dfrac{rx}{h}$. The moment of inertia about a diameter is then found using '$\frac{1}{4} \times$ mass $\times$ radius^2' (see Section 3.2), as $\frac{1}{4} \times \left(\dfrac{3M}{h^3}x^2\,\delta x\right) \times \left(\dfrac{rx}{h}\right)^2$, which is $\dfrac{3Mr^2}{4h^5}x^4\,\delta x$. Therefore, by the parallel axes rule, the moment of inertia of the disc about the y-axis is approximately

$$\frac{3Mr^2}{4h^5}x^4\,\delta x + \left(\frac{3M}{h^3}x^2\,\delta x\right) \times x^2 = \frac{3M(r^2 + 4h^2)}{4h^5}x^4\,\delta x.$$

The moment of inertia of the complete cone about the y-axis is then

$$\frac{3M(r^2 + 4h^2)}{4h^5}\int_0^h x^4\,dx = \frac{3M(r^2 + 4h^2)}{4h^5} \times \tfrac{1}{5}h^5 = \tfrac{3}{20}M(r^2 + 4h^2).$$

The moment of inertia of the cone about an axis through the vertex perpendicular to the axis of symmetry is $\tfrac{3}{20}M(r^2 + 4h^2)$.

Exercise 3D

1 Find the moment of inertia of a uniform rod AB of length 6 metres and mass 4 kg about an axis perpendicular to the rod through the point of the rod 1 metre from A.

2 Find the moment of inertia of a uniform disc of radius 30 cm and mass 2 kg about an axis perpendicular to its plane 10 cm from the centre.

3 A spherical shell has mass 3 kg and radius 20 cm. Find the moment of inertia about a tangent line.

4 A wire of mass M is bent into the circumference of a uniform ring of radius r. P is a point of the ring. Find the moment of inertia of the ring about

(a) an axis through P perpendicular to the ring,   (b) the tangent to the ring at P.

Where in your solution have you used the fact that the ring is uniform?

5 A uniform wire of mass M is bent into an L-shape with two arms each of length $2l$. Find the moment of inertia of the wire about an axis through one end perpendicular to its plane.

6 Three uniform rods, each of mass m and length $2l$, are pin-jointed together to make an equilateral triangle. Find the moment of inertia of the framework about an axis perpendicular to its plane

(a) through a vertex,   (b) through the mid-point of one rod.

7 A uniform square lamina of mass M, with sides of length $2a$, rotates about an axis perpendicular to its plane through a point halfway between the centre and one corner. Find the moment of inertia about the axis.

8 A uniform elliptic lamina of mass M has major and minor axes of length $2a$ and $2b$. The foci are points on the major axis at a distance $\sqrt{a^2 - b^2}$ from the centre. Find the moment of inertia of the lamina about a perpendicular axis through one focus.

9 A semicircular wire of radius r has ends A and B. Find the moment of inertia of the wire, assumed uniform, about an axis through A perpendicular to its plane, in terms of the mass M and the radius r.

10 A uniform semicircular lamina has mass M and radius r. It rotates about a perpendicular axis through its centre of mass. Find the moment of inertia about the axis.

11 For the cone in Example 3.9.2, find a formula for the moment of inertia about a diameter of the base.

12 A uniform solid cylinder of mass M and radius r has length $2l$. Find a formula for the moment of inertia of the cylinder about an axis through its centre perpendicular to the axis of circular symmetry. Check your answer by considering what happens when

(a) $r \to 0$,   (b) $l \to 0$.

13 For the solid defined in Exercise 3C Question 6, find the moment of inertia about a tangent at the origin.

14 A uniform pyramid of mass M has height h and a square base with sides of length $2a$. Find its moment of inertia about axes parallel to the base through

(a) the vertex,   (b) the centre of mass. (See Exercise 3A Question 11.)

15* For the solid defined in Exercise 3C Question 7, find the moment of inertia about the x-axis.

Miscellaneous exercise 3

1   A uniform circular disc has mass 1.5 kg and radius 0.4 m. The point A is on the disc at a distance 0.2 m from the centre. Calculate the moment of inertia of the disc about an axis through A perpendicular to the disc.   (OCR)

2   Calculate the kinetic energy of a square lamina of mass 2 kg and side 30 cm rotating in a horizontal plane about a vertical axis 5 cm from its centre and making 4 revolutions per second.

3   In the diagram, AC and BD are two metal strips, each of mass 3 kg and length 2 metres. They are hinged at A and B, so that each strip can rotate in a plane perpendicular to the line AB, which is horizontal. A board $EFDC$, 1 metre high and of mass 12 kg, is bolted to the strips. The whole framework is now rotated about AB until the board is horizontal, and then released. Find its angular speed when the board is again vertical.

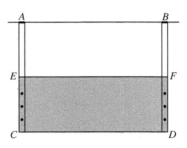

4   A lamina of mass M is bounded by parts of the curve $y = \dfrac{x^3}{a^2}$, the x-axis and the line $x = a$.

Find an expression in terms of M and a for the mass per unit area of the lamina. Hence find the moment of inertia of the lamina about

(a) the x-axis,

(b) the y-axis,

(c) a line through the origin perpendicular to the plane.

5   The diagram shows a lamina bounded by the axes and part of the curve with equation $y = \sqrt[3]{8 - x}$, the units being metres. The mass of the lamina is 3 kg. Find the moment of inertia of the lamina about the x-axis.

6   The diagram shows the frustum of a cone made of material with density 0.002 kg cm^{-3}. The base and the top are circles of radius 10 cm and 8 cm respectively, and the height is 10 cm. Find the moment of inertia about the axis of rotational symmetry.

7   A sheet of card is cut into a shape bounded by parts of the x- and y-axes and the curve $y = 3 + 2x - x^2$, the units being metres. The mass per unit area of the card is 0.5 kg m^{-2}. Find the moment of inertia of the card about the y-axis.

8 A hard-boiled egg of mass 80 grams is modelled as the interior of the region formed by rotating the curve $16x^2 + y^4 = 81$ (see diagram) about the y-axis, the units being centimetres.

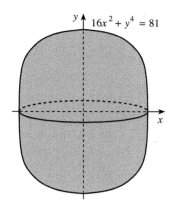

(a) Calculate the volume of the egg in cm^3.

(b) Assuming that the egg is uniform, find its density in gram cm^{-3}.

(c) Calculate the moment of inertia of the egg about the y-axis in gram cm^{-2}.

9 AB is a diagonal of one face of a cube whose sides are of length a. Prove that, if the cube is a uniform solid of mass M, its moment of inertia about AB is $\frac{5}{12}Ma^2$.

The cube is attached to a light fixed horizontal axle along the diagonal AB, so that it is free to rotate. Initially it hangs in stable equilibrium with its centre directly below the axle. It is then given an angular speed so that it starts to rotate about the axle. How large must this be if the angular speed of the cube at its highest position is one-half of the initial angular speed?

10 A uniform lamina of mass 7 kg has the shape bounded by the y-axis and that part of the graph $y = \sqrt{1 - 4x}$ for which x is positive, the units being metres. Find the kinetic energy of the lamina if it rotates about the y-axis with angular speed $5\,\text{rad s}^{-1}$.

11* Suppose that the moment of inertia of a uniform rod of mass M and length $2l$ about a perpendicular axis through its centre O is kMl^2. By imagining the rod to be made up of two rods, each of mass $\frac{1}{2}M$ and length l, with centres at a distance $\frac{1}{2}l$ from O, use the parallel axes theorem to make up an equation for k, and solve it.

12* A uniform right-angled triangular lamina has mass M, base b and height h. Let I be the moment of inertia of the lamina about the axis through its centre of mass parallel to the base. By amalgamating two such triangles to make a rectangle, and using the parallel axes theorem, make an equation for I and solve it.

13 A compound flywheel is to be constructed in the form of a circular disc with a radius of 0.25 m, a thickness of 0.05 m and a moment of inertia about its axis of $2\,\text{kg m}^2$. The flywheel is to have a central circular disc of aluminium alloy, density $2800\,\text{kg m}^{-3}$, and a steel outer rim, density $7900\,\text{kg m}^{-3}$. Denoting the radius of the junction between the alloy central disc and steel outer rim by r, find expressions for the moments of inertia of

(a) the alloy central disc about its axis,

(b) the steel outer rim about the same axis.

Hence determine the value of r.

(MEI)

14 A baseball bat is modelled as a cone of uniform density ρ, length l, and radius $r = \frac{1}{20}x$ at distance x along from the handle end. Show that its moment of inertia about an axis through $x = 0$ and perpendicular to the axis of symmetry of the bat is $I = \dfrac{1601}{32 \times 10^5}\pi\rho l^5$.

Find the value of α such that $I = \alpha M l^2$, where M is the mass of the bat. (OCR)

15 A valve lifting device is made from a uniform circular disc of radius a with a square hole cut out, as shown in the diagram. The hole has sides of length $\frac{1}{4}a$ and the centre of the hole is a distance $\frac{2}{3}a$ from the centre O of the disc. The mass of the device is m. Show that the moment of inertia I of the device about an axis perpendicular to its plane through the point O is given by $I = \dfrac{8\pi - \frac{131}{288}}{16\pi - 1}ma^2$. (MEI)

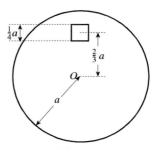

16 As part of an investigation into rotating interstellar dust clouds a simple mathematical model of such a cloud is proposed. The cloud is assumed to have a uniform density ρ and a shape defined by the volume produced by rotating the area between the curves $y = \pm be^{-x^2/a^2}$, $-\infty < x < \infty$, about the y-axis.

   (a) By considering thin cylindrical shells of radius x and thickness δx about the y-axis, find an expression for the mass M of the dust cloud in terms of ρ, a and b.

   (b) Find an expression for the moment of inertia I of the cloud about its axis of symmetry in terms of M and a. (MEI)

4 Centres of mass

The summation principle, used to find moments of inertia in Chapter 3, can also be used to locate centres of mass for shapes defined by coordinate equations. When you have completed the chapter, you should

- understand how the summation principle can be applied to the problem of locating centres of mass
- be able to find the centres of mass of rods of variable density, uniform solids of revolution and uniform laminas.

If you are working this chapter before Chapter 3, you should read Section 3.5 before continuing.

4.1 Rods of variable density

The density (more precisely, the 'line density') at a point P of a straight rod is the limiting value of $\dfrac{\delta m}{\delta x}$, where δm is the mass of a very short piece of the rod around P and δx is its length (see Fig. 4.1). It is measured in units such as kg m^{-1}. If the density is constant throughout the length of the rod, then the rod is uniform and its centre of mass is at its geometrical centre.

Fig. 4.1

The idea of a rod having variable density may seem unrealistic, but this is not so. It could well be convenient to model an object such as a javelin or the leg of a giraffe as a straight rod, even though the thickness varies along its length. This variable thickness would then be modelled as a variation in line density along the rod.

In one dimension, the centre of mass for a set of particles of mass $m_1, m_2, \ldots, m_n$ at points of the line with coordinates $x_1, x_2, \ldots, x_n$ is given in M2 Section 5.1 as having coordinate

$$\bar{x} = \frac{m_1 x_1 + m_2 x_2 + \cdots + m_n x_n}{M}, \quad \text{where } M = m_1 + m_2 + \cdots + m_n.$$

This can be written in sigma notation as

$$\bar{x} = \frac{\sum m_i x_i}{M}, \quad \text{where } M = \sum m_i.$$

For a continuous rod, the separate bits are short lengths of the rod; a typical one has length δx and mass δm, as in Fig. 4.1. If the line density is denoted by λ, then $\dfrac{\delta m}{\delta x}$ is approximately equal to λ, so $\delta m \approx \lambda \, \delta x$. The formula for the coordinate of the centre of mass then becomes

$$\bar{x} \approx \frac{\sum (\lambda \, \delta x) \times x}{M} = \frac{\sum x \lambda \, \delta x}{M}, \quad \text{where } M = \sum \lambda \, \delta x.$$

The word 'approximate' will appear a lot in this chapter. In this application it has to be used because the line density λ is not constant even within a short length of the rod; also the centre of mass of the short length is not exactly at the point with coordinate x but somewhere between x and $x + \delta x$. But these are approximations which get better as the modelling is improved by increasing the number of bits into which you split the rod, and decreasing their length. In the limit, as $\delta x \to 0$, the summation principle entitles you to replace these approximations by exact equations involving integrals. In this case, these equations are

$$\bar{x} = \frac{\displaystyle\int_a^b x\lambda \, dx}{M}, \quad \text{where } M = \int_a^b \lambda \, dx.$$

In these formulae λ is a function of x, and a and b are the coordinates of the ends of the rod.

It is not worth learning these formulae, but it is important to understand the argument which leads up to them.

Example 4.1.1
A girder 10 metres long projects horizontally from the wall of a building. It is modelled as a rod with line density $(8 - 0.3x) \, \text{kg m}^{-1}$ at a distance of x metres from the wall. What is the mass of the girder, and how far from the wall is its centre of mass?

Substituting $\lambda = 8 - 0.3x$ in the formulae above, you have to calculate the integrals

$$\int_0^{10} (8 - 0.3x) \, dx = \left[8x - 0.15x^2\right]_0^{10} = 80 - 15 = 65,$$

and $\quad \displaystyle\int_0^{10} x(8 - 0.3x) \, dx = \int_0^{10} (8x - 0.3x^2) \, dx = \left[4x^2 - 0.1x^3\right]_0^{10} = 400 - 100 = 300.$

From these you can calculate $\bar{x} = \frac{300}{65} = 4.62$, correct to 3 significant figures.

The mass of the girder is 65 kg, and its centre of mass is 4.62 metres from the wall.

4.2 Solids of revolution

If a solid is formed by rotating a region about the x-axis, you can imagine it to be split into thin discs, each of which has its centre on the x-axis. So if an object is modelled as a uniform solid of revolution, its centre of mass is on the x-axis. This means that you can find the centre of mass using a method very similar to that for a rod of variable line density; the only difference is that the mass of a short length of the rod is replaced by the mass of a thin disc.

Example 4.2.1
A machine component has the form of a uniform solid of revolution formed by rotating the region under the curve $y = \sqrt{9 - x}$ for which $x \geqslant 0$ about the x-axis, the units being centimetres. Find the position of the centre of mass.

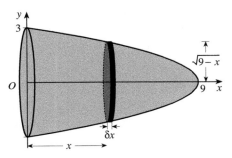

Fig. 4.2

Fig. 4.2 shows the solid, with a typical thin disc of thickness δx and radius $\sqrt{9-x}$. The volume of the disc is then $\pi\left(\sqrt{9-x}\right)^2\delta x$. You are given that the solid is uniform, so the mass per unit volume is constant; denote it by k. Then the mass of the typical disc is $k\pi(9-x)\,\delta x$, giving a total mass of $M = \sum k\pi(9-x)\,\delta x$.

The centre of mass of the disc is at a distance of $x + \frac{1}{2}\delta x$ from O. So the centre of mass formula gives

$$\bar{x} = \frac{\sum\left(k\pi(9-x)\,\delta x\right)\times\left(x+\frac{1}{2}\delta x\right)}{M}, \text{ which is approximately } \bar{x}\approx\frac{\sum k\pi\, x(9-x)\,\delta x}{M}.$$

The solid extends for values of x from 0 to 9. So, by the summation principle, the exact expression for the centre of mass of the machine component is

$$\bar{x} = \frac{\displaystyle\int_0^9 k\pi\, x(9-x)\,\mathrm{d}x}{M}, \quad \text{where } M = \int_0^9 k\pi(9-x)\,\mathrm{d}x.$$

Notice that the constant factors k and π appear in both integrals, so these cancel out in the final calculation of $\bar{x}$. All that is needed is to evaluate the integrals

$$\int_0^9 (9-x)\,\mathrm{d}x = \left[9x - \tfrac{1}{2}x^2\right]_0^9 = 9^2 - \tfrac{1}{2}\times 9^2 = \tfrac{1}{2}\times 9^2,$$

and $\displaystyle\int_0^9 x(9-x)\,\mathrm{d}x = \left[9\times\tfrac{1}{2}x^2 - \tfrac{1}{3}x^3\right]_0^9 = \tfrac{1}{2}\times 9^3 - \tfrac{1}{3}\times 9^3 = \tfrac{1}{6}\times 9^3.$

Then

$$\begin{aligned}
\bar{x} &= \frac{k\pi\times\tfrac{1}{6}\times 9^3}{k\pi\times\tfrac{1}{2}\times 9^2}\\
&= \frac{\tfrac{1}{6}\times 9^3}{\tfrac{1}{2}\times 9^2}\\
&= \tfrac{1}{3}\times 9\\
&= 3.
\end{aligned}$$

The centre of mass of the machine component is on the x-axis, 3 cm from the origin.

You can check for yourself that, if you apply the method of Example 4.2.1 to a general uniform solid of revolution, formed by rotating the region under $y = f(x)$ from $x = a$ to $x = b$ about the x-axis, the centre of mass is at $(\bar{x}, 0)$, where

$$\bar{x} = \int_a^b x(f(x))^2 \, dx \Big/ \int_a^b (f(x))^2 \, dx.$$

But again, it is not worth learning this formula. You will find that, with practice, it is easy to work it out from first principles when you need it. The advantage is that you can then adapt the method if, for example, the rotation is about the y-axis rather than the x-axis, or if there is a hole through the middle of the solid.

Two of the standard formulae for centres of mass given in M2 Chapter 10 were for solids of revolution: the hemisphere and the circular cone (see inside back cover of this book). The result for the hemisphere is proved in the next example; the circular cone is left for you to do (see Exercise 4A Question 5).

Example 4.2.2
Prove that the centre of mass of a uniform solid hemisphere of radius r is at a distance $\frac{3}{8}r$ from the centre.

This result is most often used with the plane face of the hemisphere horizontal, so Fig. 4.3 illustrates it as the solid formed by rotating the part of the circle $x^2 + y^2 = r^2$ for which $y \geqslant 0$ about the y-axis. A typical disc would then be horizontal, with thickness δy and radius $\sqrt{r^2 - y^2}$.

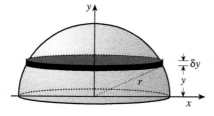

Fig. 4.3

If the mass per unit volume is k, the mass of the disc is $k\pi(r^2 - y^2)\delta y$.

You know the formula $\frac{4}{3}\pi r^3$ for the volume of a sphere, so the mass of the hemisphere is $k \times \frac{1}{2} \times \frac{4}{3}\pi\, r^3$. Applying the formula $\bar{y} = \dfrac{\sum m_i y_i}{M}$, and using the summation principle,

$$\begin{aligned}
\bar{y} &= \frac{\displaystyle\int_0^r k\pi y(r^2 - y^2)\, dy}{\frac{2}{3}k\pi\, r^3} \\
&= \frac{\left[\frac{1}{2}r^2 y^2 - \frac{1}{4}y^4\right]_0^r}{\frac{2}{3}r^3} = \frac{\frac{1}{2}r^4 - \frac{1}{4}r^4}{\frac{2}{3}r^3} = \frac{\frac{1}{4}r^4}{\frac{2}{3}r^3} = \frac{3}{8}r.
\end{aligned}$$

So the centre of mass is at $(0, \frac{3}{8}r)$.

4.3 Laminas: the symmetrical case

Another example to which the method of the preceding sections can be applied is a uniform lamina with a line of symmetry. If this is split into strips at right angles to the line of symmetry, then the centres of mass of all the strips lie on that line, and so does the centre of mass of the whole lamina.

Example 4.3.1
A uniform lamina occupies the region bounded by parts of the curve $y^2 = x$ and the line $x = 4$. Find the position of its centre of mass.

The curve $y^2 = x$ is a parabola with the x-axis as its axis of symmetry; values of y exist only where $x \geqslant 0$. You can also think of it as the combination of two graphs with equations $y = \sqrt{x}$ and $y = -\sqrt{x}$. Fig. 4.4 shows the region occupied by the lamina.

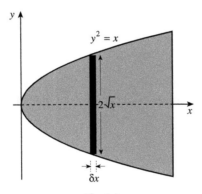

Fig. 4.4

Imagine this region to be filled with thin rectangular strips of width δx. A typical strip is shown in the figure. Its height is $2\sqrt{x}$, so its area is $2\sqrt{x}\,\delta x$. If the material of the lamina has mass k per unit area, the mass of the strip is $2k\sqrt{x}\,\delta x$, and the total mass of all the strips is $\sum 2k\sqrt{x}\,\delta x$.

There is of course a small amount of the lamina not covered by these strips, but as the width of the strips gets smaller the area of the uncovered part becomes smaller. In the limit the mass of the lamina is given by the integral

$$\int_0^4 2k\sqrt{x}\,\mathrm{d}x = \int_0^4 2kx^{\frac{1}{2}}\,\mathrm{d}x$$
$$= \left[\tfrac{4}{3}kx^{\frac{3}{2}}\right]_0^4$$
$$= \tfrac{4}{3}k \times 4^{\frac{3}{2}} = \tfrac{4}{3}k \times 8 = \tfrac{32}{3}k.$$

The symmetry of the figure shows that the centre of mass is on the x-axis, so let its coordinates be $(\bar{x}, 0)$.

The centre of mass of the strip is at the centre of the rectangle, which is $(x + \tfrac{1}{2}\delta x, 0)$. So in the formula for $\bar{x}$ the sum $\sum m_i x_i$ becomes $\sum (2k\sqrt{x}\,\delta x) \times (x + \tfrac{1}{2}\delta x)$. But since $\tfrac{1}{2}\delta x$ is small compared with x, this sum is approximately $\sum (2k\sqrt{x}\,\delta x) \times x$. This can be written more simply as $\sum 2kx\sqrt{x}\,\delta x$.

In the limit this sum becomes

$$\int_0^4 2kx\sqrt{x}\,dx = \int_0^4 2kx^{\frac{3}{2}}\,dx$$
$$= \left[\tfrac{4}{5}kx^{\frac{5}{2}}\right]_0^4$$
$$= \tfrac{4}{5}k \times 4^{\frac{5}{2}}$$
$$= \tfrac{4}{5}k \times 32$$
$$= \tfrac{128}{5}k.$$

Therefore

$$\bar{x} = \frac{\tfrac{128}{5}k}{\tfrac{32}{3}k} = \tfrac{128}{5} \times \tfrac{3}{32}$$
$$= \tfrac{12}{5}$$
$$= 2\tfrac{2}{5}.$$

The centre of mass of the lamina is $(2\tfrac{2}{5}, 0)$.

Example 4.3.2

Fig. 4.5 shows a design for a window, to be made of uniform plate glass. Its base AB is 2 metres wide, and AC and BC are arcs of circles with centres at B and A respectively. Find the height of the centre of mass of the window above the base.

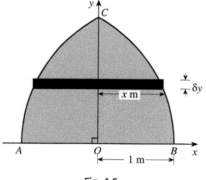

Fig. 4.5

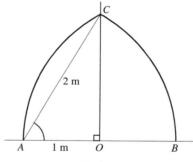

Fig. 4.6

If O is the mid-point of AB, the lamina is symmetrical about OC, so the centre of mass must lie on that line. If OB is taken as the x-axis and OC as the y-axis, then the centre of mass has coordinates $(0, \bar{y})$.

The area of the window can be calculated using Fig. 4.6. In the triangle AOC, $AO = 1$ metre and $AC = 2$ metres, so $\cos(\text{angle } OAC) = \tfrac{1}{2}$, giving angle OAC to be $\tfrac{1}{3}\pi$. The area of the circular sector ABC is given by the formula $\tfrac{1}{2}r^2\theta$, as $\tfrac{1}{2} \times 2^2 \times \tfrac{1}{3}\pi$ m^2, which is $\tfrac{2}{3}\pi$ m^2. Since $OC = \sqrt{3}$ metres, triangle OAC has area $\tfrac{1}{2}\sqrt{3}$ m^2. So the area of the window is $2 \times$ area $OBC = 2 \times \left(\tfrac{2}{3}\pi - \tfrac{1}{2}\sqrt{3}\right)$ m^2, which is $\left(\tfrac{4}{3}\pi - \sqrt{3}\right)$ m^2 $= 2.456...$ m^2.

To find the centre of mass, imagine the window to be split into strips of height δy and length $2x$. If the glass has mass k kg per square metre, the mass of the strip is $2kx\,\delta y$ kg, and its centre of mass is at $(0, y + \frac{1}{2}\delta y)$. So the position of the centre of mass is given approximately by $\bar{y} \approx \dfrac{\sum (2kx\delta y) \times y}{M}$, where M kg is the mass of the window, so $M = 2.456...k$.

The connection between x and y can be found from the circular arc BC, which has centre $(-1, 0)$ and radius 2. So its equation is $(x + 1)^2 + y^2 = 4$. It follows that $x = \sqrt{4 - y^2} - 1$. (Check for yourself that it is the positive square root that is wanted.)

Therefore, using the summation principle,

$$\bar{y} = \frac{\displaystyle\int_0^{\sqrt{3}} 2ky(\sqrt{4 - y^2} - 1)\,dy}{2.456...k}.$$

Cancelling the factor k,

$$\bar{y} = \frac{1}{2.456...} \int_0^{\sqrt{3}} (2y\sqrt{4 - y^2} - 2y)\,dy$$

$$= \frac{1}{2.456...}\left[-\tfrac{2}{3}(4 - y^2)^{\frac{3}{2}} - y^2\right]_0^{\sqrt{3}}$$

$$= \frac{1}{2.456...}\left(-\tfrac{2}{3} + \tfrac{16}{3} - 3\right) = \frac{1}{2.456...} \times \tfrac{5}{3} = 0.678, \text{ to 3 significant figures.}$$

The centre of mass of the window is 0.678 metres above the base.

Exercise 4A

1 A fir trunk, after it has been felled and trimmed, is 10 metres long. Its mass per unit length at a distance x metres from the root end is given by the formula $12(1 - 0.05x)^2$ kg m^{-1}. Find its total mass and the distance of the centre of mass from the root end.

2 A spear is modelled as a rod of length 2 metres with line density given by an expression of the form $c\sqrt{x}(2 - x)^2$ kg m^{-1}, where x metres is the distance from the user's end and c is a constant. Find the distance of the centre of mass from the user's end.

Find also the distance from that end of the point at which the line density is greatest.

3 The spike of a swordfish is modelled as the solid formed by rotating the curve $y = 1 + 0.001x^{\frac{3}{2}}$ about the x-axis for $0 \leqslant x \leqslant 100$, the units being centimetres. How far from the end is the centre of mass of the spike?

4 A spinning top has a shape obtained by rotating the graph of $y = \frac{1}{2}x\sqrt{4 - x}$ for $0 \leqslant x \leqslant 4$, the units being centimetres. It is made of wood of uniform density. Find the distance of the centre of mass from the pointed end.

5 Show that the centre of mass of a uniform solid circular cone is on the axis of symmetry, three-quarters of the distance from the vertex to the base. (You may wish to use the notation of Example 3.7.2.)

6 A uniform solid pyramid has height 20 metres and a square base of side 15 metres. Find the height of its centre of mass above the base.

7 The barrel of a cannon is 3 metres long. The internal diameter is 0.18 metres, and the thickness of the metal decreases steadily from 0.06 metres at the breech end to 0.03 metres at the muzzle end. Find the distance of the centre of mass of the barrel from the breech end.

8 A uniform lamina occupies the region bounded by parts of the curve $y = x^4$ and the line $y = 1$. Find the coordinates of its centre of mass.

9 A uniform lamina occupies the region bounded by parts of the curve $y = \dfrac{1}{x^2}$ and the lines $y = 1$ and $y = 4$. Find the coordinates of its centre of mass.

10 The diagram shows the flap of a table which is hinged about the line AB. The flap is 144 cm long and 36 cm wide. At a distance of x cm from AB the width, w cm , of the flap is given by $w = 24\sqrt{36 - x}$. The flap is made of wood 1 cm thick, of density 0.001 kg cm^{-3}. Find

(a) the mass of the flap,

(b) the distance from AB of the centre of mass of the flap,

(c) the moment about the hinge of the weight of the flap when it is raised to the horizontal position.

11 Show that the graph of $y^2 = x^3(a - x)^2$ for $0 \leqslant x \leqslant a$ encloses a finite region. Find the coordinates of the centre of mass of a uniform lamina occupying the region inside the loop.

12 Find the centre of mass of a uniform lamina bounded by the graph of $y^2 = e^{-x}$, the y-axis and the line $x = K$, where $K > 0$.

Find also the centre of mass of the uniform solid of revolution formed by rotating the region about the x-axis through four right angles.

What can you say about these centres of mass when K becomes large?

13 The semicircular region defined by $x^2 + y^2 \leqslant a^2$ and $y \geqslant 0$ (where a is a positive constant) is occupied by a uniform lamina. Show by integration that the centre of mass of the lamina is at a distance $\dfrac{4a}{3\pi}$ from the origin O. (OCR)

4.4   General laminas

If a lamina doesn't have an axis of symmetry, finding the centre of mass involves calculating two coordinates $(\bar{x}, \bar{y})$. You do this as before by drawing thin rectangular strips parallel to one of the axes; but you will need both coordinates of the centre of a typical strip. Apart from this, the method is in principle the same as in the one-dimensional case.

Example 4.4.1
A uniform lamina is bounded by the x- and y-axes and the part of the curve $y = \cos x$ for which $0 \leqslant x \leqslant \frac{1}{2}\pi$. Find the coordinates of its centre of mass.

Fig. 4.7 shows the region occupied by the lamina, and a typical strip of width δx and height $\cos x$.

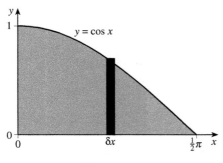

Fig. 4.7

The area of the strip is $\cos x \, \delta x$ and the coordinates of its centre of mass are at $\left(x + \frac{1}{2}\delta x, \frac{1}{2}\cos x\right)$. So, if the mass per unit area is k, the equations

$$\bar{x} = \frac{\sum m_i x_i}{M}, \quad \bar{y} = \frac{\sum m_i y_i}{M}, \text{ where } M = \sum m_i \quad \text{(M2 Section 5.2)},$$

are used with $m_i = k \cos x \, \delta x$, $x_i = x + \frac{1}{2}\delta x$ and $y_i = \frac{1}{2}\cos x$.

This gives

$$\bar{x} = \frac{\sum (k \cos x \, \delta x)\left(x + \frac{1}{2}\delta x\right)}{M},$$

which is approximately

$$\frac{\sum kx \cos x \, \delta x}{M},$$

and

$$\bar{y} = \frac{\sum (k \cos x \, \delta x) \times \frac{1}{2}\cos x}{M}$$

$$= \frac{\sum \frac{1}{2}k \cos^2 x \, \delta x}{M},$$

where $M = \sum k \cos x \, \delta x$.

In the limit, by the summation principle, the centre of mass of the given lamina has coordinates

$$\bar{x} = \dfrac{\displaystyle\int_0^{\frac{1}{2}\pi} kx\cos x\,dx}{M}, \quad \bar{y} = \dfrac{\displaystyle\int_0^{\frac{1}{2}\pi} \tfrac{1}{2}k\cos^2 x\,dx}{M}, \quad \text{where } M = \int_0^{\frac{1}{2}\pi} k\cos x\,dx.$$

So you have to find the integrals

$$\int_0^{\frac{1}{2}\pi}\cos x\,dx = \left[\sin x\right]_0^{\frac{1}{2}\pi} = 1,$$

$$\int_0^{\frac{1}{2}\pi} x\cos x\,dx = \left[x\sin x\right]_0^{\frac{1}{2}\pi} - \int_0^{\frac{1}{2}\pi}\sin x\,dx = \tfrac{1}{2}\pi + \left[\cos x\right]_0^{\frac{1}{2}\pi} = \tfrac{1}{2}\pi - 1,$$

$$\int_0^{\frac{1}{2}\pi} \tfrac{1}{2}\cos^2 x\,dx = \int_0^{\frac{1}{2}\pi} \tfrac{1}{4}(1 + \cos 2x)\,dx = \left[\tfrac{1}{4}(x + \tfrac{1}{2}\sin 2x)\right]_0^{\frac{1}{2}\pi} = \tfrac{1}{8}\pi.$$

As usual, the constant k cancels:

$$\bar{x} = \frac{(\tfrac{1}{2}\pi - 1)k}{k} = \tfrac{1}{2}\pi - 1, \quad \bar{y} = \frac{\tfrac{1}{8}\pi k}{k} = \tfrac{1}{8}\pi.$$

The coordinates of the centre of mass are $(\tfrac{1}{2}\pi - 1, \tfrac{1}{8}\pi)$.

Try for yourself to find where this point would lie on Fig. 4.7. Does it look a reasonable position for the centre of mass?

You may sometimes find it simpler to take the strips parallel to the x-axis, but the method is essentially the same. You can also extend it to laminas whose boundary is defined by more than one curve. Both these possibilities are explored in the next example.

Example 4.4.2
A uniform lamina occupies the closed region bounded by parts of the x-axis, the line $y = x$ and the curve $y = \sqrt{2 - x}$ shown in Fig. 4.8. Find the coordinates of its centre of mass.

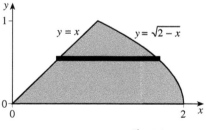

Fig. 4.8

Because the x-axis forms part of the boundary, you might think that it would be simplest to take thin strips parallel to the y-axis. But notice that, if you do this, you would have to express each of the integrals in two parts, because the formula for y in terms of x would be $y = x$ for $0 \leqslant x < 1$ and $y = \sqrt{2 - x}$ for $1 \leqslant x \leqslant 2$.

So it is worth investigating whether it would be possible to solve the problem by splitting the region into strips parallel to the x-axis. The complication would then be that neither the left end nor the right end of the strip would be constant; but this isn't a serious difficulty. For a given value of y, the left and right ends of the strip would be given by $x = y$ and $x = 2 - y^2$, so its length is $2 - y^2 - y$. And by taking $0 \leqslant y \leqslant 1$, strips like this would fill up the whole region.

The strip is a rectangle of thickness δy, and the mass per unit area is k, so its mass is $k(2 - y^2 - y)\delta y$. Also the centre of mass would be at the centre of the rectangle, with x-coordinate $\frac{1}{2}(2 - y^2 + y)$ and y-coordinate approximately y. So the centre of mass of the region would be given by

$$\bar{x} = \frac{\sum (k(2 - y^2 - y)\delta y) \times \frac{1}{2}(2 - y^2 + y)}{M}, \quad \bar{y} \approx \frac{\sum (k(2 - y^2 - y)\delta y) \times y}{M},$$

where $M = \sum k(2 - y^2 - y)\delta y$.

For the given lamina, the exact position of the centre of mass therefore has coordinates

$$\bar{x} = \frac{\int_0^1 \frac{1}{2}k(2 - y^2 - y)(2 - y^2 + y)\,dy}{M}, \quad \bar{y} = \frac{\int_0^1 ky(2 - y^2 - y)\,dy}{M},$$

where $M = \int_0^1 k(2 - y^2 - y)\,dy$.

Notice that the integrand for x contains a product of the form $(A - B)(A + B)$, where $A = 2 - y^2$ and $B = y$. So it can be multiplied out as $A^2 - B^2$, which is

$$(2 - y^2)^2 - y^2 = (4 - 4y^2 + y^4) - y^2 = 4 - 5y^2 + y^4.$$

It is now a simple matter to evaluate the integrals

$$\int_0^1 \frac{1}{2}k(4 - 5y^2 + y^4)\,dy = \left[\frac{1}{2}k(4y - \frac{5}{3}y^3 + \frac{1}{5}y^5)\right]_0^1$$
$$= \frac{1}{2}k(4 - \frac{5}{3} + \frac{1}{5}) = \frac{19}{15}k,$$

$$\int_0^1 k(2y - y^3 - y^2)\,dy = \left[k(y^2 - \frac{1}{4}y^4 - \frac{1}{3}y^3)\right]_0^1$$
$$= k(1 - \frac{1}{4} - \frac{1}{3}) = \frac{5}{12}k,$$

and $\quad \int_0^1 k(2 - y^2 - y)\,dy = \left[k(2y - \frac{1}{3}y^3 - \frac{1}{2}y^2)\right]_0^1$
$$= k(2 - \frac{1}{3} - \frac{1}{2}) = \frac{7}{6}k.$$

So $\bar{x} = \dfrac{\frac{19}{15}k}{\frac{7}{6}k} = \frac{19}{15} \times \frac{6}{7} = \frac{38}{35}$ and $\bar{y} = \dfrac{\frac{5}{12}k}{\frac{7}{6}k} = \frac{5}{12} \times \frac{6}{7} = \frac{5}{14}$.

The centre of mass of the lamina is at $\left(1\frac{3}{35}, \frac{5}{14}\right)$.

1 Find the centres of mass of uniform laminas occupying the regions enclosed between the following lines and curves:

   (a) the axes and the curve $y = 3 + 2x - x^2$ between $x = 0$ and $x = 3$,

   (b) the x-axis, the lines $x = -1$ and $x = 1$, and the curve $y = e^x$,

   (c) the y-axis and the curves $y = \cos x$ and $y = \sin x$ between $x = 0$ and $x = \frac{1}{4}\pi$,

   (d) the curves $y = \frac{1}{2}x^2$ and $y = 3x - x^2$ between $x = 0$ and $x = 2$,

   (e) the x-axis between $x = 0$ and $x = 1$, the line $y = \frac{1}{2}x$ between $x = 0$ and $x = 2$, and the curve $y = \sqrt{x - 1}$.

2 A uniform board is cut from a piece of plywood. It has vertices at $O(0, 0)$, $A(1, 0)$ and $B(1, 1)$, the units being metres. OA and AB are straight cuts, and OB is part of the curve $y = x^n$ where n is a positive integer. Find the coordinates of the centre of mass.

   If n is a large number, show that the centre of mass is close to the point which divides AB in the ratio $1 : 3$.

3 A metal template is cut out in the shape of the region contained between the curve $y = x^2 (1 - x)$ and the part of the x-axis between $x = 0$ and $x = 1$, the units being metres. If it is hung up from a hook at the origin, what angle will the x-axis make with the vertical?

4 A circle of radius r has its centre at the origin. Find the coordinates of the centre of mass of a uniform lamina occupying the region inside the circle which lies in the first quadrant. Check that your answer agrees with the formula $\dfrac{2r \sin \alpha}{3\alpha}$ given in M2 Section 10.2 for the distance from O of the centre of mass of a sector of angle α.

5 Find the centre of mass of the lamina in Example 4.4.2 by using strips parallel to the y-axis.

6 Use integration, with strips parallel to the y-axis, to find the centre of mass of a uniform triangular lamina whose sides are segments of the y-axis and the lines $y = cx$ and $y = ax + b$, where $b > 0$ and $c > a$.

   Check that your answer agrees with the statement in M2 Section 10.2 that the centre of mass of a uniform triangular lamina is at the centroid of the triangle.

1 A skyscraper 500 metres high is modelled as a vertical column for which the line density at a height of h metres is given by the formula $10(1 + 4e^{-0.02h})$ kilotonnes m^{-1}.

   Find its total mass, and the height of the centre of mass above ground level.

2 The region bounded by the curve $y = x^2 + 2$, the lines $x = 0$ and $x = 3$, and the x-axis is rotated completely about the x-axis to form a uniform solid of revolution. Find the x-coordinate of the centre of mass of this solid.   (OCR)

③ The figure shows a uniform solid pendulum. Its shape can be described by rotating the region between $y = \frac{1}{10}x^2\sqrt{1-x}$ and the x-axis through 2π radians about the x-axis for $0 \leqslant x \leqslant 1$. Calculate the volume of the pendulum and the x-coordinate of its centre of mass.

(MEI)

4 A uniform lamina occupies the region bounded by the x-axis, the line $x = 2$, and the curve $y = 3x^2$ for $0 \leqslant x \leqslant 2$. Find the coordinates of the centre of mass of this lamina. (OCR)

5 A region R is bounded by parts of the x- and y-axes, the line $x = 1$ and the curve $y = e^x$. Find the centres of mass of

(a) a uniform lamina occupying R,

(b) a uniform solid of revolution formed by rotating R about the x-axis.

⑥ Find the centre of mass of a uniform lamina occupying the region under the graph of $y = \ln x$ from $x = 1$ to $x = e$.

7 A uniform triangular lamina OAB has vertices $(0, 0)$, $(0, 2)$ and $(3, 4)$ respectively. VW is a line segment parallel to OA at a distance x from OA, where V is on OB, W is on AB and $0 \leqslant x \leqslant 3$. Find the length and the coordinates of the mid-point of VW. Hence use integration to find the centre of mass of the lamina.

8* The diagram shows a uniform wire AB in the shape of an arc of a circle with centre O and radius r. The mass per unit length of the wire is k. The wire is placed symmetrically about the x-axis with the radii OA and OB at an angle α to the positive x-axis. Suppose the wire to be made up of a large number of small arcs; the diagram shows a typical arc PQ of length $r\,\delta\theta$ with OP at an angle θ to the x-axis. Use the summation principle to show that the x-coordinate of the centre of mass is given by

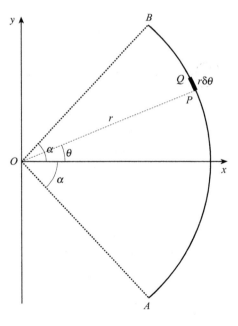

$$\bar{x} = \frac{\displaystyle\int_{-\alpha}^{\alpha} kr^2 \cos\theta \, d\theta}{M},$$

where

$$M = \int_{-\alpha}^{\alpha} kr \, d\theta.$$

Hence show that $\bar{x} = \dfrac{r \sin\alpha}{\alpha}$.

9 The shield in the diagram is bounded by the y-axis and the curves $y = \pm \left(1 - \frac{1}{4}x^2\right)$ for $0 \leqslant x \leqslant 2$, the units being metres. It is hinged along the y-axis, which is horizontal, and hangs with the x-axis vertically downwards.

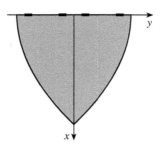

The shield is made of sheet metal with area density $6\,\text{kg}\,\text{m}^{-2}$. Find the increase in the potential energy of the shield when it is rotated about the y-axis until it is horizontal.

10 A draughtsman uses a metal template to draw sine and cosine curves. It covers the region between the axes and the part of the curve $y = 1 + \cos x$ for which $0 \leqslant x \leqslant \pi$. He hangs it from a hook at the point $(0, 2)$. What angle does the y-axis make with the vertical?

11 (a) The region P of a uniform lamina is a quadrant of a circle of radius 1 and centre $(1, 0)$, making up the regions labelled Q and R in the diagram. Use a standard centre of mass formula to show that the coordinates of the centre of mass of P are $\left(\dfrac{3\pi - 4}{3\pi}, \dfrac{4}{3\pi}\right)$.

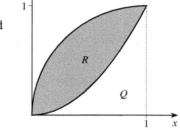

(b) The region Q of the lamina satisfies the inequalities $y \leqslant x^2$, $0 \leqslant x \leqslant 1$ and $y \geqslant 0$, as shown in the diagram. Find the coordinates of the centre of mass of Q.

(c) The uniform lamina R is obtained by taking the region P and then removing the region Q. Find the coordinates of the centre of mass of R.

(MEI, adapted)

12 (a) A uniform lamina is bounded by the parabola $y = 1 - x^2$ and the x-axis. Units are metres. Show that the centre of mass of the lamina is at the point with coordinates $(0, 0.4)$.

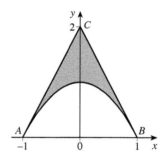

(b) A piece in the shape of the lamina in part (a) is removed from a uniform triangular lamina to form a shop sign as shown shaded in the diagram. The vertices of the triangle are at the points $A(-1, 0)$, $B(1, 0)$ and $C(0, 2)$. Calculate the y-coordinate of the centre of mass of the shop sign.

(c) The sign is suspended by vertical strings attached to the points B and C, and hangs in equilibrium with AC horizontal. The weight of the sign is $50\,\text{N}$. Calculate the tension in the string attached to the point B.

(MEI)

1 An aircraft is flying horizontally in an airstream. The velocity of the airstream relative to the ground is $65\,\mathrm{m\,s^{-1}}$ in the direction with bearing $160°$. The velocity of the aircraft relative to the ground has direction with bearing $030°$, and the velocity of the aircraft relative to the airstream has magnitude $180\,\mathrm{m\,s^{-1}}$.

   (a) Find the bearing of the velocity of the aircraft relative to the airstream.

   (b) Find the magnitude of the velocity of the aircraft relative to the ground.   (OCR)

2 A uniform solid of revolution is formed by rotating the region bounded by the x-axis, the line $x = 1$ and the curve $y = x^2$ for $0 \leqslant x \leqslant 1$, about the x-axis. The units are metres, and the density of the solid is $5400\,\mathrm{kg\,m^3}$. Find the moment of inertia of this solid about the x-axis.   (OCR)

3 A straight rod AB of length a has variable density, and at a distance x from A its mass per unit length is $k\left(1 + \dfrac{x^2}{a^2}\right)$, where k is a constant. Find the distance of the centre of mass of the rod from A.   (OCR)

4 A lamina of mass $6\,\mathrm{kg}$ lies in the xy-plane. Its centre of mass is at the point $(0.9, 1.3)$, where the units are metres. The moment of inertia of the lamina about the line $x = 0.9$ is $3.8\,\mathrm{kg\,m^2}$, and the moment of inertia of the lamina about the line $y = 1.3$ is $5.2\,\mathrm{kg\,m^2}$. Find the moment of inertia of the lamina about an axis perpendicular to the lamina and passing through the origin.   (OCR)

5 An unidentified object U is flying horizontally due east at a constant speed of $220\,\mathrm{m\,s^{-1}}$. An aircraft is $15\,000\,\mathrm{m}$ from U and is at the same height as U. The bearing of U from the aircraft is $310°$. The aircraft flies in a straight line at a constant speed of $160\,\mathrm{m\,s^{-1}}$.

   (a) Find the bearings of the two possible directions in which the aircraft could fly to intercept U.

   (b) Given that the interception occurs in the shorter of the two possible times, find the time taken to make the interception.   (OCR)

6 The region bounded by the x-axis, the y-axis, and the curve $y = 4 - x^2$ for $0 \leqslant x \leqslant 2$, is occupied by a uniform lamina of mass $35\,\mathrm{kg}$. The unit of length is the metre.

   (a) Show that the moment of inertia of the lamina about the y-axis is $28\,\mathrm{kg\,m^2}$.

   (b) You are given that the moment of inertia of the lamina about the x-axis is $128\,\mathrm{kg\,m^2}$ and the centre of mass of the lamina is at the point $G(0.75, 1.6)$. Find the moment of inertia of the lamina about an axis perpendicular to the lamina and passing through G.   (OCR)

7 The region bounded by the x-axis, the y-axis, the line $x = \ln 5$ and the curve $y = e^x$ for $0 \leqslant x \leqslant \ln 5$, is occupied by a uniform lamina.

   (a) Show that the centre of mass of this lamina has x-coordinate $\frac{5}{4}\ln 5 - 1$.

   (b) Find the y-coordinate of the centre of mass.   (OCR)

8 At midnight, ship A is 70 km due north of ship B. Ship A travels with constant velocity $20\,\text{km}\,\text{h}^{-1}$ in the direction with bearing 140°. Ship B travels with constant velocity $15\,\text{km}\,\text{h}^{-1}$ in the direction with bearing 025°.

(a) Find the magnitude and direction of the velocity of A relative to B.

(b) Find the distance between the ships when they are at their closest, and find the time when this occurs. (OCR)

9 An arm on a fairground ride is modelled as a uniform rod AB, of mass 75 kg and length 7.2 m, with a particle of mass 124 kg attached at B. The arm can rotate about a fixed horizontal axis perpendicular to the rod and passing through the point P on the rod, where $AP = 1.2\,\text{m}$.

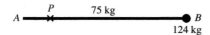

(a) Show that the moment of inertia of the arm about the axis is $5220\,\text{kg}\,\text{m}^2$

(b) The arm is released from rest with AB horizontal, and a frictional couple of constant moment 850 N m opposes the motion. Find the angular speed of the arm when B is first vertically below P. (OCR)

10 The region enclosed by the x-axis, the line $x = 2$ and the curve $y = 3x - x^2$ for $0 \leqslant x \leqslant 2$, is occupied by a uniform lamina. Find the coordinates of the centre of mass of this lamina. (OCR)

11 A light aircraft is flying at $80\,\text{km}\,\text{h}^{-1}$ in still air on a bearing of 040°. It suddenly flies into a stream of air, and as a result its velocity changes to $100\,\text{km}\,\text{h}^{-1}$ on a bearing of 025°. Find the speed and direction of the airstream.

12 A uniform solid of density k occupies the region formed by rotating about the x-axis the region under the curve $y = a\sqrt{\sin x}$ between $x = 0$ and $x = \pi$. Find, in terms of k and a, expressions for its mass m and the moment of inertia I about the axis of rotation. Hence find an expression for I in terms of m and a.

Deduce an expression for the moment of inertia of a uniform solid of mass m occupying the region formed by rotating about the x-axis the region under the curve $y = a\sqrt{\sin bx}$ between $x = 0$ and $x = \dfrac{\pi}{b}$.

13 A uniform sheet of plywood is cut into the shape bounded by the x- and y-axes and the part of the curve with equation $y = 1 - 4x^2$ which lies in the first quadrant, the units being metres. Its mass is 2 kg. Find

(a) the coordinates of its centre of mass,

(b) the moments of inertia about the x- and y-axes,

(c) the moment of inertia about an axis through its centre of mass perpendicular to its plane.

14 A motor boat, which can travel at $7\,\text{m}\,\text{s}^{-1}$ in still water, wants to reach harbour which is on a bearing of 070°. There is a tide running at $3\,\text{m}\,\text{s}^{-1}$ from the north. In what direction should the boat be steered, and what speed will it make towards the harbour?

15 Two children, Pat and Sam, play a chasing game on an open playing field. One child starts at A and the other at B, 50 metres away. The one who starts at B runs in a straight line towards C, where angle $ABC = 60°$; the one who starts at A runs in a straight line to try to catch the other. Pat can run at $3\,\mathrm{m\,s}^{-1}$, Sam at $2\,\mathrm{m\,s}^{-1}$.

   (a) If Pat starts at A and Sam at B, in which direction should Pat run to catch Sam? How long will this take?

   (b) If the children change places, show that Sam can't catch Pat. In what direction should Sam run to get as close as possible to Pat? How close together will the children then come?

16 A uniform solid of revolution of mass m is formed by rotating about the x-axis the portion of the curve with equation $y^2 = \dfrac{x(a^2 - x^2)}{a}$ between $x = 0$ and $x = a$. Find, in terms of m and a, expressions for the moment of inertia of the solid about

   (a) the axis of rotation,

   (b) an axis through the centre of mass perpendicular to the axis of rotation.

17* This question is about estimating the position of the centre of mass and the moment of inertia of the wing of a delta-wing aircraft. The distribution of mass of the wing structure is modelled by that of the thin triangular solid whose plan and end views are shown in the diagrams. The wing tips A and B are at the points $(a, 0)$ and $(-a, 0)$ respectively, and the apex C of the delta is at the point $(0, a)$ in the xy-plane. The thickness of the wing is given by $b = \lambda(a - x)$ for $x > 0$, where λ is constant, and the wing is symmetrical about the axis Oy. The density ρ of the material of the wing is uniform.

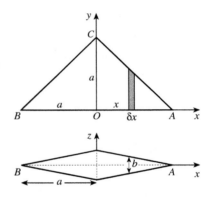

By considering the elementary strip between x and $x + \delta x$, or otherwise, find the position $(0, \bar{y})$ of the centre of mass of the wing. Find also the moment of inertia of the wing about the axis Oy in terms of M and a, where M is the mass of the wing.

What constant couple L about the axis Oy will result in the wing reaching a rate of rotation of $10\,\mathrm{rad\,s}^{-1}$ from rest in one revolution?   (OCR, adapted)

5 Rotation about a fixed axis

This chapter shows how to construct equations to describe the motion of a rigid object which is rotating about a fixed axis. When you have completed it, you should

- know and be able to use equations for motion with constant angular acceleration
- know the relationship between the moment of the applied force and angular acceleration, and be able to apply it
- know how to calculate the approximate period of a rigid object swinging as a compound pendulum
- know how to calculate the force on the axis of rotation
- understand how the equations describing the rotation of a rigid object can be derived by applying Newton's laws to the particle model.

5.1 Rotation with constant angular acceleration

You have already seen that there are parallels between rotation about a fixed point and motion in a straight line. Compare, for example, the equations

$$\text{(M3 Sections 5.1, 5.4)} \quad \left. \begin{array}{l} \omega = \dot{\theta}, \\ \alpha = \dot{\omega} = \ddot{\theta}, \\ \alpha = \omega \dfrac{d\omega}{d\theta}, \end{array} \right\} \quad \text{with} \quad \left\{ \begin{array}{l} v = \dot{x}, \\ a = \dot{v} = \ddot{x}, \\ a = v \dfrac{dv}{dx}. \end{array} \right. \quad \begin{array}{l} \text{(M1 Section 11.3,} \\ \text{M3 Section 1.3)} \end{array}$$

From the relations in the right column you can get the standard equations for constant acceleration, using integration and algebraic elimination. In just the same way, you can find equations for rotation with constant angular acceleration.

Consider an object rotating about a fixed point with initial angular velocity ω_0 and constant angular acceleration α. Suppose that, at time t later, the object has angular velocity ω, having rotated through an angle θ. Then ω, θ and t are connected by the equations

$$\left. \begin{array}{l} \omega = \omega_0 + \alpha t, \\ \theta = \omega_0 t + \frac{1}{2}\alpha t^2, \\ \omega^2 = \omega_0^2 + 2\alpha\theta, \\ \theta = \frac{1}{2}(\omega_0 + \omega)t, \\ \theta = \omega t - \frac{1}{2}\alpha t^2, \end{array} \right\} \quad \begin{array}{c} \text{corresponding} \\ \text{to the linear} \\ \text{equations} \end{array} \quad \left\{ \begin{array}{l} v = u + at, \\ s = ut + \frac{1}{2}at^2, \\ v^2 = u^2 + 2as, \\ s = \frac{1}{2}(u + v)t, \\ s = vt - \frac{1}{2}at^2. \end{array} \right.$$

The first two of these equations come directly by integrating $\dot{\omega} = \alpha$ and $\dot{\theta} = \omega$, in the special case when α is constant, using the initial conditions that $\omega = \omega_0$ and $\theta = 0$ when $t = 0$. The third can be got either by eliminating t between the first two equations, or directly by integrating $\alpha = \omega \dfrac{d\omega}{d\theta}$ with respect to θ. You can then get the last two equations by eliminating first α and then ω_0 between equations already obtained.

> Do this for yourself. The easiest way to remember the formulae on the left is by analogy with those on the right, which you already know.

Example 5.1.1

A potter's wheel is turning at $2 \, \mathrm{rad\, s^{-1}}$. The potter wants it to go faster, so she accelerates the wheel. After 2 revolutions it is turning at $8 \, \mathrm{rad\, s^{-1}}$. Assuming that the angular acceleration of the wheel is constant, find its value and the time that the wheel takes in gaining speed.

You must be careful to use consistent units, so begin by noting that 2 revolutions is 4π radians, and work in radian–second units throughout.

You are given that $\omega_0 = 2$ and that $\omega = 8$ when $\theta = 4\pi$. So to find α, use the equation $\omega^2 = \omega_0^2 + 2\alpha\theta$, giving

$$64 = 4 + 2\alpha \times 4\pi, \quad \text{so} \quad \alpha = \frac{60}{8\pi} = \frac{15}{2\pi} \approx 2.39.$$

You can find the time directly from the data by using $\theta = \frac{1}{2}(\omega_0 + \omega)\, t$, giving $4\pi = \frac{1}{2}(2+8)t$, so $t = \frac{4}{5}\pi$. Alternatively you could use $\omega = \omega_0 + \alpha\, t$ with the value of α already calculated, which gives

$$8 = 2 + \frac{15}{2\pi}t, \quad \text{so} \quad t = 6 \times \frac{2\pi}{15} = \tfrac{4}{5}\pi \approx 2.51.$$

The angular acceleration of the wheel is $2.59 \, \mathrm{rad\, s^{-2}}$, and the wheel takes 2.51 seconds to reach the angular speed of $8 \, \mathrm{rad\, s^{-1}}$.

Example 5.1.2

A wheel is rotating without friction at a constant angular speed of $30 \, \mathrm{rad\ s^{-1}}$. The brakes are applied for 2 seconds, producing constant angular deceleration of $10 \, \mathrm{rad\ s^{-2}}$. At what angular speed is the wheel then turning, and what angle does it turn through while slowing down?

You can answer this question either by using the equations for constant acceleration or by integration.

Using the equations It is given that $\omega_0 = 30$ and $\alpha = -10$, and you want to find ω and θ when $t = 2$. The equations

$$\omega = \omega_0 + \alpha t \quad \text{and} \quad \theta = \omega_0 t + \tfrac{1}{2}\alpha t^2$$

give

$$\omega = 30 + (-10) \times 2$$
$$= 30 - 20 = 10$$

and

$$\theta = 30 \times 2 + \tfrac{1}{2} \times (-10) \times 2^2$$
$$= 60 - 20 = 40.$$

Using integration Since $\alpha = \dfrac{d\omega}{dt}$, it is given that $\dfrac{d\omega}{dt} = -10$. This can be integrated to give

$$\omega = -10t + k.$$

Since $\omega = 30$ when $t = 0$, the constant $k = 30$. Therefore

$$\omega = -10t + 30.$$

Now write ω as $\dfrac{\mathrm{d}\theta}{\mathrm{d}t}$ and integrate a second time. This gives

$$\theta = -5t^2 + 30t + c.$$

When $t = 0$ the angle turned through is 0, so $\theta = 0$. Therefore $c = 0$, and

$$\theta = -5t^2 + 30t.$$

Putting $t = 2$ in the equations for ω and θ gives

$$\omega = -10 \times 2 + 30 = 10 \quad \text{and} \quad \theta = -5 \times 2^2 + 30 \times 2 = 40.$$

After 2 seconds the wheel has angular speed 10 rad s^{-1}, and it turns through 40 radians in that time.

Exercise 5A

1. A rotary pump achieves its maximum angular speed of 30 rad s^{-1} in 5 seconds. Find the angular acceleration, assuming it is constant, and the number of revolutions turned through in reaching maximum speed.

2. A revolving door rotating at half a revolution per second turns through 3 revolutions in coming to rest. Find the angular deceleration in rad s^{-2}, assuming that it is constant.

3. A turntable rotating at 33 revolutions per minute takes 5 seconds to come to rest. How many revolutions does it turn through in doing so?

   If instead the turntable is initially rotating at 78 revolutions per minute, and the angular deceleration is unchanged, how long will it take to come to rest, and how many revolutions will it turn through?

4. A shaft is rotating at 1500 rad s^{-1}. After a change of gear, the speed of rotation adjusts to a new angular speed of 1200 rad s^{-1}. If the change takes half a second, calculate the angular deceleration.

5. A carousel is rotating at 1 rad s^{-1}, and accelerating at 0.4 rad s^{-2}. How fast is it rotating after 5 seconds, and how many revolutions does it turn through in this time?

6. (a) A stationary wheel is accelerated at a constant rate by turning a handle. The wheel rotates through 3 revolutions in 2 seconds. Find the angular acceleration.

   (b) The wheel then rotates through one more revolution with half the angular acceleration in part (a). What is its final angular speed in revolutions per second?

7. A door is open at right angles to its frame. A child slams the door shut by giving it an angular speed of 2 rad s^{-1}. There is an angular deceleration of $\frac{1}{2}$ rad s^{-2}. What is the angular speed of the door when it hits the frame?

8. A wheel is rotating at $1\frac{1}{4}$ rad s^{-1} and slowing down at a rate of $\frac{1}{50}$ rad s^{-2}. How long will it take to turn through 6 radians?

   If the wheel continues to slow down at the same rate, what further angle will it turn through before it comes to a complete stop?

5.2   The equation of rotational motion

The similarity between rotational and linear motion can be taken further. You have met, in Sections 2.2, 2.4 and 2.5, the expressions

$$\left.\begin{array}{l} \text{kinetic energy} = \tfrac{1}{2}I\omega^2, \text{and} \\ \text{work done} = C\theta \\ \text{for rotation about an axis,} \end{array}\right\} \begin{array}{c} \text{compared} \\ \text{with} \end{array} \left\{\begin{array}{l} \text{kinetic energy} = \tfrac{1}{2}mv^2, \text{and} \\ \text{work done} = Fs \\ \text{for motion in a straight line.} \end{array}\right.$$

This suggests that there is a law for rotation about a fixed axis similar to Newton's second law $F = ma$ (often called the 'equation of motion'), in which F is replaced by C, m by I and a by α.

> **The equation of rotational motion**
>
> If forces (including couples) act on a rigid object which can rotate about a fixed axis, then the moment of the forces, C, and the angular acceleration of the rigid object, α, are connected by the equation
>
> $C = I\alpha$,
>
> where I is the moment of inertia of the object about the axis.

It is shown in Section 5.5 that this law can be deduced by applying Newton's laws to the model of a rigid object as a set of particles, as described in Section 2.2. The examples in the rest of this section show how the equation of rotational motion can be used.

When you use the equation $F = ma$ for linear motion, F stands for the net force in the given direction; that is, the accelerating forces minus any forces of resistance. Similarly, in the equation $C = I\alpha$, C must include all the forces (and couples) which have a moment about the axis. In Example 5.2.1, for example, the left side of the equation is the moment of the turning force minus the moment of the resisting couple.

Example 5.2.1

A uniform solid wheel, mounted horizontally on a vertical axle, has mass 6 kg and radius 50 cm. The wheel is initially at rest. It is turned by a handle, 40 cm from the axle, with a force of 5 newtons at right angles to the radius. The motion is opposed by a couple of moment 0.8 N m. Find the angular acceleration, and the time for the first revolution.

As always, you must be careful to use consistent units for the quantities C, I and α. Since the moment of the couple is given in newton metres, other lengths should be expressed in metres: the radius of the disc is 0.5 m, and the force is applied at 0.4 m from the axis.

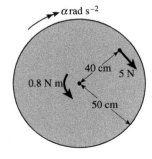

Fig. 5.1

The information in the question is summarised in Fig. 5.1. The moment of inertia of the wheel about the axle is given by the formula $\tfrac{1}{2}mr^2$ with $m = 6$ and $r = 0.5$ (in metres), so its value is $0.75\,\text{kg m}^2$.

The moment of the accelerating force is $5 \times 0.4\,\text{N m}$. So, if the angular acceleration is $\alpha\,\text{rad s}^{-2}$,

$$\mathcal{M}(\text{axle}) \qquad 5 \times 0.4 - 0.8 = 0.75\alpha, \qquad \alpha = \frac{1.2}{0.75} = 1.6.$$

Since the angular acceleration is constant, the time for the first revolution can be found from the equation $\theta = \omega_0 t + \frac{1}{2}\alpha t^2$ with $\theta = 2\pi$, $\omega_0 = 0$ and $\alpha = 1.6$. So

$$2\pi = 0.8t^2, \quad \text{which gives} \quad t = \sqrt{\frac{2\pi}{0.8}} \approx 2.80.$$

The wheel accelerates with angular acceleration $1.6\,\mathrm{rad\,s^{-2}}$, and takes 2.80 seconds to complete the first revolution.

Example 5.2.2

A light chain is placed over a sprocket wheel, which can rotate on smooth bearings about a fixed horizontal axle. The radius of the wheel is 0.1 m, and its moment of inertia about the axle is $0.02\,\mathrm{kg\,m^2}$. Loads of mass 1.4 kg and 1.5 kg are attached to the two ends of the chain. Find the acceleration with which the heavier load descends.

It was shown in M3 Chapter 5 that the tangential acceleration for an object moving round a circle is $r\dot{\omega}$, that is $r\alpha$. The tangential acceleration of any point on the circumference of the sprocket wheel is the same as that of the chain and the loads. So, if the acceleration of the loads is $a\,\mathrm{m\,s^{-2}}$, $a = 0.1\alpha$; that is, the angular acceleration of the wheel is $\dfrac{a}{0.1}\,\mathrm{rad\,s^{-2}}$.

Fig. 5.2 shows the forces on each of the loads and on the wheel. Notice that the tensions in the chain on either side of the wheel are different, because some force is required to accelerate the wheel. Let these tensions be S newtons and T newtons.

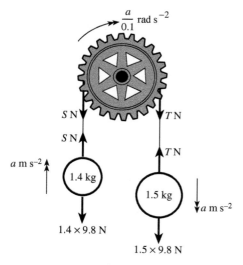

Fig. 5.2

You can now write down equations of linear motion for each of the loads, and an equation of rotational motion for the wheel.

For the heavier load:

$$\mathcal{R}(\downarrow) \qquad 1.5 \times 9.8 - T = 1.5a.$$

For the lighter load:

$\mathcal{R}(\uparrow)$ $S - 1.4 \times 9.8 = 1.4a.$

For the wheel:

$\mathcal{M}(\text{axle})$ $T \times 0.1 - S \times 0.1 = 0.02 \times \dfrac{a}{0.1}.$

Multiplying the last equation by 10 gives

$$T - S = 2a.$$

Then, adding the corresponding sides of all three equations,

$$(1.5 \times 9.8 - T) + (S - 1.4 \times 9.8) + (T - S) = 1.5a + 1.4a + 2a,$$

so $0.98 = 4.9a,$ which gives $a = 0.2.$

The heavier load has a downward acceleration of $0.2\,\mathrm{m\,s^{-2}}$.

Example 5.2.3

A uniform metal plate is in the shape of a $20\,\mathrm{cm} \times 10\,\mathrm{cm}$ rectangle. Its mass is $1.2\,\mathrm{kg}$. It is suspended from the ceiling by a cord, which is attached to the plate at its geometrical centre as shown in Fig. 5.3. The cord has the property that, when one end is twisted through an angle of θ radians, there is a couple of moment $k\theta$ N m tending to untwist it. The plate is initially at rest in a horizontal plane with the cord untwisted. An experimenter then rotates it horizontally about its centre and observes that, when he releases it, the plate oscillates with period 6 seconds. Find the value of k. (This is called a 'torsion pendulum'.)

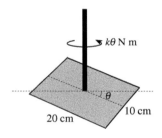

Fig. 5.3

The moment of inertia, $I\,\mathrm{kg\,m^2}$, of the plate about an axis perpendicular to its plane through the centre is given by the formula $\frac{1}{3}m(a^2 + b^2)$, where $m = 1.2$, $a = \frac{1}{2} \times 0.2 = 0.1$ and $b = \frac{1}{2} \times 0.1 = 0.05$ (in metres). This gives $I = \frac{1}{3} \times 1.2(0.1^2 + 0.05^2) = 0.005.$

If θ radians is the angular displacement of the plate after t seconds, its angular acceleration is $\ddot{\theta}\,\mathrm{rad\,s^{-2}}$, and the cord exerts on it a couple of moment $k\theta$ N m. So the equation of rotational motion about the vertical axis through the centre is

$$-k\theta = 0.005\ddot{\theta}, \quad \text{which can be written as} \quad \ddot{\theta} = -200k\theta.$$

This is an equation of simple harmonic motion with period $\dfrac{2\pi}{\sqrt{200k}}$. It is given that this is equal to 6, so

$$6 = \frac{2\pi}{\sqrt{200k}}, \quad \text{which gives} \quad k = \tfrac{1}{200}\left(\tfrac{1}{3}\pi\right)^2 \approx 0.005\,48.$$

The value of the constant k is 5.48×10^{-3}, correct to 3 significant figures.

Example 5.2.4

A uniform rod AB, of mass m and length $2a$, is hinged at A to a fixed point. A long vertical elastic string of natural length l is attached to the rod at B, and the other end is fixed to the ceiling. In equilibrium the rod is horizontal and the string is extended by a distance d. The rod is then displaced through a small angle and released, so that it oscillates about the equilibrium position. Find the period of the oscillation.

Fig. 5.4 shows the rod at an instant when it is at an angle θ above the horizontal. If θ is small, and the string is long, a reasonable approximation is that the string remains vertical during the oscillation and that the extension of the string in the position shown is $d - 2a\theta$.

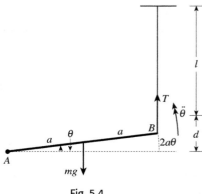

Fig. 5.4

If the string has modulus of elasticity λ, the tension in the equilibrium position is $\dfrac{\lambda d}{l}$.

Then

$$\mathcal{M}(A) \qquad \frac{\lambda d}{l}(2a) - (mg)\,a = 0, \quad \text{so} \quad \frac{\lambda}{l} = \frac{mg}{2d}.$$

Now consider the oscillating rod in the general position illustrated in Fig. 5.4. The tension is now $\dfrac{\lambda(d - a\theta)}{l}$ and the angular acceleration is $\ddot{\theta}$ anticlockwise. To form the equation of rotational motion you also need the moment of inertia of the rod about A, which for a rod of length $2a$ is $\frac{4}{3}ma^2$. So the equation $C = I\alpha$ becomes

$$\mathcal{M}(A) \qquad \frac{\lambda(d - 2a\theta)}{l}(2a) - (mg)\,a = \tfrac{4}{3}ma^2\ddot{\theta}.$$

Substituting $\dfrac{\lambda}{l} = \dfrac{mg}{2d}$, the left side is

$$\frac{mg(d - 2a\theta)}{2d}(2a) - (mg)a = mga - \frac{2mga^2}{d}\theta - mga = -\frac{2mga^2}{d}\theta.$$

So
$$-\frac{2mga^2}{d}\theta = \tfrac{4}{3}ma^2\ddot{\theta},$$

which can be simplified to

$$\ddot{\theta} = -\frac{3g}{2d}\theta.$$

Therefore, within the limits of the approximation made above, the rod makes simple harmonic oscillations with period $2\pi\sqrt{\dfrac{2d}{3g}}$.

Exercise 5B

1 A frisbee is spinning about a vertical axis with angular speed 30 rad s^{-1}. The moment of inertia about this axis is 0.0003 kg m^2. When the frisbee lands on the ground it comes to rest in one-tenth of a second. Find the angular deceleration, and the frictional couple from the ground.

2 The wheel of an exercise bike has moment of inertia 0.4 kg m^2 about the axle. The wheel is accelerated by the tension of 10 N in the chain, which passes round a sprocket wheel of radius 5 cm. The rotation is resisted by a couple of moment 0.3 N m. Calculate the angular acceleration of the wheel.

3 A uniform cylinder of mass 2 kg and radius 5 cm can rotate about its axis. A thread is wound round the cylinder and pulled with a force of 2 newtons tangentially to the cylinder at right angles to the axis. The motion is opposed by a frictional couple of moment 4 N cm. Find the angular acceleration of the cylinder.

4 A spinning top has the form of a uniform solid sphere of mass 0.5 kg and radius 4 cm, supported on a thin needle. It spins with the needle vertical, but when its angular speed drops to 40 rad s^{-1} its motion becomes unstable. The top is set spinning at an angular speed of 100 rad s^{-1}, and goes on spinning for 2 minutes before the motion becomes unstable. Find the moment of the constant frictional couple slowing the top down.

5 A uniform disc of mass 5 kg and radius 12 cm is rotating at 20 rad s^{-1}. It is brought to rest in 0.6 seconds by friction from brake pads on each side of the disc 10 cm from the axis of rotation, as shown in the diagram. Find the frictional force from each brake pad.
If the coefficient of friction is 0.8, what force must be applied normal to the surface of the disc to produce this deceleration?

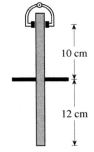

6 A carousel has seats for 20 children at a distance of 2 metres from its axis of rotation, which is vertical. When unoccupied the motor can accelerate the carousel at 0.5 rad s^{-2}. When filled with children whose average mass is 40 kg the acceleration drops to 0.4 rad s^{-2}. Find the moment of inertia of the carousel about its axis, and the couple produced by the motor.

7 Loads of mass m_1 and m_2, where $m_1 > m_2$, are attached to the two ends of a rope. The rope passes over a pulley, and friction between the rope and the edge of the pulley is large enough for the rope not to slip. The pulley has radius r and moment of inertia I about its axis. The system is released with the loads at rest. Calculate the angular acceleration of the pulley

(a) if the pulley runs on smooth bearings,

(b) if there is a frictional couple of moment C at the bearings.

What condition must C satisfy for motion to be possible?

8 The cylinder in Question 3 is mounted with its axis horizontal, and a small ball of mass 500 grams is attached to the end of the thread. If the frictional couple is unchanged, find the acceleration with which the ball descends.

9 A trolley of mass 20 kg stands on the flat roof of a building. A rope attached to the trolley runs horizontally to the edge of the roof, where it passes over a wheel of radius 2 metres. The other end of the rope hangs vertically and supports a load of mass 2 kg. It is observed that the load descends and pulls the trolley towards the wheel with acceleration $0.8\,\mathrm{m\,s^{-2}}$. Find the moment of inertia of the wheel, assuming that it runs on smooth bearings.

If in fact there is some friction at the axle of the wheel, would your answer for the moment of inertia be an underestimate or an overestimate?

10 In a torsion pendulum (see Example 5.2.3) the cord supports a uniform circular cylinder of mass 500 grams and radius 4 cm. The lower end of the cord is firmly attached to the cylinder at the centre of a plane face. The cylinder is twisted through a right angle, and held steady in this position by a couple of moment 0.8 N cm. Find the period with which the pendulum will oscillate when it is released, and the greatest angular speed during the oscillation.

11 The diagram shows a piece of apparatus made up of a spring of negligible mass, a cord, a load of mass M and a wheel which can rotate freely about a fixed horizontal axle. The spring has natural length l, and when the apparatus is in equilibrium the spring is extended by a distance d. The wheel has radius r, mass m and moment of inertia kmr^2, where $0 < k < 1$. The load is pulled down from its equilibrium position and released. Prove that it then oscillates with simple harmonic motion of period $2\pi\sqrt{\dfrac{(M + km)\,d}{Mg}}$.

12 The rotor of a helicopter consists of three blades, each modelled as a rod of mass 24 kg and length 5 metres, bolted on to a circular metal plate of mass 16 kg and radius 0.5 metres. Each rod has one end at the centre of rotation. When the motor is activated the blades take 2 seconds to complete the first revolution. Calculate the moment of the constant couple applied to the rotor.

With this couple, how long will it take for the rotor to achieve an angular speed of 10 revolutions per second from rest?

5.3   Compound pendulums

The simple pendulum described in M3 Section 6.2 consists of a small particle attached to a fixed point by a string. But the pendulums used in clocks are more substantial than this, and have to be modelled as rigid objects which can rotate about a fixed horizontal axis. To find the period of oscillation for such a pendulum, you need to use the equation of rotational motion.

Fig. 5.5 shows a rigid object which can rotate about a horizontal axis. The centre of mass is at G, at a distance h from the axis; its mass is m, and the moment of inertia about the axis is I. In its position of stable equilibrium it will rest with G vertically below a point O of the axis. The figure shows the object when it is in motion, with OG making an angle θ with the downward vertical at time t.

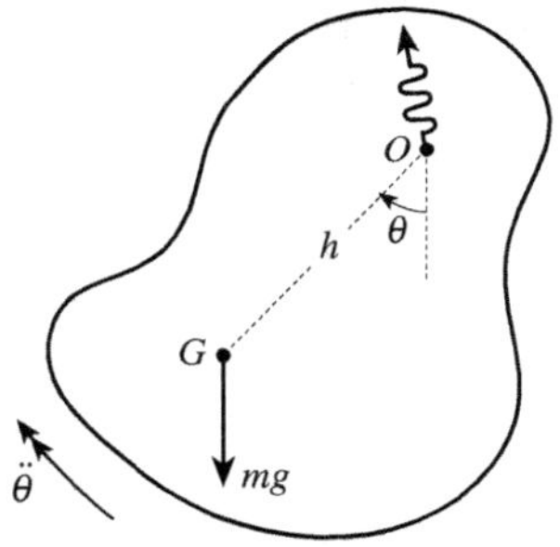

Fig. 5.5

The only forces on the object are its weight and the force from the support; you don't know anything about this force, but that doesn't matter because the force has no moment about the axis. There may also be a frictional couple at the axis, but in this model it is assumed that it is so small that it can be neglected. With θ measured clockwise from the downward vertical as in Fig. 5.5, the angular acceleration anticlockwise is $-\ddot{\theta}$. The equation of rotational motion is then

$$\mathcal{M}(\text{axis}) \qquad mg \times h\sin\theta = -I\ddot{\theta}, \quad \text{so} \quad \ddot{\theta} = -\frac{mgh\sin\theta}{I}.$$

This equation has exactly the same form as the equation $\ddot{\theta} = -\dfrac{g\sin\theta}{l}$ found in M3 Section 6.2 to describe the motion of the simple pendulum. You can therefore make the same approximation as in the simple case, that for swings through a small angle $\sin\theta$ can be replaced by θ. The equation then becomes

$$\ddot{\theta} \approx -\frac{mgh\theta}{I}.$$

So the motion of the pendulum approximates to simple harmonic oscillation with period $\dfrac{2\pi}{\sqrt{\dfrac{mgh}{I}}}$, which can be written more simply as $2\pi\sqrt{\dfrac{I}{mgh}}$.

> A rigid object free to rotate about a horizontal axis, swinging through a small angle on either side of its position of stable equilibrium, oscillates with period of approximately $2\pi\sqrt{\dfrac{I}{mgh}}$, where I is the moment of inertia about the axis, m is the mass and h is the distance of the centre of mass from the axis.

A rigid object oscillating like this is called a **compound pendulum**. The formula for the period is worth remembering.

In the examples which follow, the first obtains the period directly from the equation of rotational motion. The other three are worked by applying the formula; the second of these is suggested as an experiment which you could try, to test the theory.

Example 5.3.1

A uniform rod of mass 10 kg and length 2.1 metres can swing freely in a vertical plane round a horizontal pin at one end. Form the equation of rotational motion for the oscillation about the vertical equilibrium position. If the rod swings through a small angle, find the approximate period of the oscillation.

The weight of the rod is 98 N, and the moment of inertia is given by the formula $\frac{1}{3}Md^2$ (see Section 2.3) to be $\frac{1}{3} \times 10 \times 2.1^2$ kg m^2, which is 14.7 kg m^2. The centre of mass of the rod is 1.05 m from the hinge.

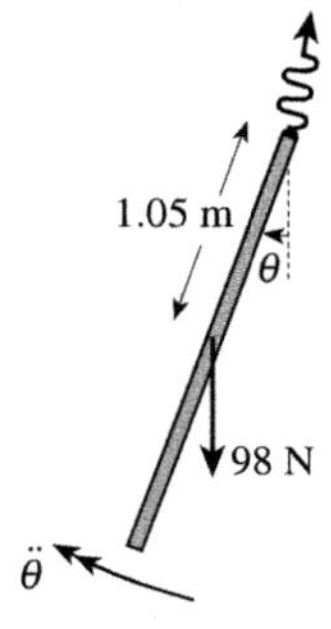

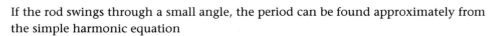

Fig. 5.6 shows the rod at a general position in its swing, when it makes an angle θ with the vertical. The equation of rotational motion, $C = I\alpha$, then takes the form

$$\mathcal{M}(\text{pin}) \qquad 98 \times 1.05 \sin \theta = -14.7\ddot{\theta},$$

which can be simplified as

$$\ddot{\theta} = -7 \sin \theta.$$

Fig. 5.6

If the rod swings through a small angle, the period can be found approximately from the simple harmonic equation

$$\ddot{\theta} = -7\theta.$$

The period of the oscillation is therefore approximately $\dfrac{2\pi}{\sqrt{7}}$ seconds, which is 2.37 seconds correct to 3 significant figures.

Example 5.3.2

A uniform circular disc of radius r is free to rotate in a vertical plane about a horizontal axis at a distance kr from the centre. It oscillates through a small angle about its position of stable equilibrium. Find the period of the oscillation, and where the axis must be placed for the period to have its smallest value.

The moment of inertia of the disc about the horizontal axis through its centre is $\frac{1}{2}mr^2$. By the parallel axes rule (Section 3.8), the moment of inertia about the axis of rotation is $\frac{1}{2}mr^2 + m(kr)^2$. Applying the compound pendulum formula with $I = m\left(\frac{1}{2} + k^2\right)r^2$ and $h = kr$, the period is $2\pi\sqrt{\dfrac{m\left(\frac{1}{2} + k^2\right)r^2}{mgkr}}$, which can be simplified to $2\pi\sqrt{\dfrac{\left(\frac{1}{2} + k^2\right)r}{gk}}$.

This will have its smallest value when the function $\mathrm{f}(k) \equiv \dfrac{\frac{1}{2} + k^2}{k}$ is a minimum, with $k > 0$. Writing $\mathrm{f}(k)$ as $\dfrac{1}{2k} + k$, $\mathrm{f}'(k) = -\dfrac{1}{2k^2} + 1$, and $\mathrm{f}'(k) = 0$ when $2k^2 = 1$, $k = \dfrac{1}{\sqrt{2}}$.

So the period has its smallest value when the axis is at a distance $\dfrac{r}{\sqrt{2}}$ from the centre.

The period is then $2\pi\sqrt{\dfrac{\sqrt{2}r}{g}}$.

Example 5.3.3

The pendulum in Fig. 5.7 is made of a strip of wood with a square board screwed to it at one end. It is hung over a nail by a small eye screwed into it at the other end. The wooden strip is 1.2 metres long and has mass 0.5 kg. The board is 0.4 metres square and has mass 1.5 kg. Find the period when the pendulum makes small oscillations about the vertical.

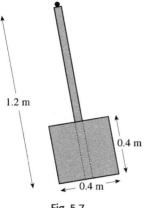

Fig. 5.7

> If you do the experiment, you must change the numbers to fit your apparatus.

You have to do two preliminary calculations to find the distance of the centre of mass from the nail and the moment of inertia about the nail.

Centre of mass   The data are set out in the usual tabular form (see M2 Section 5.1).

	Strip	Board	Pendulum
Mass (kg)	0.5	1.5	2.0
Distance from nail (m)	0.6	1.0	h

From this you can form the equation $2h = 0.5 \times 0.6 + 1.5 \times 1.0$, which gives $h = 0.9$.

Moment of inertia   This is calculated in two parts.

For the strip about its end, using $I = \frac{1}{3}md^2$ (see Section 2.3) with $d = 1.2$ gives $I = \frac{1}{3} \times 0.5 \times 1.2^2$, so the moment of inertia is $0.24\,\text{kg m}^2$.

For the board (of sides $2a$, $2b$ with $a = b = 0.2$) use $I = \frac{1}{3}m(a^2 + b^2)$, which gives $I = \frac{1}{3} \times 1.5 \times (2 \times 0.2^2) = 0.04$. So the moment of inertia about the axis through the centre of the board is $0.04\,\text{kg m}^2$. Then, by the parallel axes rule, the moment of inertia about the nail is $(0.04 + 1.5 \times 1.0^2)\,\text{kg m}^2$, which is $1.54\,\text{kg m}^2$.

The moment of inertia of the complete pendulum about the nail is therefore $(0.24 + 1.54)\,\text{kg m}^2$, which is $1.78\,\text{kg m}^2$.

The period of oscillation of the pendulum is therefore $2\pi\sqrt{\dfrac{1.78}{2.0 \times 9.8 \times 0.9}}$ seconds, which is 2.00 seconds correct to 3 significant figures.

For some compound pendulum calculations you have to begin by using integration methods to calculate I and h. The next example uses results which have already been found in this way.

Example 5.3.4

A uniform solid circular cone, of height h and radius r, hangs from a hook at the vertex. It swings as a compound pendulum through a small angle. Find an approximate expression for the period.

It was shown in Example 3.9.2, using integration, that the moment of inertia of the cone about an axis through the vertex perpendicular to the axis of symmetry is $\frac{3}{20}m(r^2 + 4h^2)$.

You know that the centre of mass is at a distance $\frac{3}{4}h$ from the vertex. This was proved using integration in Exercise 4A Question 5.

A little care is needed in using the formula $2\pi\sqrt{\dfrac{I}{mgh}}$ in this example, since the 'h' in the formula is not the height of the cone. In the notation of this example, you have to substitute $\frac{3}{4}h$ in place of h in the formula.

The approximate period of oscillation is then $2\pi\sqrt{\dfrac{\frac{3}{20}m(r^2 + 4h^2)}{mg(\frac{3}{4}h)}}$, which can be simplified to $2\pi\sqrt{\dfrac{r^2 + 4h^2}{5gh}}$.

Exercise 5C

① A uniform rod of length 1 metre and mass 3 kg has a particle of mass 2 kg attached to one end. The rod is hinged at its mid-point so that it can rotate freely in a vertical plane. It oscillates through a small angle about the equilibrium position. Form an equation of rotational motion for the oscillation, and find the approximate period.

② A wheel of radius 20 cm has moment of inertia 0.001 kg m^2 about its axis of rotational symmetry, which is fixed horizontally. A bird of mass 100 grams lands on the rim of the wheel close to its lowest point, and the wheel begins to oscillate with the bird on it. Form an equation of rotational motion for the oscillation, and find the approximate period.

③ A hoop of mass m and radius r hangs in a vertical plane over a rough horizontal nail. It is knocked sideways, so that it starts to oscillate in its plane. Show that the oscillation is described by the equation $\ddot{\theta} = -\dfrac{g}{2r}\sin\theta$. By writing $\ddot{\theta}$ as $\omega\dfrac{d\omega}{d\theta}$, where ω is the angular velocity, show that the value of $\omega^2 - \dfrac{g}{r}\cos\theta$ remains constant as the hoop oscillates.

④ The diagram shows a hemispherical bowl of radius r, which has small rings at the two ends of a diameter of the rim. A rod is passed through the two rings and placed in fixed supports on each side of the bowl, so that the bowl hangs below the level of the rod. The bowl is slightly tipped and oscillates about the rod. Find the period of the oscillation.

5 A uniform rod of length $2l$ is hinged to a fixed point at a distance a from the centre, so that it can swing freely in a vertical plane. Show that the period of small oscillations is smallest if $a = \dfrac{l}{\sqrt{3}}$.

6 A cricket bat is modelled as a thin rectangular board of length 50 cm attached to a handle of negligible mass. If the bat is held 20 cm above the bottom of the handle and allowed to swing about a horizontal axis in the plane of the bat, find its natural period of oscillation.

7 The leg of a giraffe is modelled as a uniform rod AB of length 1 metre (the upper leg), a second uniform rod BC of length 1 metre attached to the first rod (the lower leg), and a particle attached to the second rod at C (the foot). If the masses of the three components are in the ratio $6 : 3 : 1$, and they swing together from a hinge at A with ABC in a straight line, what is the natural time for the leg to swing from back to front?

8 Sit on a table and swing one leg to and fro below the knee. By making suitable modelling assumptions, estimate the natural period of a swing.

9 The seat of a child's swing is supported by two parallel metal rods, each of mass 1.5 kg and length 2 metres. The child and the seat are modelled as a solid sphere of mass 20 kg and radius 20 cm with its bottom at the level of the end of the rods. Find the period with which the swing will oscillate.

10 A uniform rectangular lamina, with sides $2a$ and $2b$, can swing as a compound pendulum in a vertical plane about a hinge at one corner. Find the period of the oscillation.

11 A uniform rectangular wire, with sides $2a$ and $2b$, can swing as a compound pendulum in a vertical plane about a hinge at one corner. Find the period of the oscillation.

12 Signboards are cut out in plywood having the shapes bounded by the x-axis and the curves
   (a) $y = x(2 - x)$ from $x = 0$ to $x = 2$,
   (b) $y = \sin x$ from $x = 0$ to $x = \pi$,

   the units being metres. They are hinged to a fixed horizontal rod along the x-axis. Find the periods with which they oscillate.

13 A uniform lamina has the shape of a quadrant of a circle with centre O and radius r. It can swing freely in a vertical plane about a hinge fixed at O. Find the period of the oscillation.

14 A uniform wire has the shape of the perimeter of a quadrant of a circle with centre O and radius r. It can swing freely in a vertical plane about a hinge fixed at O. Find the period of the oscillation.

15 G is the centre of mass of a lamina of mass m, of any shape. The moment of inertia about an axis l through G perpendicular to the plane of the lamina is I. The lamina swings as a compound pendulum about an axis parallel to l through a point X. Show that the period of oscillation is the same for all the points X which lie on a circle with its centre at G.

Show also that this period is least when the radius of this circle is $\sqrt{\dfrac{I}{m}}$.

5.4   The force on the axis

It was stated in Section 5.3 that one of the forces on a compound pendulum is the force from the axis, but that this isn't known. But it is sometimes important to be able to find it.

To do this, a new principle is needed, which extends Newton's second law from a particle to a rigid object.

> **Newton's second law (extended)**
>
> The equation $\mathbf{F} = M\mathbf{a}$ can be applied to the motion of a large object, where $\mathbf{F}$ stands for the vector sum of the external forces on the object, M is the total mass of the object and $\mathbf{a}$ is the acceleration of the centre of mass.

This section gives some examples to show how this principle can be applied. In Section 5.5 the principle is deduced from Newton's laws of motion for a particle, applied to the model of a large object as a collection of particles.

> Notice that the words 'rigid' and 'rotating about a fixed axis' don't appear in the statement. It is in fact true whether the object is rigid or not, and however it is moving. But in this book it will only be used for a rigid object rotating about a fixed axis.

Applying the principle to an object rotating about a fixed axis is especially simple, since the centre of mass then moves in a circle about the axis. The acceleration of the centre of mass is therefore made up of two components: a radial component $r\omega^2$ towards the axis and a transverse component $r\alpha$ perpendicular to the radius in the plane perpendicular to the axis.

Example 5.4.1

A power plant has a flywheel of mass 10 kg and radius 20 cm mounted on a vertical axle. The centre of mass of the wheel is one-tenth of a millimetre away from the axis of rotation. What force does this impose on the mounting when the flywheel is rotating at 1200 revolutions per minute?

The angular speed of the flywheel, $\frac{1200}{60} \times 2\pi$ rad s^{-1} = 40π rad s^{-1}, is constant, so there is no transverse acceleration. The centre of mass has acceleration towards the axis of rotation of amount $0.0001 \times (40\pi)^2$ m s^{-2}. The force on the wheel from the axle therefore acts in the direction of the vector from the centre of mass to the axis of rotation, and its magnitude, F newtons, is given by

$$F = 10 \times (0.0001 \times (40\pi)^2) \approx 15.8.$$

The force from the axle on the wheel is 15.8 newtons, correct to 3 significant figures. By Newton's third law, the force from the wheel on the axle has the same magnitude in the opposite direction. As the wheel rotates, the direction of this force rotates at the same rate.

In this example, notice that the answer does not depend on the radius of the flywheel, or on its moment of inertia. The moment of inertia affects the amount of energy stored in the flywheel, and how difficult it is to accelerate it or slow it down, but does not affect the forces in steady motion. This is like mass in linear motion: for an object such as a train travelling at speed, the mass affects the kinetic energy and how much force is needed to accelerate or decelerate it, but not the forces when it is travelling at constant speed.

Example 5.4.2

A uniform circular hoop of mass m and radius r is attached to a fixed hinge at a point C of its circumference so that it can rotate freely in a vertical plane. The hoop is raised until its centre is level with the hinge, and then released. Find the force on the hinge (a) immediately after it is released, (b) when the centre is directly below the hinge, (c) in the position halfway between.

In problems which involve the force on the axis, you need diagrams which show where both the forces and the acceleration are located. It is a good idea to draw two figures, one showing the forces and the other the acceleration of the centre of mass.

The force at C shown in Figs. 5.8 to 5.10 is the force from the hinge on the hoop, with horizontal component X and vertical component Y. The force on the hinge, which is what the question asks for, is equal to this in magnitude but in the opposite direction.

The only force on the hoop apart from the force from the hinge is its weight mg, acting at the centre of mass. The centre of mass moves round the lower half of a circle with centre C and radius r.

The moment of inertia of the hoop about its centre is mr^2, so by the parallel axes rule the moment of inertia about the axis of rotation through C is $mr^2 + mr^2 = 2mr^2$.

(a) Immediately after the hoop is released it has no angular velocity, so the centre of mass has no radial acceleration towards C. The transverse acceleration is $r\alpha$ vertically downwards (see Fig. 5.8).

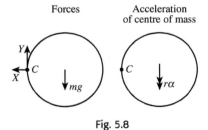

Forces   Acceleration
of centre of mass

Fig. 5.8

The angular acceleration can be found from the equation of rotational motion about C.

$$\mathcal{M}(C) \qquad mgr = (2mr^2)\alpha,$$

so the transverse acceleration $r\alpha$ is equal to $\tfrac{1}{2}g$.

You can now find the force from the hinge by applying the extended form of Newton's second law.

$$\mathcal{R}(\leftarrow) \qquad X = 0 \qquad \text{and} \qquad \mathcal{R}(\downarrow) \qquad mg - Y = m(r\alpha).$$

Substituting $\frac{1}{2}g$ for $r\alpha$ gives $Y = mg - \frac{1}{2}mg = \frac{1}{2}mg$.

(b) Fig. 5.9 shows the forces and acceleration when the centre of the hoop is directly below the hinge. In this position the weight has no moment about C, so the angular acceleration is zero. This means that the centre of mass has no transverse acceleration, so its acceleration is simply $r\omega^2$ vertically upwards.

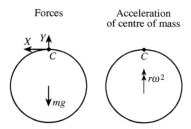

Fig. 5.9

The easiest way to find ω is with an equation of energy. In falling from the release position the centre of mass loses height equal to r, so the hoop loses potential energy mgr. This is converted into kinetic energy of amount $\frac{1}{2}(2mr^2)\omega^2$. So $mgr = mr^2\omega^2$, which gives $r\omega^2 = g$.

The extended form of Newton's second law then gives

$$\mathcal{R}(\leftarrow) \qquad X = 0 \qquad \text{and} \qquad \mathcal{R}(\uparrow) \qquad Y - mg = mg.$$

So the force from the hinge is $2mg$ vertically upwards.

(c) When the hoop has turned through 45° both components of acceleration are present (see Fig. 5.10). To find ω, the energy equation gives $mg\dfrac{r}{\sqrt{2}} = \frac{1}{2}(2mr^2)\omega^2$, so the radial component $r\omega^2$ is $\dfrac{g}{\sqrt{2}}$. The angular acceleration $r\alpha$ comes from the equation of rotational motion,

$$\mathcal{M}(C) \qquad mg \times \frac{r}{\sqrt{2}} = (2mr^2)\alpha,$$

so the transverse component $r\alpha$ is $\dfrac{g}{2\sqrt{2}}$.

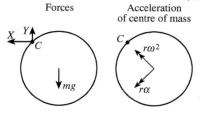

Fig. 5.10

Then, by the extended form of Newton's second law,

$$\mathcal{R}(\leftarrow) \quad X = m\left(r\omega^2 \times \frac{1}{\sqrt{2}} + r\alpha \times \frac{1}{\sqrt{2}}\right) = m\left(\frac{g}{\sqrt{2}} \times \frac{1}{\sqrt{2}} + \frac{g}{2\sqrt{2}} \times \frac{1}{\sqrt{2}}\right)$$
$$= mg\left(\tfrac{1}{2} + \tfrac{1}{4}\right) = \tfrac{3}{4}mg;$$

$$\mathcal{R}(\uparrow) \quad Y - mg = m\left(r\omega^2 \times \frac{1}{\sqrt{2}} - r\alpha \times \frac{1}{\sqrt{2}}\right) = m\left(\frac{g}{\sqrt{2}} \times \frac{1}{\sqrt{2}} - \frac{g}{2\sqrt{2}} \times \frac{1}{\sqrt{2}}\right)$$
$$= mg\left(\tfrac{1}{2} - \tfrac{1}{4}\right) = \tfrac{1}{4}mg,$$

so $Y = \tfrac{5}{4}mg$.

The force from the hoop on the hinge is (a) $\tfrac{1}{2}mg$ vertically downwards, (b) $2mg$ vertically downwards, (c) the resultant of $\tfrac{3}{4}mg$ horizontally towards the hoop and $\tfrac{5}{4}mg$ vertically downwards.

Example 5.4.3

A uniform broomstick is balanced vertically in unstable equilibrium on a rough floor. It is slightly disturbed so that it starts to fall in a vertical plane. At what angle to the vertical will it start to slip if the coefficient of friction is (a) 0.3, (b) 0.4?

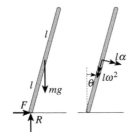

Fig. 5.11

Fig. 5.11 shows the broomstick when it is at an angle θ to the vertical, assuming that it has not yet begun to slip. Up to that time the broomstick is rotating about a fixed point, the foot of the stick. The forces are the weight, mg, and the normal and frictional forces, R and F, from the floor.

If the length of the broomstick is $2l$, the centre of mass starts to move in a circle of radius l, with acceleration components $l\omega^2$ radially and $l\alpha$ at right angles to the broomstick. The value of ω can be found from an energy equation; the potential energy lost by the broomstick is equal to the gain in kinetic energy, so

$$mgl(1 - \cos\theta) = \tfrac{1}{2}(\tfrac{4}{3}ml^2)\omega^2.$$

The value of α can be found from the equation of rotational motion

$$\mathcal{M}(\text{foot of broomstick}) \quad mg \times l\sin\theta = (\tfrac{4}{3}ml^2)\alpha.$$

These equations can be simplified to give

$$l\omega^2 = \tfrac{3}{2}g(1 - \cos\theta) \quad \text{and} \quad l\alpha = \tfrac{3}{4}g\sin\theta.$$

Notice that these two equations are not independent. If you differentiate the first equation with respect to θ you get $2l\omega\dfrac{d\omega}{d\theta} = \tfrac{3}{2}g\sin\theta$; and remembering that $\omega\dfrac{d\omega}{d\theta}$ is equal to α, this is equivalent to the second equation.

The extended form of Newton's second law then gives

$$\mathcal{R}(\rightarrow) \quad F = m(l\alpha \cos\theta - l\omega^2 \sin\theta)$$
$$= m(\tfrac{3}{4}g \sin\theta \cos\theta - \tfrac{3}{2}g(1-\cos\theta)\sin\theta)$$
$$= \tfrac{3}{4}mg \sin\theta(3\cos\theta - 2);$$

and

$$\mathcal{R}(\downarrow) \quad mg - R = m(l\alpha \sin\theta + l\omega^2 \cos\theta),$$

from which

$$R = mg - m(\tfrac{3}{4}mg \sin^2\theta + \tfrac{3}{2}g(1-\cos\theta)\cos\theta)$$
$$= \tfrac{1}{4}mg(4 - 3\sin^2\theta - 6\cos\theta + 6\cos^2\theta)$$
$$= \tfrac{1}{4}mg(1 - 6\cos\theta + 9\cos^2\theta) = \tfrac{1}{4}mg(1 - 3\cos\theta)^2.$$

The condition for the broomstick not to slip depends on the value of $\dfrac{F}{R}$, which must not exceed the coefficient of friction. In this case,

$$\frac{F}{R} = \frac{3\sin\theta(3\cos\theta - 2)}{(1 - 3\cos\theta)^2}.$$

Denote this expression by f(θ). The question of where the broomstick begins to slip can be answered from the graph of f(θ),which is drawn in Fig. 5.12.

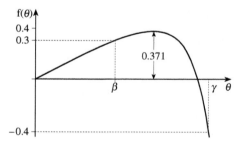

Fig. 5.12

Notice that f(θ) is positive as far as $\cos^{-1}\tfrac{2}{3}$ (about 48°), but that beyond this point the frictional force changes direction. As θ approaches $\cos^{-1}\tfrac{1}{3}$ (about 71°) f(θ) tends to $-\infty$, and the normal contact force tends to zero.

(a) You can see from the graph that f(θ) reaches the value 0.3 when θ has the value marked β in the figure. A numerical method (for example, using the sign-change rule, see C3 Section 8.1) shows that the angle β is about 24°.

(b) The standard method for finding a maximum shows that f$'(\theta) = 0$ when $\cos\theta = \tfrac{9}{11}$, and $f\left(\cos^{-1}\tfrac{9}{11}\right) = \dfrac{15\sqrt{10}}{128} \approx 0.371$. (You can work through the rather heavy details for yourself.) So f(θ) doesn't reach the value 0.4, and the broomstick won't slip until θ reaches the value γ at which f(γ) $= -0.4$, about 51°.

So, if the coefficient of friction is 0.3, the foot of the broomstick will slip to the left when it makes an angle of about 24° with the vertical. If the coefficient of friction is 0.4, it will slip to the right when it makes an angle of about 51° with the vertical.

This last example makes the basis of an interesting informal experiment. (In the absence of a broomstick, a pencil will do as well, though less spectacularly.) It is somewhat unexpected that the direction in which slipping occurs depends on whether the contact with the floor is smoothish or roughish.

Exercise 5D

1 A rattle is modelled as a circular disc of mass 200 grams and radius 5 cm connected at a point of its circumference to a stick. The stick is held upright, and the disc rotates about the top of the stick in a horizontal plane, making 2 revolutions a second (see diagram). Calculate the horizontal force on the stick.

2 In a food processor a straight blade of mass 100 grams and length 6 cm rotates at 5 revolutions per second. How large is the force on the shaft?

3 In Example 5.4.2, find the horizontal and vertical components of the force on the hinge when the radius of the hoop through C makes an angle θ with the horizontal.

4 A uniform rod of mass 10 kg and length 4 metres swings as a compound pendulum through an angle of 60° on either side of the downward vertical. Find the magnitude and direction of the force on the hinge
(a) at the extremity of the swing,   (b) in the middle of the swing.

5 A square lamina of side $2a$ and mass m is hinged to a fixed point at one corner. The square is raised until one of the sides through this corner is horizontal, and then released. Find the force on the hinge immediately after the instant of release.

6 A rod of mass m and length $2l$ is making complete revolutions about one end. Its angular velocity at the lowest point is double that at its highest point. Find the force from the hinge on the rod
(a) at its highest point,   (b) at its lowest point,   (c) when it is horizontal.

7 A gymnast is modelled as a uniform cuboid of mass 60 kg with height 1.8 metres and thickness (front to back) 0.2 metres. His arms, whose mass can be neglected, are 0.8 metres long, and attached to the cuboid 0.3 metres from the top. The diagram shows the 'gymnast' doing a hand stand on a horizontal bar. From this position he rotates rigidly in a semicircle until he is vertically below the bar. Find his angular speed in this position, and the tension in each arm.

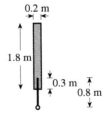

(8) A rod AB of length a has variable line density such that, at a distance x from A the line density $\lambda = k(a - x)$, where k is constant. Show that its centre of mass is at a distance $\frac{1}{3}a$ from A, and that its moment of inertia about a perpendicular axis through A is $\frac{1}{6}ma^2$, where m is its mass.

The rod is hinged to a fixed point at A, and held horizontal by a vertical string attached at a point C of the rod. Find the distance of C from A if there is no sudden change in the force on the hinge when the string is cut.

9* The rod in Question 8 is placed vertically upright, with the end A on a rough floor, and falls in a vertical plane. Investigate its fall in a manner similar to Example 5.4.3. By drawing appropriate graphs, find whether, for a given coefficient of friction, it will slip at a greater or smaller angle with the vertical than the broomstick did.

(10) A uniform shelf of length $6a$ rests symmetrically on two narrow pegs a distance $2a$ apart at the same level. The coefficient of friction between the pegs and the shelf is μ. One of the pegs falls out of its hole, so that the rod begins to turn about the other peg. Find expressions for the normal and frictional forces from the peg on the shelf when it has rotated through an angle θ. What angle does the shelf make with the horizontal when it starts to slip?

5.5* Proofs of the laws of rotational motion

This chapter has introduced two new laws which apply to the rotation of a rigid object about a fixed axis: the equation of rotational motion, and the extension of Newton's second law. Both of these can be shown to follow from corresponding laws for a particle, applied to the model of a rigid object described in Section 2.2. You may omit these proofs if you wish, but you should know that the laws have a logical basis in the theory of mechanics.

There is no exercise on this section.

Equation of rotational motion

Fig. 5.13 shows one of the particles, P_i, which make up a rigid object rotating about a fixed axis. P_iC_i is the perpendicular from P_i to the axis of rotation (compare Fig. 2.2), of length r_i. If the rigid object has angular velocity ω and angular acceleration α, the acceleration of the particle has radial and transverse components $r_i\omega^2$ and $r_i\alpha$.

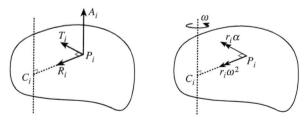

Fig. 5.13

There will be a lot of forces acting on the particle. Most will be internal forces linking it to other particles in the system, and some may be external forces (including its own weight). A_i, R_i and T_i denote the components parallel to the axis and in the radial and transverse directions of the resultant force on the particle at P_i. Applying Newton's second law in the transverse direction, $T_i = m_i(r_i\alpha)$. Multiply this by r_i to get

$$T_i r_i = m_i r_i^2 \alpha.$$

Now A_i and R_i have no moment about the axis, so $T_i r_i$ is the total moment of all the forces acting on this particular particle. There is an equation like this for each particle making up the rigid object, and these equations can be added to show that the total moment of all the forces is equal to $\sum m_i r_i^2 \alpha$; this can be written as $\left(\sum m_i r_i^2\right)\alpha = I\alpha$, where I is the moment of inertia about the axis.

You might think that 'the total moment of all the forces' is a very complicated expression. But it is greatly simplified by the fact that all the internal forces between pairs of particles occur in equal and opposite pairs acting along the same line, by Newton's third law (in the form given in M3 Section 4.1). So the moments of these forces appear in the sum as pairs which add up to zero.

This leaves only the total moment of the external forces on the object, and completes the proof that this is equal to $I\alpha$.

Extended form of Newton's second law

To prove this it is convenient to use vector notation. Again begin by considering a single particle P_i and denote the external and internal forces on that particle by $\mathbf{E}_i$ and $\mathbf{F}_i$. If the position vector of this particle is denoted by $\mathbf{r}_i$, then Newton's second law applied to the particle is

$$\mathbf{E}_i + \mathbf{F}_i = m_i \ddot{\mathbf{r}}_i.$$

As in the previous proof, when you add these equations for all the particles making up the object, the internal forces occur in opposite pairs whose sum is zero. Therefore

$$\sum \mathbf{E}_i = \sum m_i \ddot{\mathbf{r}}_i.$$

The expression on the right side should remind you of the formula for the centre of mass. In fact, in M2 Section 5.2 it was pointed out that this can be put into vector form,

$$\bar{\mathbf{r}} = \frac{m_1 \mathbf{r}_1 + m_2 \mathbf{r}_2 + \cdots + m_n \mathbf{r}_n}{M}.$$

In sigma notation, this can be written as

$$\sum m_i \mathbf{r}_i = M\bar{\mathbf{r}}, \quad \text{where } M \text{ is the total mass.}$$

Now if the object is in motion, the vectors $\mathbf{r}_i$ vary with time, and so does $\bar{\mathbf{r}}$. But the equation connecting them remains true, so you can differentiate with respect to t to get

$$\sum m_i \dot{\mathbf{r}}_i = M\dot{\bar{\mathbf{r}}}, \quad \text{and} \quad \sum m_i \ddot{\mathbf{r}}_i = M\ddot{\bar{\mathbf{r}}}.$$

The equation for $\sum \mathbf{E}_i$ above can therefore be written in the form

$$\sum \mathbf{E}_i = M\ddot{\mathbf{r}}$$

That is, the equation $\mathbf{F} = M\mathbf{a}$ can be applied to the large object, where $\mathbf{F}$ denotes the sum of all the external forces, M is the total mass and $\mathbf{a}$ is the acceleration of the centre of mass.

You will notice that nowhere in this proof has it been assumed that the object is rigid, or that it is rotating about a fixed point. That is why the law can be stated in the very general form given in the blue box in Section 5.4.

Miscellaneous exercise 5

1 A spacecraft is rotating about a fixed axis with angular speed $0.2\,\text{rad}\,\text{s}^{-1}$. By firing rocket motors, a couple of constant moment is applied to the spacecraft and, after 5 complete revolutions, the angular speed of the spacecraft is $0.5\,\text{rad}\,\text{s}^{-1}$. Find the angular acceleration of the spacecraft. (OCR)

2 A top is spinning about a fixed axis, and is slowing down with constant angular deceleration. At one instant, the angular speed of the top is $80\,\text{rad}\,\text{s}^{-1}$; in the next 25 seconds the top rotates through a total angle of 1625 radians. Calculate the angular deceleration of the top, and the angular speed at the end of the 25 seconds. (OCR)

3 A flywheel is rotating freely about its axis with angular speed $500\,\text{rad}\,\text{s}^{-1}$; its moment of inertia about the axis is $2.8\,\text{kg}\,\text{m}^2$. A constant braking couple of moment $70\,\text{N}\,\text{m}$ is applied to the flywheel.

(a) Calculate the time taken for the flywheel to come to rest.

(b) Calculate the number of revolutions made by the flywheel while it is slowing down. (OCR)

4 A uniform lamina in the shape of a semicircle of radius r has mass m. It is freely hinged along its bounding diameter to a fixed horizontal beam.

(a) Show that the moment of inertia of the lamina about the hinge is $\frac{1}{4}mr^2$.

(b) Find the period of small oscillations of the lamina about its position of stable equilibrium.

5 A uniform circular disc, of mass m and radius r, can rotate freely in a vertical plane about a point P on its circumference. Initially the disc is at rest with its centre O directly above P. It is slightly disturbed from this position of unstable equilibrium. In the subsequent motion, when PO makes an angle θ with the upward vertical, find

(a) the components of the acceleration of O in directions towards P and at right angles to PO,

(b) the components of the force on the disc at P in the directions towards O and at right angles to PO.

Hence find the largest and smallest values of the magnitude of the resultant force at P as the disc rotates, and the values of θ at which these occur.

6 A uniform ruler of mass 0.8 kg has length 1.2 metres and negligible width. A hole is made in the ruler 0.4 metres from one end. A light spike, whose underside is flat and rough, is inserted through the hole. The spike rests on a pair of parallel horizontal rails at the same level, at right angles to the rails, as shown in the diagram. The ruler then hangs vertically in equilibrium midway between the rails.

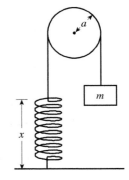

The ruler is now raised to a horizontal position and released, so that it swings in a vertical plane.

(a) Assuming that the spike does not slip on the rails, find expressions for the normal and frictional forces at each point of contact when the ruler is at an angle θ to the vertical.

(b) Find the least value of the coefficient of friction if the spike is not to slip on the rails as the ruler swings.

7 A uniform disc of radius a and mass m is freely pivoted on a horizontal axis through its centre. An inextensible string is wrapped several times round the disc (so that it does not slip). To one end of the string is tied a mass m, to the other a light spring of natural length a and modulus of elasticity λ. The bottom of the spring is fastened so that the spring is vertical. The mass m also moves vertically.

Express the angular velocity of the disc and the speed of the mass in terms of x, where x is the length of the spring at time t. Write down equations of motion for the mass and the disc, and hence show that the equation of motion of the system is

$$\frac{d^2x}{dt^2} + \frac{2\lambda}{3ma}x = \tfrac{2}{3}g + \frac{2\lambda}{3m}.$$

Write down the period of oscillation of the system. (OCR)

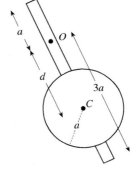

8 A pendulum is made by bolting a uniform circular disc of mass M and radius a to a uniform thin rod of mass M and length $4a$. The rod swings about a horizontal axle through a point O at distance a from one end, and the centre C of the disc is a distance d along the rod from O (see diagram). Use the parallel axes theorem to show that the moment of inertia I of the pendulum about the axis is $I = \tfrac{1}{6}M\left(17a^2 + 6d^2\right)$.

The pendulum performs small oscillations about its position of stable equilibrium. Show that the oscillations have minimum period when $d \approx 0.96a$. (OCR)

9 A sickle is modelled as a rod AB of mass m and length a rigidly joined to a semicircle BC of metal, of mass m and radius a. It hangs from a small hook at A, and swings as a pendulum about an axis through A and perpendicular to its plane. Show that the moment of inertia about this axis is $\frac{16}{3}ma^2$ and deduce that the period of small oscillations is approximately $9.034\sqrt{\dfrac{a}{g}}$.   (OCR, adapted)

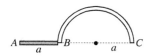

10 A machine contains a component called an 'aerospinner', illustrated in the first diagram. This is made of thin sheet metal of uniform surface density. It consists of a circular plate of radius 9 cm with a hole of radius 1 cm in the centre, to which is welded a hollow tube of radius 1 cm and height 10 cm. The total mass is 2 kg, distributed as shown in the table.

	Area (cm^2)	Mass (kg)
'Filled in' plate	81π	1.62
'Filled in' hole	π	0.02
Plate with hole	80π	1.60
Tube	20π	0.40
Aerospinner	100π	2.00

While the machine is switched off, the plate rests on a horizontal platform. When the machine is operated, compressed air is forced down the tube and it spins while supported on a cushion of air.

The machine is switched off and the spinner drops gently back onto the platform. It is brought to rest by friction. The coefficient of friction is 0.3, and it is assumed that the normal force is distributed across the surface of the plate so that, over any area, the normal force is equal to the weight of the part of the aerospinner directly above that area.

(a) Show that the frictional couple round the inner rim of the aerospinner is $0.0012g$ N m. Find the normal force on a thin ring of the plate of radius r metres and thickness δr metres (see the second diagram), and show that the frictional couple, in newton metres, on the plate is given by $120g\displaystyle\int_{0.01}^{0.09} r^2\,dr$. Hence evaluate the total frictional couple.

(b) Find the total moment of inertia of the aerospinner about the vertical axis of symmetry, and hence the angular retardation.

(c) If the aerospinner is spinning at 8 revolutions per second when the machine is switched off, how long will it take to come to rest?   (OCR)

11 A uniform circular disc has mass m and radius a. The point A is on the disc at a distance $\frac{1}{2}a$ from the centre C. The disc is rotating freely about a fixed horizontal axis perpendicular to the disc and passing through A. Find the moment of inertia of the disc about this axis.

The angular speed when C is vertically below A is three times the angular speed when C is vertically above A. At an instant when AC is at an angle $\frac{1}{6}\pi$ below the horizontal,

(a) show that the angular speed of the disc is $\sqrt{\dfrac{7g}{3a}}$,

(b) find, in terms of g and a, the angular acceleration of the disc,

(c) find, in terms of m and g, the components parallel and perpendicular to CA of the force acting on the disc at A.   (OCR)

12 An arm on a fairground ride is modelled by a uniform rod AB, of mass m and length $2a$, with a point mass m attached at B. The arm rotates freely in a vertical plane about a fixed horizontal axis through A. You may assume that air resistance is negligible. The arm is released from rest with AB horizontal.

(a) Show that the moment of inertia of the arm about the axis is $\frac{16}{3}ma^2$.

(b) Find the angular acceleration of the arm immediately after it has been released.

(c) Show that, at the instant when AB is vertical, the angular speed of the arm is $\sqrt{\dfrac{9g}{8a}}$.

(d) Find the force acting on the arm at A

(i) immediately after the arm is released (with AB horizontal),

(ii) at the instant when AB is vertical.   (OCR)

13 A uniform rod AB, of mass m and length $2a$, is free to rotate in a vertical plane about a fixed horizontal axis passing through the point C on the rod, where $AC = \frac{2}{3}a$. Find the moment of inertia of the rod about this axis.

Initially the rod is vertical with B above C. It is slightly disturbed from rest in this position. At an instant during the subsequent motion, AB makes an angle θ with the upward vertical.

(a) Show that the angular speed of the rod at this instant is $\sqrt{\dfrac{3g}{2a}(1 - \cos\theta)}$.

(b) Find the angular acceleration of the rod at this instant.

At this instant, the force acting on the rod at C has components R along $\overrightarrow{AB}$ and S perpendicular to $\overrightarrow{AB}$. Show that $R = \frac{1}{2}mg(3\cos\theta - 1)$ and find an expression for S in terms of m, g and θ.   (OCR)

14 In a fairground ride, a cabin is attached to one end of an arm of
    mass 100 kg and length 7.2 m. The total mass of the cabin and
    passengers is 300 kg. A counterweight of mass 200 kg is attached
    to the other end of the arm. The ride is modelled as a uniform
    rod AB, with particles attached at A and B, which is free to
    rotate, without resistance, in a vertical plane about a fixed
    horizontal axis through the mid-point O of AB (see diagram).

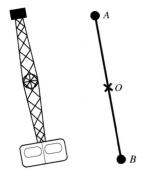

(a) Find the distance of the centre of mass of the system from O.

(b) Find the moment of inertia of the system about the
    horizontal axis through O.

Before the motor is switched on, the ride performs oscillations
with the cabin moving a short distance each side of its
equilibrium position.

(c) Find the approximate period of these small oscillations.

(d) Comment briefly on the modelling assumptions made in
    this question.   (OCR)

15 A thin rod AB of length a has variable density $\dfrac{kx}{a}$ per unit
    length where x is the distance from the end A and k is a
    constant.

(a) Find the mass m of the rod.

(b) Find the distance of the centre of mass from A, and the
    moment of inertia of the rod about an axis through A
    perpendicular to the rod, giving your answers in terms of
    a and m.

The centre of a thin uniform circular disc of radius $\frac{1}{4}a$ and
mass m is attached to the rod at the end point B, with the
rod in the plane of the disc. The compound body can rotate freely about a fixed horizontal
axis through A, which is perpendicular to the plane of the disc, as shown in the diagram.
The angle between the rod and the downward vertical is denoted by θ.

(c) Show that the moment of inertia I of the compound body about the horizontal axis
    through A is given by $I = \frac{49}{32}ma^2$.

(d) Write down, in terms of θ, a differential equation describing the motion of the
    compound body. Hence find the approximate period of small oscillations about the
    position of stable equilibrium.   (MEI)

16 A hanging basket filled with compost may be considered as a
uniform solid hemisphere of mass M and radius r suspended
from a fixed point P by three equally spaced light chains of
length $\sqrt{5}r$. The chains connect P to points on the rim of
the plane circular face of the hemisphere, as shown in the
diagram.

(a) Show that the moment of inertia of the hanging basket
about a horizontal axis through P is $\frac{59}{10}Mr^2$.

(b) The hanging basket and chains can be considered as a rigid
body which can undergo small oscillations about a
horizontal axis through P. If this body is displaced through a
small angle θ from its equilibrium position and released
from rest, show that such oscillations are approximately
simple harmonic. Find the period of these oscillations.

(c) When $\theta = 0$, the wind catches the hanging basket and gives it a small angular velocity
ω about the horizontal axis through P. Find the maximum value of θ attained in the
subsequent motion. (OCR)

6 Angular momentum

There is an equivalent of the concepts of momentum and impulse for rotation. When you have completed this chapter, you should

- understand the ideas of angular momentum and impulsive moment, and the connection between them
- know that, for objects rotating about the same axis and interacting with each other, angular momentum is conserved
- know how to find the impulse on the axis of rotation.

6.1 The rotational impulse–momentum equation

If you are taking an engine apart and have difficulty unscrewing a nut, you can sometimes shift it with a sharp tangential blow from a hammer on the handle of the spanner. This may not just overcome the resisting couple, but also give the nut an angular velocity so that it begins to unscrew.

The blow from the hammer produces an impulsive moment about the axis of the nut, and the result is to give it 'rotational momentum'. This is the equivalent of linear momentum, mv, for rotational motion. Replacing m by I, and v by ω, you would expect it to be calculated from the formula $I\omega$.

If you have a rigid object which can rotate about an axis, and if a force (or couple) with moment C acts on it from time t_1 to t_2, then the angular velocity ω satisfies the differential equation

$$C = I\dot{\omega}.$$

If $\omega = \omega_1$ when $t = t_1$, and $\omega = \omega_2$ when $t = t_2$, you can integrate this equation to get

$$\int_{t_1}^{t_2} C\,\mathrm{d}t = \left[I\omega \right]_{t_1}^{t_2} = I\omega_2 - I\omega_1.$$

The integral on the left is the **impulsive moment** of the force or couple about the axis. Since the unit of C is the newton metre, impulsive moment is measured in newton metre seconds (N m s).

The quantity $I\omega$ is called the **angular momentum** of the object about the axis. The equation therefore states that:

> The total impulsive moment applied to the object is equal to the increase in the angular momentum.

Like the linear impulse–momentum equation, this is most often used when a force with a large moment is applied for a very short time. If C is constant, the impulsive moment is simply the moment C multiplied by the time for which it acts.

Example 6.1.1
A spin drier with a full load of laundry, rotating at 1200 revolutions per minute, is brought to rest in 2 seconds. The drum is modelled as a hollow cylinder of mass 2 kg and radius 20 cm, and the contents as a solid cylinder of mass 8 kg and radius 20 cm. Find the moment of the constant couple slowing it down.

It is important to work with a consistent system of units. The angular speed is 20 revolutions per second, which is 40π rad s^{-1}. The moment of inertia of the drum is 2×0.2^2 kg m^2, which is 0.08 kg m^2, and the moment of inertia of the contents is $\frac{1}{2} \times 8 \times 0.2^2$ kg m^2, or 0.16 kg m^2. This gives a total moment of inertia of 0.24 kg m^2. So the initial angular momentum is $0.24 \times 40\pi$ N m s, which is 9.6π N m s.

If the couple bringing the drum to rest is C N m, assumed to be constant, its impulsive moment is $2C$ N m s. So $2C = 9.6\pi$, giving $C = 4.8\pi \approx 15.1$.

The couple acting on the drum has moment 15.1 N m, correct to 3 significant figures.

Example 6.1.2
A uniform rod AB, of mass 5 kg and length 1.2 metres, hangs from a fixed hinge at A. The rod is struck by a horizontal blow of impulse 20 N s at a point 0.9 metres below A. Will this be large enough to cause the rod to make complete revolutions about the hinge?

The moment of inertia of the rod is $\frac{1}{3} \times 5 \times 1.2^2$ kg m^2, which is 2.4 kg m^2. The impulsive moment of the blow is 20×0.9 N m s, which is 18 N m s. If the rod starts to rotate with angular velocity ω rad s^{-1}, then $18 = 2.4\omega$, so $\omega = \dfrac{18}{2.4} = 7.5$.

To find whether the rod will make complete revolutions, it is best to consider energy; has the blow given the rod enough kinetic energy to produce the potential energy needed to get it into the vertical position with B above A?

The kinetic energy of the rod just after the blow is $\frac{1}{2} \times 2.4 \times 7.5^2$ joules, which is 67.5 joules. The centre of mass of the rod has to move from 0.6 metres below A to 0.6 metres above A, a gain in potential energy of $5 \times 9.8 \times 1.2$ joules, which is 58.8 joules.

Since $67.5 > 58.8$, the impulse from the blow is large enough for the rod to make complete revolutions about the hinge.

Example 6.1.3
A door has moment of inertia 4 kg m^2 about its hinges. A boy kicks a football of mass 0.5 kg, which strikes the door at right angles 0.8 metres from the line of the hinges, with a speed of 9 m s^{-1}. If the coefficient of restitution is 0.5, find the angular speed with which the door starts to rotate, and the speed with which the ball rebounds.

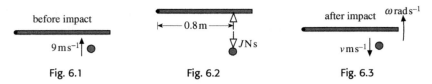

| before impact | 0.8 m | after impact ω rad s^{-1} |

Fig. 6.1   Fig. 6.2   Fig. 6.3

Figs. 6.1 to 6.3 show the situation just before the impact, at the instant of impact, and just after. The impulse between the ball and the door is J N s; after the impact the door has angular speed ω rad s^{-1} and the ball has speed v m s^{-1}.

For the ball, the impulse–momentum equation is

$$J = 0.5v - 0.5 \times (-9).$$

The rotational impulse–momentum equation for the door is

$$J \times 0.8 = 4\omega.$$

To use the information about the coefficient of restitution, the speed of approach is 9 m s^{-1}, but it is not so obvious how to calculate the speed of separation; at what point of the door should this be taken?

Remember that the coefficient of friction is the ratio of the impulses during restitution and compression at the point of contact. So this must be the point where the speed of the door is calculated. The speed of separation is therefore $v + 0.8\omega$, and the restitution equation is

$$v + 0.8\omega = 0.5 \times 9.$$

There are now three equations to be solved for the unknowns v, ω and J. Since J is not asked for, begin by eliminating this between the first two equations. Substituting $J = 0.5v + 4.5$ from the first equation in the second,

$$(0.5v + 4.5) \times 0.8 = 4\omega.$$

You now have two simultaneous equations for v and ω. You can check for yourself that they are satisfied by $v = 3.5$ and $\omega = 1.25$.

The door starts to rotate with angular speed 1.25 rad s^{-1}, and the ball rebounds with speed 3.5 m s^{-1}.

Example 6.1.4
Two gear wheels are mounted on parallel shafts. One has radius 10 cm and moment of inertia 30 kg cm^2; the other has radius 4 cm and moment of inertia 6 kg cm^2. The first wheel is rotating clockwise at 4 rad s^{-1}, the second anticlockwise at 7 rad s^{-1}. The gears then engage together. Find

(a) their subsequent angular velocities,   (b) the loss of kinetic energy.

Figs. 6.4 to 6.6 show the situation just before the gears engage, at the instant of engagement, and just after.

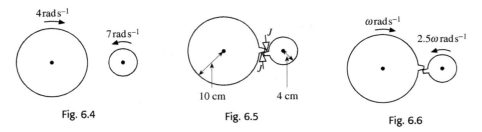

Fig. 6.4   Fig. 6.5   Fig. 6.6

It makes sense to use centimetres as the unit of length at this stage.

(a) The reason why there is an impact is that the tangential velocities of the two gear wheels are different. At the circumference of the wheels the speeds are $10 \times 4 \, \text{cm s}^{-1} = 40 \, \text{cm s}^{-1}$ and $4 \times 7 \, \text{cm s}^{-1} = 28 \, \text{cm s}^{-1}$. Although the wheels are rotating in opposite senses, the tangential velocities are in the same direction.

After the impact the two velocities must be equal. So, if the first wheel then has angular velocity $\omega \, \text{rad s}^{-1}$, its tangential speed is $10\omega \, \text{cm s}^{-1}$, so the other wheel rotates at $\frac{10}{4}\omega \, \text{cm s}^{-1} = 2.5\omega \, \text{cm s}^{-1}$.

This change of speed is produced by impulses of magnitude J units between a pair of gear teeth.

Notice that, because the moments of inertia are given in kg cm^2 the units of angular momentum are 10^{-4} times the standard units. If the moments are calculated using the radius in centimetres, this means that the units of impulse are $10^{-2} \, \text{N s}$. Since units are consistent throughout, it isn't important to specify them precisely in the calculation.

You can now write rotational impulse–momentum equations for each wheel. Taking clockwise as positive for the first, and anticlockwise for the second, these are

$$-10J = 30\omega - 30 \times 4, \quad \text{and} \quad 4J = 6(2.5\omega) - 6 \times 7.$$

Since $2 \times (-10J) + 5 \times 4J = 0$, J can be eliminated to give

$$2(30\omega - 120) + 5(15\omega - 42) = 0.$$

So $135\omega - 450 = 0$, giving $\omega = \frac{450}{135} = \frac{10}{3}$.

After the gears engage, the larger wheel has angular speed $3\frac{1}{3} \, \text{rad s}^{-1}$ clockwise, the smaller wheel has angular speed $8\frac{1}{3} \, \text{rad s}^{-1}$ anticlockwise.

(b) When the formula $\frac{1}{2}I\omega^2$ is used for kinetic energy, with the moment of inertia in units of $\text{kg cm}^2 = 10^{-4} \, \text{kg m}^2$, the energy will be in units of 10^{-4} joules. With this unit, the kinetic energy is $\frac{1}{2} \times 30 \times 4^2 + \frac{1}{2} \times 6 \times 7^2 = 387$ before the wheels engage. Afterwards the kinetic energy is $\frac{1}{2} \times 30 \times \left(\frac{10}{3}\right)^2 + \frac{1}{2} \times 6 \times \left(\frac{25}{3}\right)^2 = 375$.

The loss of kinetic energy is therefore 12×10^{-4} joules.

6.2   Conservation of angular momentum

If two objects, *A* and *B*, rotating about the same axis, come into contact with each other, there will be forces of interaction between them. Newton's third law applies to these forces. That is, to any force which *A* exerts on *B*, there corresponds a force from *B* on *A*; these forces have the same magnitude, and act in opposite directions along the same line. It follows that the moments of the two forces are equal in magnitude, but in opposite senses about the axis; and, by integrating over time, the same is true of their impulsive moments.

Now the impulsive moment of *A* on *B* is equal to the increase in the angular momentum of *B* about the axis; and the impulsive moment of *B* on *A* is equal to the increase in the angular momentum of *A*. Since the two impulsive moments have equal magnitude and opposite sense, they add up to zero. So the increase in the combined angular momentum of the two objects is zero. That is, the combined angular momentum is constant.

> **Conservation of angular momentum**
>
> If two objects rotating about the same axis interact with each other, and there is no external impulsive moment about the axis, the total angular momentum of the two objects about the axis is constant.

Notice the condition that there should be no external impulsive moment about the axis. In Example 6.1.3, the equation $(0.5v + 4.5) \times 0.8 = 4\omega$ obtained by eliminating J could in fact be interpreted as a conservation of angular momentum equation (see Example 6.3.1), even though at the instant of impact there is an external impulse from the door hinges, because this impulse has no moment about the hinges. However, conservation of angular momentum couldn't be used in Example 6.1.4 because when the gears engage there are impulses on the shafts of both gears; whichever shaft you choose, there is a moment about that shaft from the impulse on the other shaft.

Example 6.2.1

In a clutch mechanism, two half-shafts end in circular plates. The shafts are in line, rotating freely in the same sense as each other. The shafts, together with their plates, have moment of inertia 0.05 kg m^2 and 0.01 kg m^2, and they are rotating at 50 and 35 revolutions per second respectively. The two plates are pushed into contact with each other, causing the two shafts to rotate together. Find their common angular speed, and the impulsive moment of the couple which each exerts on the other.

Let the common angular speed be x revolutions per second. The situation before the plates come together is illustrated in Fig. 6.7.

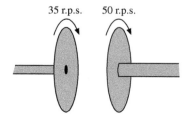

In radians per second, the angular speeds before the plates come together are 100π and 70π, and the common angular speed afterwards is $2\pi x$. So the conservation of angular momentum equation is

$$0.05 \times 100\pi + 0.01 \times 70\pi = (0.05 + 0.01) \times 2\pi x,$$

which gives $x = 47.5$.

Fig. 6.7

The angular momentum of the lighter shaft increases from $0.01 \times 70\pi$ N m s to $0.01 \times (2\pi \times 47.5)$ N m s, a gain of 0.785 N m s. Check for yourself that this is equal to the decrease in angular momentum of the other shaft.

After the shafts make contact, they rotate with common angular speed of 47.5 revolutions per second. The couple which each plate exerts on the other has impulsive moment 0.785 N m s.

In this example, notice that the common factor 2π can be cancelled from the angular momentum equation. So, if only the common angular speed is wanted, there is no need to convert the angular speeds to rad s^{-1}. But to find the impulsive moment it is essential to work in standard SI units.

6.3 Angular momentum of a particle

Suppose that a turntable is rotating freely on smooth bearings about a vertical axis; denote its moment of inertia by I and the angular speed by ω_0. A pebble of mass m, small enough to be modelled as a particle, is lowered gently on to the turntable at a distance r from the axis of rotation. The surface is so rough that the pebble scarcely slips on the turntable before both are rotating about the axis with angular speed ω.

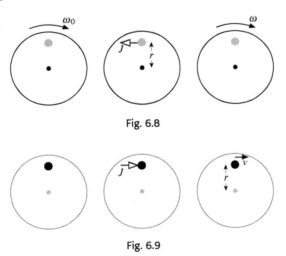

Fig. 6.8

Fig. 6.9

Fig. 6.8 and Fig. 6.9 show the speeds of the turntable and of the pebble before and after they come into contact, and the impulse J which each exerts on the other in a tangential direction. For the turntable you can write an angular momentum equation

$$-Jr = I\,\omega - I\,\omega_0;$$

and for the pebble you can write a linear equation

$$J = mv - m \times 0,$$

where $v = r\omega$.

To eliminate v, multiply the second equation by r and add it to the first, to get

$$0 = -Jr + Jr = I\omega - I\omega_0 + (mv)r,$$

so $$I\omega_0 = I\omega + (mv)r.$$

You will recognise the terms $I\omega_0$ and $I\omega$ as the angular momentum of the turntable before and after the contact. What is less familiar is the expression $(mv)r$ for the angular momentum of the pebble about the axis.

The factor mv in this expression is the linear momentum of the particle in the tangential direction, so you can think of the product $(mv)r$ as the moment of this momentum about the axis. Because of this, angular momentum is sometimes called 'moment of momentum'.

> The angular momentum of a particle about an axis of rotation is the moment about the axis of the linear momentum of the particle.

To complete the analysis, write v as $r\omega$, which changes the angular momentum equation to

$$I\omega_0 = I\omega + (mr\omega)r, \quad or \quad I\omega_0 = (I + mr^2)\omega.$$

This last equation suggests a different interpretation. The expression in brackets on the right side is the sum of the moments of inertia of the turntable and the pebble about the axis, so you can think of it as the moment of inertia of the combined object turntable-plus-pebble. The equation then states that the angular momentum of the turntable alone before contact is equal to the angular momentum of the combined object after contact.

Example 6.3.1
Verify the statement that, in Example 6.1.3, the equation $(0.5v + 4.5) \times 0.8 = 4\omega$ expresses the conservation of the total angular momentum of the football and the door.

Fig. 6.10 shows the relevant parts of Fig. 6.1 and Fig. 6.3, indicating the velocity of the football before and after the impact, and the angular speed of the door afterwards. Taking anticlockwise to be positive, expressions for the linear momentum of the ball before and after impact are 0.5×9 N s and $0.5 \times (-v)$ N s, so the moments are 4.5×0.8 N m s and $(-0.5v) \times 0.8$ N m s. The angular momentum of the door is 4ω N m s. So, using the conservation of momentum,

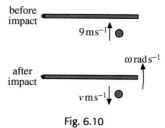

Fig. 6.10

$$4.5 \times 0.8 = 4\omega - 0.5v \times 0.8,$$

which can be rearranged as $(0.5v + 4.5) \times 0.8 = 4\omega$.

Solving some problems involves combining the principles of conservation of angular momentum and energy. As with linear motion, kinetic energy is usually lost when a collision occurs. On the other hand, angular momentum is only conserved if there is no external impulse with a moment about the axis. This is illustrated by the next example, for which different principles are applied in the two stages.

Example 6.3.2

A spiked wheel consists of nine rods, each of mass 5 kg and length 2 metres, rigidly attached to a central hub which can rotate freely about a horizontal axis. The inner end of each rod is at the centre of rotation. The moment of inertia of the central hub is 8 kg m^2. The wheel is initially stationary with one of the rods horizontal. An object of mass 3 kg falls vertically from a height of 10 metres and strikes the horizontal rod at its far end, as shown in Fig. 6.11. After the impact the object sticks to the rod.

(a) Find the angular speed with which the wheel (with the object attached) begins to rotate.

(b) Find the loss of kinetic energy when the impact occurs.

(c) Show that the wheel will come to rest again, and find the angle through which it turns before doing so.

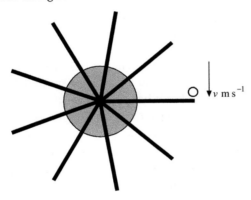

Fig. 6.11

The moment of inertia of each rod about the axis of rotation is given by $\frac{1}{3}Md^2$ with $M = 5$ and $d = 2$, that is $\frac{20}{3}$ kg m^2. So the moment of inertia of the spiked wheel is $(9 \times \frac{20}{3} + 8)$ kg m^2, which is 68 kg m^2.

(a) When the falling object strikes the rod it is moving at a speed v m s^{-1} given by $v^2 = u^2 + 2as$ with $u = 0$, $a = 9.8$ and $s = 10$. Therefore $v^2 = 2 \times 9.8 \times 10 = 196$, giving $v = 14$.

The total angular momentum of the wheel and the falling object is unchanged by the impact. Before the impact the angular momentum of the wheel is 0. The linear momentum of the falling object is 3×14 N s, and the moment of this about the axis is $(3 \times 14) \times 2$ N m s. So the angular momentum of the falling object is 84 N m s.

After the impact the wheel and the object rotate together. Their combined moment of inertia about the axis is $(68 + 3 \times 2^2)$ kg m^2, which is 80 kg m^2. If the angular speed is then ω rad s^{-1}, the angular momentum is 80ω N m s.

Therefore, since angular momentum is conserved,

$$80\omega = 84, \quad \text{which gives} \quad \omega = 1.05.$$

After the impact the wheel and the object start to rotate with angular speed 1.05 rad s^{-1}.

(b) Before the impact only the falling object has kinetic energy, of amount
$\frac{1}{2} \times 3 \times 14^2$ J, which is 294 J. (This could also be calculated as the potential energy
lost by the object in falling, which is $3 \times 9.8 \times 10$ J.) After the impact the wheel
and the object together have kinetic energy $\frac{1}{2} \times 80 \times 1.05^2$ J, or 44.1 J. The loss of
kinetic energy is therefore 249.9 J.

(c) After the impact the total angular momentum of the wheel with the object
attached is no longer conserved, because the weight of the object has a moment
about the axis. But since there are no further collisions, the total energy of the
system is conserved.

What happens after the object strikes the rod? To begin with, the object will lose
potential energy; but the centre of mass of the wheel is at the centre of rotation,
so the potential energy of the wheel remains constant. Since there is an overall
loss of potential energy, the angular speed of the wheel will increase.

But once the wheel has turned through 90° the object will begin to rise and gain
potential energy, so the wheel will slow down. When it has turned through 180°
the object will again be level with the axis, and the angular speed will again be
1.05 rad s^{-1}. The question now is whether it has enough kinetic energy for the
object to rise the further 2 metres necessary for the wheel to make complete
revolutions.

It was shown in part (b) that the total kinetic energy after the impact is 44.1 J.
This is not enough for the object to rise a further 2 metres, which requires
potential energy of $3 \times 9.8 \times 2$ J, that is 58.8 J.

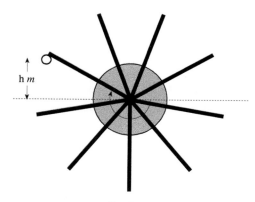

Fig. 6.12

So the wheel will come to rest when the object is at a height h metres above the
axis (see Fig. 6.12), where

$$3 \times 9.8 \times h = 44.1, \quad \text{which gives} \quad h = 1.5.$$

The wheel will then have turned through an angle equal to $180° + \sin^{-1} \dfrac{1.5}{2}$,
which is 228.6°.

6.4 The impulse on the axis

When a rigid object which can rotate about an axis is hit, the impulse from the blow will usually be accompanied by an impulse from the axis. This is calculated in much the same way as that described in Section 5.4 for the force from the axis on an accelerating object. That is, the total impulse is equated to the change of momentum located at the centre of mass. But in one respect the application is simpler, because the velocity, and therefore the momentum, has only a transverse component; there is no radial component, as there was for the acceleration.

> The impulse–momentum equation $\mathbf{J} = m\mathbf{v} - m\mathbf{u}$ can be applied to the motion of a large object, where $\mathbf{J}$ stands for the vector sum of the external forces on the object, m is the total mass, and $\mathbf{u}$, $\mathbf{v}$ are the velocities of the centre of mass before and after the impulse.

Example 6.4.1
In Example 6.1.2, find the impulse on the hinge when the rod is hit.

As in the corresponding force problems, you have to be careful to notice whether the question asks for the impulse on the hinge, or the impulse from the hinge on the rod. Fig. 6.13 shows the impulses on the rod from the hinge and from the blow; the impulse on the hinge will be in the opposite direction.

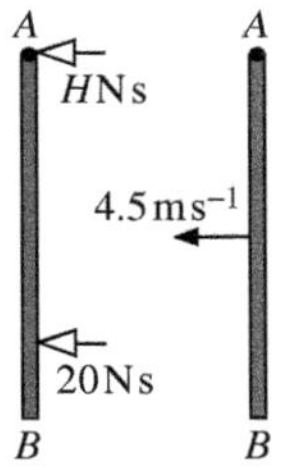

As in Section 5.4, it is best to draw two copies of the figure, one showing the impulses and the other the velocity of the centre of mass. You may even want three if the velocity is non-zero both before and after the impulse.

Fig. 6.13

It was found in Example 6.1.2 that the angular velocity is $7.5\,\mathrm{rad\,s^{-1}}$ after the rod is hit, and the centre of mass is 0.6 metres from the hinge, so the velocity of the centre of mass is $0.6 \times 7.5\,\mathrm{m\,s^{-1}} = 4.5\,\mathrm{m\,s^{-1}}$ horizontally. The impulse from the hinge on the rod is therefore also horizontal; let it have magnitude $H\,\mathrm{N\,s}$. Then

$$\mathcal{R}(\rightarrow) \quad H + 20 = 5 \times 4.5, \quad \text{so} \quad H = 2.5.$$

The impulse from the hinge on the rod is $2.5\,\mathrm{N\,s}$ in the same direction as the blow. The impulse on the hinge is therefore $2.5\,\mathrm{N\,s}$ in the opposite direction to the blow.

Example 6.4.2
A uniform square lamina $ABCD$ has mass m and sides of length a. It is placed on a smooth horizontal surface, and is free to rotate about a vertical axis at A. It is struck at C with a blow of impulse J in the direction $\overrightarrow{CD}$. Find the components X and Y of the impulse from the axis on the lamina in the directions $\overrightarrow{AB}$ and $\overrightarrow{AD}$ respectively.

The moment of inertia of the lamina about each of the edges AB and AD is $\frac{1}{3}ma^2$, so by the perpendicular axes rule the moment of inertia about the axis through A is $\frac{2}{3}ma^2$.

Fig. 6.14 shows the impulses on the lamina and the velocity of the centre of mass. If the angular speed of the lamina after the blow is ω, the rotational impulse–momentum equation about the axis is

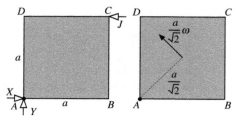

Fig. 6.14

$$Ja = \tfrac{2}{3}ma^2\omega, \quad \text{so} \quad \omega = \frac{3J}{2ma}.$$

The centre of mass of the lamina is at a distance $\dfrac{a}{\sqrt{2}}$ from A, so the velocity of the centre of mass after the blow is $\dfrac{a}{\sqrt{2}}\omega$ in the direction of the diagonal $\overrightarrow{BD}$.

This can be split into components in the directions $\overrightarrow{AB}$ and $\overrightarrow{AD}$ of

$$-\frac{a}{\sqrt{2}}\omega \times \frac{1}{\sqrt{2}} = -\tfrac{1}{2}a\omega = -\frac{3J}{4m} \quad \text{and} \quad \frac{a}{\sqrt{2}}\omega \times \frac{1}{\sqrt{2}} = \tfrac{1}{2}a\omega = \frac{3J}{4m}$$

respectively.

Impulse–momentum equations in these directions are then

$$X - J = m \times \left(-\frac{3J}{4m}\right) \quad \text{and} \quad Y = m \times \frac{3J}{4m},$$

which can be simplified as $X - J = -\tfrac{3}{4}J$ and $Y = \tfrac{3}{4}J$.

The components of the impulse from the hinge are $X = \tfrac{1}{4}J$ and $Y = \tfrac{3}{4}J$.

Exercise 6

1 Calculate the angular momentum about the axis of

 (a) an aircraft propeller with moment of inertia $12\,\text{kg m}^2$ rotating at 2500 revolutions per minute,

 (b) a solid flywheel of mass $20\,\text{kg}$ and radius $40\,\text{cm}$, rotating at 3000 revolutions per minute,

 (c) a hovering frisbee of mass 80 grams and radius $10\,\text{cm}$, rotating at 10 revolutions per second,

 (d) a stone of mass 500 grams travelling at $10\,\text{m s}^{-1}$ in a plane at right angles to the axis, along a line 2 metres from the axis.

2 A bicycle wheel with moment of inertia $1.5\,\text{kg m}^2$ is rotating freely on its axis at $8\,\text{rad s}^{-1}$, and brought to rest by a frictional force of 20 newtons applied at $30\,\text{cm}$ from the axle. How long does it take to come to rest?

3 A uniform disc of mass $4\,\text{kg}$ and radius $\tfrac{1}{4}$ metre is set in motion by a motor which produces a couple of moment $(0.5 + 2t)\,\text{N m}$ after t seconds, for $0 \leqslant t \leqslant 10$. What is its angular speed after 10 seconds?

④ A uniform rod, of mass 3 kg and length 1 metre, is hinged at a point 25 cm from one end, and hangs in stable equilibrium. It is given a horizontal blow of impulse 2 N s at its lowest point. Find the angular speed with which it starts to rotate, and the angle through which it swings before coming to rest.

⑤ A square lamina $ABCD$, of mass m and sides of length a, can rotate about a horizontal axis through A in a vertical plane. There is a fixed inelastic stop at a point E at a distance a below A. The lamina is originally resting with AB vertical and the corner B against the stop. It is then raised until AB is horizontal, and let go. Find the impulse when it is brought to rest by the stop at E.

⑥ The rotating parts of a potter's wheel have moment of inertia 1.8 kg m² about its vertical axis. It is rotating at 6 rad s⁻¹ when a lump of clay of mass 2 kg, modelled as a hemisphere of radius 5 cm, is placed on the centre of the wheel. By how much is the angular speed of the wheel decreased?

⑦ A uniform door, of mass 15 kg and width 80 cm, is free to move round vertical hinges. A bullet of mass 40 grams is fired at, and embeds itself in, the door. It hits the door at right angles, 60 cm from the hinges, moving horizontally at 500 m s⁻¹. Find the angular speed with which the door swings open.

⑧ A uniform rod AB of length 2 metres and mass 3 kg has a particle of mass 1 kg attached at the end B. It hangs from a fixed hinge at A. It is struck with a horizontal blow on the end B, and comes to rest with B at the same level as A. Calculate the impulse of the blow and the impulse on the hinge.

⑨ A turntable in a microwave oven is turning at 2 rad s⁻¹. A cake, modelled as a uniform cylinder of mass 0.8 kg and radius 10 cm, is placed centrally on the turntable, which continues to turn at the same rate. What is the impulsive moment from the motor?

10 A boy is standing on a rotating platform with his arms outstretched. His centre of mass is on the axis of rotation, and the moment of inertia of the boy and the platform about the axis is 0.72 kg m². As the boy rotates he picks up a pole in each hand, and holds the poles vertically at a distance of 0.9 metres from the axis, as shown in the diagram. As a result his angular speed is reduced by 90%. Find the mass of each pole.

⑪ A uniform rod of length a hangs from a fixed hinge at its upper end. It is struck with a horizontal blow of impulse J at a distance x below the hinge. Find the impulse on the rod from the hinge, and show that there is a value of x for which this impulse is zero.

Tubular bells are long thin tubes hung by cords from a wooden frame. Explain an application of the above result to the playing of tubular bells.

12 Two horizontal circular discs, of the same thickness and radii r and s, are made of identical uniform material. They are free to rotate at the same horizontal level about parallel vertical shafts (whose moment of inertia is negligible). The disc of radius r is rotating with angular speed ω; the other disc is stationary. The shafts are now brought together so that the rims of the discs come into contact. When slipping between the rims stops, with what angular speeds are the discs rotating?

Miscellaneous exercise 6

1 Two flywheels are rotating, in the same direction, about the same fixed axis. One wheel has moment of inertia $3.6\,\mathrm{kg\,m^2}$ about the axis, and angular speed $45\,\mathrm{rad\,s^{-1}}$. The other has moment of inertia $1.4\,\mathrm{kg\,m^2}$ about the axis, and angular speed $75\,\mathrm{rad\,s^{-1}}$. A clutch mechanism then locks the two flywheels together so that they rotate with the same angular speed $\omega\,\mathrm{rad\,s^{-1}}$. Find ω. (OCR)

2 A merry-go-round of radius 1.5 metres has moment of inertia $100\,\mathrm{kg\,m^2}$ about its vertical axis. It is rotating at $1.6\,\mathrm{rad\,s^{-1}}$ when a child of mass 24 kg steps on to the rim. How does this affect the angular speed with which it rotates? What is the impulse on the axle?

What would be the effect on the angular speed of two children of mass 24 kg stepping on to the rim at the same time?

3 The diagram shows a circular aperture of radius r in a wall, which is closed by a uniform circular door held in place by a vertical hinge at its circumference. If the door is blown in by the wind, it is prevented from opening through more than 90° by a bar which projects from the side wall at the level of the hinge. How far from the plane of the door opening should this be fixed to minimise the impulse on the hinge?

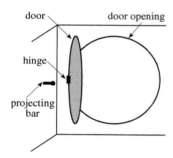

4 A uniform rod of length $2l$ is hinged to a fixed point at a distance x from its centre and hangs in stable equilibrium. The lowest point of the rod is struck horizontally with a blow of impulse J, so that it starts to rotate about the hinge. For what value of x is its angular velocity greatest?

5 A horizontal platform is rotating about a vertical axle at 0.6 revolutions per second. The moment of inertia about the axle is $150\,\mathrm{kg\,m^2}$. An engine of mass 50 kg is lowered on to the platform at 2 metres from the axle. What is the impulse on the axle?

6 A hollow sphere of mass 0.2 kg and radius 6 cm is set rotating by a motor which produces a couple of moment $0.1\sin^2 100\pi t\,\mathrm{N\,m}$ after t seconds. How long does it take to attain an angular speed of 40 revolutions per second?

7 A uniform rod of mass M and length $2l$ is rotating about its centre in a vertical plane with angular speed ω. As it passes through the horizontal position a particle of mass m is attached to one end. Find an inequality that ω must satisfy if the rod is to continue to make complete revolutions.

8 A wheel A can turn freely about a vertical shaft, and a wheel B can turn freely about a horizontal shaft. The two shafts are in the same plane. Initially A is stationary and B is rotating at 500 rad s^{-1}. B is then lowered on to A, and friction between the rim of B and the surface of A acts until there is no slipping between the two wheels. The moments of inertia of the wheels about their axes are 10 kg m^2 for A and 0.025 kg m^2 for B. The radius of B is 14 cm, and the point of contact between the wheels is 40 cm from the axis of A.

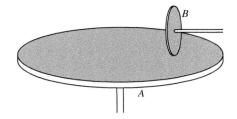

(a) Find the angular speed of each wheel when slipping stops.

(b) If this occurs after 0.7 seconds, find the frictional force between the wheels.

(c) Find the loss of kinetic energy while slipping occurs.

9 A uniform square board $ABCD$ has mass 5 kg and sides of length 60 cm. The board is hinged at A so that it can rotate freely in a vertical plane. A light string of length 1 metre is attached to B and to a point E, 80 cm above A. The board rests in equilibrium with AB horizontal and with D vertically below A. It is now raised through a right angle, so that B is vertically above A and AD is horizontal, and released from rest in this position. When the board returns to its original position the string becomes taut and the board is brought suddenly to rest. Find the impulsive tension in the string when this occurs and the horizontal and vertical components of the impulse on the hinge.

10 A gong is modelled as a uniform circular disc of radius r mounted in a vertical plane. It is supported by chains which cannot exert any horizontal impulse. When the gong is struck at a distance d below the centre, it appears to start to rotate about a horizontal axis at a height h above the centre. Find an equation connecting h, d and r.

11 AB is a diameter of a uniform circular lamina of mass m and radius r. The lamina is placed on a smooth surface, and attached to it by a hinge at A. C is a point on the circumference of the lamina such that angle $CBA = \theta$. The lamina is hit at C with a blow of impulse J in the direction $\overrightarrow{CB}$. Find the angular speed with which the lamina starts to rotate, and the impulse on the hinge at A.

12 A machine to simulate the behaviour of a golf putter consists of a weighted rod AB of length 90 cm and mass 200 grams. The rod is hinged at the end A and hangs so that B is just clear of the ground. Its centre of mass is 80 cm from A, and its moment of inertia about A is 0.147 kg m^2. A ball of mass 45 grams is placed on the ground alongside the rod at B. The end B is then raised until it is $7\frac{1}{2}$ cm clear of the ground, and let go. The coefficient of restitution between the rod and the ball is $\frac{3}{4}$. Find the speed with which the ball starts to move along the ground, and the height to which B rises in the follow-through.

13 A triangle ABC is made up of three uniform rods, each of mass m. The lengths $AB = AC = l$ and $BC = \sqrt{2}l$. The framework hangs from A by a smooth hinge, and it is struck at C with a blow of impulse J. Find the angular speed with which it starts to move, and the horizontal and vertical components of the impulse on the framework at A if the blow is

(a) in the direction $\overrightarrow{CB}$,   (b) perpendicular to AC.

14 Some of the features of a cricket bat hitting a ball are modelled in this question.

(a) A uniform rod AB (the bat) of mass $6m$ and length l is freely pivoted to a fixed point at A. Initially it is held with AB horizontal. It is then released from rest. Find the angular velocity ω of AB when it first becomes vertical.

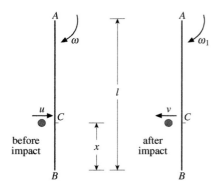

When AB first becomes vertical it strikes a particle P of mass m (the ball). Just before impact P is travelling horizontally towards AB with speed u, in the vertical plane in which AB is swinging. The point of impact C is at a distance x from B, as shown in the first diagram. Just after impact AB has angular velocity ω_1 and P has a horizontal velocity v in the direction away from AB, as shown in the second diagram.

(b) If I is the magnitude of the impulse given to P by the bat, write down two equations for I. If $x = \frac{1}{3}l$, show that there is no impulse at the pivot A.

(c) If $x = \frac{1}{3}l$ and the impact is fully elastic (that is, there is no loss in the total kinetic energy of the system), show that $v = \frac{7}{11}u + \frac{12}{11}\sqrt{3lg}$ and find a corresponding expression for ω_1. (OCR)

7 Stability and oscillation

This chapter develops an approach in which mechanical systems are treated as a whole rather than as a set of interacting components. When you have completed it, you should

- know that positions of equilibrium are associated with stationary values of the potential energy
- know that the nature of the stationary point determines the stability or instability of the equilibrium
- be able to obtain an equation of motion for a system by differentiating the equation of conservation of energy
- be able to find equations of approximate simple harmonic motion for oscillation about a position of stable equilibrium.

7.1 Equilibrium and potential energy

Imagine a small ball which can roll on a path with a section like Fig. 7.1. If you place the ball at most points of the path, it will immediately start to roll downhill. But if you place it at the points marked A, B, C or D, the ball will stay there in equilibrium. This is because the tangents at these points are horizontal, so the normal contact force on the ball is vertical, and acts along the same line as the weight of the ball.

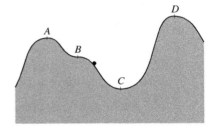

Fig. 7.1

In C1 Section 11.1 points of a graph where the gradient is 0 were called 'stationary points'. So you could say that the points of the path where the ball can rest in equilibrium are the stationary points on the path, regarded as a graph. Now if the ball has weight W, and its height at a point of the path (above some base level) is y, it has potential energy Wy. So you get the potential energy from the height by multiplying by W. That is, the potential energy graph (x, Wy) is the height graph (x, y) stretched by a constant factor W. It follows that stationary points on the height graph correspond (for the same values of x) to stationary points on the potential energy graph.

This suggests a general principle which can be applied to a wide variety of situations in mechanics.

> If a mechanical system has the freedom to take many different positions, and if all the forces which do work in the system are conservative, then the possible positions of equilibrium are those for which the potential energy is stationary.

There are several points to make about this statement.

* You have met many problems on equilibrium applied to systems which are geometrically rigid. The principle does not deal with these. Where it can be used is for systems which include components such as springs, hinged rods, pulleys, etc. which enable them to take a variety of geometrical configurations.

* For many such systems the geometry can be described in terms of a single variable, perhaps a length or an angle. The system is then said to have **one degree of freedom**. Some systems need more than one variable to describe them, in which case they have more than one degree of freedom. The principle still applies to these, but almost all the examples in this chapter have just one degree of freedom.

* The principle applies only if all the forces which do work are conservative (see M2 Section 3.3). That is, they produce energy which can later be recovered in another form. This means that systems in which work has to be done against frictional forces are excluded. For example, if in Fig. 7.1 the ball is replaced by a small cube and the path is rough, then there are other points on the path where it can rest which aren't stationary points.

* The potential energy referred to is not only gravitational; it includes also, for example, elastic potential energy. The total potential energy is usually denoted by V.

Example 7.1.1
A load of mass m hangs from the ceiling by an elastic string of natural length l and modulus of elasticity λ. Write down an expression for the potential energy when the string has extension x, and deduce the value of x when the load is in equilibrium.

When the string has extension x, the load is $l + x$ below the ceiling. Taking the level of the ceiling as the fixed level, the gravitational potential energy is

$mg \times (-(l + x)) = -mgl - mgx$. The elastic potential energy is $\dfrac{\lambda x^2}{2l}$. So the total potential energy is given by

$$V = -mgl - mgx + \frac{\lambda x^2}{2l}.$$

The potential energy is stationary when $\dfrac{dV}{dx} = 0$, that is when

$$-mg + \frac{\lambda x}{l} = 0.$$

This is of course the equation you get by resolving vertically for the forces on the load. The weight is mg, and the tension in the string is $\dfrac{\lambda x}{l}$.

The load is in equilibrium when $x = \dfrac{mgl}{\lambda}$.

Example 7.1.2

A string 2 metres long has particles of weight 5 newtons attached at each end. The string is hung symmetrically over a pair of smooth pegs at the same level 0.8 metres apart. A third particle, of weight 6 newtons, is now attached to the middle of the string, and eased down until it reaches its equilibrium position. How far is this below the level of the pegs?

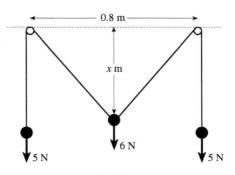

Fig. 7.2

To answer this question by the potential energy method, begin by finding the potential energy when the middle particle is x metres below the level of the pegs, as in Fig. 7.2. The portion of the string between this particle and either peg then has length $\sqrt{0.4^2 + x^2}$ metres, so that each of the other particles is at a depth $(1 - \sqrt{0.16 + x^2})$ metres below the pegs. Taking the level of the pegs as the fixed level, the total potential energy is then V joules, where

$$V = 6 \times (-x) + 2 \times 5 \times (-(1 - \sqrt{0.16 + x^2}))$$
$$= -6x - 10 + 10\sqrt{0.16 + x^2}.$$

Differentiating to find where this is stationary,

$$\frac{dV}{dx} = -6 + 10 \times \frac{1}{2\sqrt{0.16 + x^2}} \times 2x$$
$$= -6 + \frac{10x}{\sqrt{0.16 + x^2}}.$$

So $\dfrac{dV}{dx} = 0$ when

$$\frac{10x}{\sqrt{0.16 + x^2}} = 6,$$
$$100x^2 = 36(0.16 + x^2),$$
$$64x^2 = 36 \times 0.16,$$

giving $x = \dfrac{6 \times 0.4}{8} = 0.3$, since x must be positive.

The system is in equilibrium when the middle particle is 0.3 metres below the level of the pegs.

Example 7.1.3

Fig. 7.3 shows a uniform rod AB of mass $2m$ and length a, hinged to a fixed point at A. A cord of length l attached to B passes through a small smooth eye at a point C, at a height a above A, and carries a particle of mass m at its other end. Find an expression for the potential energy of the system above A, in terms of the angle $CAB = \theta$, and deduce the positions in which it can rest in equilibrium.

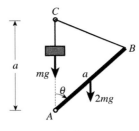

Fig. 7.3

Since the triangle ABC is isosceles, the length of cord between B and the peg is $2a\sin\frac{1}{2}\theta$, so the length hanging down below the eye is $l - 2a\sin\frac{1}{2}\theta$. The height of the hanging particle above A is therefore $a - (l - 2a\sin\frac{1}{2}\theta)$.

The total potential energy is therefore

$$V = 2mg \times \tfrac{1}{2}a\cos\theta + mg(a - l + 2a\sin\tfrac{1}{2}\theta).$$

The system is in equilibrium when $\dfrac{\mathrm{d}V}{\mathrm{d}\theta} = 0$. This gives the equation

$$-mga\sin\theta + mga\cos\tfrac{1}{2}\theta = 0, \quad \text{or more simply} \quad \sin\theta - \cos\tfrac{1}{2}\theta = 0.$$

To solve this, write $\sin\theta$ in terms of $\frac{1}{2}\theta$, which gives

$$2\sin\tfrac{1}{2}\theta\cos\tfrac{1}{2}\theta - \cos\tfrac{1}{2}\theta = 0, \quad \text{or in factors} \quad \cos\tfrac{1}{2}\theta(2\sin\tfrac{1}{2}\theta - 1) = 0.$$

Therefore either $\cos\frac{1}{2}\theta = 0$ or $\sin\frac{1}{2}\theta = \frac{1}{2}$, so $\frac{1}{2}\theta = \frac{1}{2}\pi$ or $\frac{1}{2}\theta = \frac{1}{6}\pi$, giving $\theta = \pi$ or $\theta = \frac{1}{3}\pi$.

Check for yourself the answers to this example by the usual method, taking moments about A. You should have no difficulty getting the answer $\theta = \frac{1}{3}\pi$, but you might well have missed the other possibility $\theta = \pi$. (Of course the cord must have length more than $2a$ for this to be a realistic answer.)

Example 7.1.4
Illustrate the principle for two particles, of mass m and $2m$, connected by a light inextensible string and placed over the surface of a smooth cylinder.

The situation will be investigated in two ways, first by the method you are used to, then using the potential energy principle.

Resolving method   Fig. 7.4 shows the forces on each particle, with the string exerting tension T at each end. Suppose that in the equilibrium position the radii to the two particles make angles α, β with the vertical.

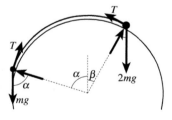

Fig. 7.4

You are not interested in the normal force, so resolve in the tangential direction for each particle. This gives equations

$$T = mg\sin\alpha \quad \text{and} \quad T = 2mg\sin\beta,$$

so $\sin\alpha = 2\sin\beta$.

Potential energy method   It is geometrically possible for the particles to occupy a range of positions on the surface of the cylinder; some of these are drawn in Fig. 7.5. The chords joining the particles in the various positions all have the same length, and the centre of mass of the two particles in any position divides the chord in the ratio 2 : 1. The locus of the centre of mass is the circular arc with its centre on the axis of the cylinder, shown by the bold line in Fig. 7.5.

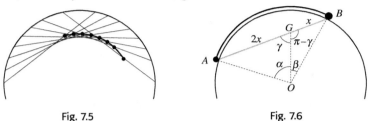

Fig. 7.5   Fig. 7.6

The potential energy of the particles is proportional to the height of the centre of mass. So the potential energy is stationary when the centre of mass is at the highest point of the circular arc.

Fig. 7.6 shows the particles A and B in this position, with their centre of mass G vertically above the point O on the axis of the cylinder. Suppose that the radii OA and OB then make angles α, β with the vertical. Denote the radius of the cylinder by r, the lengths $AG = 2x$ and $GB = x$, and the angle $AGO = \gamma$, so that angle $BGO = \pi - \gamma$.

Using the sine rule in triangles OAG and OBG,

$$\frac{r}{\sin \gamma} = \frac{2x}{\sin \alpha} \quad \text{and} \quad \frac{r}{\sin(\pi - \gamma)} = \frac{x}{\sin \beta}.$$

Since $\sin(\pi - \gamma) = \sin \gamma$, it follows that $\sin \alpha = 2 \sin \beta$.

The point of Example 7.1.4 is not to suggest that one method is better than the other, but to show that you can reach the same answer by two completely different approaches. What is interesting about the potential energy method is that it treats the system as a whole, rather than by breaking it into its component parts.

7.2 Stable and unstable equilibrium

All the examples in Section 7.1 could have been solved by using equations of resolving or moments. So what is the point of the potential energy method? One answer is that it provides a way of deciding whether equilibrium is stable or unstable.

There have been many references during the course to positions of stable and unstable equilibrium. It is time to try to define these ideas more precisely.

What distinguishes them is how the system behaves if it is displaced very slightly from the equilibrium position and then released. If the equilibrium is stable, the system will tend to move back towards the equilibrium position. If it is unstable, it will tend to move further away. You can see this in Fig. 7.1; C is a position of stable equilibrium, A and D are positions of unstable equilibrium.

A typical example of stable equilibrium is a ball sitting in the bottom of a hemispherical bowl. The ball has two degrees of freedom on the surface of the bowl, but to displace it in any direction you have to exert some force. That is, you have to do work, and this increases the potential energy of the ball. So in the equilibrium position the potential energy is a minimum.

This is a simple example of a very general principle, which can be applied to any mechanical system of the kind described in Section 7.1.

> A configuration of a system in which the potential energy is a minimum is a position of **stable equilibrium**. A configuration in which the potential energy is a maximum is a position of **unstable equilibrium**.

To show this, look at Fig. 7.7 which shows the graph of the potential energy for different positions of a system with one degree of freedom. The point M, corresponding to a value m of the independent variable x, is a minimum. Suppose that the system is displaced slightly to a position where $x = p$, corresponding to the point P on the graph, and released from rest in this position. How will the system then behave?

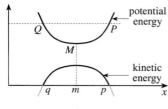

Fig. 7.7

The clue is to consider the kinetic energy. Since the forces in the system are conservative, the sum of the kinetic and potential energy is constant. The system is released from rest, so the kinetic energy where $x = p$ is 0. So the graph of the kinetic energy is a mirror image of the potential energy graph, passing through the point $(p, 0)$.

But kinetic energy can't be negative, so only the part of the kinetic energy graph shown with a black line represents a possible motion of the system. It will therefore start to move back towards the equilibrium value $x = m$. In fact, it will oscillate between $x = p$ and $x = q$, where the point Q on the potential energy graph corresponding to $x = q$ is at the same level as P.

Contrast this with Fig. 7.8, which shows what happens at a point M where the potential energy is a maximum. If the system is released from rest where $x = p$, the only possible motion is away from the equilibrium position $x = m$.

Equilibrium is therefore stable at positions of minimum potential energy, and unstable at positions of maximum potential energy.

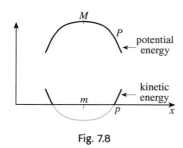

Fig. 7.8

Example 7.2.1
Verify the stability condition for the load hanging by an elastic string in Example 7.1.1.

The expression found in Example 7.1.1 for the potential energy was

$$V = -mgl - mgx + \frac{\lambda x^2}{2l}.$$

This is the equation of a quadratic function for which the coefficient of x^2 is positive.

The graph is therefore a parabola for which the vertex is a minimum point, so the equilibrium position is stable.

This agrees with what you know, that if the load is displaced through a small distance from its equilibrium position, it will oscillate with simple harmonic motion.

Example 7.2.2
For the system in Example 7.1.3, find whether the positions of equilibrium are stable or unstable.

It was shown in Example 7.1.3 that

$$V = mga\cos\theta + mg(a - l + 2a\sin\tfrac{1}{2}\theta), \qquad \frac{dV}{d\theta} = mga(-\sin\theta + \cos\tfrac{1}{2}\theta)$$

and that $\dfrac{dV}{d\theta} = 0$ when $\theta = \tfrac{1}{3}\pi$ or $\theta = \pi$.

To find whether the potential energy in these positions is minimum or maximum, one method is to consider the second derivative. So find

$$\frac{d^2V}{d\theta^2} = mga(-\cos\theta - \tfrac{1}{2}\sin\tfrac{1}{2}\theta).$$

When $\theta = \tfrac{1}{3}\pi$, the expression in brackets has value $-\tfrac{1}{2} - \tfrac{1}{2} \times \tfrac{1}{2} = -\tfrac{3}{4}$, so $\dfrac{d^2V}{d\theta^2}$ is negative and the potential energy is at a maximum. So the equilibrium is unstable.

When $\theta = \pi$, the expression in brackets has value $-(-1) - \tfrac{1}{2} \times 1 = \tfrac{1}{2}$, the potential energy is at a minimum and equilibrium is stable.

Example 7.2.3
A uniform plank of weight W, length $2l$ and thickness $2a$ rests symmetrically across a fixed cylinder of radius r, whose axis is horizontal. The contact between the plank and the cylinder is rough. Investigate whether the equilibrium is stable.

Fig. 7.9 shows the plank in its equilibrium position, and Fig. 7.10 shows it displaced from this position, at an angle θ to the horizontal. Because the surfaces are rough, the plank rolls on the cylinder, so in the displaced position the line of contact is a distance $r\theta$ from the central plane of the plank.

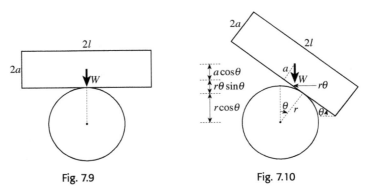

Fig. 7.9   Fig. 7.10

Notice that in this example the potential energy method can be used even though the surfaces are rough. This is because the motion involves rolling rather than sliding, so that no work is done against the friction.

Taking the level of the axis of the cylinder as the base, the potential energy V in the displaced position is given by

$$V = W(r\cos\theta + r\theta\sin\theta + a\cos\theta) = W((r+a)\cos\theta + r\theta\sin\theta).$$

To find whether equilibrium is stable, differentiate to obtain

$$\frac{dV}{d\theta} = W(-(r+a)\sin\theta + r(\sin\theta + \theta\cos\theta)) = W(r\theta\cos\theta - a\sin\theta),$$

and $$\frac{d^2V}{d\theta^2} = W(r(\cos\theta - \theta\sin\theta) - a\cos\theta) = W((r-a)\cos\theta - r\theta\sin\theta).$$

The symmetrical equilibrium position is given by $\theta = 0$, in which case $\frac{dV}{d\theta} = 0$ (as you would expect) and $\frac{d^2V}{d\theta^2} = W(r - a)$. So the potential energy is a minimum if $a < r$, and a maximum if $a > r$.

The symmetrical position of equilibrium is stable if $a < r$, and unstable if $a > r$.

The special case $a = r$ is more tricky to decide. See Example 7.3.2.

7.3 Some calculus techniques

In Examples 7.2.2 and 7.2.3 it was quite simple to use the second derivative to find whether the potential energy is a minimum or maximum. But sometimes this method doesn't work, or it involves heavy algebra, in which case you need to use a different approach. This section suggests two other methods which are sometimes useful.

Sign of the derivative
In C1 Section 11.2 the method described for distinguishing minimum and maximum points on the graph of $y = f(x)$ is to find the sign of $f'(x)$ just to the left and right of a stationary point. If these signs are $-$, $+$ the point is a minimum, and if they are $+$, $-$ the point is a maximum. Before finding the second derivative, it is always worth looking to see whether this method will produce the information you want more easily.

Example 7.3.1
In Example 7.1.2, is equilibrium stable or unstable?

In this example it was found that

$$\frac{dV}{dx} = -6 + \frac{10x}{\sqrt{0.16 + x^2}}$$

and that, for positive x, $\dfrac{\mathrm{d}V}{\mathrm{d}x} = 0$ only when $x = 0.3$. Differentiating this expression to find $\dfrac{\mathrm{d}^2 V}{\mathrm{d}x^2}$ would involve unpleasant algebra. But it is easy to calculate that, when $x = 0.2$,

$$\begin{aligned}
\frac{\mathrm{d}V}{\mathrm{d}x} &= -6 + \frac{10 \times 0.2}{\sqrt{0.16 + 0.04}} \\
&= -6 + \frac{2}{\sqrt{0.2}} \\
&= -1.52\ldots;
\end{aligned}$$

and when $x = 0.4$,

$$\begin{aligned}
\frac{\mathrm{d}V}{\mathrm{d}x} &= -6 + \frac{10 \times 0.4}{\sqrt{0.16 + 0.16}} \\
&= -6 + \frac{4}{\sqrt{0.32}} \\
&= 1.07\ldots .
\end{aligned}$$

This shows that V has a minimum when $x = 0.3$, so that equilibrium is stable.

Example 7.3.2
In Example 7.2.3, investigate whether there are any non-symmetrical positions of equilibrium, and if so whether they are stable or unstable.

The expression $\dfrac{\mathrm{d}V}{\mathrm{d}\theta} = W(r\theta \cos\theta - a \sin\theta)$ in Example 7.2.3 could be written as

$$\frac{\mathrm{d}V}{\mathrm{d}\theta} = Wa \cos\theta \left(\frac{r}{a}\theta - \tan\theta \right).$$

For a position of equilibrium this has to be equal to 0, and there will be a root which might be relevant to the problem if the equation

$$\frac{r}{a}\theta = \tan\theta$$

has roots between $-\tfrac{1}{2}\pi$ and $\tfrac{1}{2}\pi$ other than $\theta = 0$.

Fig. 7.11 shows the graphs of $\dfrac{r}{a}\theta$ and $\tan\theta$ in the two cases $a \geqslant r$ and $a < r$.

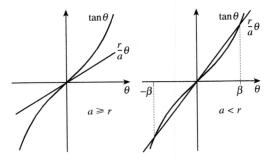

Fig. 7.11

You can see that in the first case the graphs intersect only where $\theta = 0$, so there are no unsymmetrical positions of equilibrium. Notice that $\frac{r}{a}\theta > \tan\theta$ if $\theta < 0$, and $\frac{r}{a}\theta < \tan\theta$ if $\theta > 0$, so the sign of $\frac{dV}{d\theta}$ changes from $+$ to $-$; this shows that $\theta = 0$ gives a maximum for the potential energy, so equilibrium is unstable. This agrees with the conclusion reached in Example 7.2.3 using the second derivative.

But if $a < r$, there are two other points of intersection, corresponding to roots of the equation given by $\theta = \pm\beta$. So, if the plank is not too thick, and if it is long enough (if $l > r\beta$, to be precise), it can rest in equilibrium at an angle β to the horizontal on either side of the symmetrical position.

To find if this position is stable or unstable, it would not be too easy to substitute $\theta = \beta$ in the expression for $\frac{d^2V}{d\theta^2}$ and to decide whether this is positive or negative.

But you can see from Fig. 7.11 that, as θ passes through the value β from left to right, the factor $\left(\frac{r}{a}\theta - \tan\theta\right)$ changes sign from $+$ to $-$; and since $\cos\theta$ is positive throughout, the sign of $\frac{dV}{d\theta}$ changes from $+$ to $-$. The potential energy therefore is a maximum, and equilibrium is unstable.

It is interesting to summarise these results by comparing the forms of the (θ, V) graph for the cases $a < r$, $a = r$ and $a > r$. These are drawn in Fig. 7.12.

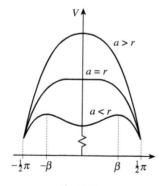

Fig. 7.12

Polynomial approximations*

Another technique which is sometimes useful is to approximate to the potential energy by a polynomial. The most commonly used approximations are those given by the first few terms of a binomial expansion, and the Maclaurin polynomials for small values of θ,

$$\sin\theta \approx \theta - \tfrac{1}{6}\theta^3 \quad \text{and} \quad \cos\theta \approx 1 - \tfrac{1}{2}\theta^2 + \tfrac{1}{24}\theta^4$$

described in FP2 Section 3.2.

Examples 7.3.3 and 7.3.4 show the method applied to the same situations as in Examples 7.3.1 and 7.3.2.

Example 7.3.3

In Example 7.1.2, is equilibrium stable or unstable?

The potential energy is given by

$$V = -6x - 10 + 10\sqrt{0.16 + x^2},$$

and the system is in equilibrium when $x = 0.3$. So the question is, if you make a small displacement from this value, does V get larger or smaller? To answer this, write x as $x = 0.3 + y$, and express V in terms of y as a polynomial approximation when y is small.

Then

$$
\begin{aligned}
V &= -6(0.3 + y) - 10 + 10\sqrt{0.16 + (0.3 + y)^2} \\
&= -1.8 - 6y - 10 + 10\sqrt{0.25 + 0.6y + y^2} \\
&= -11.8 - 6y + 5(1 + 2.4y + 4y^2)^{\frac{1}{2}} \\
&= -11.8 - 6y + 5\left(1 + \tfrac{1}{2}(2.4y + 4y^2) + \frac{\tfrac{1}{2} \times (-\tfrac{1}{2})}{2}(2.4y + 4y^2)^2 + \ldots\right),
\end{aligned}
$$

using the binomial expansion. It will probably be good enough to retain powers of y as far as y^2, so write

$$
\begin{aligned}
V &\approx -11.8 - 6y + 5(1 + 1.2y + 2y^2 - \tfrac{1}{8}(2.4y)^2) \\
&= -11.8 - 6y + 5 + 6y + 10y^2 - 3.6y^2 \\
&= -6.8 + 6.4y^2.
\end{aligned}
$$

This shows that V is a minimum when $y = 0$, that is when $x = 0.3$. So the equilibrium is stable.

Example 7.3.4

In Example 7.2.3, investigate the stability of the symmetrical equilibrium position of the plank.

If you make a small displacement from the symmetrical equilibrium position, θ is small. so you can use the Maclaurin polynomial approximations for $\sin \theta$ and $\cos \theta$ to write

$$
\begin{aligned}
V &= W((r + a)\cos\theta + r\theta \sin\theta) \\
&\approx W((r + a)(1 - \tfrac{1}{2}\theta^2 + \tfrac{1}{24}\theta^4) + r\theta(\theta - \tfrac{1}{6}\theta^3)) \\
&= W(r + a) + W(-\tfrac{1}{2}(r + a) + r)\theta^2 + W(\tfrac{1}{24}(r + a) - \tfrac{1}{6}r)\theta^4 \\
&= W(r + a) + \tfrac{1}{2}W(r - a)\theta^2 + \tfrac{1}{24}W(a - 3r)\theta^4.
\end{aligned}
$$

The first term $W(r + a)$ is simply a constant which depends on the base from which the potential energy is calculated. For small values of θ, the next term in θ^2 is the most important. You can see that if $a < r$ this term is positive, so potential energy is a minimum and equilibrium is stable; if $a > r$ it is negative, potential energy is a maximum and equilibrium is unstable.

For the case $a = r$ the θ^2 term is zero, and you must go on to the next term involving θ^4. With $a = r$ this term is $-\frac{1}{12}Wr\theta^4$, which is negative. This shows that potential energy is a maximum and equilibrium is unstable. You can see that this agrees with the evidence from the graph in Fig. 7.12.

In this example the method is especially simple because you are interested in the potential energy around $\theta = 0$. But in a case such as Example 7.2.2, where

$$V = mga \cos\theta + mg(a - l + 2a \sin\tfrac{1}{2}\theta)$$

and equilibrium occurs at $\theta = \frac{1}{3}\pi$, you need to begin by writing θ as $\frac{1}{3}\pi + \phi$, where ϕ is small. To simplify the algebra, denote the part involving the variable, $\cos\theta + 2\sin\tfrac{1}{2}\theta$, by $\mathrm{f}(\theta)$. Then

$$\mathrm{f}(\tfrac{1}{3}\pi + \phi) = \cos\left(\tfrac{1}{3}\pi + \phi\right) + 2\sin\tfrac{1}{2}\left(\tfrac{1}{3}\pi + \phi\right)$$
$$= \tfrac{1}{2}\cos\phi - \tfrac{1}{2}\sqrt{3}\sin\phi + 2\left(\tfrac{1}{2}\cos\tfrac{1}{2}\phi + \tfrac{1}{2}\sqrt{3}\sin\tfrac{1}{2}\phi\right).$$

In this case it is enough to take the approximations as far as the terms involving ϕ^2, that is $\cos\phi \approx 1 - \tfrac{1}{2}\phi^2$ and $\sin\phi \approx \phi$. Then

$$\mathrm{f}(\tfrac{1}{3}\pi + \phi) \approx \tfrac{1}{2}\left(1 - \tfrac{1}{2}\phi^2\right) - \tfrac{1}{2}\sqrt{3}\phi + 1 - \tfrac{1}{2}\left(\tfrac{1}{2}\phi\right)^2 + \sqrt{3}\left(\tfrac{1}{2}\phi\right)$$
$$= \tfrac{3}{2} - \tfrac{3}{8}\phi^2.$$

This shows that, at $\theta = \frac{1}{3}\pi$, the potential energy is a maximum, so this position of equilibrium is unstable.

Exercise 7A

1 A uniform cylinder with elliptic cross-section is placed with its curved surface in contact with the floor. Describe the equilibrium positions, and distinguish the stable from the unstable positions.

2 Find the positions of
   (a) stable equilibrium,   (b) unstable equilibrium
   for a 50p coin placed upright on its edge on a horizontal table.

3 Is a configuration in which the potential energy has a stationary point of inflexion stable or unstable?

4 Are the connected particles in Example 7.1.4 in stable or unstable equilibrium when $\sin\alpha = 2\sin\beta$?

5 AB and AC are two fixed smooth rails making angles 25° and 65° with the downward vertical, one on either side of it. A uniform rod XY has rings at X and Y, which can move along AB and AC respectively. Show that, in any position of the rod, the centre of mass is at a constant distance from A. Hence find the angle which the rod makes with the vertical in its equilibrium position. Is the equilibrium stable or unstable?

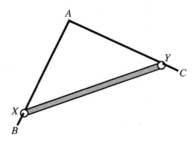

6 A small smooth peg is at a distance 3 metres from a fixed smooth vertical wire. A ring of mass 4 kg is free to slide on the wire. It is attached to one end of a string, which passes over the peg and carries a load of mass 5 kg hanging from the other end.

By expressing the potential energy in terms of a suitable variable, find how far the ring is below the peg in the equilibrium position, and whether the equilibrium is unstable or stable.

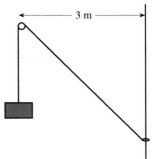

7 An elastic band has natural length 0.8 metres and modulus of elasticity 4 newtons. It is stretched round two pegs at the same level which are 0.8 metres apart. A particle of weight 6 newtons is attached to the band at a point halfway between the pegs; this particle is eased down until it is at rest in its equilibrium position. Taking the level of the pegs as the fixed level, find an expression for the total potential energy when the particle is x metres below the level of the pegs. Use this to find the depth of the particle below the pegs in the equilibrium position. Is the equilibrium stable or unstable?

8 A fixed smooth surface has the shape of a quadrant of a circle of radius 2 metres. A string of length 3 metres, with particles attached at each end, lies partly on the surface and partly hangs vertically, as shown in the diagram. The particle on the surface has weight 5 newtons, and the hanging particle has weight 4 newtons. Taking the centre of the circle as the fixed level, write an expression for the potential energy when a length 2θ metres of the string is on the surface. Hence find the value of θ when the system is in equilibrium, and determine whether the equilibrium is stable or unstable.

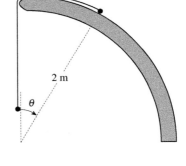

9 A uniform rod OA of weight 12 newtons and length 1 metre can turn freely about the end O in a vertical plane. A peg P is fixed at the same level as O and 1 metre from it, as shown in the diagram. A string of length 2 metres has one end attached to the rod at A. The string passes over the peg and supports a load of weight 1 newton at its other end. Find an expression for the potential energy of the system when OA is at an angle 2θ below the horizontal, taking OP as the fixed level. Hence find the angle that OA makes with the horizontal when the system is in equilibrium, and determine whether equilibrium is stable or unstable.

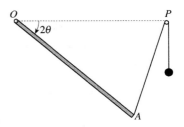

Show that, if the rod can make a complete revolution about O, so that $0 < \theta < \pi$, there is another position of equilibrium with A above the level of O. Find the angle that the rod makes with the horizontal in this position, and determine whether this position of equilibrium is stable or unstable. Draw a diagram to illustrate this position.

10 A fixed sphere of radius r has a smooth outer surface. An elastic band of weight W, of natural length πr and modulus of elasticity λ, lies on the surface in a horizontal plane. Show that, if the band is at a height $r\cos\theta$ above the centre of the sphere (where $\theta > \frac{1}{6}\pi$), the total potential energy is $Wr\cos\theta + \frac{1}{2}\lambda\pi r(2\sin\theta - 1)^2$.

If the band can rest in equilibrium at a height $\frac{1}{2}r$ above the centre of the sphere, find an expression for λ in terms of W.

Show also that, with this value of λ, there is another position of equilibrium with the band about $0.7r$ above the centre of the sphere.

11 A and B are two fixed points at different heights above the ground. A string, whose length l is greater than AB, has one end attached to A and the other to B. A smooth ring is threaded on to the string. Describe the position of the ring in its equilibrium position, with reference to an ellipse having A and B as its foci.

Give a reason why, when the ring is in its equilibrium position, the two parts of the string make equal angles with the horizontal. What geometrical property of an ellipse does this demonstrate?

12 A bead of mass m is threaded on a smooth circular wire of radius r, which is fixed in a vertical plane. An elastic string, of natural length r and modulus of elasticity kmg, is attached at one end to the bead and at the other end to the highest point of the wire.

(a) Investigate whether the equilibrium position with the bead at the lowest point of the wire is stable or unstable.

(b) Investigate whether there are equilibrium positions with the bead at some other point of the wire, and whether this position is stable or unstable.

Illustrate your answers with graphs of the potential energy for $k = \frac{1}{2}, 1, 1\frac{1}{2}, 2, 2\frac{1}{2}, 3$.

13* For the system in Example 7.2.2, use Maclaurin approximations to show that the position of equilibrium with $\theta = \pi$ is stable.

14 A hollow hemispherical bowl of radius a is placed on top of a fixed sphere of radius r. The surfaces are rough, so that the bowl can roll on the surface of the sphere. Find the condition which a must satisfy for the bowl to be in stable equilibrium.

15 Two smooth planes are at angles α, β with the horizontal, where $\alpha > \beta$. A uniform brick, of length $2l$ and height $2h$, is placed on the planes as shown in the diagram. If the sides of length $2l$ make an angle θ with the horizontal, express the lengths labelled x and y in terms of l, θ, α and β. Hence find an expression for the height of the centre of mass of the brick above the line of intersection of the planes. Show that, if the brick is in equilibrium,

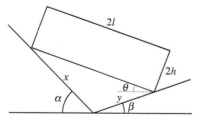

$$\tan\theta = \frac{l\sin(\alpha - \beta)}{2l\sin\alpha\sin\beta + h\sin(\alpha + \beta)}.$$

Determine whether the equilibrium is stable or unstable.

16 Sketch the curve with equation $y^2 = 1 - \frac{1}{4}x^2$, and show that the normals to the curve at the points $(1.2, \pm 0.8)$ cut the x-axis at the point $(0.9, 0)$.

A lamina having the curve as its boundary has its centre of mass at $(0.9, 0)$. The lamina is placed in a vertical plane on a horizontal surface. Find the positions of equilibrium, and which of these are stable.

17 The diagram shows a rhombus $ABCD$ formed from four light rods, each of length a, pin-jointed together and hung from a fixed point at A. A load of 36 newtons is hung from C, and B and D are connected by a light spring of natural length a and modulus of elasticity 65 newtons. Show that the rhombus can rest in equilibrium with each rod at an angle of $\sin^{-1} \frac{5}{13}$ to the vertical.

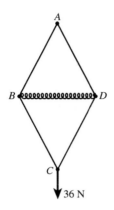

7.4 Differentiating the energy equation

Consider the motion of a particle at the end of a string of length l moving in a vertical circle with centre O. Fig. 7.13 shows the situation when the string makes an angle θ with the upward vertical. You know that, if the angular velocity is ω, the acceleration has components $l\omega^2$ towards O and $l\dot{\omega}$ in the direction of the tangent. The magnitude of the component $l\omega^2$ is best found by using the conservation of energy, from the equation

$$\tfrac{1}{2}m(l\omega)^2 + mgl\cos\theta = \text{constant}.$$

Fig. 7.13

The tangential component can be found by resolving in the tangential direction, giving the equation

$$mg\sin\theta = ml\dot{\omega}.$$

These appear to be two quite different equations, but in fact the second can be deduced from the first. If you differentiate the energy equation with respect to t, you get

$$\tfrac{1}{2}ml^2\frac{\mathrm{d}}{\mathrm{d}t}\omega^2 + mgl\frac{\mathrm{d}}{\mathrm{d}t}\cos\theta = 0.$$

Now by the chain rule $\dfrac{\mathrm{d}}{\mathrm{d}t}\omega^2 = 2\omega \times \dfrac{\mathrm{d}\omega}{\mathrm{d}t} = 2\omega\dot{\omega}$ and $\dfrac{\mathrm{d}}{\mathrm{d}t}\cos\theta = -\sin\theta \times \dfrac{\mathrm{d}\theta}{\mathrm{d}t} = -\omega\sin\theta$, since $\dfrac{\mathrm{d}\theta}{\mathrm{d}t} = \omega$. So the equation can be written as

$$ml^2\omega\dot{\omega} - mgl\omega\sin\theta = 0.$$

Dividing by $l\omega$ and rearranging, this is

$$mg\sin\theta = ml\dot{\omega},$$

which is the tangential resolving equation given above.

> A similar procedure was carried out in Example 5.4.3 by differentiating with respect to θ rather than t, and using $\alpha = \omega\dfrac{d\omega}{d\theta}$ rather than $\alpha = \dot{\omega}$. Both methods work equally well, but for the purposes of this chapter differentiating with respect to t is more convenient.

This idea can be applied much more widely. A simple example is the oscillation of a load hanging by an elastic string. Adding a kinetic energy term to the expression for potential energy in Example 7.1.1 gives the conservation of energy equation

$$\tfrac{1}{2}m\dot{x}^2 - mgl - mgx + \frac{\lambda x^2}{2l} = \text{constant}.$$

This equation holds for all values of t, so you can differentiate it with respect to t. Note that, by the chain rule, $\dfrac{d}{dt}x^2 = 2x \times \dfrac{dx}{dt} = 2x\dot{x}$ and that $\dfrac{d}{dt}\dot{x}^2 = 2\dot{x} \times \dfrac{d\dot{x}}{dt} = 2\dot{x}\ddot{x}$, so this gives

$$m\dot{x}\ddot{x} - mg\dot{x} + \frac{\lambda x\dot{x}}{l} = 0.$$

Notice that $\dot{x}$ is a factor of each term, so it can be cancelled to give

$$m\ddot{x} = mg - \frac{\lambda x}{l}.$$

This is just the equation of motion: the right side is the weight minus the tension, which equals mass times acceleration on the left.

In more complicated examples, it can be much simpler to find an equation of motion by differentiating the conservation of energy equation than by considering forces and accelerations for the various components.

This is illustrated by the next example, which would be difficult to solve by Newton's second law. You may omit this example if you wish.

Example 7.4.1*

A chain AB of length $\tfrac{1}{2}\pi r$ is placed over a fixed smooth cylinder of radius r with its axis horizontal. Initially the end A is at the top of the cylinder, and the end B is level with the axis. As the chain slides off the cylinder, after a time t the radius OA is at an angle θ to the vertical. Find an expression for the angular acceleration of A about the axis.

When OA makes an angle θ with the vertical, a length $r\theta$ has come off the surface and is hanging vertically. A length $2r\phi$, where $\phi = \frac{1}{2}(\frac{1}{2}\pi - \theta)$, is still in contact with the surface of the cylinder, as shown in Fig. 7.14.

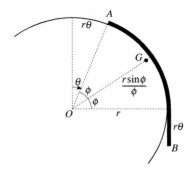

The potential energy of the chain can be found in two parts. The part still on the cylinder can be modelled as a circular arc, and you know from M2 Section 10.1 that the centre of mass G is at a distance $\dfrac{r \sin \phi}{\phi}$ from O. If the mass per unit length of the chain is k, then its mass is $2r\phi k$, so the potential energy of this part of the chain above O is

Fig. 7.14

$$(2r\phi k)g \times \left(\frac{r \sin \phi}{\phi} \sin \phi\right) = r^2 kg(2 \sin^2 \phi) = r^2 kg(1 - \cos 2\phi)$$
$$= r^2 kg\left(1 - \cos\left(\tfrac{1}{2}\pi - \theta\right)\right) = r^2 kg(1 - \sin \theta).$$

The vertical part of the chain has mass $r\theta k$, and its centre of mass is $\frac{1}{2}r\theta$ below O, so its potential energy is $(r\theta k)g \times \left(-\frac{1}{2}r\theta\right) = -\frac{1}{2}r^2 kg\theta^2$.

Although different parts of the chain are moving in different directions, they are all moving at the same speed $r\dot{\theta}$. Therefore, since the mass of the whole chain is $\frac{1}{2}\pi r k$, its kinetic energy is $\frac{1}{2}\left(\frac{1}{2}\pi r k\right) \times (r\dot{\theta})^2 = \frac{1}{4}\pi r^3 k\dot{\theta}^2$.

Putting all this together gives the conservation of energy equation

$$\tfrac{1}{4}\pi r^3 k\dot{\theta}^2 + r^2 kg\left(1 - \sin \theta - \tfrac{1}{2}\theta^2\right) = \text{constant}.$$

Now differentiate with respect to t. This gives

$$\tfrac{1}{2}\pi r^3 k\dot{\theta}\ddot{\theta} + r^2 kg(-\cos \theta - \theta)\dot{\theta} = 0,$$

which can be written more simply as

$$\ddot{\theta} = \frac{2g}{\pi r}(\cos \theta + \theta).$$

7.5 Small oscillations

The method described in the last section is often a good way of investigating the oscillation of a system about a position of stable equilibrium. For a system with one degree of freedom, choose a variable which measures the displacement from the equilibrium position, and express the conservation of energy in terms of this variable. Differentiating with respect to time then gives an equation for the acceleration. Often you will recognise this as an equation which, for small values of the variable, is approximately simple harmonic. If so, then you can write down an approximate expression for the period of the oscillation.

Example 7.5.1

A light inextensible chain hangs over a sprocket wheel of radius 0.4 metres which can turn freely about a horizontal axis. The moment of inertia of the wheel about the axis is $0.32\,\text{kg m}^2$ and the ends of the chain are 2 metres above the floor. A light elastic cord with natural length 2 metres and modulus of elasticity 350 newtons attaches one end of the chain to the point on the floor directly beneath it. A load of mass 5 kg is then attached to the other end of the chain. Show that the load will perform simple harmonic oscillations, and find the period and amplitude.

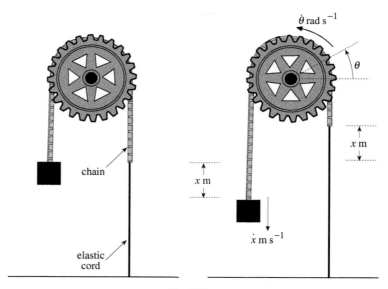

Fig. 7.15

In Fig. 7.15 the diagram on the left shows the situation as the load is attached, before it starts to move. The diagram on the right shows the state of the system t seconds later, when the load is x metres below its initial position, that is $(2 - x)$ metres above the floor. The cord is then stretched by x metres, so the elastic potential energy is $\dfrac{350x^2}{2 \times 2}$ joules. The total potential energy is therefore V joules, where

$$V = 5 \times 9.8 \times (2 - x) + 87.5x^2.$$

The depth at which the load could rest in equilibrium is given by $\dfrac{\mathrm{d}V}{\mathrm{d}x} = 0$, that is

$$-49 + 175x = 0, \quad \text{which gives} \quad x = \frac{49}{175} = 0.28.$$

To investigate the oscillation, introduce a new variable y defined by $x = 0.28 + y$, so that the load is y metres below the equilibrium position. In terms of y,

$$\begin{aligned}
V &= 5 \times 9.8 \times (1.72 - y) + 87.5(0.28 + y)^2 \\
&= 84.28 - 49y + 6.86 + 49y + 87.5y^2 \\
&= 91.14 + 87.5y^2.
\end{aligned}$$

You also need an expression for the kinetic energy of the system. The velocity of the load is $\dot{x}$ m s^{-1} downwards. Also, when the load has descended x metres, the wheel has turned through $\dfrac{x}{0.4}$ radians, so the angular velocity of the wheel is $\dfrac{\dot{x}}{0.4}$ rad s^{-1}. The total kinetic energy is therefore W joules, where

$$W = \tfrac{1}{2} \times 5 \times \dot{x}^2 + \tfrac{1}{2} \times 0.32 \times \left(\dfrac{\dot{x}}{0.4}\right)^2$$
$$= 3.5\dot{x}^2.$$

Since $x = 0.28 + y$, $\dot{x} = \dot{y}$, so that W can be written as $3.5\dot{y}^2$. The conservation of energy equation for the system is therefore

$$91.14 + 87.5y^2 + 3.5\dot{y}^2 = \text{constant}.$$

This can be differentiated with respect to t, using $\dfrac{d}{dt}y^2 = 2y\dot{y}$ and $\dfrac{d}{dt}\dot{y}^2 = 2\dot{y}\ddot{y}$, to give

$$175y\dot{y} + 7\dot{y}\ddot{y} = 0.$$

Dividing this by $7\dot{y}$,

$$\ddot{y} = -25y.$$

This is an equation of simple harmonic motion with period $\dfrac{2\pi}{\sqrt{25}} \approx 1.26$ seconds, correct to 3 significant figures.

Note also that, since the load is stationary when the cord is unstretched, the extension of the cord never becomes negative. The amplitude is equal to the depth of the load in the equilibrium position.

The system therefore oscillates with amplitude 0.28 metres and period 1.26 seconds.

Example 7.5.2
A rod AB, of mass m and length $2a$, is attached to a fixed hinge at A. An elastic string, of natural length $2a$ and modulus of elasticity $5mg$, has one end attached to the hinge and passes through a small eye at B. The other end is then fixed to a point C, at a distance $3a$ below A. The rod is displaced through a small angle from its position of stable equilibrium and oscillates about the downward vertical through A. Find an approximate expression for the period of oscillation.

Fig. 7.16 shows the system when the rod makes an angle θ with the downward vertical. In this position the centre of mass is a distance $a\cos\theta$ below the level of A, so the gravitational potential energy (with the level of A as base) is $-mg(a\cos\theta)$. Because the natural length of the string is equal to the length of the rod, the extension x of the string is equal to BC, so the elastic potential energy is $\dfrac{5mgx^2}{2(2a)}$, where

$$x^2 = (2a)^2 + (3a)^2 - 2(2a)(3a)\cos\theta$$
$$= (13 - 12\cos\theta)a^2.$$

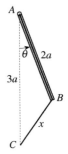

Fig. 7.16

The moment of inertia of the rod about A is $\frac{4}{3}ma^2$, so the kinetic energy of the rod is $\frac{1}{2}\left(\frac{4}{3}ma^2\right)\dot{\theta}^2$. The conservation of energy equation is therefore

$$\frac{2}{3}ma^2\dot{\theta}^2 - mga\cos\theta + \frac{5mg}{4a}(13 - 12\cos\theta)a^2 = \text{constant},$$

which can be written more simply as

$$\frac{2}{3}ma^2\dot{\theta}^2 - 16mga\cos\theta = \text{constant}.$$

Differentiating with respect to t gives

$$\frac{4}{3}ma^2\dot{\theta}\,\ddot{\theta} + 16mga\sin\theta\,\dot{\theta} = 0.$$

Cancelling $\dot{\theta}$ and rearranging gives

$$\ddot{\theta} = -12\frac{g}{a}\sin\theta.$$

You will recognise that this is like the equations you get for the oscillation of a pendulum. It is not an exact simple harmonic equation, but since the displacement is small you can use the approximation $\sin\theta \approx \theta$ to write

$$\ddot{\theta} \approx -12\frac{g}{a}\theta.$$

The system therefore oscillates with period of approximately

$$2\pi \div \sqrt{\frac{12g}{a}}, \quad \text{which is} \quad \pi\sqrt{\frac{a}{3g}}.$$

Example 7.5.3

Axes are laid out on a horizontal plane, with coordinates measured in metres. A bead of mass 0.01 kg is free to move on a smooth wire along the x-axis, as shown in Fig. 7.17. It is connected by elastic strings, each of natural length 1 metre and modulus of elasticity 2 newtons, to points $(4, 3)$ and $(-4, -3)$, so that it can rest in equilibrium at the origin. If the bead is displaced by a small distance along the wire and then released, find an approximation to the period of oscillation.

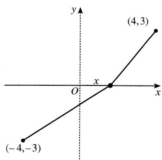

Fig. 7.17

When the bead is at $(x, 0)$, the extension of the string joining it to $(-4, -3)$ is $\left(\sqrt{(4 + x)^2 + 3^2} - 1\right)$ metres, so the elastic energy (in joules) is

$$\frac{2 \times \left(\sqrt{(4 + x)^2 + 3^2} - 1\right)^2}{2 \times 1} = (4 + x)^2 + 9 - 2\sqrt{(4 + x)^2 + 3^2} + 1$$

$$= 26 + 8x + x^2 - 2\sqrt{25 + 8x + x^2}.$$

In this example it is simplest to make an approximation at this stage, rather than leaving it until after differentiating as was done in Example 7.5.2. Since x is small, the square root in this expression can be approximated using the binomial expansion as

$$\sqrt{25 + 8x + x^2} = 5\left(1 + \tfrac{8}{25}x + \tfrac{1}{25}x^2\right)^{\frac{1}{2}}$$
$$= 5\left(1 + \tfrac{1}{2}\left(\tfrac{8}{25}x + \tfrac{1}{25}x^2\right) + \frac{\tfrac{1}{2} \times \left(-\tfrac{1}{2}\right)}{2}\left(\tfrac{8}{25}x + \tfrac{1}{25}x^2\right)^2 + \ldots\right)$$
$$\approx 5\left(1 + \tfrac{4}{25}x + \left(\tfrac{1}{50} - \tfrac{8}{625}\right)x^2\right)$$
$$= 5 + 0.8x + 0.036x^2.$$

Notice that in this approximation the terms involving x^2 have been retained, but terms of higher degree have been omitted. This needs to be justified, but it will be clearer to continue with the solution at this stage and to review the decision later on.

Substituting this approximation in the formula for the elastic energy gives

$$26 + 8x + x^2 - 2\sqrt{25 + 8x + x^2} = 26 + 8x + x^2 - 2(5 + 0.8x + 0.036x^2)$$
$$= 16 + 6.4x + 0.928x^2.$$

In a similar way, you can find the elastic energy of the string joining the bead to $(4, 3)$ as

$$\frac{2x\left(\sqrt{(4 - x)^2 + 3^2} - 1\right)^2}{2 \times 1}.$$

Notice that this differs from the previous expression only by having $-x$ in place of x, so you can write down straight away an approximation for this elastic energy as

$$16 - 6.4x + 0.928x^2.$$

The total elastic energy (in joules) is therefore approximately

$$32 + 1.856x^2.$$

As the bead oscillates the velocity of the bead is $\dot{x}$, so its kinetic energy is $\tfrac{1}{2} \times 0.01\dot{x}^2$ joules.

Conservation of energy can therefore be expressed by the approximation

$$0.005\dot{x}^2 + 32 + 1.856x^2 \approx \text{constant}.$$

Differentiating with respect to t,

$$0.01\dot{x}\ddot{x} + 3.712x\dot{x} \approx 0, \quad \text{so} \quad \ddot{x} + 371.2x \approx 0.$$

This shows that the oscillation is approximately simple harmonic, with period approximately $\dfrac{2\pi}{\sqrt{371.2}}$ seconds, which is 0.326 seconds.

You can now see the justification for taking the binomial expansion as far as the term in x^2 but no further. In this example, when the elastic energy of the two strings is combined, the next term would involve the power x^4. If this is included in the approximation, differentiation with respect to t will give a term of the form constant $\times x^3\dot{x}$, which would become constant $\times x^3$

after dividing through by $\dot{x}$. For small values of x, this would be very small compared with the term proportional to x on the right side of the expression for $\ddot{x}$. So omitting the x^4 term in the expansion introduces only a small error into the calculation of the period.

7.6* A general formula for the period

The examples in the last section are fairly simple, because the expression for the kinetic energy has the form constant $\times \dot{x}^2$ or constant $\times \dot{\theta}^2$. But it quite often happens that the multiplier of $\dot{x}^2$ is not constant but a function of x, and this makes the algebra more complicated. Fortunately, when the oscillations have small amplitude, the extra terms are small enough to be neglected in calculating the approximate period.

Consider first the simplest case when the position of stable equilibrium is given by $x = 0$. This means that, if the potential energy is $V(x)$, then $V'(0) = 0$ and $V''(0) > 0$.

> Occasionally $V''(0) = 0$ at a position of stable equilibrium, in which case the theory which follows doesn't apply, and the oscillation is not approximately simple harmonic. For an example see M3 Miscellaneous exercise 6, Question 12.

Suppose that the kinetic energy is given by a formula $K(x) \times \dot{x}^2$. Kinetic energy cannot be negative, so the function $K(x)$ is always positive. Then the conservation of energy equation has the form

$$V(x) + K(x) \times \dot{x}^2 = \text{constant}.$$

This equation is exact. But now consider what approximations you could make if the oscillations are small and approximately simple harmonic.

You will remember that, in simple harmonic motion, the velocity $v = \dot{x}$ and the displacement x are connected by the equation

$$\dot{x}^2 + n^2 x^2 = n^2 a^2$$

(see M3 Section 3.3). The largest values of x and $\dot{x}$ are a and na respectively, so for small oscillations the maximum values of x and $\dot{x}$ are of comparable degrees of smallness.

The aim of the argument is to show how the conservation of energy equation can be approximated by an equation of the simple harmonic form. Consider the two terms in turn.

The potential energy term   Since $x = 0$ is a position of stable equilibrium, the graph of $V(x)$ has a minimum at $x = 0$, like Fig. 7.18. This suggests that it has a form very much like a graph of $a + bx^2$ near $x = 0$. To get the best possible approximation, choose a and b so that the two graphs agree as far as the second derivative (so that both bend at the same rate). In that case $a = V(0)$ and $2b = V''(0)$. So you could replace $V(x)$ by $V(0) + \frac{1}{2}V''(0)x^2$.

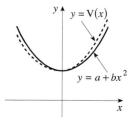

Fig. 7.18

If you have already covered FP2 Chapter 3, you will recognise this as the second degree Maclaurin polynomial for V(x).

The kinetic energy term   This already has a factor $\dot{x}^2$, which is very small. So the error which would result by replacing the multiplier K(x) by its value at $x = 0$, which is K(0), would be very small indeed.

If you make these suggested approximations, the conservation of energy equation becomes

$$V(0) + \tfrac{1}{2}V''(0)x^2 + K(0)\dot{x}^2 \approx \text{constant}.$$

Since V(0) and K(0) are both constant, they can be combined with the constant on the right to give

$$\dot{x}^2 + \frac{V''(0)}{2K(0)}x^2 \approx \text{constant}.$$

Now compare this with the equation $\dot{x}^2 + n^2x^2 = n^2a^2$ for exact simple harmonic motion. You can see that, for small oscillations, the general equation leads to approximate simple harmonic motion with $n^2 = \dfrac{V''(0)}{2K(0)}$.

Finally, this has to be modified for the case where the position of stable equilibrium is not given by $x = 0$, but by $x = s$. All you need to do in that case is to replace x by $s + y$, where $y = 0$ corresponds to the position of stable equilibrium. Then $\dot{x} = \dot{y}$, and the values of V''(x) and K(x) have to be evaluated at $y = 0$, that is $x = s$. So the approximation becomes simple harmonic with $n^2 = \dfrac{V''(s)}{2K(s)}$.

> If, for a system with one degree of freedom, the potential and kinetic energy are given by the functions V(x) and K(x) $\dot{x}^2$, then oscillation about a position of stable equilibrium $x = s$ (where V''(s) $\neq$ 0) is approximately simple harmonic with period $2\pi\sqrt{\dfrac{2K(s)}{V''(s)}}$.

Example 7.6.1
For the system in Example 7.1.3 find approximately the period of oscillation about the position of stable equilibrium.

The potential energy function is

$$V(\theta) = mga\cos\theta + mg(a - l + 2a\sin\tfrac{1}{2}\theta),$$

and it was shown in Example 7.2.2 that

$$V''(\theta) = -mga\cos\theta - \tfrac{1}{2}mga\sin\tfrac{1}{2}\theta.$$

The kinetic energy of the rod is $\frac{1}{2} \times \frac{1}{3}(2m)\,a^2 \times \dot{\theta}^2 = \frac{1}{3}ma^2\dot{\theta}^2$. To find the kinetic energy of the hanging load, note that its height above the hinge is $a - l + 2a\sin\frac{1}{2}\theta$, so its velocity vertically upwards is the derivative of this, which is $a\cos\frac{1}{2}\theta\,\dot{\theta}$. The kinetic energy of the hanging load is therefore $\frac{1}{2}ma^2\cos^2\frac{1}{2}\theta\,\dot{\theta}^2$. This gives the total kinetic energy to be $ma^2(\frac{1}{3} + \frac{1}{2}\cos^2\frac{1}{2}\theta)\,\dot{\theta}^2$, which can be written as $K(\theta)\,\dot{\theta}^2$, where

$$K(\theta) = ma^2\left(\tfrac{1}{3} + \tfrac{1}{2}\cos^2\tfrac{1}{2}\theta\right).$$

It was shown in Example 7.2.2 that the position of stable equilibrium is given by $\theta = \pi$, so the period of small oscillations about this position is approximately $2\pi\sqrt{\dfrac{2K(\pi)}{V''(\pi)}}$. Since

$$K(\pi) = ma^2\left(\tfrac{1}{3} + \tfrac{1}{2}\cos^2\tfrac{1}{2}\pi\right) = \tfrac{1}{3}ma^2,$$

and $\quad V''(\pi) = -mga\cos\pi - \tfrac{1}{2}mga\sin\tfrac{1}{2}\pi = mga - \tfrac{1}{2}mga = \tfrac{1}{2}mga,$

this period is $2\pi\sqrt{\dfrac{2 \times \frac{1}{3}ma^2}{\frac{1}{2}mga}} = 2\pi\sqrt{\dfrac{4a}{3g}} = 4\pi\sqrt{\dfrac{a}{3g}}.$

Exercise 7B

1 In the diagram AB and CD are identical light springs with natural length l and modulus of elasticity λ, and BC is a light chain which engages with a sprocket wheel of radius r and moment of inertia I. Initially the springs are both in tension, with extension d. The point B is then moved away from A and released from rest. Write an equation of energy, and deduce the period of oscillation of the system.

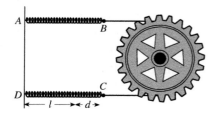

2 An elastic band has natural length $2a$ and modulus of elasticity λ. It is stretched between two fixed nails at the same level which are a distance $2a$ apart. A particle of mass m is attached to the band which oscillates in the vertical line halfway between the nails. At time t the particle is a distance x below the nails. By differentiating an equation of energy, find the period of oscillation, and the depth of the centre of oscillation below the nails.

3 A thin tube is bent into a circle of radius r and fixed in a vertical plane. There is a smooth uniform chain of length $2r\alpha$ inside the tube which rests in equilibrium in the lowest part of the tube. It is slightly displaced from this position and released. Find the approximate period with which it will oscillate.

4 Find the period of oscillation of the system in Miscellaneous exercise 5 Question 7 by differentiating an equation of energy.

5 In Exercise 7A Question 12, the bead is displaced slightly from its position at the lowest point of the wire and released from rest. By differentiating an energy equation, find an equation of motion for the bead. Deduce that, if the equilibrium is stable, the bead will

oscillate about the lowest point of the wire with period of approximately $2\pi\sqrt{\dfrac{2r}{(2-k)g}}$.

6 An acrobat of mass 50 kg hangs from two points A and B at the same level, 24 metres apart, by two elastic cords which have natural length 3.2 metres and modulus of elasticity 208 newtons. Find an equation for the depth, x metres, below AB at which she is in equilibrium by

(a) resolving the forces,

(b) finding where the potential energy is stationary.

Show that this equation is satisfied by $x = 5$.

She now oscillates vertically about this equilibrium position. By writing a conservation of energy equation and using a binomial approximation, find the period of her oscillation.

7* For the system in Exercise 7A Question 6, use the method of Section 7.6 to find an expression for the approximate period of oscillation about the equilibrium position.

8* A smooth wire in the shape of the parabola $ay = x^2$ is set up in a vertical plane with the y-axis vertically upwards. A bead of mass m is threaded on the wire and makes small oscillations about the origin. Show that the conservation of energy equation can be written as $\dfrac{mg}{a}x^2 + \tfrac{1}{2}m\left(1 + \dfrac{4x^2}{a^2}\right)\dot{x}^2 = \text{constant}$.
Find the approximate period of the oscillation.

9* Two children, each of mass m, sit at the ends of a plank of length $2l$ which is balanced over a log of radius r. This see-saw is modelled as shown in the diagram; the mass and the thickness of the plank can be neglected.

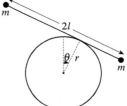

(a) Taking the origin at the centre of the log, write down the coordinates of the two ends of the plank.

(b) By differentiating your answers to part (a), find expressions for the velocities of the two ends of the plank. Show that these are consistent with the suggestion that the plank is instantaneously rotating about the point of contact of the plank with the log. (This point is called the *instantaneous centre of rotation*.)

(c) Write down a conservation of energy equation for the oscillation and deduce an approximate expression for the period.

(d) Choose suitable numerical values for the mass of the children, the length of the plank and the radius of the log, and substitute these in your answer to part (c). Does this suggest that the model is a reasonable one?

10* The plank in Example 7.2.3 has mass m, so that $W = mg$, and a is less than r. It rocks through a small angle about the position of stable equilibrium. Use the idea of the instantaneous centre of rotation (see Question 9(b)) to find an expression for the kinetic energy of the plank when it is at an angle θ to the horizontal. Hence find an approximate expression for the period of the oscillation.

1 A particle P of mass m can move inside a smooth circular tube with centre O, which is fixed in a vertical plane. The particle is attached to the end of an elastic string of natural length $\frac{1}{2}\pi r$ and modulus of elasticity $\frac{3}{2}mg$. The other end of the string is fixed to a point inside the tube at the same level as O, as shown in the diagram.

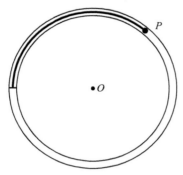

Show that the particle can rest in stable equilibrium with the radius OP at an angle $\frac{1}{6}\pi$ to the vertical.

The particle is slightly displaced from this position of equilibrium and released. By writing the angle of the radius with the vertical as $\frac{1}{6}\pi + \phi$ and using the approximations $\sin\phi \approx \phi$ and $\cos\phi \approx 1 - \frac{1}{2}\phi^2$, find the approximate period of small oscillations about the position of equilibrium.

2 A smooth circular wire of radius 2 metres is fixed in a vertical plane. A bead of weight 1 newton is threaded on to the wire. A small ring is fixed 1 metre above the centre of the wire. An inextensible string of length 4 metres, with one end attached to the bead, passes through the ring; a particle of weight w newtons, attached to the other end of the string, hangs vertically below the ring, as shown in the diagram.

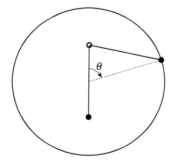

Find the total potential energy of the bead and the particle when the radius to the bead is at an angle θ to the upward vertical. (Take the centre of the wire as the fixed level.)

Show that the bead can always rest in equilibrium at the top and bottom of the wire, and that there are also other positions of equilibrium if $1 < w < 3$. By considering the graph of the potential energy as a function of θ, investigate the stability of the possible positions of equilibrium

(a) if $w < 1$,   (b) if $w > 3$,   (c) if $1 < w < 3$.

3 A uniform rod AB of mass m and length $2a$ is smoothly hinged at a fixed point A. A light inextensible string BCD is attached to B and carries a mass M at D. The string passes over a smooth pulley at the fixed point C with the portion CD of the string hanging vertically.

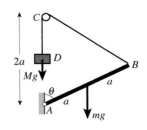

The total length of the string is l. As shown in the diagram, C is vertically above A and $CA = 2a$. The angle between AB and the upward vertical is denoted by θ, where $0 < \theta \leqslant \pi$.

(a) Show that the potential energy V of the system relative to C can be written

$$V = -mga(2 - \cos\theta) - Mg(l - 4a\sin\tfrac{1}{2}\theta).$$

(b) Show that, if $m > M$, there are two positions of equilibrium. Investigate their stability.

(c) Show that, if $m < M$, or if $m = M$, there is only one equilibrium position. Show that this position is always unstable. (MEI)

4 A particle of mass m moves along the positive x-axis under the influence of a force. The potential energy at a point with coordinate x is $k\dfrac{e^{ax}}{x}$; k and a are positive constants.

(a) Find the position of equilibrium of the particle and show that it is stable.

(b) Find the approximate periodic time of small oscillations of the particle about this position of stable equilibrium. (MEI)

5 A particle is subject to an attractive force of magnitude kx^2 towards a fixed point, where k is a constant and x is the distance of the particle from the fixed point. Show that the potential energy of the particle relative to the fixed point is $\tfrac{1}{3}kx^3$.

A particle lies on the line segment joining two fixed points, A and B, which are a distance d apart. The particle is subject to forces of attraction towards each of the points, the magnitude of each force being proportional to the square of the distance of the particle from the point. The constants of proportion are a^2 and b^2 respectively.

(a) Write down an expression for the potential energy of the particle as a function of its distance x from the point A.

(b) Show that there is a single point of equilibrium, determine its position, and show that the equilibrium is stable.

(c) Given that the mass of the particle is m, find the period of small oscillations about this point of stable equilibrium in terms of a, b, d and m. (MEI)

6 An electrically charged particle of mass m is free to move along a straight tube of length $2l$. When it is a distance x from either end of the tube, it experiences a force of repulsion from that end of the tube of magnitude kx^{-2}. Originally the particle is in equilibrium at the mid-point of the tube. Show that, if it is slightly displaced, it will oscillate about the mid-point with motion which is approximately simple harmonic. Find an expression for the approximate period of the oscillation.

7 A particle of mass m hangs by two elastic strings from pegs which are at the same horizontal level at a distance $2a$ apart. Each string has natural length l and modulus of elasticity λ. In equilibrium the particle is a distance b below the level of the pegs. Show that $\dfrac{1}{l} - \dfrac{1}{c} = \dfrac{mg}{2\lambda b}$, where $c = \sqrt{a^2 + b^2}$.

The particle is pulled down a small distance and then released. Show that its oscillation is described approximately by the simple harmonic motion equation $\ddot{x} = -\left(\dfrac{g}{b} + \dfrac{2\lambda b^2}{mc^3}\right)x$.

8* A rod AB, of mass $4m$ and length a, is hinged to a fixed point at A. A peg is fixed at a distance $2a$ from A at the same horizontal level. A thread is attached to the rod at B, which passes over the peg and carries a particle of mass m at its other end. Find the angle which the rod makes with the horizontal when the system is in equilibrium.

Show that the equilibrium is stable, and find the approximate period of small oscillations about the position of equilibrium.

9 Four light rods each of length $2a$ are freely hinged at their ends to form a rhombus $ABCD$ which is suspended at A from a fixed point.

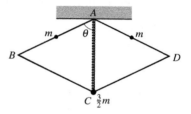

A light spring of natural length $2a$ and modulus of elasticity $6mg$ connects the points A and C. A particle of mass $\frac{3}{2}m$ is attached at the point C and each of the rods AB and AD carries a particle of mass m at its mid-point, as shown in the diagram. The point C can move freely in the vertical line through A. The angle between AB and the downward vertical is θ.

(a) Show that the potential energy V of the system relative to the zero level through A is given by $V = mga(24\cos^2\theta - 32\cos\theta + 6)$. Deduce that there are two positions of equilibrium and show that only one of these is stable.

(b) The system now performs small oscillations about the position of stable equilibrium where $\theta = \alpha$. Show that the kinetic energy T is given by $T = ma^2\dot{\theta}^2(13 - 12\cos^2\theta)$.

(c) By putting $\theta = \alpha + \phi$ and assuming both ϕ and $\dot{\phi}$ remain very small, show that $T \approx \frac{23}{3}ma^2\dot{\phi}^2$.

(d) Show that, near the equilibrium position, $V \approx \frac{1}{3}mga(-14 + 40\phi^2)$. Find the approximate period of small oscillations about the position of stable equilibrium.   (MEI, adapted)

Revision exercise 4

1 A wheel rotating about a fixed axis is slowing down with constant angular deceleration. Initially the angular speed is $24\,\mathrm{rad\,s}^{-1}$. In the first 5 seconds the wheel turns through 96 radians.

   (a) Find the angular deceleration.

   (b) Find the total angle the wheel turns through before corning to rest. (OCR)

2 A circular flywheel of radius 0.2 m is rotating freely about a fixed axis through its centre and perpendicular to its plane. The moment of inertia of the flywheel about the axis is $0.37\,\mathrm{kg\,m}^2$. When the angular speed of the flywheel is $8\,\mathrm{rad\,s}^{-1}$ a particle of mass 0.75 kg, initially at rest, sticks to a point on the circumference of the flywheel. Find the angular speed of the flywheel immediately after the particle has stuck to it. (OCR)

3 A cylinder with radius a is fixed with its axis horizontal. A uniform rod, of mass m and length $2b$, moves in a vertical plane perpendicular to the axis of the cylinder, maintaining contact with the cylinder and not slipping (see diagram). When the rod is horizontal, its mid-point G is in contact with the cylinder. You are given that, when the rod makes an angle θ with the horizontal, the height of G above the axis of the cylinder is $a(\theta\sin\theta + \cos\theta)$.

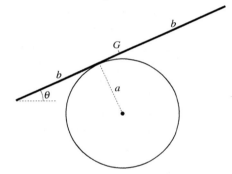

   (a) By considering the potential energy of the rod, show that $\theta = 0$ is a position of stable equilibrium.

   (b) You are also given that, when θ is small, the kinetic energy of the rod is approximately $\frac{1}{6}mb^2\dot{\theta}^2$. Show that the approximate period of small oscillations about the position $\theta = 0$ is $\dfrac{2\pi b}{\sqrt{3ga}}$. (OCR)

4 (a) Prove by integration that the moment of inertia of a uniform rod, of mass m and length $2a$, about a perpendicular axis through its centre G, is $\frac{1}{3}ma^2$.

   The point A on the rod is such that $GA = x$. The rod makes small oscillations in a vertical plane about a fixed horizontal axis through A. All resistances to motion may be neglected.

   (b) Find the approximate period of these oscillations, in terms of a, x and g. (OCR)

5 A uniform rectangular lamina $ABCD$ of mass 0.6 kg has sides $AB = 0.4\,\mathrm{m}$ and $AD = 0.3\,\mathrm{m}$. The lamina is free to rotate about a fixed horizontal axis which passes through A and is perpendicular to the lamina.

   (a) Find the moment of inertia of the lamina about the axis.

   (b) Find the approximate period of small oscillations in a vertical plane. (OCR)

6 A uniform solid sphere, of mass 4 kg and radius 0.1 m, is rotating freely about a fixed axis with angular speed 20 rad s^{-1}. The axis is a diameter of the sphere. A couple, having constant moment 0.36 N m about the axis and acting in the direction of rotation, is then applied for 6 seconds. For this time interval, find

   (a) the angular acceleration of the sphere,

   (b) the angle through which the sphere turns,

   (c) the work done by the couple.   (OCR)

7 Four uniform rods AB, BC, CD and DA, each of mass m and length $2a$, are freely jointed at A, B, C and D. Also, A is freely jointed to a fixed point. The points A and C are joined by a light elastic string with natural length $2a$ and modulus of elasticity $10mg$. The angle BAC is denoted by θ, and C is vertically below A (see diagram).

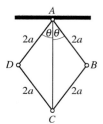

   (a) By considering potential energy, find the non-zero value of θ for which the system is in equilibrium.

   (b) Determine whether this position of equilibrium is stable or unstable.   (OCR)

8 A wheel is rotating freely about a fixed axis with angular speed 15 rad s^{-1}. A couple with constant moment 3.2 N m about the axis, acting in the direction of rotation, is applied to the wheel for 8 seconds. In this time the wheel turns through 45 revolutions.

   (a) Find the work done by the couple.

   (b) Find the moment of inertia of the wheel about the axis.   (OCR)

9 A uniform circular disc has mass m, radius a and centre C. The disc is free to rotate in a vertical plane about a fixed horizontal axis passing through a point A on the disc, where $CA = \frac{1}{3}a$.

   (a) Find the moment of inertia of the disc about this axis.

   The disc is released from rest with CA horizontal.

   (b) Find the initial angular acceleration of the disc.

   (c) State the direction of the force acting on the disc at A immediately after release, and find its magnitude.   (OCR)

10 A uniform rod AB, of mass m and length $2a$, is free to rotate in a vertical plane about a fixed horizontal axis through A. The rod is released from rest with AB horizontal. Air resistance may be neglected. For the instant when the rod has rotated through an angle $\frac{1}{6}\pi$,

   (a) show that the angular acceleration of the rod is $\dfrac{(3\sqrt{3})g}{8a}$,

   (b) find the angular speed of the rod,

   (c) show that the force acting on the rod at A has magnitude $\dfrac{\sqrt{103}}{8}mg$.   (OCR)

11 The diagram shows a uniform rod AB, of mass m and length $2a$, free to rotate in a vertical plane about a fixed horizontal axis through A. A light elastic string has natural length a and modulus of elasticity $\frac{1}{2}mg$. The string joins B to a light ring R which slides along a smooth horizontal wire fixed at a height a above A and in the same vertical plane as AB. The string BR remains vertical. The angle between AB and the horizontal is denoted by θ, where $0 < \theta < \pi$.

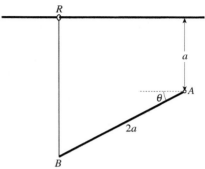

(a) Taking the reference level for gravitational potential energy to be the horizontal through A, show that the total potential energy of the system is $mga(\sin^2\theta - \sin\theta)$.

(b) Find the three values of θ for which the system is in equilibrium.

(c) For each position of equilibrium, determine whether it is stable or unstable.   (OCR)

12 A uniform solid sphere with centre C, mass m and radius a, is gently pushed over the edge E of a table. The sphere begins to rotate about a fixed horizontal axis through E. When EC makes an angle θ with the vertical, the angular speed of the sphere is ω, the normal reaction is R and the frictional force is F (see diagram). At the start C is vertically above E, with $\omega = 0$. It may be assumed that the only forces acting on the sphere are R, F and its weight.

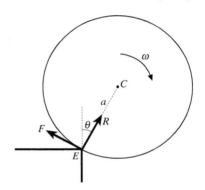

(a) Find the moment of inertia of the sphere about the axis through E.

(b) Show that $\omega^2 = \dfrac{10g(1 - \cos\theta)}{7a}$.

(c) Find the angular acceleration of the sphere, in terms of g, a and θ.

(d) Find R and F, in terms of m, g and θ.

(e) Assuming that the sphere rotates about the axis through E until it loses contact with the edge of the table, find the value of θ at the instant when contact is lost.

(f) What does the assumption in part (e) imply about the nature of the contact between the sphere and the edge E? Describe briefly what will happen in reality.   (OCR)

13 A uniform rectangular piece of card $ABCD$, with $AB = 40$ cm and $BC = 30$ cm, is pinned to a door at a point E on the diagonal AC such that $AE = 10$ cm. It hangs in stable equilibrium in a vertical plane. If it is slightly disturbed from this position, calculate the period with which it will oscillate.

14 A cylindrical drum of radius 0.2 metres can rotate with its axis horizontal on smooth bearings. A rope, whose mass can be neglected, has one end fixed to a point on the circumference of the drum. It winds several times round the drum, and then supports a sack of mass 36 kg at its free end. If the sack descends with acceleration 4.8 m s^{-2}, find the moment of inertia of the drum about its axis.

What would the acceleration be if the mass of the sack were 50 kg?

15 A square plate has mass 5 kg and edges of length 1.2 metres. It hangs in a vertical plane from a horizontal axle along one edge. It is struck with a blow perpendicular to its plane, at the mid-point of the opposite edge. The plate comes to rest in its position of unstable equilibrium. Assuming that the effect of friction can be neglected, find the impulse of the blow.

16 A child is sitting on a stool which can rotate about a vertical axis. His friends set the stool rotating at an angular speed of 0.8 revolutions per second. It is then brought to rest by a frictional couple of constant moment 0.06 N m. If it turns through 4 revolutions while coming to rest, find the combined moment of inertia of the child and the stool about the axis of rotation.

Find also the time that it takes for the stool to come to rest.

17 A particle P of mass 0.25 kg moves in a straight line AOB on a horizontal surface. At time t seconds, the displacement of P from O towards B is x metres. The only horizontal forces acting on P are:

a force of constant magnitude 1 N in the direction $\overrightarrow{AB}$;

a force of variable magnitude $\sqrt{1+x}$ N in the direction $\overrightarrow{BA}$.

Obtain an expression for $\dfrac{\text{d}^2 x}{\text{d}t^2}$ in terms of x. It is given that, in the motion, x remains small.

(a) Write down the first two terms of the binomial expansion of $\sqrt{1+x}$.

(b) Hence obtain and simplify an equation for the approximate acceleration of P.

(c) For the approximate motion of P, state its type, and find the period.

Explain why the force of magnitude 1 N cannot be a frictional force.   (OCR)

18 A clockwork motor is wound up by 15 turns of a key, each of angle 120°, against a couple of moment 2 N cm. How much energy is then stored in the spring?

This energy is expended in applying a couple to a wheel with moment of inertia 0.1 kg cm². The magnitude of the couple decreases linearly to zero over a period of 5 seconds.

What is the angular speed of the wheel at the end of this period, and how many revolutions has the wheel made in that time?

19 A uniform piece of plywood is cut so that it occupies the region between the curve $y = x^2$ and the line $y = 1\frac{1}{4}$, the units being metres. Show that it can rest in equilibrium in a vertical plane with the point $(\frac{1}{2}, \frac{1}{4})$ in contact with the floor.

Show that there are three possible positions of equilibrium in which the curved edge is in contact with the floor. State which are stable and which are unstable.

20 A uniform rod has length $2a$ and mass m. It swings in a vertical plane on a smooth horizontal axle through one end. Show that the period of small oscillations is $2\pi\sqrt{\dfrac{4a}{3g}}$.

The rod is hanging vertically and at rest when it is struck a horizontal blow at its mid-point; the blow is perpendicular to the plane of the axle and the vertical, and has impulse J. Find the initial angular velocity of the rod.

If the result of the blow is an oscillation whose amplitude is not small, find an expression for that amplitude.   (OCR)

21 A ring R of mass 0.25 kg is threaded on a smooth horizontal wire. P is a fixed point in the same vertical plane as the wire, and O is the point on the wire such that OP is perpendicular to the wire. The distance OP is 1 m. The ring is connected to P by a light elastic string of natural length 0.75 m and modulus of elasticity 27 N. The ring is projected from O along the wire. After t seconds the displacement of R from O is x metres (see diagram). In a simple model for the subsequent motion, air resistance is ignored. Show that

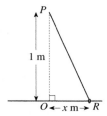

$$\frac{\mathrm{d}^2x}{\mathrm{d}t^2} = -108x\left(\frac{4}{3} - \frac{1}{\sqrt{1+x^2}}\right).$$

It is given that x remains small, and that in the binomial expansion of $(1 + x^2)^{-\frac{1}{2}}$ terms involving x^2 and higher powers of x can be ignored. Show that R moves with approximate simple harmonic motion of period $\frac{1}{3}\pi$ seconds.

Given that the amplitude of the motion is 0.05 m, find the approximate position of the ring 1.9 s after it is projected from O.   (OCR)

22 AB and BC are uniform planks of equal length $2a$ and equal weight W, hinged together at B. They rest in equilibrium on two smooth pegs at the same level a distance a apart, with B above the pegs and on the vertical line halfway between them. Find the angle which the planks make with the downward vertical, and whether the equilibrium is stable.

A and C are now connected by an elastic cord of natural length a. The planks then rest in equilibrium at 45° to the downward vertical. Find the modulus of elasticity of the cord. Does the presence of the cord affect the stability of the equilibrium?

Investigate what happens if B is below the level of the pegs.

23 (a) Show that the area of the region OAB shown
in the diagram, bounded by the parabola
$hy = x^2$ and the line $y = h$, is equal to $\frac{4}{3}h^2$.

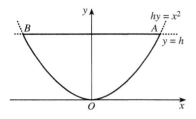

(b) The shape OAB is cut from thin sheet material of
uniform thickness and density. The mass of this
lamina is M. By considering strips parallel to AB, or
otherwise, find the coordinates of the centre of
mass of the lamina.

(c) Show that the moment of inertia of the lamina about the line $y = 0$ is $\frac{3}{7}Mh^2$, and
hence find the moment of inertia about a parallel line through the centre of mass.

(d) The lamina is freely suspended from a horizontal axis along AB and is disturbed from
its equilibrium position. Write down the equation of motion in terms of θ, the angle
which the plane of the lamina makes with the vertical at time t. Find the period of
small oscillations about AB.   (OCR)

24 A mechanism for ringing a gong consists of a uniform metal rod of mass 2 kg and length
90 cm, with a solid wooden ball of radius 10 cm and mass 3 kg attached at its lower end, so
that the centre of the ball is in line with the rod. The rod is hinged to a fixed point at its
upper end. When not in use, the ball rests against the vertical surface of the gong, with the
rod vertical. To ring the gong, the mechanism is raised until the rod is at 15° to the
vertical, and then released. The ball doesn't rebound after hitting the gong.

(a) Find the impulse which the gong receives from the ball.

(b) Find the impulse on the hinge when the ball hits the gong.

(c) Approximately how much time elapses from the release of the mechanism until the
ball hits the gong?

25 A square beer-mat of side $2a$ and mass m is placed on a
horizontal table with one edge parallel to a side of the table
and overhanging the table by a distance $\frac{1}{2}a$. The centre of
the overhanging edge is then struck a blow which gives the
mat an initial angular velocity Ω.

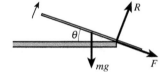

(a) Modelling the beer-mat as a rigid body with negligible thickness, find its moment of
inertia about the edge of the table.

Assume that immediately after the blow the mat remains in contact with the edge of
the table and does not slip. As it rotates, there are force components F (friction) and
R (normal reaction) as shown in the diagram.

(b) Find a formula for the angular acceleration $\ddot\theta$ during rotation.

(c) Find the initial values of R and F.

(d) Show that the mat will indeed rotate without slipping initially if $\Omega^2 < \dfrac{8\mu g}{7a}$, where μ is
the coefficient of friction.

(e) Discuss whether F will increase or decrease as the mat starts to rotate.   (OCR)

26 A uniform plane lamina *OAB* has mass *m* and is in the shape of an equilateral triangle of side *a*. Find the moment of inertia of the elementary strip in the first diagram about an axis through *O* and perpendicular to the plane *OAB*. Use integration to show that the moment of inertia of the lamina about this axis is $\frac{5}{12}ma^2$.

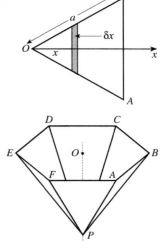

The second diagram shows a lampshade *PABCDEF* made from six uniform isosceles triangles having a common vertex *P*. *ABCDEF* lies in a horizontal plane and forms a regular hexagon of side *a*. *P* is a distance *h* below the centre *O* of the hexagon. Explain why the moment of inertia of the lampshade about *OP* is independent of *h* and is equal to $\frac{5}{12}Ma^2$, where *M* is the mass of the lampshade.

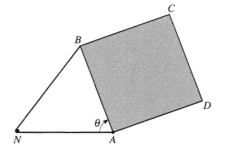

The lampshade is suspended from a ceiling fixture by light chains. When the lampshade rotates through a small angle θ about the vertical axis *OP*, the centre of mass of the lampshade rises through a distance $\lambda a\theta^2$, where λ is a small constant. Write down an equation for work and kinetic energy of rotation (you may neglect the small kinetic energy associated with the vertical motion); differentiate it with respect to time to derive the equation of motion of the lampshade for rotation about the vertical axis. If the lampshade is twisted through a small angle θ_0 about *OP* from its equilibrium position, and then released from rest, find the period of the subsequent oscillations in terms of λ, *a* and *g*. (OCR)

27 A uniform square lamina *ABCD* has mass *m* and sides of length *a*. It is hinged to a fixed point of a wall at *A* so that it can rotate in a vertical plane. There is a nail *N* in the wall at a distance *a* from *A* and at the same horizontal level, so that the angle *NAB* $(= \theta)$ can take values between 0 and $\frac{3}{2}\pi$. An elastic string, of natural length *a* and modulus $\frac{1}{4}mg$, has its ends attached to the square at *A* and *B*, and passes round the nail, as shown in the diagram. By considering the graph of the potential energy, show that there are two possible positions of equilibrium, one stable and one unstable.

Investigate what happens if the square is slightly displaced from a position of equilibrium. If the equilibrium is stable, find the period of small oscillations about this position. If it is unstable, find the angular speed with which the lamina hits the nail.

What happens if the elastic string is replaced by a string of the same natural length and modulus $\frac{3}{4}mg$?

Practice examination 1 for M4

Time 1 hour 30 minutes

Answer all the questions.

Graphic calculators are permitted.

1 A flywheel whose moment of inertia about its axis is $1.6\,\mathrm{kg\,m^2}$ is accelerated by means of a couple of constant moment $10\,\mathrm{N\,m}$. The angular speed of the flywheel increases from $5\,\mathrm{rad\,s^{-1}}$ to $20\,\mathrm{rad\,s^{-1}}$. Find

 (i) the time taken and the total angle turned through by the flywheel, [6]

 (ii) the work done by the couple. [1]

2 A uniform rod AB of mass $2\,\mathrm{kg}$ and length $1\,\mathrm{m}$ is free to rotate in a vertical plane about a fixed horizontal axis through its mid-point. Initially the rod is at rest in a horizontal position. A particle of mass $1\,\mathrm{kg}$ is dropped from rest at a distance of $0.5\,\mathrm{m}$ vertically above the end A of the rod. The particle falls freely, and adheres to A when it strikes the rod. Calculate

 (i) the angular speed with which the rod begins to rotate, [6]

 (ii) the energy lost as a result of the impact between the particle and the rod. [2]

3 The diagram shows the uniform solid cone of base radius r and height h formed by rotating part of the line $y = \dfrac{rx}{h}$ about the x-axis. The centre of the thin vertical disc shown is at $(x, 0)$, and the disc has thickness δx. The density of the cone is ρ.

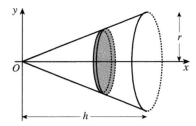

 (i) Explain why the moment of inertia of the disc about the y-axis is given (approximately) by $\frac{1}{4}\pi\rho\,\dfrac{r^4 x^4}{h^4}\delta x + \pi\rho\,\dfrac{r^2 x^4}{h^2}\delta x$. [4]

 (ii) Hence show that the moment of inertia of the cone about the y-axis is $\frac{3}{20}M(r^2 + 4h^2)$, where M is the mass of the cone. [4]

4 A river of width d flows between straight parallel banks with speed $3u$. A boat crossing the river travels at speed $5u$ in still water.

  (i) The boat travels directly across the river. Find the angle with the bank at which the boat heads, and the time it takes to cross the river. [4]

  (ii) On another journey the boat takes a time $\dfrac{d}{3u}$ to cross the river, travelling in a straight line.

    (a) Write down the components, parallel and perpendicular to the banks, of the velocity of the boat relative to the water. [2]

    (b) Hence show that the boat finishes its crossing either upstream or downstream of its starting point. [4]

5 A uniform lamina of mass M is in the shape of a semicircle of radius a. The mid-point of the straight edge of the lamina is O.

  (i) Use integration to show that the centre of mass of the lamina is at a distance $\dfrac{4a}{3\pi}$ from O. [6]

  (ii) You are given that the moment of inertia of a circular disc of mass m and radius r about an axis through its centre and perpendicular to its plane is $\frac{1}{2}mr^2$. Explain how you can deduce that the moment of inertia of the lamina about its straight edge is $\frac{1}{4}Ma^2$. [3]

  (iii) The lamina is smoothly hinged to a horizontal axis along its straight edge. Find the period of the small oscillations that the lamina can make about this axis. [2]

6 A uniform circular disc of mass m and radius a is free to rotate in a vertical plane about a fixed horizontal axis through its centre O. A particle P, also of mass m, is attached to the circumference of the disc. The system is released from rest with P at the same horizontal level as O. At time t later, OP has turned through an angle θ (see diagram).

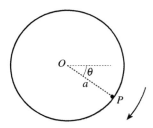

  (i) Show that $a\dot\theta^2 = \frac{4}{3}g\sin\theta$ and $a\ddot\theta = \frac{2}{3}g\cos\theta$. [6]

  (ii) The force acting on the disc at O has components of magnitude X parallel to PO and Y perpendicular to PO. Find expressions, in terms of m, g and θ, for X and Y. [6]

7 A uniform rod AB of mass $2m$ and length $2a$ is smoothly hinged to a fixed point at A so that it can rotate in a vertical plane. The end B of the rod is attached to A by means of a light elastic string of natural length $2a$ and modulus of elasticity mg. The string passes over a small smooth peg P which is fixed at the same horizontal level as A, with $AP = 2a$. The string and the rod lie in the same vertical plane (see diagram).

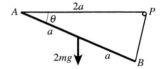

(i) Taking AP as the reference level for gravitational potential energy, show that the total potential energy of the system can be expressed in the form $2mga(1 - \sin\theta - \cos\theta)$, where θ denotes angle PAB. [4]

(ii) Deduce that there is a position of stable equilibrium where $\theta = \frac{1}{4}\pi$. [4]

(iii) The system makes small oscillations about this equilibrium position. Use the substitution $\theta = \frac{1}{4}\pi + \phi$, where ϕ is a small angle, to show that the energy equation for the system may be written as $2a\dot{\phi}^2 - 3\sqrt{2}\,g\cos\phi = $ constant. [4]

(iv) Hence find the approximate period of these small oscillations. [4]

Time 1 hour 30 minutes

Answer all the questions.

Graphic calculators are permitted.

1 The diagram shows a body formed from two uniform rods AB and CD, each of mass m and length $2a$. The end B of the rod AB is rigidly fixed to the mid-point of CD, with AB and CD at right angles. The body is free to rotate in a vertical plane about a horizontal axis through A.

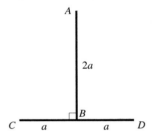

   (i) Show that the moment of inertia of the body about the axis through A is $\frac{17}{3}ma^2$. [3]

   (ii) Find the period of small oscillations about the axis through A. [3]

2 A horizontal uniform disc, of mass 5 kg and radius 0.8 m, is rotating with angular speed 30 rad s^{-1} about a vertical axis through its centre. A circular hoop, of mass 2 kg and radius 0.4 m, is at rest and is placed gently onto the surface of the disc, so that the disc and the hoop are concentric. When slipping between the hoop and the disc stops, the hoop and the disc are rotating together with angular speed ω rad s^{-1}.

   (i) Use the principle of conservation of angular momentum to calculate ω. [3]

   (ii) While slipping is occurring, a frictional couple of constant moment may be assumed to be acting on the disc. Given that the disc turns through one revolution while slipping is occurring, find the moment of this couple and the angular deceleration of the disc. [5]

3 A uniform lamina is bounded by the x-axis, the y-axis, the line $x = a$ and the curve $y = ae^{x/a}$, where a is a positive constant. Show that the centre of mass of the lamina is at the point with coordinates $\left(\dfrac{a}{e-1}, \dfrac{a(e+1)}{4} \right)$. [9]

4 A uniform lamina OAB of mass m is a right-angled isosceles triangle with equal sides of length a. The side OA lies along the x-axis, with O at the origin (see diagram).

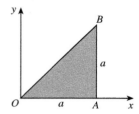

(i) Prove by integration that the moment of inertia of the lamina about the side OA is $\frac{1}{6}ma^2$. [4]

(ii) Use perpendicular and parallel axes theorems to deduce the moment of inertia of the lamina

   (a) about an axis through A perpendicular to the plane, [2]

   (b) about an axis through the mid-point of OB perpendicular to the plane. [4]

5 At noon, two ships A and B are a distance of 25 km apart, with B on a bearing of 050° from A. Ship B travels due east at a steady speed of $10\,\mathrm{km\,h^{-1}}$. Ship A travels at a steady speed of $20\,\mathrm{km\,h^{-1}}$.

(i) Find the direction in which ship A must travel in order to intercept ship B. [4]

(ii) If instead ship A travels on a bearing of 050°, find the closest approach between the ships, and find also the time at which this occurs. [8]

6 A uniform rod has mass m and length $4a$. The rod is initially held at rest with a length a of the rod in contact with a rough horizontal table and with the remaining length $3a$ projecting over the edge of the table. The rod is released and it begins to rotate, without slipping, about the point P at the edge of the table. At time t, the rod makes an angle θ with the horizontal, and the force acting on the rod at P has components X and Y parallel and perpendicular to the rod (see diagram).

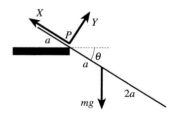

(i) Find expressions, in terms of m, g and θ, for $a\dot{\theta}^2$ and $a\ddot{\theta}$. [6]

(ii) Show that $\dfrac{X}{Y} = \frac{13}{4}\tan\theta$. [7]

7 A particle A of mass $2m$ is fixed to a point on the circumference of a light circular disc of radius a, which is free to rotate in a vertical plane about a horizontal axis through its centre O. One end of a light inextensible string is attached to A. The string is in contact with part of the circumference of the disc and passes over a small smooth peg P fixed level with the highest point of the disc. A particle B of mass m hangs freely from the other end of the string (see diagram).

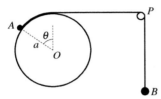

When A is at the highest point of the disc, B is a distance a below the level of the lowest point of the disc. In a general position, the angle between OA and the upwards vertical at O is θ, where $0 < \theta < \pi$.

(i) Show that there are two values of θ for which the system is in equilibrium, and determine in each case whether the equilibrium is stable or unstable.   [7]

(ii) Show that the period of small oscillations of the system about the position of stable equilibrium is approximately $2\pi \sqrt{\dfrac{a\sqrt{3}}{g}}$.   [7]

Answers to M3

Most non-exact numerical answers are given correct to 3 significant figures.

1 Linear motion with variable forces

Exercise 1A (page 9)

1 $2\,\mathrm{m\,s^{-1}}$, $26\frac{2}{3}\,\mathrm{m}$

2 $80\,\mathrm{m\,s^{-1}}$, $600\,\mathrm{m}$

3 $(2 - 2\cos 2t)\,\mathrm{m\,s^{-1}}$, $(2t - \sin 2t)\,\mathrm{m}$

4 75, 63 m

5 $\dfrac{K}{mc}(1 - \mathrm{e}^{-ct})$, $\dfrac{K}{mc^2}(ct + \mathrm{e}^{-ct} - 1)$

6 $5.36\,\mathrm{m\,s^{-1}}$, $132\,\mathrm{m}$

7 6.4 s, 129 m; speed never becomes zero with parachute and air brakes alone

8 1.54 s, 3.88 m; 1.5 s, 3.75 m

9 6 s, 65 m, $10.8\,\mathrm{m\,s^{-1}}$; 8.20 s

10 118 s, 1.15 km

11 $\displaystyle\int_0^{80} \dfrac{500\,000v}{25\,000\,000 - 0.8v^3}\,\mathrm{d}v$, 64 s

12 54.9 s; 288 m

Exercise 1B (page 18)

1 (a) $v = 8t + 1$, $v^2 = 16x + 1$
   (b) $v = 6\cos 2t$, $v^2 = 36 - 4x^2$
   (c) $v = -10\mathrm{e}^{-2t}$, $v = -2x$
   (d) $v = -\dfrac{1}{(t+1)^2}$, $v = -x^2$

2 (a) $x = \tan t$, $v = 1 + x^2$
      (i) $2x(1 + x^2)$ (ii) $2v\sqrt{v-1}$
   (b) $x = 4\mathrm{e}^{\frac{1}{4}t} - 4$, $v = 1 + \frac{1}{4}x$
      (i) $\frac{1}{4}(1 + \frac{1}{4}x)$ (ii) $\frac{1}{4}v$
   (c) $x = 2(1 - \cos\frac{1}{2}t)$, $v^2 = x - \frac{1}{4}x^2$
      (i) $\frac{1}{2}(1 - \frac{1}{2}x)$ (ii) $\pm\frac{1}{2}\sqrt{1 - v^2}$
   (d) $x = \mathrm{e}^t - \mathrm{e}^{-t}$, $v^2 = 4 + x^2$
      (i) x (ii) $\sqrt{v^2 - 4}$

3 $v = 8 - 0.02x$

4 129 m

5 1.15 km

6 288 m

7 79.8 m

8 3.44 km

9 204 m

10 3.45 km

11 $x = 10\dfrac{\mathrm{e}^{2t} - 1}{\mathrm{e}^{2t} + 1}$; $\dfrac{40\mathrm{e}^{2t}}{(\mathrm{e}^{2t} + 1)^2}$

12 $x = \frac{1}{4}qt^2 + \sqrt{p}\,t$; $p = u^2$, $q = 2a$

13 $v^2 = n^2(c^2 - x^2)$, $-n^2x$

14 1.6 N s

15 54 000 N s

16 23.0 J

17 24 J

Exercise 1C (page 25)

1 (a) $50\,\mathrm{m\,s^{-1}}$ (b) $44.5\,\mathrm{m\,s^{-1}}$ (c) 7.25 s

2 (a) 1.84 km   (b) $225\,\mathrm{m\,s^{-1}}$ (c) 14.3 s

3 (a) 21.9 m   (b) $16.9\,\mathrm{m\,s^{-1}}$ (c) 4.27 s

4 (a) 25.8 m   (b) $20.3\,\mathrm{m\,s^{-1}}$ (c) 4.59 s

Miscellaneous exercise 1 (page 26)

1 $22.5\,\mathrm{m\,s^{-1}}$; the particle will not start to move until $2t$ exceeds the limiting friction.

2 (b) 10;
   the force decays exponentially with time.

3 (b) $2\sqrt{x^2 - 4}$

5 $0.001\,42\,\mathrm{m\,s^{-1}}$; the speed increases to a terminal value of $4.9\,\mathrm{m\,s^{-1}}$ when t becomes large.

6 14.7; $9.90\,\mathrm{m\,s^{-1}}$; k would be smaller.

7 0.275 s; x approaches $\dfrac{4}{\ln 2}$

8 3.7 s

9 2125 m

10 21.4

11 $12.5\,\mathrm{m\,s^{-1}}$

12 (a) $v = 50(1 - \mathrm{e}^{-0.196t})$ (b) $14.6\,\mathrm{m\,s^{-1}}$

13 $14\sqrt{1 - \mathrm{e}^{-0.05x}}$

2 Elastic strings and springs

Exercise 2A (page 36)

1 0.12 m

2 24.5 N

3 3.06×10^8 N

4 25.7 cm

5 115 N

6 0.375 kg

7 (a) 4 cm   (b) 5 cm

8 24 cm

9 75 N

10 $1\frac{1}{3}$ N

12 $\frac{\sqrt{3}\lambda}{l}(2a - l)$

13 (a) 21 cm   (b) 15 cm

14 (a) $\frac{2\lambda x}{l}$ (b) $\frac{\lambda(l + x)}{l}$ (c) $\frac{2\lambda(x - l)}{l}$

15 2λ

16 0.976 m

Exercise 2B (page 43)

1 40 J

2 $11\frac{1}{4}$ J

3 75 N, 48 J

4 $7.5\,\mathrm{m\,s^{-1}}$; 2.5 m (on the other side of O); particle oscillates through 2.5 m on either side of O.

5 $7.5\,\mathrm{m\,s^{-1}}$; 1.5 m; particle oscillates between 1.5 m and 2.5 m on the same side of O.

6 $5.6\,\mathrm{m\,s^{-1}}$

7 (a) 3.3 J   (b) $2.90\,\mathrm{m\,s^{-1}}$

8 $\frac{1}{2}mgx$

9 10.6 kN

10 1.73 m

11 $20.5\,\mathrm{m\,s^{-1}}$

12 $12.6\,\mathrm{m\,s^{-1}}$

13 294 N, $8.82\,\mathrm{m\,s^{-1}}$

14 (a) $\sqrt{u^2 + 2gx - \dfrac{\lambda x^2}{ml}}$

(b) $\dfrac{mgl + \sqrt{ml(mg^2l + \lambda u^2)}}{\lambda}$

(c) The resultant force is downwards/upwards when the particle is above/below the equilibrium position.

15 $mg(l + \frac{1}{2}a)$

Miscellaneous exercise 2 (page 44)

1 2.695 cm

2 0.170 m; 0.125 m

3 $14\,\mathrm{m\,s^{-1}}$

5 (a) 0.0637 m   (b) 0.0718 J

6 3.27 N; 0.163 J

7 no friction   (a) $2.42\,\mathrm{m\,s^{-1}}$ (b) 1.38 m

8 (a) 0.9, 0.6   (b) 2.2 m

9 (b) 17.6 N

10 $945x^2$ J; 7 m

11 0.196 m   (b) $0.620\,\mathrm{m\,s^{-1}}$

12 0.8 m; $98(x - 0.5)$ N, $98(2 - x)$ N, 39.7 J, 17.6 J; $0.808\,\mathrm{m\,s^{-1}}$

13 33.8 N   (a) 58.5 J   (b) 19.2 N

14 14.7 N; 0.660

15 $\frac{1}{8}x^2$ N cm, 8.58 N cm

16 (c) $7.34\,\mathrm{m\,s^{-1}}$

17 $\dfrac{\lambda\sqrt{a^2 + h^2}}{a}$ (a) λa (c) $g\sqrt{\dfrac{ma}{2\lambda}}$

18 $30r(5r - 1)$; 0.6 m

3 Simple harmonic motion

Exercise 3A (page 56)

1 (a) 3 m, $\frac{2}{5}\pi$ s, $15\,\mathrm{m\,s^{-1}}$
   (b) 2 m, 6 s, $\frac{2}{3}\pi\,\mathrm{m\,s^{-1}}$
   (c) 5 m, 2 s, $5\pi\,\mathrm{m\,s^{-1}}$

2 (a) $x = 4\cos\frac{2}{5}\pi t$ (b) $x = \dfrac{4}{\pi}\sin\frac{1}{2}\pi t$
   (c) $x = 2\cos 3t$

3 4π s, $1.5\,\mathrm{m\,s^{-2}}$

4 10.3 cm, $32.4\,\mathrm{cm\,s^{-1}}$

5 10π s, $6\,\mathrm{cm\,s^{-1}}$, $1.6\,\mathrm{cm\,s^{-2}}$

6 10 m, $5\,\mathrm{m\,s^{-1}}$

7 $x = 10\cos\left(\frac{1}{2}t - 0.6435\right)$; the point (8, 3) corresponds to $t = 0$.

8 (a) 4π s, $x = 1$, $\frac{1}{2}\sqrt{3}\,\mathrm{m\,s^{-1}}$, -2 and 2
   (b) 2 s, $x = \frac{3}{2}\sqrt{2}$, $\frac{3}{2}\pi\sqrt{2}\,\mathrm{m\,s^{-1}}$, -3 and 3
   (c) $\frac{2}{3}\pi$ s, $x = 7$, 0, -3 and 7
   (d) π s, $x = 0.793$, $-5.40\,\mathrm{m\,s^{-1}}$, 0 and 10
   (e) 2 s, $x = -4$, 0, -4 and 4
   (f) $\dfrac{2\pi}{n}$, $x = c + a\cos\varepsilon$, $-na\sin\varepsilon$, $c - a$ and $c + a$

9 -11 and 15, $12.8\,\mathrm{m\,s^{-1}}$

10 (a) 5.21 mm, 4.59 s   (b) 4.17 mm, 3.75 s
   (c) 3.12 mm, 2.65 s

11 3.85 m s^{-1}; 60.76 kg

12 2.36 m s^{-1}, 1.85 m s^{-2}
   (a) 159 N   (b) 233 N   (c) 196 N

Exercise 3B (page 63)

1 0.1π s, 0.1 m

2 0.1π s

3 (a) One-quarter of a simple harmonic
     oscillation until the string becomes slack,
     then constant speed until it hits the wall.
   (b) 7.5 m s^{-1} (c) 0.895 s

4 $\frac{1}{15}\pi$ s, 4 cm

5 2 m   (a) 0.5 m   (b) 0.1π s   (c) 10 m s^{-1}

6 $\frac{2}{7}\pi$ s, 0.1 m, $(0.2 + 0.1 \sin 7t)$ m

7 0.018 m, 0.359 s

8 7.04 m and 9 m, 1.99 s

9 0.126 s

11 $\pi\sqrt{\dfrac{M}{250Arg}}$

12 0.9 m, 11.6 m; 19.1 m, 10.6 m s^{-1}

Exercise 3C (page 74)

1 3.40 s

2 0.535

3 2.35 s

4 1.29 s

5 0.0665 s, 54.5 cm s^{-1}

7 (a) $x = 1.6 + 4.4 \cos 5t$
   (b) $x = 3(\cos 2t - 1)$

8 6 N s

9 The block will make 5 half-oscillations,
   coming to rest at 0.478 m, 0.694 m, 0.534 m,
   0.638 m and finally 0.59 m from A, taking in
   all $\frac{1}{2}\pi$ s before coming to rest in its final
   position.

10 $\frac{1}{3}\pi$ s, 27.2 cm

11 $(0.4 - 0.008 \cos 50t)$ cm

12 3.84 s, 21.7 m s^{-1}

13 157 s; 44.8 s

14 $\pi\sqrt{\dfrac{ml}{\lambda}}$

15 $\frac{1}{2}mn^2(a^2 - x^2)$

Miscellaneous exercise 3 (page 76)

1 3.29 m s^{-1}, 2 m

2 4π s

3 0.4 m s^{-1}, 0.24 N

4 (a) $\frac{1}{3}\pi$, $-\frac{1}{6}\pi$
   (b) $2\sqrt{3}$ cm, $\frac{1}{3}\pi\sqrt{3}$ cm s^{-1}
   (c) $\frac{2}{9}\pi^2\sqrt{3}$ cm s^{-2}

5 Symmetry about $t = 0$ implies that 1 full
   cycle $= (2 \times 2.5 + 10)$ s.
   0.2 m; $\frac{2}{7}\pi$ s

6 $(80 + 4x)$ N; 1.2 m s^{-1}, 0.0141 m

7 2.24 m s^{-1}, 0.0841 s; 2.65 m s^{-1}

8 (a) $k(y - l)$, $2k(4l - y)$ (b) $\ddot{y} = -\dfrac{3k}{m}(y - 3l)$
   (c) $2\pi\sqrt{\dfrac{m}{3k}}$, $\frac{1}{2}l$

9 (b) $2\pi\sqrt{\dfrac{l}{g}}$, $\frac{1}{2}l$; because $4l - \frac{1}{2}l > 3l$ (c) $\frac{3}{2}l$

10 0.510   (b) $\sqrt{3}$ m s^{-1} (c) 0.451 s

11 (b) 0.4   (c) 0.497 s
   No, since the direction of the frictional force
   reverses.

12 (c) $x = 0.041 \sin(14t - 1.79)$ (d) 0.224 s

13 3.01, 0.784 m s^{-1}

14 0.0848 m; 0.426 N, 1.53 N

Revision exercise 1 (page 84)

1 3π m s^{-1} $\approx$ 9.42 m s^{-1}

2 2220 m

3 (a) 55 kg   (b) 1850 N
   (c) 23.8 m s^{-2} upwards

4 (c) $\frac{2}{7}\pi$ s $\approx$ 0.898 s

5 (a) $v = 28(1 - e^{-0.35t})$ (b) 32.0 m

6 (a) 0.74 m   (b) 3.43 J   (c) 24.5

7 (a) $\dfrac{k}{(3a - x)^2} - \dfrac{4k}{x^2}$
   (c) $\sqrt{\dfrac{2k}{3a - x} + \dfrac{8k}{x} - \dfrac{k}{a}}$ (d) $\sqrt{\dfrac{5k}{a}}$

8 (a) 147 N   (c) $x = 0.4 \sin 7t$
   (d) $\frac{1}{6}\pi$ s $\approx$ 0.524 s

9 (a) 270 N   (b) 59.4 m s^{-2} (c) 3.18 m s^{-1}
   (d) no air resistance, rock modelled as
       particle, Hooke's law applies

10 (a) 256 N   (b) 1160 N   (c) 210 N, 147 N

11 (a) $mv\dfrac{dv}{dx} = \dfrac{k}{x}$

$mv\dfrac{dv}{dx} = \dfrac{k}{x} - F$

12 2.21 cm

13 (b) 0.9 m   (c) 1.04 m   (d) 1.21 m

14 $3.6\,\mathrm{m\,s^{-1}}$, $4.4\,\mathrm{m\,s^{-1}}$

15 2.31 m   (a) 1.02 N   (b) 2.90 s

16 $6\,\mathrm{m\,s^{-1}}$ (c) 0.819 s

17 (a) 87.4 cm   (b) 0.117 N s

18 72.6 N   (a) $85v\dfrac{dv}{dx} = \dfrac{150}{v}$

$1.36\,\mathrm{m\,s^{-2}}$

19 The height will oscillate with simple

harmonic motion with period $\pi\sqrt{\dfrac{2m}{kg}}$;

the speed will vary according to a law

$v = \sqrt{v_0^2 - A\sin\sqrt{\dfrac{2kg}{m}}\,t}$, where A is a constant

depending on the strength of the turbulence.

20 (a) $\frac{2}{3}mg\sqrt{3}$

21 137 m

22 (a) $14.6\,\mathrm{m\,s^{-1}}$ (b) 25.1 m (c) $-16.5\,\mathrm{m\,s^{-2}}$

23 $0.5v\dfrac{dv}{dx} = 10(4-x) - \dfrac{80}{x^2}$; $2.58\,\mathrm{m\,s^{-1}}$

25 (a) $\dfrac{v_T}{g}\ln\dfrac{1}{1-\lambda}$, $\dfrac{v_T}{2g}\ln\dfrac{1+\lambda}{1-\lambda}$, $t_1 > t_2$

(b) $\dfrac{v_T^2}{g}\left(\ln\dfrac{1}{1-\lambda} - \lambda\right)$, $\dfrac{v_T^2}{2g}\ln\dfrac{1}{1-\lambda^2}$, $x_1 > x_2$

(c) Model 1 predicts the greater time,
Model 2 predicts the greater speed.

4   Systems of rigid objects

Exercise 4A (page 97)

1 On AB: 50 N upwards at A; 150 N upwards,
100 N downwards at B; 100 N downwards at
mid-point.
On BC: 100 N upwards at B; 100 N upwards
at C; 200 N downwards at mid-point.

2 $\frac{3}{2}W$ downwards; the contact force from the
support at F on BC is then zero.

4 (a) $200x + 350$ for $0 < x < 3$,
$1850 - 300x$ for $3 < x < 5$

(b) 150 for $0 < x < 3$,
$1650 - 300x$ for $3 < x < 5$

5 (a) A vertical force would destroy symmetry.

(b) 0.375

6 12.5 N

7 20 N

8 5 N in the direction $\overrightarrow{XZ}$, 1 N downwards

9 30 N in the direction $\overrightarrow{BC}$, 15 N upwards

10 vertically upwards, half the weight of BC

12 0.692, 0.409

14 A vertical force would destroy symmetry;
126.9°

15 (a) $\frac{1}{3}\sqrt{3}$ (b) $\frac{1}{9}\sqrt{3}$
Equilibrium is possible.

16 (a) $\dfrac{2\mu W}{\sqrt{3} - \mu}$ if $\mu < \sqrt{3}$, otherwise no limit

(b) $\dfrac{W}{\sqrt{3} - 1}$

17 1, $\frac{1}{5}$, $\frac{1}{13}$

Exercise 4B (page 109)

1 On AC: 50 N upwards at A, 50 N upwards
at C.
On BC: 110 N upwards at B, 50 N downwards
at C.

2 $1.32W$ at 49.1° to the horizontal

3 0.563; 0.466

4 (a) Yes; $\frac{1}{6}\sqrt{3}kl$; $\frac{1}{6}\sqrt{3}kl$, 0

(b) Yes; 0; 0, $\frac{1}{2}\sqrt{2}kl$

(c) No, tension would have to be negative.

(d) No, moment about C is clockwise.

5 (a) 0.75   (b) 0.5

6 6.22 N, 0.059

7 1.61 m

8 203 N

9 2.46 m

10 AC tension, BC compression

(a) Both 0.781 m; both 23.0 N

(b) 1.17 m, 0.6 m; 34.3 N, 17.6 N

11 (a) $24X$, $15X$ (b) $4.5L$

12 AD: 1300 N compression;
BC: 1300 N tension;
BD: 1200 N tension;
DC: 500 N compression.
At A: 1300 N in direction $\overrightarrow{AD}$;
At B: 2450 N at 11.8° to the upward vertical

Miscellaneous exercise 4 (page 112)

1 (a) 8.26 N   (b) 0.652

2 (a) 9.8 N   (b) 0.808

3 (a) $\frac{9}{4}mg$

(b) $1.69mg$ at $81.5°$ to the vertical

4 0.385; $480\,\text{N}$

5 0.577, 0.268

6 $\frac{1}{4}(W+w)\tan\theta$

7 (b) $290\,\text{N}$ at $43.6°$ to the horizontal

8 $-200\,\text{N}$, $500\,\text{N}$; $200\,\text{N}$, $50\,\text{N}$

9 (b) 200, 100

(c) AB: $150\,\text{N}$, tension

BC: $150\sqrt{5}\,\text{N}$, compression

AC: $50\sqrt{5}\,\text{N}$, tension

10 (b) AB: $\frac{125}{3}\sqrt{3}\,\text{N}$, tension

BC: $\frac{200}{3}\sqrt{3}\,\text{N}$, compression

CD: $\frac{100}{3}\sqrt{3}\,\text{N}$, tension

AD: $\frac{250}{3}\sqrt{3}\,\text{N}$, compression

DB: $150\,\text{N}$, compression

5 Motion round a circle with variable speed

Exercise 5A (page 123)

1 (a) $3.6\,\text{m s}^{-2}$ in the direction of motion

(b) $6.10\,\text{m s}^{-2}$ at $72.8°$ to the direction of motion

(c) $10.4\,\text{m s}^{-2}$ towards the centre

2 $1.6\cos 5t\,\text{m s}^{-1}$; $1.6\cos^2 5t\,\text{m s}^{-2}$, $-8\sin 5t\,\text{m s}^{-2}$; oscillation, $0.32\,\text{m}$ measured along the arc either side of the centre, period $\frac{2}{5}\pi$ s; motion of a pendulum bob.

3 $a = 5$, $b = 0.1$, $8.74\,\text{s}$; $101.3°$

4 $\omega = \dfrac{\omega_0}{1 + \mu\omega_0 t}$, $\theta = \dfrac{1}{\mu}\ln(1 + \mu\omega_0 t)$; $\omega > 0$ for all $t > 0$

5 (a) $9.8\,\text{m s}^{-2}$ vertically upwards, $0.98\,\text{N}$

(b) $8.49\,\text{m s}^{-2}$ tangentially, $0.245\,\text{N}$

6 (a) 5.6 (b) 6.26

7 (a) $1.4\,\text{m s}^{-1}$ (b) $41.4°$

8 $9.65\,\text{m s}^{-1}$, $4.70\,\text{N}$

9 (a) $\sqrt{4.9\cos\theta - 0.9}\,\text{m s}^{-1}$, $(0.588\cos\theta - 0.072)$ N; the ball moves up the groove until the radius makes an angle $79.4°$ with the downward vertical, then returns down the groove to the starting point.

(b) $\sqrt{4.9\cos\theta + 4.1}\,\text{m s}^{-1}$, $(0.588\cos\theta + 0.328)$ N; the ball stays in the groove until the radius makes an angle $56.1°$ with the upward vertical, then separates from the groove with a speed of $1.17\,\text{m s}^{-1}$ and follows a projectile trajectory until it again lands in the groove.

(c) $\sqrt{4.9\cos\theta + 11.1}\,\text{m s}^{-1}$, $(0.588\cos\theta + 0.888)$ N; the ball remains in the groove as far as the end, then follows a projectile trajectory until it again lands in the groove.

10 $96.6\,\text{N s}$

(a) $487\,\text{N}$, tension   (b) $96.5\,\text{N}$, thrust

11 (a) $\dfrac{mu^2}{l} - 2mg + 3mg\cos\theta$

(b) $mg\left(1 - \dfrac{u^2}{2gl}\right)$

If $u = \sqrt{3gl}$, the string is taut until $\cos\theta = -\frac{1}{3}$, when the speed is $\sqrt{\frac{1}{3}gl}$, after which the string becomes slack.

12 (a) $19.8\,\text{m s}^{-1}$ (b) $0.95\,\text{m}$

13 (a) $\sqrt{\frac{3}{2}gl - 2gl\cos\theta}$, $mg(\frac{3}{2} - 3\cos\theta)$

(b) $\frac{1}{3}\pi$, $\sqrt{\frac{1}{2}gl}$

Exercise 5B (page 129)

2 (a) $Mg - T = Mr\ddot{\theta}$, $T - mg\cos\theta = mr\ddot{\theta}$, $mg\sin\theta - R = mr\dot{\theta}^2$

(b) $\frac{1}{2}Mr^2\dot{\theta}^2 + \frac{1}{2}mr^2\dot{\theta}^2 = Mgr\theta - mgr\sin\theta$

3 $\sqrt{gr(\sin\theta + \cos\theta - 1)}$; $\frac{1}{2}g(\cos\theta - \sin\theta)$; $\frac{1}{2}\sqrt{2}T - mg\sin\theta = m\dot{v}$, $mg\cos\theta - \frac{1}{2}\sqrt{2}T = m\dot{v}$; $\frac{1}{2}\sqrt{2}mg(\cos\theta + \sin\theta)$;

(a) When $\theta = \frac{1}{4}\pi$ (b) When $\theta = 0$ or $\frac{1}{2}\pi$

$\frac{1}{2}mg(5\cos\theta + 3\sin\theta - 2)$, $\frac{1}{2}mg(3\cos\theta + 5\sin\theta - 2)$

4 $mgr(\cos\alpha - \cos\theta) - Fr(\theta - \alpha) = \frac{1}{2}mr^2\omega^2$, $mg\sin\theta - F = mr\dot{\omega}$; it is not possible.

5 $\dfrac{u}{r}\sec\theta$, $\dfrac{r}{2u}$; $\dfrac{u^2}{r}\sec^3\theta$

6 $3.00\,\text{rad}$

7 The velocity has radial component $\dot{r}$, transverse component $r\dot{\omega}$.

$(\ddot{r} - r\omega^2)\mathbf{p} + (r\dot{\omega} + 2\dot{r}\omega)\mathbf{q}$

The acceleration has radial component $\ddot{r} - r\omega^2$, transverse component $r\dot{\omega} + 2\dot{r}\omega$.

Miscellaneous exercise 5 (page 130)

1 $4\,\text{m s}^{-2}$

2 $7.38\,\text{N}$

3 $1.71\,\mathrm{m\,s^{-1}}$

4 (b) $146.8°$, $5.37\,\mathrm{m\,s^{-2}}$ at $56.8°$ to the downward vertical
  (c) $123.9°$

5 $2.57\,\mathrm{N}$

6 (a) $2gr(1-\cos\theta)$
  $1.81\,\mathrm{m\,s^{-1}}$

7 $14.7\,\mathrm{N}$; greatest $9.8\,\mathrm{m\,s^{-2}}$ at the same horizontal level as O, least 0 vertically above and below O.

8 (a) $2\sqrt{ga}$ (c) $mg(2-3\cos\theta)$
  (d) $\frac{1}{3}\sqrt{\frac{10}{3}ga}$

9 (a) $5.42\,\mathrm{m\,s^{-1}}$, $8.97\,\mathrm{m\,s^{-1}}$
  There would be no change.
  The speed would be less, so the normal contact force would be greater.

10 $\cos\theta$ and v are both greatest when $\theta=0$.
  (a) 14.0 (b) $0.132\,\mathrm{m}$

11 (a) $gl(2\cos\theta-1)$ (c) $2mg$ when $\theta=0$
  (d) Perpendicular to AB (e) $\frac{1}{6}\pi$

12 (a) $0<\alpha<\frac{1}{4}\pi$ (b) $1.176(3-2\cos\alpha)\,\mathrm{N}$
  (c) Would be smaller, because the speed (and therefore the upward acceleration) would be smaller.

13 (b) $6.26\,\mathrm{N}$
  (c) $7.17\,\mathrm{m\,s^{-2}}$, $4.9\,\mathrm{m\,s^{-2}}$, $8.69\,\mathrm{m\,s^{-2}}$
  Would be smaller.

6 Oscillations with small amplitude

Exercise 6 (page 144)

1 $0.993\,\mathrm{m}$

2 $24.8\,\mathrm{m}$

3 $4.95\,\mathrm{s}$

4 (a) Increase   (b) Increase
  (c) Neither   (d) Neither
  (e) Decrease   (f) Doesn't swing;
  The clock runs slow.

5 $0.561\,\mathrm{s}$, $0.611\,\mathrm{m\,s^{-1}}$; $0.610\,\mathrm{m\,s^{-1}}$

6 $0.6\,\mathrm{m}$, $\frac{1}{12}$ rad $= 4.77°$, $2.69\,\mathrm{s}$

7 $4.54\,\mathrm{m}$, $1.6\,\mathrm{m\,s^{-1}}$

8 (a) $4.04\,\mathrm{s}$ (b) $21.8\,\mathrm{m\,s^{-1}}$ (c) $617\,\mathrm{N}$

9 Swings with period approximately $\frac{1}{5}\pi$ s

10 $\phi=-0.0997$, $\dot{\phi}=0$; 0.0997 rad $=5.71°$, $2.83\,\mathrm{s}$

11 $mg(3-2\cos a)$; $mg(1+a^2)$, overestimate

Miscellaneous exercise 6 (page 146)

1 $\ddot{\theta}=-2.45\sin\theta$, $4.01\,\mathrm{s}$

2 $82\,\mathrm{m}$, $9.09\,\mathrm{s}$

3 $12\,\mathrm{cm}$, $0.449\,\mathrm{s}$

4 $6°$, $2.24\,\mathrm{s}$

5 The periods of oscillation are equal, and collisions occur at intervals of half a period.
  $2°$, $6°$

6 $26.4\,\mathrm{s}$, $20.3\,\mathrm{m\,s^{-1}}$; $405\,\mathrm{m}$

7 $2\pi\sqrt{\dfrac{2l}{\sqrt{3}g}}$; $\dfrac{1}{\sqrt{3}}mg\cos\theta$

8 (a) It doesn't oscillate.
  (b) Oscillates with period approximately $3.36\,\mathrm{s}$.
  (c) Oscillates with period approximately $0.947\,\mathrm{s}$.

9 $2\pi\sqrt{\dfrac{l\cos\beta}{g}}$

10 $0.536...\pi$, 6.8%

11 $500a^2-800\sqrt{1+a^2}$; $v^2+100x^2=100a^2$;
  $800+500a^2-800\sqrt{1+a^2}$, $100a^2$;
  overestimates

12 $v^2=100(a^4-x^4)$
  If displaced a small distance, the tension in the string is very small, and at a large angle to the direction PM, so the restoring effect is very small. If displaced a large distance, the particle will acquire some speed in the early stages, which will then vary very little as it passes through the equilibrium position.

7 Impulse and momentum in two dimensions

Exercise 7A (page 154)

1 $14.1\,\mathrm{m\,s^{-1}}$, $9.85\,\mathrm{N\,s}$

2 $16.6\,\mathrm{m\,s^{-1}}$, $3.75\,\mathrm{N\,s}$

3 $4.41\,\mathrm{N\,s}$ at $55°$ to the line of the wickets

4 $4.91\,\mathrm{N\,s}$ at $6.7°$ to the direction from which the ball was received

5 $4.93\,\mathrm{kN\,s}$ from the direction of $313.1°$

6 $2.41\,\mathrm{N\,s}$, $3.41\,\mathrm{N\,s}$

7 $7.2°$; at $82.8°$ to the direction from which the puck came

8 $8.70\,\mathrm{m\,s^{-1}}$ at $24.5°$ to the direction the heavier acrobat was moving

9 $1.89\,\mathrm{m\,s^{-1}}$ at $61.9°$ to the direction of the plate conveyor

10 $0.75°$, reduced to $7.94\,\mathrm{km\,s^{-1}}$

11 $2\,\mathrm{m\,s^{-1}}$ at $36.9°$ to the direction in which the stone is thrown

12 Parallel to the original line of the string

Exercise 7B (page 163)

1 (a) $11.9, 0.520$ (b) $46.5°, 0.738$
 (c) $0.686, 41.7$ (d) $33.7°, 6.01, 0.386$
 (e) $69.1°, 13.0$

2 (a) $0.2, 180°, 5.12, 51.3°$
 (b) $4.71, 3.68, 0.531, 2.33, 0.319$
 (c) $0.195, 0.628$
 (d) $3.05, 5.42, 100.8°, 39.7°, 18.5$

4 $\cot^{-1}\sqrt{e}$

5 $\tan^{-1}\dfrac{be}{ae+c}$

6 $R=\dfrac{2pq}{g}$; $\dfrac{R}{1-e}$; it slides along the floor with speed p.

9 $23.4°$

Miscellaneous exercise 7 (page 164)

1 (a) $27.0\,\mathrm{m\,s^{-1}}$ (b) 0.217

3 (b) $0.233u\,\mathrm{N\,s}$ (c) No resistance to motion

4 (a) $12.1\,\mathrm{m\,s^{-1}}$ (b) $\frac{1}{14}$

5 (b) 0.674 (c) $3.12\,\mathrm{N\,s}$ (d) $0.142\,\mathrm{s}$

7 $\tan\phi = e\tan\theta$; $26.6°, 18.4°$

8 $1\,\mathrm{m\,s^{-1}}$ in the reverse direction to its original velocity, $4\sqrt{2}\,\mathrm{m\,s^{-1}}$ at $45°$ to the line of centres

11 (a) The total momentum of the two objects
 (b) The impulse from object 1 on object 2

Revision exercise 2 (page 168)

1 $5.2\,\mathrm{N\,s}$

2 $53\,\mathrm{N}$ at $31.9°$ above the horizontal

3 (a) $\frac{1}{2}$ (b) $26.6°$

4 $3\,\mathrm{N\,s}$ vertically upwards

5 $5.3\,\mathrm{N}$

6 $\sqrt{5ag}$

7 $16.8\,\mathrm{N}, 7.4\,\mathrm{N}$

8 $5.75\,\mathrm{m\,s^{-1}}$ at $41.4°$ to the line of centres

9 (a) $28.2\,\mathrm{m\,s^{-2}}, 6.30\,\mathrm{m\,s^{-2}}$
 (c) $(3.95+8.82\cos\theta)\,\mathrm{N}$ (d) $116.6°$

10 (a) $33.6\,\mathrm{N}, 30\,\mathrm{N}$
 (b) at B, where the normal force is smaller; 0.187

11 $6.47\,\mathrm{m\,s^{-1}}$

12 (b) $2.24\,\mathrm{s}$ (c) $0.368\,\mathrm{s}$

13 (a) $7.53\,\mathrm{kN\,s}$ (b) $1.74\,\mathrm{s}$ (c) $22.0\,\mathrm{kN}$

14 $\dfrac{mg(2h-5r)}{r}$

15 $13.0\,\mathrm{N}; 28.1\,\mathrm{N}$

16 (b) $0.993\,\mathrm{m}$ (c) (i) $2\,\mathrm{s}$ (ii) $2.83\,\mathrm{s}$

17 $0.38, 2.0\,\mathrm{N}; 0.615$

18 (b) $m\sqrt{\frac{1}{2}ag}$
 $\frac{1}{2}\sqrt{3g}; \frac{7}{2}mg$

19 (a) $200\,\mathrm{N}, 200\,\mathrm{N}, 150\,\mathrm{N}, 150\,\mathrm{N}$ (b) $400\,\mathrm{N}$

20 (a) $1.5\,\mathrm{m\,s^{-1}}$ (b) $2.5\,\mathrm{N\,s}$ (c) $0.5\,\mathrm{m\,s^{-1}}$
 (d) $2\,\mathrm{N\,s}$ (e) $\frac{3}{4}$

21 $\frac{1}{4}(3-e)u, \frac{1}{4}\sqrt{3}(1+e)u$

22 (a) In applying Newton's second law to the motion of the machine, the vertical component mg of the contact force has been neglected in comparison with the horizontal component $\dfrac{mv^2}{R}$.

 (b) $\left(\dfrac{PR}{\mu m}\right)^{\frac{1}{3}}$ (c) $\left(\dfrac{PR}{\mu m}(1-\mathrm{e}^{-3\mu s/R})\right)^{\frac{1}{3}}$

 (d) $\dfrac{VR}{R+\mu Vt}$

 There must be other forces, since (d) shows that with this model it takes an infinite time to stop; at low speeds the rolling resistance may be more important than the friction from the sideways force from the rails; initially $\dfrac{P}{v}$ is infinite, so the machine can't run at constant power to start with.

23 $2a\sin\frac{1}{2}\theta$; all the forces which contribute to the energy equation are conservative;
 $mg\left(\dfrac{3c}{k}-2+3\cos\theta\left(1-\dfrac{c}{k}\right)\right)$

24 (b) $(0.2\sqrt{3}, 0.2)$

 (c) $\begin{pmatrix} -0.7 \\ 0.7\sqrt{3}-9.8t \end{pmatrix}\mathrm{m\,s^{-1}}$,

 $\begin{pmatrix} 0.2\sqrt{3}-0.7t \\ 0.2+0.7\sqrt{3}t-4.9t^2 \end{pmatrix}\mathrm{m}$

 (d) The lowest point of the drum
 (e) $0.42\,\mathrm{N\,s}$ at $60°$ to the horizontal

Practice examinations

Practice examination 1 for M3 (page 175)

1 (i) 2.25 m   (ii) 0.680 m h^{-1}

3 (i) 4.04   (ii) 54.2 m s^{-2}

4 (i) $mv\dfrac{\mathrm{d}v}{\mathrm{d}x} = kx^{-\frac{3}{2}}$

  (ii) 2.90 × 10^5 m s^{-2}

5 (i) $\sqrt{2gr}$ (ii) $\frac{1}{2}m\sqrt{2gr}$

6 (i) 0.02 m

  (ii) $T - 245(0.02 + x) = 0.5\ddot{x}$,
     $4.9 - T = 0.5\ddot{x}$

  (iii) 0.04 m

7 (iii) $\dfrac{100}{2 + \sqrt{2}} \approx 29.3$ (iv) $\dfrac{1}{3 + 2\sqrt{2}} \approx 0.172$

Practice examination 2 for M3 (page 178)

1 (ii) $\sqrt{2g} \approx 4.43\,\mathrm{m\,s}^{-1}$

2 (i) $4W$ (ii) $6W, 5W$

3 (i) π s, $\sqrt{5}$ m
  (ii) $4\sqrt{5}\,\mathrm{m\,s}^{-2} \approx 8.94\,\mathrm{m\,s}^{-2}$

4 (i) 30°   (ii) $\frac{2}{3}\sqrt{3}\,mu$ (iii) $\frac{2}{3}$

5 (ii) $\dfrac{\pi}{3}\sqrt{\dfrac{l}{g}}$

6 (i) 3.125   (iii) $v = 80\sqrt{1 - \mathrm{e}^{-\frac{1}{120}t}}$
  (iv) 0.322 m s^{-2}

7 (ii) $2mg - T = 2ma\ddot{\theta}$, $\ddot{\theta} = \dfrac{g}{3a}(2 - \cos\theta)$
  (iv) $\frac{1}{3}mg(5\sin\theta - 4\theta)$

Answers to M4

Most non-exact numerical answers are given correct to 3 significant figures.

1 Relative motion

Exercise 1A (page 189)

1 $3.16\,\text{m}\,\text{s}^{-1}$ at $18.4°$ to velocity of bus

2 $30.3\,\text{m}\,\text{s}^{-1}$ at $7.6°$ to velocity of aircraft

3 (a) 18 m   (b) 49.5 m

4 $10.4\,\text{m}\,\text{s}^{-1}$ at $9.4°$ to the horizontal in liner's forward direction

5 5.13 m

6 $056.2°$ at $11.0\,\text{m}\,\text{s}^{-1}$

7 (a) 36 m, 60 s   (b) $126.9°$, 75 s

8 (a) $160.9°$ (b) 3 h 38 min

9 $29.5\,\text{km}\,\text{h}^{-1}$ from $235°$

10 $13.4\,\text{km}\,\text{h}^{-1}$

Exercise 1B (page 195)

1 $4.0°$

2 (a) $16\,\text{km}\,\text{h}^{-1}$
(b) $27.7\,\text{km}\,\text{h}^{-1}$, $32\,\text{km}\,\text{h}^{-1}$

3 2.5 km at $53.1°$ to x-axis, $17\,\text{km}\,\text{h}^{-1}$ at $241.9°$ to x-axis; 382 m; (7.18, 7.73), (7.52, 7.55)

4 28.3 m; $25.5°$ east of north, 104 s (or $64.5°$, 219 s)

5 $72.3°$

6 $4.66\,\text{m}\,\text{s}^{-1}$; $50.9°$

7 191 m

8 $163.2°$, 13.6 min

9 At $56.5°$ to the side on which the children are

10 2.73 nautical miles, $163.1°$

11 $130.4°$

12 $019.6°$ to $071.4°$, and $271.7°$ to $277.3°$

Exercise 1C (page 200)

1 $48.2°$

2 $1.06\,\text{m}\,\text{s}^{-1}$

3 (a) perpendicular to AB
(b) $3\frac{3}{4}\,\text{m}\,\text{s}^{-1}$ (c) $\frac{5}{8}\,\text{rad}\,\text{s}^{-1}$
(d) $1\frac{1}{4}\,\text{m}\,\text{s}^{-1}$ perpendicular to BC
(e) $-1\,\text{m}\,\text{s}^{-1}$, $4\frac{1}{4}\,\text{m}\,\text{s}^{-1}$; $4.37\,\text{m}\,\text{s}^{-1}$ at $13.2°$ to OY

4 (a) $2\sqrt{3}\,\text{m}\,\text{s}^{-1}$ (b) $2\sqrt{3}\,\text{m}\,\text{s}^{-1}$ at $30°$ to $\overrightarrow{AB}$

5 (a) $\frac{5}{3}u$, $\frac{2}{3}u$ (b) $\frac{2}{3}u$, $\frac{1}{3}u$, $\frac{4}{3}u$

6 $81.8°$ to $\overrightarrow{AB}$

7 $k\cos\theta$, $k\sin\theta$ where $k=\sqrt{2gl(1-\cos\theta)}$; $48.2°$

Exercise 1D (page 204)

1 (a) 0
(b) Each moves directly away from the other at constant speed.

2 $\sqrt{\dfrac{2h}{g-f}}$

Miscellaneous exercise 1 (page 204)

1 $27.1°$

3 30 s

4 $41.8°$

5 $(500\mathbf{i})\,\text{km}\,\text{h}^{-1}$, $(521.9...\mathbf{i}+92.0...\mathbf{j})\,\text{km}\,\text{h}^{-1}$; $(21.9...\mathbf{i}+92.0...\mathbf{j})\,\text{km}\,\text{h}^{-1}$, $94.6\,\text{km}\,\text{h}^{-1}$

6 $2\sqrt{3}$

7 $61.3°$, 45.6 s

8 (a) $(5\mathbf{i}-10\mathbf{j})\,\text{m}\,\text{s}^{-1}$
(b) $(5t\,\mathbf{i}+(200-10t)\mathbf{j})\,\text{m}$ (c) 89.4 m

9 $(9\mathbf{i}-12\mathbf{j})\,\text{km}\,\text{h}^{-1}$, $(-5\mathbf{i}+12\mathbf{j})\,\text{km}\,\text{h}^{-1}$, $(-14\mathbf{i}+24\mathbf{j})\,\text{km}\,\text{h}^{-1}$; 8.57 km

10 (a) $(4\mathbf{i}+(16-\alpha)\mathbf{j})\,\text{km}\,\text{h}^{-1}$
(b) 16   (c) $2\frac{1}{2}\,\text{h}$

11 (a) $14\,\text{km}\,\text{h}^{-1}$, $188.2°$ (b) $6.46\,\text{km}\,\text{h}^{-1}$

12 $82.1°$, $11.5\,\text{m}\,\text{s}^{-1}$

13 (a) $293.6°$ (b) 6.21 km

14 $301.3°$; 6.93 km

15 6.51 km, $10.8\,\text{m}\,\text{s}^{-1}$; $32.0°$, 2.81 km

16 $5\,\text{m}\,\text{s}^{-1}$ from $030°$

17 (b) $(b+Wt\cos\theta)\mathbf{i}+Wt\sin\theta\,\mathbf{j}$
(d) $\dfrac{aV}{\sqrt{a^2+b^2}}$ at $\tan^{-1}\dfrac{b}{a}$

2   Rotational energy

Exercise 2A (page 215)

1 (a) $32\,\text{kg}\,\text{m}^2$ (b) $4 \times 10^7\,\text{kg}\,\text{m}^2$
   (c) $1.25 \times 10^{-3}\,\text{kg}\,\text{m}^2$ (d) $1.5 \times 10^{-3}\,\text{kg}\,\text{m}^2$

2 (a) $7.90 \times 10^4\,\text{J}$ (b) $0.592\,\text{J}$
   (c) $0.790\,\text{J}$

3 (a) $704\,\text{gram}\,\text{cm}^2$ (b) $7.04 \times 10^{-5}\,\text{kg}\,\text{m}^2$

4 $0.75\,\text{kg}\,\text{m}^2$

5 The disc; particles of the sphere are clustered more closely round the axis.

6 $2.56\,\text{kg}\,\text{m}^2$

7 $84.3\,\text{rad}\,\text{s}^{-1}$

8 $\sqrt{\tfrac{4}{3}gh}$

9 $4.99\,\text{m}\,\text{s}^{-1}$, $49.9\,\text{rad}\,\text{s}^{-1}$

10 $\sqrt{\omega^2 + \dfrac{2g}{r}}$

11 $\tfrac{2}{5}mr^2$

12 $\tfrac{2}{5}mr^2$

13 $\tfrac{1}{7}m$, $\tfrac{31}{70}mr^2$

14 $a = 0$

15 $2ml^2 + ma^2$, independent of θ

Exercise 2B (page 222)

1 39.8

2 $0.289\,\text{rad}\,\text{s}^{-1}$

3 $251\,\text{N}\,\text{m}$

4 $7.47\,\text{N}$; 15.9

5 $0.0025\,\text{kg}\,\text{m}^2$; 9.82

6 (a) $7090\,\text{J}$ (b) $2260\,\text{N}\,\text{m}$

7 $61.2\,\text{rad}\,\text{s}^{-1}$

8 $0.603\,\text{W}$

9 $127\,\text{N}\,\text{m}$

10 $2.18\,\text{N}\,\text{m}$, 4.26

11 $36.9\,\text{rad}\,\text{s}^{-1}$

12 $\dfrac{2P}{\sqrt{3}}$

Miscellaneous exercise 2 (page 223)

1 $4.26 \times 10^6\,\text{J}$

2 $62.0\,\text{rad}\,\text{s}^{-1}$

3 $0.346\,\text{rad}\,\text{s}^{-1}$

4 $24\,\text{rad}\,\text{s}^{-1}$

5 (a) $1.03\,\text{N}\,\text{m}$ (b) $6\,\text{rad}\,\text{s}^{-1}$

6 (a) $560\,\text{kg}\,\text{m}^2$ (b) $0.990\,\text{rad}\,\text{s}^{-1}$
   (c) $24.4\,\text{N}\,\text{m}$

7 (a) $\dfrac{3mgr}{2\pi}$ (b) $\sqrt{\dfrac{3gr}{\pi}}$

8 $\sqrt{\dfrac{33g}{16r}}$

9 $\sqrt{\dfrac{3ga}{l^2 + 3a^2}}$, $\dfrac{l}{\sqrt{3}}$

10 $17.5\,\text{N}\,\text{m}$; $39.5°$; $1.87\,\text{rad}\,\text{s}^{-1}$, it won't swing back

11 (a) $66.1\,\text{J}$ (b) $10.912\,\text{kg}\,\text{m}^2$
    (c) $5.00\,\text{m}\,\text{s}^{-1}$

3   Moment of inertia

Exercise 3A (page 231)

1 $\tfrac{1}{2}Mr^2$; mass distribution is no longer uniform

2 $\tfrac{1}{2}mr^2$

3 $\tfrac{1}{4}M(a^2 + b^2)$

4 (a) $\tfrac{1}{3}Ma^2$ (b) $\tfrac{2}{3}Ma^2$ (c) $\tfrac{1}{3}Ma^2$

5 (a) $\tfrac{1}{6}Mq^2$ (b) $\tfrac{1}{6}M(p^2 + q^2)$

6 (a) $\tfrac{1}{6}mh^2$ (b) $\tfrac{1}{6}m(c^2 + h^2)$

7 $\tfrac{2}{3}Ma^2$

9 $\tfrac{1}{3}Mh^2$

11 (a) The square has fourfold rotation symmetry about the centre.
    (b) Polygons for which the number of sides is a multiple of 4

Exercise 3B (page 238)

1 (a) $\tfrac{2}{3}\,\text{kg}\,\text{m}^2$ (b) $(\tfrac{3}{4}\pi^2 - 6)\,\text{kg}\,\text{m}^2$

2 (a) $\tfrac{32}{35}\,\text{kg}\,\text{m}^2$ (b) $\tfrac{4}{5}\,\text{kg}\,\text{m}^2$ (c) $\tfrac{12}{7}\,\text{kg}\,\text{m}^2$

3 (a) $\tfrac{1}{9}ka^4(1 - e^{-3})$ (b) $ka^4(2 - 5e^{-1})$

4 $1\tfrac{1}{12}\,\text{kg}$, $\tfrac{1}{5}\,\text{kg}\,\text{m}^2$

5 $\tfrac{1}{3}Ma^2 \sin^2 \alpha$; $\tfrac{1}{6}Ma^2\omega^2 \sin^2 \alpha$

6 $\tfrac{2}{3}Ma^2$

7 $\tfrac{1}{16}\pi r^4$, $\tfrac{1}{4}Mr^2$

8 (a) $\tfrac{1}{6}Mh^2$ (b) $\tfrac{1}{6}Mc^2$

9 $\displaystyle\int_a^b \tfrac{1}{3}k(\mathrm{f}(x))^3\,\mathrm{d}x$, $\displaystyle\int_a^b kx^2\mathrm{f}(x)\,\mathrm{d}x$

Exercise 3C (page 242)

1 $0.102\,\text{kg}\,\text{cm}^2$

2 $17.4 \, \text{kg cm}^2$

3 $0.201 \, \text{kg cm}^2$

4 $13.8 \, \text{gram cm}^2$

5 $8.50 \, \text{grams}, 2.66 \, \text{gram cm}^2$

6 $\frac{1}{3}Ma^2$

7 $\frac{2}{5}Ma^2$; because of the stretch rule.

8 $7.96 \, \text{kg}, 9.45 \times 10^{-3} \, \text{kg m}^2$

Exercise 3D (page 248)

1 $28 \, \text{kg m}^2$

2 $1100 \, \text{kg cm}^2$

3 $2000 \, \text{kg cm}^2$

4 (a) $2Mr^2$ (b) $\frac{3}{2}Mr^2$
   In both (a) and (b) the answer depends
   on the centre of mass being at the centre
   of the ring. Also, in (b), you can't assume
   that $I_x = I_y$ if the ring is not uniform.

5 $\frac{10}{3}Ml^2$

6 (a) $6ml^2$ (b) $3ml^2$

7 $\frac{7}{6}Ma^2$

8 $\frac{1}{4}M(5a^2 - 3b^2)$

9 $2Mr^2$

10 $\left(\frac{1}{2} - \frac{16}{9\pi^2}\right)Mr^2$

11 $\frac{1}{20}M(3r^2 + 2h^2)$

12 $\frac{1}{4}Mr^2 + \frac{1}{3}Ml^2$;
    cylinder becomes (a) a rod, (b) a disc.

13 $\frac{2}{3}Ma^2$

14 (a) $\frac{1}{5}M(a^2 + 3h^2)$ (b) $\frac{1}{5}Ma^2 + \frac{3}{80}Mh^2$

15 $\frac{1}{5}M(a^2 + b^2)$

Miscellaneous exercise 3 (page 250)

1 $0.18 \, \text{kg m}^2$

2 $11.1 \, \text{J}$

3 $3.61 \, \text{rad s}^{-1}$

4 $\frac{4M}{a^2}$; (a) $\frac{2}{15}Ma^2$ (b) $\frac{2}{3}Ma^2$ (c) $\frac{4}{5}Ma^2$

5 $2\frac{2}{3} \, \text{kg m}^2$

6 $211 \, \text{kg cm}^2$

7 $9.45 \, \text{kg m}^2$

8 (a) $76.3 \, \text{cm}^3$
   (b) $1.05 \, \text{gram cm}^{-3}$
   (c) $180 \, \text{gram cm}^2$

9 $\sqrt{\dfrac{32g}{5a}}$

10 $1.25 \, \text{J}$

11 $kMl^2 = 2\left(k\left(\frac{1}{2}M\right)\left(\frac{1}{2}l\right)^2 + \left(\frac{1}{2}M\right)\left(\frac{1}{2}l\right)^2\right), k = \frac{1}{3}$

12 $2\left(I + M\left(\frac{1}{6}h\right)^2\right) = \frac{1}{3}(2M)\left(\frac{1}{2}h\right)^2, I = \frac{1}{18}Mh^2$

13 (a) $70\pi r^4 \, \text{kg m}^2$
    (b) $197.5\pi\left(\left(\frac{1}{4}\right)^4 - r^4\right) \, \text{kg m}^2$
    $0.180 \, \text{m}$

14 $\frac{4803}{8000}$

16 (a) $2\pi \rho a^2 b$ (b) Ma^2

4   Centres of mass

Exercise 4A (page 259)

1 $70 \, \text{kg}, 3.93 \, \text{m}$

2 $\frac{2}{3}\text{m}; \frac{2}{5}\text{m}$

3 $62.0 \, \text{cm}$

4 $2.4 \, \text{cm}$

5 $5 \, \text{m}$

6 ...

7 $1.30 \, \text{m}$

8 $\left(0, \frac{5}{9}\right)$

9 $\left(0, 2\frac{1}{3}\right)$

10 (a) $3.456 \, \text{kg}$ (b) $14.4 \, \text{cm}$ (c) $4.88 \, \text{N m}$

11 $\left(\frac{5}{9}a, 0\right)$

12 $\left(2 - \dfrac{K}{e^{\frac{1}{2}K} - 1}, 0\right); \left(1 - \dfrac{K}{e^K - 1}, 0\right)$; they
    approach $(2, 0), (1, 0)$ respectively.

Exercise 4B (page 264)

1 (a) $(1.25, 1.7)$ (b) $\left(\dfrac{2}{e^2 - 1}, \dfrac{e^2 + 1}{4e}\right)$
   (c) $(0.267, 0.604)$ (d) $(1, 1.2)$ (e) $\left(\frac{4}{5}, \frac{1}{4}\right)$

2 $\left(\dfrac{n+1}{n+2}, \dfrac{n+1}{2(2n+1)}\right)$

3 $5.4°$

4 $\left(\dfrac{4r}{3\pi}, \dfrac{4r}{3\pi}\right)$

5 $\left(1\frac{3}{35}, \frac{5}{14}\right)$

6 $\left(\dfrac{b}{3(c-a)}, \dfrac{b(2c-a)}{3(c-a)}\right)$

Miscellaneous exercise 4 (page 264)

1 $7000 \, \text{kilotonnes}, 193 \, \text{m}$

2 2.28

3 $\frac{1}{3000}\pi$, $\frac{5}{7}$

4 $(1.5, 3.6)$

5 (a) $\left(\dfrac{1}{e-1}, \frac{1}{4}(e+1)\right)$ (b) $\left(\dfrac{e^2+1}{2(e^2-1)}, 0\right)$

6 $(\frac{1}{4}(e^2+1), \frac{1}{2}e-1)$

7 $2 - \frac{2}{3}x$, $(x, x+1)$; $(1, 2)$

9 118 J

10 36.8°

11 (b) $(\frac{3}{4}, \frac{3}{10})$ (c) $\left(\dfrac{3\pi-7}{3\pi-4}, \dfrac{14}{5(3\pi-4)}\right)$

12 (b) 1.2   (c) $\frac{80}{3}$ N

Revision exercise 3 (page 267)

1 (a) 013.9°   (b) 131 m s^{-1}

2 300π kg m$^2 \approx 942$ kg m^2

3 $\frac{9}{16}a$

4 24 kg m^2

5 (a) 012.1°, 067.9°   (b) 61.6 s

6 (b) 46.7125 kg m^2

7 (b) $\frac{3}{2}$

8 (a) 29.6 m s^{-1}, 167.3°
   (b) 15.4 km, 2.18 a.m.

9 (b) 1.72 rad s^{-1}

10 $(1.2, 0.96)$

11 30.7 km h^{-1}, 343°

12 $2\pi a^2 k$, $\frac{1}{4}\pi^2 a^4 k$; $\frac{1}{8}\pi m a^2$; $\frac{1}{8}\pi m a^2$

13 (a) $(\frac{3}{16}, \frac{2}{5})$ (b) $\frac{16}{35}$ kg m^2, $\frac{1}{10}$ kg m^2
   (c) 0.167 kg m^2

14 046.3°, 5.38 m s^{-1}

15 (a) at 35.3° to $\overrightarrow{AB}$, 14.5 s
   (b) at 71.8° to $\overrightarrow{AB}$, 15.6 m

16 (a) $\frac{16}{105} m a^2$ (b) $\frac{197}{1575} m a^2$

17 $(0, \frac{3}{8}a)$; $\frac{1}{20}Ma^2(2+\lambda^2)$; $\dfrac{5Ma^2}{4\pi}(2+\lambda^2)$

5 Rotation about a fixed axis

Exercise 5A (page 272)

1 6 rad s^{-2}, 11.9

2 0.262 rad s^{-2}

3 1.375; 11.8 s, 7.68

4 600 rad s^{-2}

5 3 rad s^{-1}, 1.59

6 (a) 9.42 rad s^{-2} $(= 1\frac{1}{2}$ rev s$^{-2})$
   (b) 3.24 rev s^{-1}

7 1.56 rad s^{-1}

8 5 s; 33.1 rad

Exercise 5B (page 277)

1 300 rad s^{-2}, 0.09 N m

2 0.5 rad s^{-2}

3 24 rad s^{-2}

4 1.6×10^{-4} N m

5 6 N; 7.5 N

6 12 800 kg m^2, 6400 N m

7 (a) $\dfrac{(m_1 - m_2)gr}{(m_1 + m_2)r^2 + I}$

   (b) $\dfrac{(m_1 - m_2)gr - C}{(m_1 + m_2)r^2 + I}$

   $C < (m_1 - m_2)gr$

8 2.73 m s^{-2}

9 10 kg m^2; an overestimate

10 1.76 s, 5.60 rad s^{-1}

12 1890 N m; 20 s

Exercise 5C (page 282)

1 $-9.8\sin\theta = \frac{3}{4}\ddot{\theta}$, 1.74 s

2 $-0.196\sin\theta = 0.005\ddot{\theta}$, 1.00 s

4 $4\pi\sqrt{\dfrac{r}{3g}}$

6 1.41 s

7 1.17 s

9 2.67 s

10 $4\pi\dfrac{(a^2+b^2)^{\frac{1}{4}}}{(3g)^{\frac{1}{2}}}$

11 $2\pi\sqrt{\dfrac{2(2a^2 + ab + 2b^2)}{3g\sqrt{a^2+b^2}}}$

12 (a) 1.52 s   (b) 1.51 s

13 $5.73\sqrt{\dfrac{r}{g}}$

14 $6.45\sqrt{\dfrac{r}{g}}$

Exercise 5D (page 289)

1 1.58 N

2 2.96 N

3 $\frac{3}{4}mg\sin 2\theta$, $\frac{1}{4}mg(5 - 3\cos 2\theta)$

4 (a) 53.4 N at 53.4° to the horizontal
   (b) 171.5 N vertically downwards

5 $\frac{3}{8}mg$ horizontally, $\frac{5}{8}mg$ vertically downwards

6 (a) 0   (b) $5mg$ vertically upwards
(c) $\frac{1}{4}mg$ vertically upwards, $\frac{5}{2}mg$ horizontally

7 $4.96\,\mathrm{rad\,s^{-1}}$, 1330 N

8 $\frac{1}{2}a$

9 $f(\theta) = \dfrac{2\sin\theta(3\cos\theta - 2)}{1 - 4\cos\theta + 6\cos^2\theta}$; it will slip at a greater angle than the broomstick for any coefficient of friction, and will never slip if $\mu > \frac{5}{3}\sqrt{15}$.

10 $\frac{3}{4}mg\cos\theta$, $\frac{3}{2}mg\sin\theta$; $\tan^{-1}\frac{1}{2}\mu$

Miscellaneous exercise 5 (page 292)

1 $3.34 \times 10^{-3}\,\mathrm{rad\,s^{-2}}$

2 $1.2\,\mathrm{rad\,s^{-2}}$, $50\,\mathrm{rad\,s^{-1}}$

3 (a) 20 s   (b) 796

4 (b) $\frac{1}{2}\pi\sqrt{\dfrac{3\pi r}{g}}$

5 (a) $\frac{4}{3}g(1 - \cos\theta)$, $\frac{2}{3}g\sin\theta$
(b) $\frac{1}{3}mg(7\cos\theta - 4)$,
$\frac{1}{3}mg\sin\theta$ $\frac{11}{3}mg$ when $\theta = \pi$,
$\frac{1}{3}\sqrt{\frac{2}{3}}mg$ when $\theta = \cos^{-1}\frac{7}{12}$

6 (a) $0.98(4 - \sin^2\theta + 2\cos^2\theta)\,\mathrm{N}$,
$2.94\sin\theta\cos\theta\,\mathrm{N}$
(b) $\frac{1}{4}\sqrt{2} \approx 0.354$

7 $\dfrac{\dot{x}}{a}$, $\dot{x}$;
$mg - T = m\ddot{x}$,
$\left(T - \dfrac{\lambda(x - a)}{a}\right)a = \frac{1}{2}ma^2 \times \dfrac{\ddot{x}}{a}$;
$2\pi\sqrt{\dfrac{3ma}{2\lambda}}$

10 (a) $0.297\,\mathrm{N\,m}$
(b) $0.0066\,\mathrm{kg\,m^2}$, $45.0\,\mathrm{rad\,s^{-2}}$
(c) 1.12 s

11 $\frac{3}{4}ma^2$;   (b) $\dfrac{g}{a\sqrt{3}}$ (c) $\frac{5}{3}mg$, $\dfrac{mg}{\sqrt{3}}$

12 (b) $\dfrac{9g}{16a}$
(d) (i) $\frac{5}{16}mg$ vertically upwards
(ii) $\frac{43}{8}mg$ vertically upwards

13 $\frac{4}{9}ma^2$ (b) $\dfrac{3g}{4a}\sin\theta$
$\frac{3}{4}mg\sin\theta$

14 (a) 0.6 m   (b) $6912\,\mathrm{kg\,m^2}$ (c) 8.79 s
(d) The cabin and the counterweight are not point masses, the central section is not a uniform rod, resistances are ignored.

15 (a) $\frac{1}{2}ka$ (b) $\frac{2}{3}a$, $\frac{1}{2}ma^2$
(d) $\ddot{\theta} = -\dfrac{160g}{147a}\sin\theta$, $\frac{7}{2}\pi\sqrt{\dfrac{3a}{10g}}$

16 (b) $2\pi\sqrt{\dfrac{236r}{95g}}$ (c) $\cos^{-1}\left(1 - \dfrac{118r\omega^2}{95g}\right)$

6   Angular momentum

Exercise 6 (page 308)

1 (a) $3140\,\mathrm{N\,m\,s}$
(b) $503\,\mathrm{N\,m\,s}$
(c) $0.0251\,\mathrm{N\,m\,s}$
(d) $10\,\mathrm{N\,m\,s}$

2 2 s

3 $840\,\mathrm{rad\,s^{-1}}$

4 $3\frac{3}{7}\,\mathrm{rad\,s^{-1}}$, 49.4°

5 $2m\sqrt{\frac{1}{3}ag}$

6 decreases by $6.66 \times 10^{-3}\,\mathrm{rad\,s^{-1}}$

7 $3.73\,\mathrm{rad\,s^{-1}}$

8 $14\,\mathrm{N\,s}$, $3.5\,\mathrm{N\,s}$ in the direction of the blow

9 $0.008\,\mathrm{N\,m\,s}$

10 4 kg

11 $\dfrac{3x - 2a}{2a}J$; if struck $\frac{2}{3}$ of the way down, they will swing about the top of the tube where the cord is attached

12 $\dfrac{r^2\omega}{r^2 + s^2}$, $\dfrac{r^3\omega}{s(r^2 + s^2)}$

Miscellaneous exercise 6 (page 310)

1 53.4

2 drops to $1.04\,\mathrm{rad\,s^{-1}}$, $37.4\,\mathrm{N\,s}$ in the direction opposite to that in which the child starts to move; would drop to $0.769\,\mathrm{rad\,s^{-1}}$.

3 $\frac{5}{4}r$

4 $0.155l$

5 $162\,\mathrm{N\,s}$

6 2.41 s

7 $\omega > \dfrac{3}{M}\sqrt{\dfrac{2mg(\frac{1}{3}M + m)}{l}}$

8 (a) $3.5\,\mathrm{rad\,s^{-1}}$, $10\,\mathrm{rad\,s^{-1}}$
(b) 125 N   (c) 3062.5 J

9 17.5 N s; 21 N s, 3.5 N s in directions $\overrightarrow{AB}$, $\overrightarrow{AD}$

10 $4hd = r^2$

11 $\dfrac{4J}{3mr}\sin\theta$; $J\cos\theta$ in direction $\overrightarrow{BA}$, $\frac{1}{3}J\sin\theta$ perpendicular to AB

12 $1.68\,\mathrm{m\,s^{-1}}$, 3.19 cm

13 (a) $\dfrac{3J}{4\sqrt{2}ml}$, $\frac{1}{4}J$, 0 (b) $\dfrac{3J}{4ml}$, $\dfrac{J}{2\sqrt{2}}$, $\dfrac{J}{\sqrt{2}}$

14 (a) $\sqrt{\dfrac{3g}{l}}$

   (b) $I = m(u+v)$, $-I(l-x) = 2ml^2(\omega_1 - \omega)$

   (c) $\frac{7}{11}\sqrt{\dfrac{3g}{l}} - \frac{6}{11}\dfrac{u}{l}$

7 Stability and oscillation

Exercise 7A (page 324)

1 stable with the minor axis, unstable with the major axis in contact with the ground

2 (a) with the centre of a curved arc on the table

   (b) with a corner on the table

3 unstable

4 unstable

5 $50°$, stable

6 4 m, stable

7 $(10x^2 - 6x + 1.6)\,\mathrm{J}$, 0.3 m, stable

8 $(10\cos\theta + 8\theta - 4)\,\mathrm{J}$, $\sin^{-1}0.8 \approx 0.927$ rad, unstable

9 $(2\sin\theta - 6\sin 2\theta - 2)\,\mathrm{J}$; $2\cos^{-1}\frac{3}{4} \approx 1.45$ rad, stable; $2\cos^{-1}\left(-\frac{2}{3}\right) - \pi$, unstable

10 $\dfrac{3+\sqrt{3}}{4\pi}W$

11 The locus of points P such that $AP + PB = l$ is an ellipse with foci at A and B. The equilibrium position of the ring is the lowest point of the ellipse, where the tangent is horizontal. The lines PA, PB make equal angles with the tangent at P.

12 (a) stable if $k \leqslant 2$, unstable if $k > 2$.

   (b) If $k > 2$, there are stable positions with the string at an angle $\cos^{-1}\dfrac{k}{2(k-1)}$ to the downward vertical.

14 $a < r$

15 $2l\dfrac{\sin(\beta+\theta)}{\sin(\alpha+\beta)}$, $2l\dfrac{\sin(\alpha-\theta)}{\sin(\alpha+\beta)}$;

   $\dfrac{l}{\sin(\alpha+\beta)}(2\sin\alpha\sin\beta\cos\theta + \sin(\alpha-\beta)\sin\theta)$
   $+ h\cos\theta$;   unstable

16 stable with $(1.2, \pm 0.8)$ in contact with the surface, unstable with $(\pm 2, 0)$ in contact

Exercise 7B (page 336)

1 $\dfrac{\lambda}{2l}((d+x)^2 + (d-x)^2) + \frac{1}{2}I\left(\dfrac{\dot{x}}{r}\right)^2 = $ constant, $\dfrac{2\pi}{r}\sqrt{\dfrac{Il}{2\lambda}}$

2 $2\pi\sqrt{\dfrac{ma}{2\lambda}}$, $\dfrac{mga}{2\lambda}$

3 $2\pi\sqrt{\dfrac{r\alpha}{g\sin\alpha}}$

4 $2\pi\sqrt{\dfrac{3ma}{2\lambda}}$

5 $\ddot{\theta} = -\dfrac{g}{4r}(-2k\sin 2\theta + 2k\sin\theta + 2\sin 2\theta)$

6 $13x\left(1 - \dfrac{3.2}{\sqrt{144 + x^2}}\right) = 49$; 4.38 s

7 $\frac{20}{7}\pi$ s ≈ 8.98 s

8 $\pi\sqrt{\dfrac{2a}{g}}$

9 (a) $(r\sin\theta + (l-r\theta)\cos\theta, r\cos\theta - (l-r\theta)\sin\theta)$,
   $(r\sin\theta - (l+r\theta)\cos\theta, r\cos\theta + (l+r\theta)\sin\theta)$

   (b) $(l - r\theta)\dot{\theta}$, $(l + r\theta)\dot{\theta}$,
   both perpendicular to the plank

   (c) $mgr(\cos\theta + \theta\sin\theta) + \frac{1}{2}m((l-r\theta)^2$
   $+ (l+r\theta)^2)\dot{\theta}^2 = $ constant,

   $2\pi l\sqrt{\dfrac{2}{gr}}$

10 $\frac{1}{2}I\dot{\theta}^2$, where $I = \frac{1}{3}m(l^2 + a^2) + ma^2 + mr^2\theta^2$;

   $2\pi\sqrt{\dfrac{l^2 + 4a^2}{3g(r-a)}}$

Miscellaneous exercise 7 (page 338)

1 $2\pi\sqrt{\dfrac{2\pi r}{g(6 - \pi\sqrt{3})}}$

2 $(2\cos\theta - (3 - \sqrt{5 - 4\cos\theta})w)\,\mathrm{J}$;

   (a) stable if $\theta = \pi$, unstable if $\theta = 0$

   (b) stable if $\theta = 0$, unstable if $\theta = \pi$

   (c) stable if $\theta = 0$ or $\theta = \pi$, unstable if
   $\theta = \pm\cos^{-1}\dfrac{5 - w^2}{4}$.

3 (b) $\theta = \pi$ stable, $\theta = 2\sin^{-1}\dfrac{M}{m}$ unstable

   (c) $\theta = \pi$

4 (a) $x = \dfrac{1}{a}$

   (b) $2\pi\sqrt{\dfrac{m}{kea^3}}$

5 (a) $\frac{1}{3}a^2x^3 + \frac{1}{3}b^2(d-x)^3$

(b) $x = \dfrac{bd}{a+b}$

(c) $2\pi\sqrt{\dfrac{m}{2abd}}$

6 $\pi\sqrt{\dfrac{ml^3}{k}}$

8 $\frac{1}{3}\pi$; $2\pi\sqrt{\dfrac{7a}{3\sqrt{3}g}}$

9 (a) $\theta = 0$ unstable, $\theta = \cos^{-1}\frac{2}{3}$ stable

(d) $2\pi\sqrt{\dfrac{23a}{40g}}$

Revision exercise 4 (page 341)

1 (a) $1.92\,\text{rad}\,\text{s}^{-2}$ (b) 150 rad

2 $7.4\,\text{rad}\,\text{s}^{-1}$

4 (b) $2\pi\sqrt{\dfrac{a^2 + 3x^2}{3gx}}$

5 (a) $0.05\,\text{kg}\,\text{m}^2$ (b) 1.16 s

6 (a) $22.5\,\text{rad}\,\text{s}^{-2}$ (b) 525 rad   (c) 189 J

7 (a) $0.927 (= \cos^{-1} 0.6)$ (b) stable

8 (a) 905 J   (b) $0.629\,\text{kg}\,\text{m}^2$

9 (a) $\frac{11}{18}ma^2$ (b) $\dfrac{6g}{11a}$

(c) vertically upwards, $\frac{9}{11}mg$

10 (b) $\sqrt{\dfrac{3g}{4a}}$

11 (b) $\frac{1}{6}\pi$, $\frac{1}{2}\pi$, $\frac{5}{6}\pi$

(c) stable, unstable, stable

12 (a) $\frac{7}{5}ma^2$ (c) $\dfrac{5g}{7a}\sin\theta$

(d) $mg\left(\dfrac{17\cos\theta - 10}{7}\right)$, $\frac{2}{7}mg\sin\theta$

(e) $0.942 (= \cos^{-1}\frac{10}{17})$

(f) Perfectly rough; in reality it will slip before contact is lost.

13 1.08 s

14 $1.5\,\text{kg}\,\text{m}^2$; $5.6\,\text{m}\,\text{s}^{-2}$

15 14 N s

16 $0.119\,\text{kg}\,\text{m}^2$; 10 s

17 $4(1 - \sqrt{1+x})$ (a) $1 + \frac{1}{2}x$ (b) $\ddot{x} = -2x$
(c) simple harmonic, $\pi\sqrt{2}$ s
A frictional force would change sign when the velocity changes direction.

18 0.628 J; $354\,\text{rad}\,\text{s}^{-1}$, 188

19 stable at $(\pm\frac{1}{2}, \frac{1}{4})$, unstable at $(0, 0)$

20 $\dfrac{3J}{4ma}$; $\cos^{-1}\left(1 - \dfrac{3J^2}{8m^2ga}\right)$

21 0.0460 m in the direction opposite to the direction of projection

22 $52.5°$, stable; $0.113W$, still stable;
If B is below the pegs, equilibrium is at $52.5°$ to the upward vertical, unstable; with the elastic cord attached, equilibrium occurs when the planks make a larger angle with the upward vertical, still unstable.

23 (b) $(0, \frac{3}{5}h)$ (c) $\frac{12}{175}Mh^2$

(d) $-\frac{2}{5}Mgh\sin\theta = \frac{8}{35}Mh^2\ddot{\theta}$, $2\pi\sqrt{\dfrac{4h}{7g}}$

24 (a) $3.04\,\text{N}\,\text{s}$ (b) $0.298\,\text{N}\,\text{s}$ (c) 0.479 s

25 (a) $\frac{7}{12}ma^2$ (b) $-\dfrac{6g}{7a}\cos\theta$

(c) $\frac{4}{7}mg$, $\frac{1}{2}ma\Omega^2$ (e) decrease

26 $\dfrac{80m}{27a^2}x^3\delta x$; moment of inertia of PAB is the same as OAB (shear rule), then total moment of inertia is $6 \times \frac{5}{12}ma^2 = \frac{5}{12}(6m)a^2$;
$\frac{5}{24}Ma^2\dot{\theta}^2 + Mg\lambda a\theta^2 = $ constant,

$\frac{5}{12}Ma^2\ddot{\theta} + 2Mg\lambda a\theta = 0$, $\pi\sqrt{\dfrac{5a}{6g\lambda}}$

27 Unstable when $\theta = \tan^{-1} 2$, hits nail with angular speed $\sqrt{\dfrac{3g}{4a}}(\sqrt{5} - 1)$ or $\sqrt{\dfrac{3g}{4a}}(\sqrt{5} + 2)$; stable when $\theta = \pi + \tan^{-1} 2$, period $2\pi\sqrt{\dfrac{8a}{3\sqrt{5}g}}$.
Only one equilibrium position, unstable when $\theta = \pi - \tan^{-1} 2$, hits nail with angular speed $\sqrt{\dfrac{3g}{4a}}(\sqrt{5} + 1)$ or $\sqrt{\dfrac{3g}{4a}}(\sqrt{5} + 2)$.

Practice examinations

Practice examination 1 for M4 (page 348)

1 (i) 2.4 s, 30 rad   (ii) 300 J

2 (i) $3.76\,\text{rad}\,\text{s}^{-1}$ (ii) 1.96 J

4 (i) $\cos^{-1}\frac{3}{5} \approx 53.1°$, $\dfrac{d}{4u}$

(ii) (a) $4u$, $3u$

5 (iii) $\frac{1}{2}\pi\sqrt{\dfrac{3\pi a}{g}}$

6 (ii) $X = \frac{10}{3}mg\sin\theta$, $Y = \frac{4}{3}mg\cos\theta$

7 (iv) $2\pi\sqrt{\dfrac{4a}{3\sqrt{2}g}}$

Practice examination 2 for M4 (page 351)

1 (ii) $2\pi\sqrt{\dfrac{17a}{9g}}$

2 (i) 25   (ii) 35.0 N m, 21.9 rad s^{-2}

4 (ii) (a) $\frac{1}{3}ma^2$ (b) $\frac{1}{6}ma^2$

5 (i) 068.7°
    (ii) 11.5 km, at 1.36 p.m.

6 (i) $a\dot{\theta}^2 = \frac{6}{7}g\sin\theta$, $a\ddot{\theta} = \frac{3}{7}g\cos\theta$

7 (i) $\theta = \frac{1}{6}\pi$, unstable; $\theta = \frac{5}{6}\pi$, stable

Index

The page numbers refer to the first mention of each term, or the blue box if there is one.

Formulae

Motion in a circle

Transverse velocity: $v = r\dot{\theta}$

Transverse acceleration: $\dot{v} = r\ddot{\theta}$

Radial acceleration: $-r\dot{\theta}^2 = -\dfrac{v^2}{r}$

Centres of mass

For uniform bodies

Triangular lamina: $\frac{2}{3}$ along median from vertex

Solid hemisphere, radius r : $\frac{3}{8}r$ from centre

Hemispherical shell, radius r : $\frac{1}{2}r$ from centre

Circular arc, radius r, angle at centre 2α : $\dfrac{r\sin\alpha}{\alpha}$ from centre

Sector of circle, radius r, angle at centre 2α : $\dfrac{2r\sin\alpha}{3\alpha}$ from centre

Solid cone or pyramid of height h : $\frac{1}{4}h$ above the base on the line from centre of base to vertex

Conical shell of height h : $\frac{1}{3}h$ above the base on the line from centre of base to vertex

Moments of inertia

For uniform bodies of mass m

Thin rod, length $2l$, about perpendicular axis through centre: $\frac{1}{3}ml^2$

Rectangular lamina about axis in plane bisecting edges of length $2l$: $\frac{1}{3}ml^2$

Thin rod, length $2l$, about perpendicular axis through end: $\frac{4}{3}ml^2$

Rectangular lamina about edge perpendicular to edges of length $2l$: $\frac{4}{3}ml^2$

Rectangular lamina, sides $2a$ and $2b$, about perpendicular axis through centre: $\frac{1}{3}m(a^2 + b^2)$

Hoop or cylindrical shell of radius r about axis: mr^2

Hoop of radius r about a diameter: $\frac{1}{2}mr^2$

Disc or solid cylinder of radius r about axis: $\frac{1}{2}mr^2$

Disc of radius r about a diameter: $\frac{1}{4}mr^2$

Solid sphere, radius r, about a diameter: $\frac{2}{5}mr^2$

Spherical shell of radius r about a diameter: $\frac{2}{3}mr^2$

Parallel axes theorem: $I_A = I_G + m(AG)^2$

Perpendicular axes theorem: $I_z = I_x + I_y$ (for a lamina in the xy-plane)